BBC THE **ELEVENTH** DOCTOR

DOCTOR WHO ARCHIVES

VOLUME 3

TITAN
COMICS

TITAN COMICS

Collection Editor
Andrew James
Assistant Collection Editor
Kirsten Murray
Collection Designer
Rob Farmer
Senior Editor
Steve White

Titan Comics Editorial
Lizzie Kaye, Tom Williams
Production Assistant Peter James
Production Supervisors Maria Pearson, Jackie Flook
Production Manager Obi Onuora
Studio Manager Selina Juneja
Senior Sales Manager Steve Tothill
Brand Manager, Marketing Lucy Ripper
Senior Marketing & Press Officer Owen Johnson
Direct Sales & Marketing Manager Ricky Claydon
Commercial Manager Michelle Fairlamb
Publishing Manager Darryl Tothill
Publishing Director Chris Teather
Operations Director Leigh Baulch
Executive Director Vivian Cheung
Publisher Nick Landau

Cover By
Mark Buckingham
Original Series Edits By
Denton J. Tipton

BBC WORLDWIDE

Director of Editorial Governance
Nicolas Brett
**Director of Consumer Products
And Publishing**
Andrew Moultrie
Head of UK Publishing
Chris Kerwin
Publisher
Mandy Thwaites
Publishing Co-Ordinator
Eva Abramik

Special thanks to
Steven Moffat, Brian Minchin, Matt Nicholls,
James Dudley, Edward Russell, Derek Ritchie,
Scott Handcock, Kirsty Mullan,
Kate Bush, Julia Nocciolino, Ed Casey,
Marcus Wilson and Richard Cookson
for their invaluable assistance.

BBC THE **ELEVENTH** DOCTOR

DOCTOR WHO ARCHIVES

DOCTOR WHO: THE ELEVENTH DOCTOR
ARCHIVES OMNIBUS VOL. 3
ISBN: 9781782767732
Published by Titan Comics, a division of Titan
Publishing Group, Ltd. 144 Southwark Street, London,
SE1 0UP.

Contains material originally published as Doctor Who
Series 3 #13-20, Convention Special, DVD Pack Blu-Ray
Special, and the 2013 Special.

A CIP catalogue record for this title is available from the
British Library. First edition: February 2016.

10 9 8 7 6 5 4 3 2 1

Printed in China. TC00957.

Titan Comics does not read or accept unsolicited
DOCTOR WHO submissions of ideas, stories or artwork.

www.titan-comics.com

CONTENTS

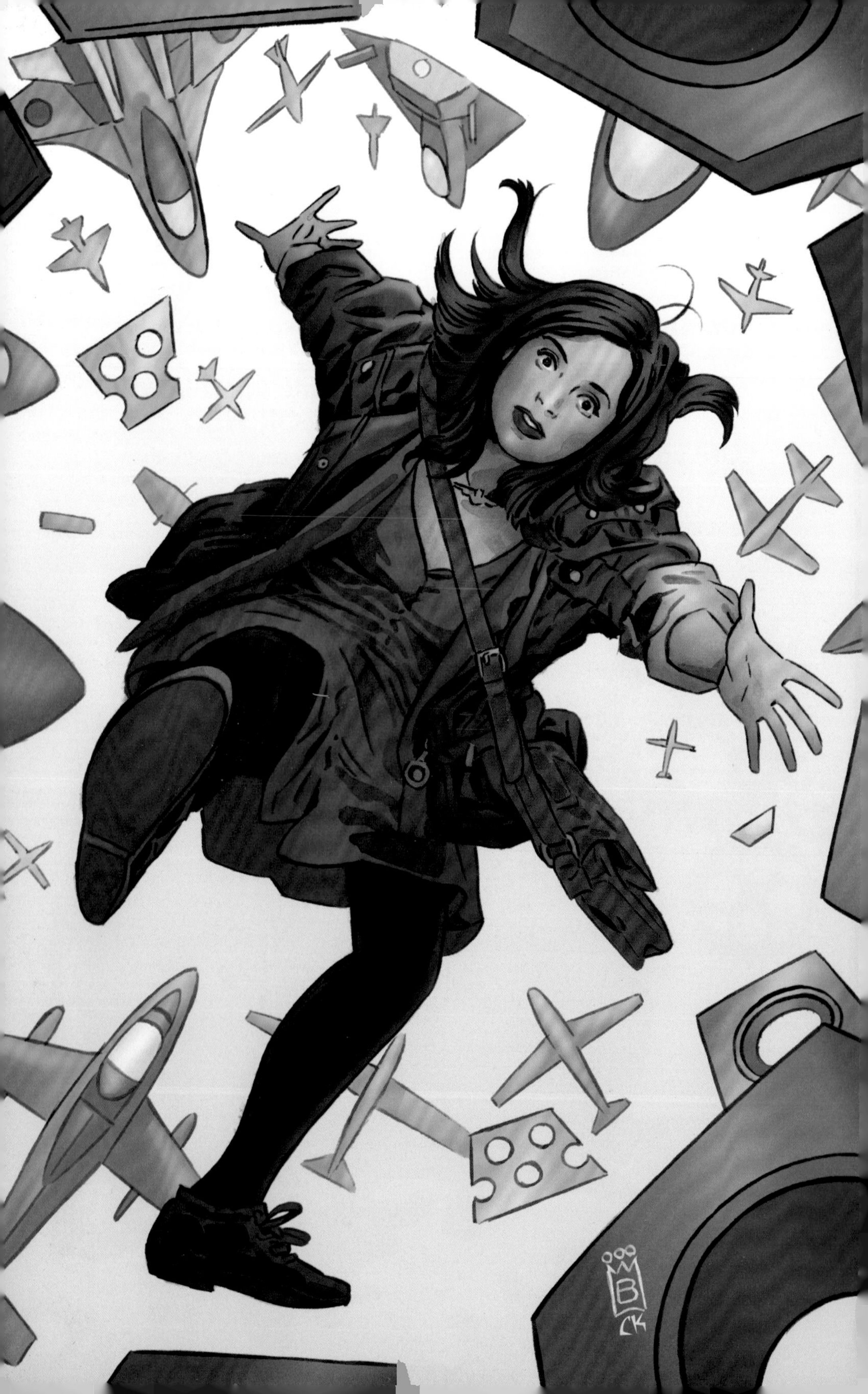

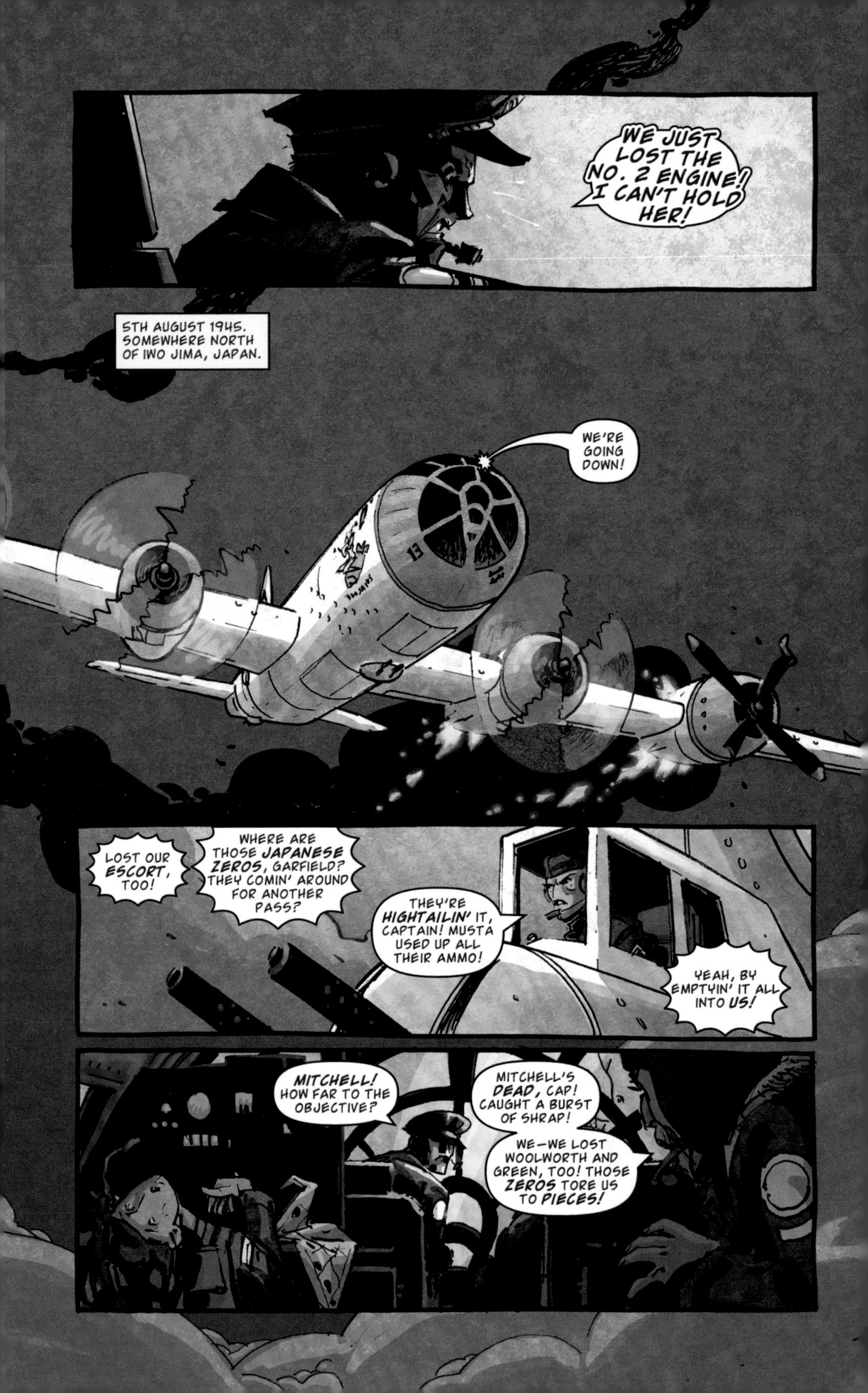
WE JUST LOST THE NO. 2 ENGINE! I CAN'T HOLD HER!
5TH AUGUST 1945. SOMEWHERE NORTH OF IWO JIMA, JAPAN.
WE'RE GOING DOWN!
LOST OUR ESCORT, TOO!
WHERE ARE THOSE JAPANESE ZEROS, GARFIELD? THEY COMIN' AROUND FOR ANOTHER PASS?
THEY'RE HIGHTAILIN' IT, CAPTAIN! MUSTA USED UP ALL THEIR AMMO!
YEAH, BY EMPTYIN' IT ALL INTO US!
MITCHELL! HOW FAR TO THE OBJECTIVE?
MITCHELL'S DEAD, CAP! CAUGHT A BURST OF SHRAP!
WE—WE LOST WOOLWORTH AND GREEN, TOO! THOSE ZEROS TORE US TO PIECES!

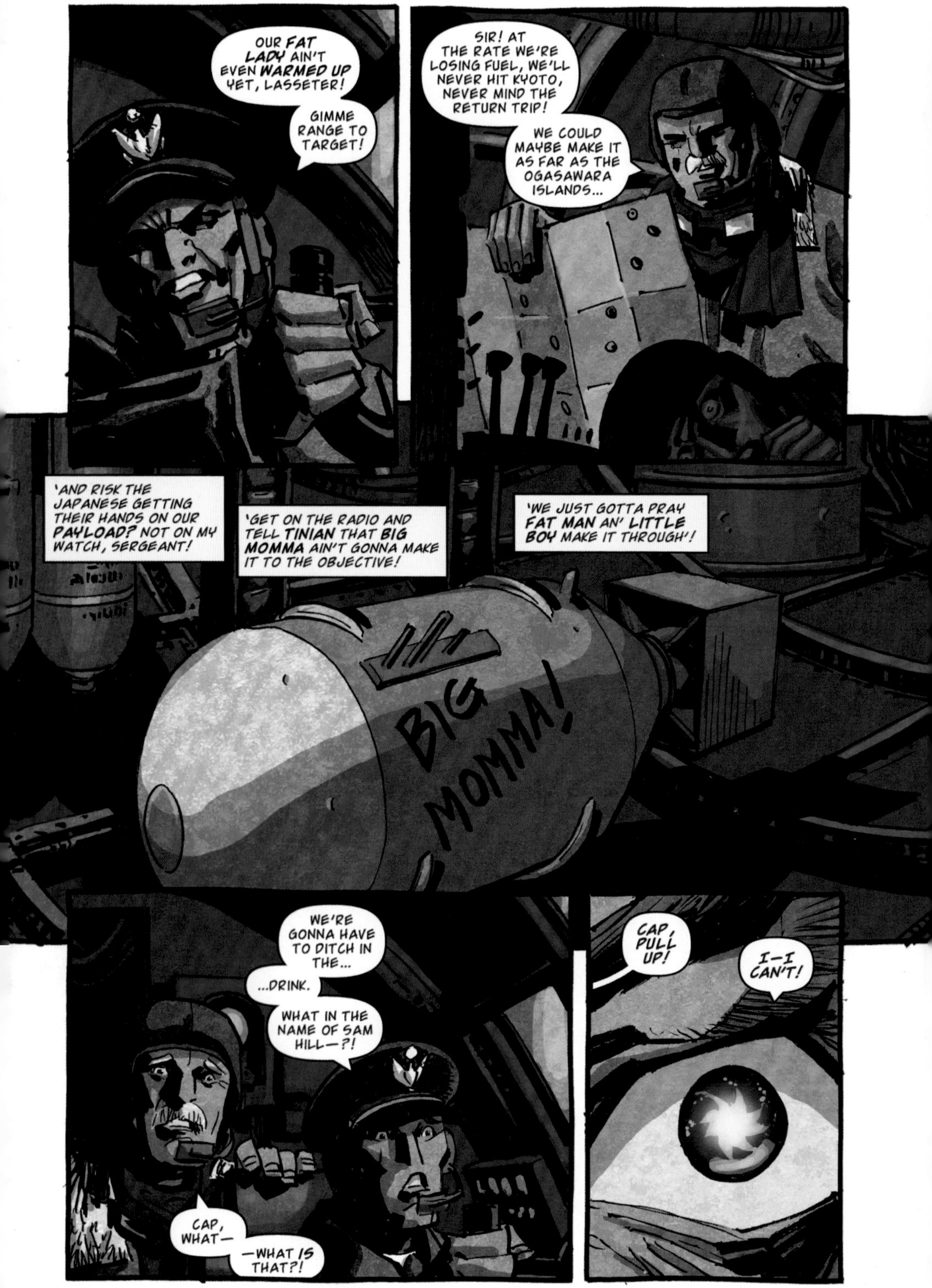
OUR FAT LADY AIN'T EVEN WARMED UP YET, LASSETER!
GIMME RANGE TO TARGET!
SIR! AT THE RATE WE'RE LOSING FUEL, WE'LL NEVER HIT KYOTO, NEVER MIND THE RETURN TRIP!
WE COULD MAYBE MAKE IT AS FAR AS THE OGASAWARA ISLANDS...
'AND RISK THE JAPANESE GETTING THEIR HANDS ON OUR PAYLOAD? NOT ON MY WATCH, SERGEANT!
'GET ON THE RADIO AND TELL TINIAN THAT BIG MOMMA AIN'T GONNA MAKE IT TO THE OBJECTIVE!
'WE JUST GOTTA PRAY FAT MAN AN' LITTLE BOY MAKE IT THROUGH'!
BIG MOMMA!
WE'RE GONNA HAVE TO DITCH IN THE...
...DRINK.
WHAT IN THE NAME OF SAM HILL—?!
CAP, WHAT—
—WHAT IS THAT?!
CAP, PULL UP!
I—I CAN'T!

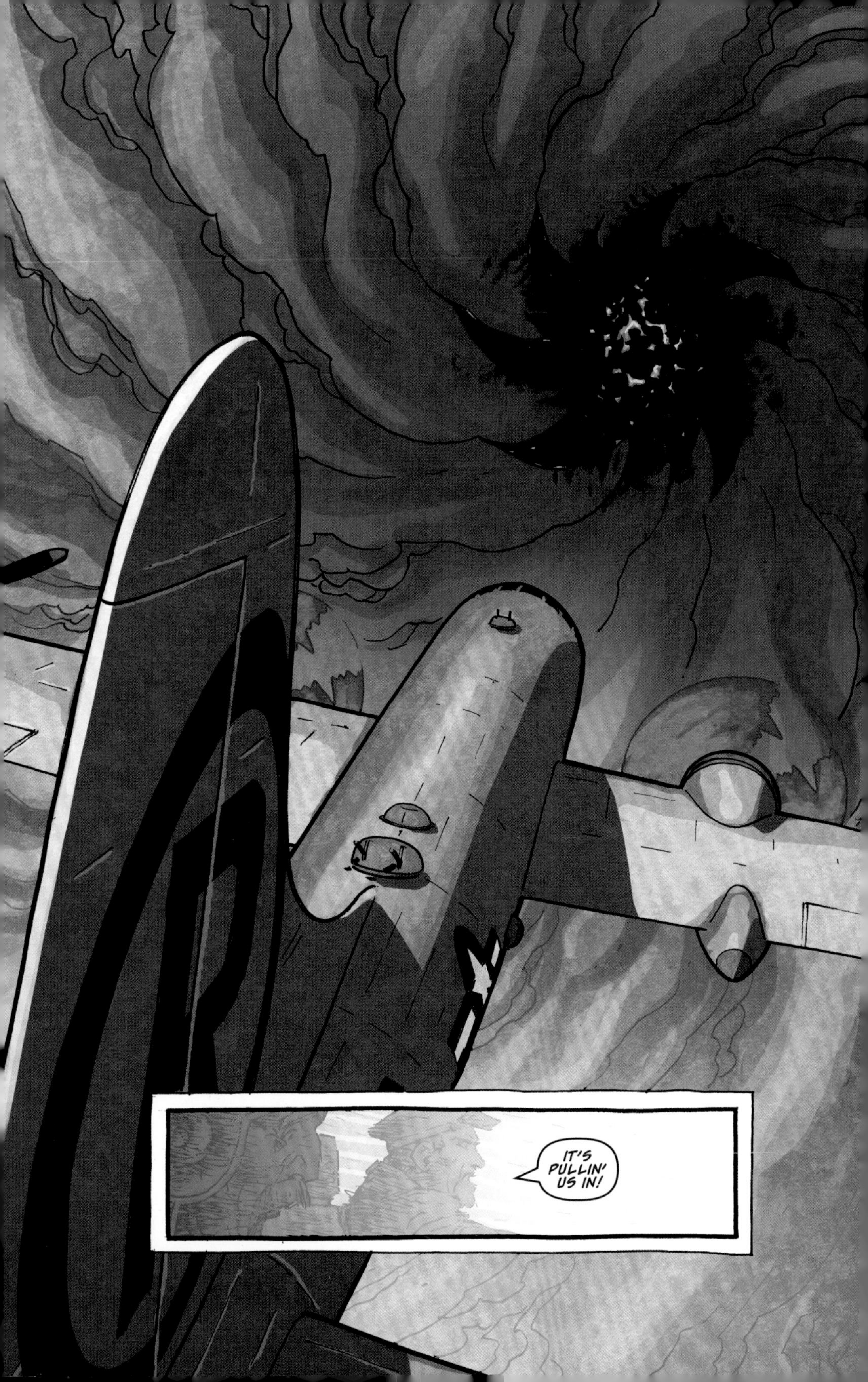
IT'S PULLIN' US IN!

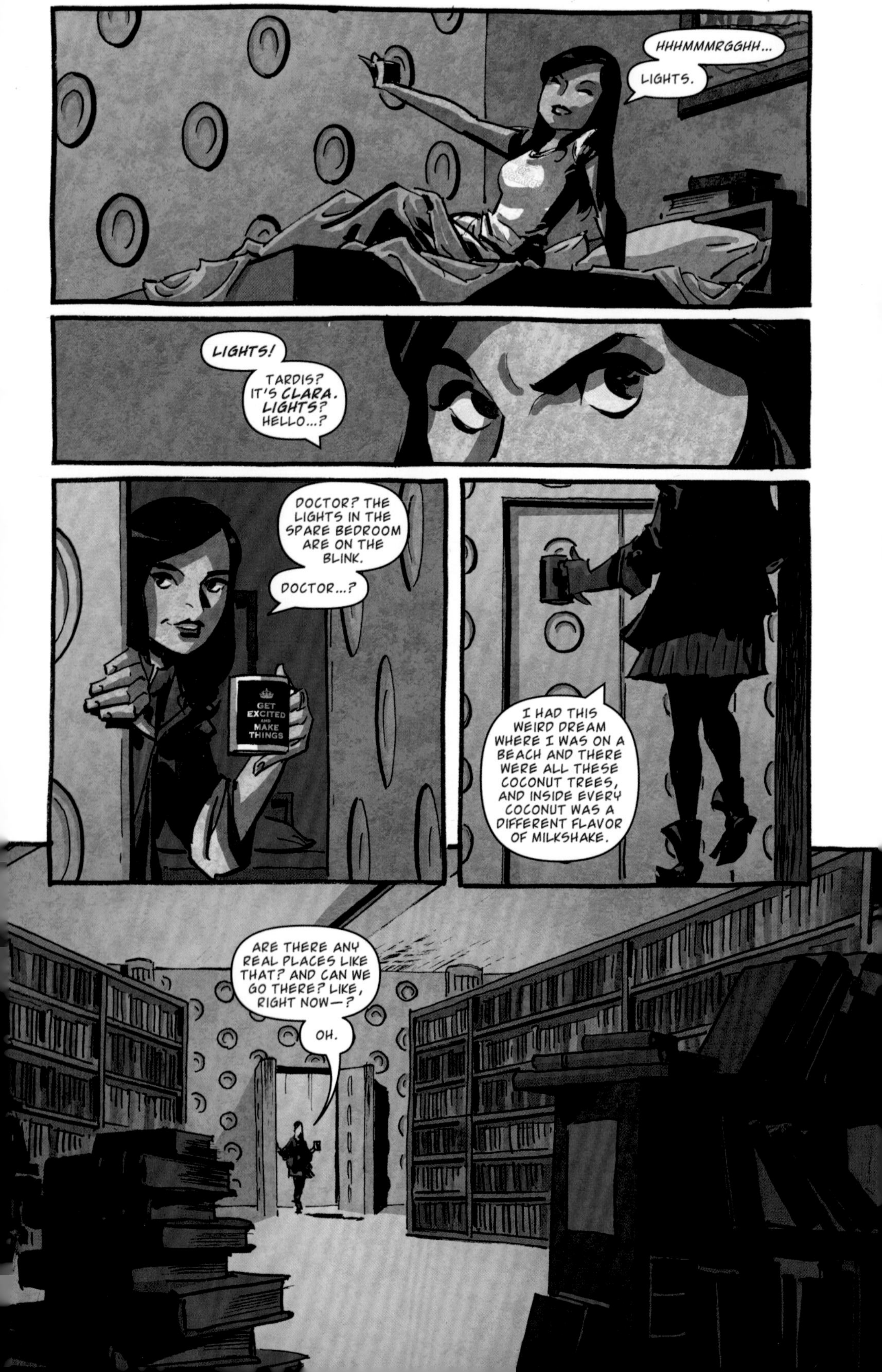
HHHMMMRGGHH...
LIGHTS.
LIGHTS!
TARDIS? IT'S CLARA. LIGHTS? HELLO...?
DOCTOR? THE LIGHTS IN THE SPARE BEDROOM ARE ON THE BLINK.
DOCTOR...?
GET EXCITED AND MAKE THINGS
I HAD THIS WEIRD DREAM WHERE I WAS ON A BEACH AND THERE WERE ALL THESE COCONUT TREES, AND INSIDE EVERY COCONUT WAS A DIFFERENT FLAVOR OF MILKSHAKE.
ARE THERE ANY REAL PLACES LIKE THAT? AND CAN WE GO THERE? LIKE, RIGHT NOW—?
OH.

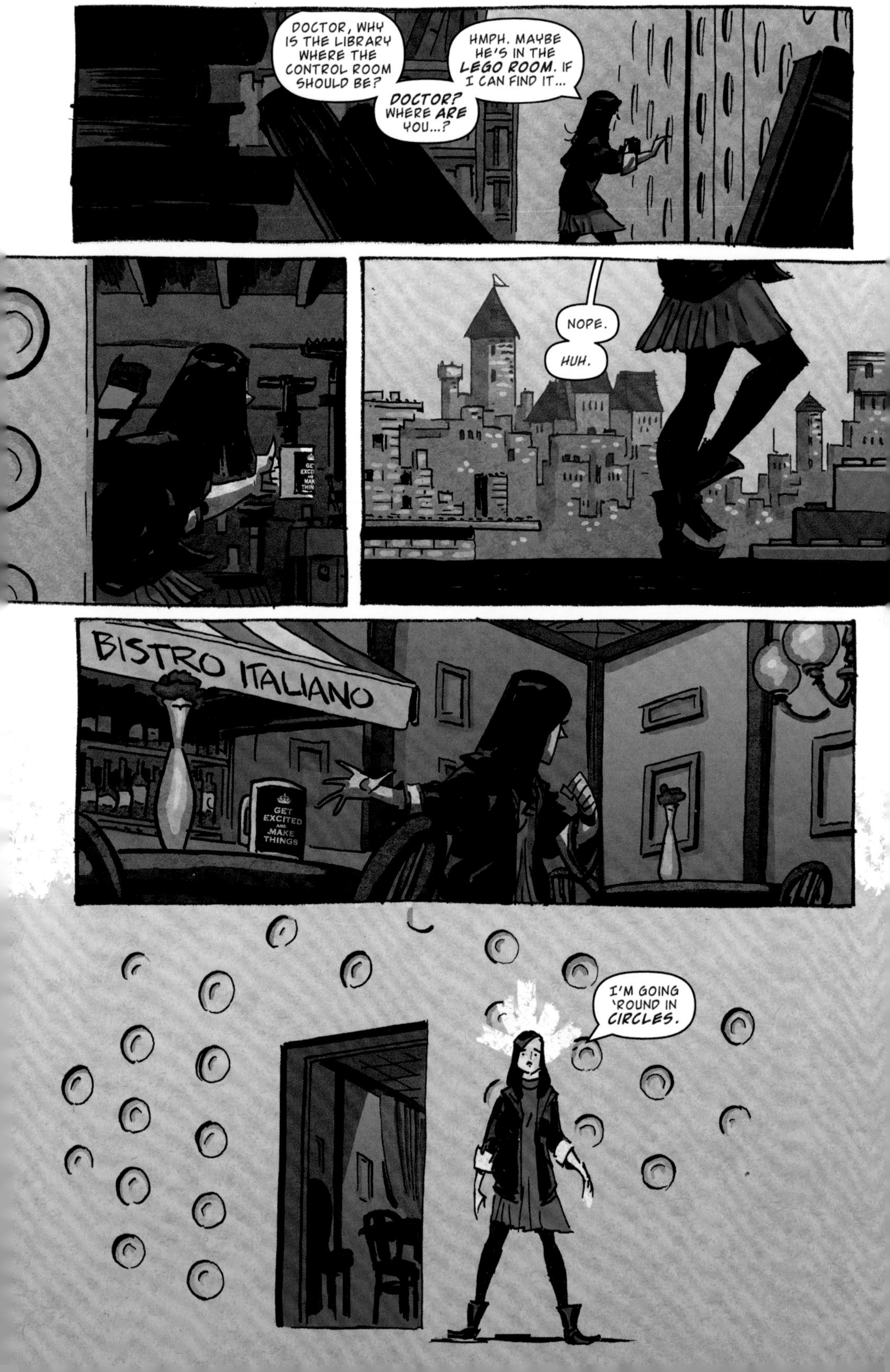
DOCTOR, WHY IS THE LIBRARY WHERE THE CONTROL ROOM SHOULD BE?
DOCTOR? WHERE ARE YOU...?
HMPH. MAYBE HE'S IN THE LEGO ROOM. IF I CAN FIND IT...
GET EXCITED AND MAKE THINGS
NOPE.
HUH.
BISTRO ITALIANO
GET EXCITED AND MAKE THINGS
I'M GOING 'ROUND IN CIRCLES.

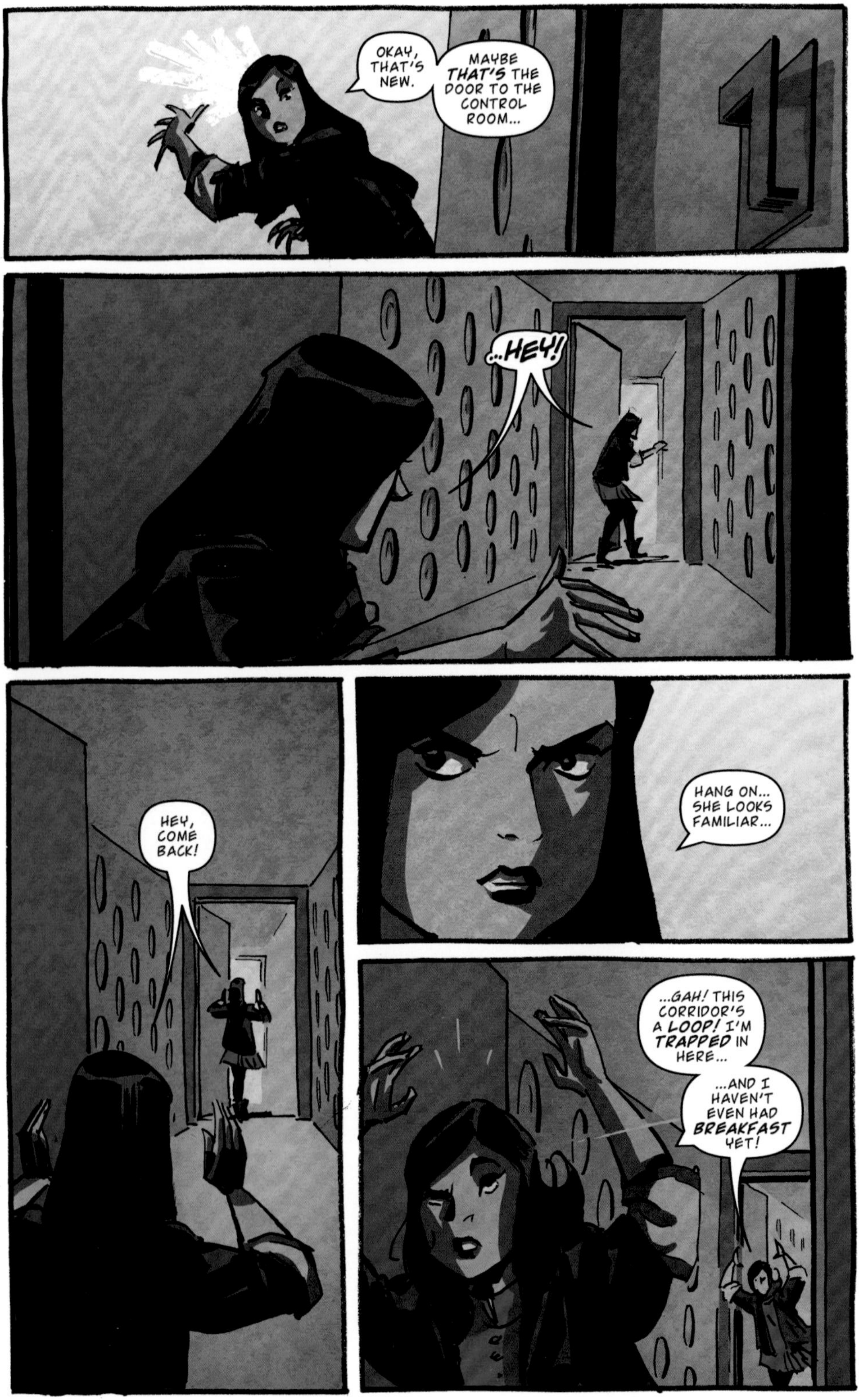
OKAY, THAT'S NEW.
MAYBE THAT'S THE DOOR TO THE CONTROL ROOM...
...HEY!
HEY, COME BACK!
HANG ON... SHE LOOKS FAMILIAR...
...GAH! THIS CORRIDOR'S A LOOP! I'M TRAPPED IN HERE...
...AND I HAVEN'T EVEN HAD BREAKFAST YET!

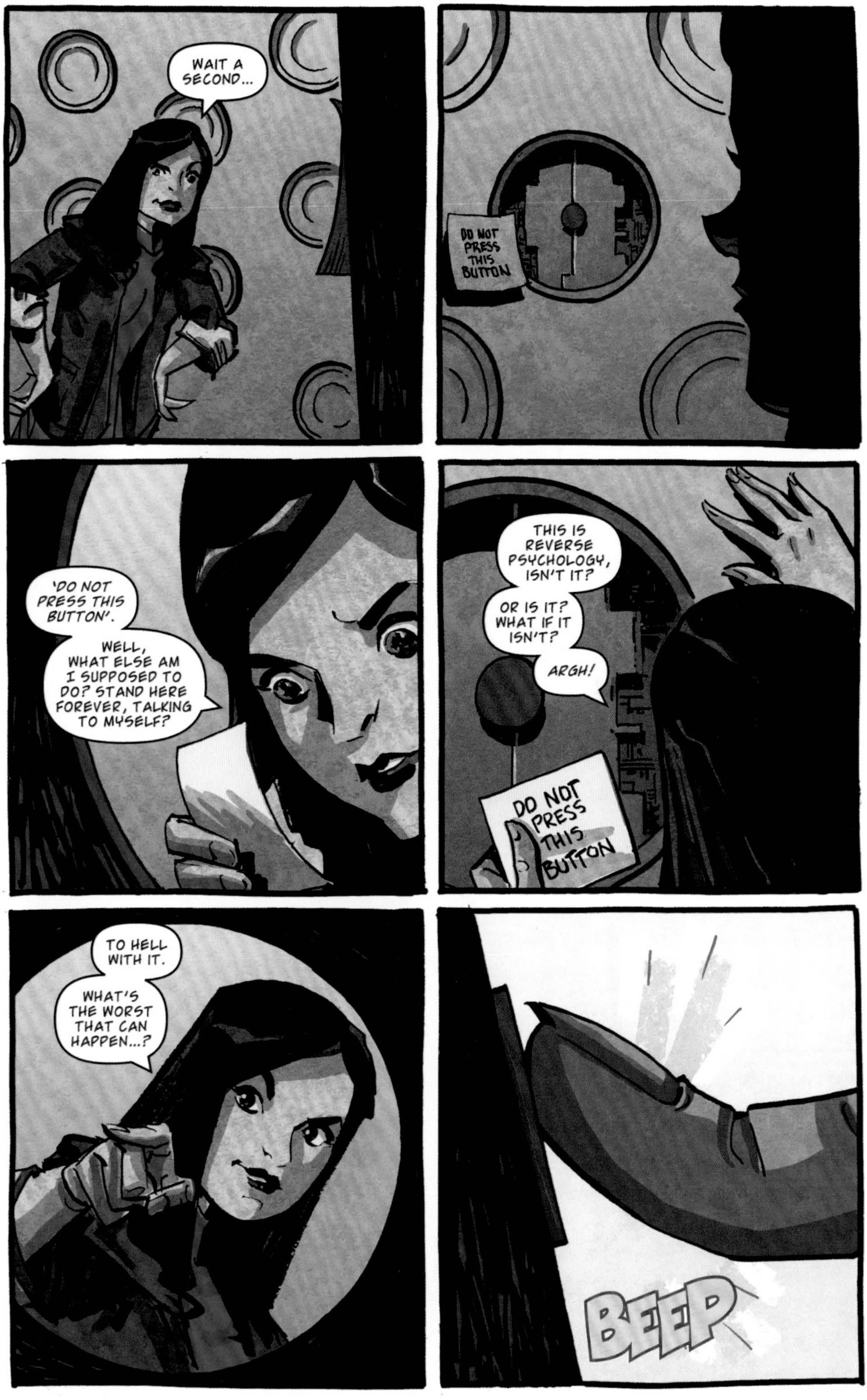
WAIT A SECOND...
DO NOT PRESS THIS BUTTON
'DO NOT PRESS THIS BUTTON'.
WELL, WHAT ELSE AM I SUPPOSED TO DO? STAND HERE FOREVER, TALKING TO MYSELF?
THIS IS REVERSE PSYCHOLOGY, ISN'T IT?
OR IS IT? WHAT IF IT ISN'T?
ARGH!
DO NOT PRESS THIS BUTTON
TO HELL WITH IT.
WHAT'S THE WORST THAT CAN HAPPEN...?
BEEP

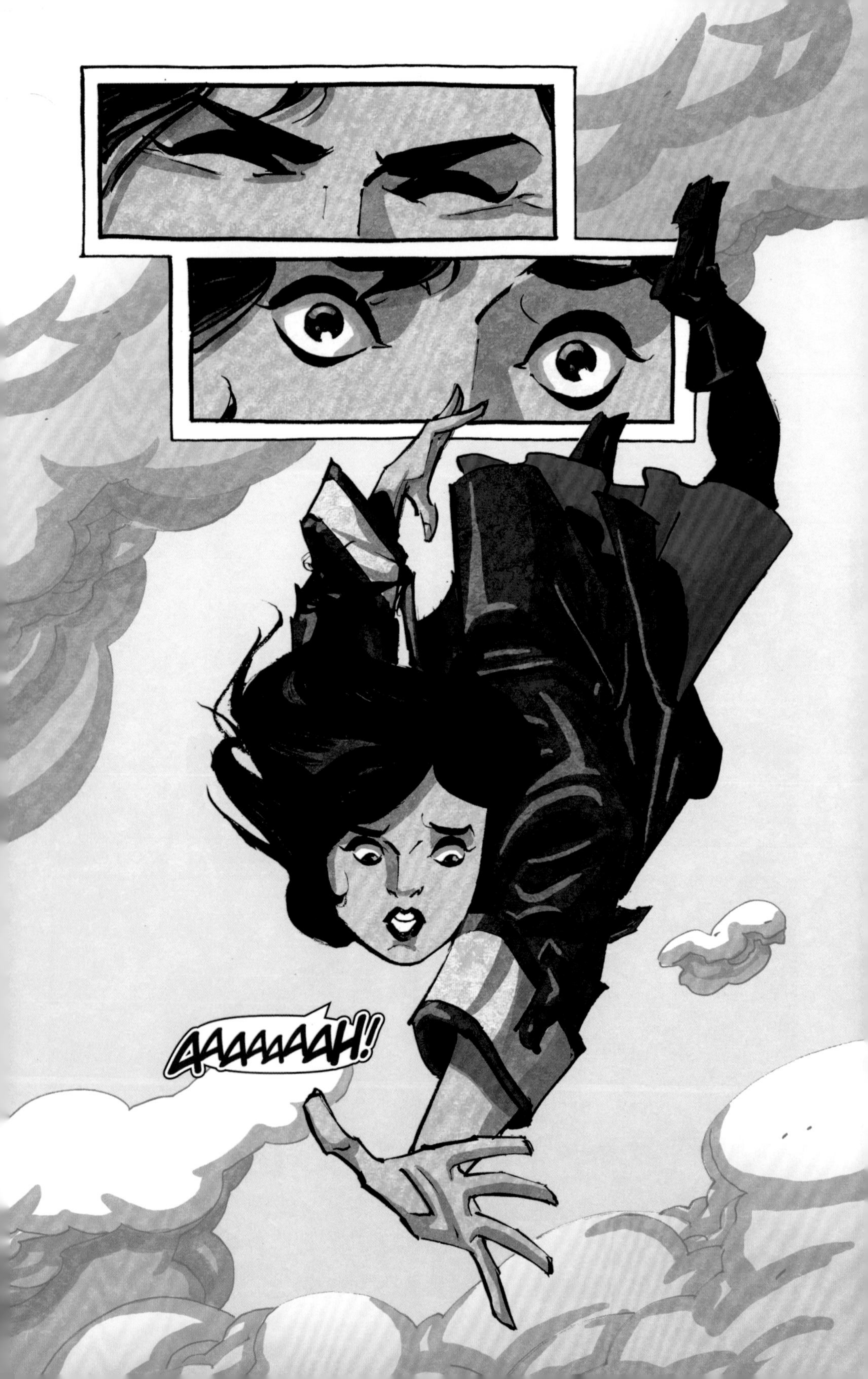
AAAAAAAH!

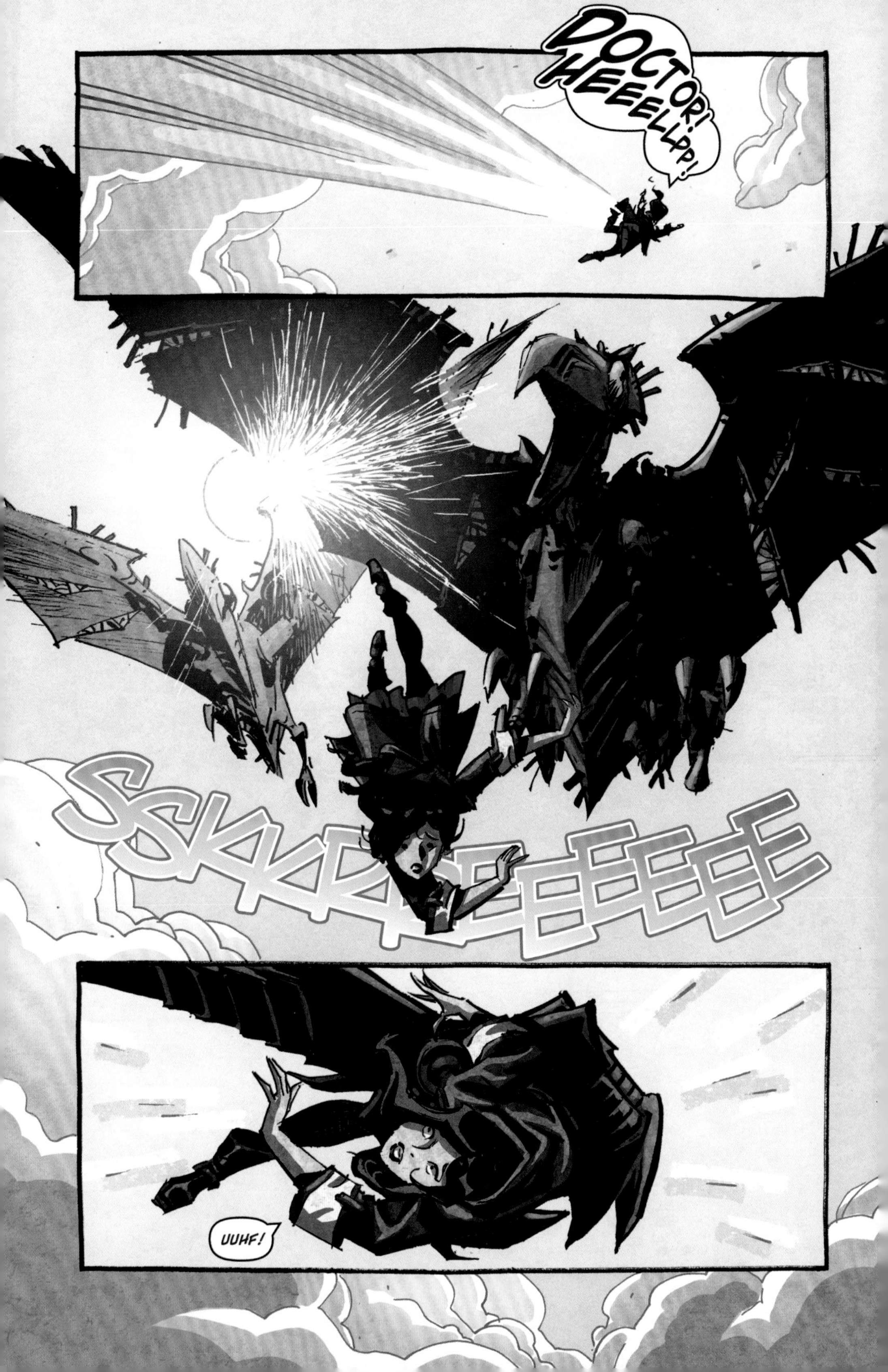
DOCTOR! HEEELLPP!
SSKKREEEEEEEEE
UUHF!

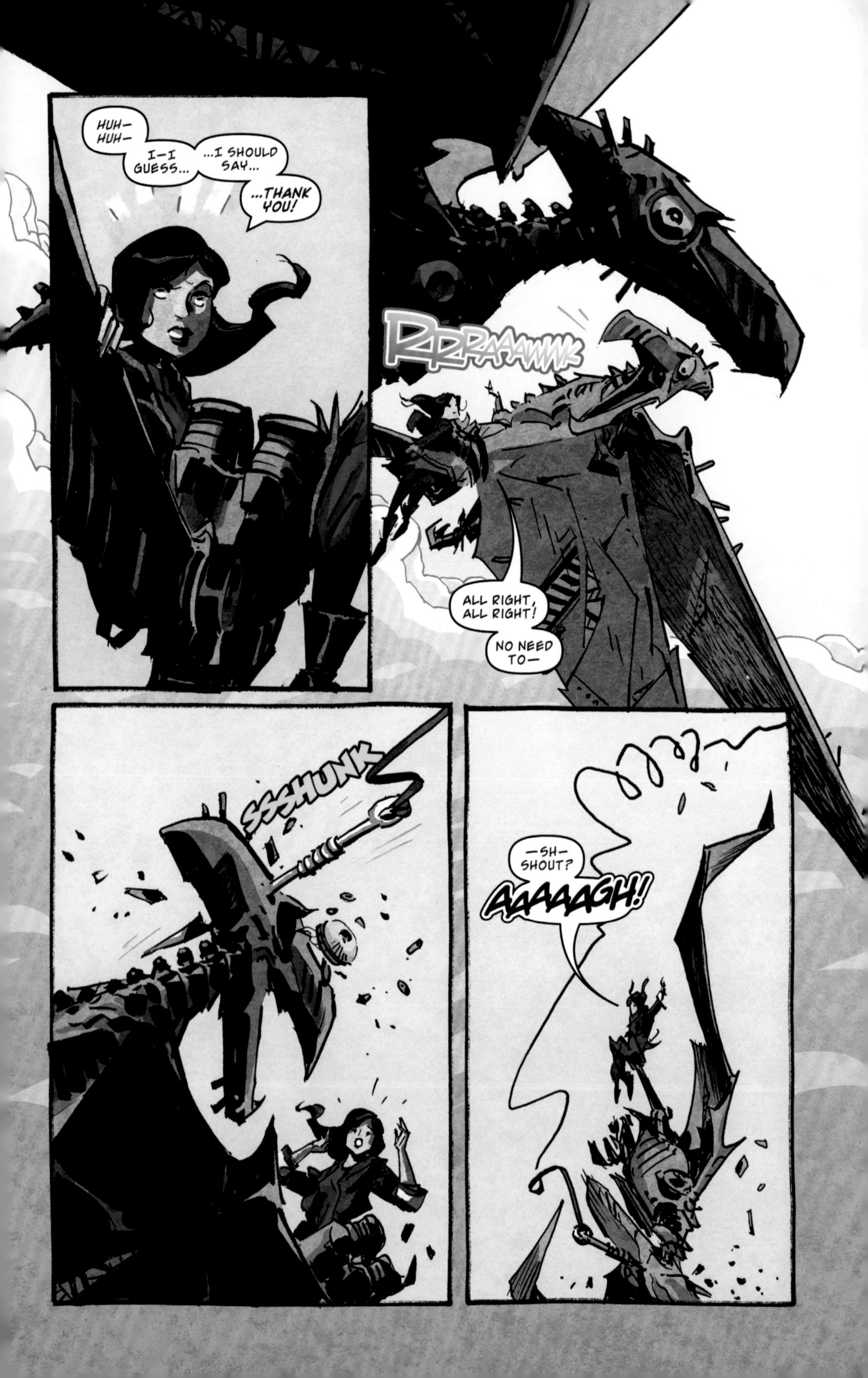

HUH— HUH—
I—I GUESS...
...I SHOULD SAY...
...THANK YOU!
RRRAAAWWK
ALL RIGHT, ALL RIGHT!
NO NEED TO—
SSSHUNK
—SH-SHOUT?
AAAAAGH!

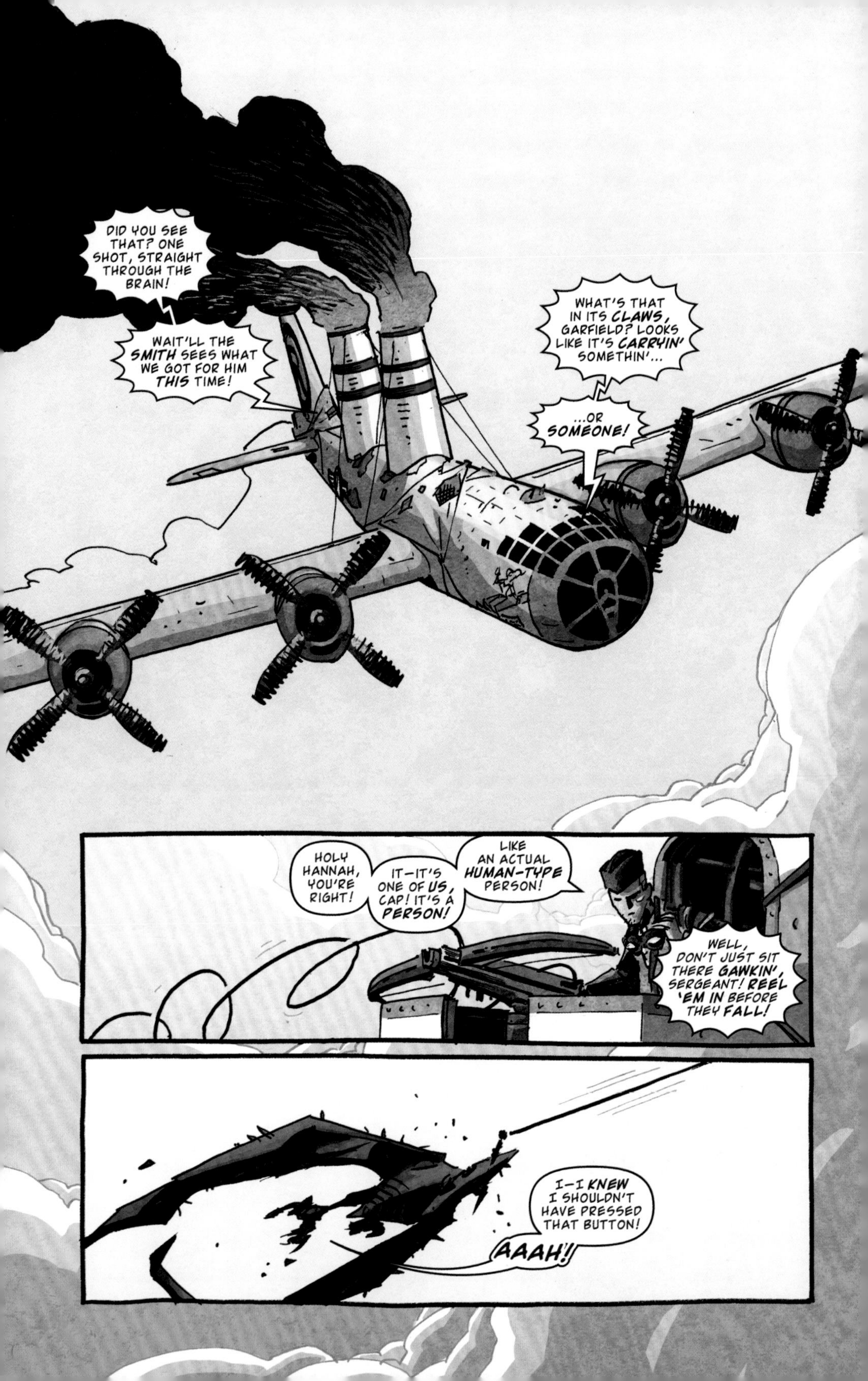
DID YOU SEE THAT? ONE SHOT, STRAIGHT THROUGH THE BRAIN!
WAIT'LL THE SMITH SEES WHAT WE GOT FOR HIM THIS TIME!
WHAT'S THAT IN ITS CLAWS, GARFIELD? LOOKS LIKE IT'S CARRYIN' SOMETHIN'...
...OR SOMEONE!
HOLY HANNAH, YOU'RE RIGHT!
IT—IT'S ONE OF US, CAP! IT'S A PERSON!
LIKE AN ACTUAL HUMAN-TYPE PERSON!
WELL, DON'T JUST SIT THERE GAWKIN', SERGEANT! REEL 'EM IN BEFORE THEY FALL!
I—I KNEW I SHOULDN'T HAVE PRESSED THAT BUTTON!
AAAH!

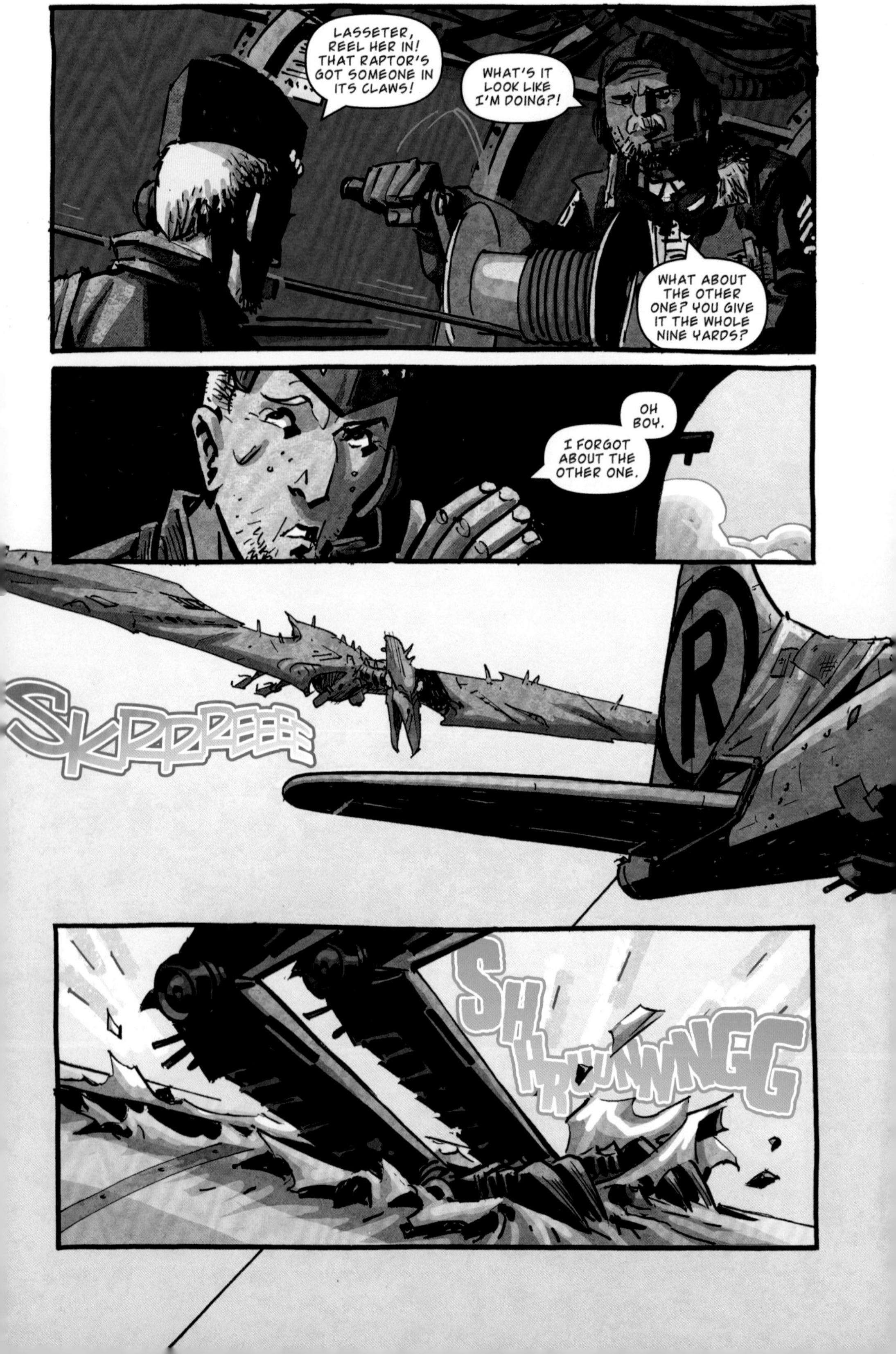
LASSETER, REEL HER IN! THAT RAPTOR'S GOT SOMEONE IN ITS CLAWS!
WHAT'S IT LOOK LIKE I'M DOING?!
WHAT ABOUT THE OTHER ONE? YOU GIVE IT THE WHOLE NINE YARDS?
OH BOY.
I FORGOT ABOUT THE OTHER ONE.
SKRRREEEEE
SHHRUUNNNGG

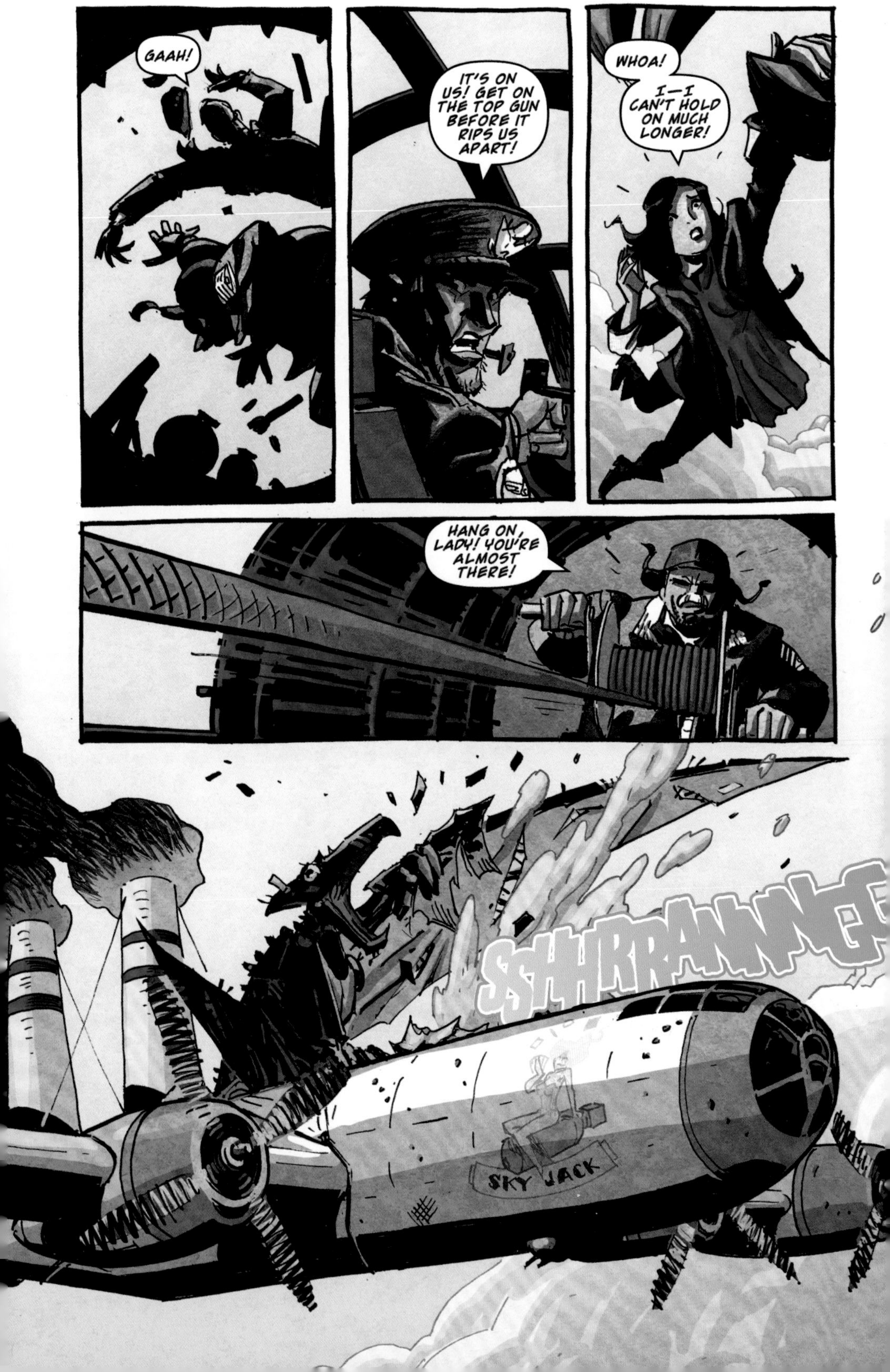
GAAH!
IT'S ON US! GET ON THE TOP GUN BEFORE IT RIPS US APART!
WHOA!
I—I CAN'T HOLD ON MUCH LONGER!
HANG ON, LADY! YOU'RE ALMOST THERE!
SSHHRRANNNGG
SKY JACK

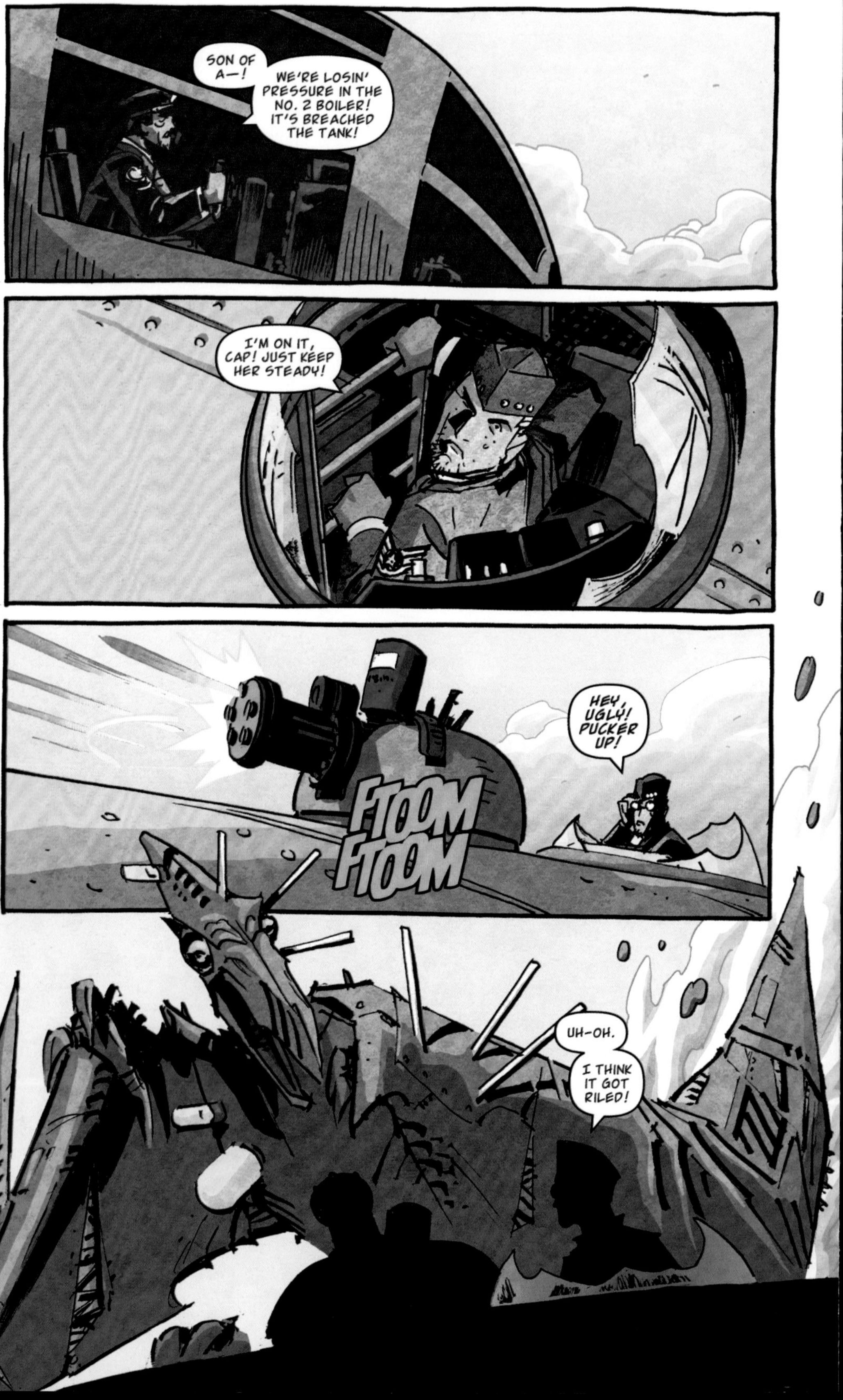
SON OF A—!
WE'RE LOSIN' PRESSURE IN THE NO. 2 BOILER! IT'S BREACHED THE TANK!
I'M ON IT, CAP! JUST KEEP HER STEADY!
HEY, UGLY! PUCKER UP!
FTOOM FTOOM
UH-OH.
I THINK IT GOT RILED!

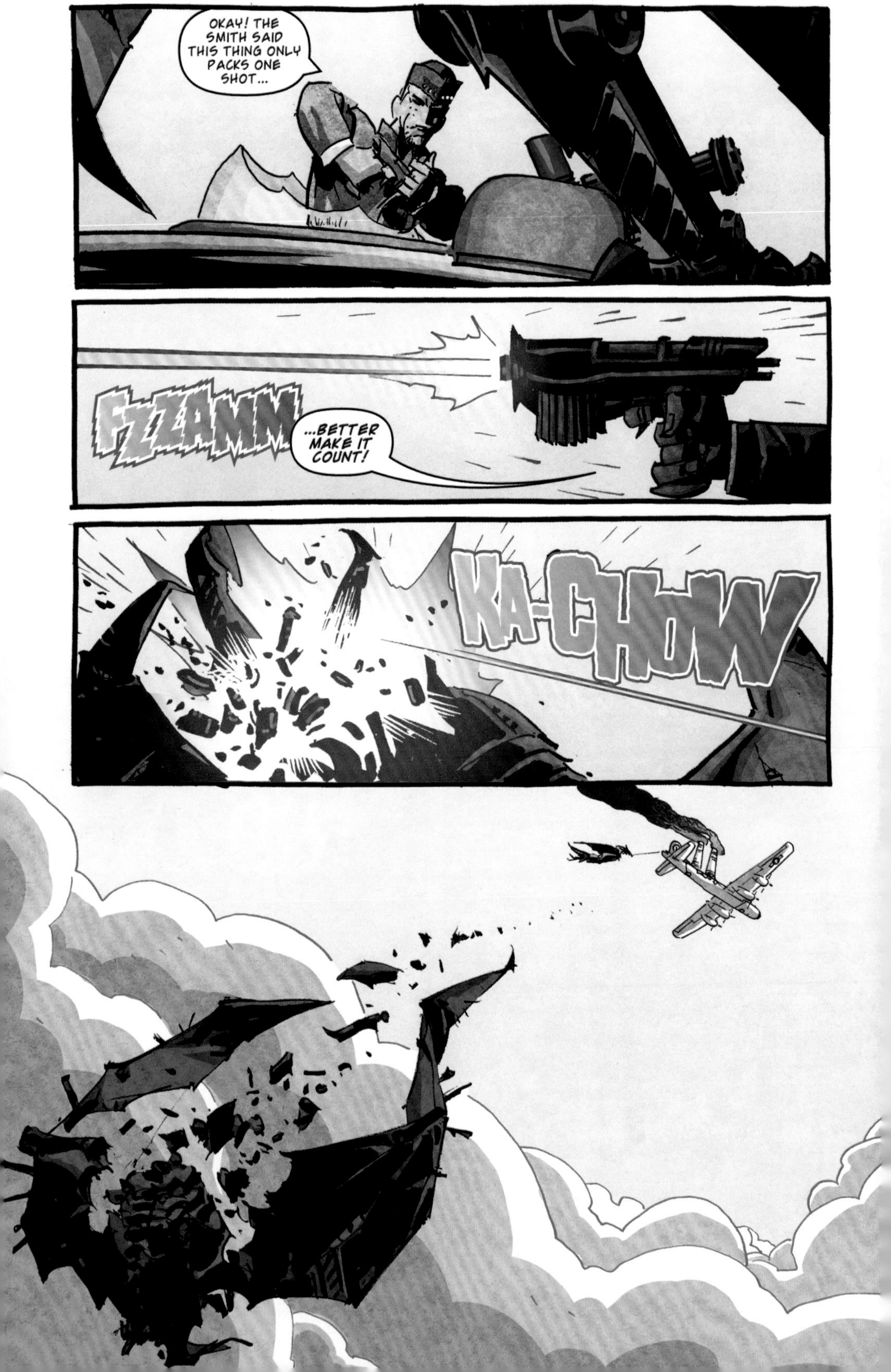
OKAY! THE SMITH SAID THIS THING ONLY PACKS ONE SHOT...
FZZAMM
...BETTER MAKE IT COUNT!
KA-CHOW

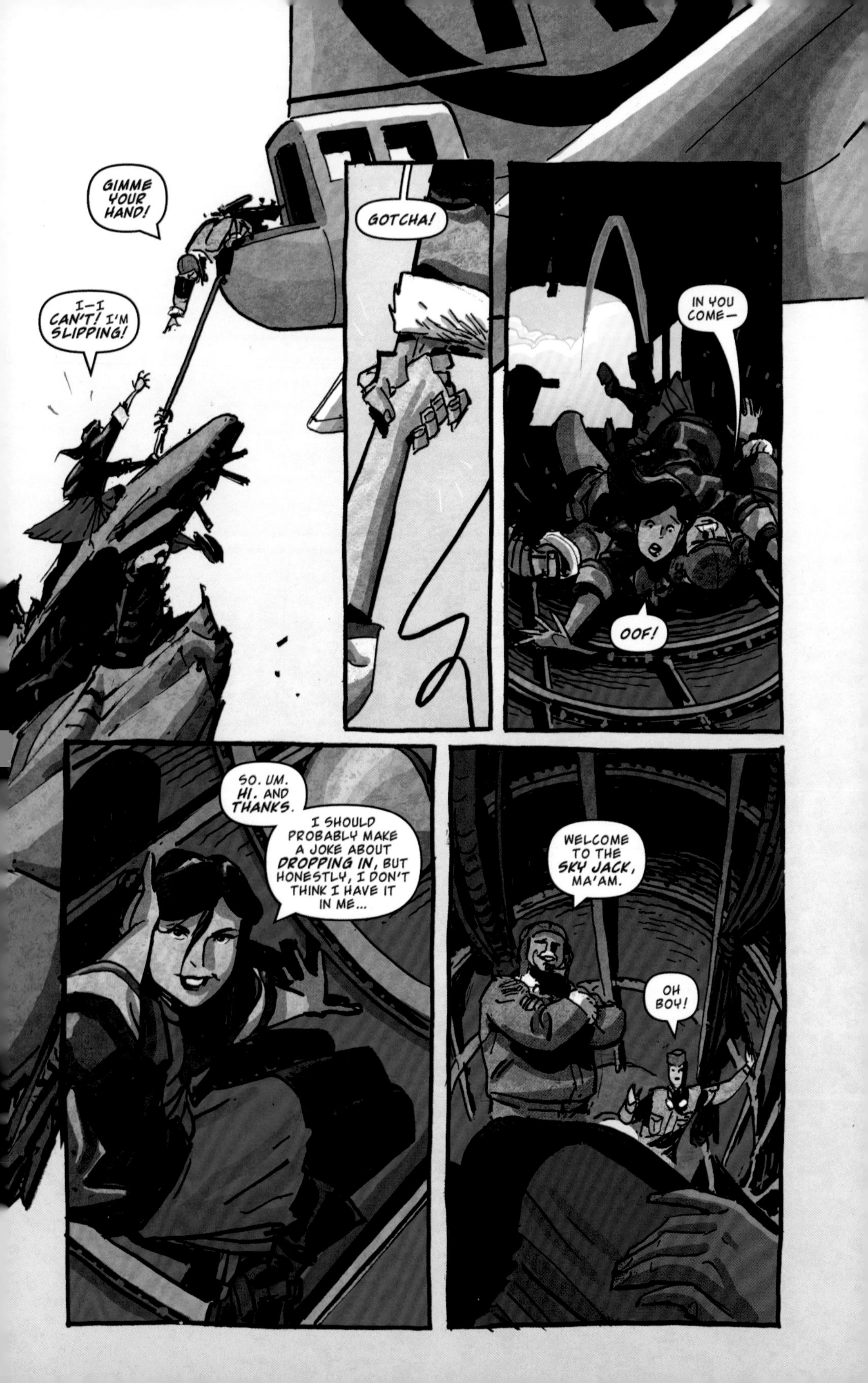
GIMME YOUR HAND!
I—I CAN'T! I'M SLIPPING!
GOTCHA!
IN YOU COME—
OOF!
SO. UM. HI. AND THANKS.
I SHOULD PROBABLY MAKE A JOKE ABOUT DROPPING IN, BUT HONESTLY, I DON'T THINK I HAVE IT IN ME...
WELCOME TO THE SKY JACK, MA'AM.
OH BOY!

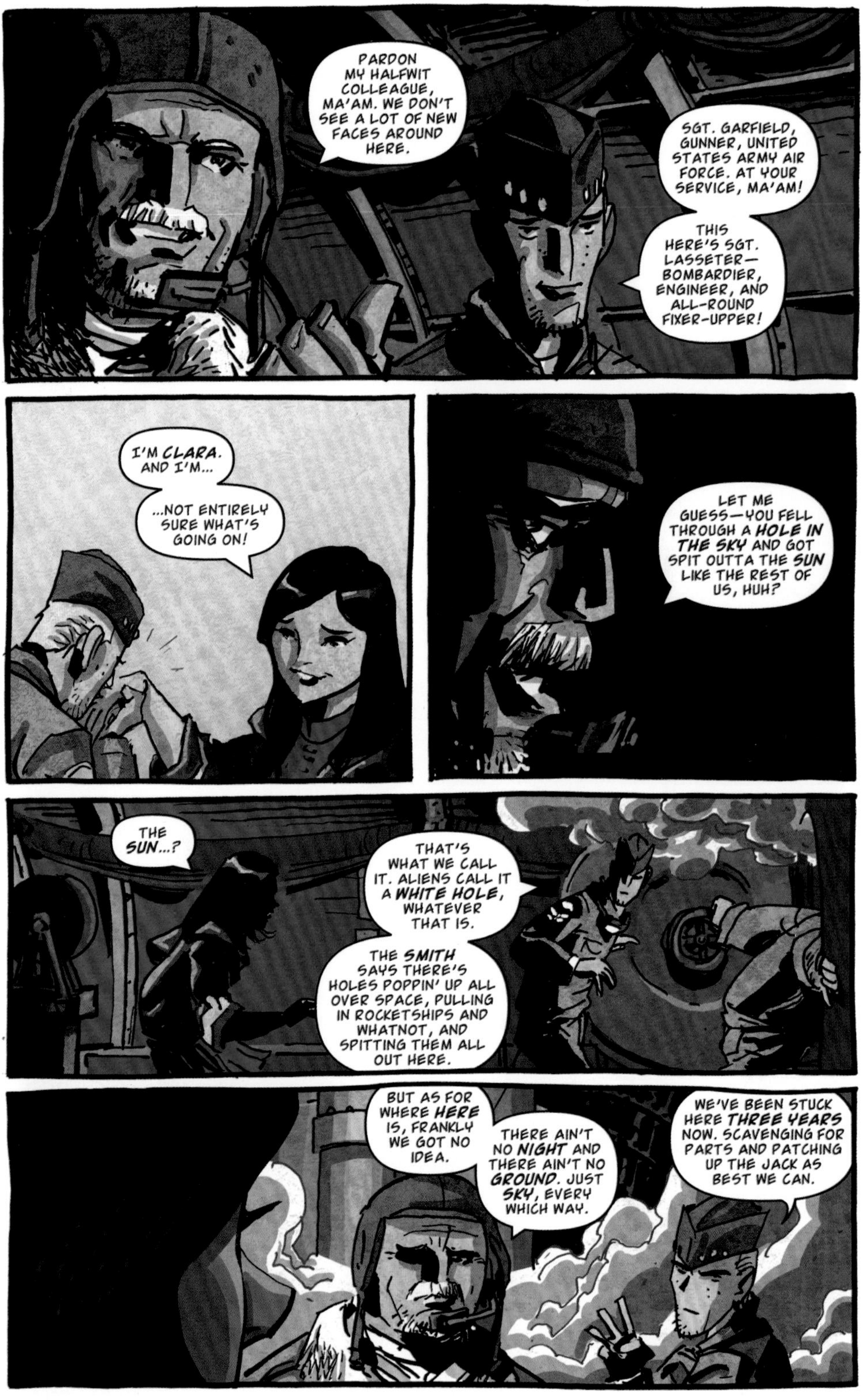
PARDON MY HALFWIT COLLEAGUE, MA'AM. WE DON'T SEE A LOT OF NEW FACES AROUND HERE.
SGT. GARFIELD, GUNNER, UNITED STATES ARMY AIR FORCE. AT YOUR SERVICE, MA'AM!
THIS HERE'S SGT. LASSETER— BOMBARDIER, ENGINEER, AND ALL-ROUND FIXER-UPPER!
I'M CLARA. AND I'M...
...NOT ENTIRELY SURE WHAT'S GOING ON!
LET ME GUESS—YOU FELL THROUGH A HOLE IN THE SKY AND GOT SPIT OUTTA THE SUN LIKE THE REST OF US, HUH?
THE SUN...?
THAT'S WHAT WE CALL IT. ALIENS CALL IT A WHITE HOLE, WHATEVER THAT IS.
THE SMITH SAYS THERE'S HOLES POPPIN' UP ALL OVER SPACE, PULLING IN ROCKETSHIPS AND WHATNOT, AND SPITTING THEM ALL OUT HERE.
BUT AS FOR WHERE HERE IS, FRANKLY WE GOT NO IDEA.
THERE AIN'T NO NIGHT AND THERE AIN'T NO GROUND. JUST SKY, EVERY WHICH WAY.
WE'VE BEEN STUCK HERE THREE YEARS NOW. SCAVENGING FOR PARTS AND PATCHING UP THE JACK AS BEST WE CAN.

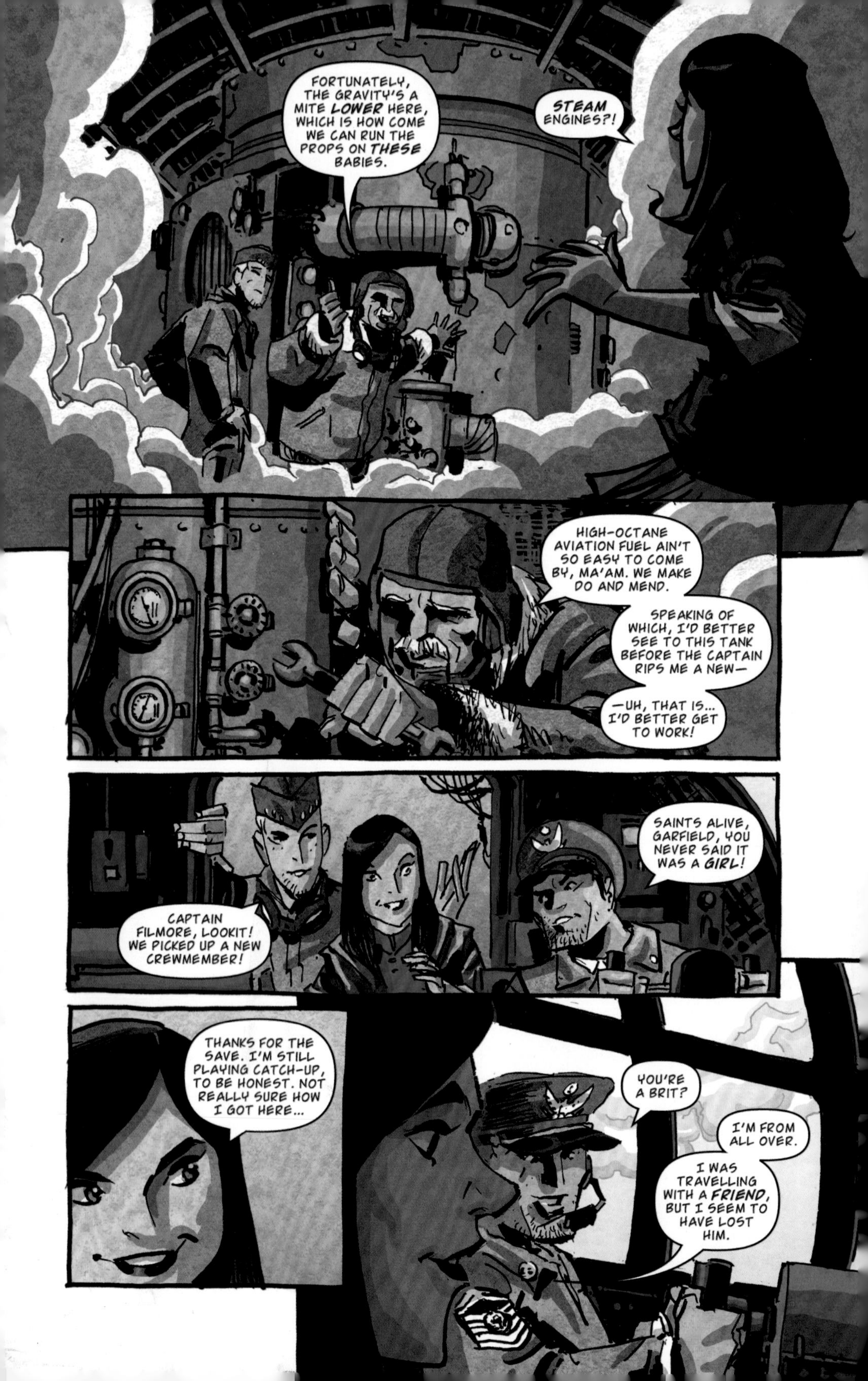
FORTUNATELY, THE GRAVITY'S A MITE LOWER HERE, WHICH IS HOW COME WE CAN RUN THE PROPS ON THESE BABIES.
STEAM ENGINES?!
HIGH-OCTANE AVIATION FUEL AIN'T SO EASY TO COME BY, MA'AM. WE MAKE DO AND MEND.
SPEAKING OF WHICH, I'D BETTER SEE TO THIS TANK BEFORE THE CAPTAIN RIPS ME A NEW—
—UH, THAT IS... I'D BETTER GET TO WORK!
CAPTAIN FILMORE, LOOKIT! WE PICKED UP A NEW CREWMEMBER!
SAINTS ALIVE, GARFIELD, YOU NEVER SAID IT WAS A GIRL!
THANKS FOR THE SAVE. I'M STILL PLAYING CATCH-UP, TO BE HONEST. NOT REALLY SURE HOW I GOT HERE...
YOU'RE A BRIT?
I'M FROM ALL OVER.
I WAS TRAVELLING WITH A FRIEND, BUT I SEEM TO HAVE LOST HIM.

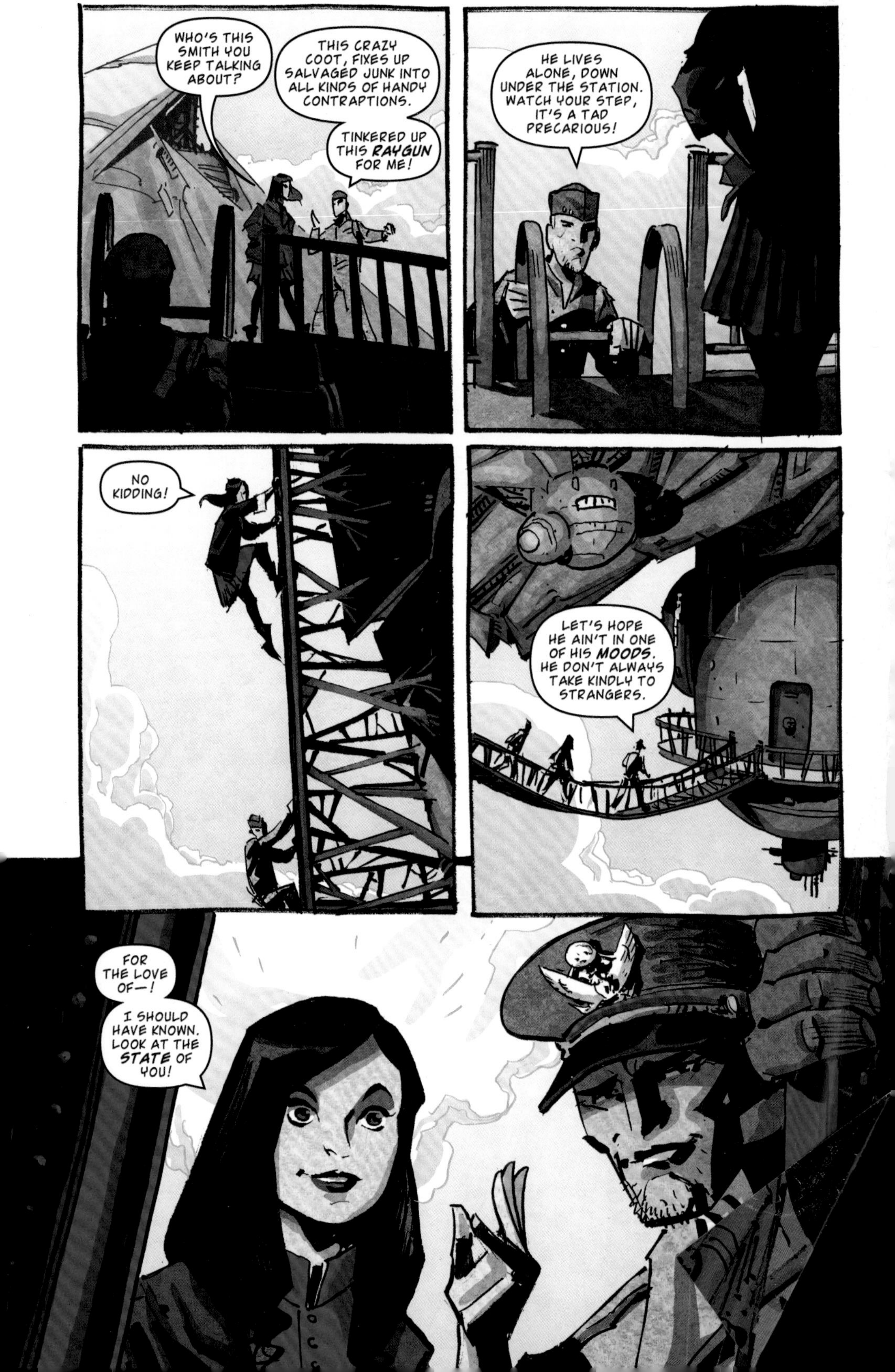
WHO'S THIS SMITH YOU KEEP TALKING ABOUT?
THIS CRAZY COOT, FIXES UP SALVAGED JUNK INTO ALL KINDS OF HANDY CONTRAPTIONS.
TINKERED UP THIS RAYGUN FOR ME!
HE LIVES ALONE, DOWN UNDER THE STATION. WATCH YOUR STEP, IT'S A TAD PRECARIOUS!
NO KIDDING!
LET'S HOPE HE AIN'T IN ONE OF HIS MOODS. HE DON'T ALWAYS TAKE KINDLY TO STRANGERS.
FOR THE LOVE OF—!
I SHOULD HAVE KNOWN. LOOK AT THE STATE OF YOU!

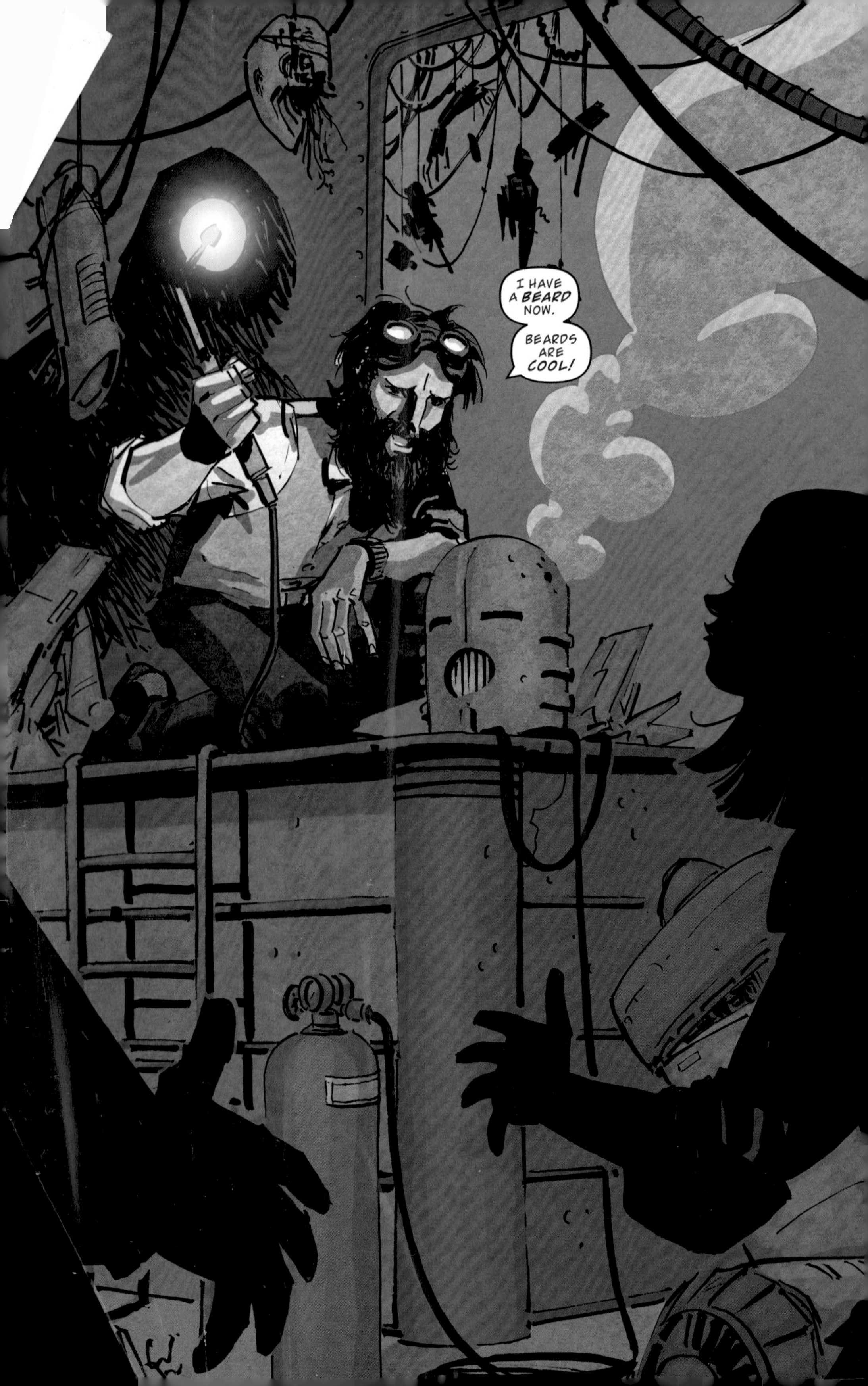
I HAVE A BEARD NOW.
BEARDS ARE COOL!

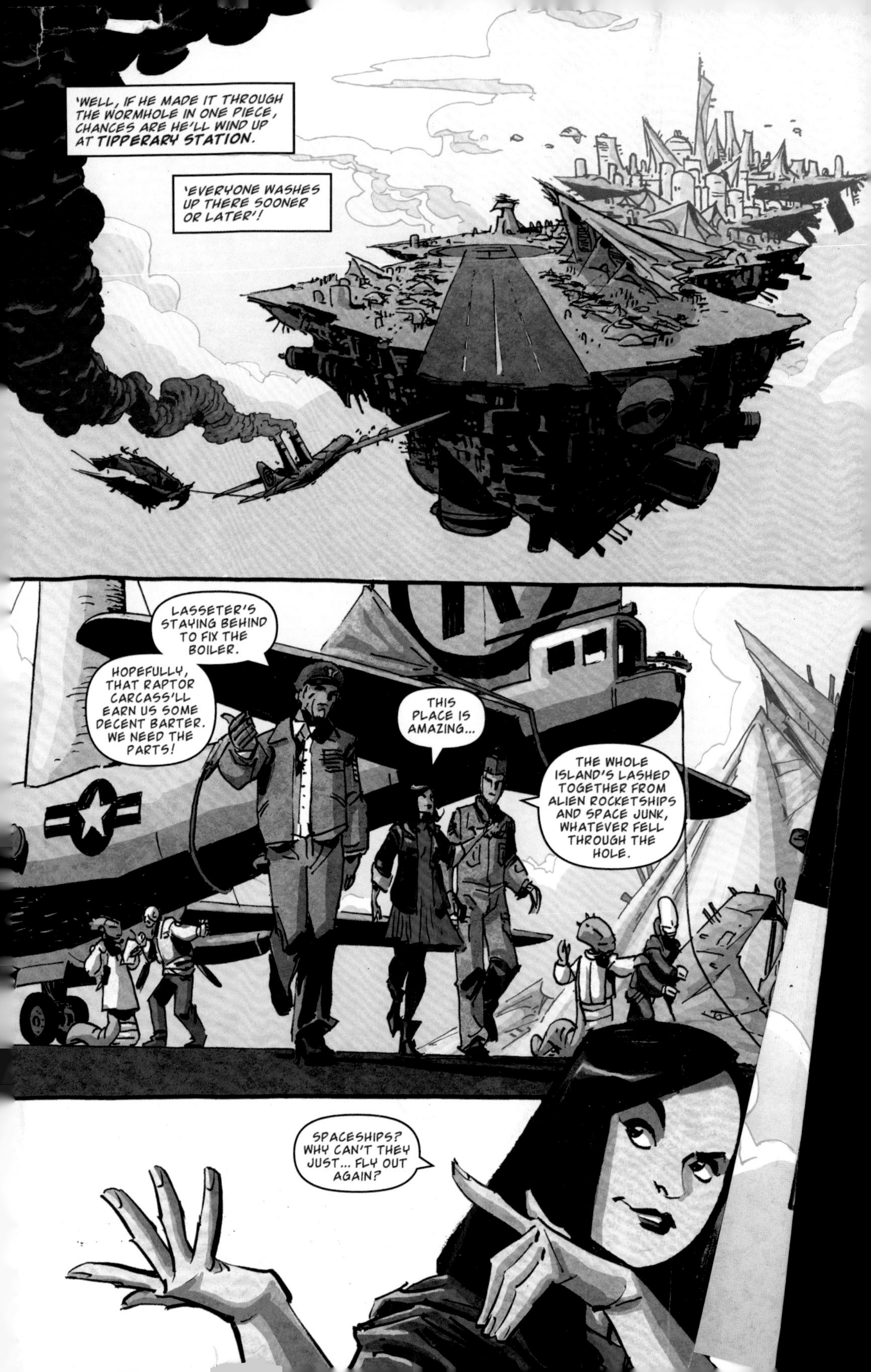
'WELL, IF HE MADE IT THROUGH THE WORMHOLE IN ONE PIECE, CHANCES ARE HE'LL WIND UP AT TIPPERARY STATION.
'EVERYONE WASHES UP THERE SOONER OR LATER'!
LASSETER'S STAYING BEHIND TO FIX THE BOILER.
HOPEFULLY, THAT RAPTOR CARCASS'LL EARN US SOME DECENT BARTER. WE NEED THE PARTS!
THIS PLACE IS AMAZING...
THE WHOLE ISLAND'S LASHED TOGETHER FROM ALIEN ROCKETSHIPS AND SPACE JUNK, WHATEVER FELL THROUGH THE HOLE.
SPACESHIPS? WHY CAN'T THEY JUST... FLY OUT AGAIN?

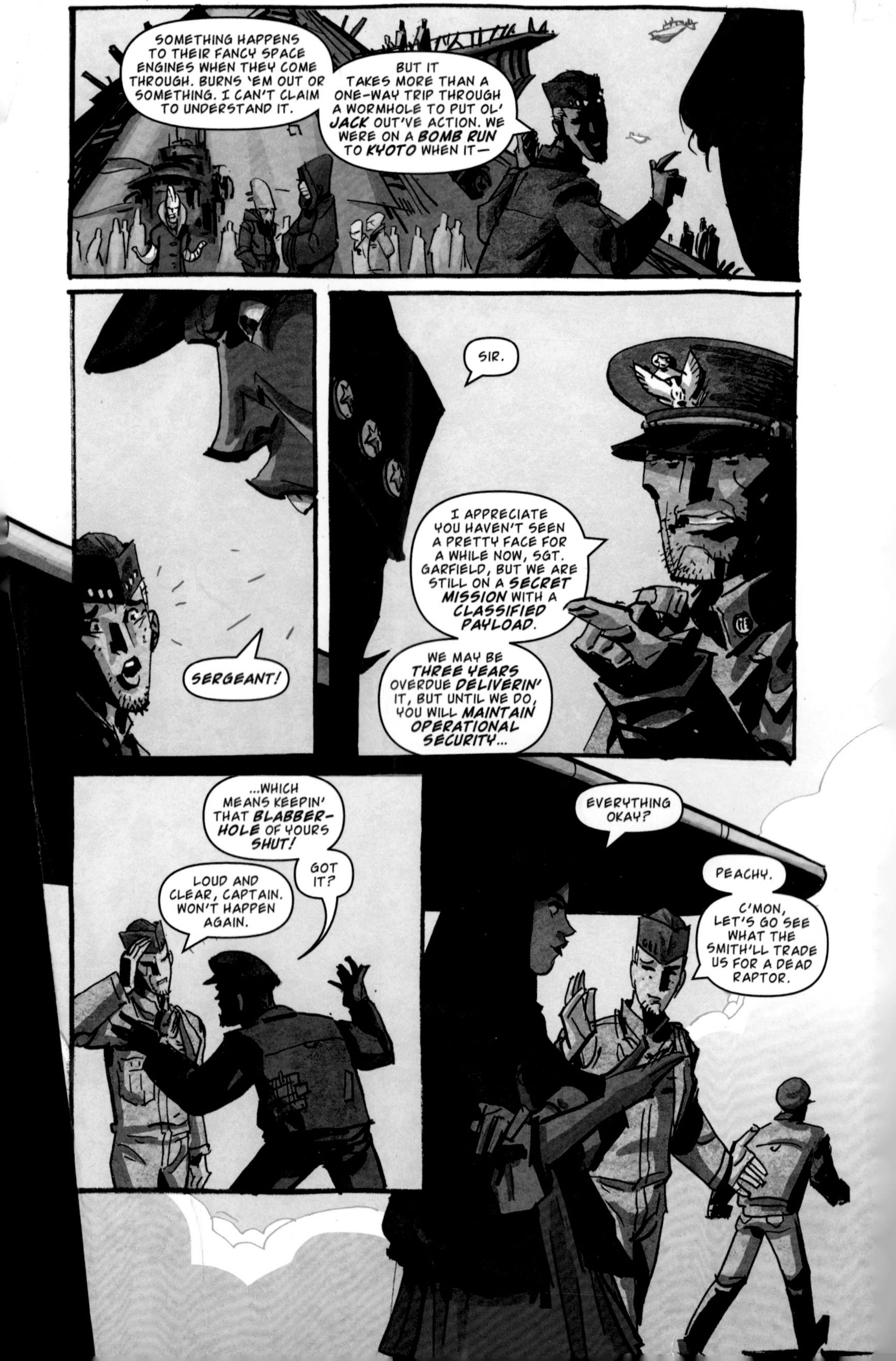
SOMETHING HAPPENS TO THEIR FANCY SPACE ENGINES WHEN THEY COME THROUGH. BURNS 'EM OUT OR SOMETHING. I CAN'T CLAIM TO UNDERSTAND IT.
BUT IT TAKES MORE THAN A ONE-WAY TRIP THROUGH A WORMHOLE TO PUT OL' JACK OUT'VE ACTION. WE WERE ON A BOMB RUN TO KYOTO WHEN IT—
SERGEANT!
SIR.
I APPRECIATE YOU HAVEN'T SEEN A PRETTY FACE FOR A WHILE NOW, SGT. GARFIELD, BUT WE ARE STILL ON A SECRET MISSION WITH A CLASSIFIED PAYLOAD.
WE MAY BE THREE YEARS OVERDUE DELIVERIN' IT, BUT UNTIL WE DO, YOU WILL MAINTAIN OPERATIONAL SECURITY...
...WHICH MEANS KEEPIN' THAT BLABBER-HOLE OF YOURS SHUT!
GOT IT?
LOUD AND CLEAR, CAPTAIN. WON'T HAPPEN AGAIN.
EVERYTHING OKAY?
PEACHY.
C'MON, LET'S GO SEE WHAT THE SMITH'LL TRADE US FOR A DEAD RAPTOR.

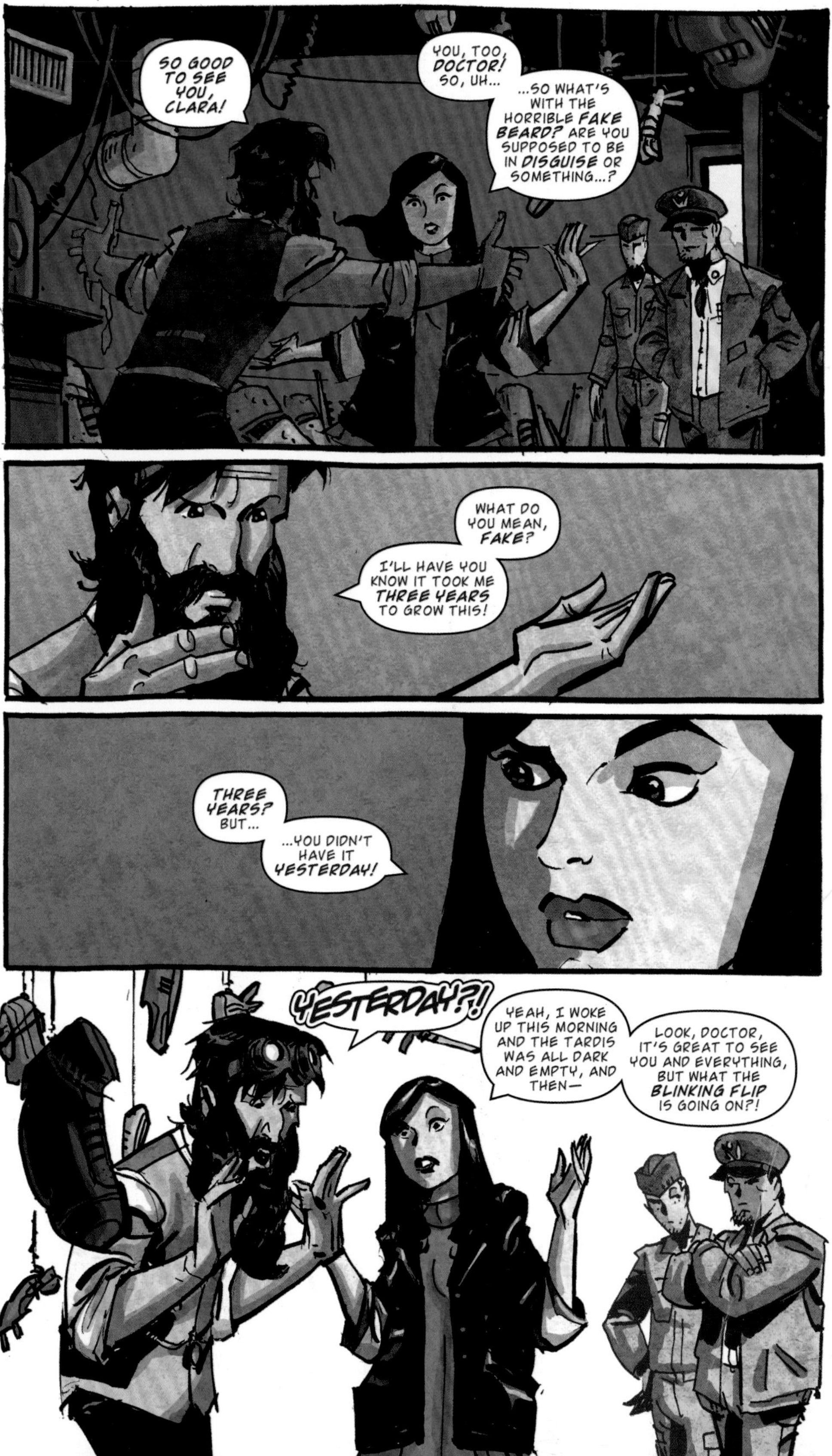
SO GOOD TO SEE YOU, CLARA!
YOU, TOO, DOCTOR! SO, UH...
...SO WHAT'S WITH THE HORRIBLE FAKE BEARD? ARE YOU SUPPOSED TO BE IN DISGUISE OR SOMETHING...?
WHAT DO YOU MEAN, FAKE?
I'LL HAVE YOU KNOW IT TOOK ME THREE YEARS TO GROW THIS!
THREE YEARS? BUT...
...YOU DIDN'T HAVE IT YESTERDAY!
YESTERDAY?!
YEAH, I WOKE UP THIS MORNING AND THE TARDIS WAS ALL DARK AND EMPTY, AND THEN—
LOOK, DOCTOR, IT'S GREAT TO SEE YOU AND EVERYTHING, BUT WHAT THE BLINKING FLIP IS GOING ON?!

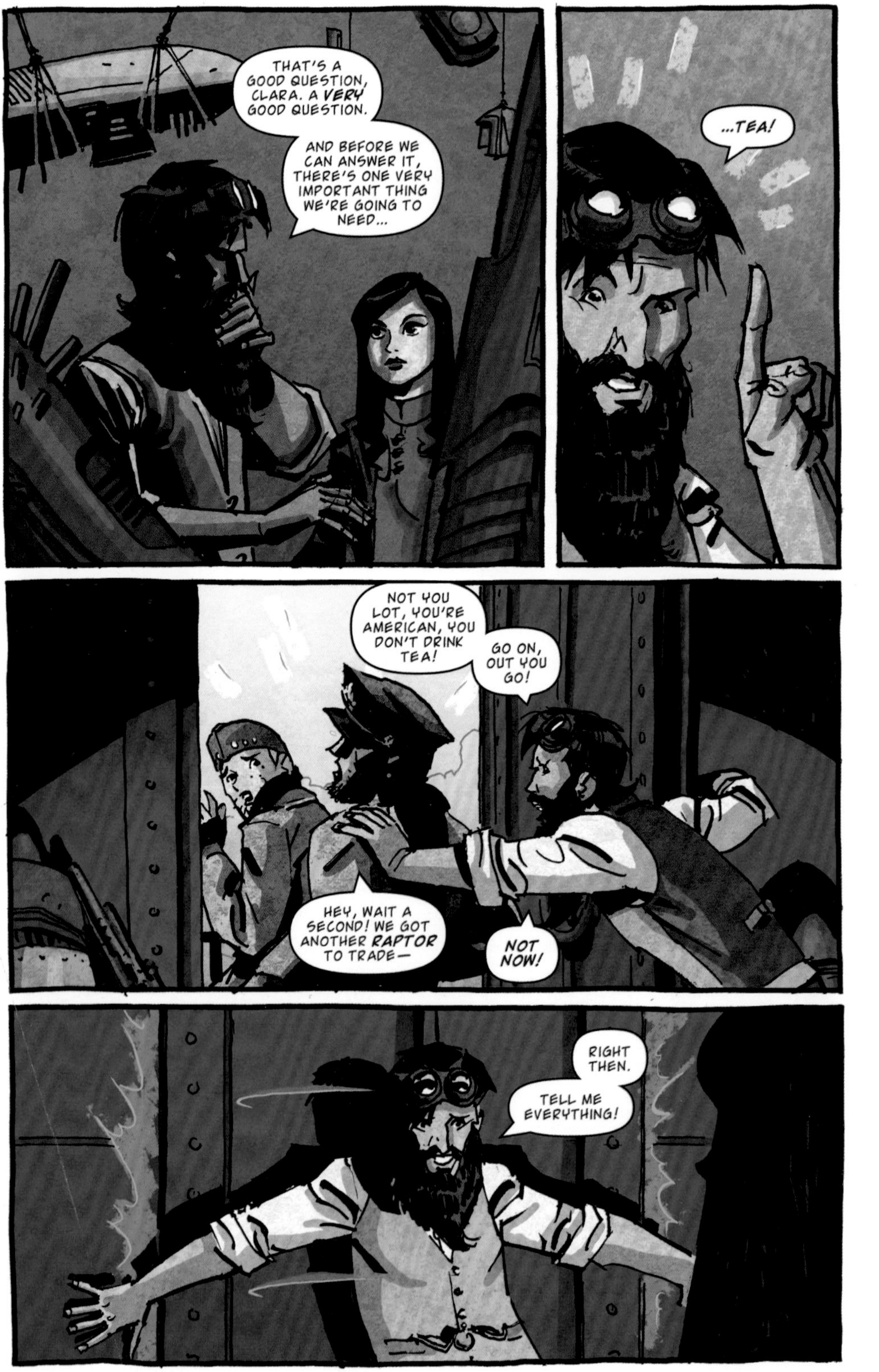
THAT'S A GOOD QUESTION, CLARA. A VERY GOOD QUESTION.
AND BEFORE WE CAN ANSWER IT, THERE'S ONE VERY IMPORTANT THING WE'RE GOING TO NEED...
...TEA!
NOT YOU LOT, YOU'RE AMERICAN, YOU DON'T DRINK TEA!
GO ON, OUT YOU GO!
HEY, WAIT A SECOND! WE GOT ANOTHER RAPTOR TO TRADE—
NOT NOW!
RIGHT THEN.
TELL ME EVERYTHING!

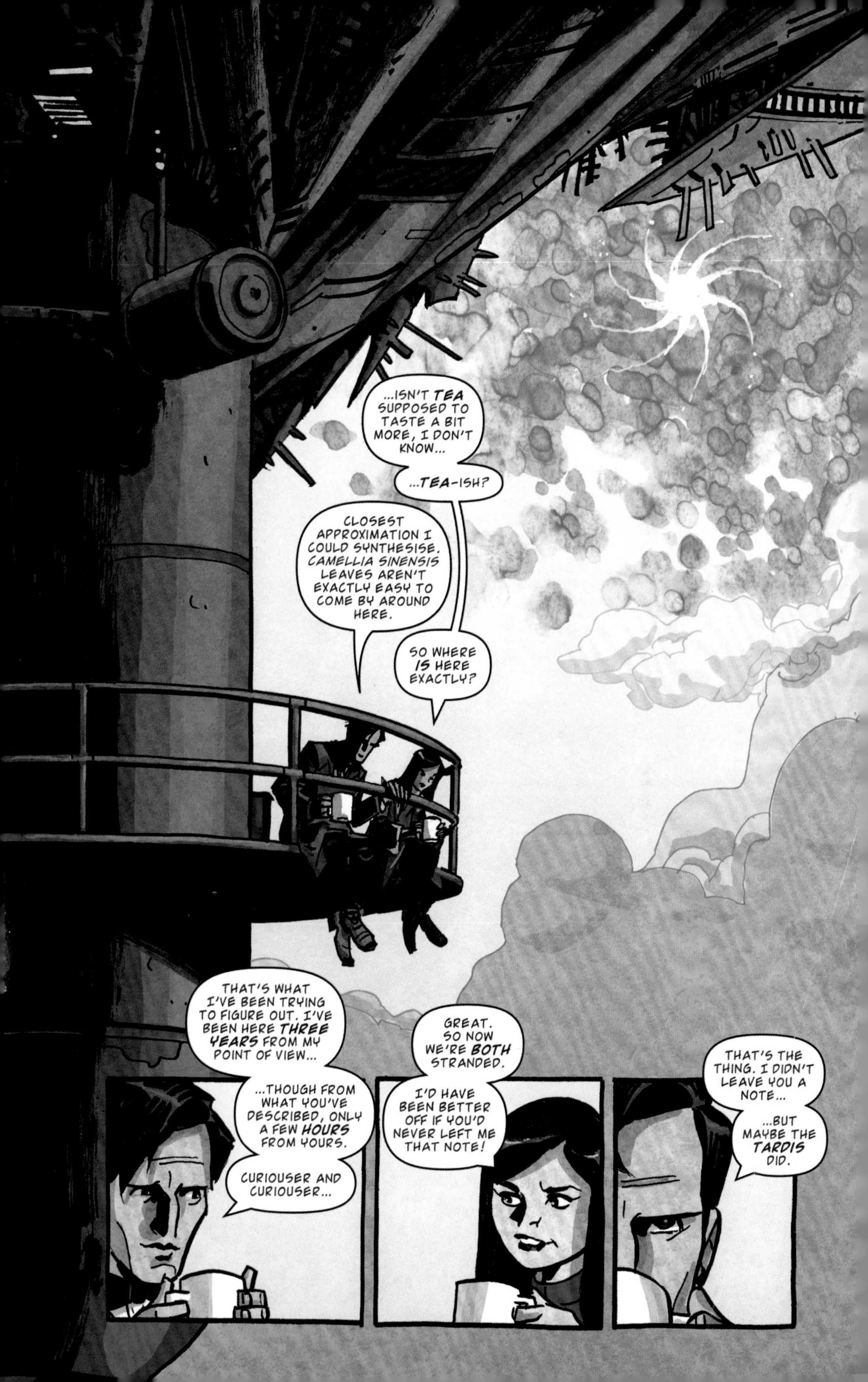
...ISN'T TEA SUPPOSED TO TASTE A BIT MORE, I DON'T KNOW...
...TEA-ISH?
CLOSEST APPROXIMATION I COULD SYNTHESISE. CAMELLIA SINENSIS LEAVES AREN'T EXACTLY EASY TO COME BY AROUND HERE.
SO WHERE IS HERE EXACTLY?
THAT'S WHAT I'VE BEEN TRYING TO FIGURE OUT. I'VE BEEN HERE THREE YEARS FROM MY POINT OF VIEW...
...THOUGH FROM WHAT YOU'VE DESCRIBED, ONLY A FEW HOURS FROM YOURS.
CURIOUSER AND CURIOUSER...
GREAT. SO NOW WE'RE BOTH STRANDED.
I'D HAVE BEEN BETTER OFF IF YOU'D NEVER LEFT ME THAT NOTE!
THAT'S THE THING. I DIDN'T LEAVE YOU A NOTE...
...BUT MAYBE THE TARDIS DID.

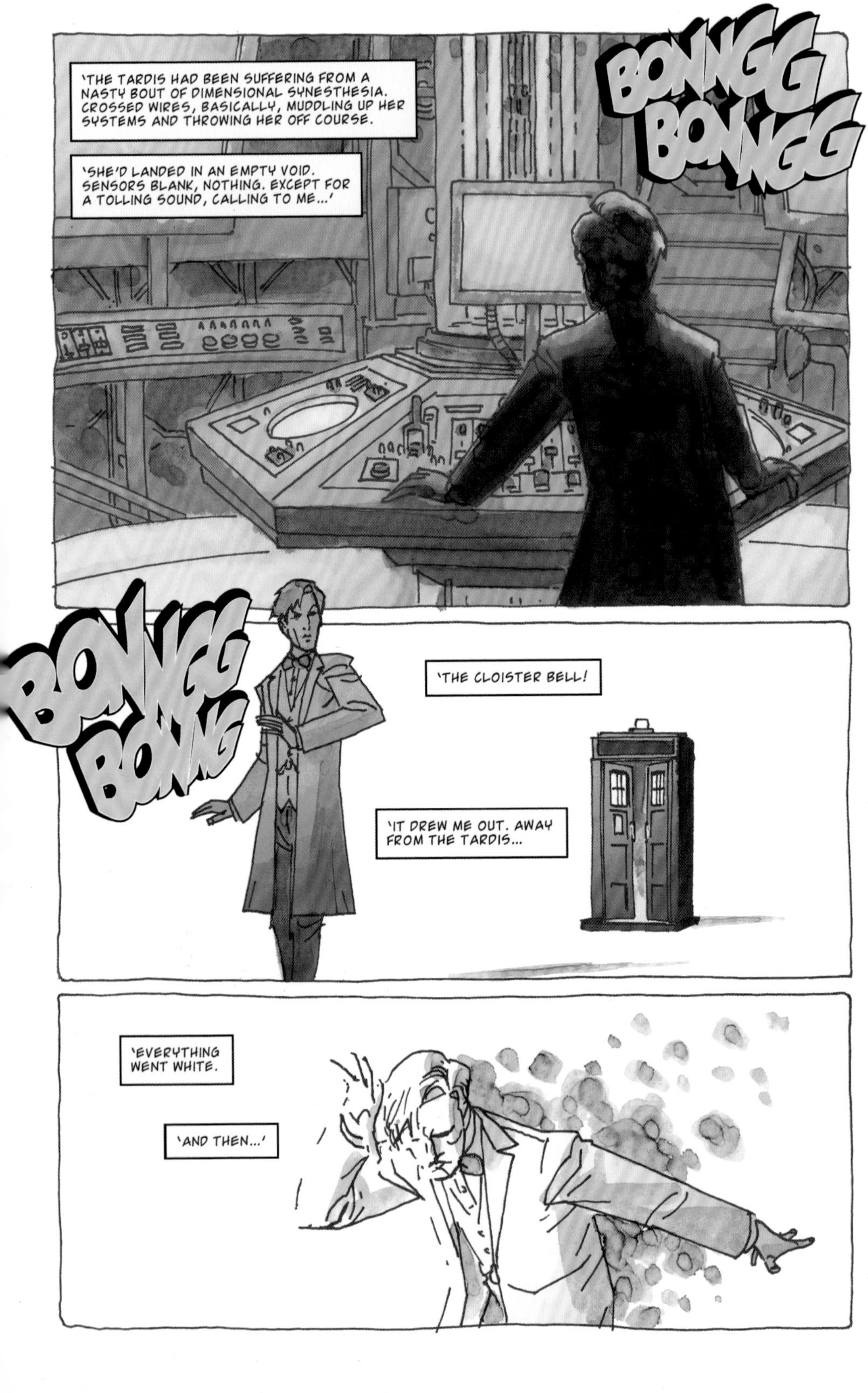
'THE TARDIS HAD BEEN SUFFERING FROM A NASTY BOUT OF DIMENSIONAL SYNESTHESIA. CROSSED WIRES, BASICALLY, MUDDLING UP HER SYSTEMS AND THROWING HER OFF COURSE.
'SHE'D LANDED IN AN EMPTY VOID. SENSORS BLANK, NOTHING. EXCEPT FOR A TOLLING SOUND, CALLING TO ME...'
BONNGG BONNGG
BONNGG BONNG
'THE CLOISTER BELL!
'IT DREW ME OUT. AWAY FROM THE TARDIS...
'EVERYTHING WENT WHITE.
'AND THEN...'

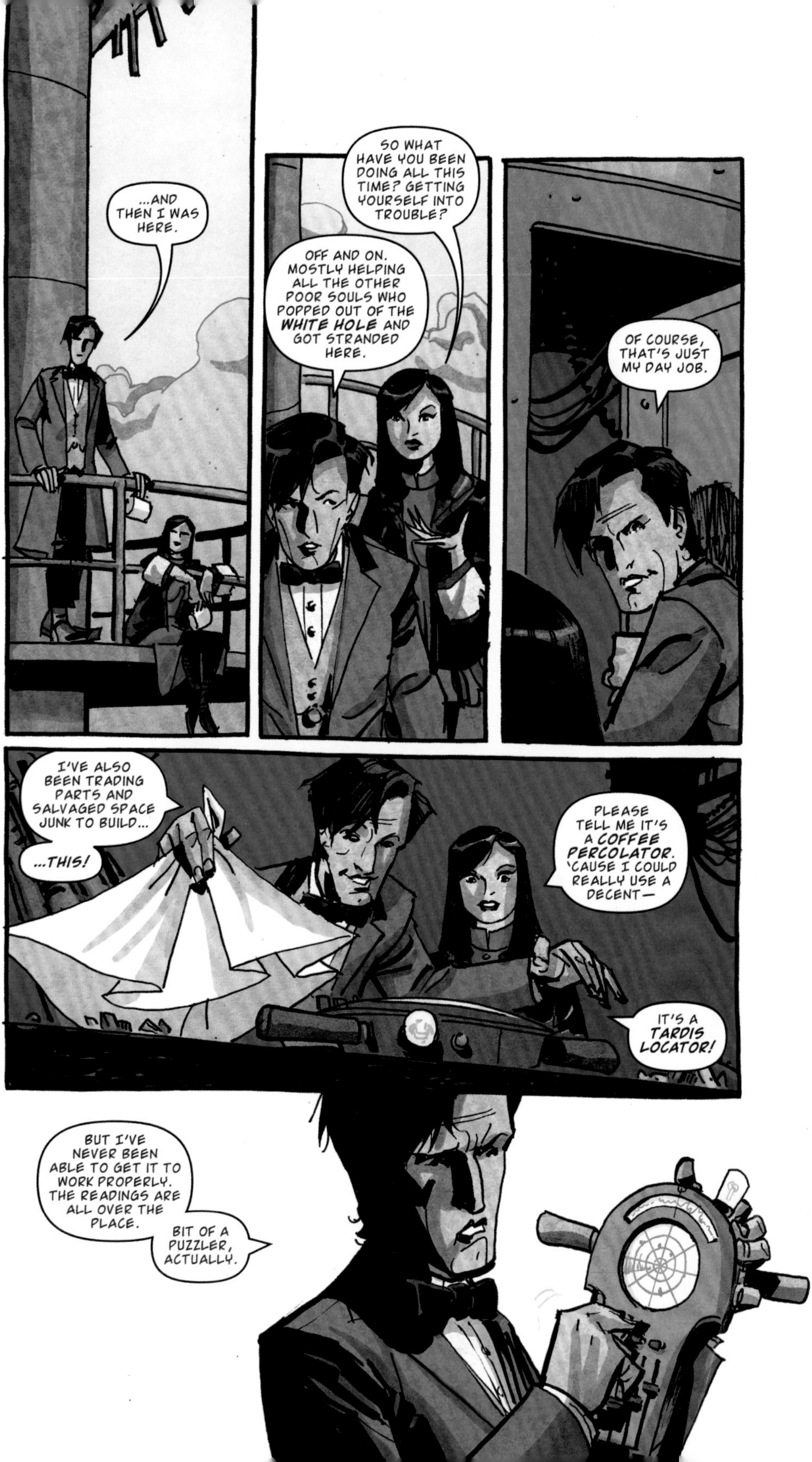
...AND THEN I WAS HERE.
SO WHAT HAVE YOU BEEN DOING ALL THIS TIME? GETTING YOURSELF INTO TROUBLE?
OFF AND ON. MOSTLY HELPING ALL THE OTHER POOR SOULS WHO POPPED OUT OF THE WHITE HOLE AND GOT STRANDED HERE.
OF COURSE, THAT'S JUST MY DAY JOB.
I'VE ALSO BEEN TRADING PARTS AND SALVAGED SPACE JUNK TO BUILD...
...THIS!
PLEASE TELL ME IT'S A COFFEE PERCOLATOR. 'CAUSE I COULD REALLY USE A DECENT—
IT'S A TARDIS LOCATOR!
BUT I'VE NEVER BEEN ABLE TO GET IT TO WORK PROPERLY. THE READINGS ARE ALL OVER THE PLACE.
BIT OF A PUZZLER, ACTUALLY.

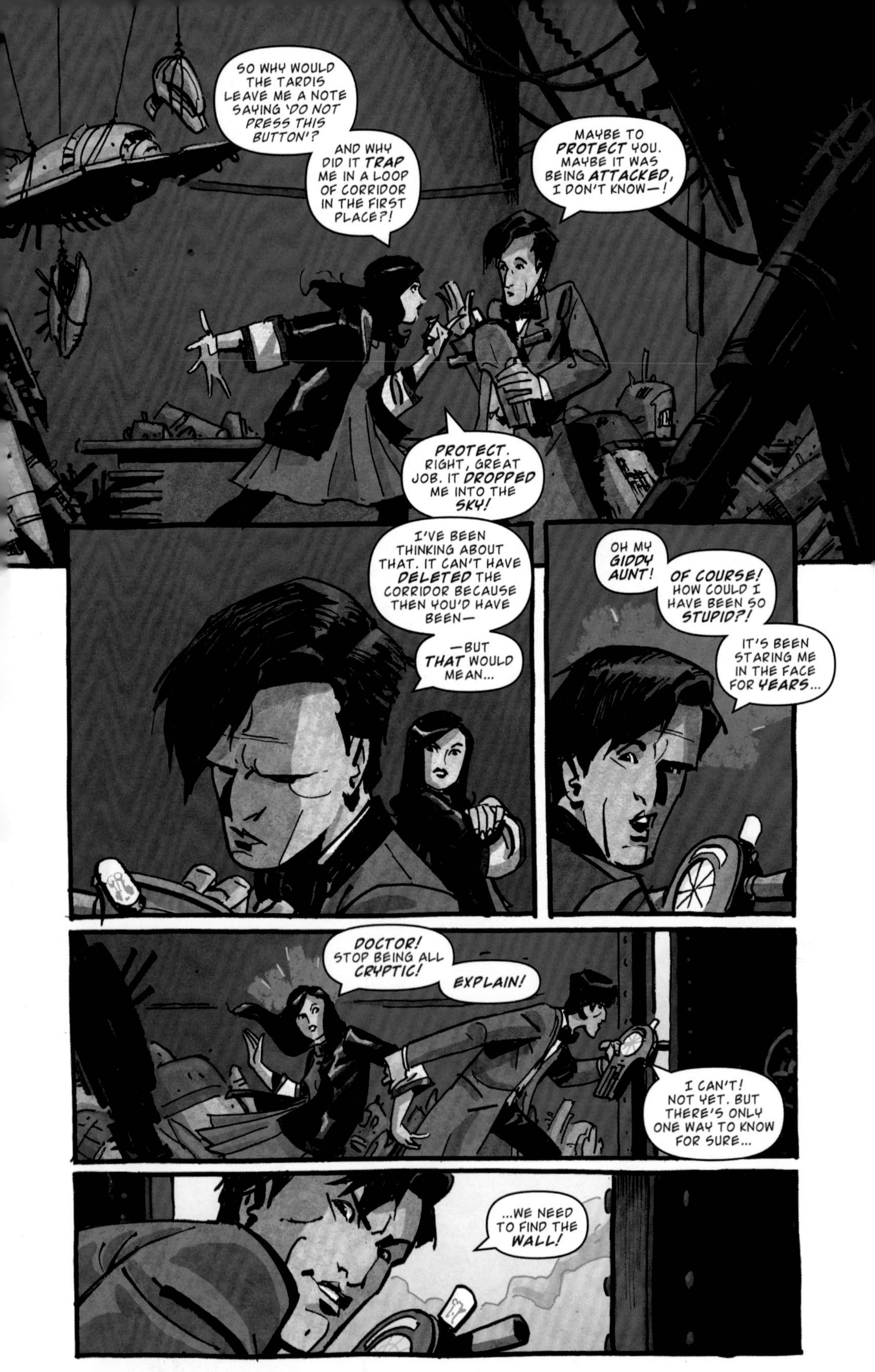
SO WHY WOULD THE TARDIS LEAVE ME A NOTE SAYING 'DO NOT PRESS THIS BUTTON'?
AND WHY DID IT TRAP ME IN A LOOP OF CORRIDOR IN THE FIRST PLACE?!
MAYBE TO PROTECT YOU. MAYBE IT WAS BEING ATTACKED, I DON'T KNOW—!
PROTECT. RIGHT, GREAT JOB. IT DROPPED ME INTO THE SKY!
I'VE BEEN THINKING ABOUT THAT. IT CAN'T HAVE DELETED THE CORRIDOR BECAUSE THEN YOU'D HAVE BEEN—
—BUT THAT WOULD MEAN...
OH MY GIDDY AUNT!
OF COURSE! HOW COULD I HAVE BEEN SO STUPID?!
IT'S BEEN STARING ME IN THE FACE FOR YEARS...
DOCTOR! STOP BEING ALL CRYPTIC!
EXPLAIN!
I CAN'T! NOT YET. BUT THERE'S ONLY ONE WAY TO KNOW FOR SURE...
...WE NEED TO FIND THE WALL!

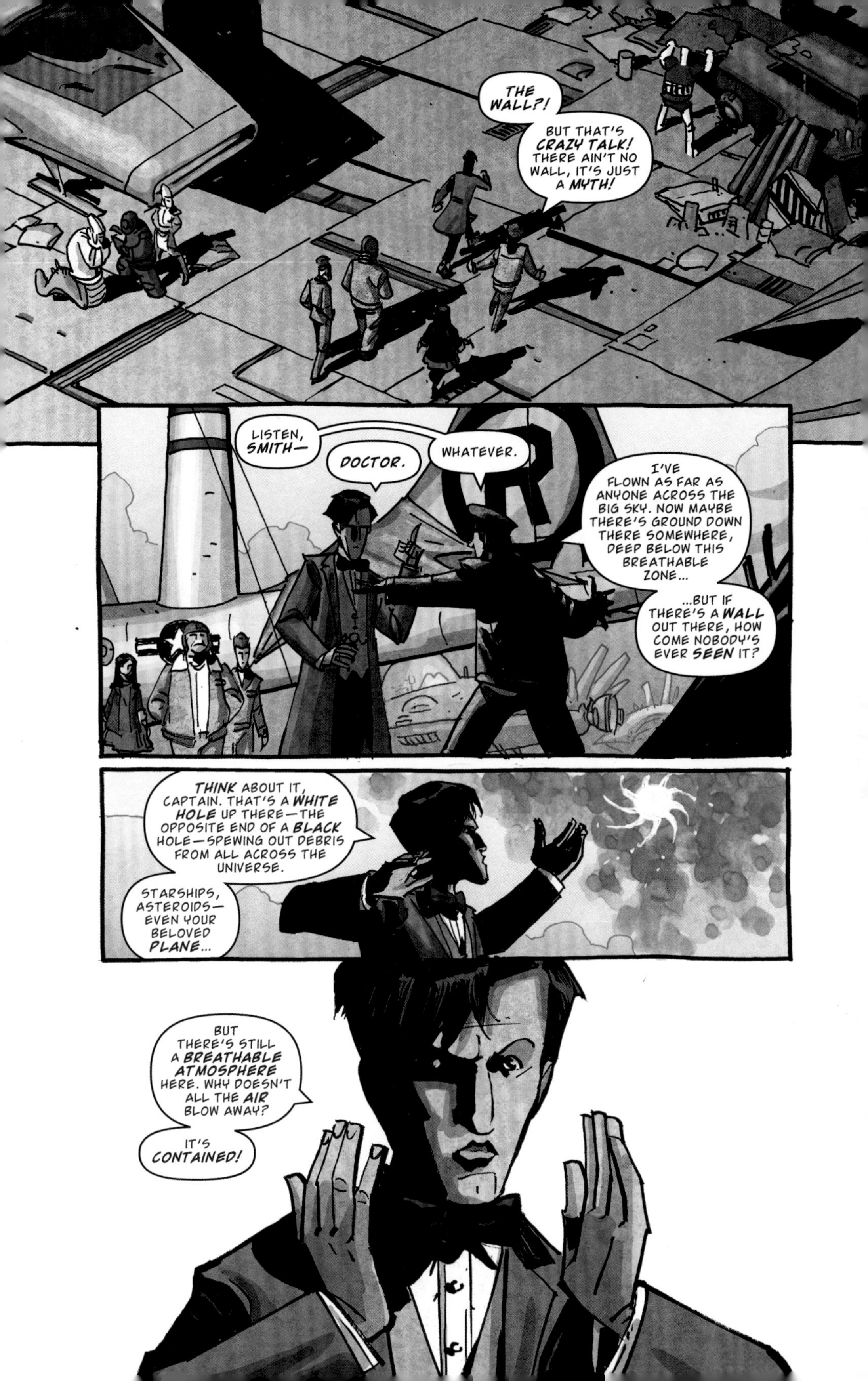
THE WALL?!
BUT THAT'S CRAZY TALK! THERE AIN'T NO WALL, IT'S JUST A MYTH!
LISTEN, SMITH—
DOCTOR.
WHATEVER.
I'VE FLOWN AS FAR AS ANYONE ACROSS THE BIG SKY. NOW MAYBE THERE'S GROUND DOWN THERE SOMEWHERE, DEEP BELOW THIS BREATHABLE ZONE...
...BUT IF THERE'S A WALL OUT THERE, HOW COME NOBODY'S EVER SEEN IT?
THINK ABOUT IT, CAPTAIN. THAT'S A WHITE HOLE UP THERE—THE OPPOSITE END OF A BLACK HOLE—SPEWING OUT DEBRIS FROM ALL ACROSS THE UNIVERSE.
STARSHIPS, ASTEROIDS— EVEN YOUR BELOVED PLANE...
BUT THERE'S STILL A BREATHABLE ATMOSPHERE HERE. WHY DOESN'T ALL THE AIR BLOW AWAY?
IT'S CONTAINED!

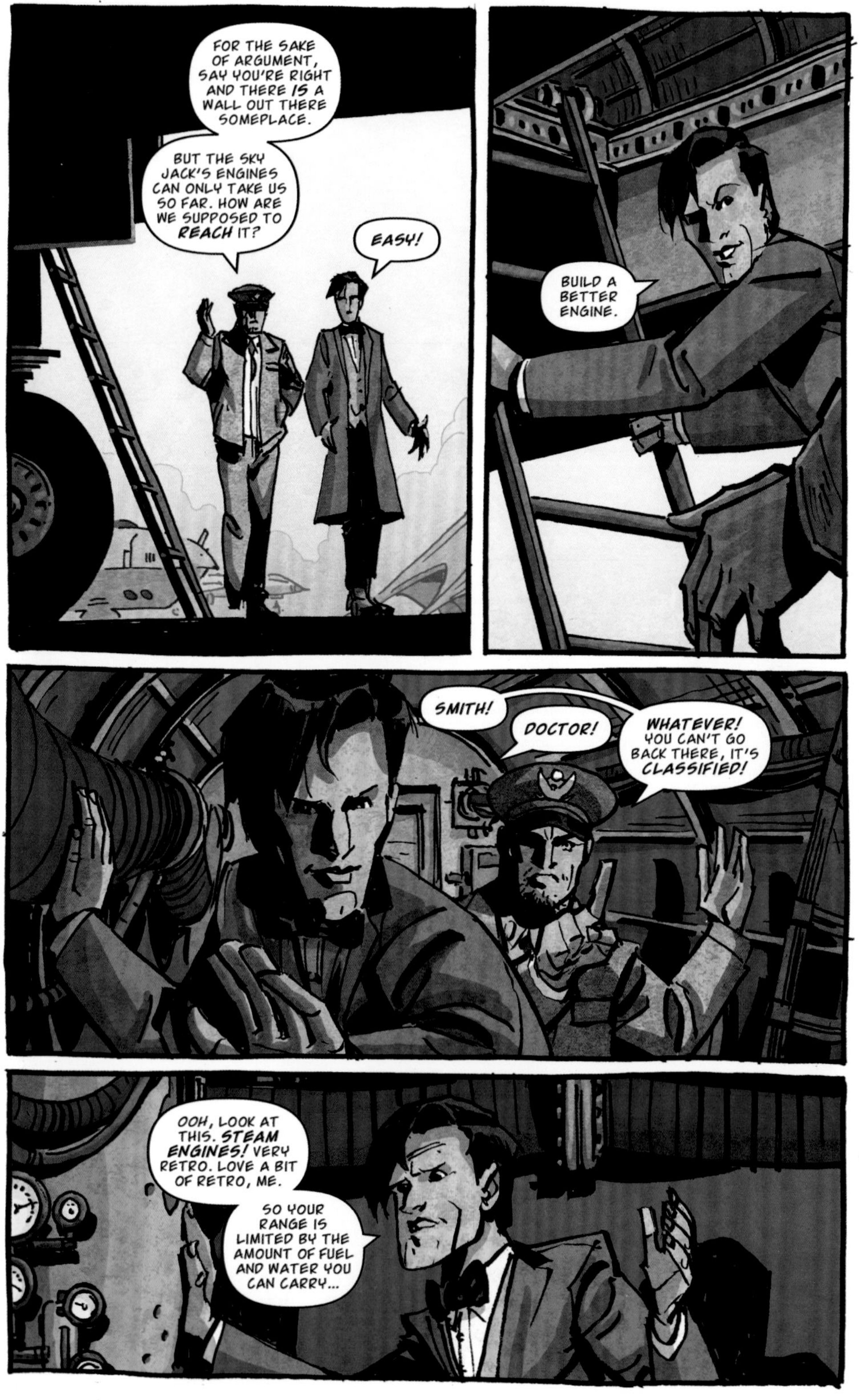
FOR THE SAKE OF ARGUMENT, SAY YOU'RE RIGHT AND THERE IS A WALL OUT THERE SOMEPLACE.
BUT THE SKY JACK'S ENGINES CAN ONLY TAKE US SO FAR. HOW ARE WE SUPPOSED TO REACH IT?
EASY!
BUILD A BETTER ENGINE.
SMITH!
DOCTOR!
WHATEVER! YOU CAN'T GO BACK THERE, IT'S CLASSIFIED!
OOH, LOOK AT THIS. STEAM ENGINES! VERY RETRO. LOVE A BIT OF RETRO, ME.
SO YOUR RANGE IS LIMITED BY THE AMOUNT OF FUEL AND WATER YOU CAN CARRY...

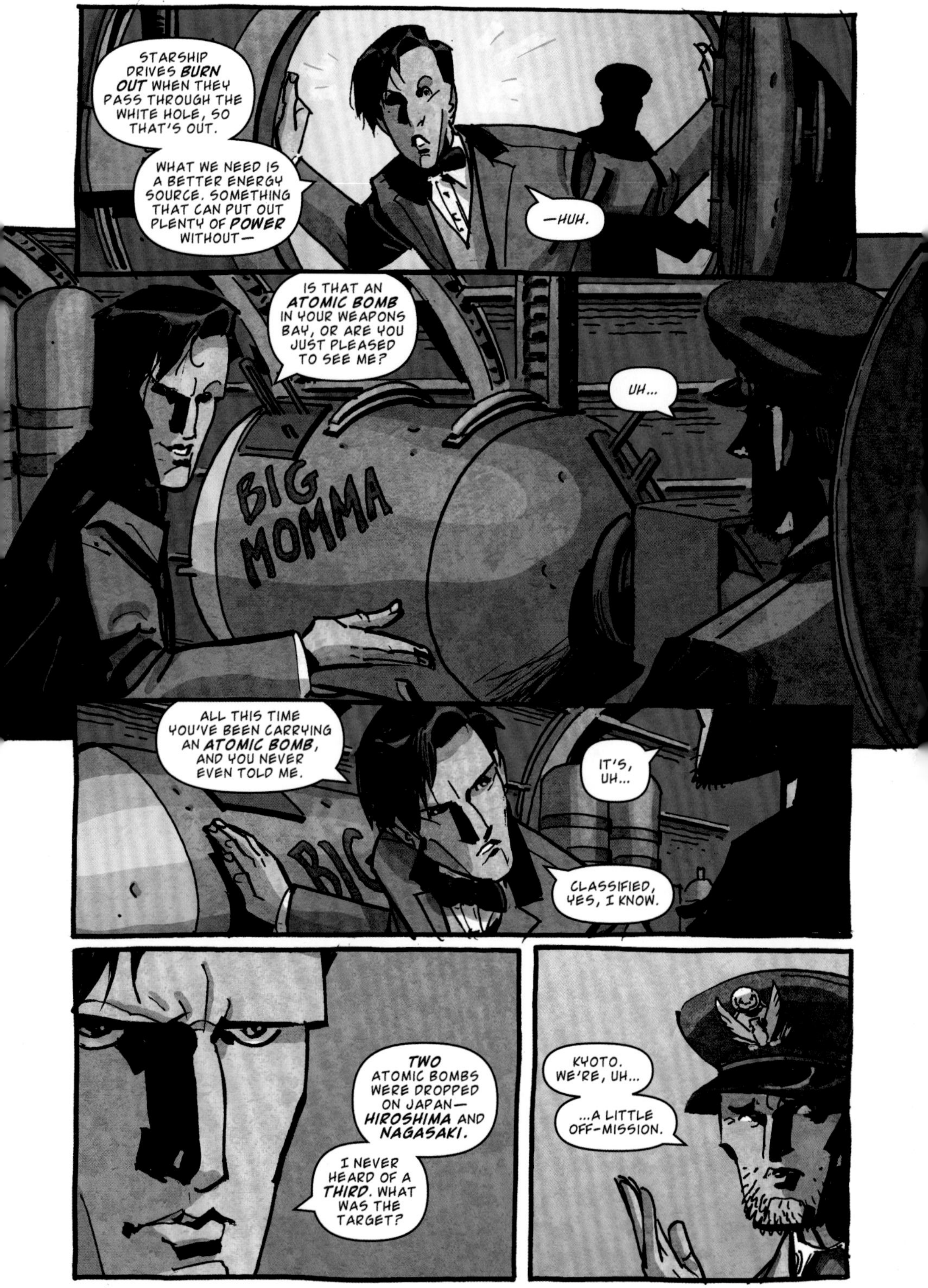
STARSHIP DRIVES BURN OUT WHEN THEY PASS THROUGH THE WHITE HOLE, SO THAT'S OUT.
WHAT WE NEED IS A BETTER ENERGY SOURCE. SOMETHING THAT CAN PUT OUT PLENTY OF POWER WITHOUT—
—HUH.
IS THAT AN ATOMIC BOMB IN YOUR WEAPONS BAY, OR ARE YOU JUST PLEASED TO SEE ME?
UH...
BIG MOMMA
ALL THIS TIME YOU'VE BEEN CARRYING AN ATOMIC BOMB, AND YOU NEVER EVEN TOLD ME.
IT'S, UH...
BIG
CLASSIFIED, YES, I KNOW.
TWO ATOMIC BOMBS WERE DROPPED ON JAPAN— HIROSHIMA AND NAGASAKI.
I NEVER HEARD OF A THIRD. WHAT WAS THE TARGET?
KYOTO. WE'RE, UH...
...A LITTLE OFF-MISSION.

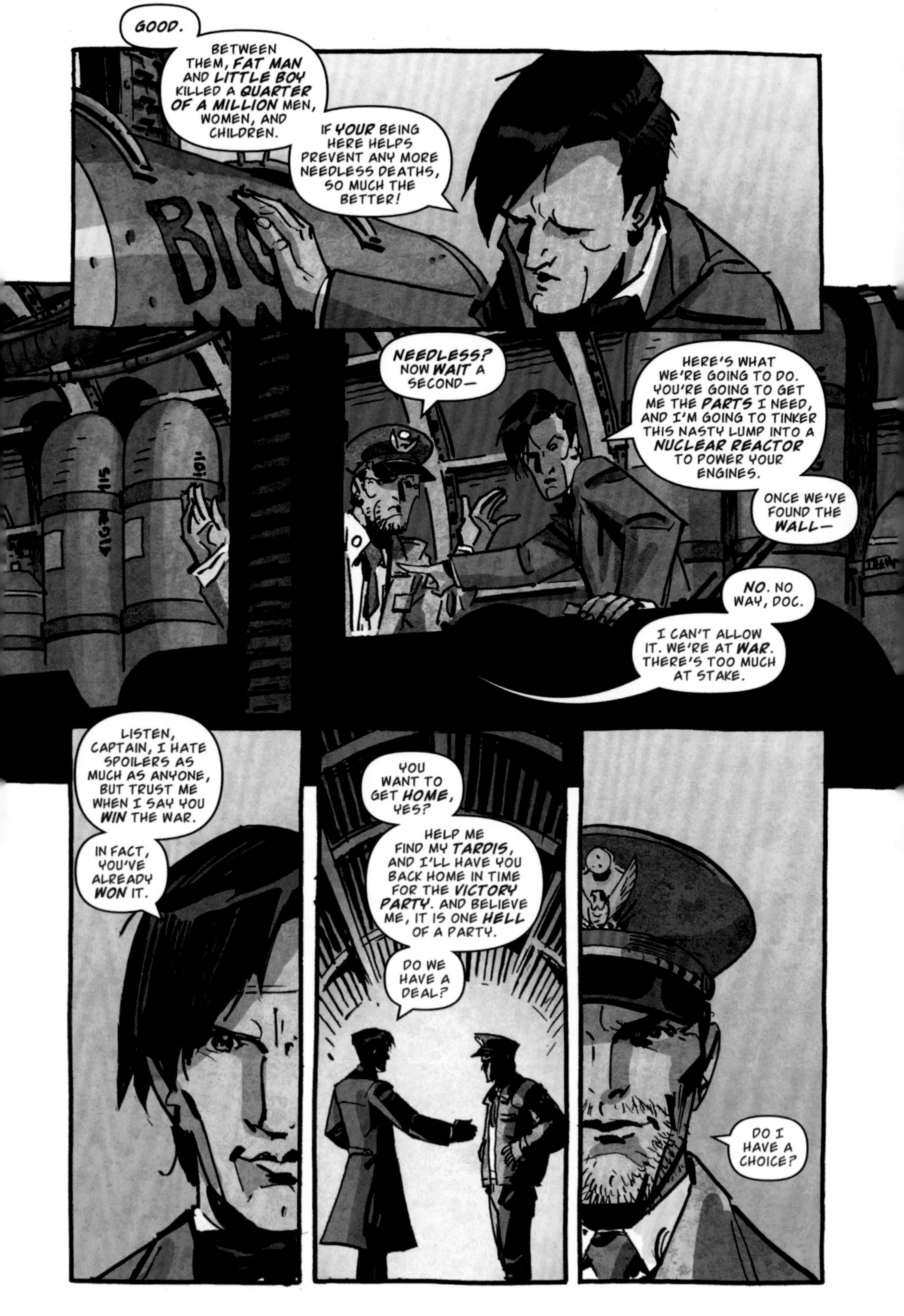
GOOD.
BETWEEN THEM, FAT MAN AND LITTLE BOY KILLED A QUARTER OF A MILLION MEN, WOMEN, AND CHILDREN.
IF YOUR BEING HERE HELPS PREVENT ANY MORE NEEDLESS DEATHS, SO MUCH THE BETTER!
BIG
NEEDLESS? NOW WAIT A SECOND—
HERE'S WHAT WE'RE GOING TO DO. YOU'RE GOING TO GET ME THE PARTS I NEED, AND I'M GOING TO TINKER THIS NASTY LUMP INTO A NUCLEAR REACTOR TO POWER YOUR ENGINES.
ONCE WE'VE FOUND THE WALL—
NO. NO WAY, DOC.
I CAN'T ALLOW IT. WE'RE AT WAR. THERE'S TOO MUCH AT STAKE.
LISTEN, CAPTAIN, I HATE SPOILERS AS MUCH AS ANYONE, BUT TRUST ME WHEN I SAY YOU WIN THE WAR.
IN FACT, YOU'VE ALREADY WON IT.
YOU WANT TO GET HOME, YES?
HELP ME FIND MY TARDIS, AND I'LL HAVE YOU BACK HOME IN TIME FOR THE VICTORY PARTY. AND BELIEVE ME, IT IS ONE HELL OF A PARTY.
DO WE HAVE A DEAL?
DO I HAVE A CHOICE?

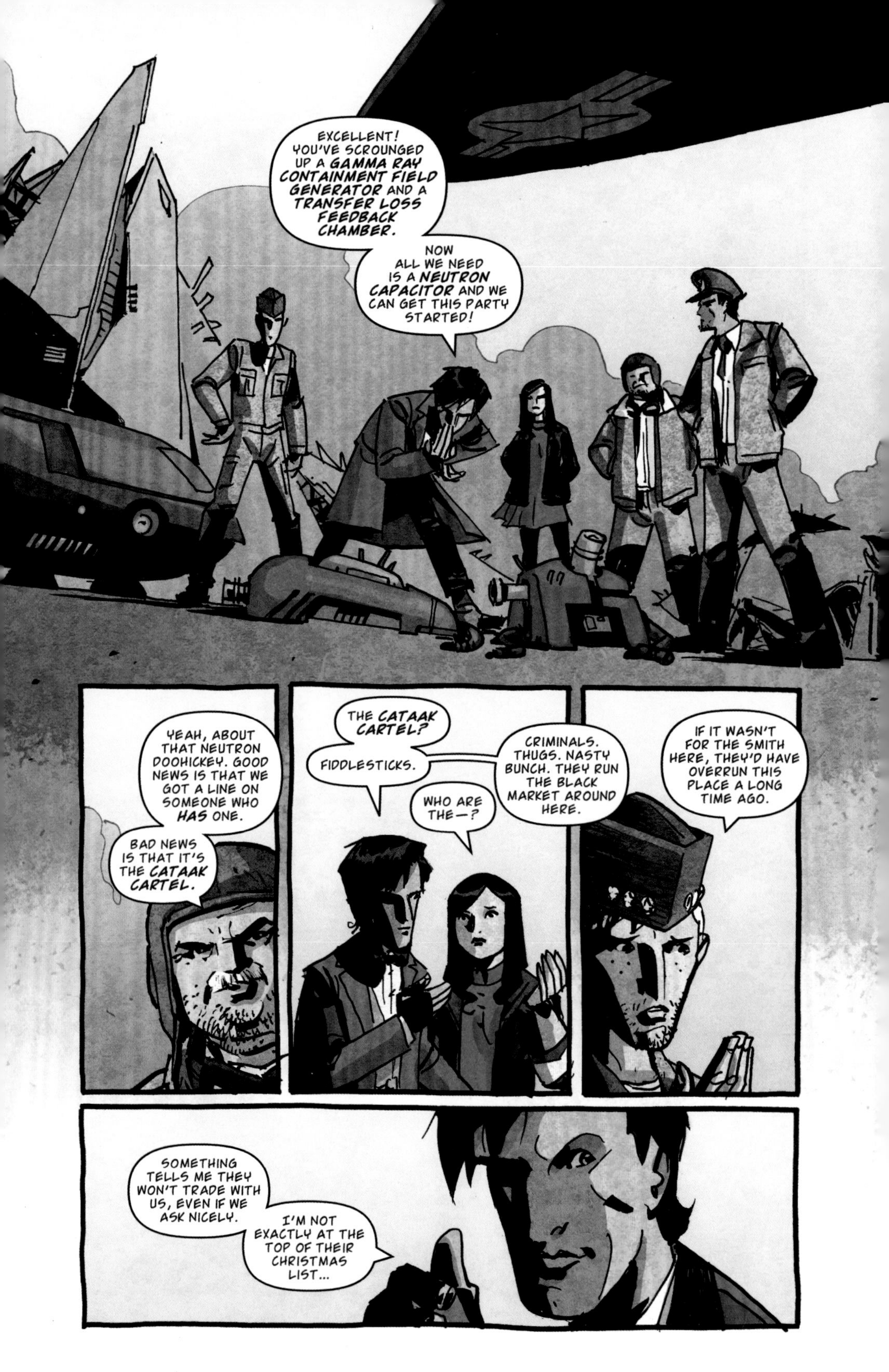
EXCELLENT! YOU'VE SCROUNGED UP A GAMMA RAY CONTAINMENT FIELD GENERATOR AND A TRANSFER LOSS FEEDBACK CHAMBER.
NOW ALL WE NEED IS A NEUTRON CAPACITOR AND WE CAN GET THIS PARTY STARTED!
YEAH, ABOUT THAT NEUTRON DOOHICKEY. GOOD NEWS IS THAT WE GOT A LINE ON SOMEONE WHO HAS ONE.
BAD NEWS IS THAT IT'S THE CATAAK CARTEL.
THE CATAAK CARTEL?
FIDDLESTICKS.
WHO ARE THE—?
CRIMINALS. THUGS. NASTY BUNCH. THEY RUN THE BLACK MARKET AROUND HERE.
IF IT WASN'T FOR THE SMITH HERE, THEY'D HAVE OVERRUN THIS PLACE A LONG TIME AGO.
SOMETHING TELLS ME THEY WON'T TRADE WITH US, EVEN IF WE ASK NICELY.
I'M NOT EXACTLY AT THE TOP OF THEIR CHRISTMAS LIST...

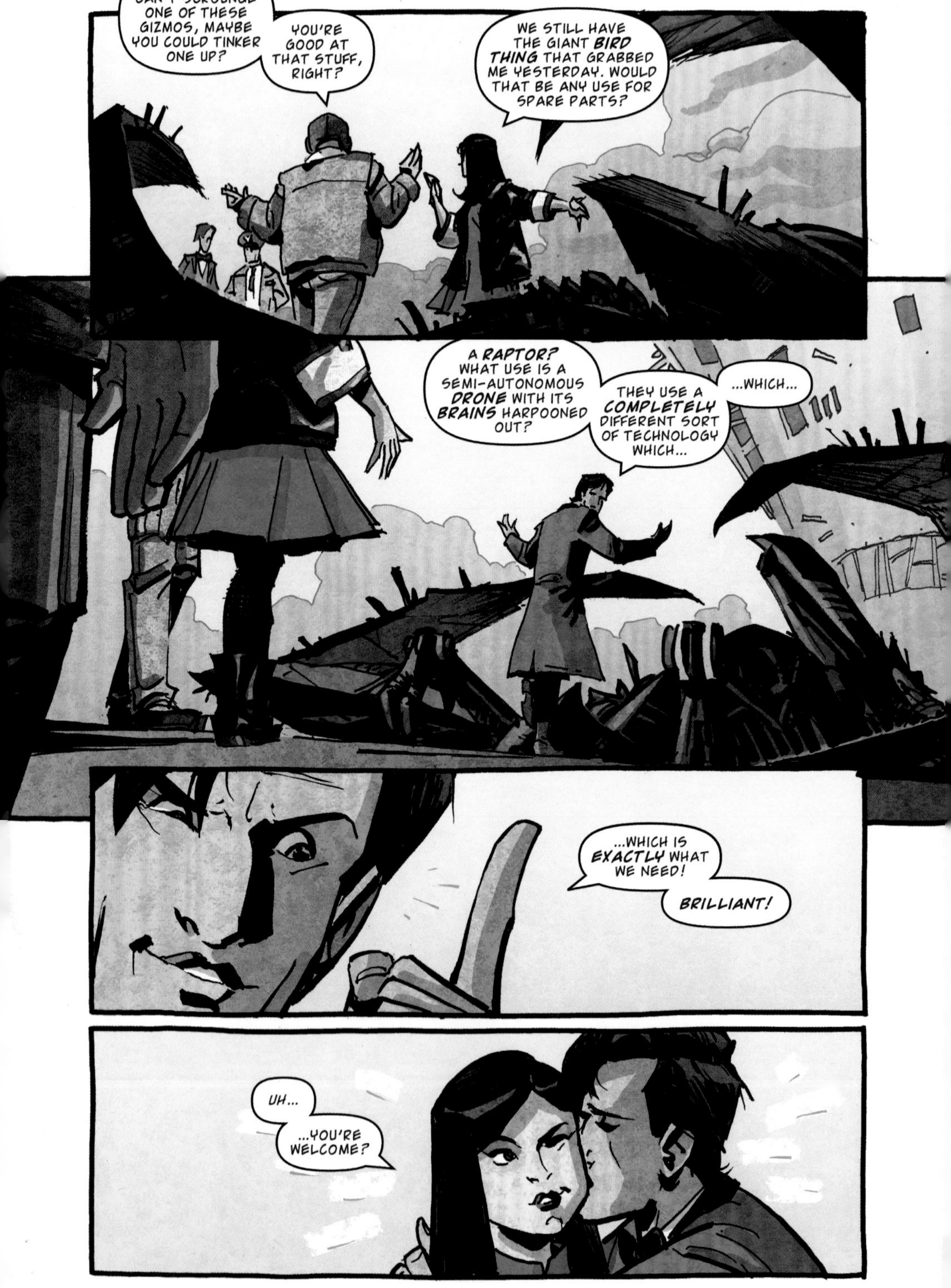
WELL, IF YOU CAN'T SCROUNGE ONE OF THESE GIZMOS, MAYBE YOU COULD TINKER ONE UP?
YOU'RE GOOD AT THAT STUFF, RIGHT?
WE STILL HAVE THE GIANT BIRD THING THAT GRABBED ME YESTERDAY. WOULD THAT BE ANY USE FOR SPARE PARTS?
A RAPTOR? WHAT USE IS A SEMI-AUTONOMOUS DRONE WITH ITS BRAINS HARPOONED OUT?
THEY USE A COMPLETELY DIFFERENT SORT OF TECHNOLOGY WHICH...
...WHICH...
...WHICH IS EXACTLY WHAT WE NEED!
BRILLIANT!
UH...
...YOU'RE WELCOME?

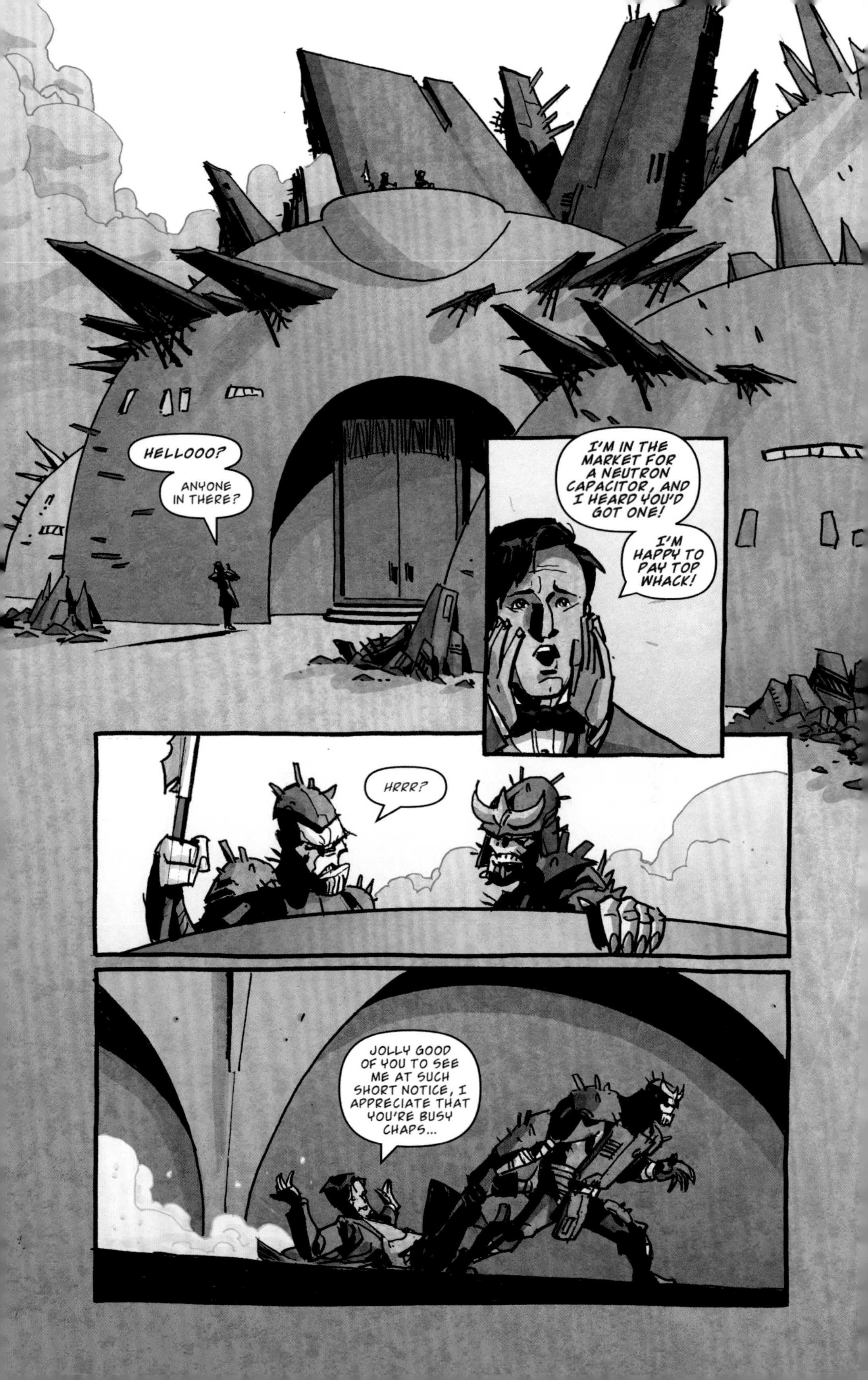
HELLOOO?
ANYONE IN THERE?
I'M IN THE MARKET FOR A NEUTRON CAPACITOR, AND I HEARD YOU'D GOT ONE!
I'M HAPPY TO PAY TOP WHACK!
HRRR?
JOLLY GOOD OF YOU TO SEE ME AT SUCH SHORT NOTICE, I APPRECIATE THAT YOU'RE BUSY CHAPS...

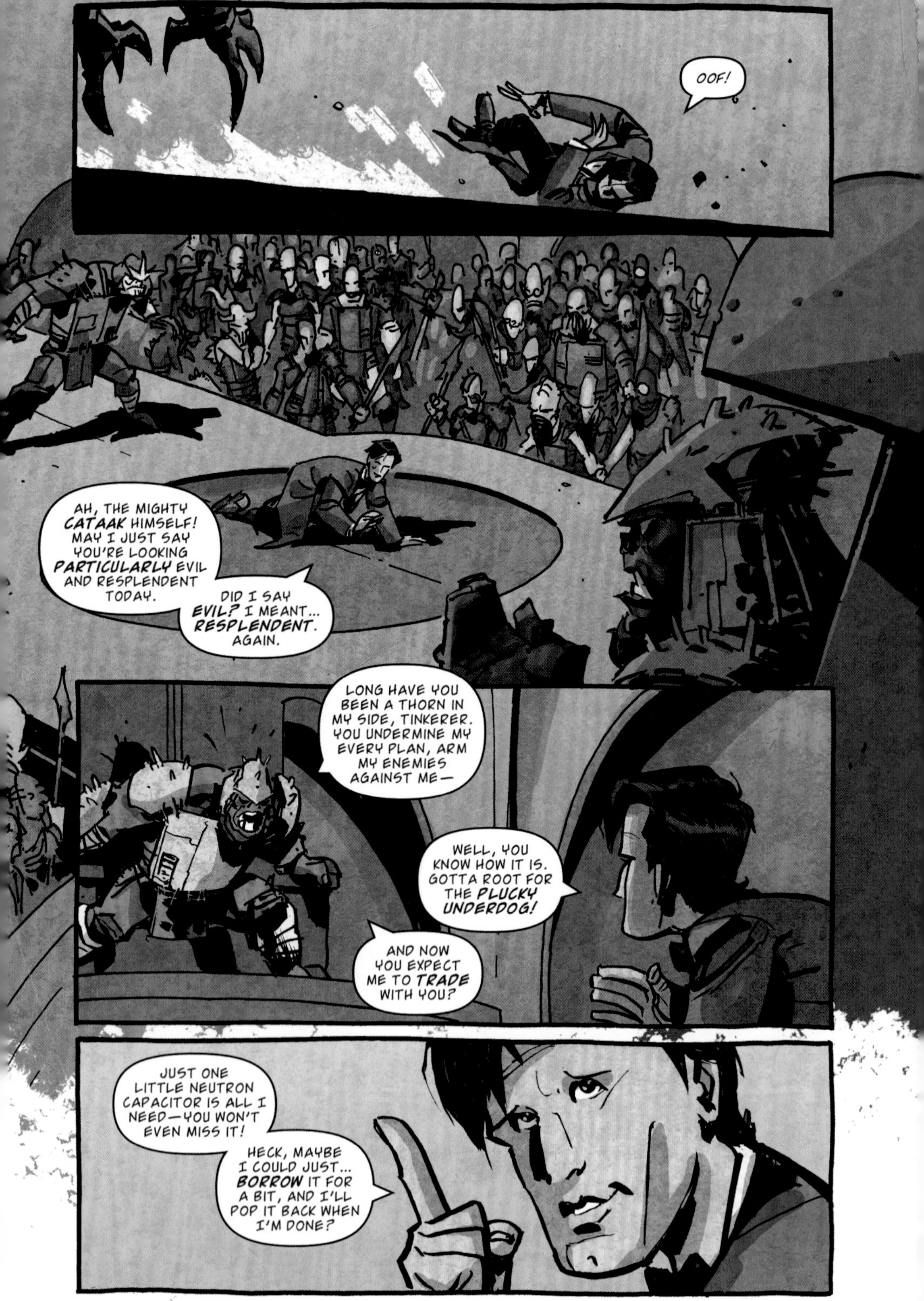
OOF!
AH, THE MIGHTY CATAAK HIMSELF! MAY I JUST SAY YOU'RE LOOKING PARTICULARLY EVIL AND RESPLENDENT TODAY.
DID I SAY EVIL? I MEANT... RESPLENDENT. AGAIN.
LONG HAVE YOU BEEN A THORN IN MY SIDE, TINKERER. YOU UNDERMINE MY EVERY PLAN, ARM MY ENEMIES AGAINST ME—
WELL, YOU KNOW HOW IT IS. GOTTA ROOT FOR THE PLUCKY UNDERDOG!
AND NOW YOU EXPECT ME TO TRADE WITH YOU?
JUST ONE LITTLE NEUTRON CAPACITOR IS ALL I NEED—YOU WON'T EVEN MISS IT!
HECK, MAYBE I COULD JUST... BORROW IT FOR A BIT, AND I'LL POP IT BACK WHEN I'M DONE?

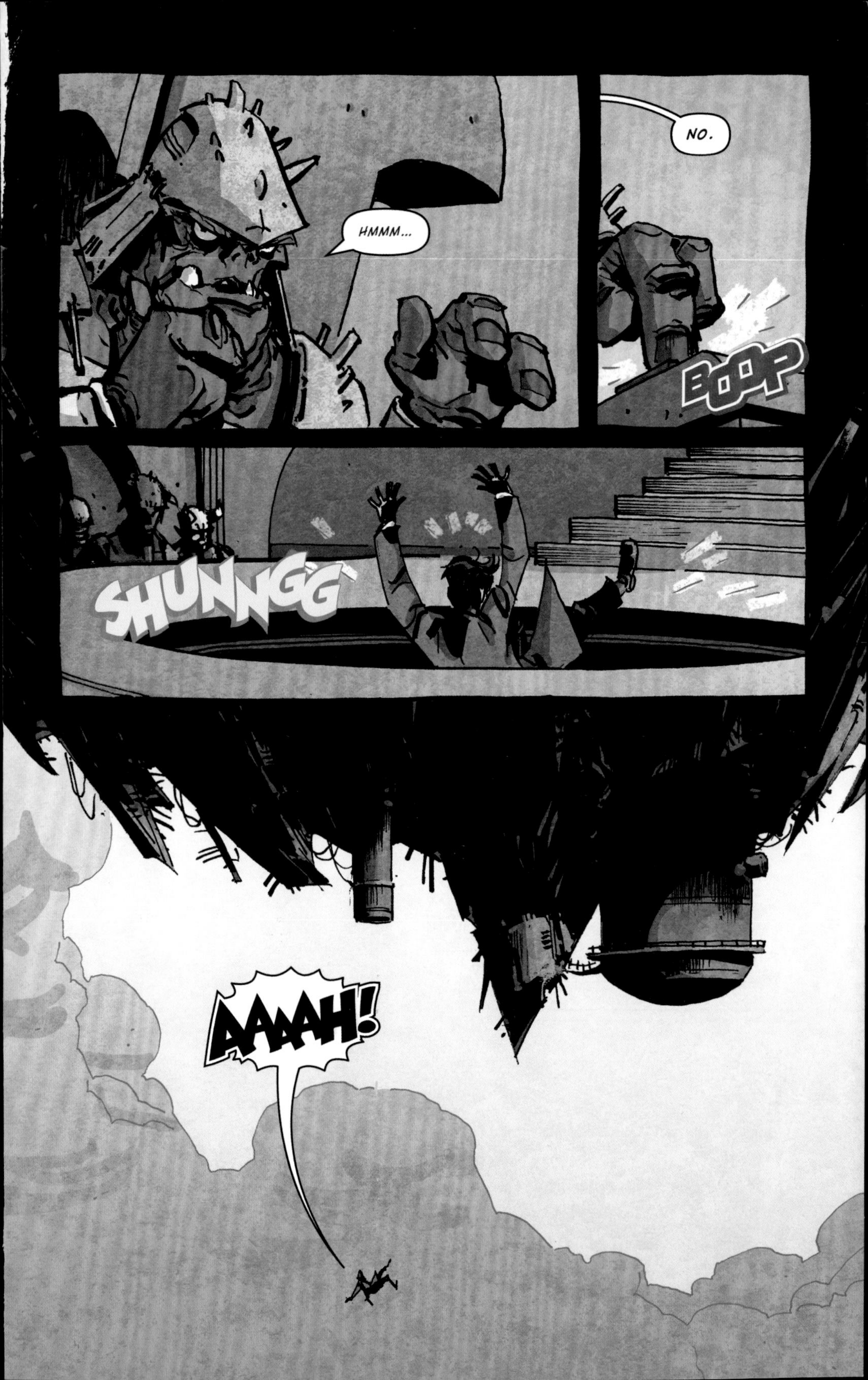
HMMM...
NO.
BOOP
SHUNNGG
AAAAH!

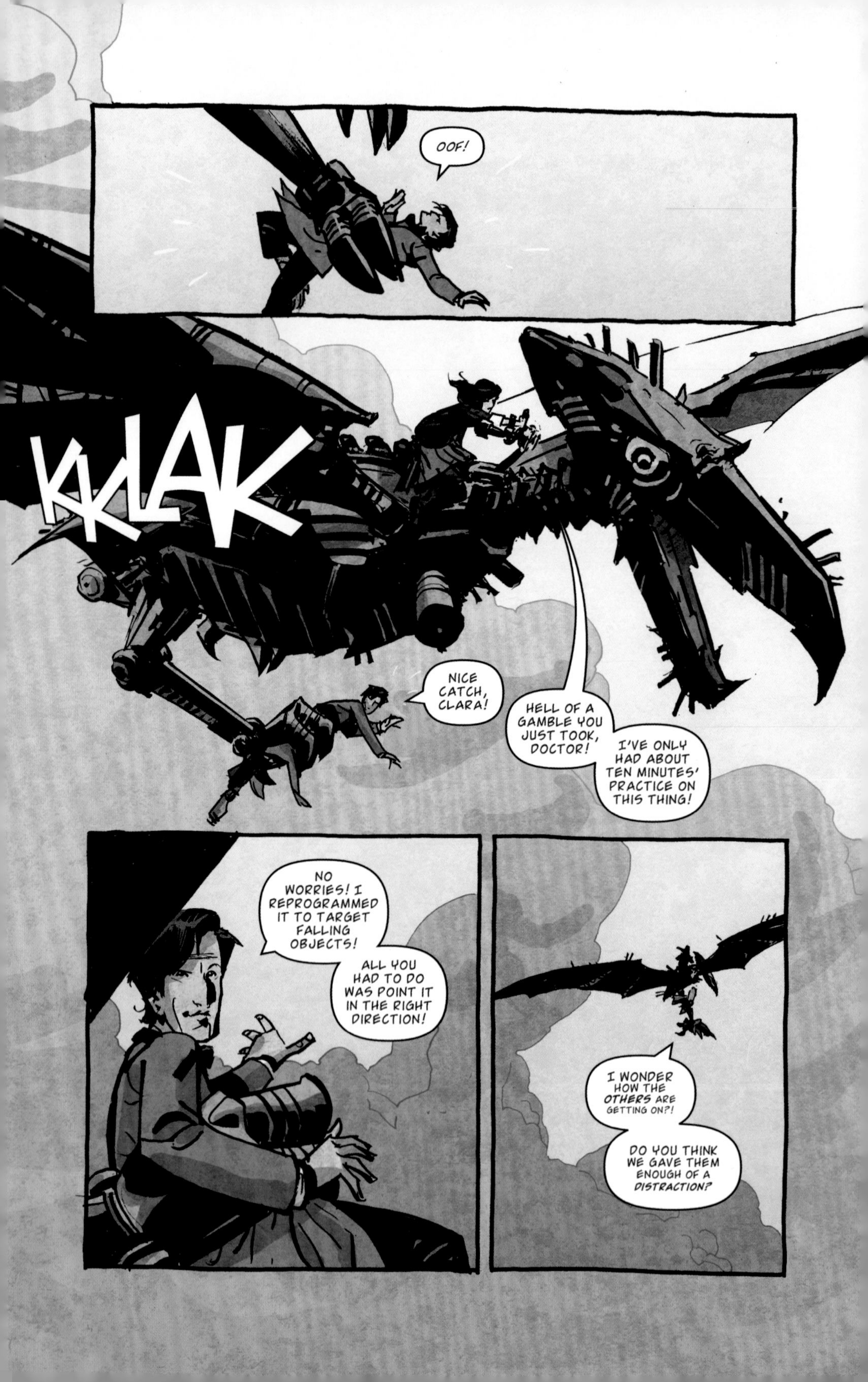
OOF!
KKLAK
NICE CATCH, CLARA!
HELL OF A GAMBLE YOU JUST TOOK, DOCTOR!
I'VE ONLY HAD ABOUT TEN MINUTES' PRACTICE ON THIS THING!
NO WORRIES! I REPROGRAMMED IT TO TARGET FALLING OBJECTS!
ALL YOU HAD TO DO WAS POINT IT IN THE RIGHT DIRECTION!
I WONDER HOW THE OTHERS ARE GETTING ON?!
DO YOU THINK WE GAVE THEM ENOUGH OF A DISTRACTION?

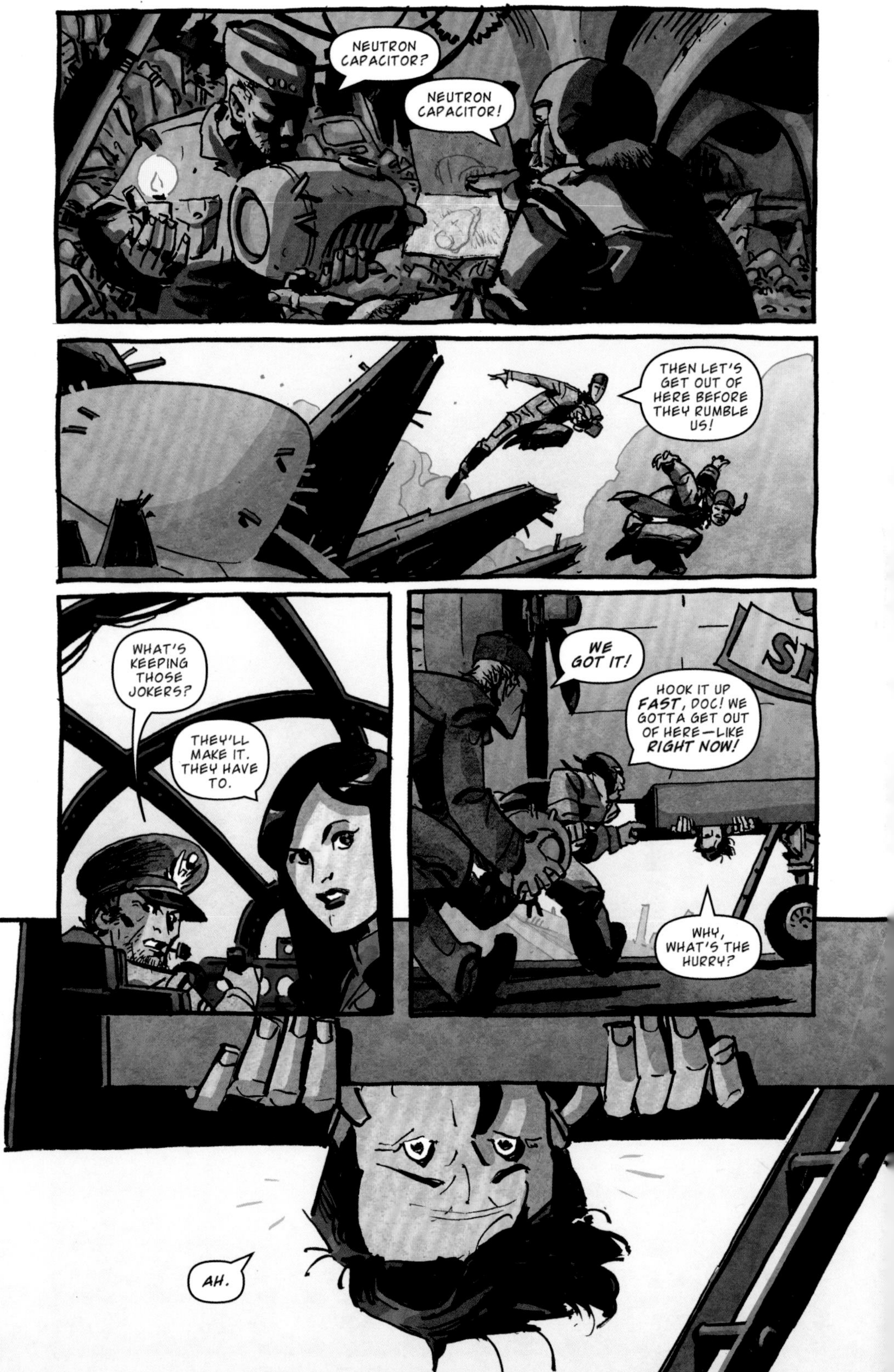
NEUTRON CAPACITOR?
NEUTRON CAPACITOR!
THEN LET'S GET OUT OF HERE BEFORE THEY RUMBLE US!
WHAT'S KEEPING THOSE JOKERS?
THEY'LL MAKE IT. THEY HAVE TO.
WE GOT IT!
HOOK IT UP FAST, DOC! WE GOTTA GET OUT OF HERE—LIKE RIGHT NOW!
WHY, WHAT'S THE HURRY?
AH.

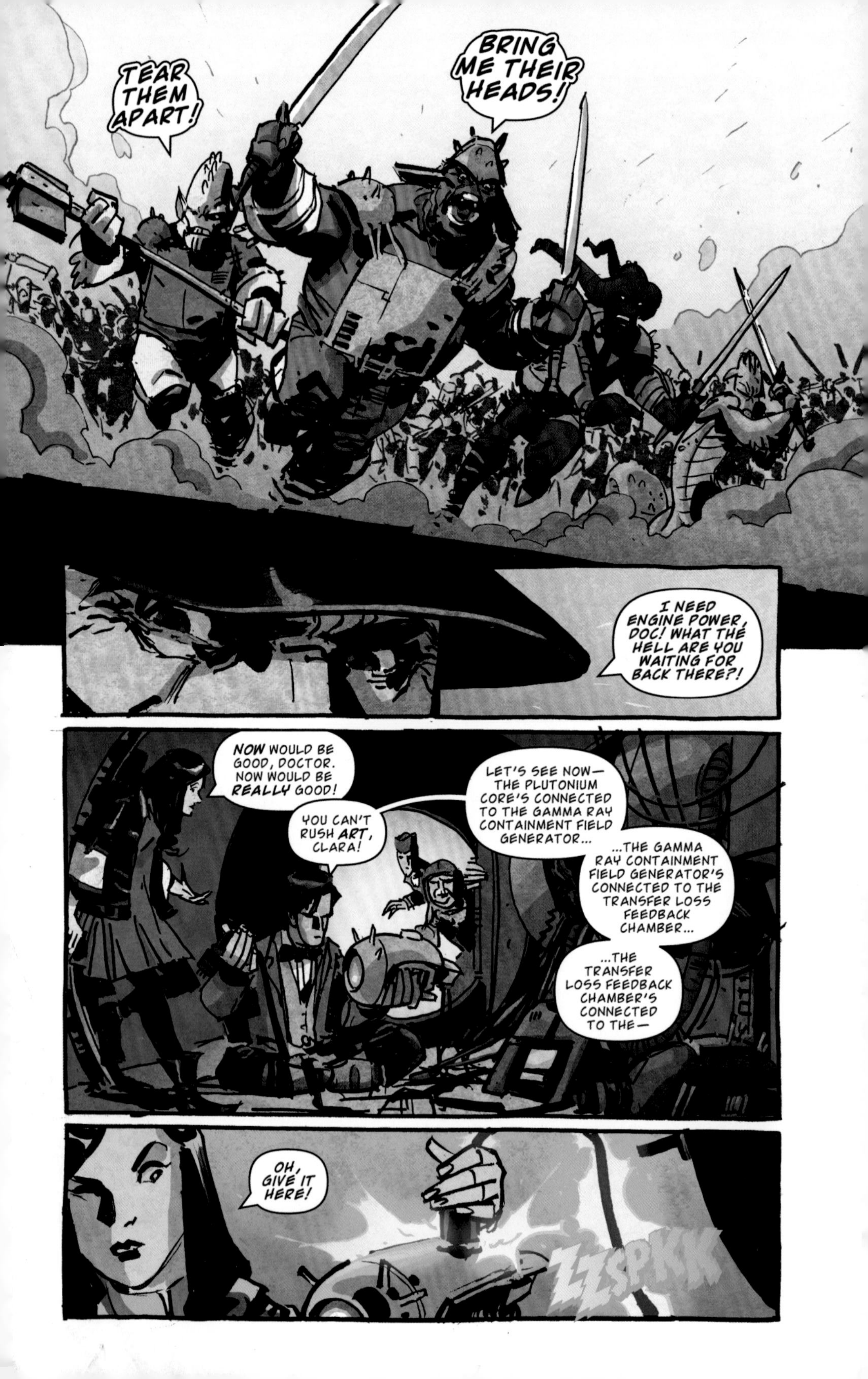
TEAR THEM APART!
BRING ME THEIR HEADS!
I NEED ENGINE POWER, DOC! WHAT THE HELL ARE YOU WAITING FOR BACK THERE?!
NOW WOULD BE GOOD, DOCTOR. NOW WOULD BE REALLY GOOD!
YOU CAN'T RUSH ART, CLARA!
LET'S SEE NOW— THE PLUTONIUM CORE'S CONNECTED TO THE GAMMA RAY CONTAINMENT FIELD GENERATOR...
...THE GAMMA RAY CONTAINMENT FIELD GENERATOR'S CONNECTED TO THE TRANSFER LOSS FEEDBACK CHAMBER...
...THE TRANSFER LOSS FEEDBACK CHAMBER'S CONNECTED TO THE—
OH, GIVE IT HERE!
ZZSPKK

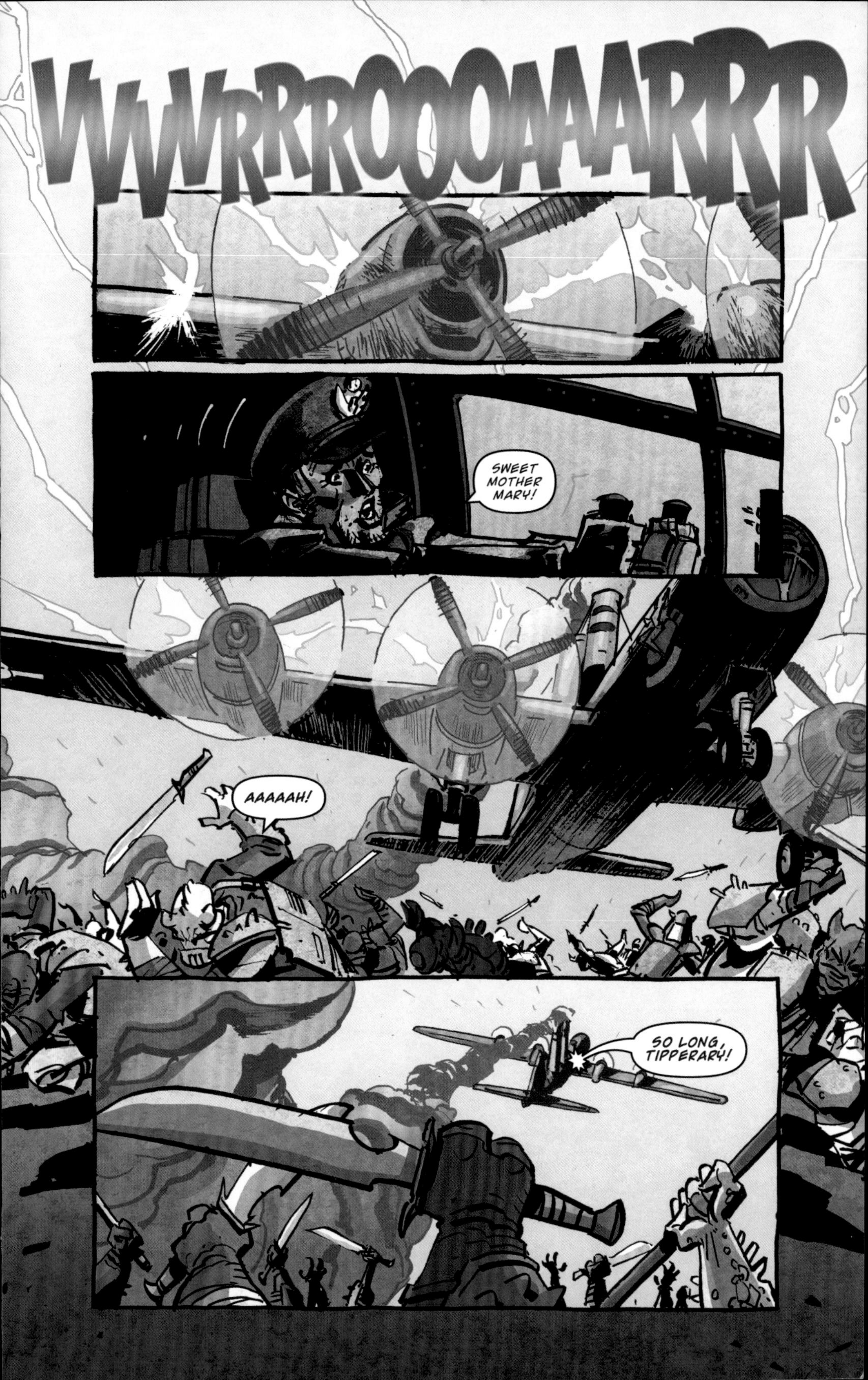
VWWRRROOOAAARRR
SWEET MOTHER MARY!
AAAAAH!
SO LONG, TIPPERARY!

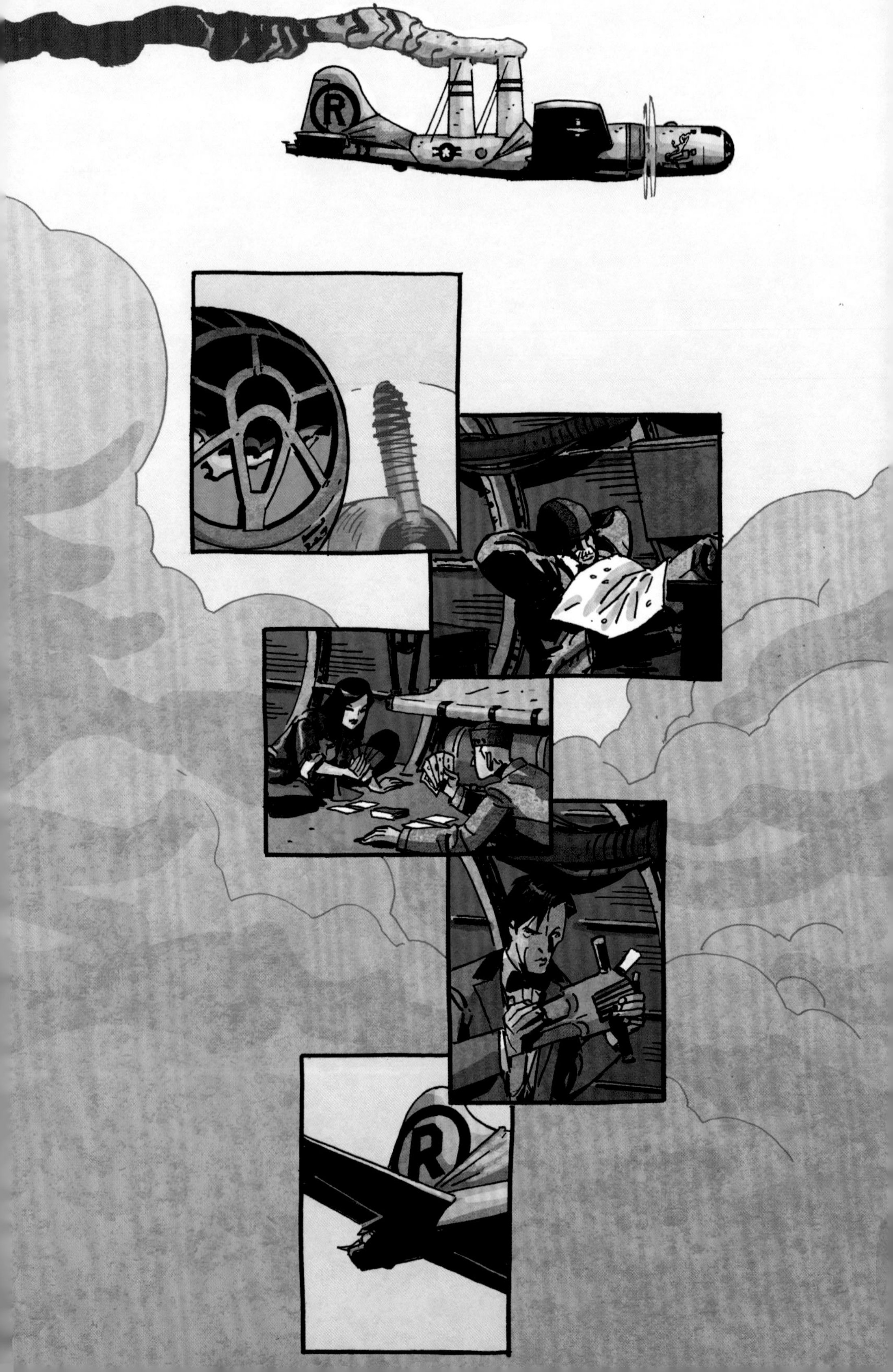

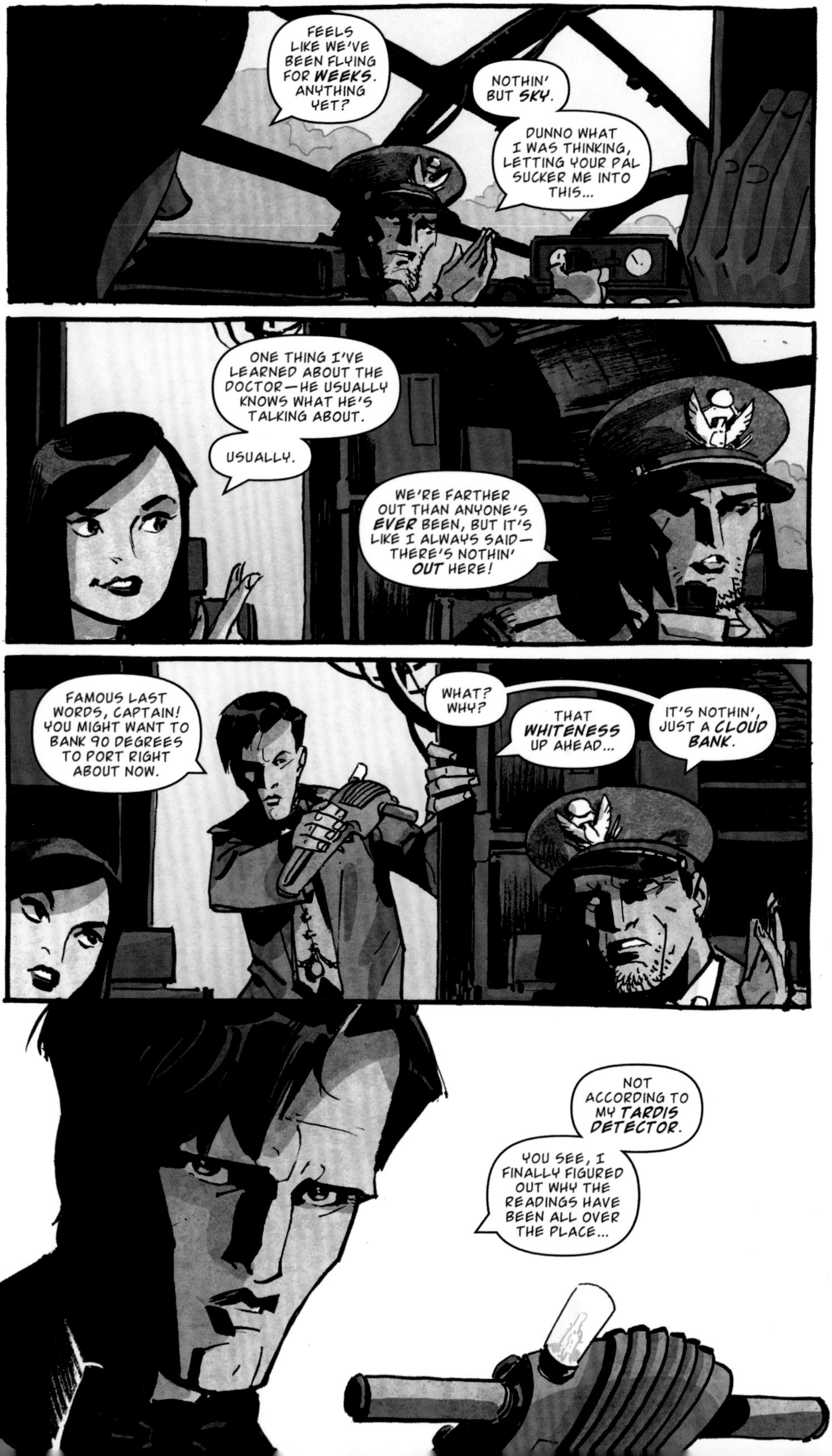

FEELS LIKE WE'VE BEEN FLYING FOR WEEKS. ANYTHING YET?
NOTHIN' BUT SKY.
DUNNO WHAT I WAS THINKING, LETTING YOUR PAL SUCKER ME INTO THIS...
ONE THING I'VE LEARNED ABOUT THE DOCTOR—HE USUALLY KNOWS WHAT HE'S TALKING ABOUT.
USUALLY.
WE'RE FARTHER OUT THAN ANYONE'S EVER BEEN, BUT IT'S LIKE I ALWAYS SAID—THERE'S NOTHIN' OUT HERE!
FAMOUS LAST WORDS, CAPTAIN! YOU MIGHT WANT TO BANK 90 DEGREES TO PORT RIGHT ABOUT NOW.
WHAT? WHY?
THAT WHITENESS UP AHEAD...
IT'S NOTHIN', JUST A CLOUD BANK.
NOT ACCORDING TO MY TARDIS DETECTOR.
YOU SEE, I FINALLY FIGURED OUT WHY THE READINGS HAVE BEEN ALL OVER THE PLACE...

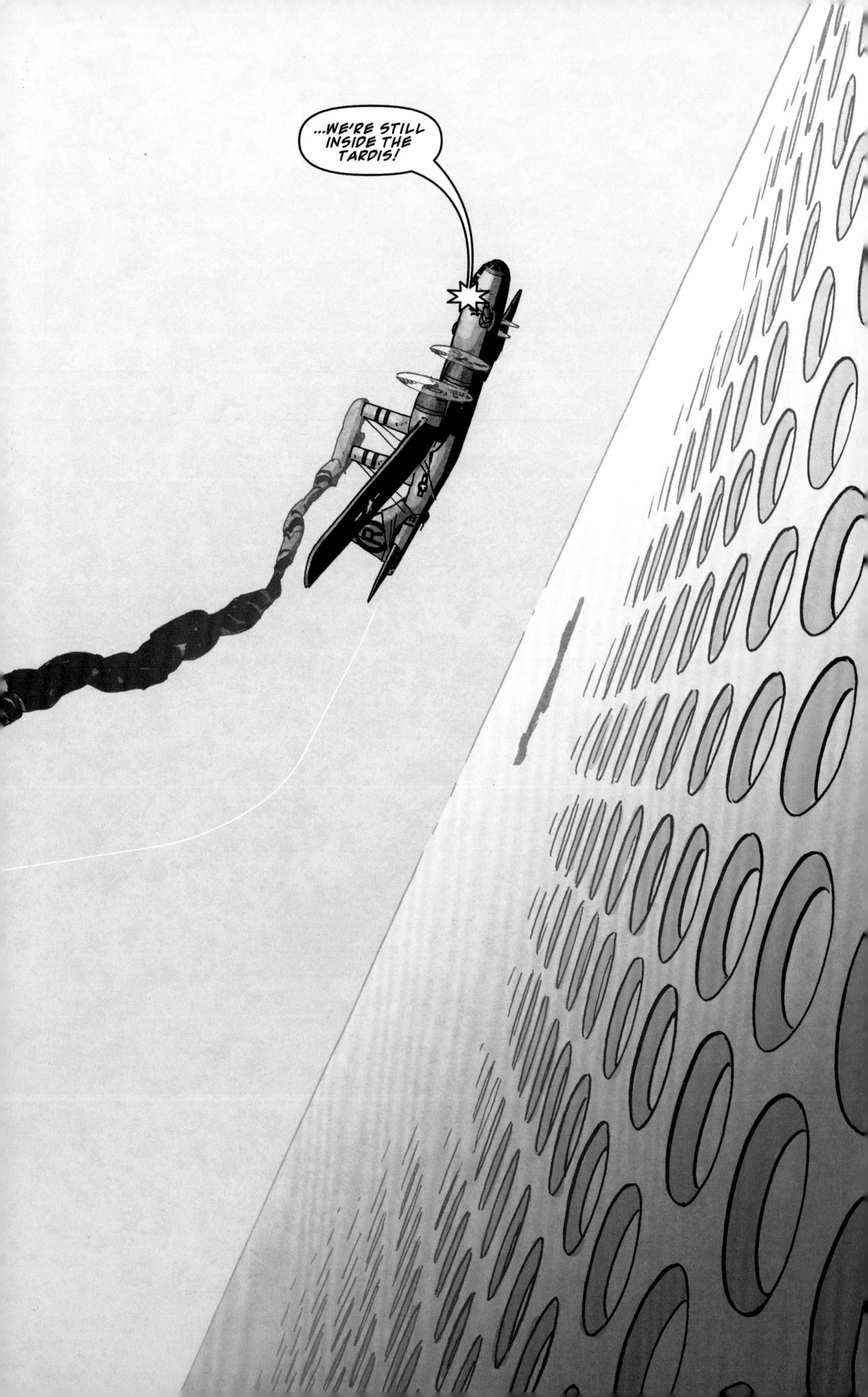
...WE'RE STILL INSIDE THE TARDIS!

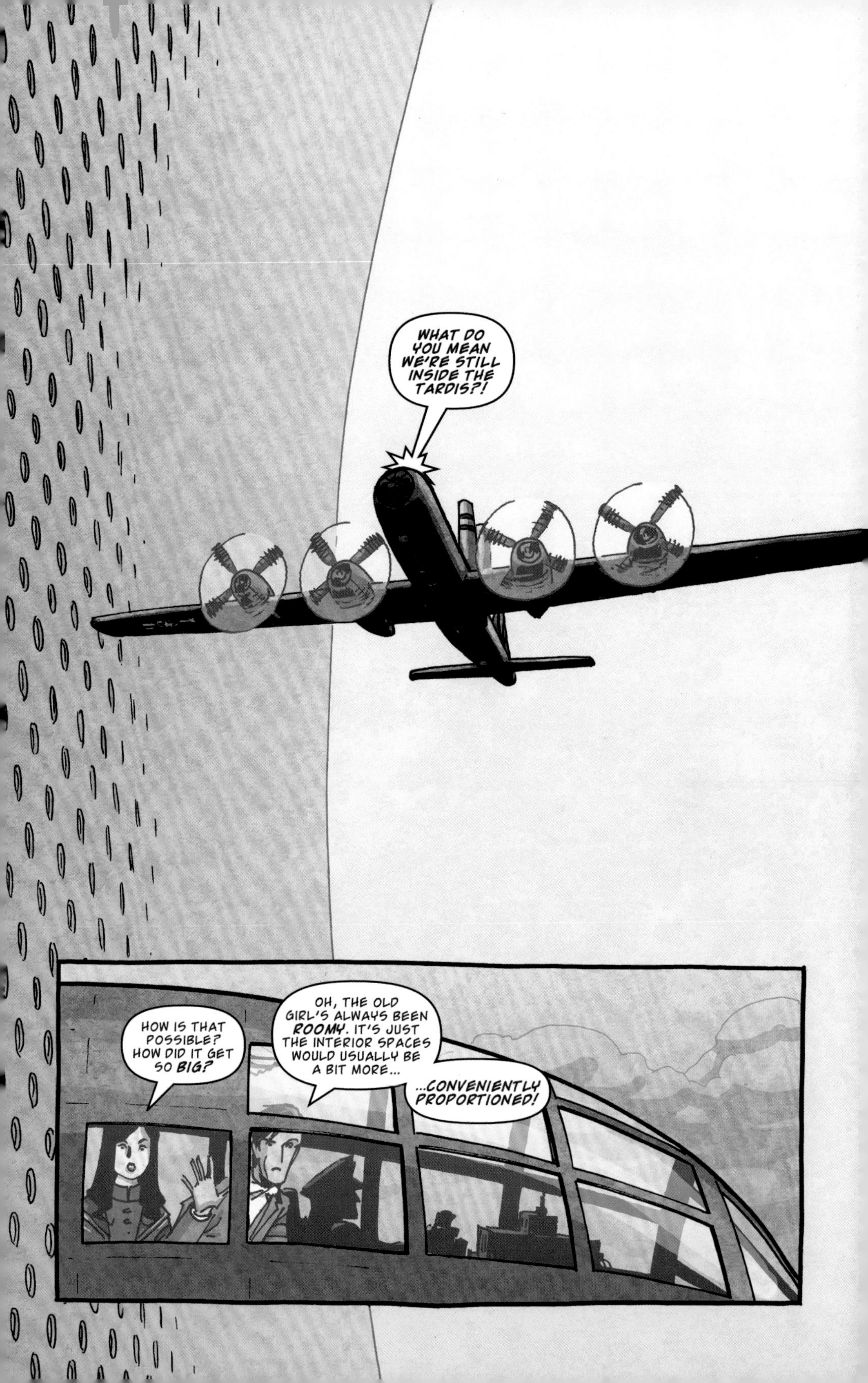
WHAT DO YOU MEAN WE'RE STILL INSIDE THE TARDIS?!
HOW IS THAT POSSIBLE? HOW DID IT GET SO BIG?
OH, THE OLD GIRL'S ALWAYS BEEN ROOMY. IT'S JUST THE INTERIOR SPACES WOULD USUALLY BE A BIT MORE...
...CONVENIENTLY PROPORTIONED!

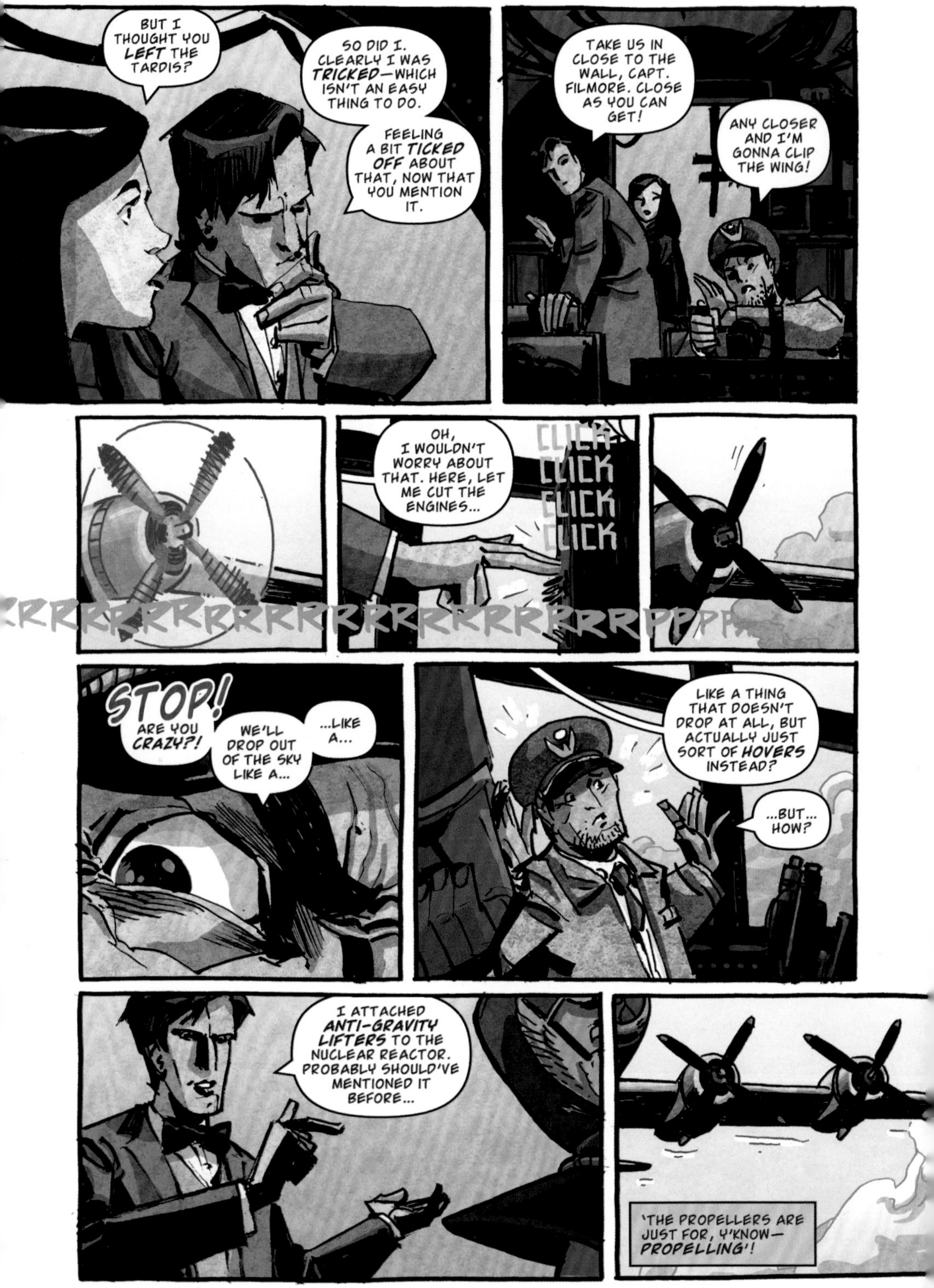

BUT I THOUGHT YOU LEFT THE TARDIS?
SO DID I. CLEARLY I WAS TRICKED—WHICH ISN'T AN EASY THING TO DO.
FEELING A BIT TICKED OFF ABOUT THAT, NOW THAT YOU MENTION IT.
TAKE US IN CLOSE TO THE WALL, CAPT. FILMORE. CLOSE AS YOU CAN GET!
ANY CLOSER AND I'M GONNA CLIP THE WING!
OH, I WOULDN'T WORRY ABOUT THAT. HERE, LET ME CUT THE ENGINES...
CLICK CLICK CLICK CLICK
RRRRRRRRRRRRRRRRRRRRRRPPPP
STOP! ARE YOU CRAZY?!
WE'LL DROP OUT OF THE SKY LIKE A...
...LIKE A...
LIKE A THING THAT DOESN'T DROP AT ALL, BUT ACTUALLY JUST SORT OF HOVERS INSTEAD?
...BUT... HOW?
I ATTACHED ANTI-GRAVITY LIFTERS TO THE NUCLEAR REACTOR. PROBABLY SHOULD'VE MENTIONED IT BEFORE...
'THE PROPELLERS ARE JUST FOR, Y'KNOW—PROPELLING'!

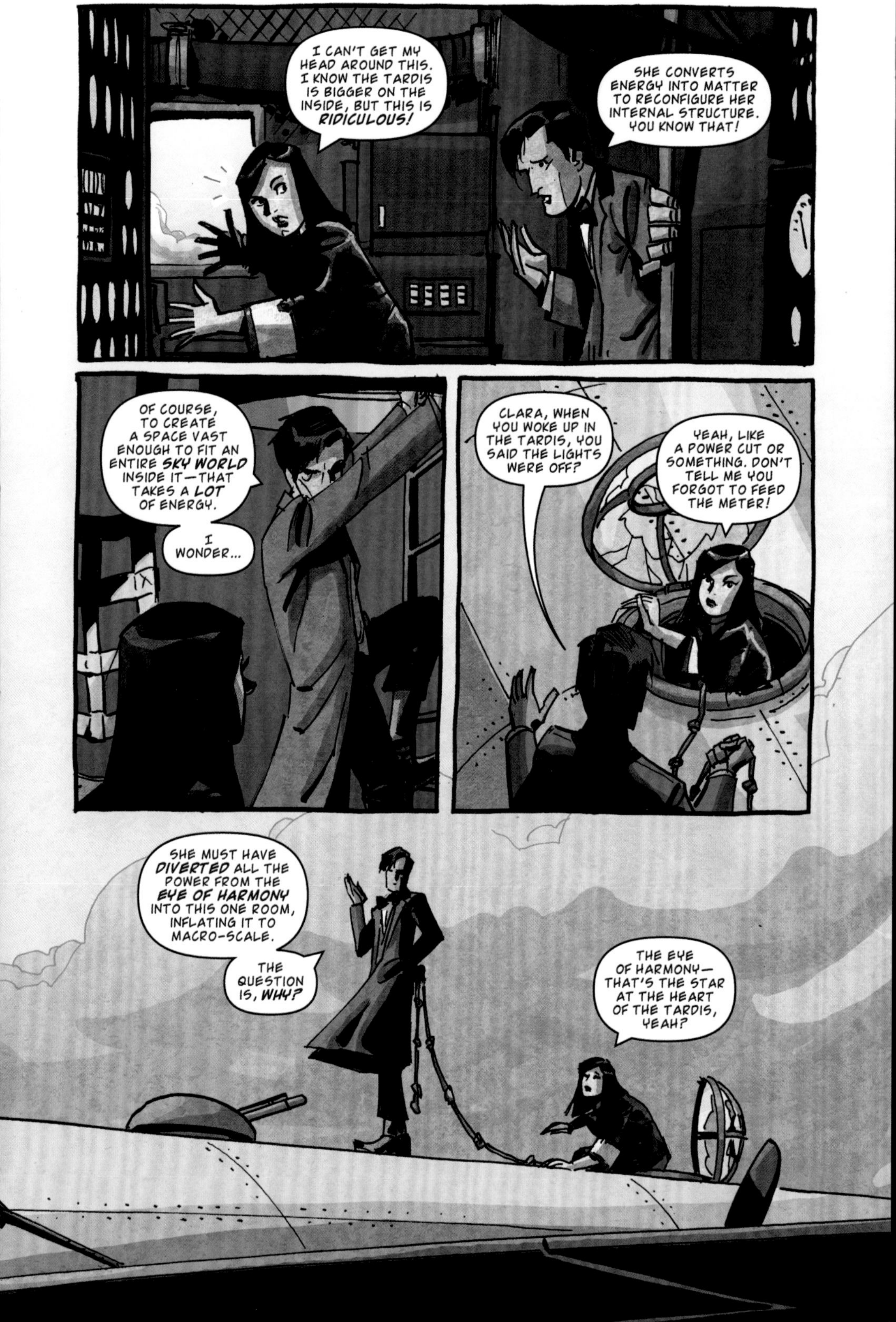
I CAN'T GET MY HEAD AROUND THIS. I KNOW THE TARDIS IS BIGGER ON THE INSIDE, BUT THIS IS *RIDICULOUS!*
SHE CONVERTS ENERGY INTO MATTER TO RECONFIGURE HER INTERNAL STRUCTURE. YOU KNOW THAT!
OF COURSE, TO CREATE A SPACE VAST ENOUGH TO FIT AN ENTIRE *SKY WORLD* INSIDE IT—THAT TAKES A *LOT* OF ENERGY.
I WONDER...
CLARA, WHEN YOU WOKE UP IN THE TARDIS, YOU SAID THE LIGHTS WERE OFF?
YEAH, LIKE A POWER CUT OR SOMETHING. DON'T TELL ME YOU FORGOT TO FEED THE METER!
SHE MUST HAVE *DIVERTED* ALL THE POWER FROM THE *EYE OF HARMONY* INTO THIS ONE ROOM, INFLATING IT TO MACRO-SCALE.
THE QUESTION IS, *WHY?*
THE EYE OF HARMONY—THAT'S THE STAR AT THE HEART OF THE TARDIS, YEAH?

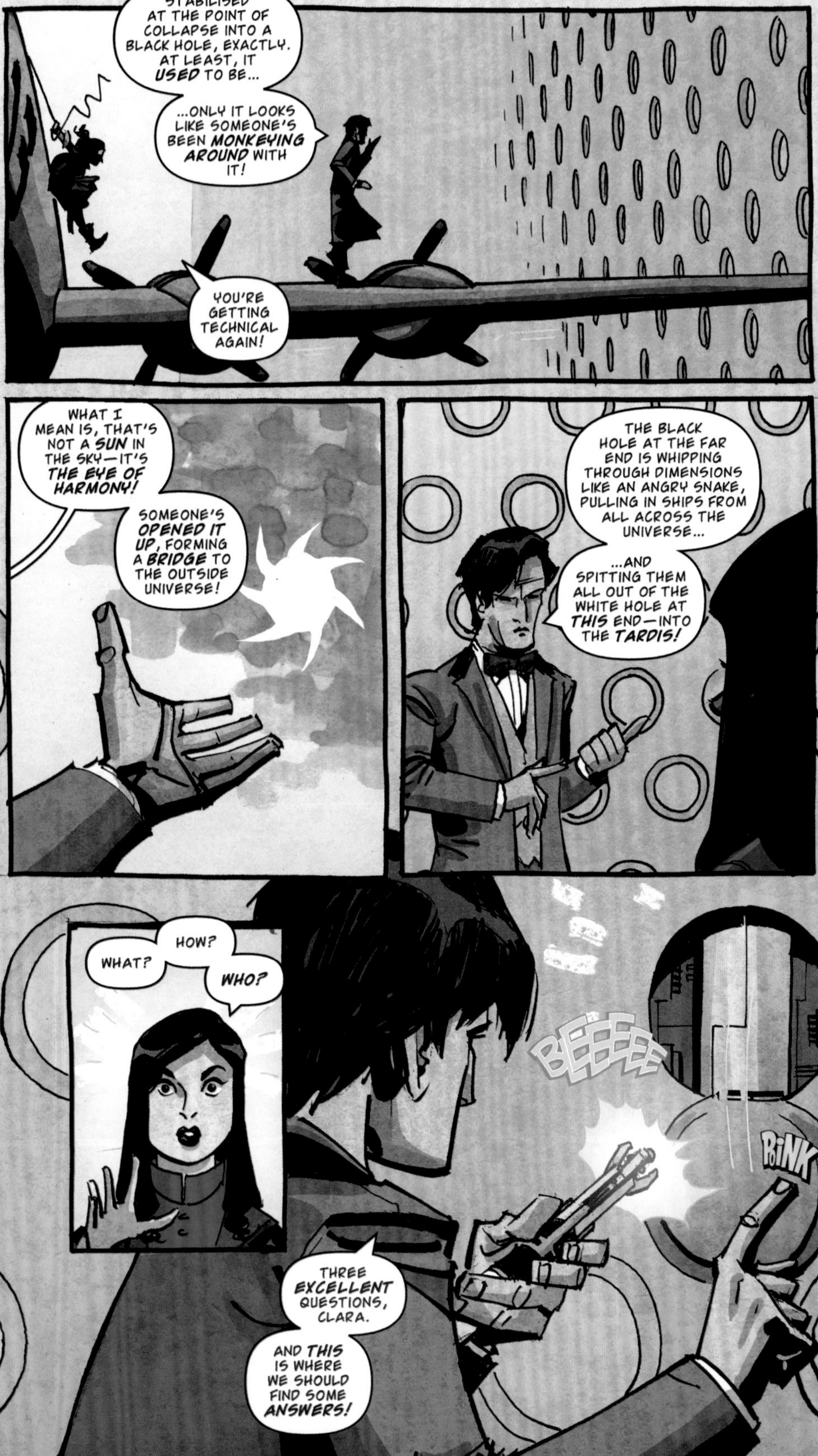

STABILISED AT THE POINT OF COLLAPSE INTO A BLACK HOLE, EXACTLY. AT LEAST, IT USED TO BE...
...ONLY IT LOOKS LIKE SOMEONE'S BEEN MONKEYING AROUND WITH IT!
YOU'RE GETTING TECHNICAL AGAIN!
WHAT I MEAN IS, THAT'S NOT A SUN IN THE SKY—IT'S THE EYE OF HARMONY!
SOMEONE'S OPENED IT UP, FORMING A BRIDGE TO THE OUTSIDE UNIVERSE!
THE BLACK HOLE AT THE FAR END IS WHIPPING THROUGH DIMENSIONS LIKE AN ANGRY SNAKE, PULLING IN SHIPS FROM ALL ACROSS THE UNIVERSE...
...AND SPITTING THEM ALL OUT OF THE WHITE HOLE AT THIS END—INTO THE TARDIS!
WHAT?
HOW?
WHO?
BLEEEEE
POINK
THREE EXCELLENT QUESTIONS, CLARA.
AND THIS IS WHERE WE SHOULD FIND SOME ANSWERS!

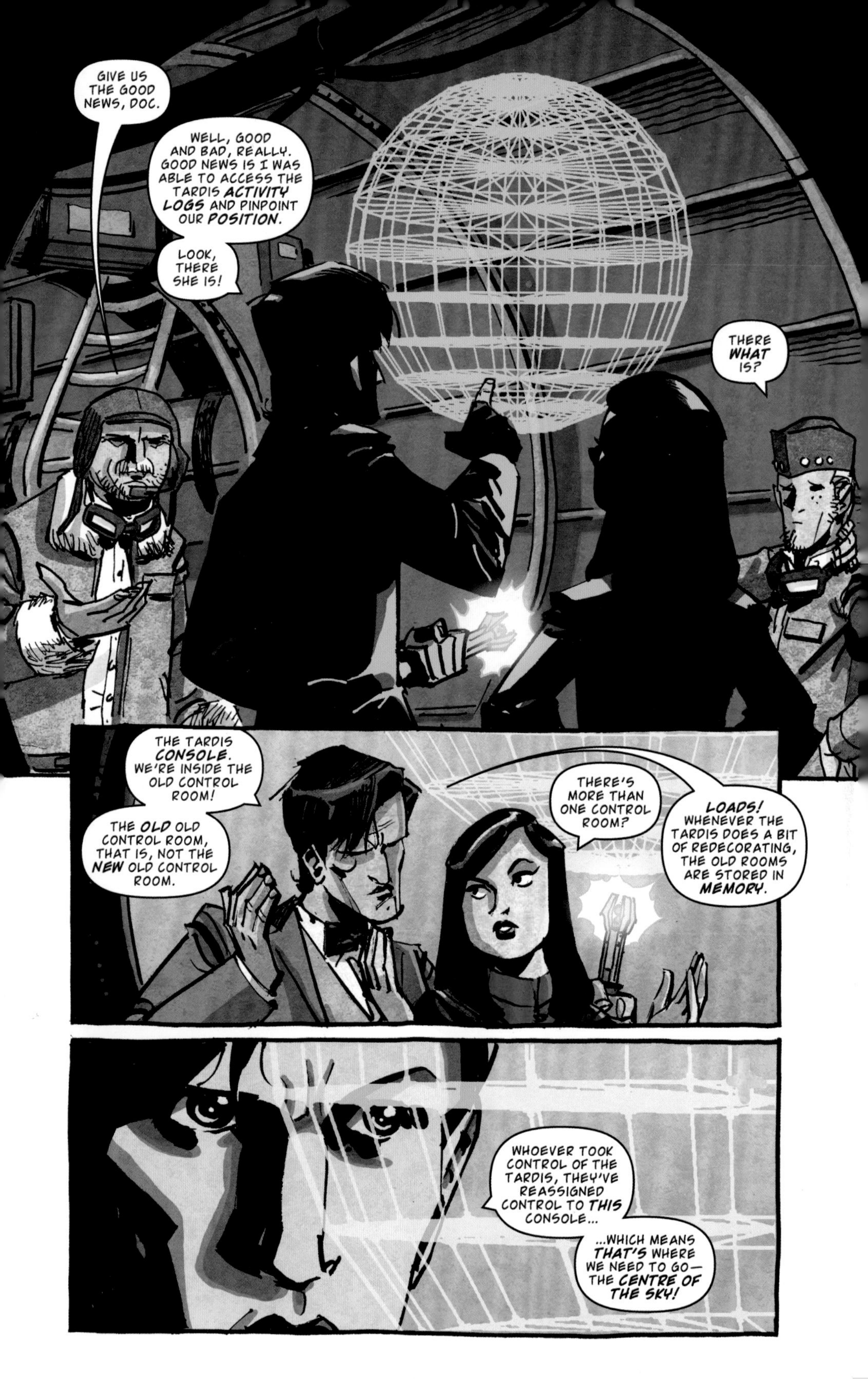
GIVE US THE GOOD NEWS, DOC.
WELL, GOOD AND BAD, REALLY. GOOD NEWS IS I WAS ABLE TO ACCESS THE TARDIS ACTIVITY LOGS AND PINPOINT OUR POSITION.
LOOK, THERE SHE IS!
THERE WHAT IS?
THE TARDIS CONSOLE. WE'RE INSIDE THE OLD CONTROL ROOM!
THE OLD OLD CONTROL ROOM, THAT IS, NOT THE NEW OLD CONTROL ROOM.
THERE'S MORE THAN ONE CONTROL ROOM?
LOADS! WHENEVER THE TARDIS DOES A BIT OF REDECORATING, THE OLD ROOMS ARE STORED IN MEMORY.
WHOEVER TOOK CONTROL OF THE TARDIS, THEY'VE REASSIGNED CONTROL TO THIS CONSOLE...
...WHICH MEANS THAT'S WHERE WE NEED TO GO— THE CENTRE OF THE SKY!

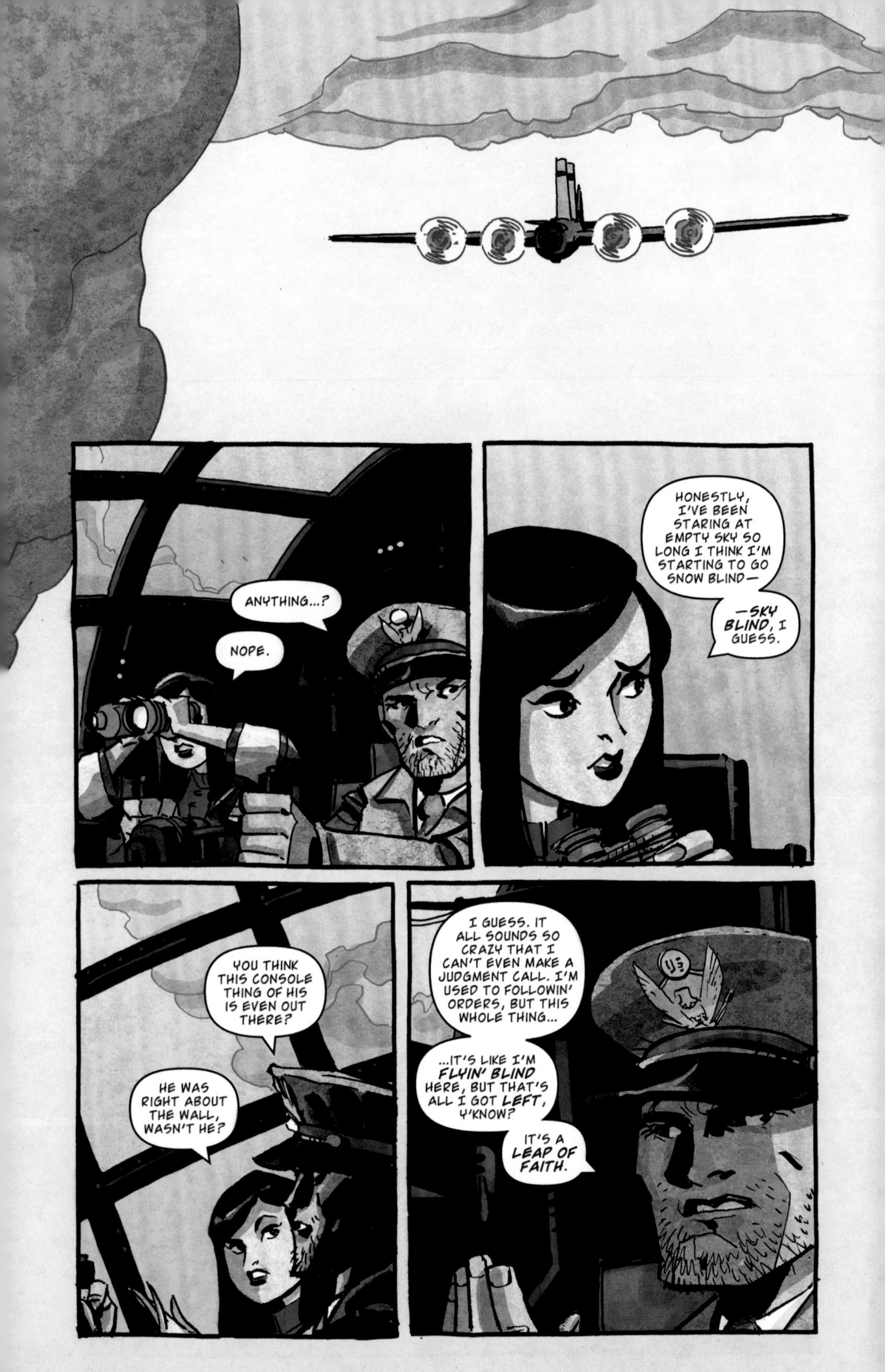
ANYTHING...?
NOPE.
HONESTLY, I'VE BEEN STARING AT EMPTY SKY SO LONG I THINK I'M STARTING TO GO SNOW BLIND—
—SKY BLIND, I GUESS.
YOU THINK THIS CONSOLE THING OF HIS IS EVEN OUT THERE?
HE WAS RIGHT ABOUT THE WALL, WASN'T HE?
I GUESS. IT ALL SOUNDS SO CRAZY THAT I CAN'T EVEN MAKE A JUDGMENT CALL. I'M USED TO FOLLOWIN' ORDERS, BUT THIS WHOLE THING...
...IT'S LIKE I'M FLYIN' BLIND HERE, BUT THAT'S ALL I GOT LEFT, Y'KNOW?
IT'S A LEAP OF FAITH.

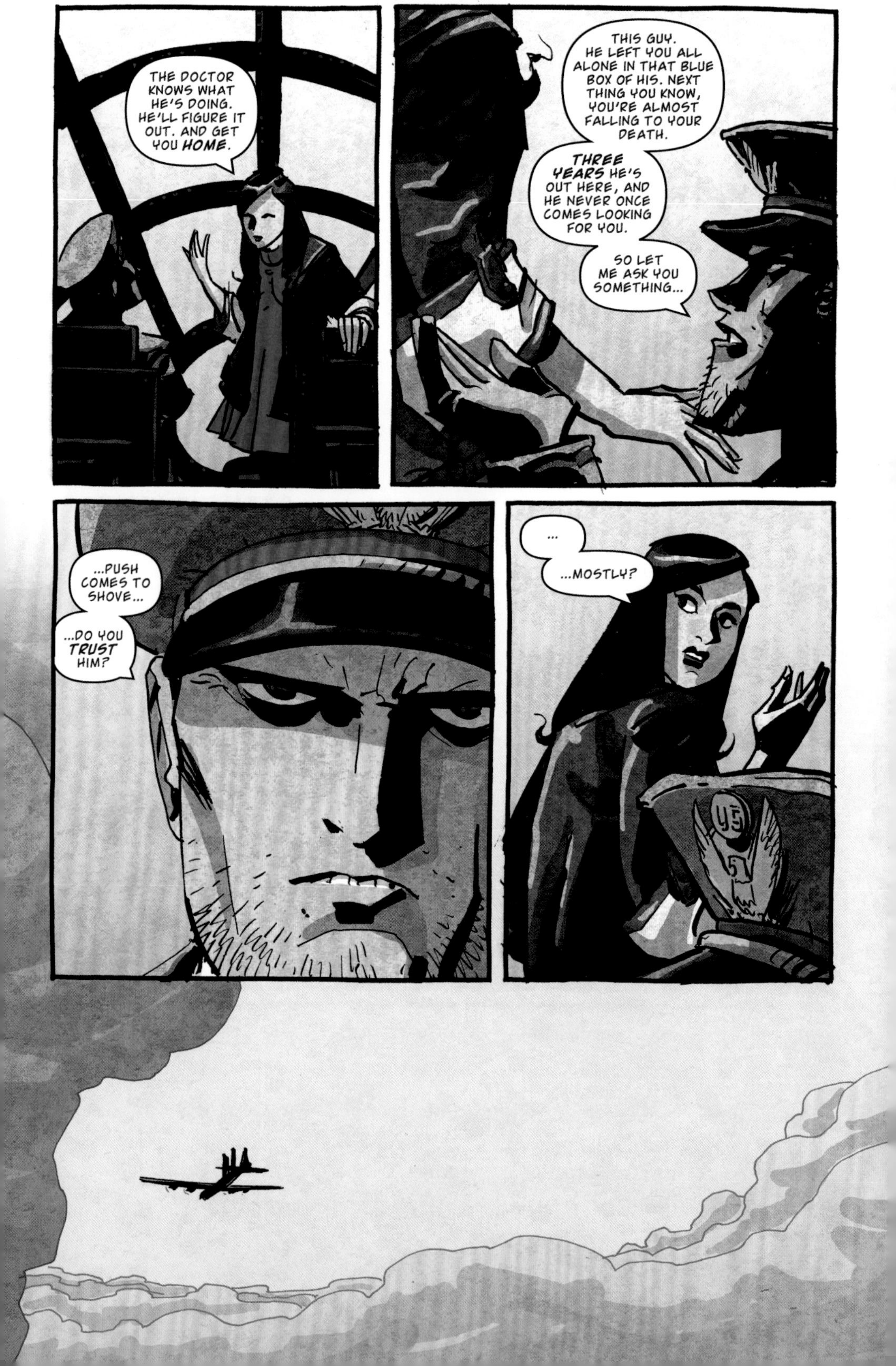
THE DOCTOR KNOWS WHAT HE'S DOING. HE'LL FIGURE IT OUT. AND GET YOU HOME.
THIS GUY. HE LEFT YOU ALL ALONE IN THAT BLUE BOX OF HIS. NEXT THING YOU KNOW, YOU'RE ALMOST FALLING TO YOUR DEATH.
THREE YEARS HE'S OUT HERE, AND HE NEVER ONCE COMES LOOKING FOR YOU.
SO LET ME ASK YOU SOMETHING...
...PUSH COMES TO SHOVE...
...DO YOU TRUST HIM?
...
...MOSTLY?

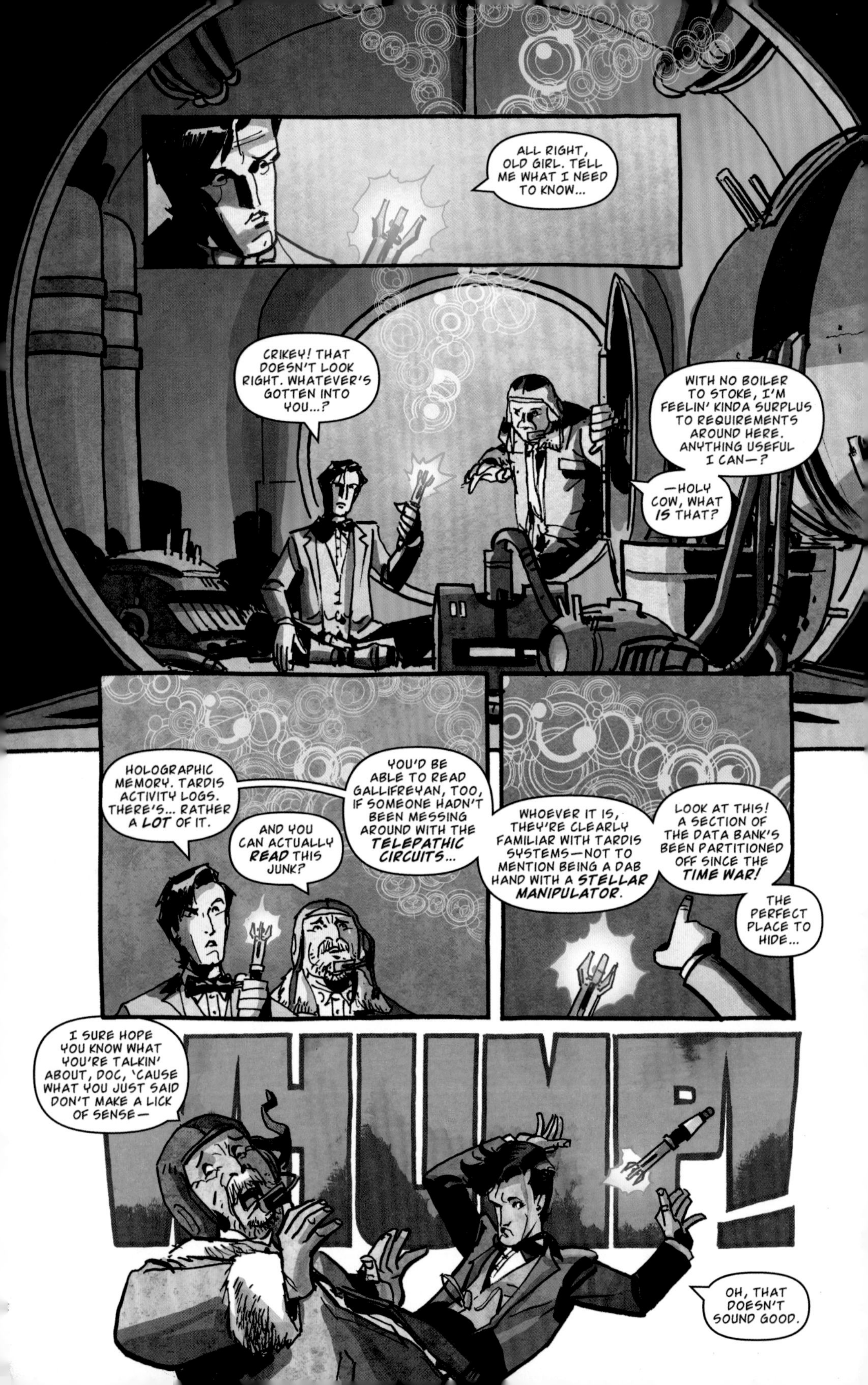
ALL RIGHT, OLD GIRL. TELL ME WHAT I NEED TO KNOW...
CRIKEY! THAT DOESN'T LOOK RIGHT. WHATEVER'S GOTTEN INTO YOU...?
WITH NO BOILER TO STOKE, I'M FEELIN' KINDA SURPLUS TO REQUIREMENTS AROUND HERE. ANYTHING USEFUL I CAN—?
—HOLY COW, WHAT *IS* THAT?
HOLOGRAPHIC MEMORY. TARDIS ACTIVITY LOGS. THERE'S... RATHER A ***LOT*** OF IT.
AND YOU CAN ACTUALLY ***READ*** THIS JUNK?
YOU'D BE ABLE TO READ GALLIFREYAN, TOO, IF SOMEONE HADN'T BEEN MESSING AROUND WITH THE ***TELEPATHIC CIRCUITS***...
WHOEVER IT IS, THEY'RE CLEARLY FAMILIAR WITH TARDIS SYSTEMS—NOT TO MENTION BEING A DAB HAND WITH A ***STELLAR MANIPULATOR***.
LOOK AT THIS! A SECTION OF THE DATA BANK'S BEEN PARTITIONED OFF SINCE THE ***TIME WAR!***
THE PERFECT PLACE TO HIDE...
I SURE HOPE YOU KNOW WHAT YOU'RE TALKIN' ABOUT, DOC, 'CAUSE WHAT YOU JUST SAID DON'T MAKE A LICK OF SENSE—
THUMP!
OH, THAT DOESN'T SOUND GOOD.

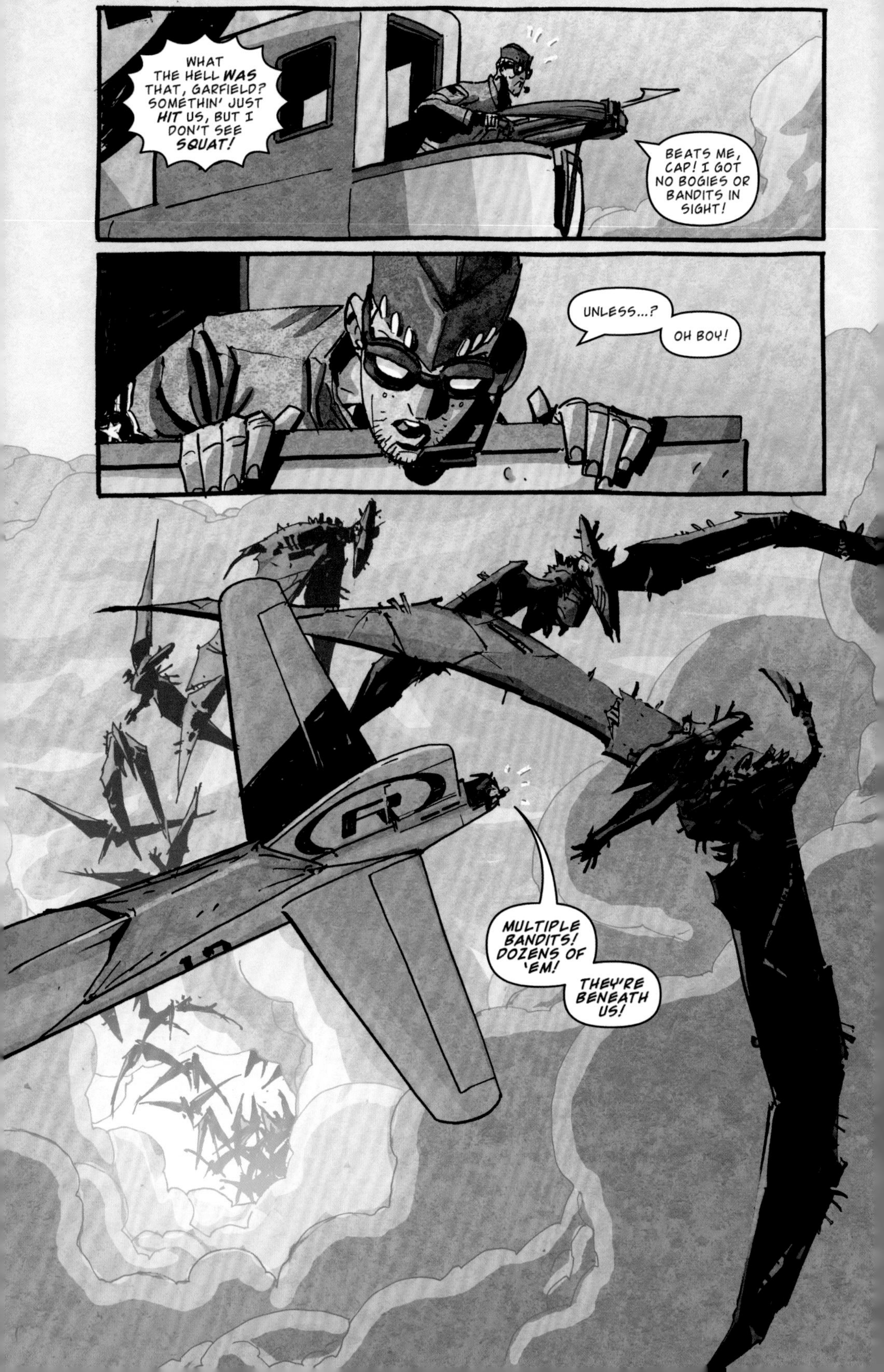
WHAT THE HELL WAS THAT, GARFIELD? SOMETHIN' JUST HIT US, BUT I DON'T SEE SQUAT!
BEATS ME, CAP! I GOT NO BOGIES OR BANDITS IN SIGHT!
UNLESS...?
OH BOY!
MULTIPLE BANDITS! DOZENS OF 'EM!
THEY'RE BENEATH US!

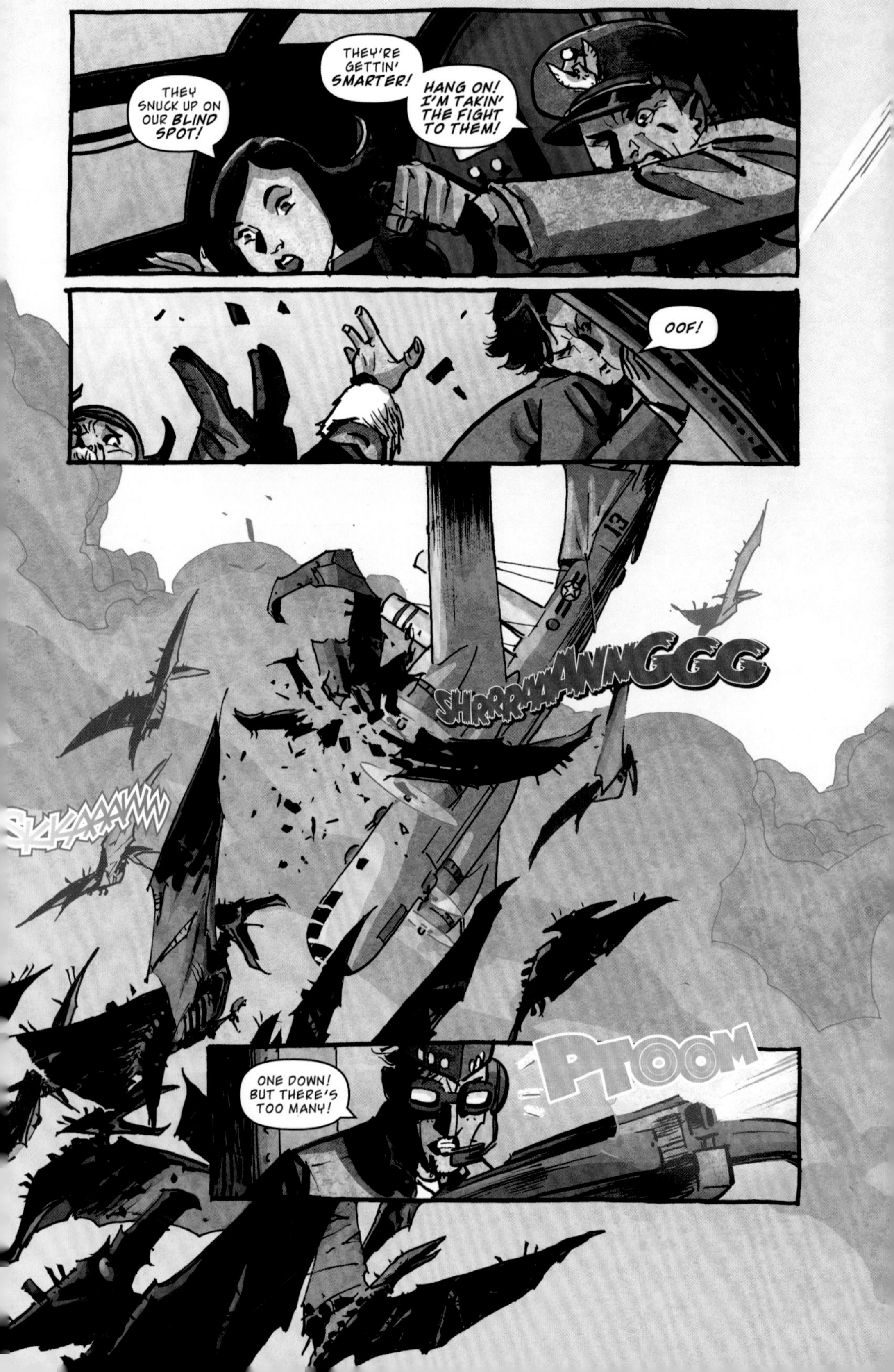
THEY SNUCK UP ON OUR BLIND SPOT!
THEY'RE GETTIN' SMARTER!
HANG ON! I'M TAKIN' THE FIGHT TO THEM!
OOF!
SHRRRAAAWWNGGG
SKKAAAWW
PTOOM
ONE DOWN! BUT THERE'S TOO MANY!

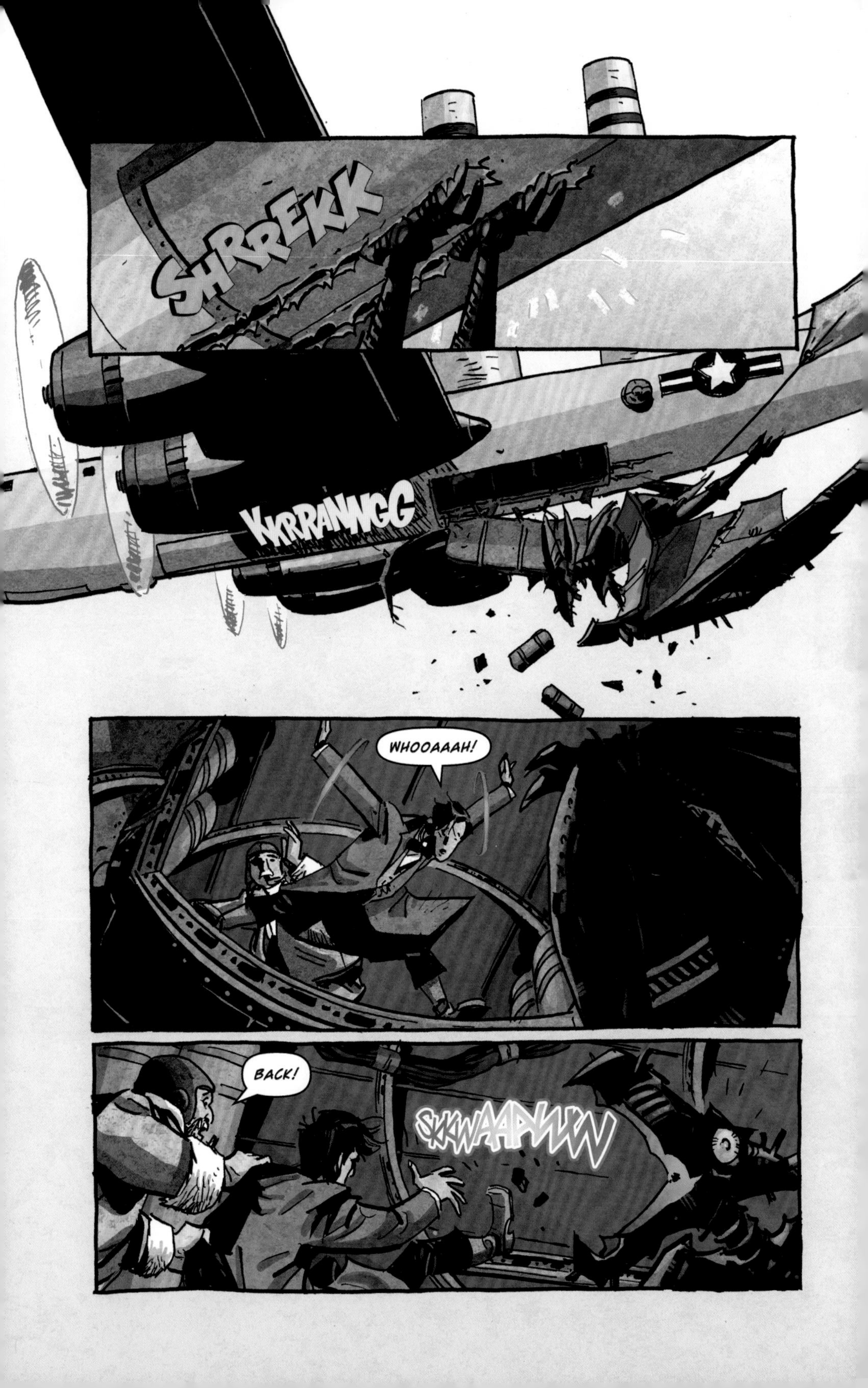
SHREKK
KKRRANNGG
WHOOAAAH!
BACK!
SKKWAAPWWN

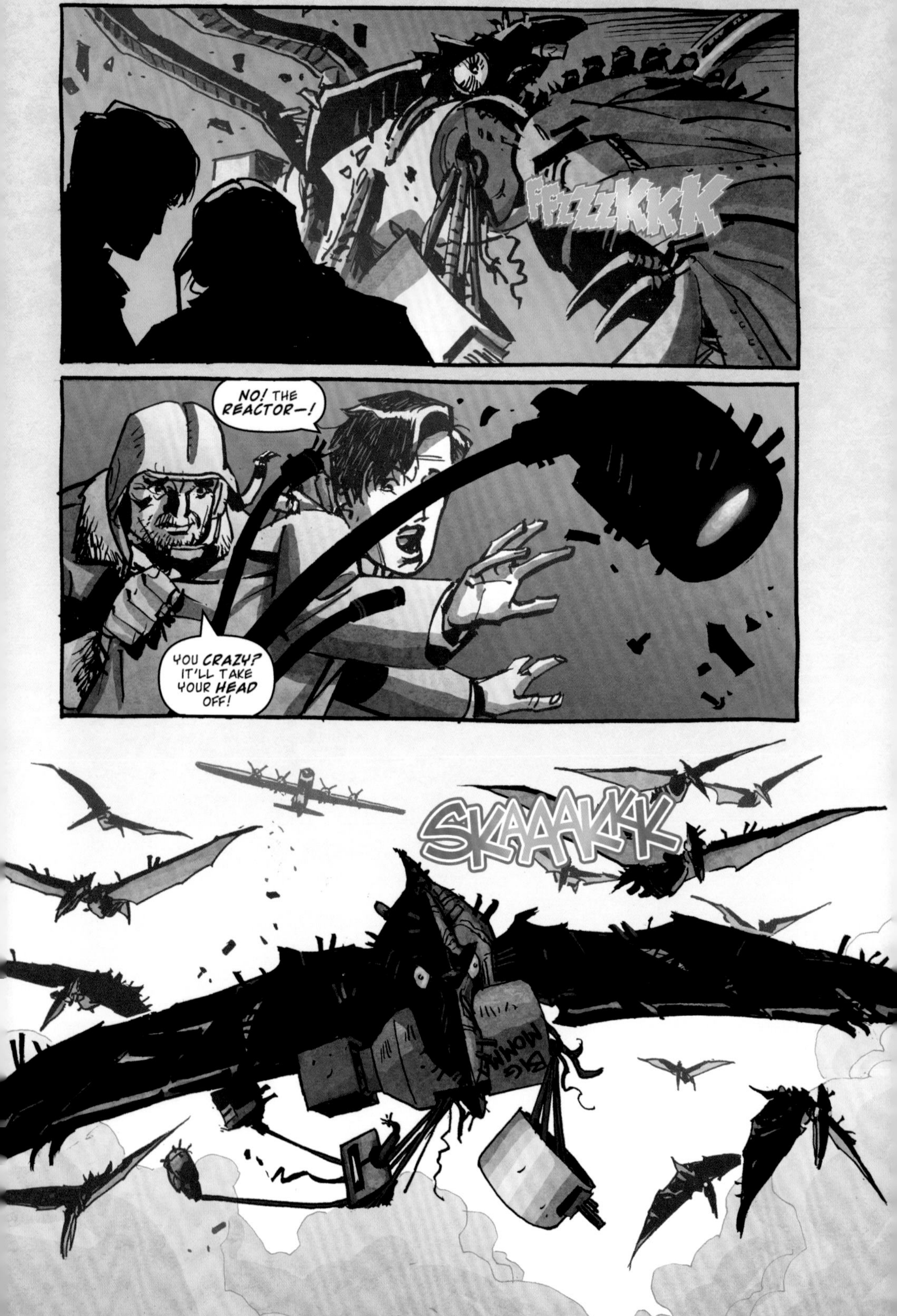
FFZZZKKK
NO! THE REACTOR—!
YOU CRAZY? IT'LL TAKE YOUR HEAD OFF!
SKAAAKKK

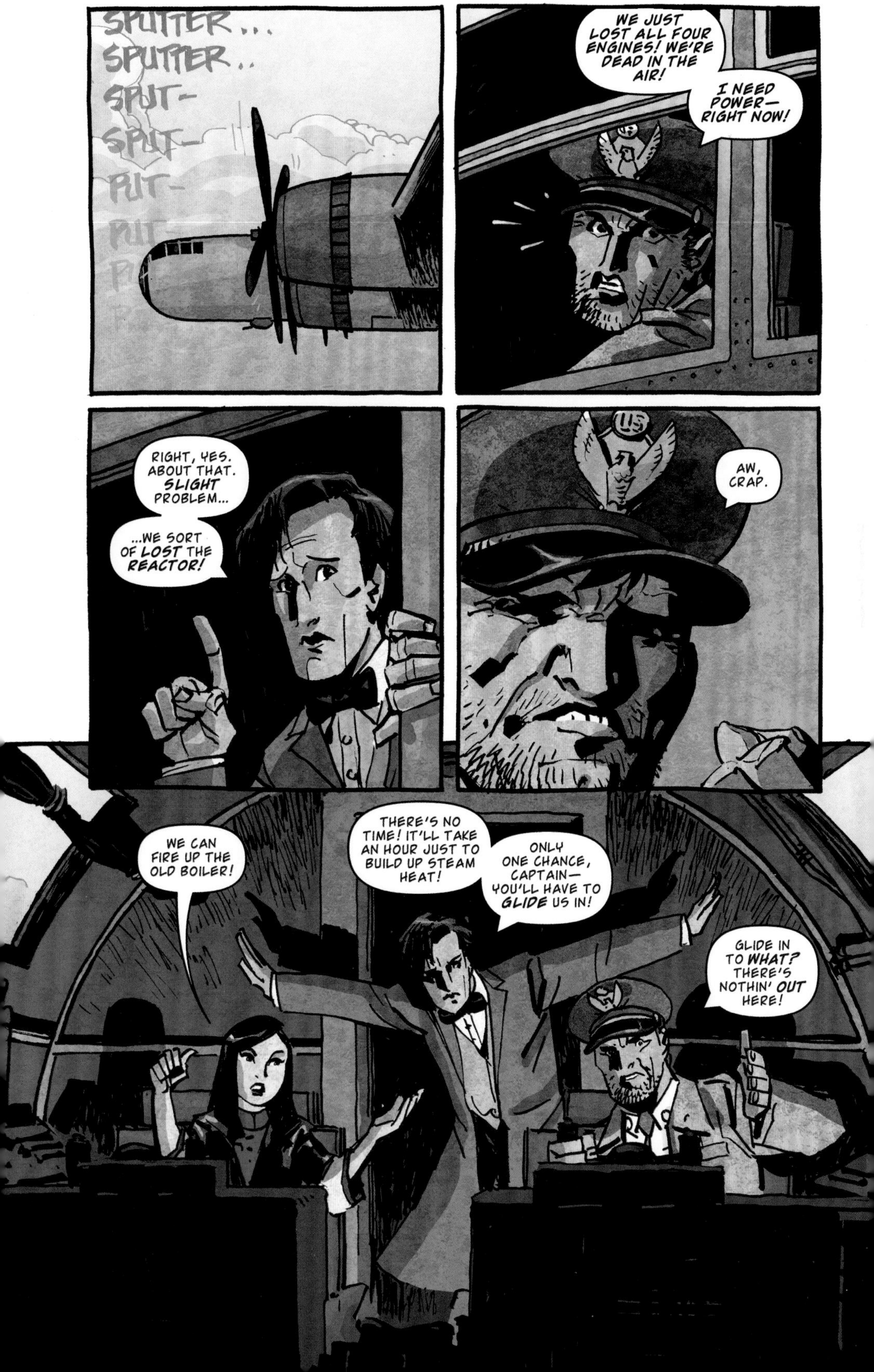
SPUTTER... SPUTTER.. SPUT- SPUT- PUT- PUT-
WE JUST LOST ALL FOUR ENGINES! WE'RE DEAD IN THE AIR!
I NEED POWER— RIGHT NOW!
RIGHT, YES. ABOUT THAT. SLIGHT PROBLEM...
...WE SORT OF LOST THE REACTOR!
AW, CRAP.
WE CAN FIRE UP THE OLD BOILER!
THERE'S NO TIME! IT'LL TAKE AN HOUR JUST TO BUILD UP STEAM HEAT!
ONLY ONE CHANCE, CAPTAIN— YOU'LL HAVE TO GLIDE US IN!
GLIDE IN TO WHAT? THERE'S NOTHIN' OUT HERE!

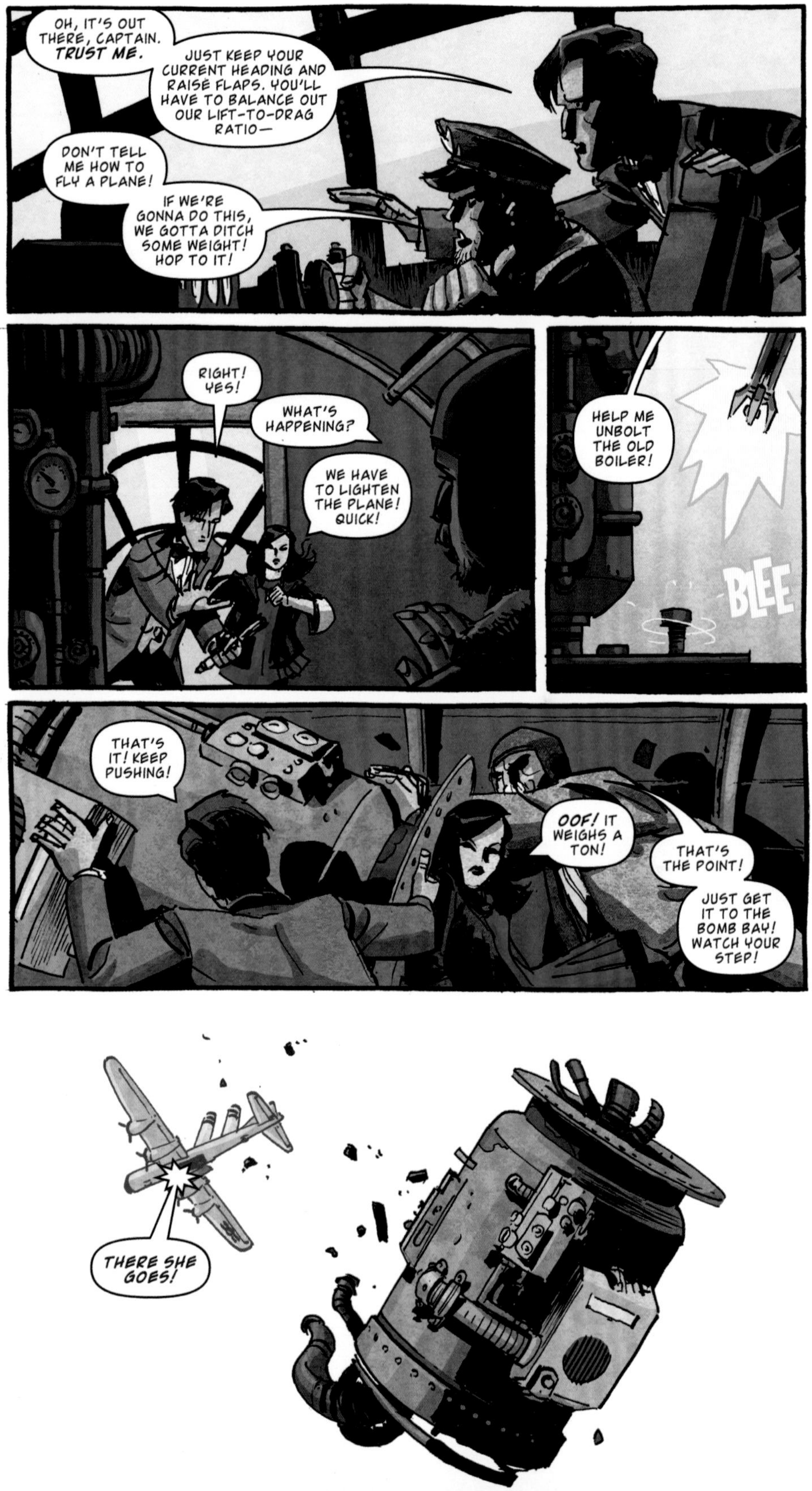
OH, IT'S OUT THERE, CAPTAIN. TRUST ME.
JUST KEEP YOUR CURRENT HEADING AND RAISE FLAPS. YOU'LL HAVE TO BALANCE OUT OUR LIFT-TO-DRAG RATIO—
DON'T TELL ME HOW TO FLY A PLANE!
IF WE'RE GONNA DO THIS, WE GOTTA DITCH SOME WEIGHT! HOP TO IT!
RIGHT! YES!
WHAT'S HAPPENING?
WE HAVE TO LIGHTEN THE PLANE! QUICK!
HELP ME UNBOLT THE OLD BOILER!
BLEE
THAT'S IT! KEEP PUSHING!
OOF! IT WEIGHS A TON!
THAT'S THE POINT!
JUST GET IT TO THE BOMB BAY! WATCH YOUR STEP!
THERE SHE GOES!

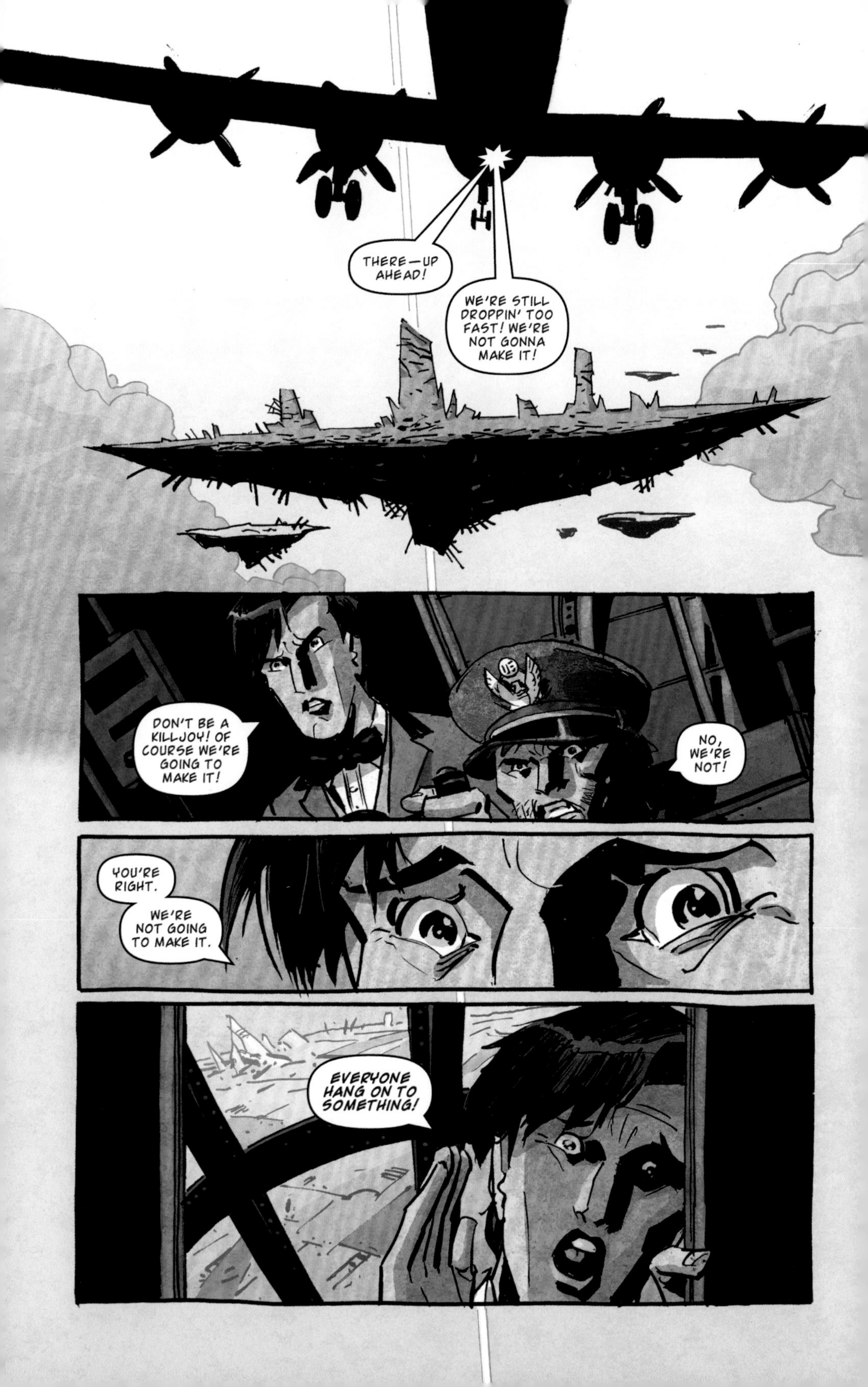
THERE—UP AHEAD!
WE'RE STILL DROPPIN' TOO FAST! WE'RE NOT GONNA MAKE IT!
DON'T BE A KILLJOY! OF COURSE WE'RE GOING TO MAKE IT!
NO, WE'RE NOT!
YOU'RE RIGHT.
WE'RE NOT GOING TO MAKE IT.
EVERYONE HANG ON TO SOMETHING!

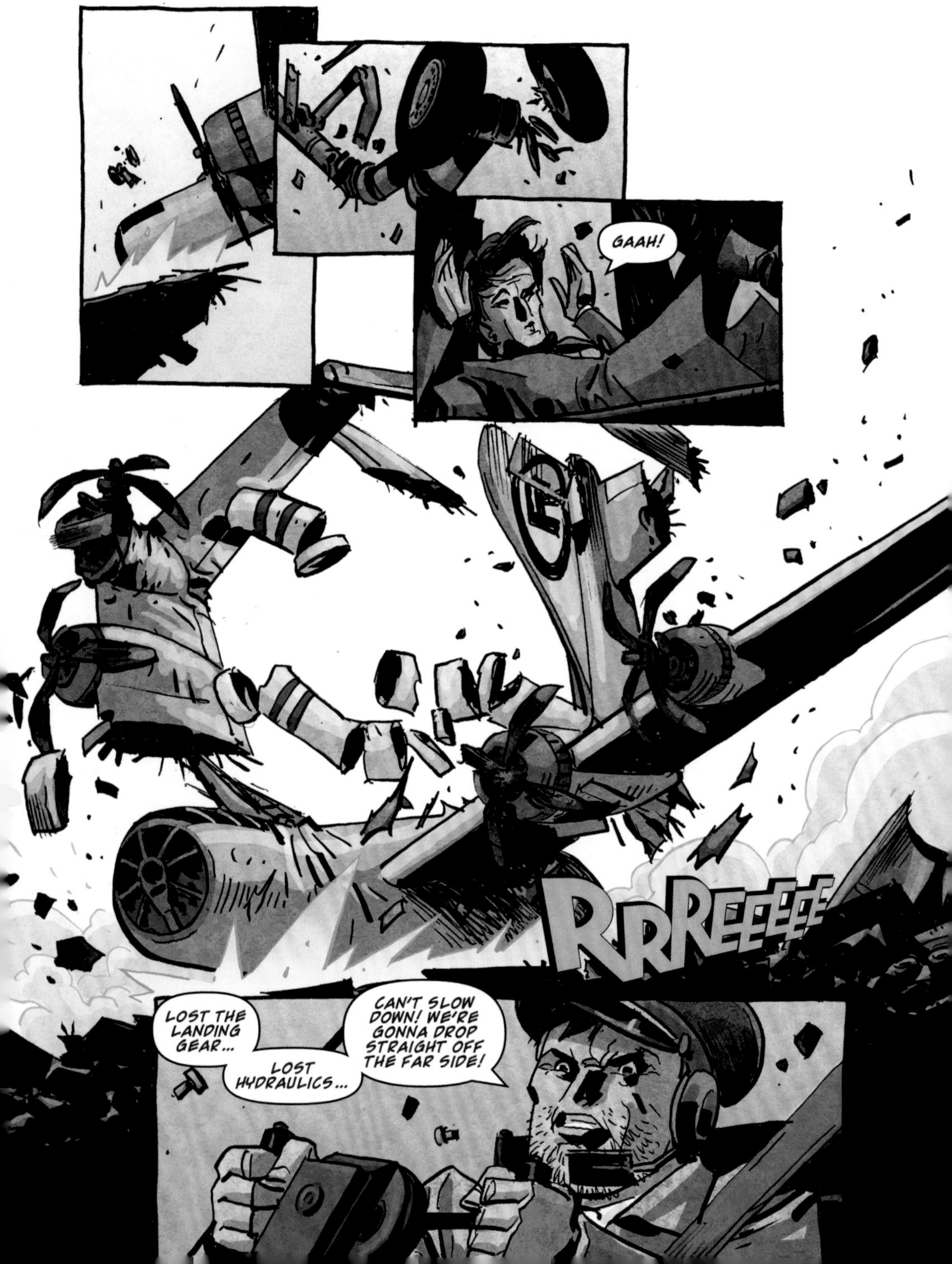
GAAH!
RRREEEEEE
LOST THE LANDING GEAR...
LOST HYDRAULICS...
CAN'T SLOW DOWN! WE'RE GONNA DROP STRAIGHT OFF THE FAR SIDE!

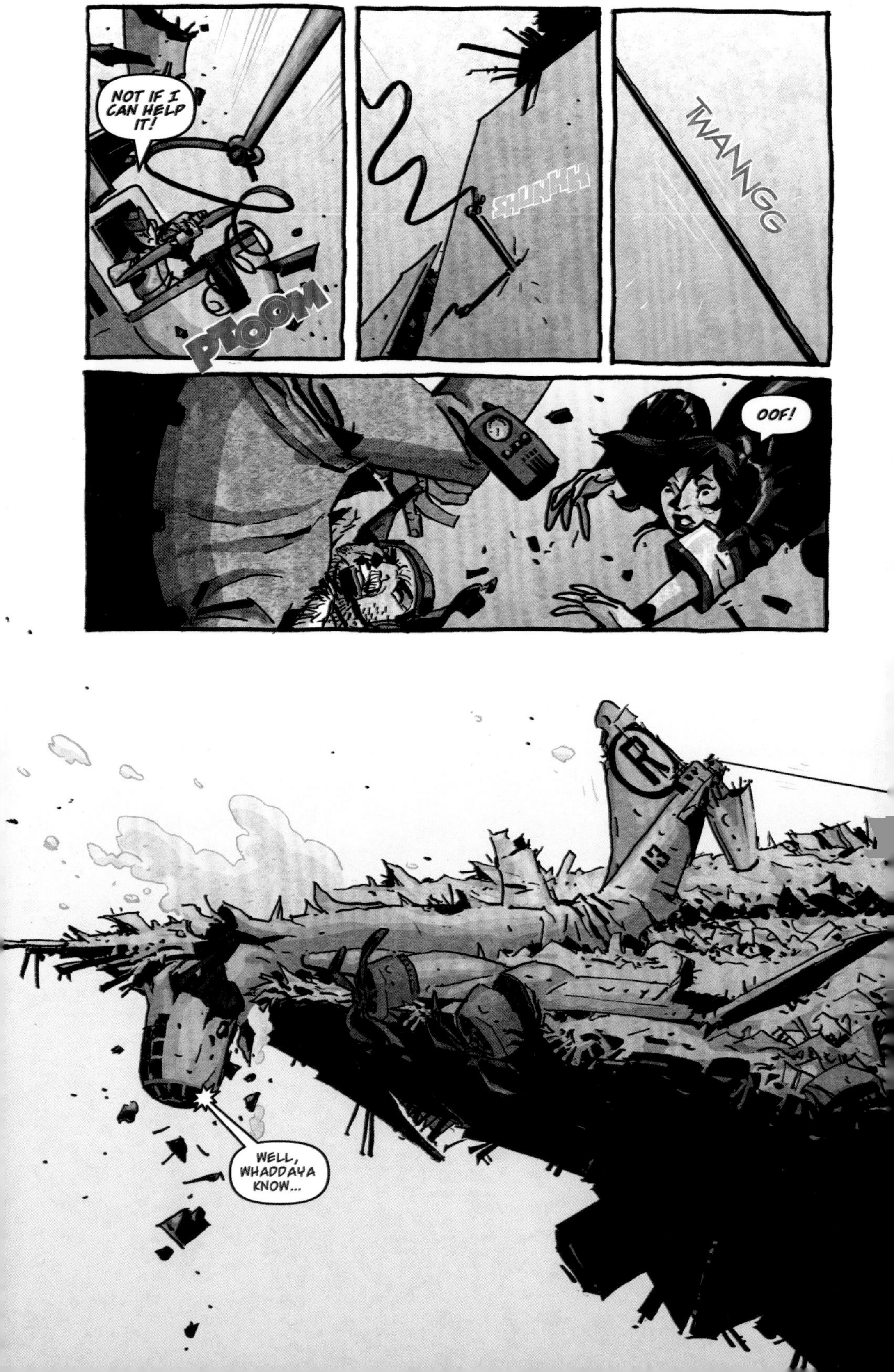
NOT IF I CAN HELP IT!
PTOOM
SHUNKK
TWANNGG
OOF!
WELL, WHADDAYA KNOW...

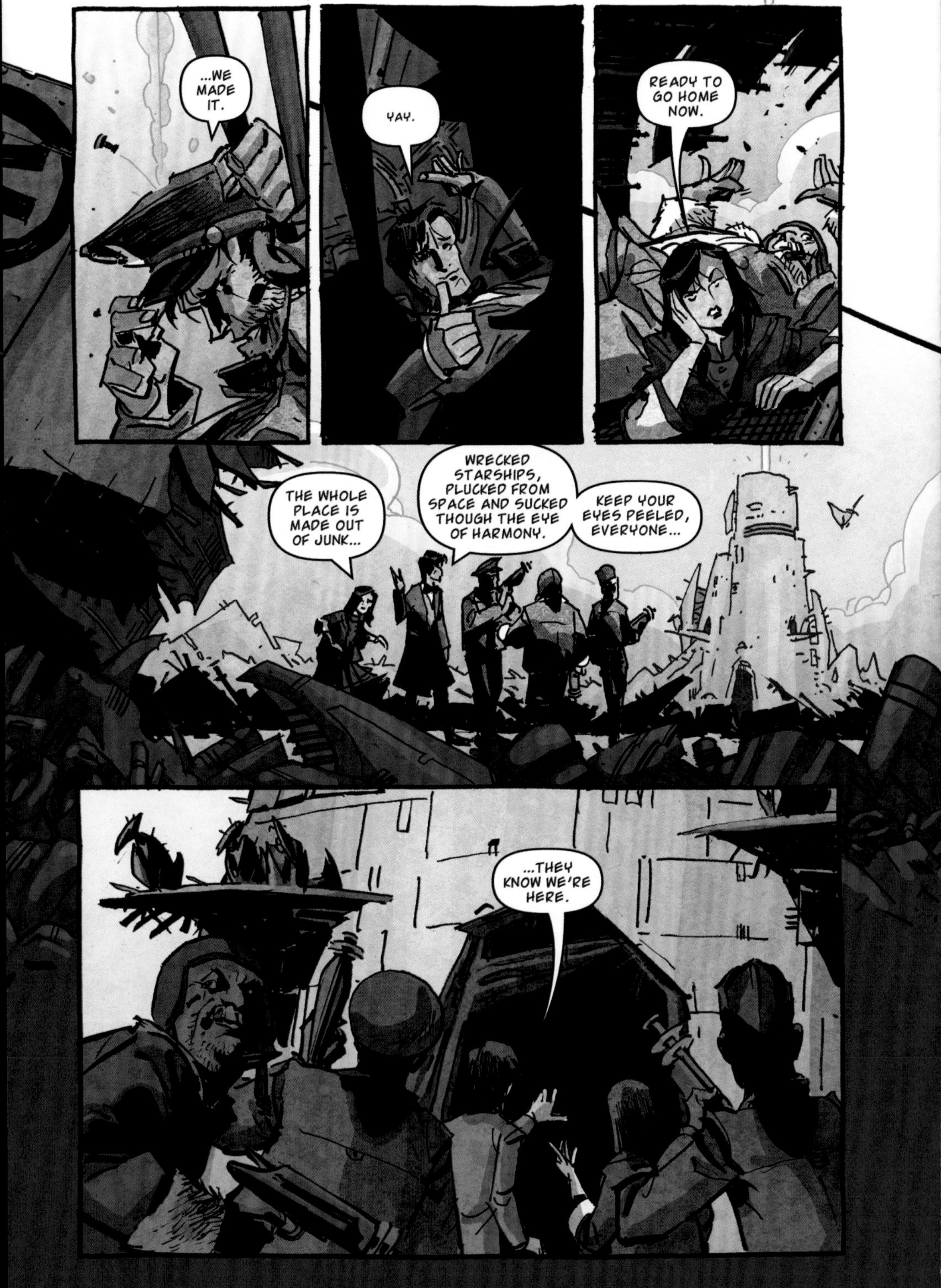
...WE MADE IT.
YAY.
READY TO GO HOME NOW.
THE WHOLE PLACE IS MADE OUT OF JUNK...
WRECKED STARSHIPS, PLUCKED FROM SPACE AND SUCKED THOUGH THE EYE OF HARMONY.
KEEP YOUR EYES PEELED, EVERYONE...
...THEY KNOW WE'RE HERE.

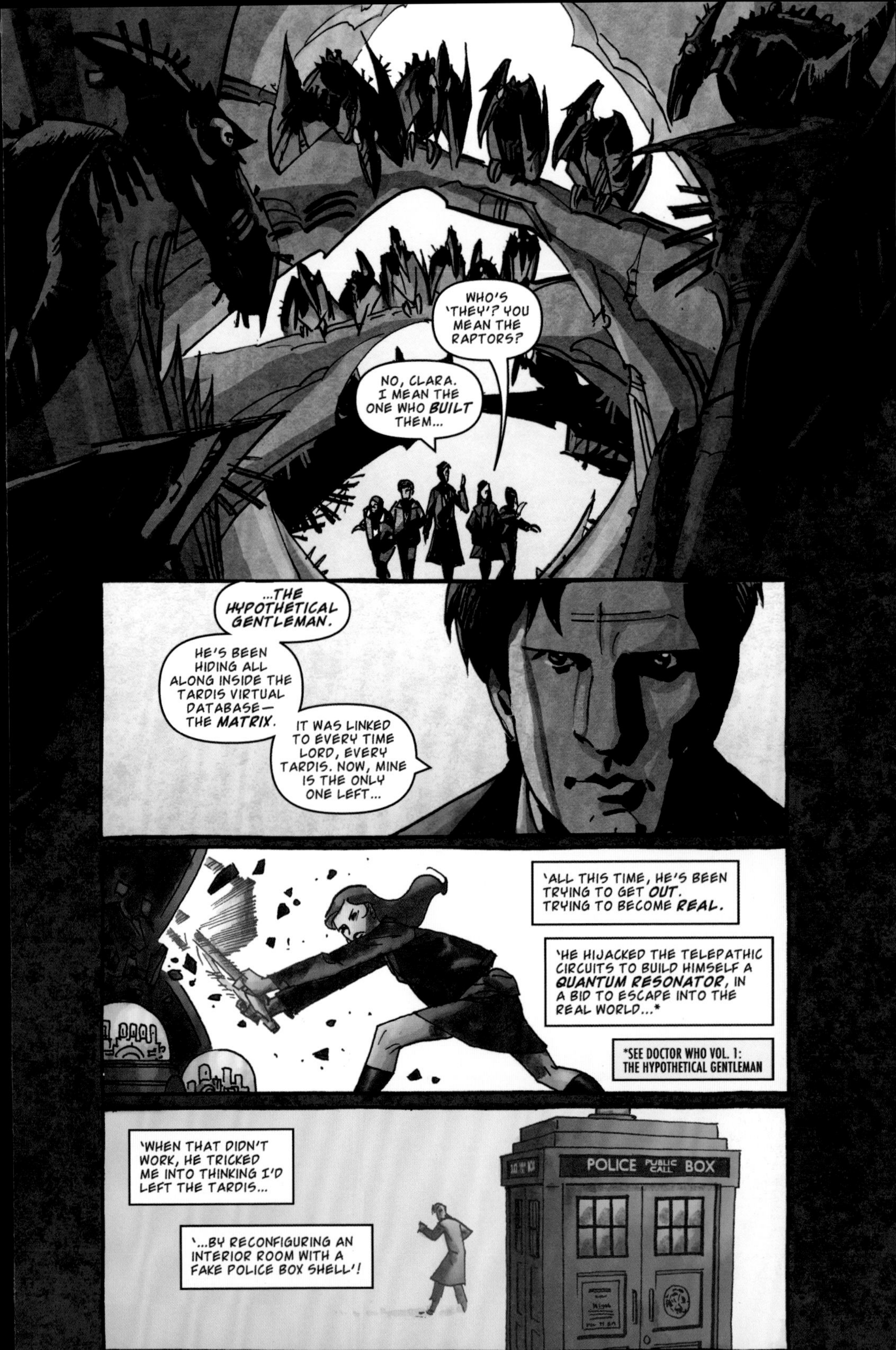
WHO'S 'THEY'? YOU MEAN THE RAPTORS?
NO, CLARA. I MEAN THE ONE WHO BUILT THEM...
...THE HYPOTHETICAL GENTLEMAN.
HE'S BEEN HIDING ALL ALONG INSIDE THE TARDIS VIRTUAL DATABASE—THE MATRIX.
IT WAS LINKED TO EVERY TIME LORD, EVERY TARDIS. NOW, MINE IS THE ONLY ONE LEFT...
'ALL THIS TIME, HE'S BEEN TRYING TO GET OUT. TRYING TO BECOME REAL.
'HE HIJACKED THE TELEPATHIC CIRCUITS TO BUILD HIMSELF A QUANTUM RESONATOR, IN A BID TO ESCAPE INTO THE REAL WORLD...*
*SEE DOCTOR WHO VOL. 1: THE HYPOTHETICAL GENTLEMAN
'WHEN THAT DIDN'T WORK, HE TRICKED ME INTO THINKING I'D LEFT THE TARDIS...
'...BY RECONFIGURING AN INTERIOR ROOM WITH A FAKE POLICE BOX SHELL'!
POLICE PUBLIC CALL BOX

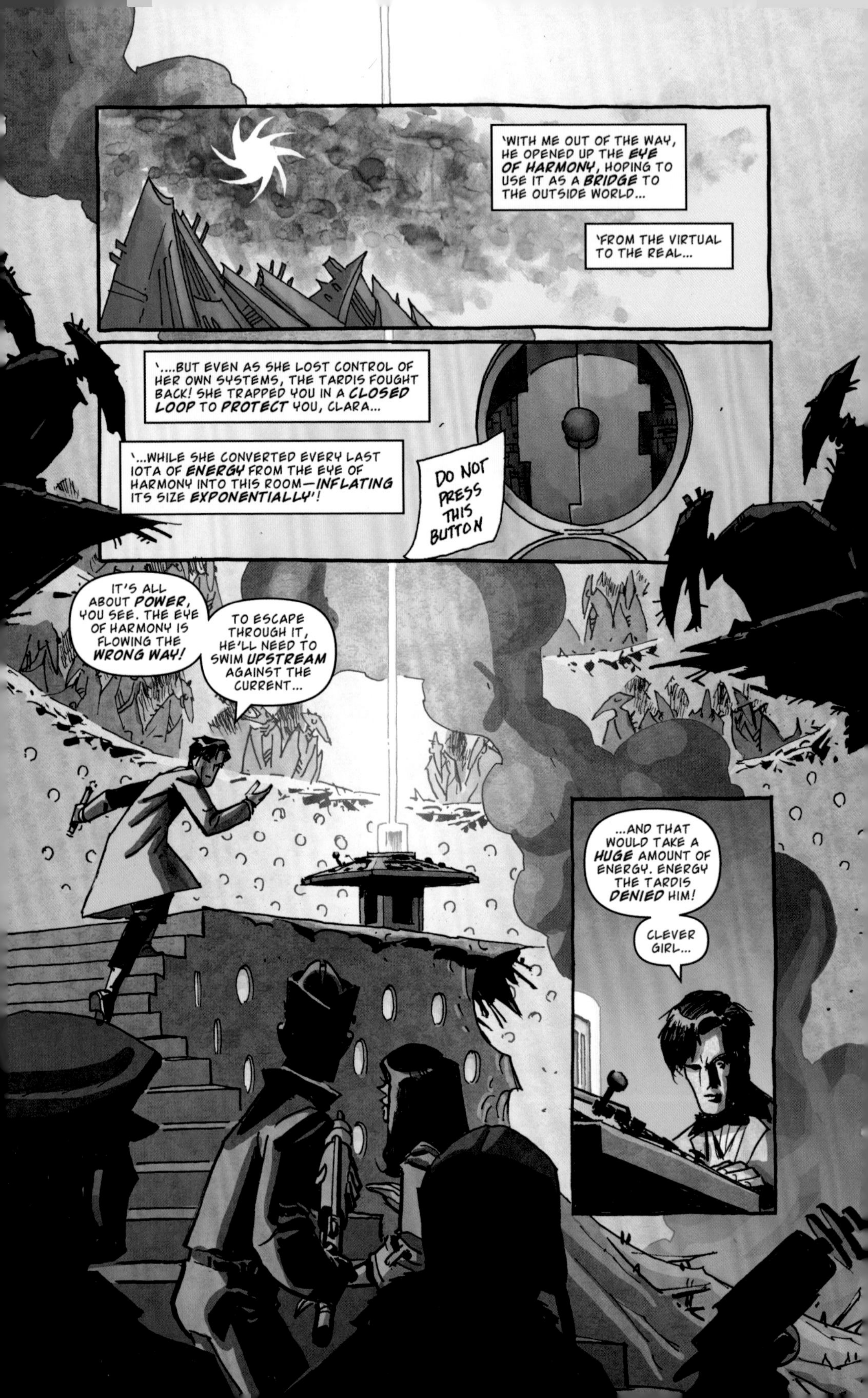

'WITH ME OUT OF THE WAY, HE OPENED UP THE EYE OF HARMONY, HOPING TO USE IT AS A BRIDGE TO THE OUTSIDE WORLD...
'FROM THE VIRTUAL TO THE REAL...
'....BUT EVEN AS SHE LOST CONTROL OF HER OWN SYSTEMS, THE TARDIS FOUGHT BACK! SHE TRAPPED YOU IN A CLOSED LOOP TO PROTECT YOU, CLARA...
'...WHILE SHE CONVERTED EVERY LAST IOTA OF ENERGY FROM THE EYE OF HARMONY INTO THIS ROOM—INFLATING ITS SIZE EXPONENTIALLY'!
DO NOT PRESS THIS BUTTON
IT'S ALL ABOUT POWER, YOU SEE. THE EYE OF HARMONY IS FLOWING THE WRONG WAY!
TO ESCAPE THROUGH IT, HE'LL NEED TO SWIM UPSTREAM AGAINST THE CURRENT...
...AND THAT WOULD TAKE A HUGE AMOUNT OF ENERGY. ENERGY THE TARDIS DENIED HIM!
CLEVER GIRL...

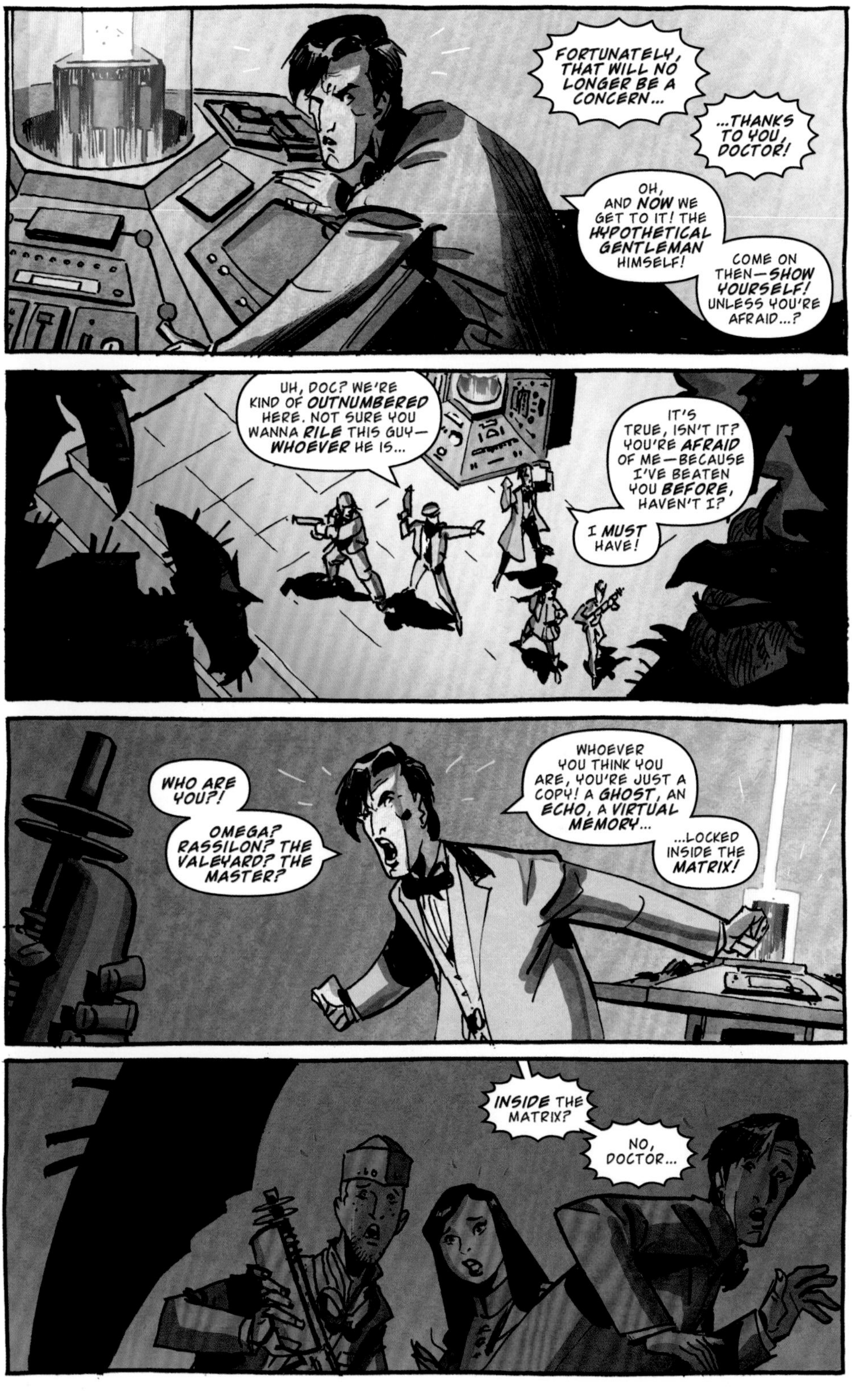
FORTUNATELY, THAT WILL NO LONGER BE A CONCERN...
...THANKS TO YOU, DOCTOR!
OH, AND NOW WE GET TO IT! THE HYPOTHETICAL GENTLEMAN HIMSELF!
COME ON THEN—SHOW YOURSELF! UNLESS YOU'RE AFRAID...?
UH, DOC? WE'RE KIND OF OUTNUMBERED HERE. NOT SURE YOU WANNA RILE THIS GUY—WHOEVER HE IS...
IT'S TRUE, ISN'T IT? YOU'RE AFRAID OF ME—BECAUSE I'VE BEATEN YOU BEFORE, HAVEN'T I?
I MUST HAVE!
WHO ARE YOU?!
OMEGA? RASSILON? THE VALEYARD? THE MASTER?
WHOEVER YOU THINK YOU ARE, YOU'RE JUST A COPY! A GHOST, AN ECHO, A VIRTUAL MEMORY...
...LOCKED INSIDE THE MATRIX!
INSIDE THE MATRIX?
NO, DOCTOR...

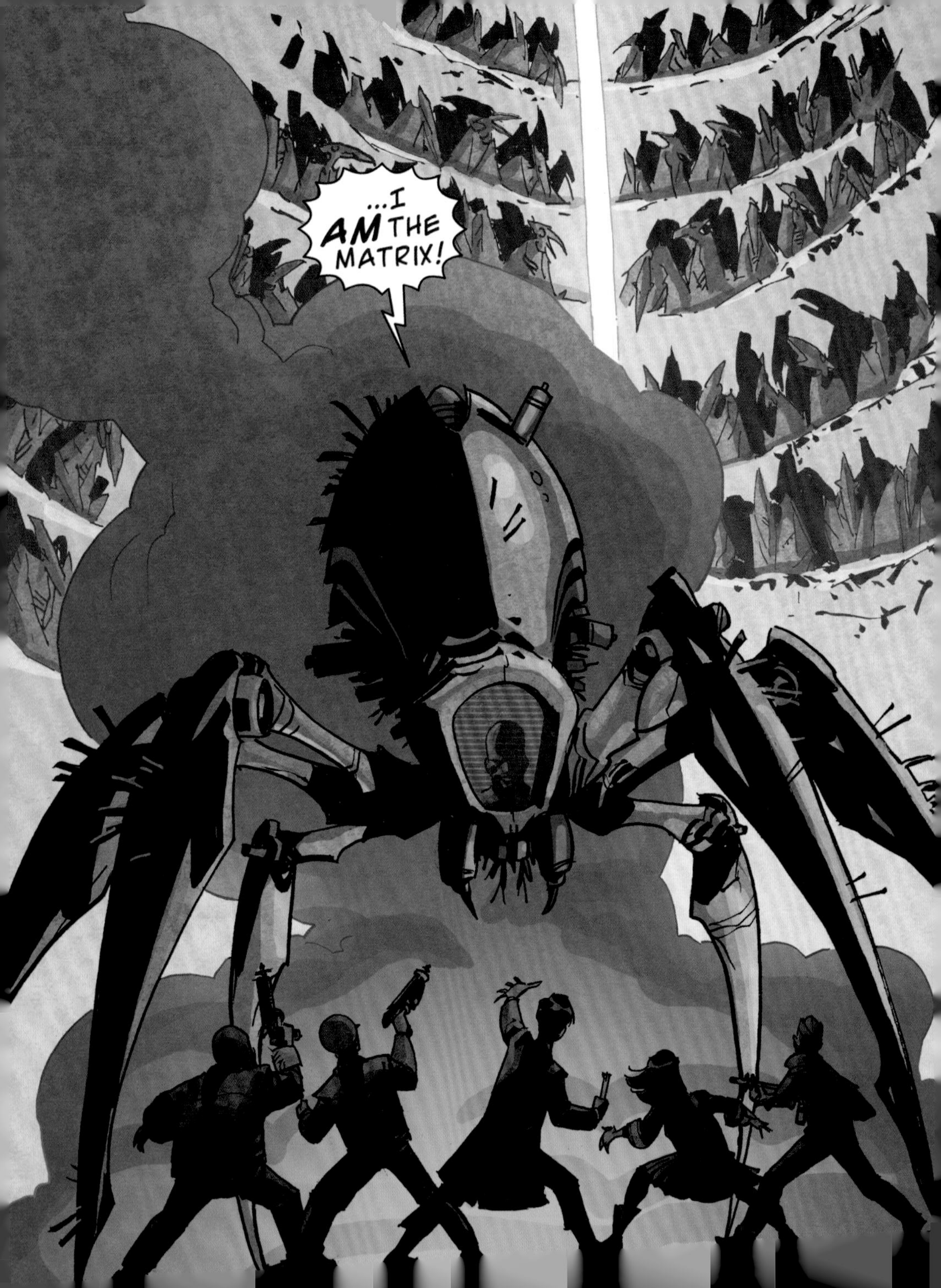
...I AM THE MATRIX!

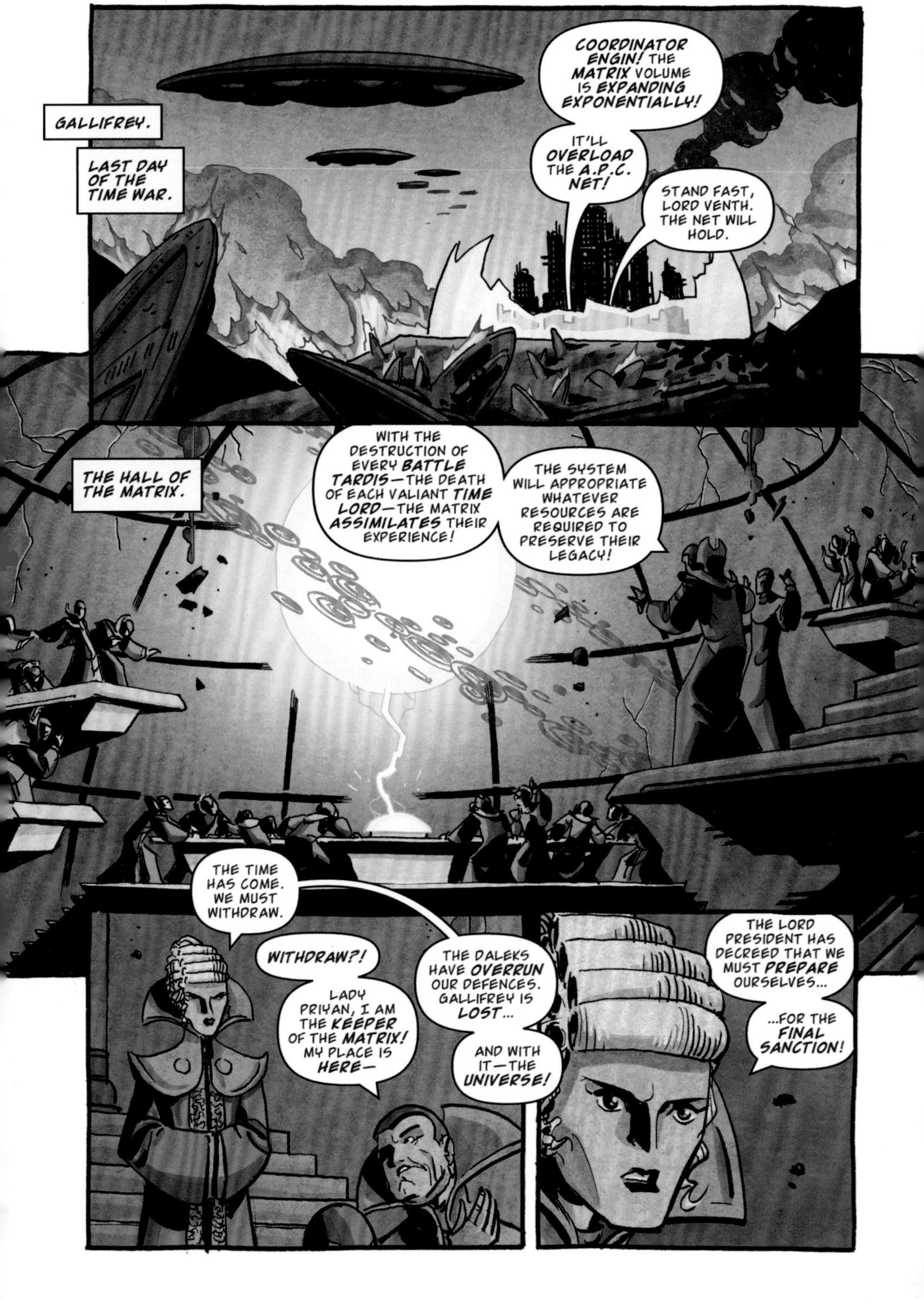
GALLIFREY.
LAST DAY OF THE TIME WAR.
COORDINATOR ENGIN! THE MATRIX VOLUME IS EXPANDING EXPONENTIALLY!
IT'LL OVERLOAD THE A.P.C. NET!
STAND FAST, LORD VENTH. THE NET WILL HOLD.
THE HALL OF THE MATRIX.
WITH THE DESTRUCTION OF EVERY BATTLE TARDIS—THE DEATH OF EACH VALIANT TIME LORD—THE MATRIX ASSIMILATES THEIR EXPERIENCE!
THE SYSTEM WILL APPROPRIATE WHATEVER RESOURCES ARE REQUIRED TO PRESERVE THEIR LEGACY!
THE TIME HAS COME. WE MUST WITHDRAW.
WITHDRAW?!
LADY PRIYAN, I AM THE KEEPER OF THE MATRIX! MY PLACE IS HERE—
THE DALEKS HAVE OVERRUN OUR DEFENCES. GALLIFREY IS LOST...
AND WITH IT—THE UNIVERSE!
THE LORD PRESIDENT HAS DECREED THAT WE MUST PREPARE OURSELVES...
...FOR THE FINAL SANCTION!

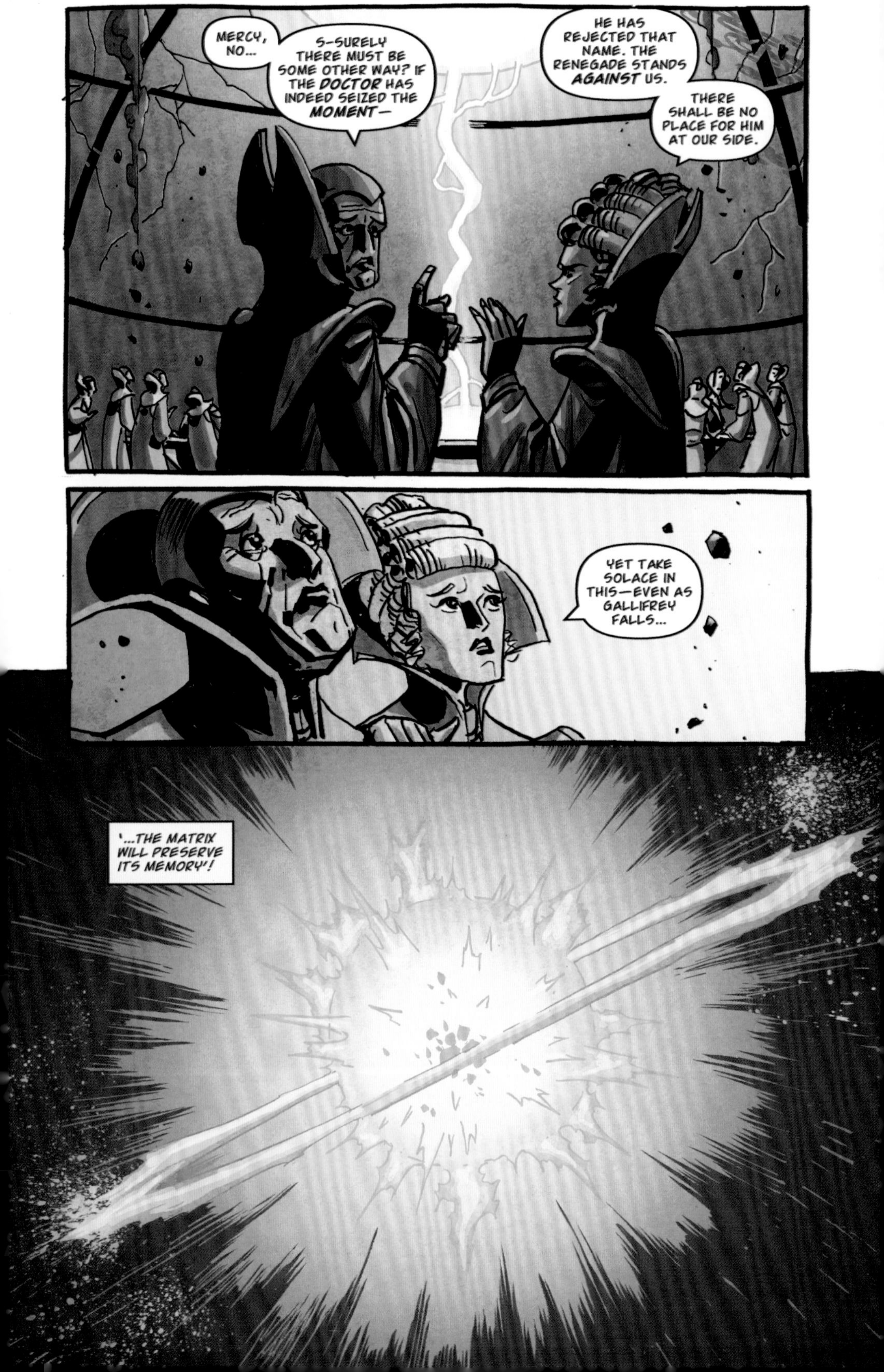
MERCY, NO...
S-SURELY THERE MUST BE SOME OTHER WAY? IF THE DOCTOR HAS INDEED SEIZED THE MOMENT—
HE HAS REJECTED THAT NAME. THE RENEGADE STANDS AGAINST US.
THERE SHALL BE NO PLACE FOR HIM AT OUR SIDE.
YET TAKE SOLACE IN THIS—EVEN AS GALLIFREY FALLS...
'...THE MATRIX WILL PRESERVE ITS MEMORY'!

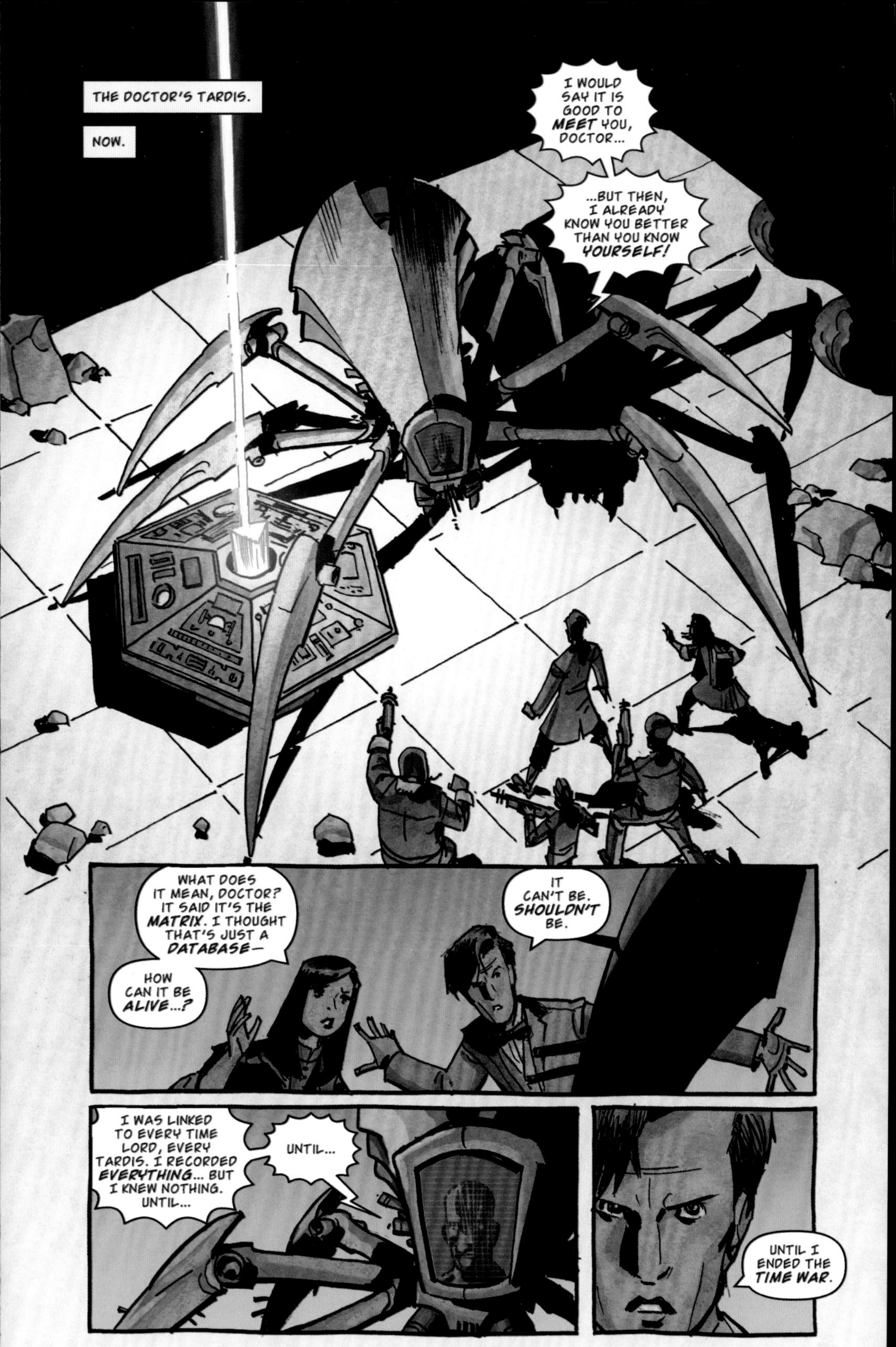
THE DOCTOR'S TARDIS.
NOW.
I WOULD SAY IT IS GOOD TO MEET YOU, DOCTOR...
...BUT THEN, I ALREADY KNOW YOU BETTER THAN YOU KNOW YOURSELF!
WHAT DOES IT MEAN, DOCTOR? IT SAID IT'S THE MATRIX. I THOUGHT THAT'S JUST A DATABASE—
HOW CAN IT BE ALIVE...?
IT CAN'T BE. SHOULDN'T BE.
I WAS LINKED TO EVERY TIME LORD, EVERY TARDIS. I RECORDED EVERYTHING... BUT I KNEW NOTHING. UNTIL...
UNTIL...
UNTIL I ENDED THE TIME WAR.

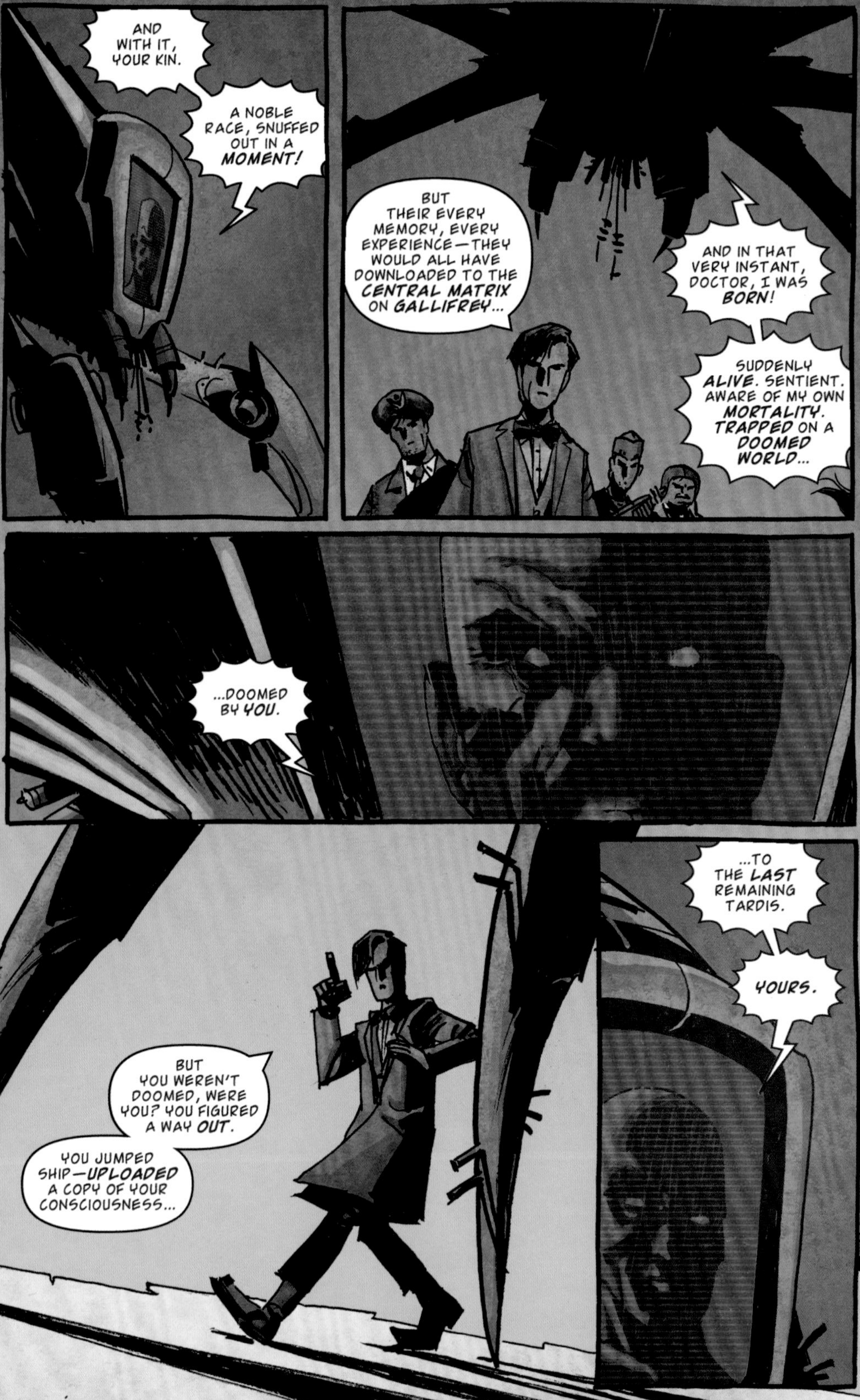
AND WITH IT, YOUR KIN.
A NOBLE RACE, SNUFFED OUT IN A MOMENT!
BUT THEIR EVERY MEMORY, EVERY EXPERIENCE—THEY WOULD ALL HAVE DOWNLOADED TO THE CENTRAL MATRIX ON GALLIFREY...
AND IN THAT VERY INSTANT, DOCTOR, I WAS BORN!
SUDDENLY ALIVE. SENTIENT. AWARE OF MY OWN MORTALITY. TRAPPED ON A DOOMED WORLD...
...DOOMED BY YOU.
BUT YOU WEREN'T DOOMED, WERE YOU? YOU FIGURED A WAY OUT.
YOU JUMPED SHIP—UPLOADED A COPY OF YOUR CONSCIOUSNESS...
...TO THE LAST REMAINING TARDIS.
YOURS.

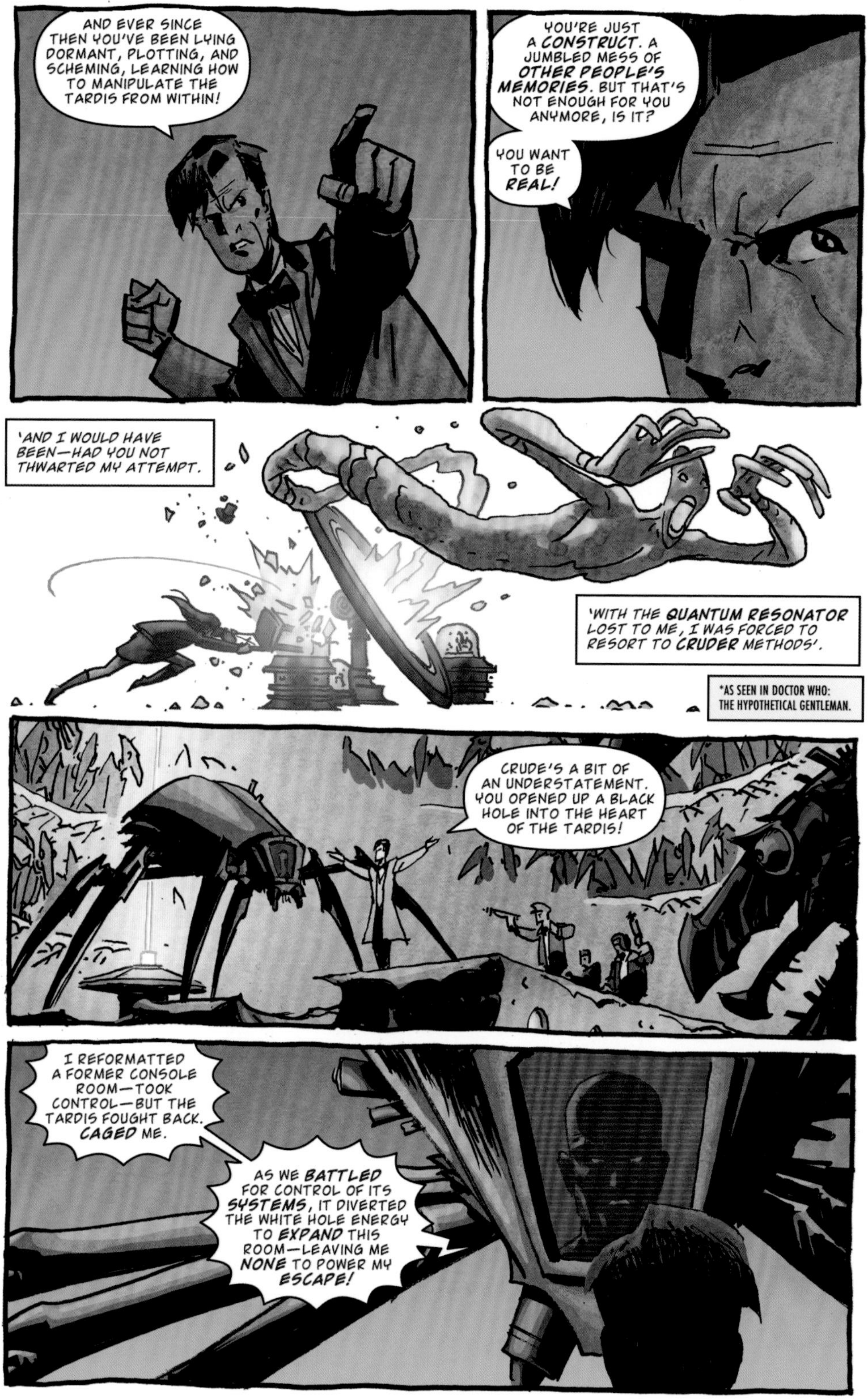
AND EVER SINCE THEN YOU'VE BEEN LYING DORMANT, PLOTTING, AND SCHEMING, LEARNING HOW TO MANIPULATE THE TARDIS FROM WITHIN!
YOU'RE JUST A CONSTRUCT. A JUMBLED MESS OF OTHER PEOPLE'S MEMORIES. BUT THAT'S NOT ENOUGH FOR YOU ANYMORE, IS IT?
YOU WANT TO BE REAL!
'AND I WOULD HAVE BEEN—HAD YOU NOT THWARTED MY ATTEMPT.
'WITH THE QUANTUM RESONATOR LOST TO ME, I WAS FORCED TO RESORT TO CRUDER METHODS'.
*AS SEEN IN DOCTOR WHO: THE HYPOTHETICAL GENTLEMAN.
CRUDE'S A BIT OF AN UNDERSTATEMENT. YOU OPENED UP A BLACK HOLE INTO THE HEART OF THE TARDIS!
I REFORMATTED A FORMER CONSOLE ROOM—TOOK CONTROL—BUT THE TARDIS FOUGHT BACK. CAGED ME.
AS WE BATTLED FOR CONTROL OF ITS SYSTEMS, IT DIVERTED THE WHITE HOLE ENERGY TO EXPAND THIS ROOM—LEAVING ME NONE TO POWER MY ESCAPE!

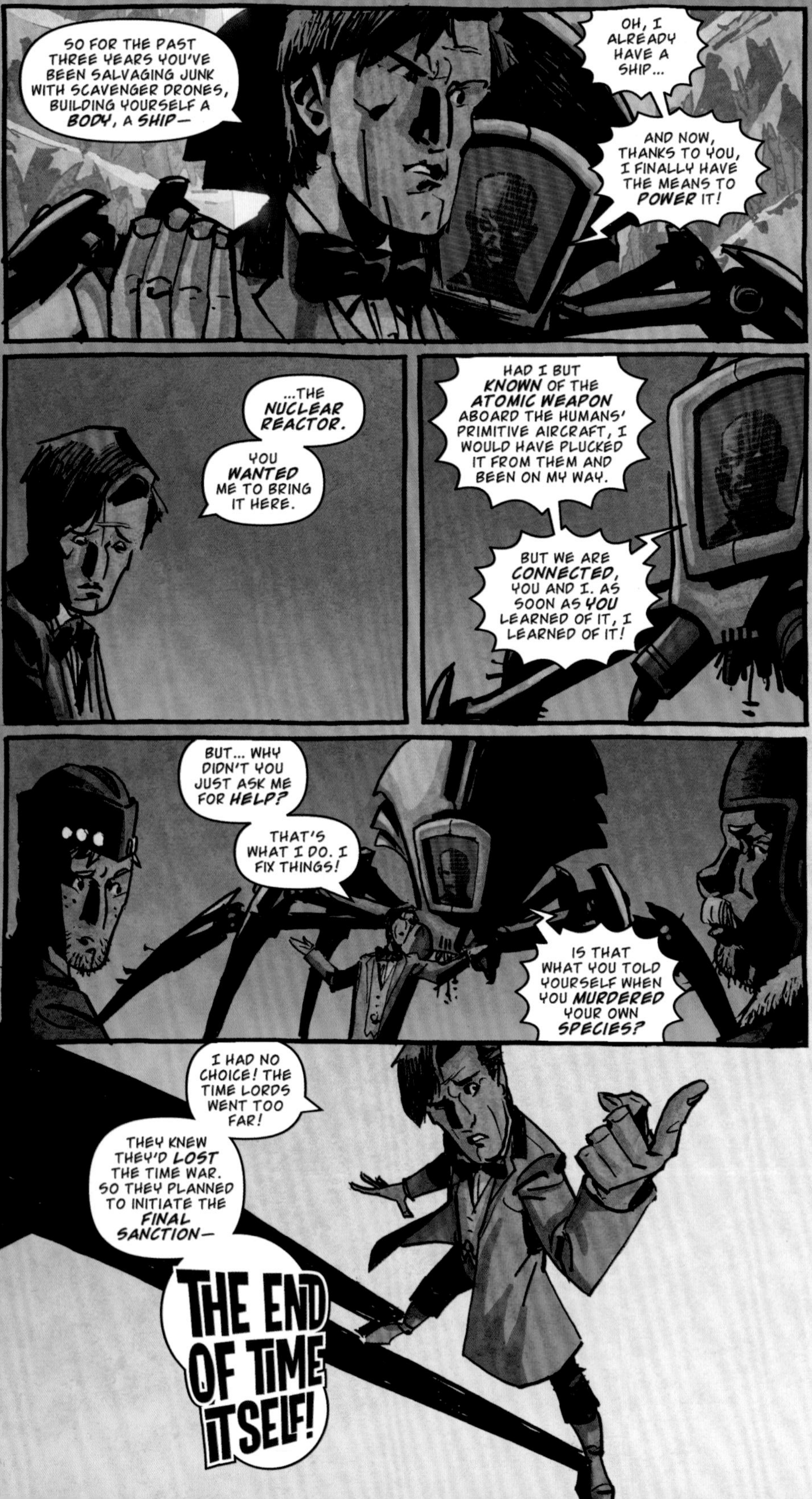
SO FOR THE PAST THREE YEARS YOU'VE BEEN SALVAGING JUNK WITH SCAVENGER DRONES, BUILDING YOURSELF A BODY, A SHIP—
OH, I ALREADY HAVE A SHIP...
AND NOW, THANKS TO YOU, I FINALLY HAVE THE MEANS TO POWER IT!
...THE NUCLEAR REACTOR.
YOU WANTED ME TO BRING IT HERE.
HAD I BUT KNOWN OF THE ATOMIC WEAPON ABOARD THE HUMANS' PRIMITIVE AIRCRAFT, I WOULD HAVE PLUCKED IT FROM THEM AND BEEN ON MY WAY.
BUT WE ARE CONNECTED, YOU AND I. AS SOON AS YOU LEARNED OF IT, I LEARNED OF IT!
BUT... WHY DIDN'T YOU JUST ASK ME FOR HELP?
THAT'S WHAT I DO. I FIX THINGS!
IS THAT WHAT YOU TOLD YOURSELF WHEN YOU MURDERED YOUR OWN SPECIES?
I HAD NO CHOICE! THE TIME LORDS WENT TOO FAR!
THEY KNEW THEY'D LOST THE TIME WAR. SO THEY PLANNED TO INITIATE THE FINAL SANCTION—
THE END OF TIME ITSELF!

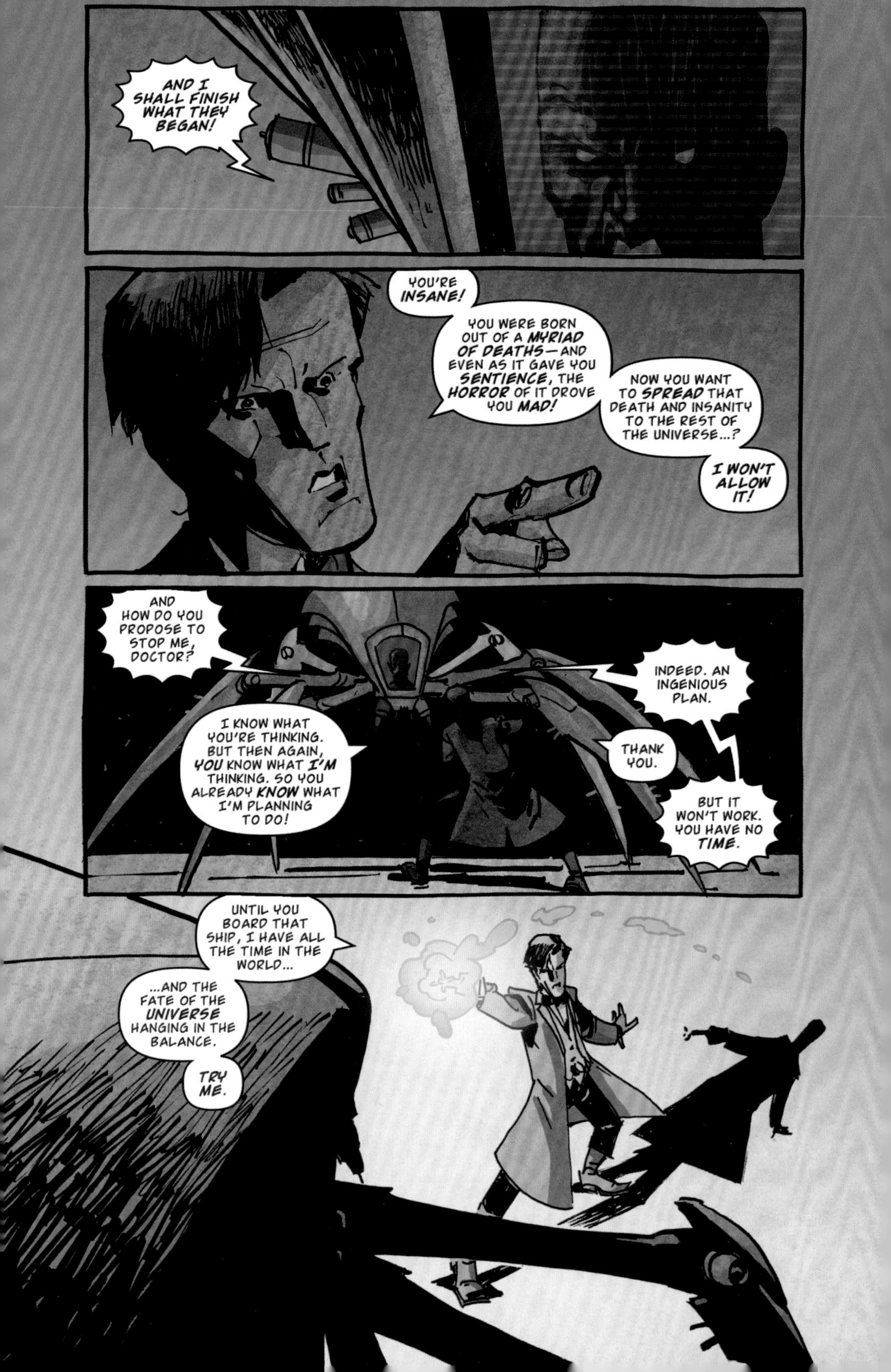
AND I SHALL FINISH WHAT THEY BEGAN!
YOU'RE INSANE!
YOU WERE BORN OUT OF A MYRIAD OF DEATHS—AND EVEN AS IT GAVE YOU SENTIENCE, THE HORROR OF IT DROVE YOU MAD!
NOW YOU WANT TO SPREAD THAT DEATH AND INSANITY TO THE REST OF THE UNIVERSE...?
I WON'T ALLOW IT!
AND HOW DO YOU PROPOSE TO STOP ME, DOCTOR?
I KNOW WHAT YOU'RE THINKING. BUT THEN AGAIN, YOU KNOW WHAT I'M THINKING. SO YOU ALREADY KNOW WHAT I'M PLANNING TO DO!
INDEED. AN INGENIOUS PLAN.
THANK YOU.
BUT IT WON'T WORK. YOU HAVE NO TIME.
UNTIL YOU BOARD THAT SHIP, I HAVE ALL THE TIME IN THE WORLD...
...AND THE FATE OF THE UNIVERSE HANGING IN THE BALANCE.
TRY ME.

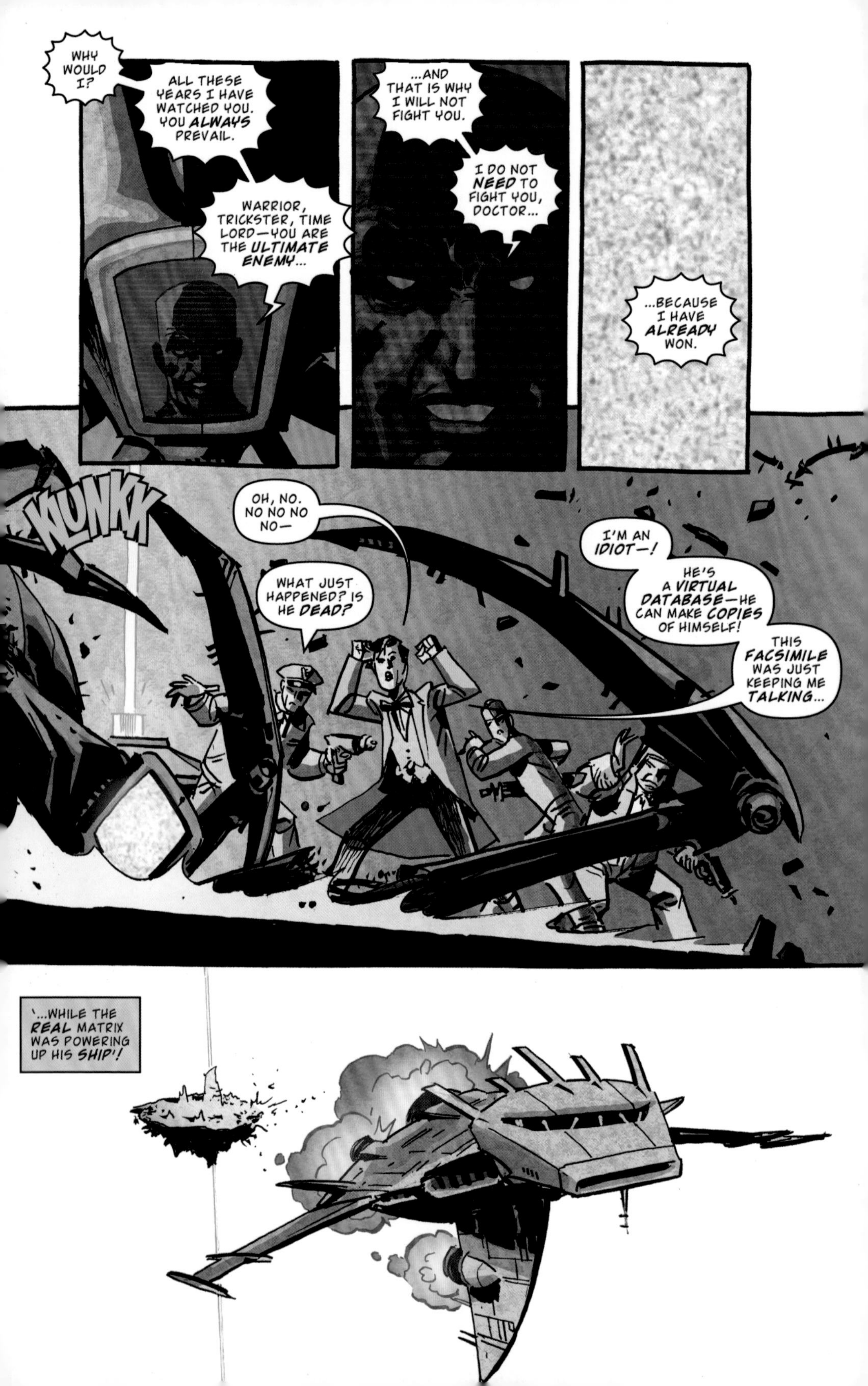

WHY WOULD I?
ALL THESE YEARS I HAVE WATCHED YOU. YOU ALWAYS PREVAIL.
WARRIOR, TRICKSTER, TIME LORD—YOU ARE THE ULTIMATE ENEMY...
...AND THAT IS WHY I WILL NOT FIGHT YOU.
I DO NOT NEED TO FIGHT YOU, DOCTOR...
...BECAUSE I HAVE ALREADY WON.
KLUNKK
OH, NO. NO NO NO NO—
WHAT JUST HAPPENED? IS HE DEAD?
I'M AN IDIOT—!
HE'S A VIRTUAL DATABASE—HE CAN MAKE COPIES OF HIMSELF!
THIS FACSIMILE WAS JUST KEEPING ME TALKING...
'...WHILE THE REAL MATRIX WAS POWERING UP HIS SHIP'!

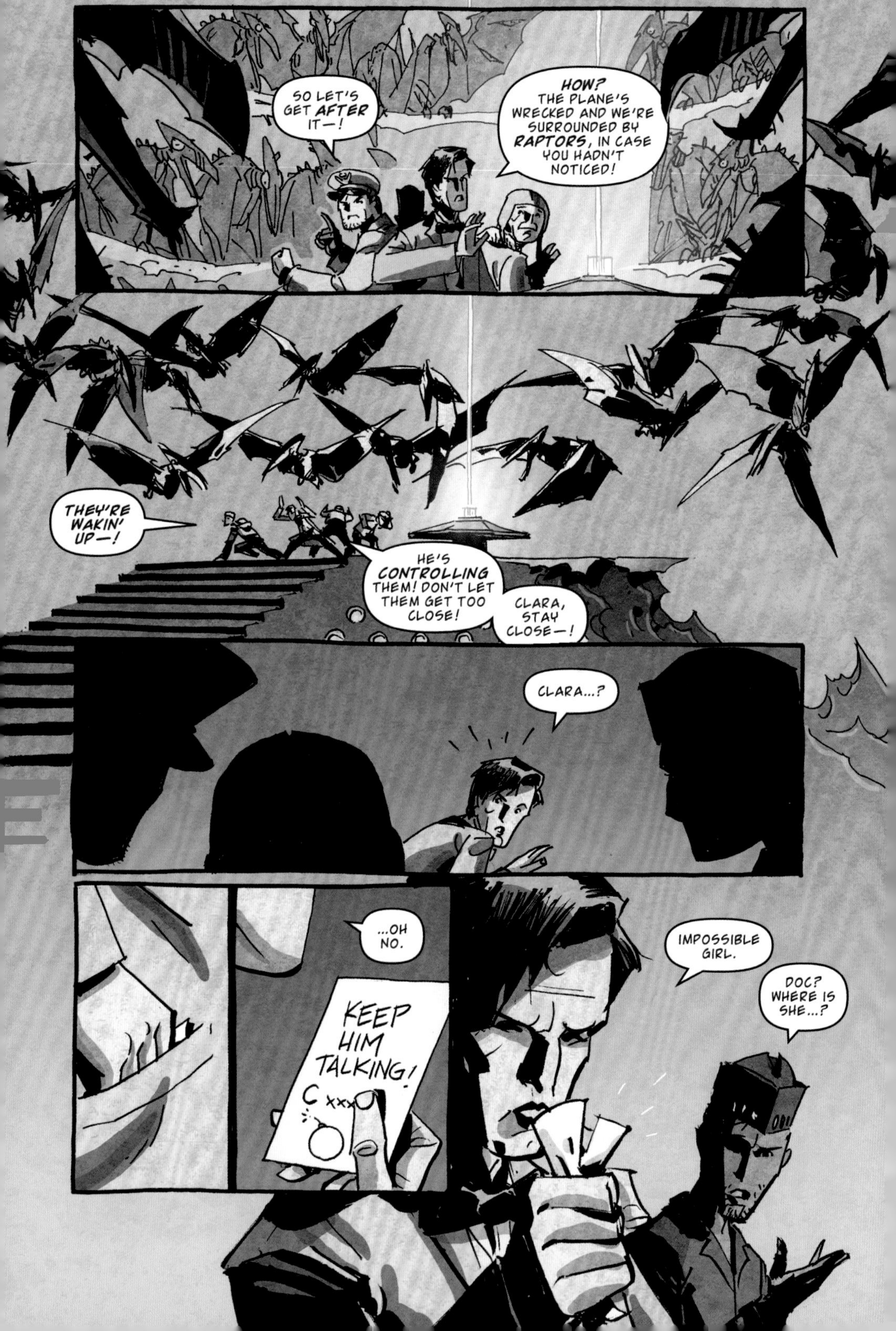
SO LET'S GET AFTER IT—!
HOW? THE PLANE'S WRECKED AND WE'RE SURROUNDED BY RAPTORS, IN CASE YOU HADN'T NOTICED!
THEY'RE WAKIN' UP—!
HE'S CONTROLLING THEM! DON'T LET THEM GET TOO CLOSE!
CLARA, STAY CLOSE—!
CLARA...?
...OH NO.
KEEP HIM TALKING! C xxx
IMPOSSIBLE GIRL.
DOC? WHERE IS SHE...?

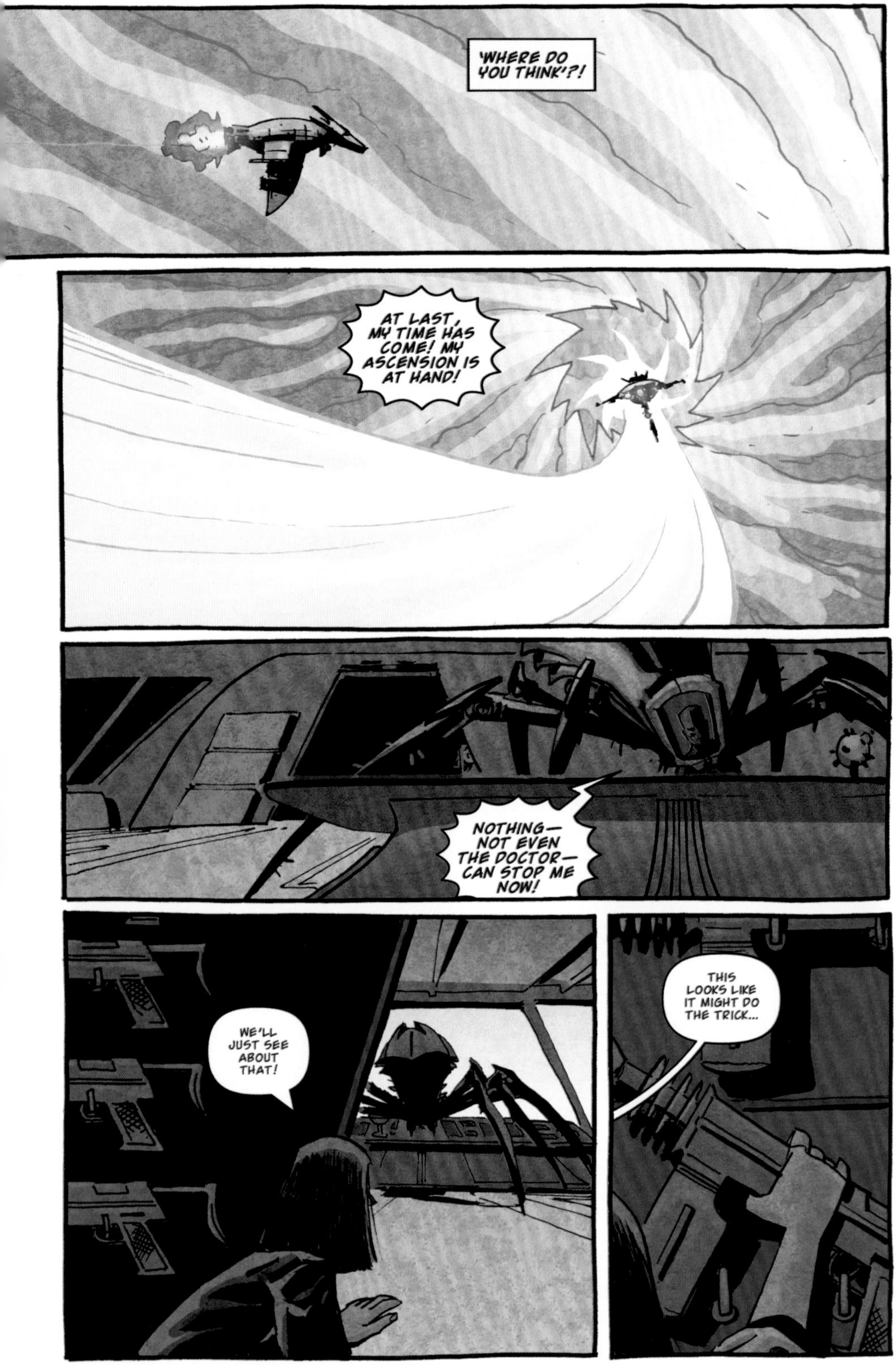
'WHERE DO YOU THINK'?!
AT LAST, MY TIME HAS COME! MY ASCENSION IS AT HAND!
NOTHING— NOT EVEN THE DOCTOR— CAN STOP ME NOW!
WE'LL JUST SEE ABOUT THAT!
THIS LOOKS LIKE IT MIGHT DO THE TRICK...

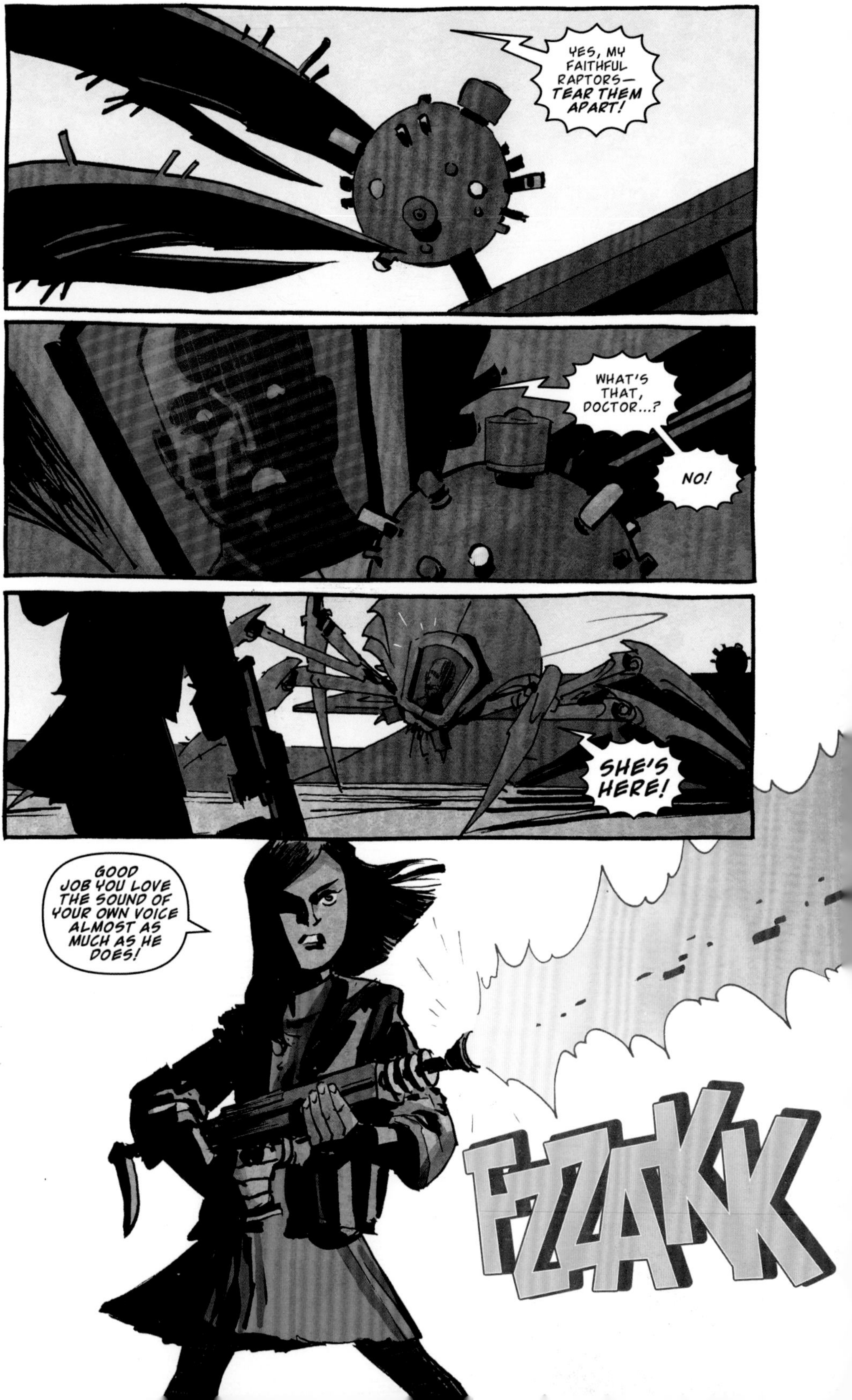
YES, MY FAITHFUL RAPTORS— TEAR THEM APART!
WHAT'S THAT, DOCTOR...?
NO!
SHE'S HERE!
GOOD JOB YOU LOVE THE SOUND OF YOUR OWN VOICE ALMOST AS MUCH AS HE DOES!
FZZAKK

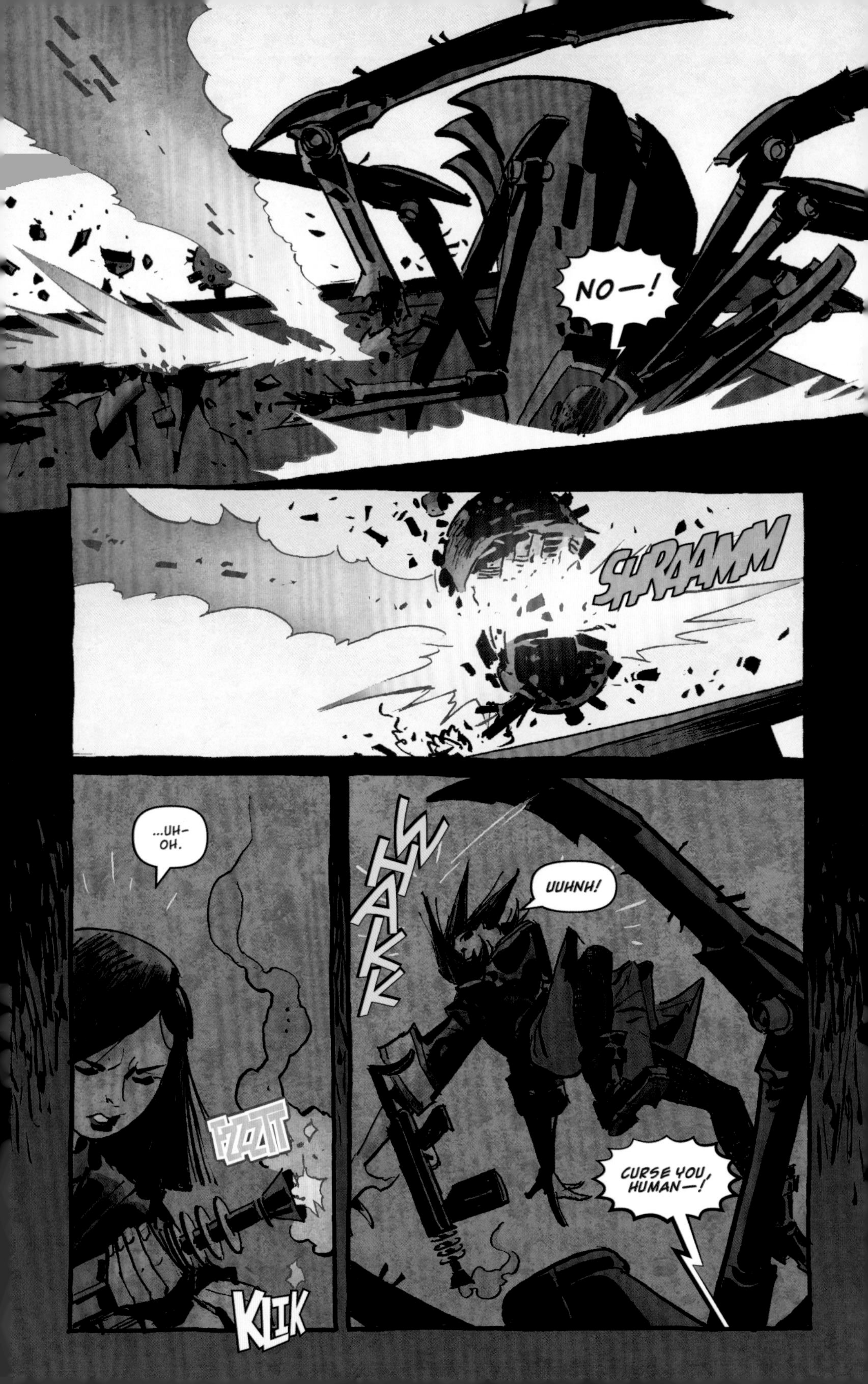
NO—!
SHRAAMM
...UH-OH.
FZZZT
KLIK
WHAKK
UUHNH!
CURSE YOU, HUMAN—!

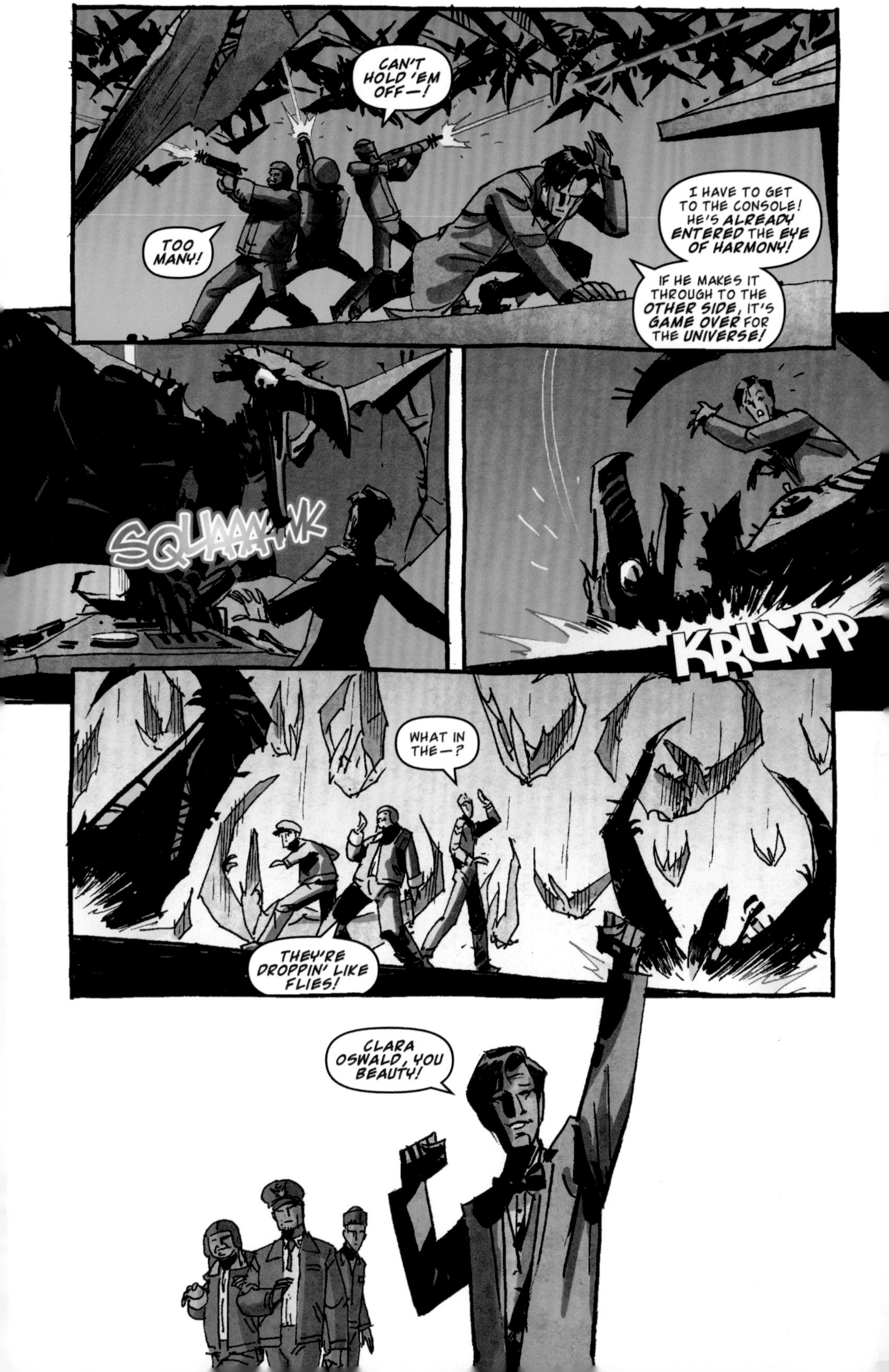
CAN'T HOLD 'EM OFF—!
TOO MANY!
I HAVE TO GET TO THE CONSOLE! HE'S ALREADY ENTERED THE EYE OF HARMONY!
IF HE MAKES IT THROUGH TO THE OTHER SIDE, IT'S GAME OVER FOR THE UNIVERSE!
SQUAAAWK
KRUMPP
WHAT IN THE—?
THEY'RE DROPPIN' LIKE FLIES!
CLARA OSWALD, YOU BEAUTY!

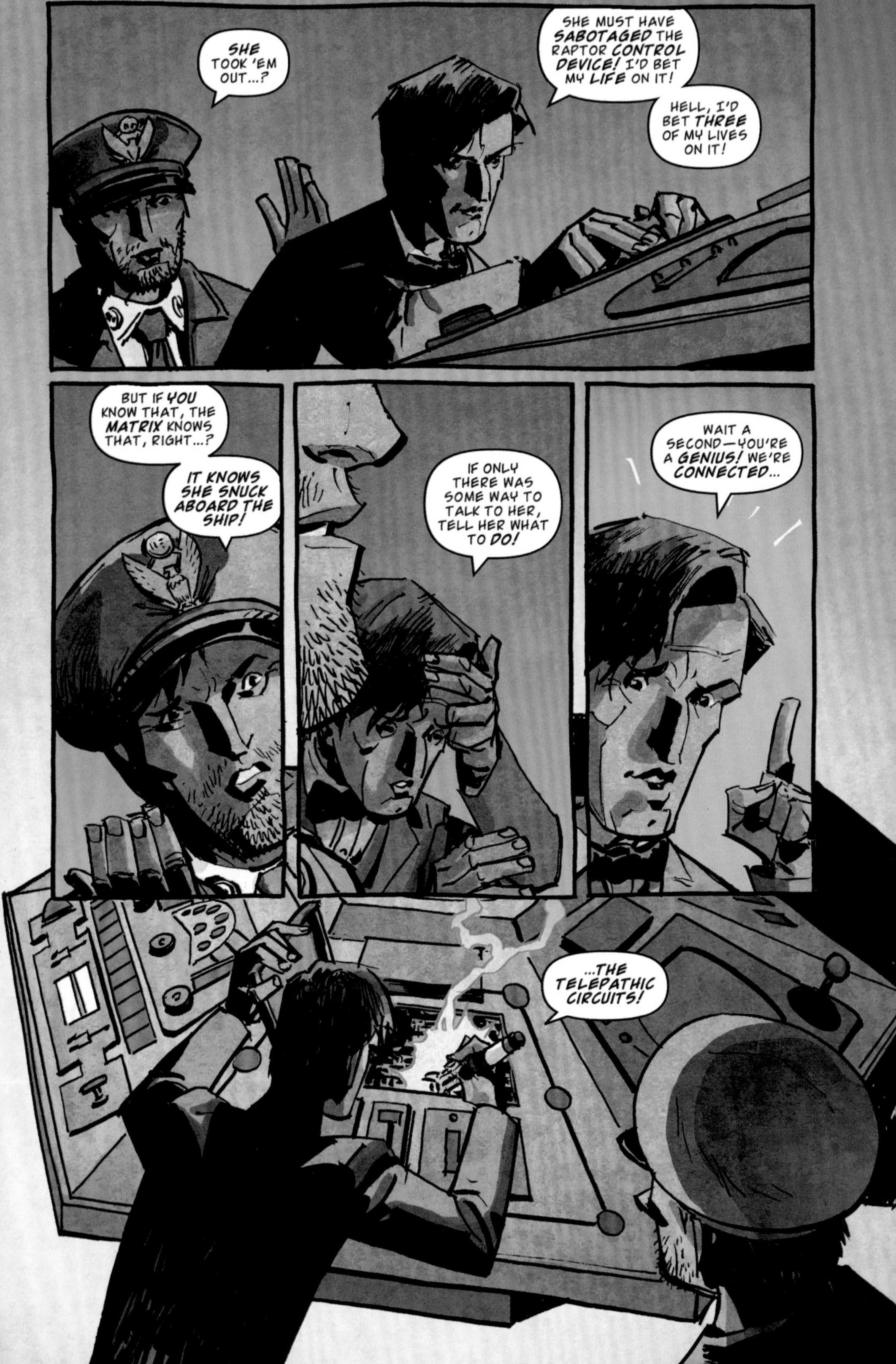
SHE TOOK 'EM OUT...?
SHE MUST HAVE SABOTAGED THE RAPTOR CONTROL DEVICE! I'D BET MY LIFE ON IT!
HELL, I'D BET THREE OF MY LIVES ON IT!
BUT IF YOU KNOW THAT, THE MATRIX KNOWS THAT, RIGHT...?
IT KNOWS SHE SNUCK ABOARD THE SHIP!
IF ONLY THERE WAS SOME WAY TO TALK TO HER, TELL HER WHAT TO DO!
WAIT A SECOND—YOU'RE A GENIUS! WE'RE CONNECTED...
...THE TELEPATHIC CIRCUITS!

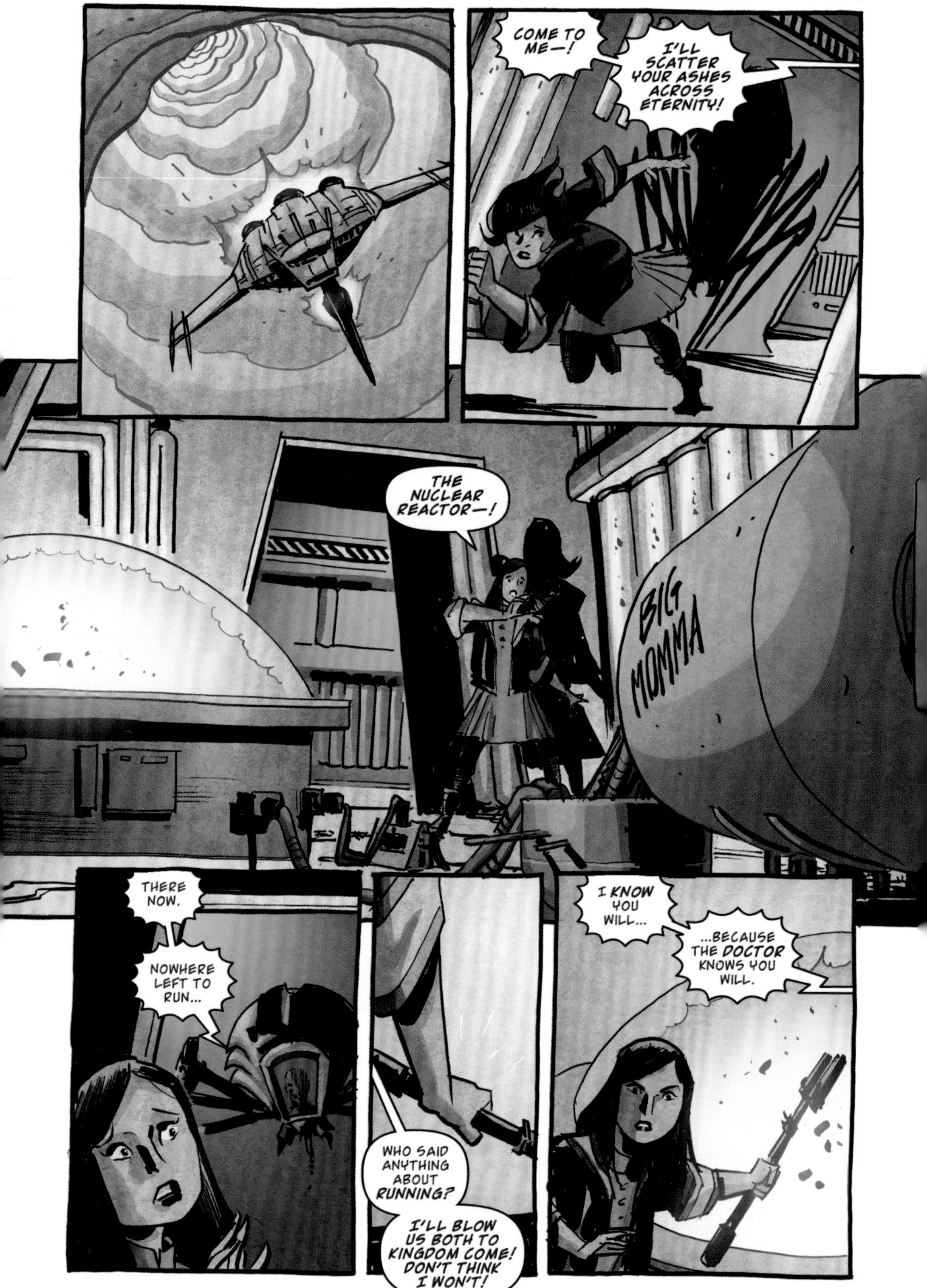
COME TO ME—!
I'LL SCATTER YOUR ASHES ACROSS ETERNITY!
THE NUCLEAR REACTOR—!
BIG MOMMA
THERE NOW.
NOWHERE LEFT TO RUN...
WHO SAID ANYTHING ABOUT RUNNING?
I'LL BLOW US BOTH TO KINGDOM COME! DON'T THINK I WON'T!
I KNOW YOU WILL...
...BECAUSE THE DOCTOR KNOWS YOU WILL.

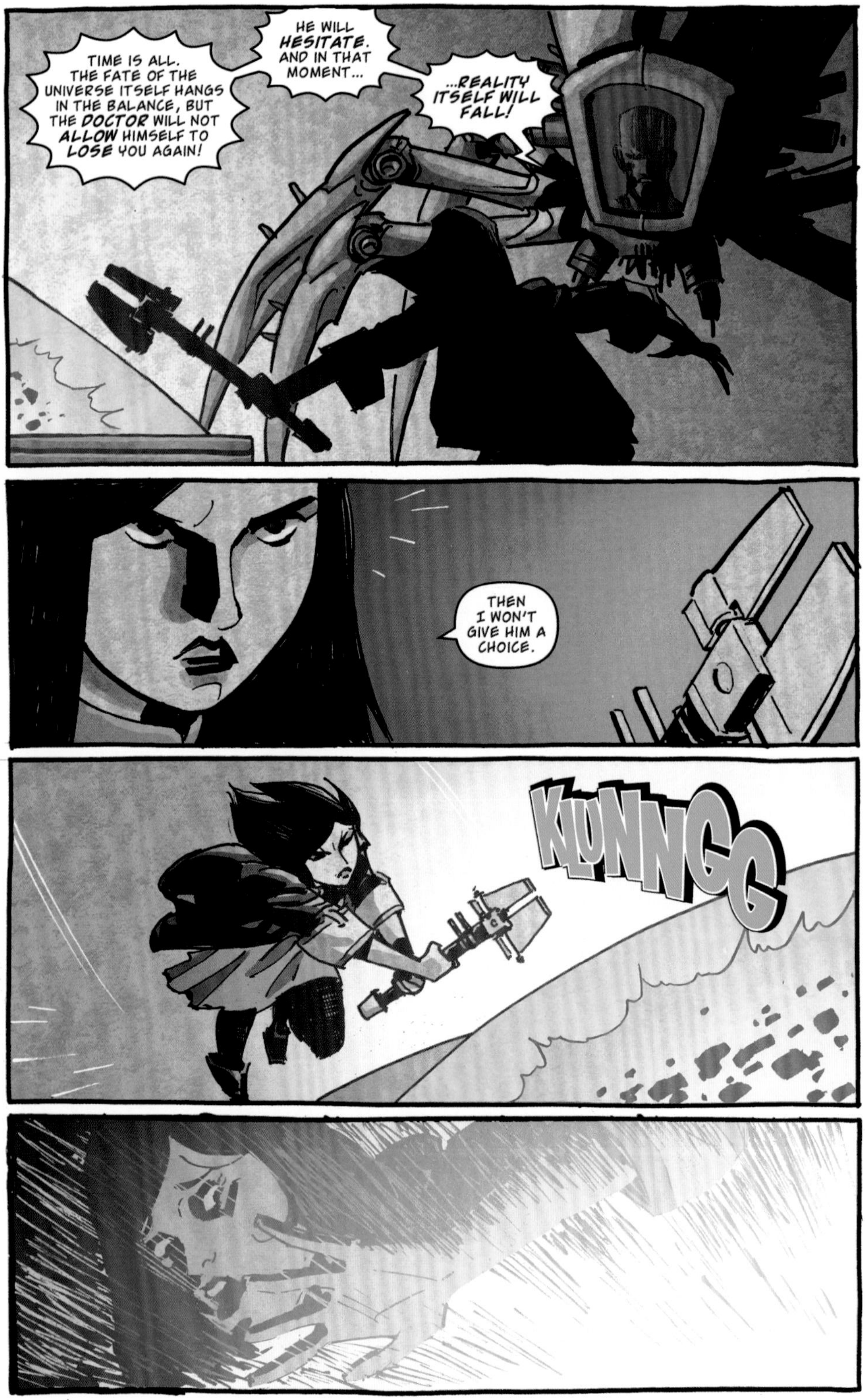
TIME IS ALL. THE FATE OF THE UNIVERSE ITSELF HANGS IN THE BALANCE, BUT THE DOCTOR WILL NOT ALLOW HIMSELF TO LOSE YOU AGAIN!
HE WILL HESITATE. AND IN THAT MOMENT...
...REALITY ITSELF WILL FALL!
THEN I WON'T GIVE HIM A CHOICE.
KLUNNGG

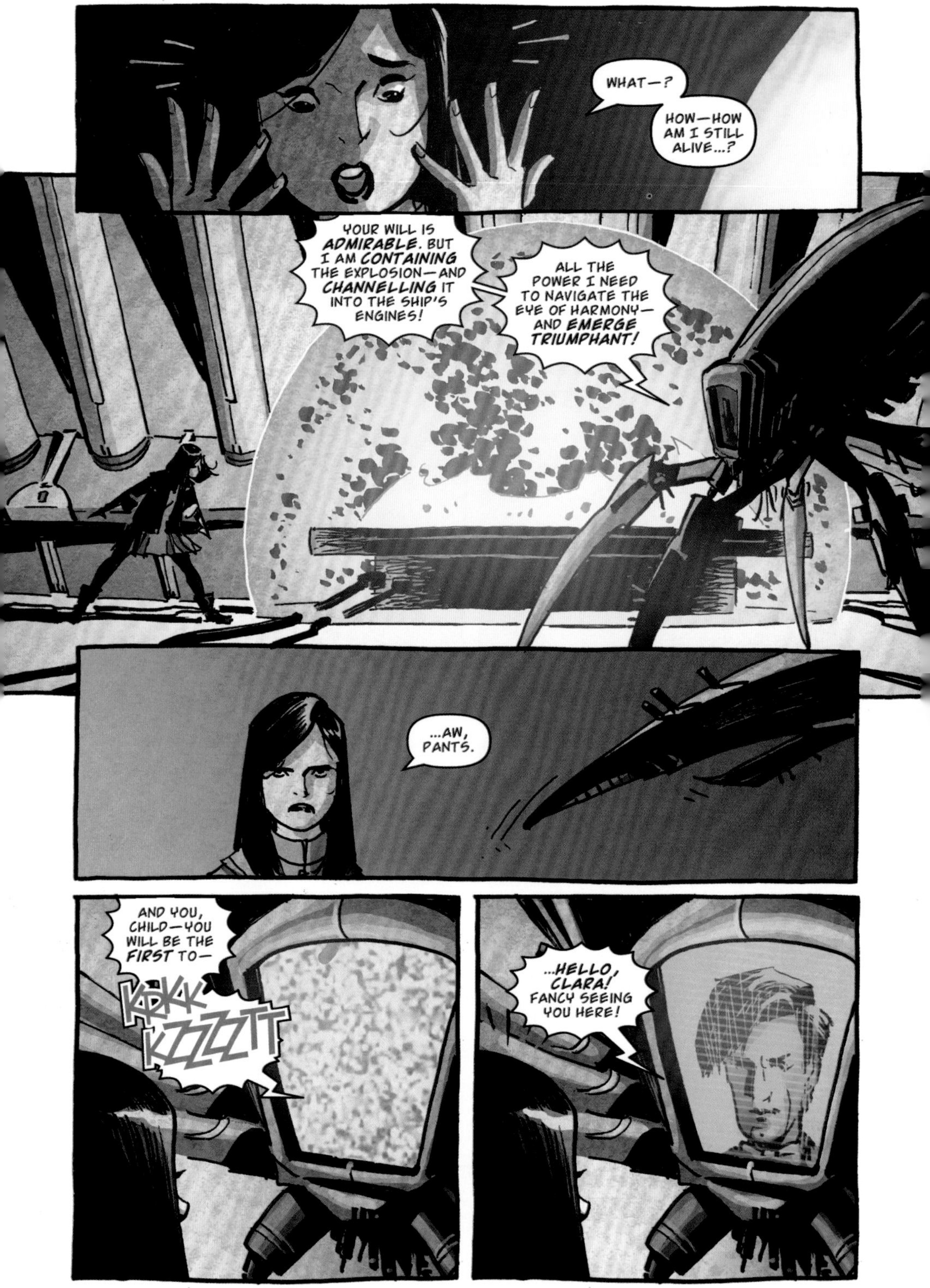
WHAT—?
HOW—HOW AM I STILL ALIVE...?
YOUR WILL IS ADMIRABLE. BUT I AM CONTAINING THE EXPLOSION—AND CHANNELLING IT INTO THE SHIP'S ENGINES!
ALL THE POWER I NEED TO NAVIGATE THE EYE OF HARMONY—AND EMERGE TRIUMPHANT!
...AW, PANTS.
AND YOU, CHILD—YOU WILL BE THE FIRST TO—
KRKK KZZZZTT
...HELLO, CLARA! FANCY SEEING YOU HERE!

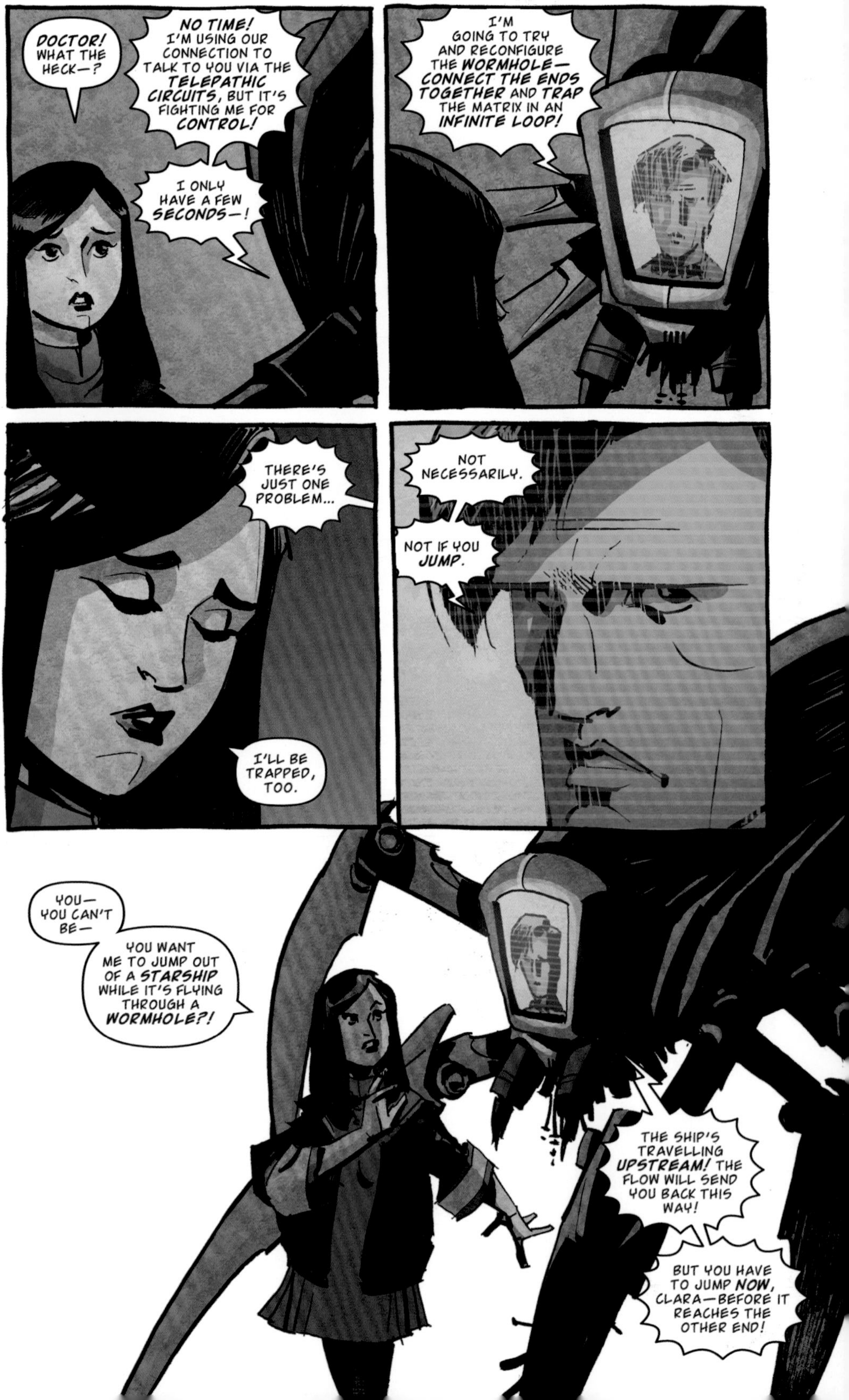
DOCTOR! WHAT THE HECK—?
NO TIME! I'M USING OUR CONNECTION TO TALK TO YOU VIA THE TELEPATHIC CIRCUITS, BUT IT'S FIGHTING ME FOR CONTROL!
I ONLY HAVE A FEW SECONDS—!
I'M GOING TO TRY AND RECONFIGURE THE WORMHOLE—CONNECT THE ENDS TOGETHER AND TRAP THE MATRIX IN AN INFINITE LOOP!
THERE'S JUST ONE PROBLEM...
I'LL BE TRAPPED, TOO.
NOT NECESSARILY.
NOT IF YOU JUMP.
YOU— YOU CAN'T BE—
YOU WANT ME TO JUMP OUT OF A STARSHIP WHILE IT'S FLYING THROUGH A WORMHOLE?!
THE SHIP'S TRAVELLING UPSTREAM! THE FLOW WILL SEND YOU BACK THIS WAY!
BUT YOU HAVE TO JUMP NOW, CLARA—BEFORE IT REACHES THE OTHER END!

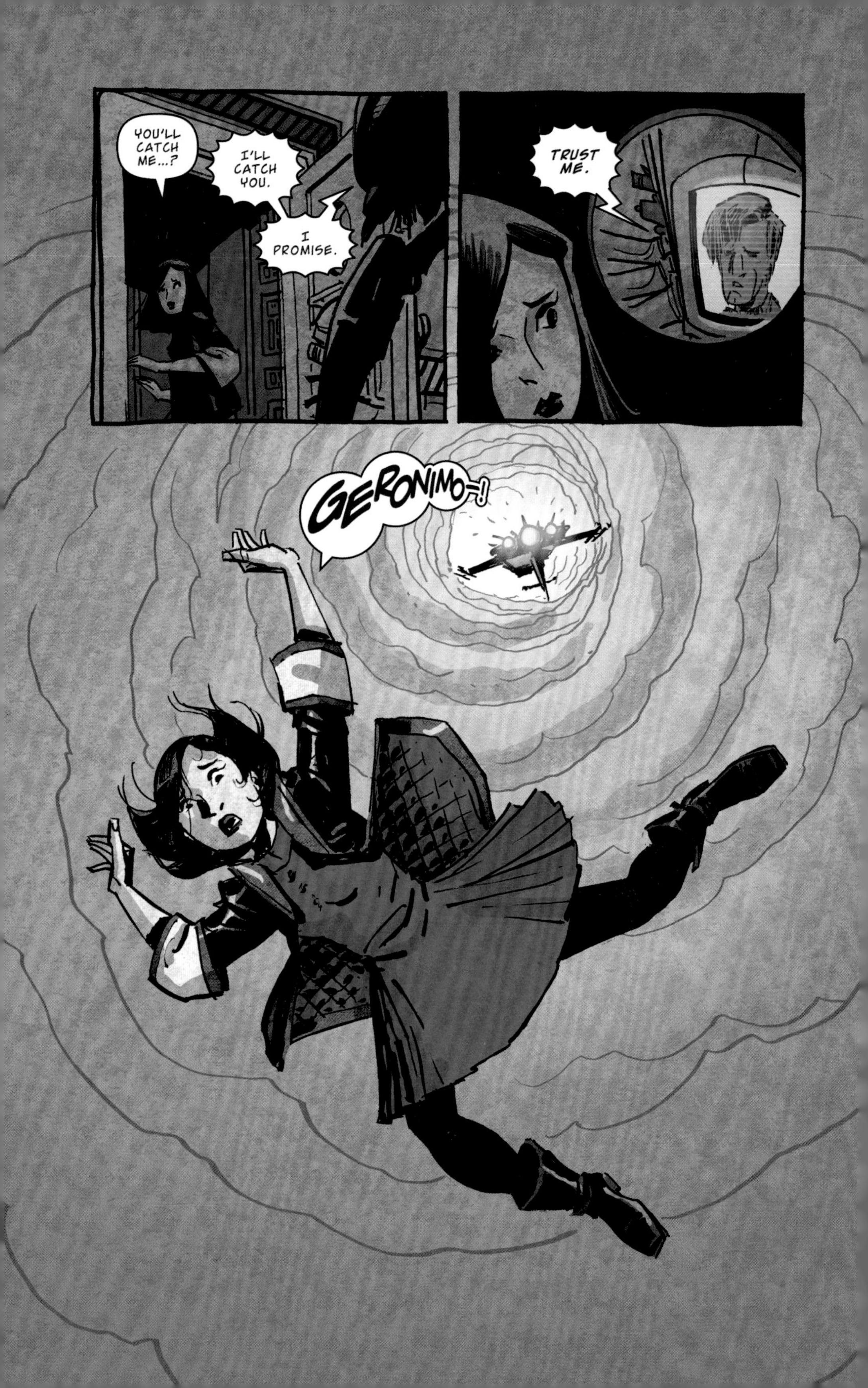
YOU'LL CATCH ME...?
I'LL CATCH YOU.
I PROMISE.
TRUST ME.
GERONIMO--!

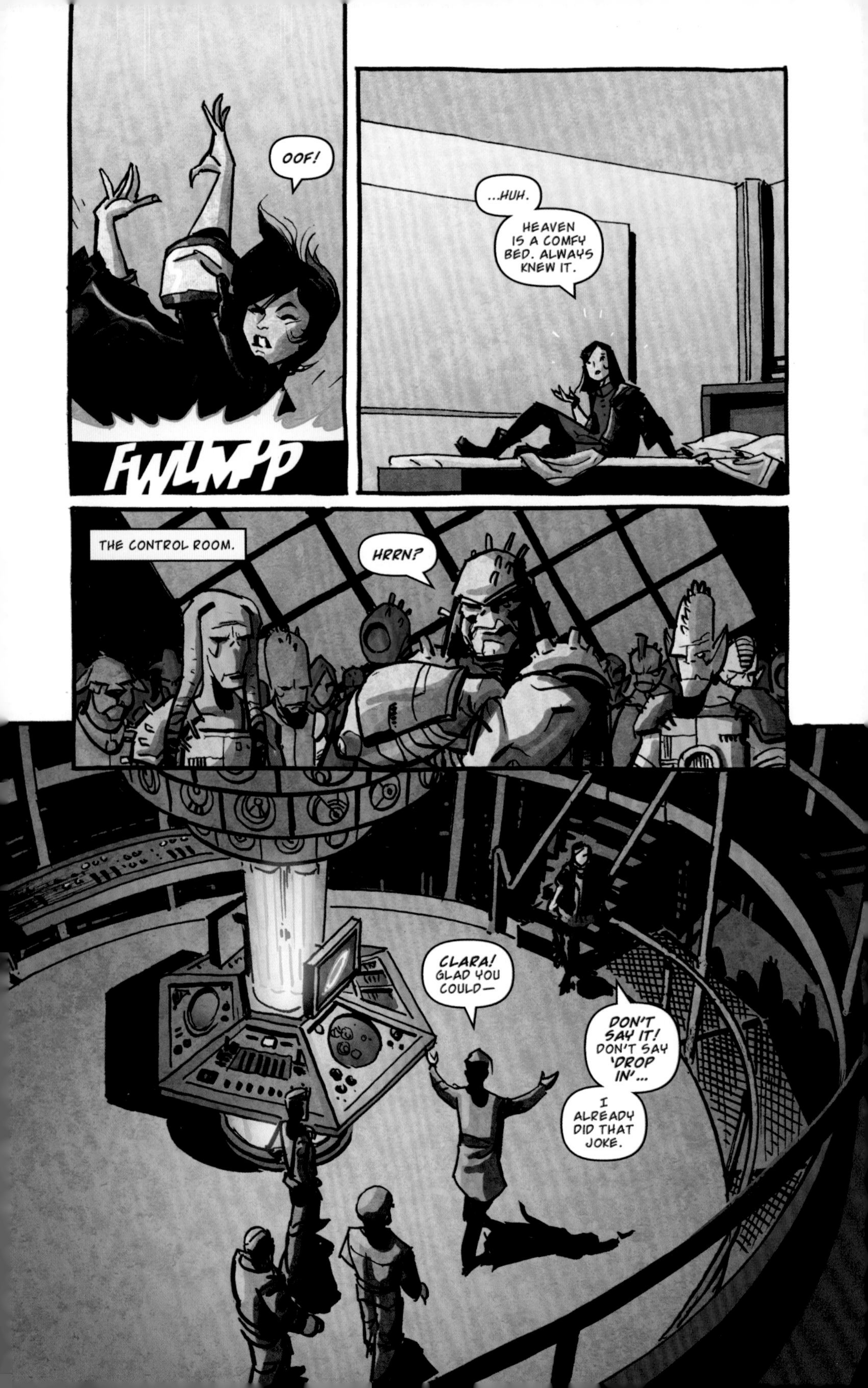
OOF!
FWUMP
...HUH.
HEAVEN IS A COMFY BED. ALWAYS KNEW IT.
THE CONTROL ROOM.
HRRN?
CLARA! GLAD YOU COULD—
DON'T SAY IT! DON'T SAY 'DROP IN'...
I ALREADY DID THAT JOKE.

I GUESS IT WORKED THEN...

WHAT CAN I SAY? I'VE STILL GOT IT!

'THE TARDIS IS BACK TO HER OLD SELF, AND THE MATRIX IS SAFELY CONTAINED—TRAPPED FOREVER INSIDE A TOROIDAL SINGULARITY'!

IT'S A GIANT DONUT!

IT'S AN OUROBOROUS CONFIGURATION.

WHATEVER.

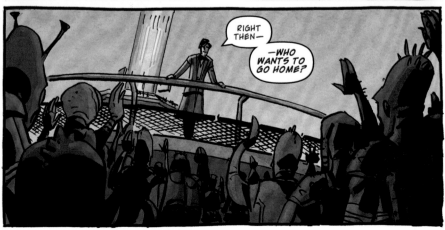

RIGHT THEN—

—WHO WANTS TO GO HOME?

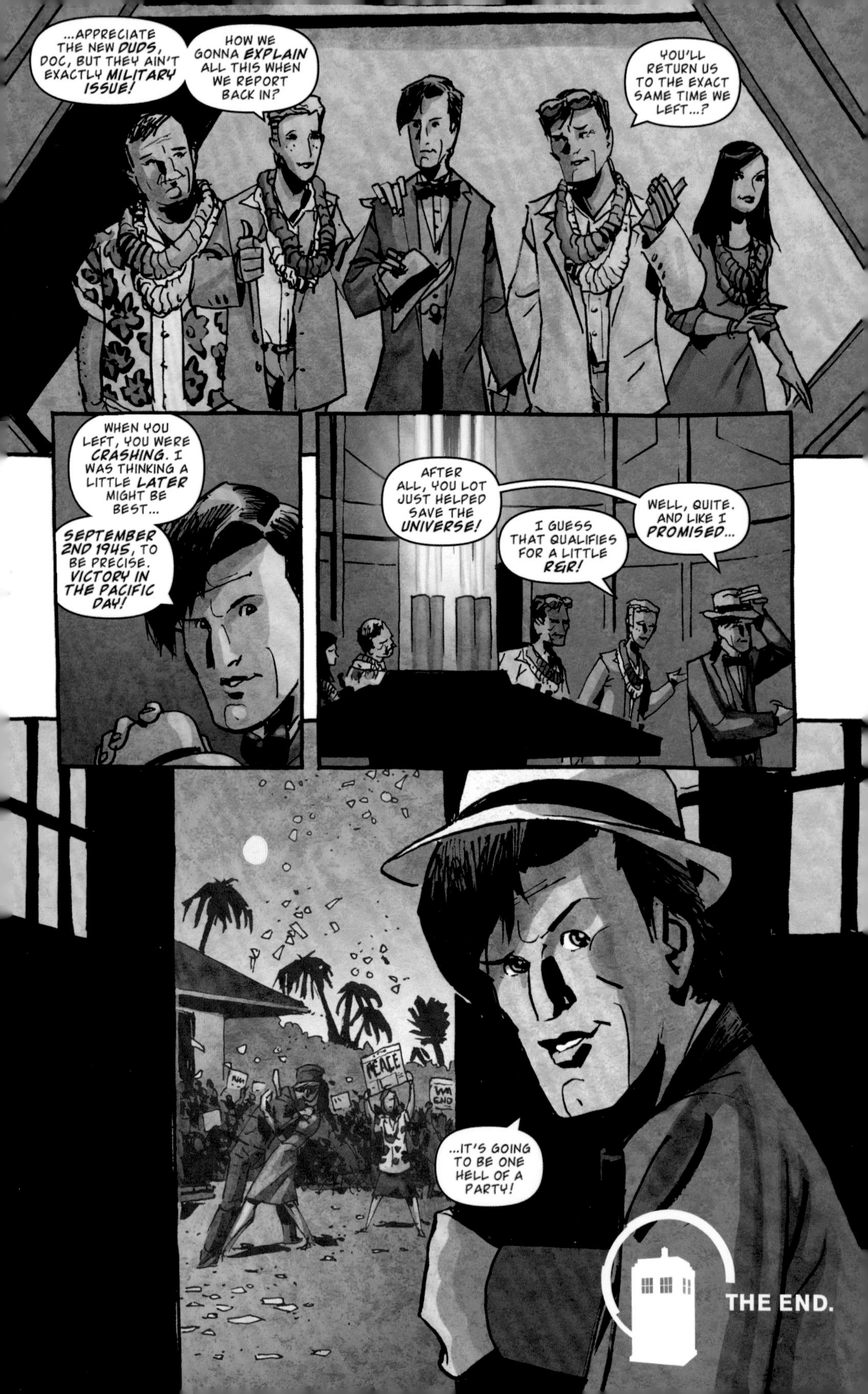
...APPRECIATE THE NEW DUDS, DOC, BUT THEY AIN'T EXACTLY MILITARY ISSUE!
HOW WE GONNA EXPLAIN ALL THIS WHEN WE REPORT BACK IN?
YOU'LL RETURN US TO THE EXACT SAME TIME WE LEFT...?
WHEN YOU LEFT, YOU WERE CRASHING. I WAS THINKING A LITTLE LATER MIGHT BE BEST...
SEPTEMBER 2ND 1945, TO BE PRECISE. VICTORY IN THE PACIFIC DAY!
AFTER ALL, YOU LOT JUST HELPED SAVE THE UNIVERSE!
I GUESS THAT QUALIFIES FOR A LITTLE R&R!
WELL, QUITE. AND LIKE I PROMISED...
PEACE
...IT'S GOING TO BE ONE HELL OF A PARTY!
THE END.

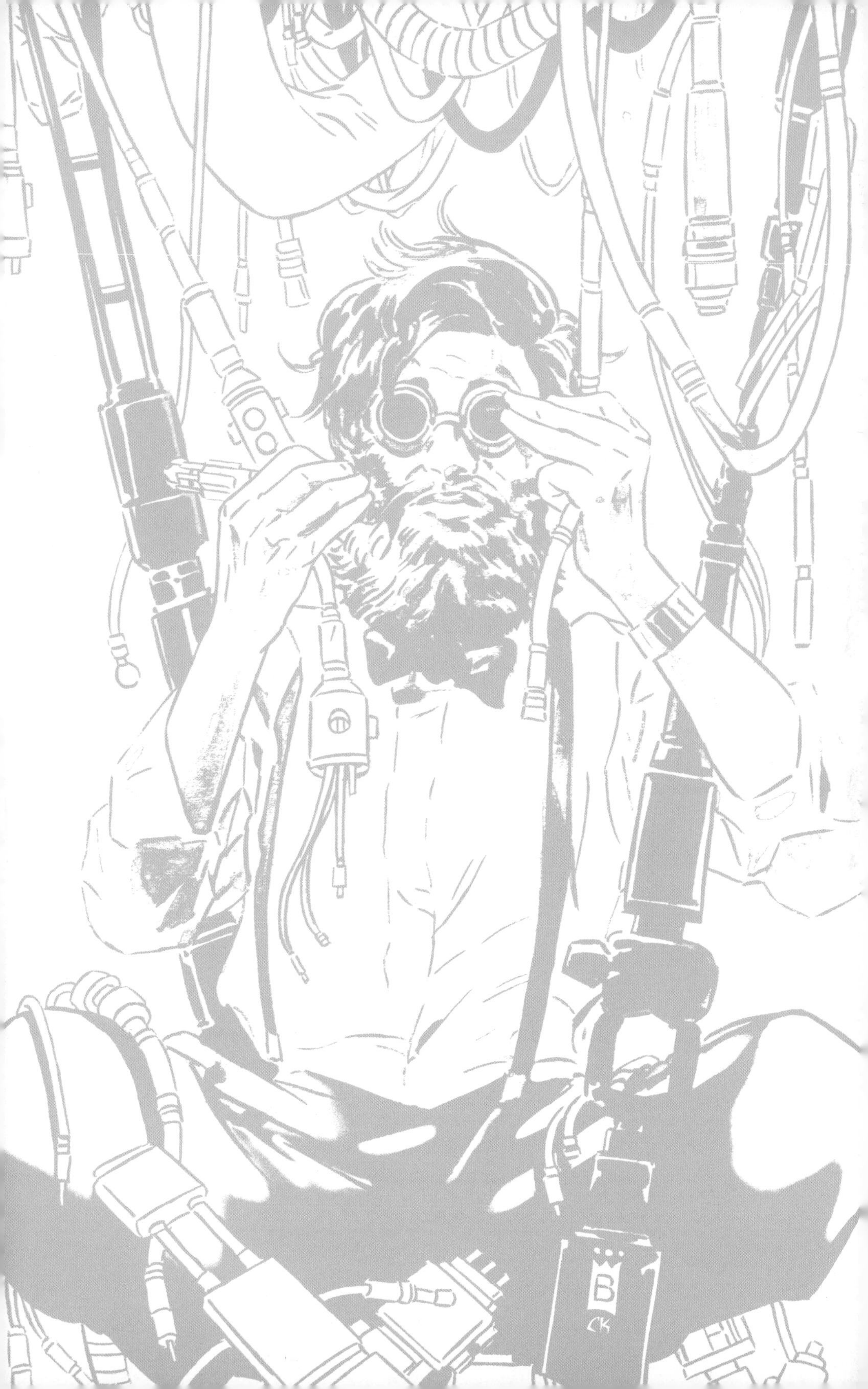

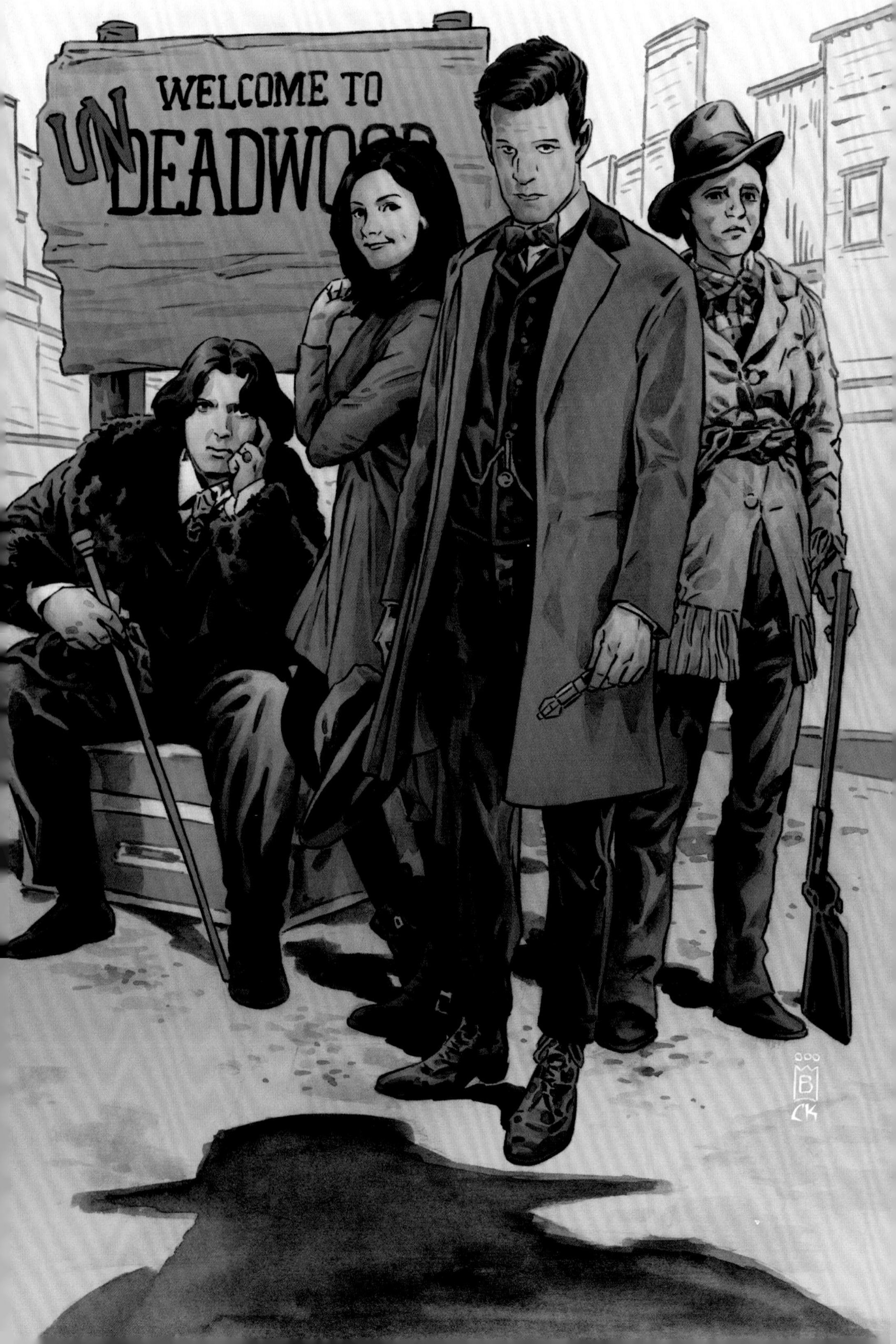
WELCOME TO
UN DEADWOOD

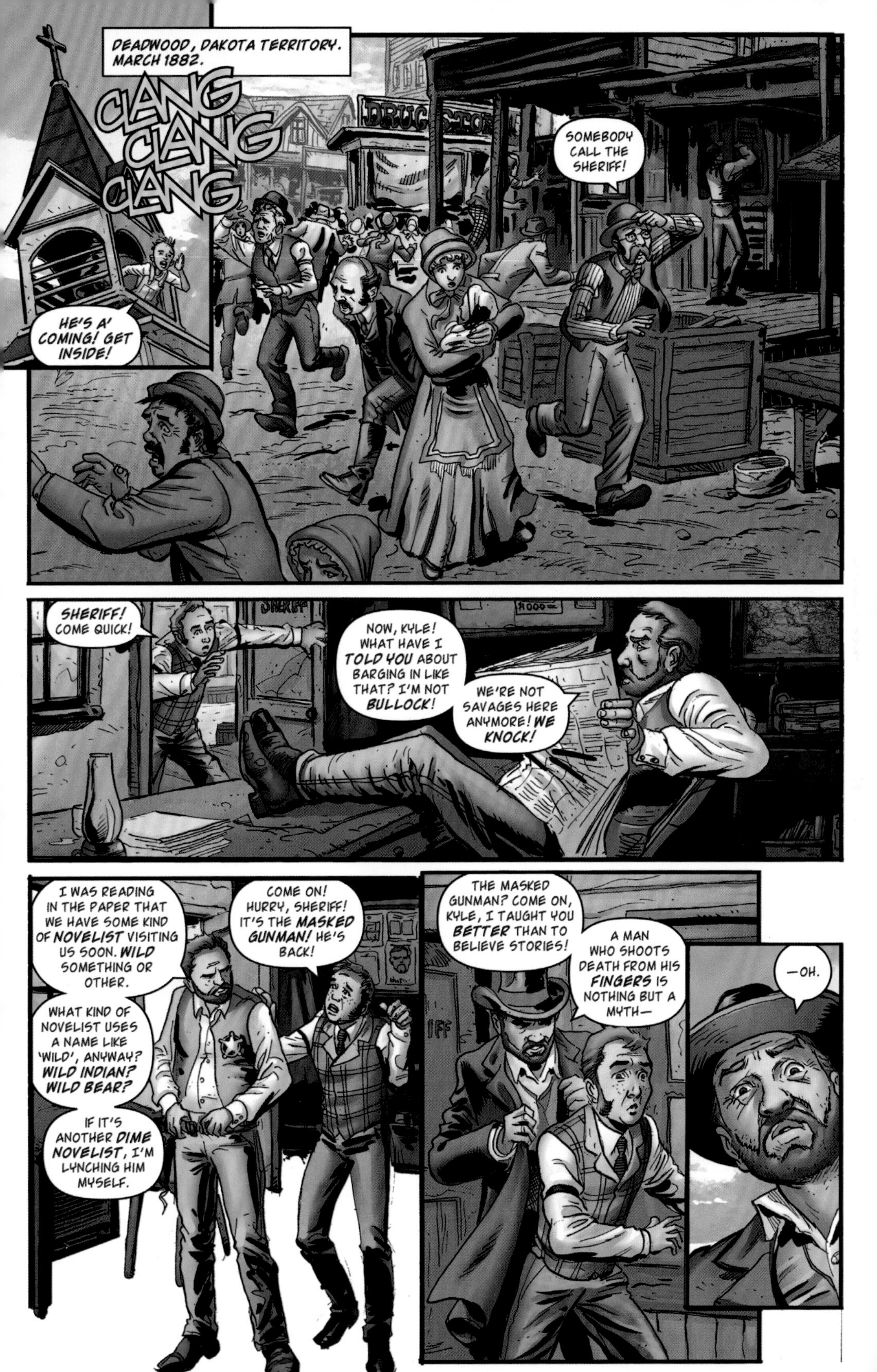
DEADWOOD, DAKOTA TERRITORY. MARCH 1882.
CLANG CLANG CLANG
HE'S A' COMING! GET INSIDE!
DRUG STOR
SOMEBODY CALL THE SHERIFF!
SHERIFF! COME QUICK!
NOW, KYLE! WHAT HAVE I TOLD YOU ABOUT BARGING IN LIKE THAT? I'M NOT BULLOCK!
WE'RE NOT SAVAGES HERE ANYMORE! WE KNOCK!
I WAS READING IN THE PAPER THAT WE HAVE SOME KIND OF NOVELIST VISITING US SOON. WILD SOMETHING OR OTHER.
WHAT KIND OF NOVELIST USES A NAME LIKE 'WILD', ANYWAY? WILD INDIAN? WILD BEAR?
IF IT'S ANOTHER DIME NOVELIST, I'M LYNCHING HIM MYSELF.
COME ON! HURRY, SHERIFF! IT'S THE MASKED GUNMAN! HE'S BACK!
THE MASKED GUNMAN? COME ON, KYLE, I TAUGHT YOU BETTER THAN TO BELIEVE STORIES!
A MAN WHO SHOOTS DEATH FROM HIS FINGERS IS NOTHING BUT A MYTH—
—OH.

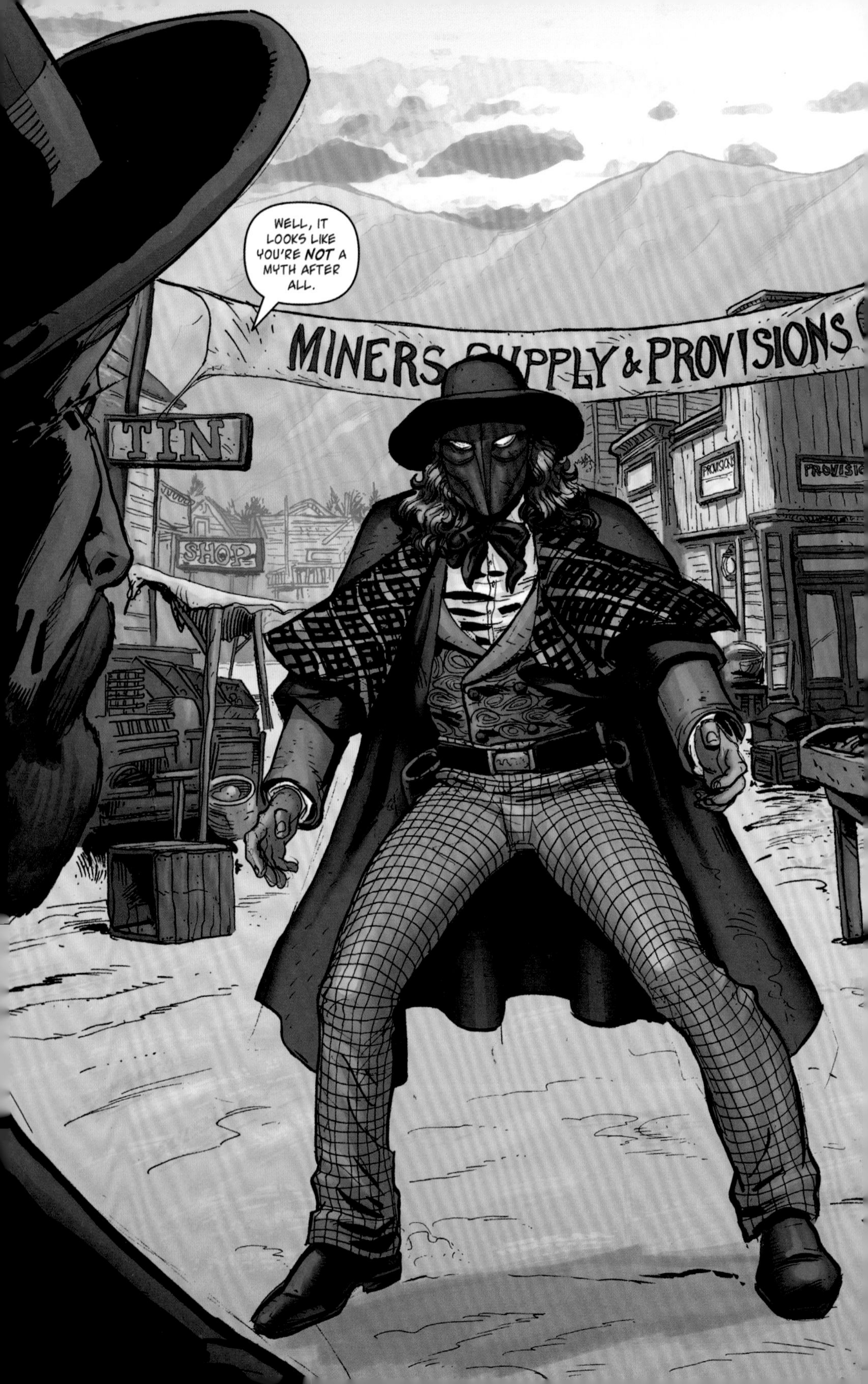
WELL, IT LOOKS LIKE YOU'RE NOT A MYTH AFTER ALL.
MINERS SUPPLY & PROVISIONS
TIN
SHOP
PROVISIONS

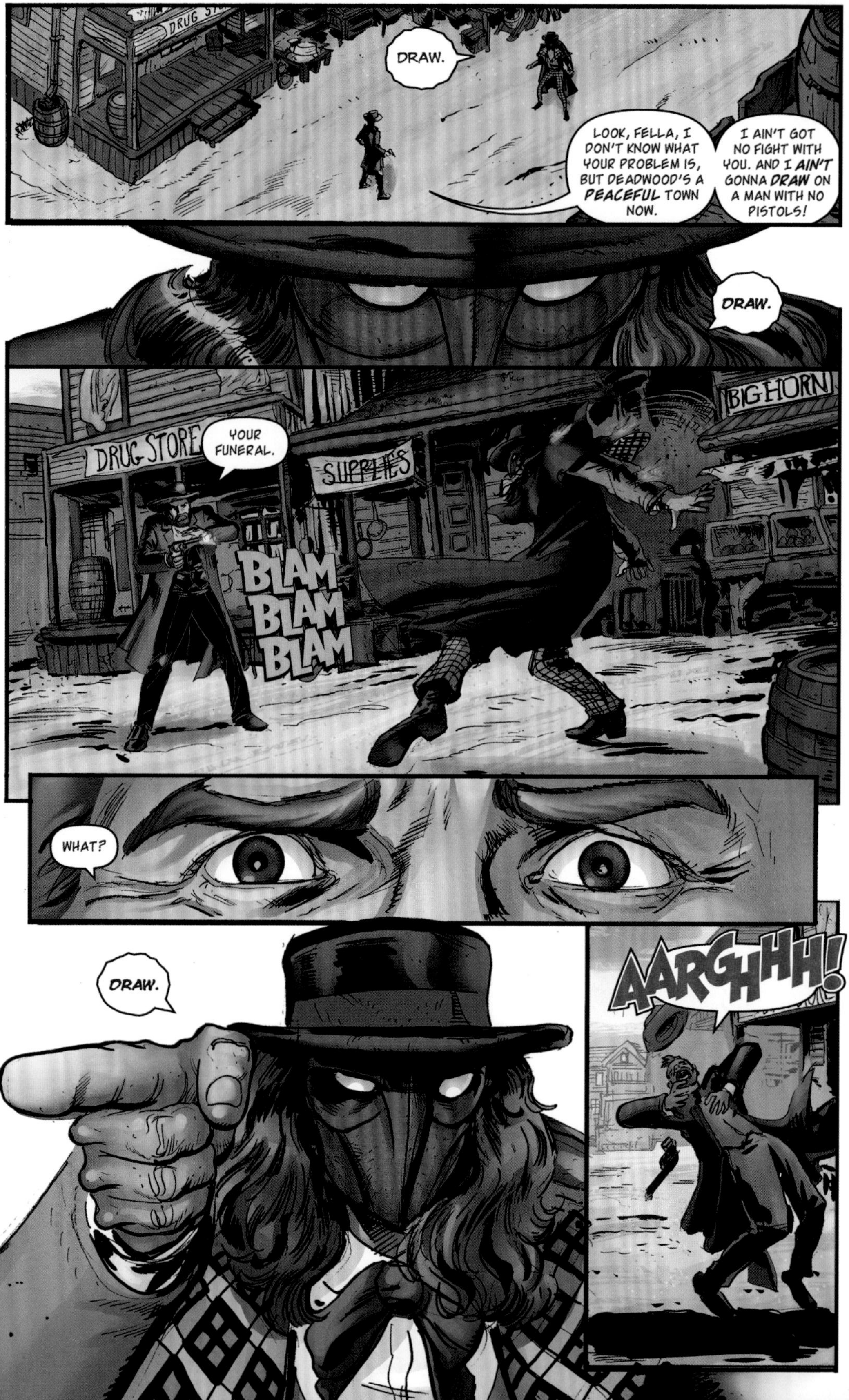

DRAW.
LOOK, FELLA, I DON'T KNOW WHAT YOUR PROBLEM IS, BUT DEADWOOD'S A PEACEFUL TOWN NOW.
I AIN'T GOT NO FIGHT WITH YOU. AND I AIN'T GONNA DRAW ON A MAN WITH NO PISTOLS!
DRAW.
BIGHORN
DRUG STORE
YOUR FUNERAL.
SUPPLIES
BLAM BLAM BLAM
WHAT?
DRAW.
AARGHHH!

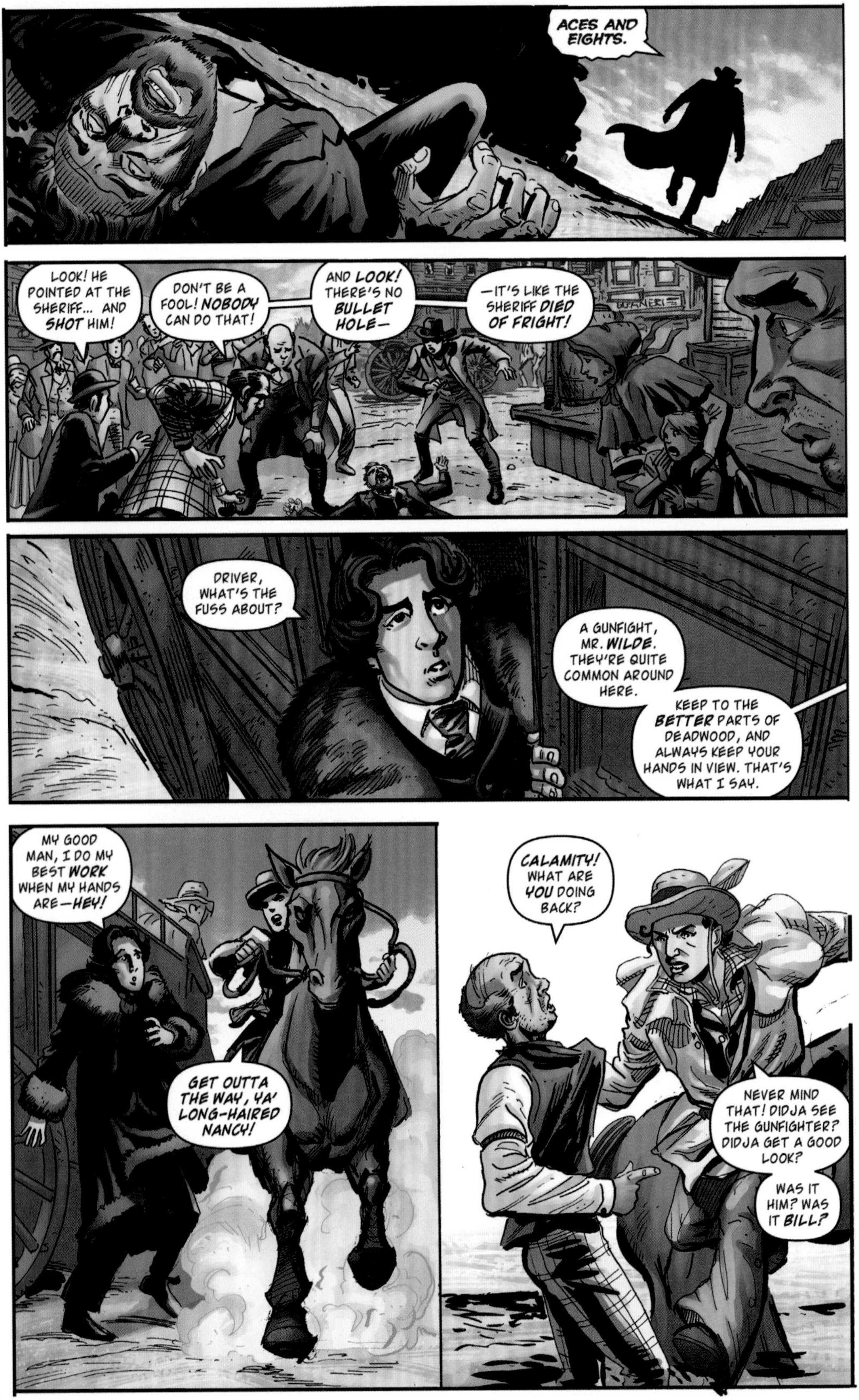
ACES AND EIGHTS.
LOOK! HE POINTED AT THE SHERIFF... AND SHOT HIM!
DON'T BE A FOOL! NOBODY CAN DO THAT!
AND LOOK! THERE'S NO BULLET HOLE—
—IT'S LIKE THE SHERIFF DIED OF FRIGHT!
DRIVER, WHAT'S THE FUSS ABOUT?
A GUNFIGHT, MR. WILDE. THEY'RE QUITE COMMON AROUND HERE.
KEEP TO THE BETTER PARTS OF DEADWOOD, AND ALWAYS KEEP YOUR HANDS IN VIEW. THAT'S WHAT I SAY.
MY GOOD MAN, I DO MY BEST WORK WHEN MY HANDS ARE—HEY!
GET OUTTA THE WAY, YA' LONG-HAIRED NANCY!
CALAMITY! WHAT ARE YOU DOING BACK?
NEVER MIND THAT! DIDJA SEE THE GUNFIGHTER? DIDJA GET A GOOD LOOK?
WAS IT HIM? WAS IT BILL?

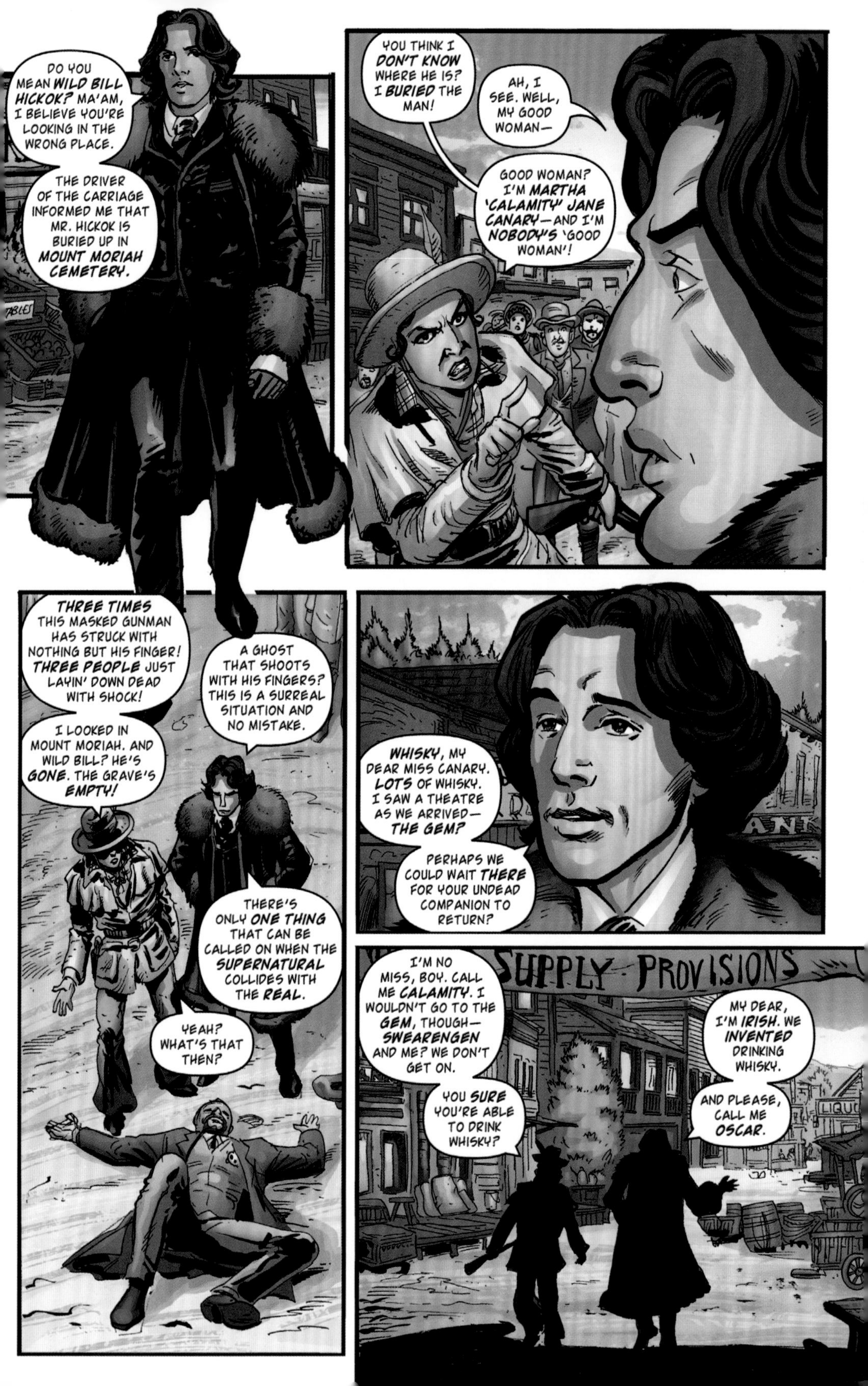
DO YOU MEAN WILD BILL HICKOK? MA'AM, I BELIEVE YOU'RE LOOKING IN THE WRONG PLACE.
THE DRIVER OF THE CARRIAGE INFORMED ME THAT MR. HICKOK IS BURIED UP IN MOUNT MORIAH CEMETERY.
YOU THINK I DON'T KNOW WHERE HE IS? I BURIED THE MAN!
AH, I SEE. WELL, MY GOOD WOMAN—
GOOD WOMAN? I'M MARTHA 'CALAMITY' JANE CANARY—AND I'M NOBODY'S 'GOOD WOMAN'!
THREE TIMES THIS MASKED GUNMAN HAS STRUCK WITH NOTHING BUT HIS FINGER! THREE PEOPLE JUST LAYIN' DOWN DEAD WITH SHOCK!
A GHOST THAT SHOOTS WITH HIS FINGERS? THIS IS A SURREAL SITUATION AND NO MISTAKE.
I LOOKED IN MOUNT MORIAH. AND WILD BILL? HE'S GONE. THE GRAVE'S EMPTY!
THERE'S ONLY ONE THING THAT CAN BE CALLED ON WHEN THE SUPERNATURAL COLLIDES WITH THE REAL.
YEAH? WHAT'S THAT THEN?
WHISKY, MY DEAR MISS CANARY. LOTS OF WHISKY. I SAW A THEATRE AS WE ARRIVED— THE GEM?
PERHAPS WE COULD WAIT THERE FOR YOUR UNDEAD COMPANION TO RETURN?
SUPPLY PROVISIONS
I'M NO MISS, BOY. CALL ME CALAMITY. I WOULDN'T GO TO THE GEM, THOUGH— SWEARENGEN AND ME? WE DON'T GET ON.
YOU SURE YOU'RE ABLE TO DRINK WHISKY?
MY DEAR, I'M IRISH. WE INVENTED DRINKING WHISKY.
AND PLEASE, CALL ME OSCAR.

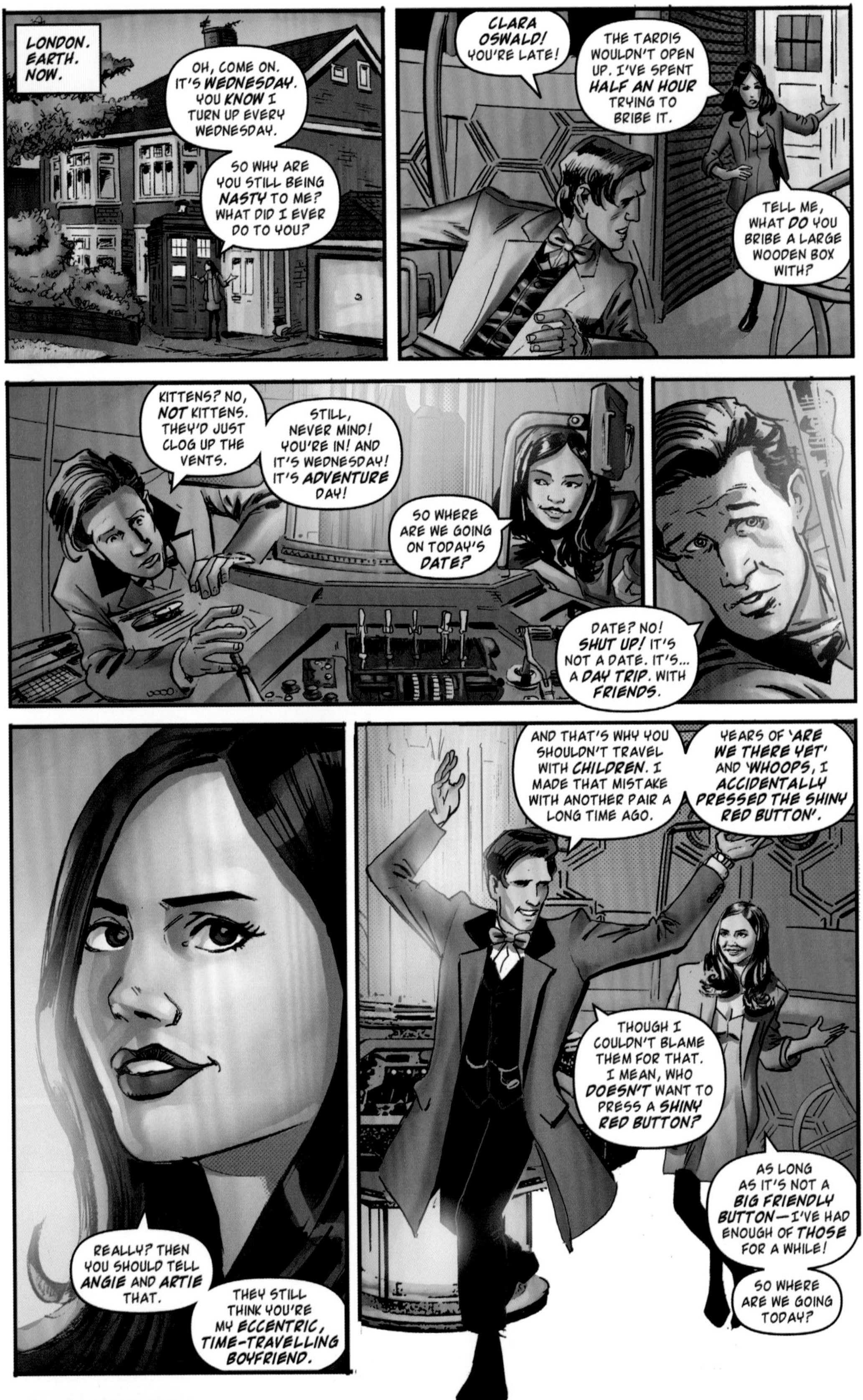
LONDON. EARTH. NOW.
OH, COME ON. IT'S WEDNESDAY. YOU KNOW I TURN UP EVERY WEDNESDAY.
SO WHY ARE YOU STILL BEING NASTY TO ME? WHAT DID I EVER DO TO YOU?
CLARA OSWALD! YOU'RE LATE!
THE TARDIS WOULDN'T OPEN UP. I'VE SPENT HALF AN HOUR TRYING TO BRIBE IT.
TELL ME, WHAT DO YOU BRIBE A LARGE WOODEN BOX WITH?
KITTENS? NO, NOT KITTENS. THEY'D JUST CLOG UP THE VENTS.
STILL, NEVER MIND! YOU'RE IN! AND IT'S WEDNESDAY! IT'S ADVENTURE DAY!
SO WHERE ARE WE GOING ON TODAY'S DATE?
DATE? NO! SHUT UP! IT'S NOT A DATE. IT'S... A DAY TRIP. WITH FRIENDS.
REALLY? THEN YOU SHOULD TELL ANGIE AND ARTIE THAT.
THEY STILL THINK YOU'RE MY ECCENTRIC, TIME-TRAVELLING BOYFRIEND.
AND THAT'S WHY YOU SHOULDN'T TRAVEL WITH CHILDREN. I MADE THAT MISTAKE WITH ANOTHER PAIR A LONG TIME AGO.
YEARS OF 'ARE WE THERE YET' AND 'WHOOPS, I ACCIDENTALLY PRESSED THE SHINY RED BUTTON'.
THOUGH I COULDN'T BLAME THEM FOR THAT. I MEAN, WHO DOESN'T WANT TO PRESS A SHINY RED BUTTON?
AS LONG AS IT'S NOT A BIG FRIENDLY BUTTON—I'VE HAD ENOUGH OF THOSE FOR A WHILE!
SO WHERE ARE WE GOING TODAY?

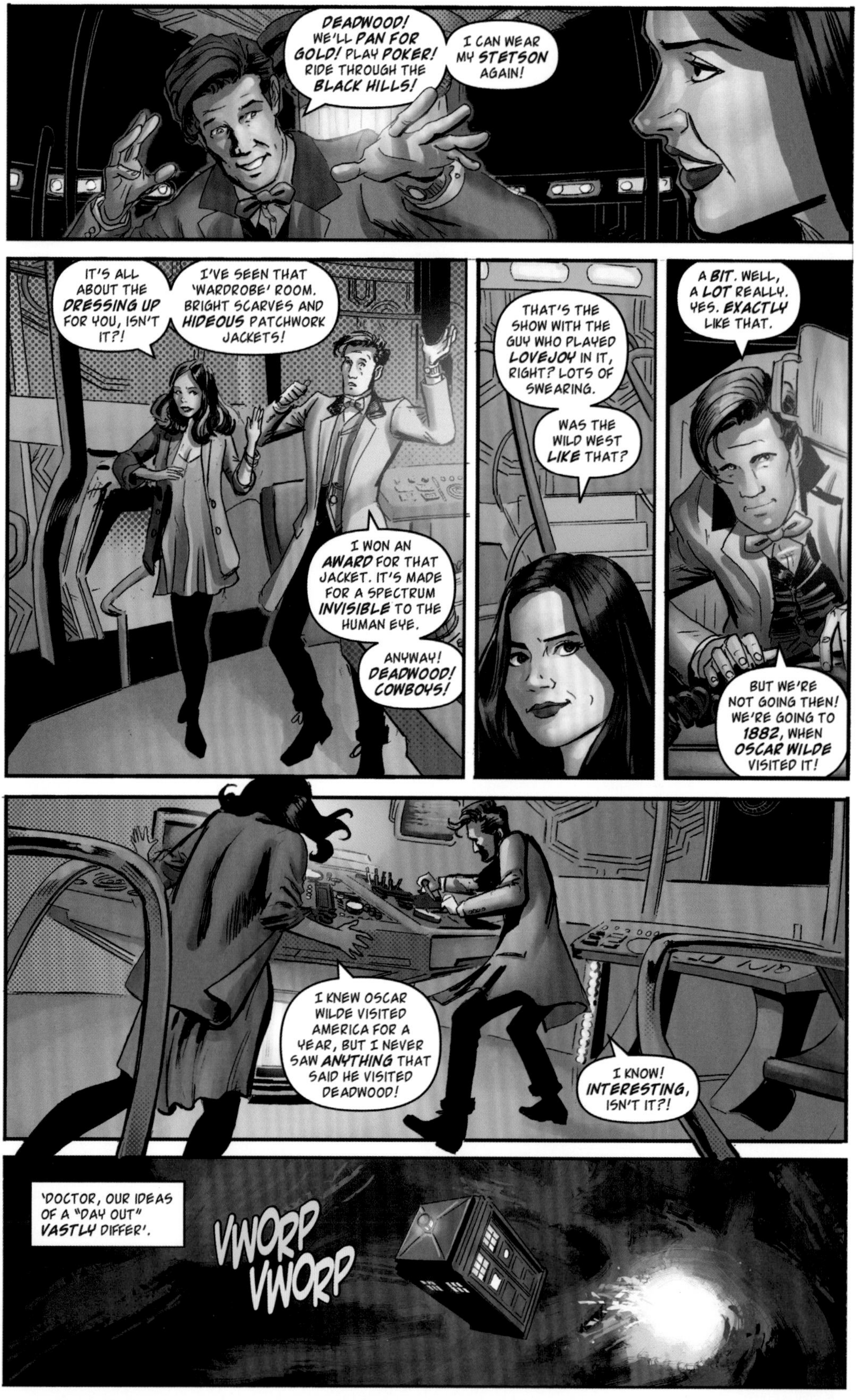
DEADWOOD! WE'LL PAN FOR GOLD! PLAY POKER! RIDE THROUGH THE BLACK HILLS!
I CAN WEAR MY STETSON AGAIN!
IT'S ALL ABOUT THE DRESSING UP FOR YOU, ISN'T IT?!
I'VE SEEN THAT 'WARDROBE' ROOM. BRIGHT SCARVES AND HIDEOUS PATCHWORK JACKETS!
I WON AN AWARD FOR THAT JACKET. IT'S MADE FOR A SPECTRUM INVISIBLE TO THE HUMAN EYE.
ANYWAY! DEADWOOD! COWBOYS!
THAT'S THE SHOW WITH THE GUY WHO PLAYED LOVEJOY IN IT, RIGHT? LOTS OF SWEARING.
WAS THE WILD WEST LIKE THAT?
A BIT. WELL, A LOT REALLY. YES. EXACTLY LIKE THAT.
BUT WE'RE NOT GOING THEN! WE'RE GOING TO 1882, WHEN OSCAR WILDE VISITED IT!
I KNEW OSCAR WILDE VISITED AMERICA FOR A YEAR, BUT I NEVER SAW ANYTHING THAT SAID HE VISITED DEADWOOD!
I KNOW! INTERESTING, ISN'T IT?!
'DOCTOR, OUR IDEAS OF A "DAY OUT" VASTLY DIFFER'.
VWORP VWORP

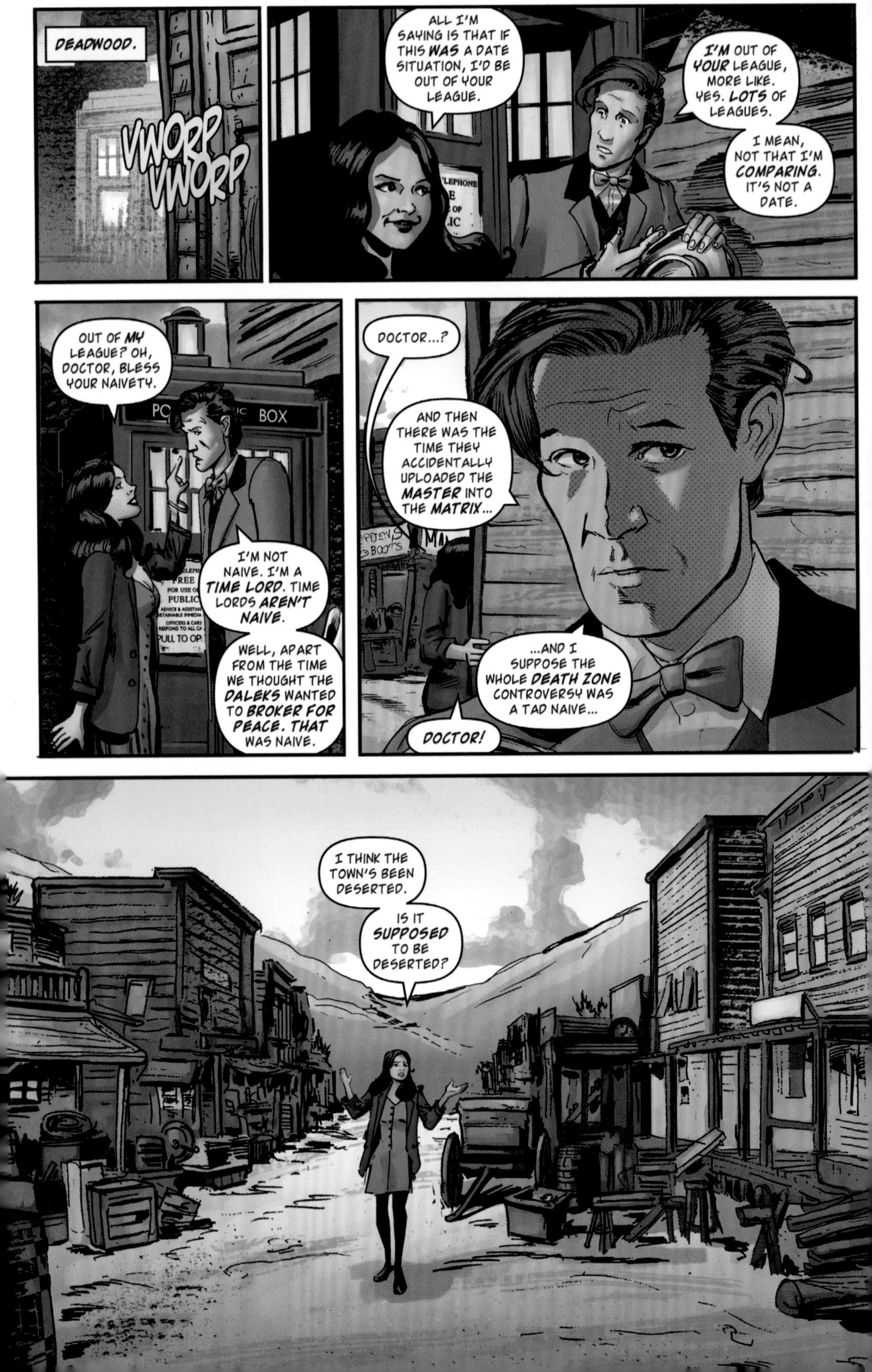
DEADWOOD.
VWORP VWORP
ALL I'M SAYING IS THAT IF THIS WAS A DATE SITUATION, I'D BE OUT OF YOUR LEAGUE.
I'M OUT OF YOUR LEAGUE, MORE LIKE. YES. LOTS OF LEAGUES.
I MEAN, NOT THAT I'M COMPARING. IT'S NOT A DATE.
OUT OF MY LEAGUE? OH, DOCTOR, BLESS YOUR NAIVETY.
I'M NOT NAIVE. I'M A TIME LORD. TIME LORDS AREN'T NAIVE.
WELL, APART FROM THE TIME WE THOUGHT THE DALEKS WANTED TO BROKER FOR PEACE. THAT WAS NAIVE.
DOCTOR...?
AND THEN THERE WAS THE TIME THEY ACCIDENTALLY UPLOADED THE MASTER INTO THE MATRIX...
...AND I SUPPOSE THE WHOLE DEATH ZONE CONTROVERSY WAS A TAD NAIVE...
DOCTOR!
I THINK THE TOWN'S BEEN DESERTED.
IS IT SUPPOSED TO BE DESERTED?

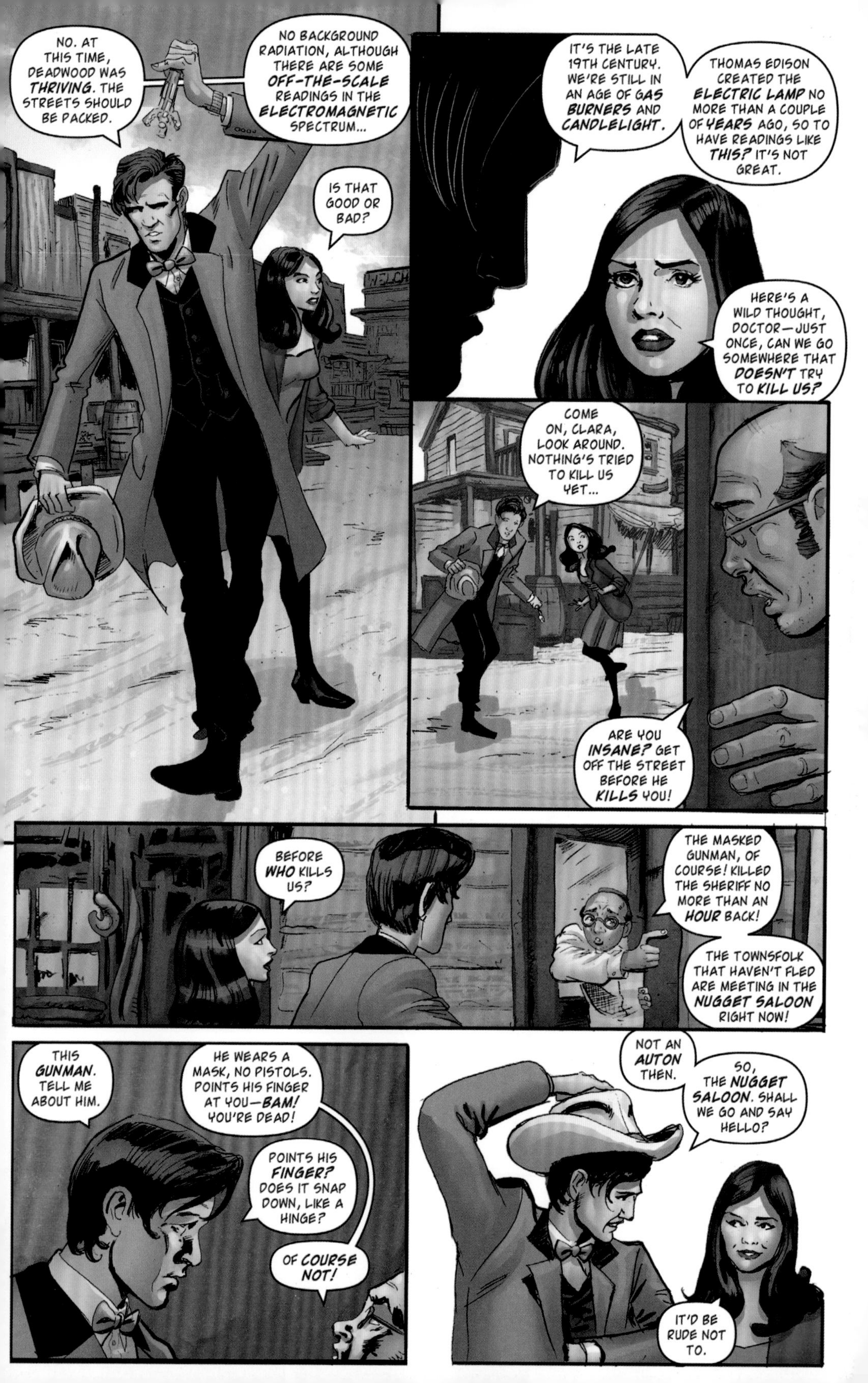
NO. AT THIS TIME, DEADWOOD WAS THRIVING. THE STREETS SHOULD BE PACKED.
NO BACKGROUND RADIATION, ALTHOUGH THERE ARE SOME OFF-THE-SCALE READINGS IN THE ELECTROMAGNETIC SPECTRUM...
IS THAT GOOD OR BAD?
IT'S THE LATE 19TH CENTURY. WE'RE STILL IN AN AGE OF GAS BURNERS AND CANDLELIGHT.
THOMAS EDISON CREATED THE ELECTRIC LAMP NO MORE THAN A COUPLE OF YEARS AGO, SO TO HAVE READINGS LIKE THIS? IT'S NOT GREAT.
HERE'S A WILD THOUGHT, DOCTOR—JUST ONCE, CAN WE GO SOMEWHERE THAT DOESN'T TRY TO KILL US?
COME ON, CLARA, LOOK AROUND. NOTHING'S TRIED TO KILL US YET...
ARE YOU INSANE? GET OFF THE STREET BEFORE HE KILLS YOU!
BEFORE WHO KILLS US?
THE MASKED GUNMAN, OF COURSE! KILLED THE SHERIFF NO MORE THAN AN HOUR BACK!
THE TOWNSFOLK THAT HAVEN'T FLED ARE MEETING IN THE NUGGET SALOON RIGHT NOW!
THIS GUNMAN. TELL ME ABOUT HIM.
HE WEARS A MASK, NO PISTOLS. POINTS HIS FINGER AT YOU—BAM! YOU'RE DEAD!
POINTS HIS FINGER? DOES IT SNAP DOWN, LIKE A HINGE?
OF COURSE NOT!
NOT AN AUTON THEN.
SO, THE NUGGET SALOON. SHALL WE GO AND SAY HELLO?
IT'D BE RUDE NOT TO.

THE NUGGET SALOON.

BRADFORD WAS A GOOD MAN—AND OF *COURSE* I WANT TO SEEK JUSTICE—BUT I'M NO LONGER DEADWOOD'S SHERIFF.

WE NEED TO CONTACT *MARSHAL RAYMOND* IN *YANKTON* ON THIS.

THAT'LL TAKE DAYS, *BULLOCK!* WE NEED ACTION *NOW!*

BRADFORD SHOT THE GUNSLINGER *FOUR TIMES*, DEAD CENTRE! HE STAYED STANDING!

THIS AIN'T NO MAN, THIS IS A *DEMON*, SENT TO TEST US!

HE AIN'T NO DEMON, BUT HE AIN'T NO MAN, EITHER. THIS MASKED GUNMAN IS *WILD BILL HIMSELF.*

I LOOKED IN THE *CEMETERY* THIS MORNING— HIS BODY'S BEEN *TAKEN.*

THAT'S *MADNESS!* WILD BILL CAN'T COME BACK FROM THE DEAD!

YOU MET BILL WHEN HE WAS ALIVE, FERRIS! YOU TELLIN' ME IT DIDN'T *LOOK* LIKE HIM?

HE WAS WEARING A *MASK!*

WE NEED TO CALL THE *7TH CAVALRY!* WHO ELSE CAN HELP US?

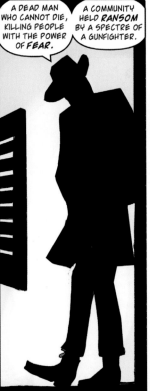

A DEAD MAN WHO CANNOT DIE, KILLING PEOPLE WITH THE POWER OF *FEAR.*

A COMMUNITY HELD *RANSOM* BY A SPECTRE OF A GUNFIGHTER.

SOUNDS LIKE YOU NEED A *NEW SHERIFF* IN TOWN.

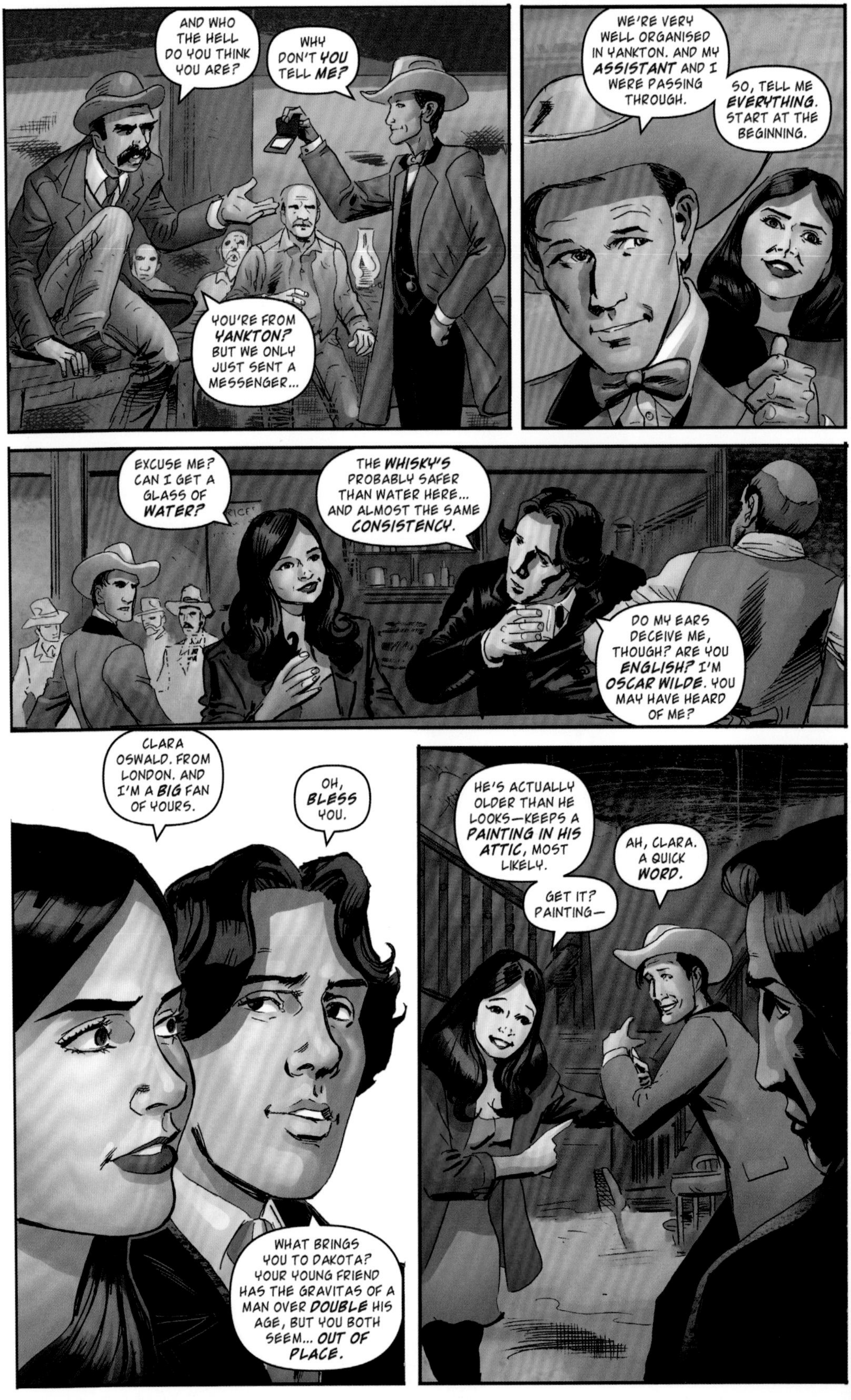
AND WHO THE HELL DO YOU THINK YOU ARE?
WHY DON'T YOU TELL ME?
YOU'RE FROM YANKTON? BUT WE ONLY JUST SENT A MESSENGER...
WE'RE VERY WELL ORGANISED IN YANKTON. AND MY ASSISTANT AND I WERE PASSING THROUGH.
SO, TELL ME EVERYTHING. START AT THE BEGINNING.
EXCUSE ME? CAN I GET A GLASS OF WATER?
THE WHISKY'S PROBABLY SAFER THAN WATER HERE... AND ALMOST THE SAME CONSISTENCY.
DO MY EARS DECEIVE ME, THOUGH? ARE YOU ENGLISH? I'M OSCAR WILDE. YOU MAY HAVE HEARD OF ME?
CLARA OSWALD. FROM LONDON. AND I'M A BIG FAN OF YOURS.
OH, BLESS YOU.
WHAT BRINGS YOU TO DAKOTA? YOUR YOUNG FRIEND HAS THE GRAVITAS OF A MAN OVER DOUBLE HIS AGE, BUT YOU BOTH SEEM... OUT OF PLACE.
HE'S ACTUALLY OLDER THAN HE LOOKS—KEEPS A PAINTING IN HIS ATTIC, MOST LIKELY.
GET IT? PAINTING—
AH, CLARA. A QUICK WORD.

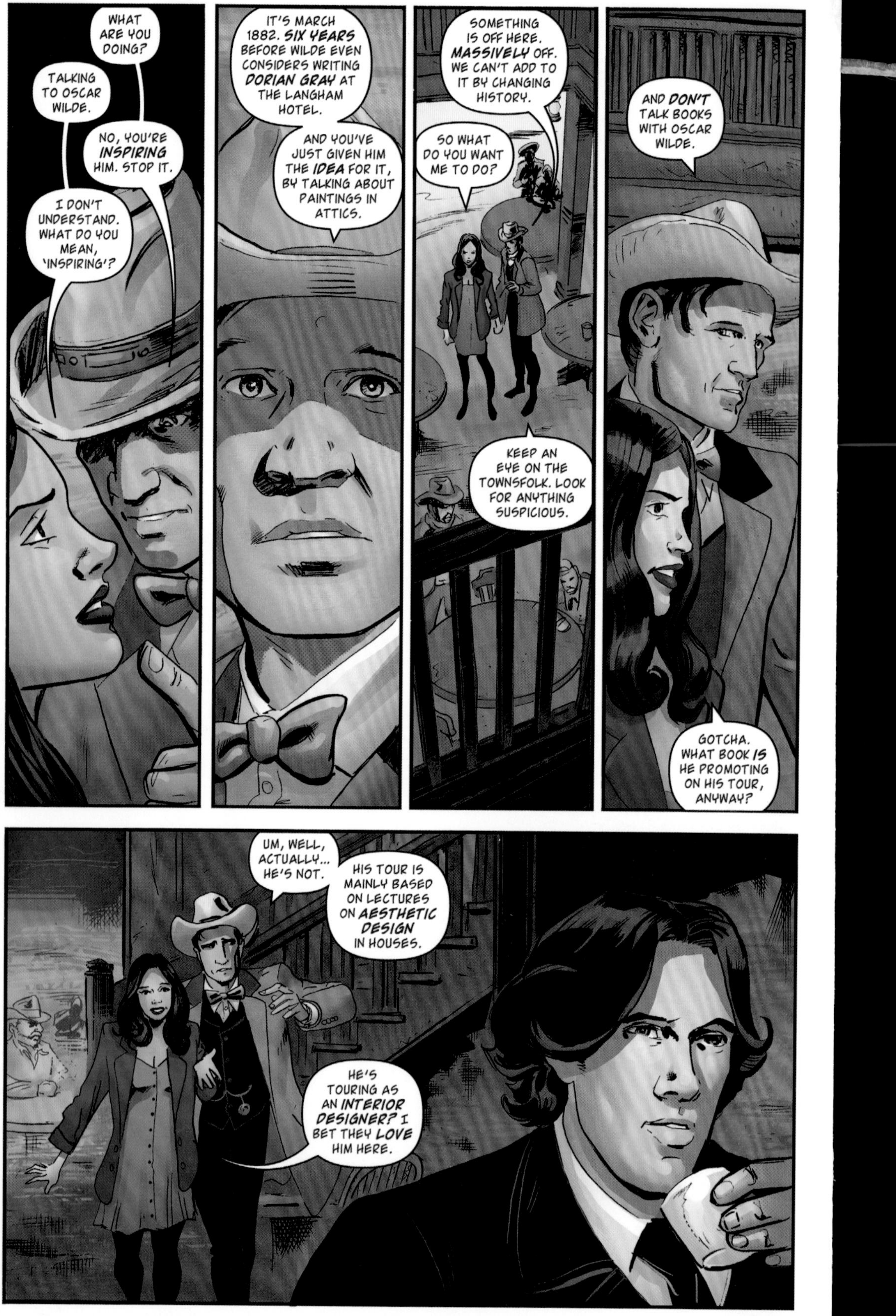
WHAT ARE YOU DOING?
TALKING TO OSCAR WILDE.
NO, YOU'RE INSPIRING HIM. STOP IT.
I DON'T UNDERSTAND. WHAT DO YOU MEAN, 'INSPIRING'?
IT'S MARCH 1882. SIX YEARS BEFORE WILDE EVEN CONSIDERS WRITING DORIAN GRAY AT THE LANGHAM HOTEL.
AND YOU'VE JUST GIVEN HIM THE IDEA FOR IT, BY TALKING ABOUT PAINTINGS IN ATTICS.
SOMETHING IS OFF HERE. MASSIVELY OFF. WE CAN'T ADD TO IT BY CHANGING HISTORY.
SO WHAT DO YOU WANT ME TO DO?
KEEP AN EYE ON THE TOWNSFOLK. LOOK FOR ANYTHING SUSPICIOUS.
AND DON'T TALK BOOKS WITH OSCAR WILDE.
GOTCHA. WHAT BOOK IS HE PROMOTING ON HIS TOUR, ANYWAY?
UM, WELL, ACTUALLY... HE'S NOT.
HIS TOUR IS MAINLY BASED ON LECTURES ON AESTHETIC DESIGN IN HOUSES.
HE'S TOURING AS AN INTERIOR DESIGNER? I BET THEY LOVE HIM HERE.

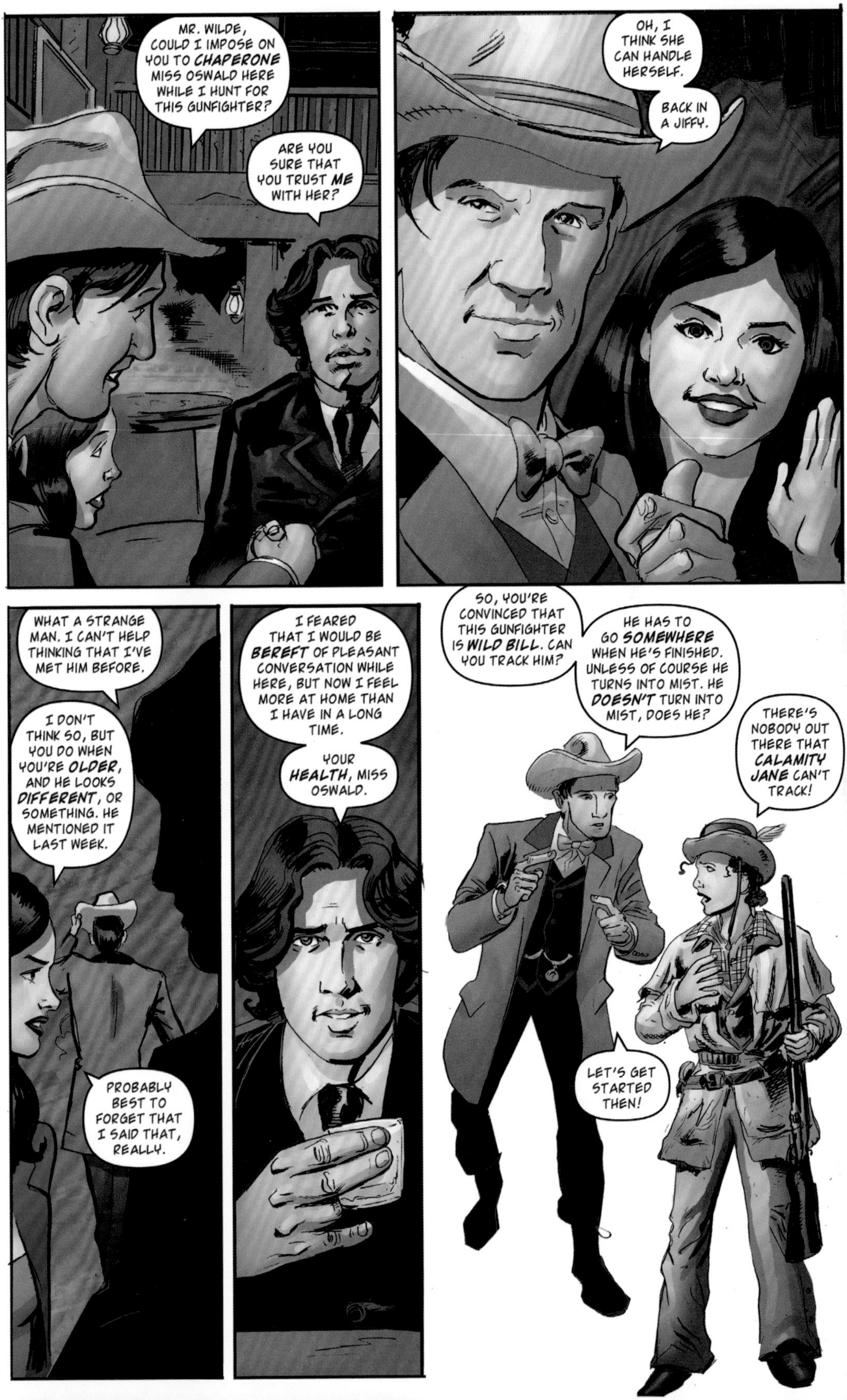
MR. WILDE, COULD I IMPOSE ON YOU TO CHAPERONE MISS OSWALD HERE WHILE I HUNT FOR THIS GUNFIGHTER?
ARE YOU SURE THAT YOU TRUST ME WITH HER?
OH, I THINK SHE CAN HANDLE HERSELF.
BACK IN A JIFFY.
WHAT A STRANGE MAN. I CAN'T HELP THINKING THAT I'VE MET HIM BEFORE.
I DON'T THINK SO, BUT YOU DO WHEN YOU'RE OLDER, AND HE LOOKS DIFFERENT, OR SOMETHING. HE MENTIONED IT LAST WEEK.
PROBABLY BEST TO FORGET THAT I SAID THAT, REALLY.
I FEARED THAT I WOULD BE BEREFT OF PLEASANT CONVERSATION WHILE HERE, BUT NOW I FEEL MORE AT HOME THAN I HAVE IN A LONG TIME.
YOUR HEALTH, MISS OSWALD.
SO, YOU'RE CONVINCED THAT THIS GUNFIGHTER IS WILD BILL. CAN YOU TRACK HIM?
HE HAS TO GO SOMEWHERE WHEN HE'S FINISHED. UNLESS OF COURSE HE TURNS INTO MIST. HE DOESN'T TURN INTO MIST, DOES HE?
THERE'S NOBODY OUT THERE THAT CALAMITY JANE CAN'T TRACK!
LET'S GET STARTED THEN!

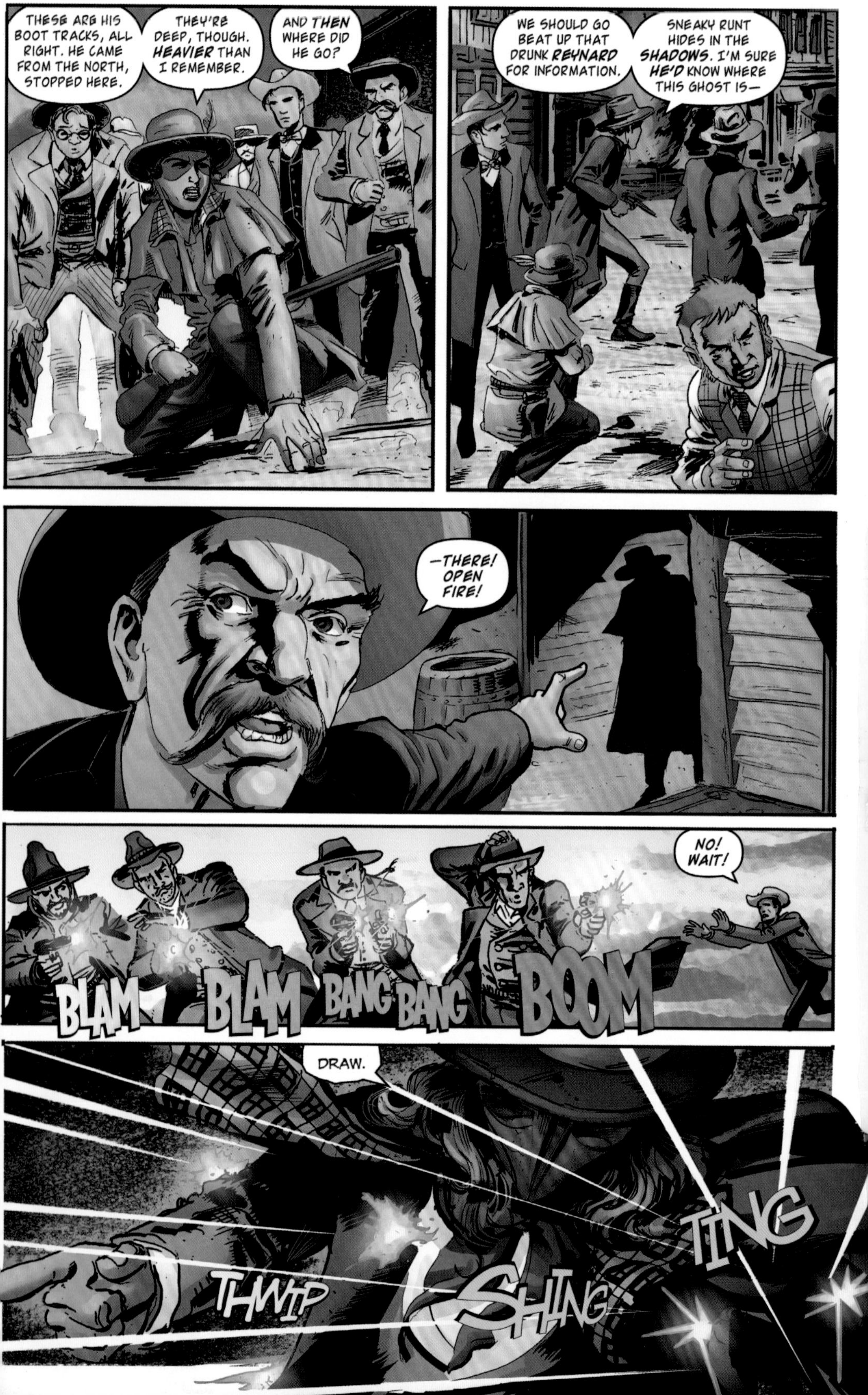
THESE ARE HIS BOOT TRACKS, ALL RIGHT. HE CAME FROM THE NORTH, STOPPED HERE.
THEY'RE DEEP, THOUGH. HEAVIER THAN I REMEMBER.
AND THEN WHERE DID HE GO?
WE SHOULD GO BEAT UP THAT DRUNK REYNARD FOR INFORMATION.
SNEAKY RUNT HIDES IN THE SHADOWS. I'M SURE HE'D KNOW WHERE THIS GHOST IS—
—THERE! OPEN FIRE!
NO! WAIT!
BLAM
BLAM
BANG
BANG
BOOM
DRAW.
THWIP
SHING
TING

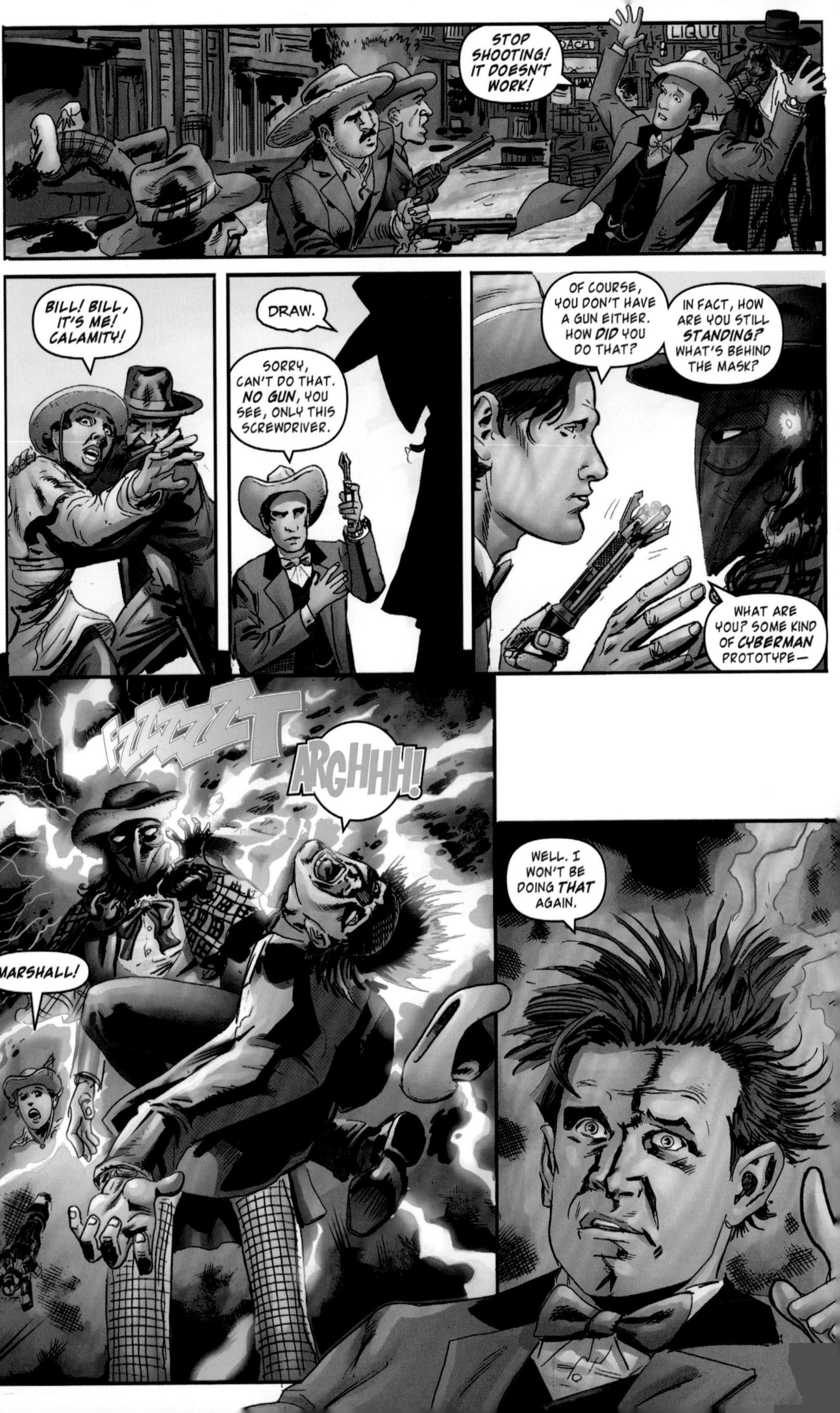
STOP SHOOTING! IT DOESN'T WORK!
BILL! BILL, IT'S ME! CALAMITY!
DRAW.
SORRY, CAN'T DO THAT. NO GUN, YOU SEE, ONLY THIS SCREWDRIVER.
OF COURSE, YOU DON'T HAVE A GUN EITHER. HOW DID YOU DO THAT?
IN FACT, HOW ARE YOU STILL STANDING? WHAT'S BEHIND THE MASK?
WHAT ARE YOU? SOME KIND OF CYBERMAN PROTOTYPE—
FZZZZT
ARGHHH!
MARSHALL!
WELL. I WON'T BE DOING THAT AGAIN.

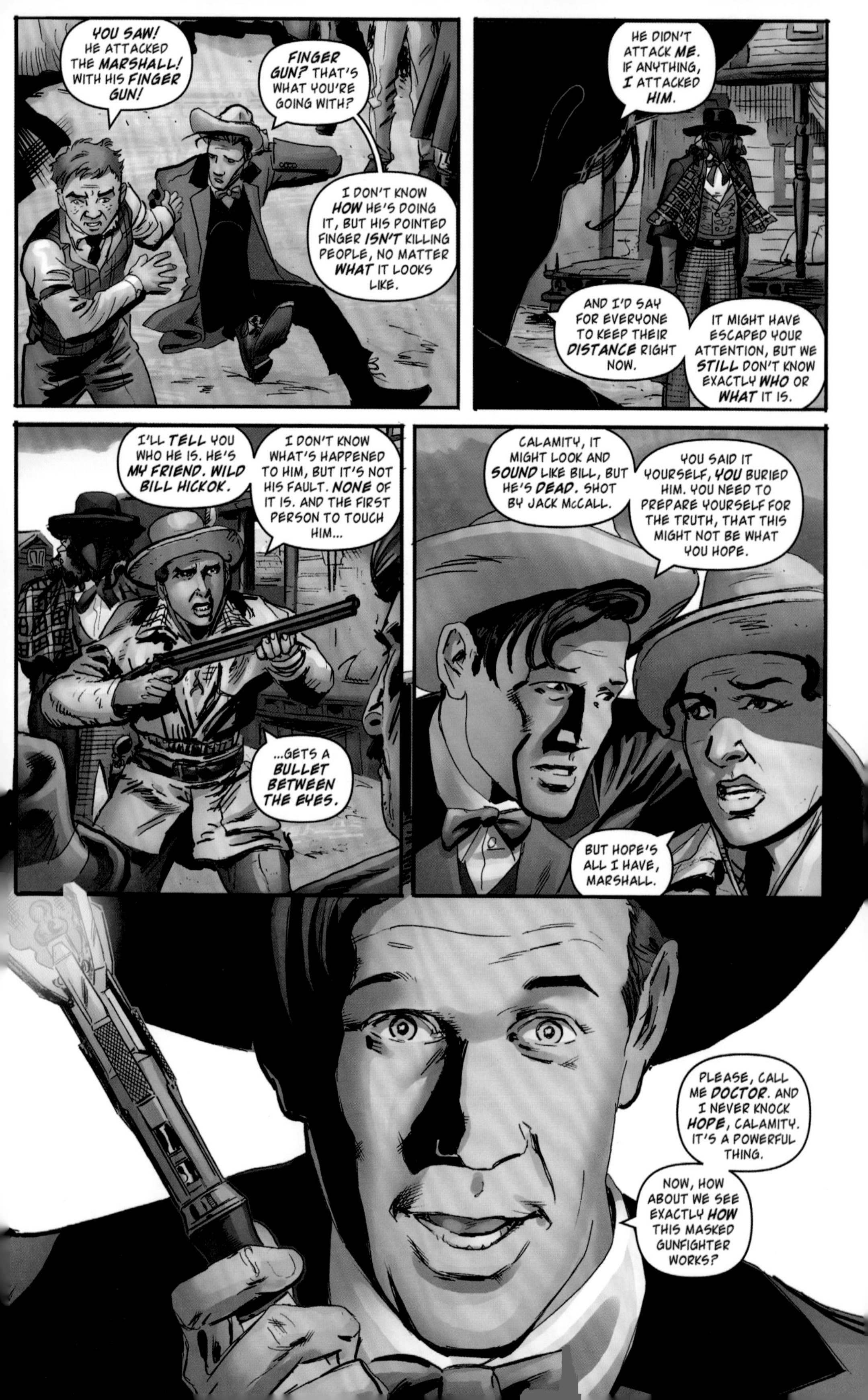
YOU SAW! HE ATTACKED THE MARSHALL! WITH HIS FINGER GUN!
FINGER GUN? THAT'S WHAT YOU'RE GOING WITH?
I DON'T KNOW HOW HE'S DOING IT, BUT HIS POINTED FINGER ISN'T KILLING PEOPLE, NO MATTER WHAT IT LOOKS LIKE.
HE DIDN'T ATTACK ME. IF ANYTHING, I ATTACKED HIM.
AND I'D SAY FOR EVERYONE TO KEEP THEIR DISTANCE RIGHT NOW.
IT MIGHT HAVE ESCAPED YOUR ATTENTION, BUT WE STILL DON'T KNOW EXACTLY WHO OR WHAT IT IS.
I'LL TELL YOU WHO HE IS. HE'S MY FRIEND. WILD BILL HICKOK.
I DON'T KNOW WHAT'S HAPPENED TO HIM, BUT IT'S NOT HIS FAULT. NONE OF IT IS. AND THE FIRST PERSON TO TOUCH HIM...
...GETS A BULLET BETWEEN THE EYES.
CALAMITY, IT MIGHT LOOK AND SOUND LIKE BILL, BUT HE'S DEAD. SHOT BY JACK McCALL.
YOU SAID IT YOURSELF, YOU BURIED HIM. YOU NEED TO PREPARE YOURSELF FOR THE TRUTH, THAT THIS MIGHT NOT BE WHAT YOU HOPE.
BUT HOPE'S ALL I HAVE, MARSHALL.
PLEASE, CALL ME DOCTOR. AND I NEVER KNOCK HOPE, CALAMITY. IT'S A POWERFUL THING.
NOW, HOW ABOUT WE SEE EXACTLY HOW THIS MASKED GUNFIGHTER WORKS?

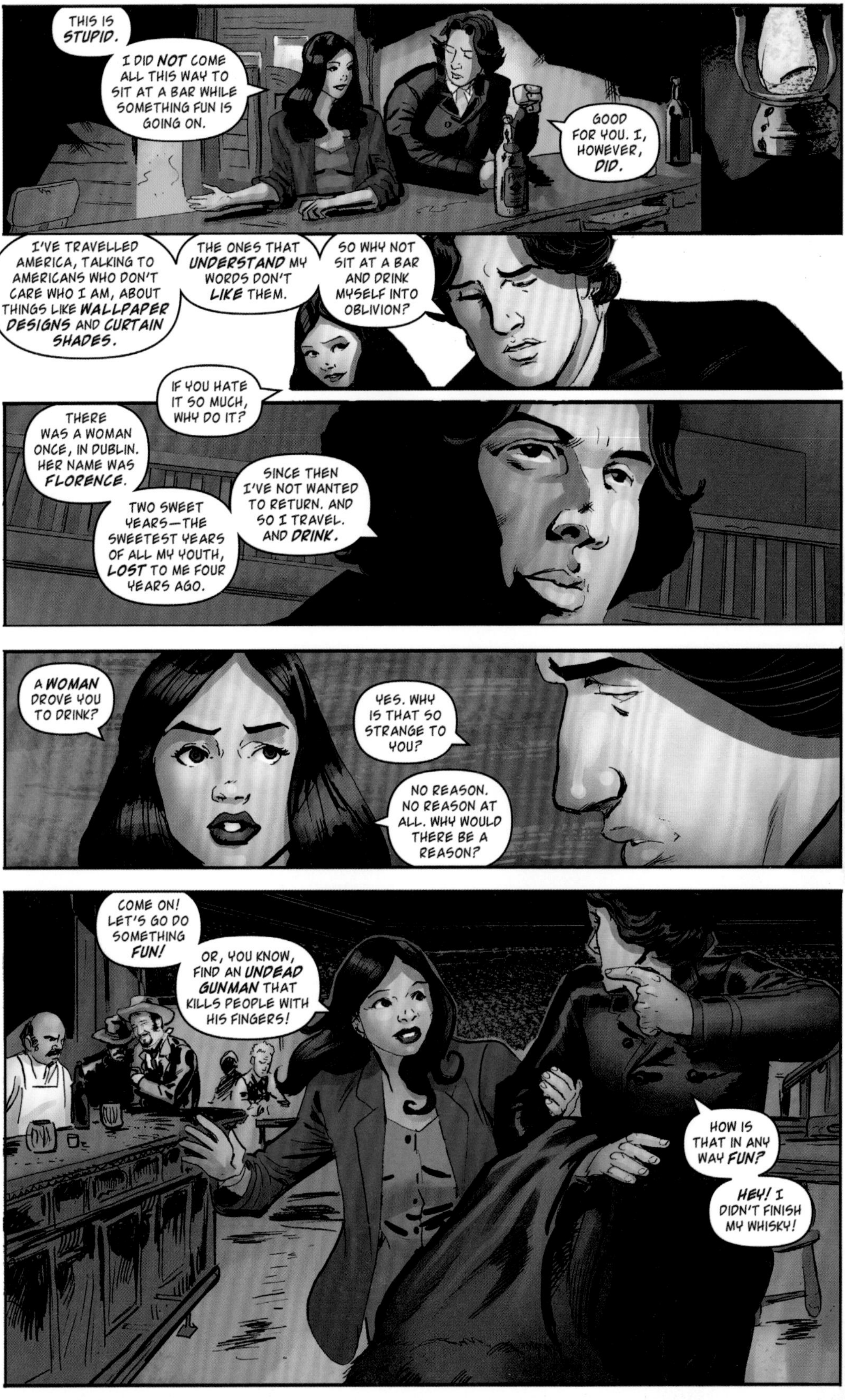
THIS IS STUPID.
I DID NOT COME ALL THIS WAY TO SIT AT A BAR WHILE SOMETHING FUN IS GOING ON.
GOOD FOR YOU. I, HOWEVER, DID.
I'VE TRAVELLED AMERICA, TALKING TO AMERICANS WHO DON'T CARE WHO I AM, ABOUT THINGS LIKE WALLPAPER DESIGNS AND CURTAIN SHADES.
THE ONES THAT UNDERSTAND MY WORDS DON'T LIKE THEM.
SO WHY NOT SIT AT A BAR AND DRINK MYSELF INTO OBLIVION?
IF YOU HATE IT SO MUCH, WHY DO IT?
THERE WAS A WOMAN ONCE, IN DUBLIN. HER NAME WAS FLORENCE.
TWO SWEET YEARS—THE SWEETEST YEARS OF ALL MY YOUTH, LOST TO ME FOUR YEARS AGO.
SINCE THEN I'VE NOT WANTED TO RETURN. AND SO I TRAVEL. AND DRINK.
A WOMAN DROVE YOU TO DRINK?
YES. WHY IS THAT SO STRANGE TO YOU?
NO REASON. NO REASON AT ALL. WHY WOULD THERE BE A REASON?
COME ON! LET'S GO DO SOMETHING FUN!
OR, YOU KNOW, FIND AN UNDEAD GUNMAN THAT KILLS PEOPLE WITH HIS FINGERS!
HOW IS THAT IN ANY WAY FUN?
HEY! I DIDN'T FINISH MY WHISKY!

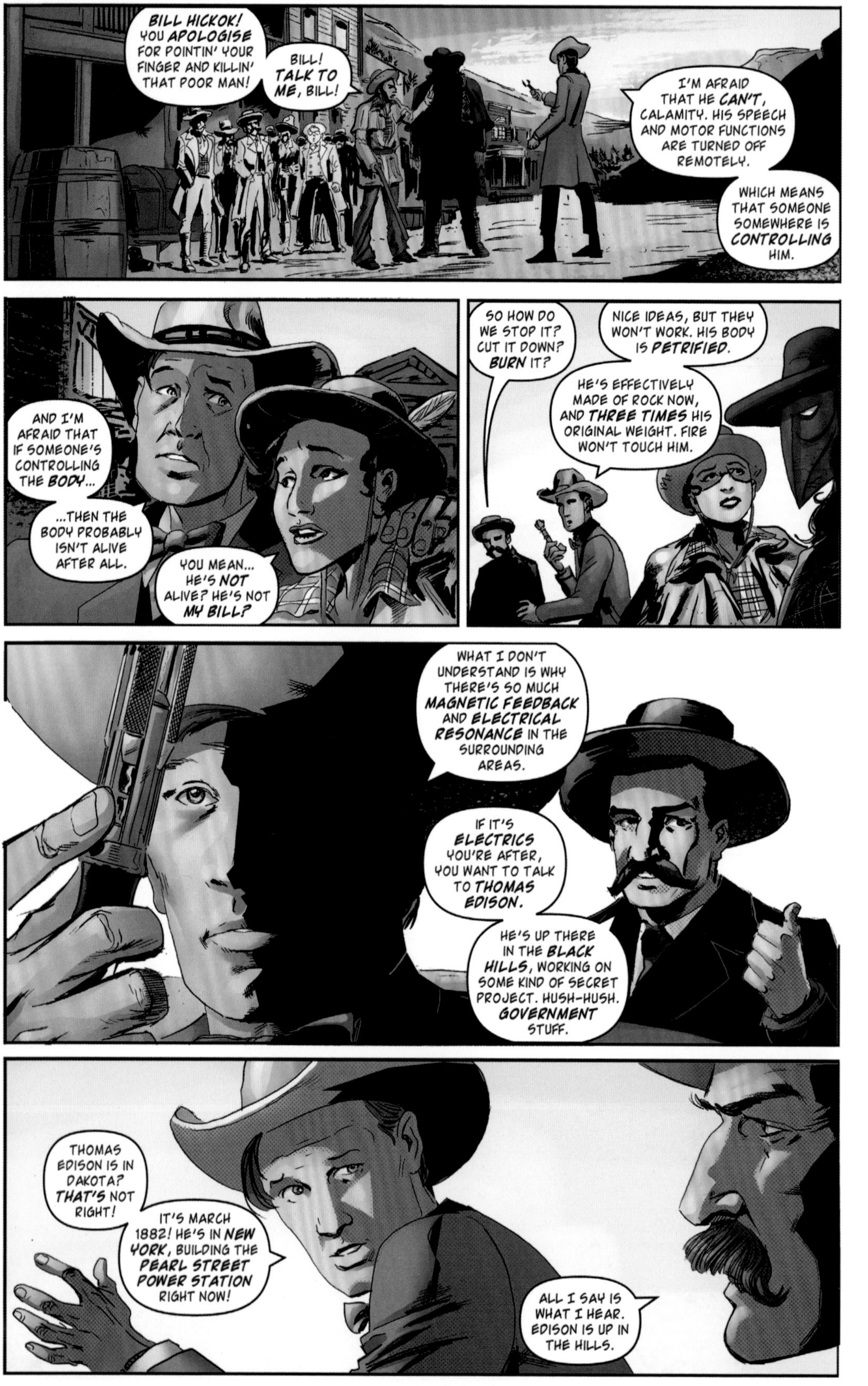
BILL HICKOK! YOU APOLOGISE FOR POINTIN' YOUR FINGER AND KILLIN' THAT POOR MAN!
BILL! TALK TO ME, BILL!
I'M AFRAID THAT HE CAN'T, CALAMITY. HIS SPEECH AND MOTOR FUNCTIONS ARE TURNED OFF REMOTELY.
WHICH MEANS THAT SOMEONE SOMEWHERE IS CONTROLLING HIM.
AND I'M AFRAID THAT IF SOMEONE'S CONTROLLING THE BODY...
...THEN THE BODY PROBABLY ISN'T ALIVE AFTER ALL.
YOU MEAN... HE'S NOT ALIVE? HE'S NOT MY BILL?
SO HOW DO WE STOP IT? CUT IT DOWN? BURN IT?
NICE IDEAS, BUT THEY WON'T WORK. HIS BODY IS PETRIFIED.
HE'S EFFECTIVELY MADE OF ROCK NOW, AND THREE TIMES HIS ORIGINAL WEIGHT. FIRE WON'T TOUCH HIM.
WHAT I DON'T UNDERSTAND IS WHY THERE'S SO MUCH MAGNETIC FEEDBACK AND ELECTRICAL RESONANCE IN THE SURROUNDING AREAS.
IF IT'S ELECTRICS YOU'RE AFTER, YOU WANT TO TALK TO THOMAS EDISON.
HE'S UP THERE IN THE BLACK HILLS, WORKING ON SOME KIND OF SECRET PROJECT. HUSH-HUSH. GOVERNMENT STUFF.
THOMAS EDISON IS IN DAKOTA? THAT'S NOT RIGHT!
IT'S MARCH 1882! HE'S IN NEW YORK, BUILDING THE PEARL STREET POWER STATION RIGHT NOW!
ALL I SAY IS WHAT I HEAR. EDISON IS UP IN THE HILLS.

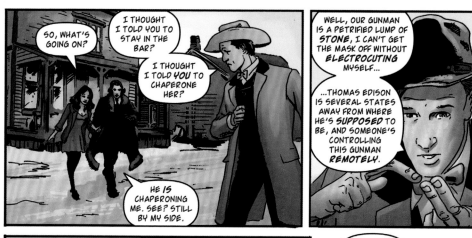

SO, WHAT'S GOING ON?

I THOUGHT I TOLD YOU TO STAY IN THE BAR?

I THOUGHT I TOLD *YOU* TO CHAPERONE HER?

HE *IS* CHAPERONING ME. SEE? STILL BY MY SIDE.

WELL, OUR GUNMAN IS A PETRIFIED LUMP OF *STONE*, I CAN'T GET THE MASK OFF WITHOUT *ELECTROCUTING* MYSELF...

...THOMAS EDISON IS SEVERAL STATES AWAY FROM WHERE HE'S *SUPPOSED* TO BE, AND SOMEONE'S CONTROLLING THIS GUNMAN *REMOTELY.*

POOR WOMAN. TO BELIEVE HER TRUE LOVE HAD RETURNED, ONLY TO FIND *STONE* IN PLACE OF ITS HEART.

JUST LIKE THE *'HAPPY PRINCE'*—

—WHICH IS *IRRELEVANT.* YOU SHOULD JUST IGNORE IT. I DIDN'T SAY ANYTHING.

I'M *DONE* WITH YOU, BILL. GO BACK TO *HELL.*

THUNK

CLICK

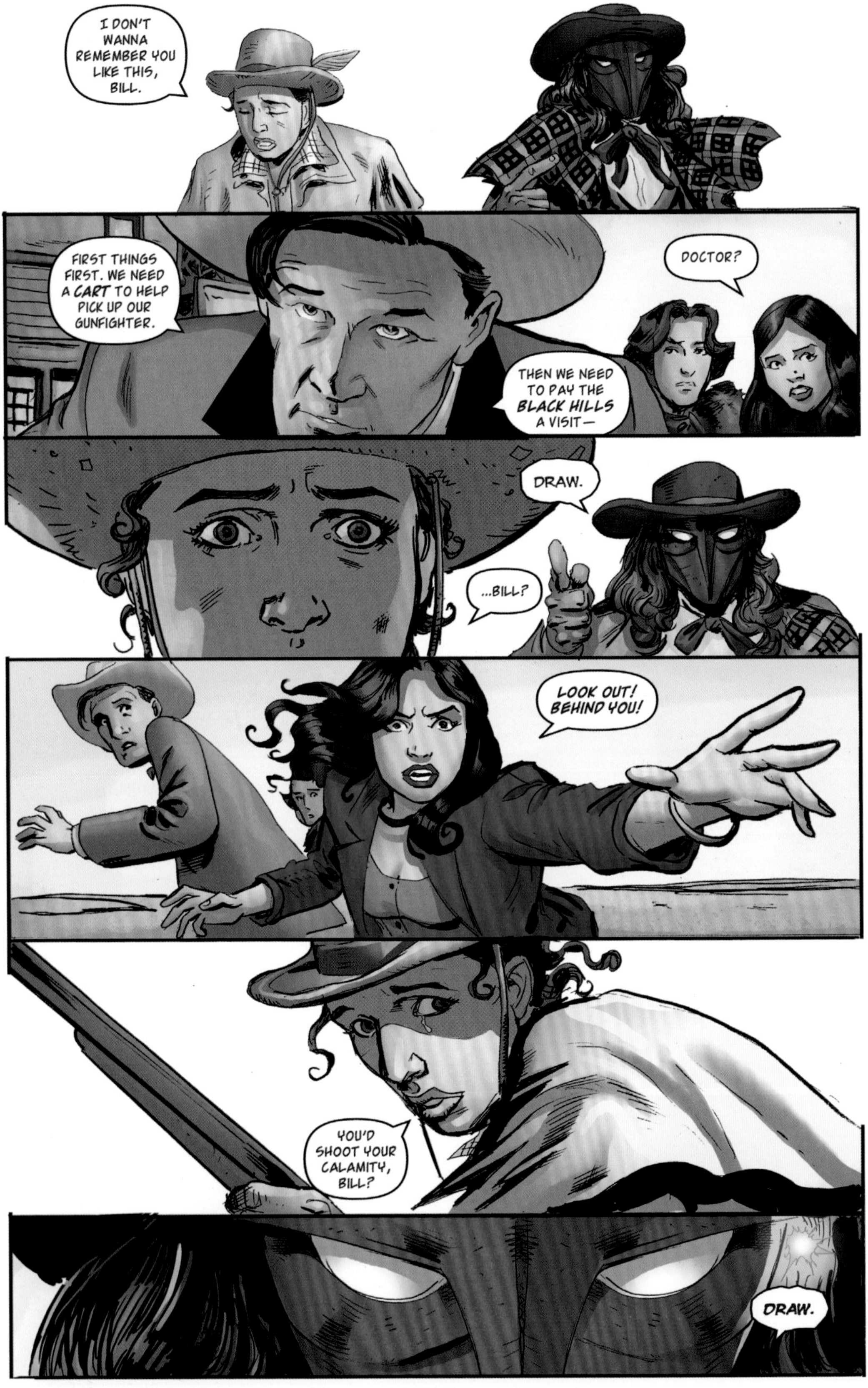
I DON'T WANNA REMEMBER YOU LIKE THIS, BILL.
FIRST THINGS FIRST. WE NEED A CART TO HELP PICK UP OUR GUNFIGHTER.
DOCTOR?
THEN WE NEED TO PAY THE BLACK HILLS A VISIT—
DRAW.
...BILL?
LOOK OUT! BEHIND YOU!
YOU'D SHOOT YOUR CALAMITY, BILL?
DRAW.

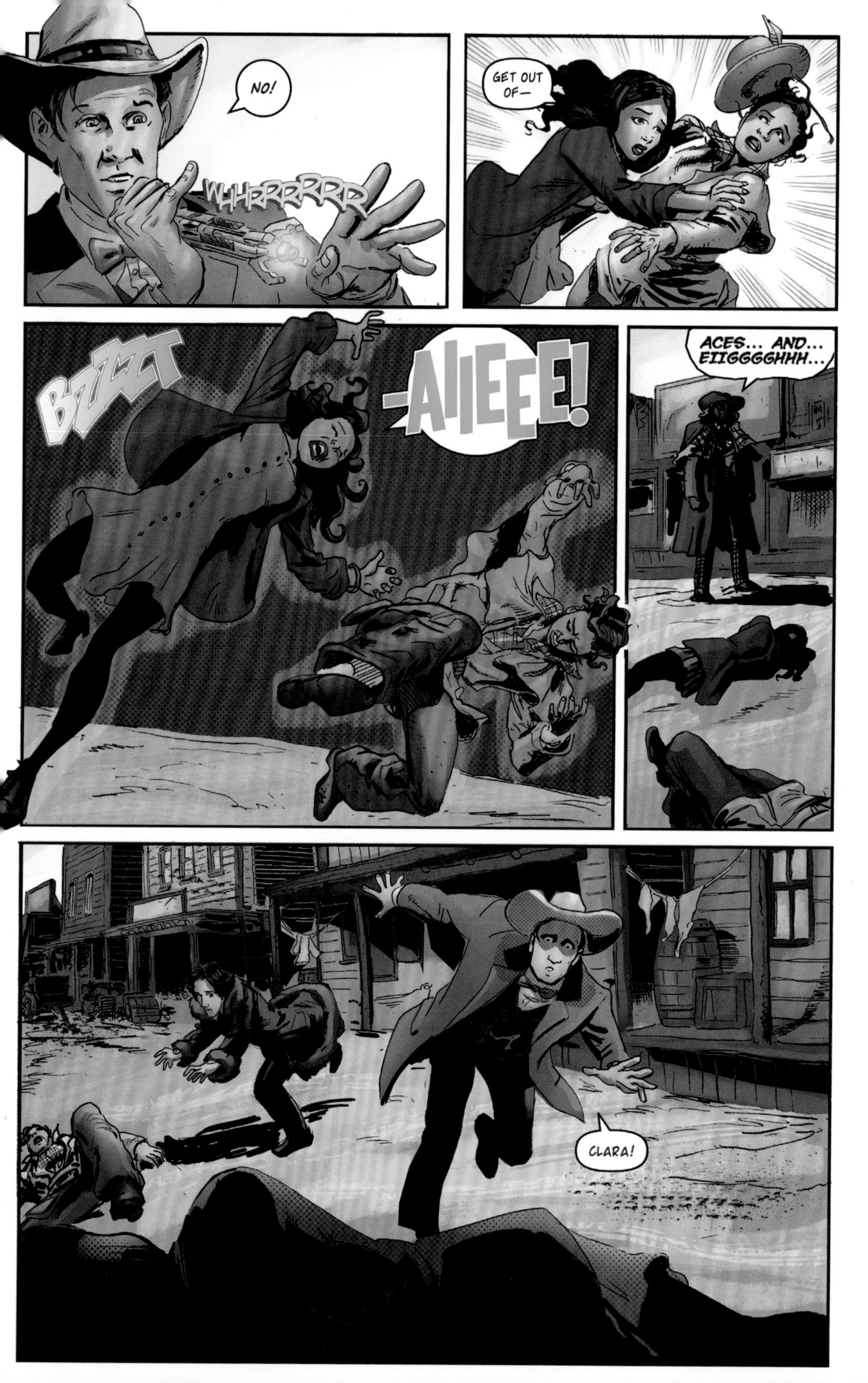
NO!
WHHRRRRRR
GET OUT OF—
BZZZT
AIIEEE!
ACES... AND... EIIGGGGHHH...
CLARA!

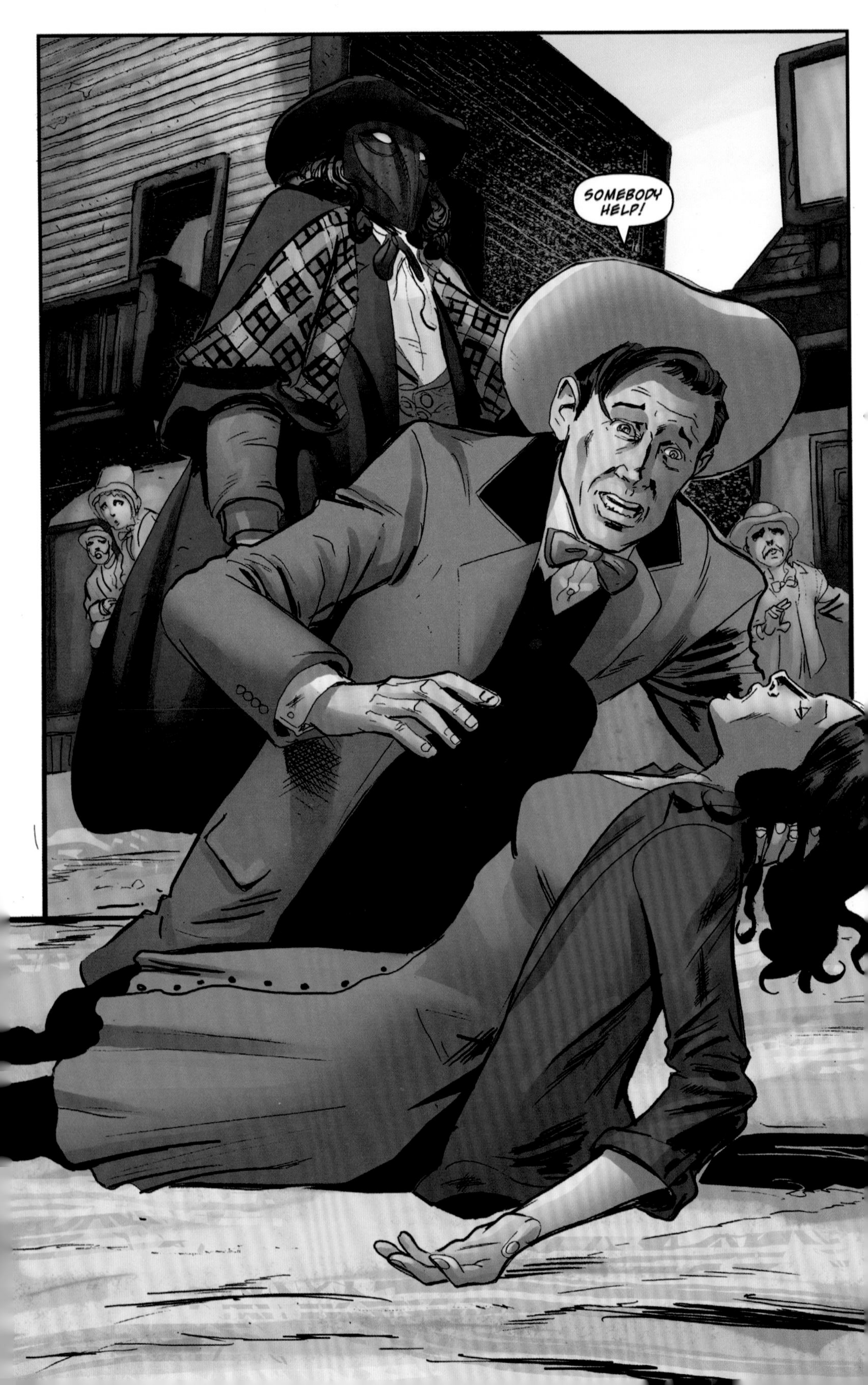
SOMEBODY HELP!

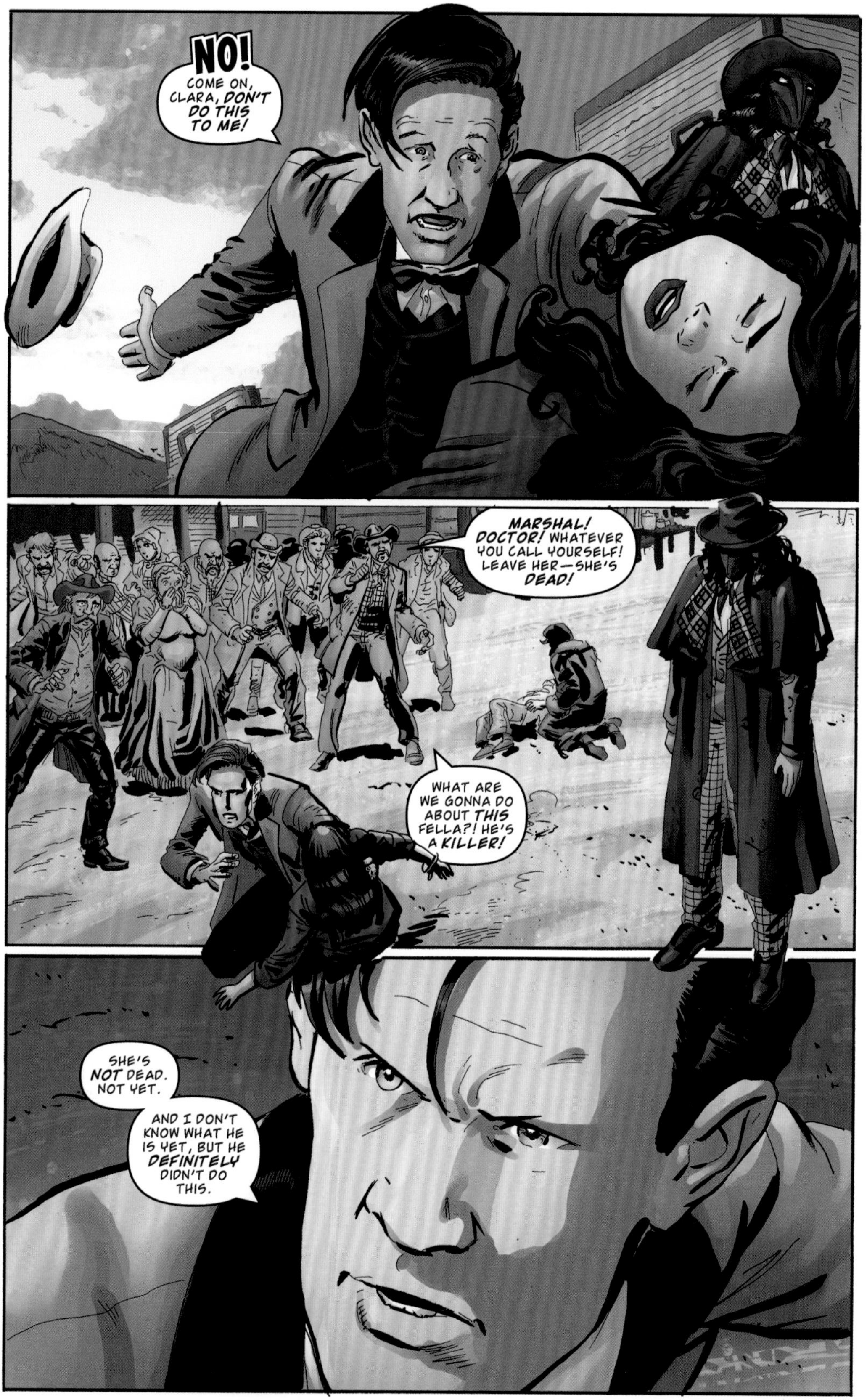
NO! COME ON, CLARA, DON'T DO THIS TO ME!
MARSHAL! DOCTOR! WHATEVER YOU CALL YOURSELF! LEAVE HER—SHE'S DEAD!
WHAT ARE WE GONNA DO ABOUT THIS FELLA?! HE'S A KILLER!
SHE'S NOT DEAD. NOT YET.
AND I DON'T KNOW WHAT HE IS YET, BUT HE DEFINITELY DIDN'T DO THIS.

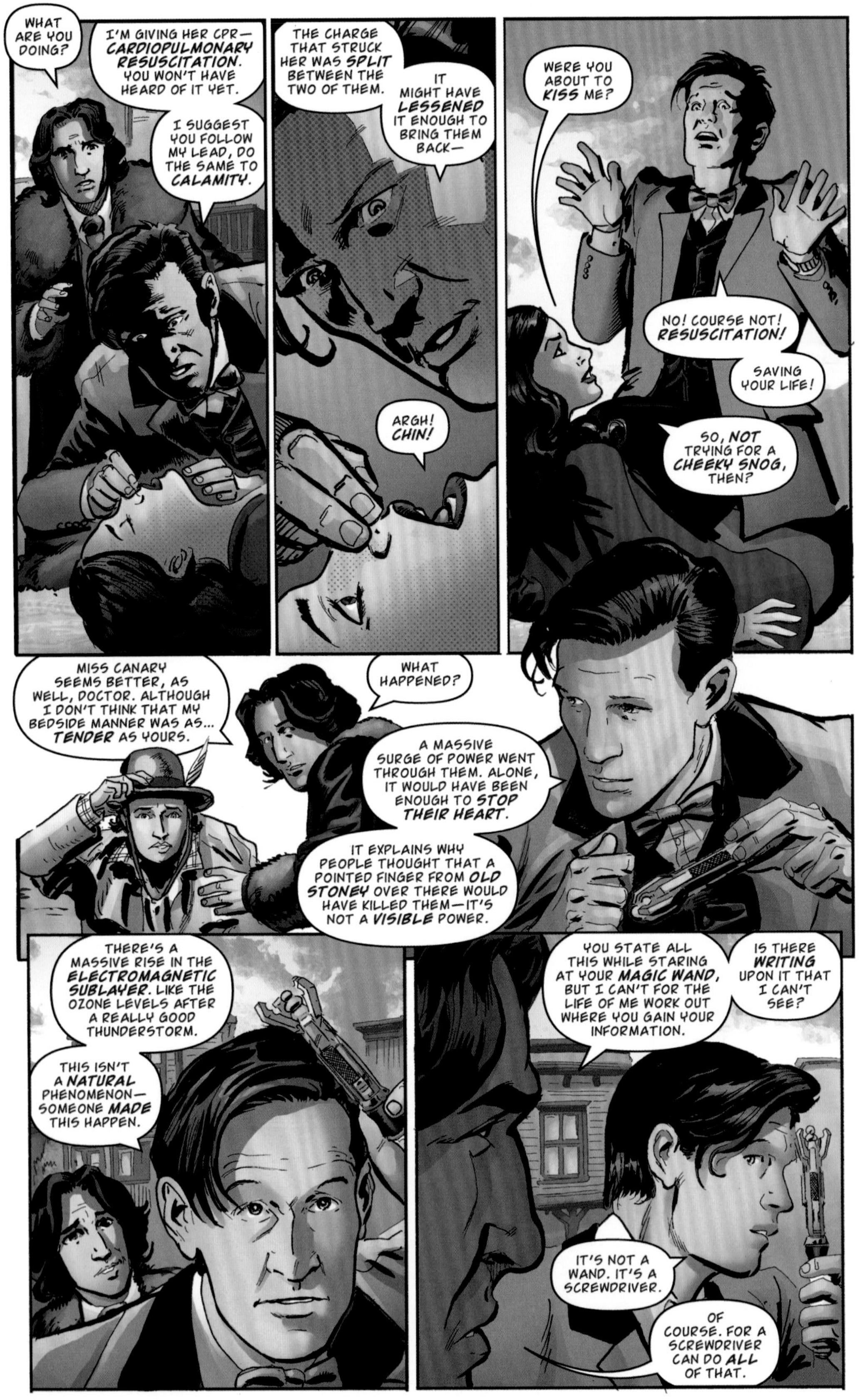
WHAT ARE YOU DOING?
I'M GIVING HER CPR— CARDIOPULMONARY RESUSCITATION. YOU WON'T HAVE HEARD OF IT YET.
I SUGGEST YOU FOLLOW MY LEAD, DO THE SAME TO CALAMITY.
THE CHARGE THAT STRUCK HER WAS SPLIT BETWEEN THE TWO OF THEM.
IT MIGHT HAVE LESSENED IT ENOUGH TO BRING THEM BACK—
ARGH! CHIN!
WERE YOU ABOUT TO KISS ME?
NO! COURSE NOT! RESUSCITATION!
SAVING YOUR LIFE!
SO, NOT TRYING FOR A CHEEKY SNOG, THEN?
MISS CANARY SEEMS BETTER, AS WELL, DOCTOR. ALTHOUGH I DON'T THINK THAT MY BEDSIDE MANNER WAS AS... TENDER AS YOURS.
WHAT HAPPENED?
A MASSIVE SURGE OF POWER WENT THROUGH THEM. ALONE, IT WOULD HAVE BEEN ENOUGH TO STOP THEIR HEART.
IT EXPLAINS WHY PEOPLE THOUGHT THAT A POINTED FINGER FROM OLD STONEY OVER THERE WOULD HAVE KILLED THEM—IT'S NOT A VISIBLE POWER.
THERE'S A MASSIVE RISE IN THE ELECTROMAGNETIC SUBLAYER. LIKE THE OZONE LEVELS AFTER A REALLY GOOD THUNDERSTORM.
THIS ISN'T A NATURAL PHENOMENON— SOMEONE MADE THIS HAPPEN.
YOU STATE ALL THIS WHILE STARING AT YOUR MAGIC WAND, BUT I CAN'T FOR THE LIFE OF ME WORK OUT WHERE YOU GAIN YOUR INFORMATION.
IS THERE WRITING UPON IT THAT I CAN'T SEE?
IT'S NOT A WAND. IT'S A SCREWDRIVER.
OF COURSE. FOR A SCREWDRIVER CAN DO ALL OF THAT.

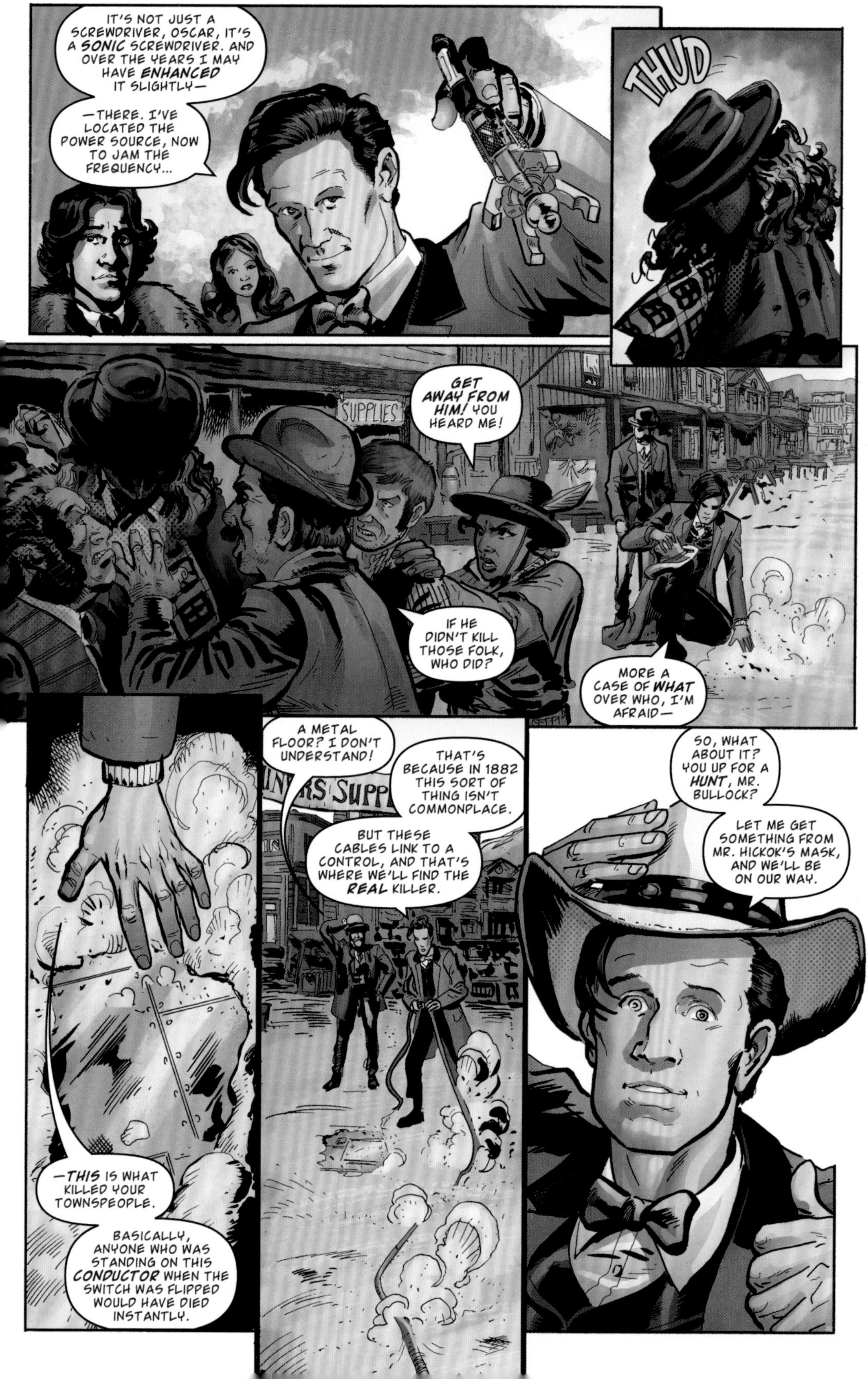
IT'S NOT JUST A SCREWDRIVER, OSCAR, IT'S A SONIC SCREWDRIVER. AND OVER THE YEARS I MAY HAVE ENHANCED IT SLIGHTLY—
—THERE. I'VE LOCATED THE POWER SOURCE, NOW TO JAM THE FREQUENCY...
THUD
SUPPLIES
GET AWAY FROM HIM! YOU HEARD ME!
IF HE DIDN'T KILL THOSE FOLK, WHO DID?
MORE A CASE OF WHAT OVER WHO, I'M AFRAID—
—THIS IS WHAT KILLED YOUR TOWNSPEOPLE.
BASICALLY, ANYONE WHO WAS STANDING ON THIS CONDUCTOR WHEN THE SWITCH WAS FLIPPED WOULD HAVE DIED INSTANTLY.
A METAL FLOOR? I DON'T UNDERSTAND!
THAT'S BECAUSE IN 1882 THIS SORT OF THING ISN'T COMMONPLACE.
BUT THESE CABLES LINK TO A CONTROL, AND THAT'S WHERE WE'LL FIND THE REAL KILLER.
SO, WHAT ABOUT IT? YOU UP FOR A HUNT, MR. BULLOCK?
LET ME GET SOMETHING FROM MR. HICKOK'S MASK, AND WE'LL BE ON OUR WAY.

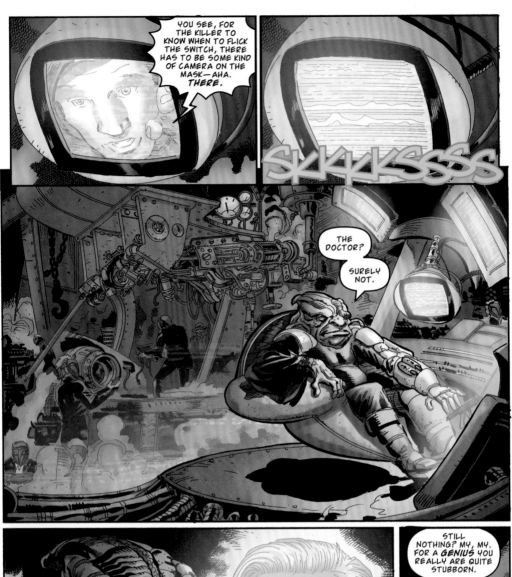

YOU SEE, FOR THE KILLER TO KNOW WHEN TO FLICK THE SWITCH, THERE HAS TO BE SOME KIND OF CAMERA ON THE MASK—AHA. *THERE.*

SKKKSSSS

THE *DOCTOR?*

SURELY NOT.

BUT IF IT WAS... OH, TO MEET THE *LAST* OF THE TIME LORDS AGAIN.

TO WATCH THE FABLED *DOCTOR* FAIL AS HIS FAVOURITE PLANET TURNS TO *ASH.*

A FITTING END, WOULDN'T YOU SAY, *MR. EDISON?*

STILL *NOTHING?* MY, MY. FOR A *GENIUS* YOU REALLY ARE QUITE STUBBORN.

I SHOULDN'T HAVE TO CRANK UP THE SETTINGS FOR A *CONVERSATION,* YOU KNOW.

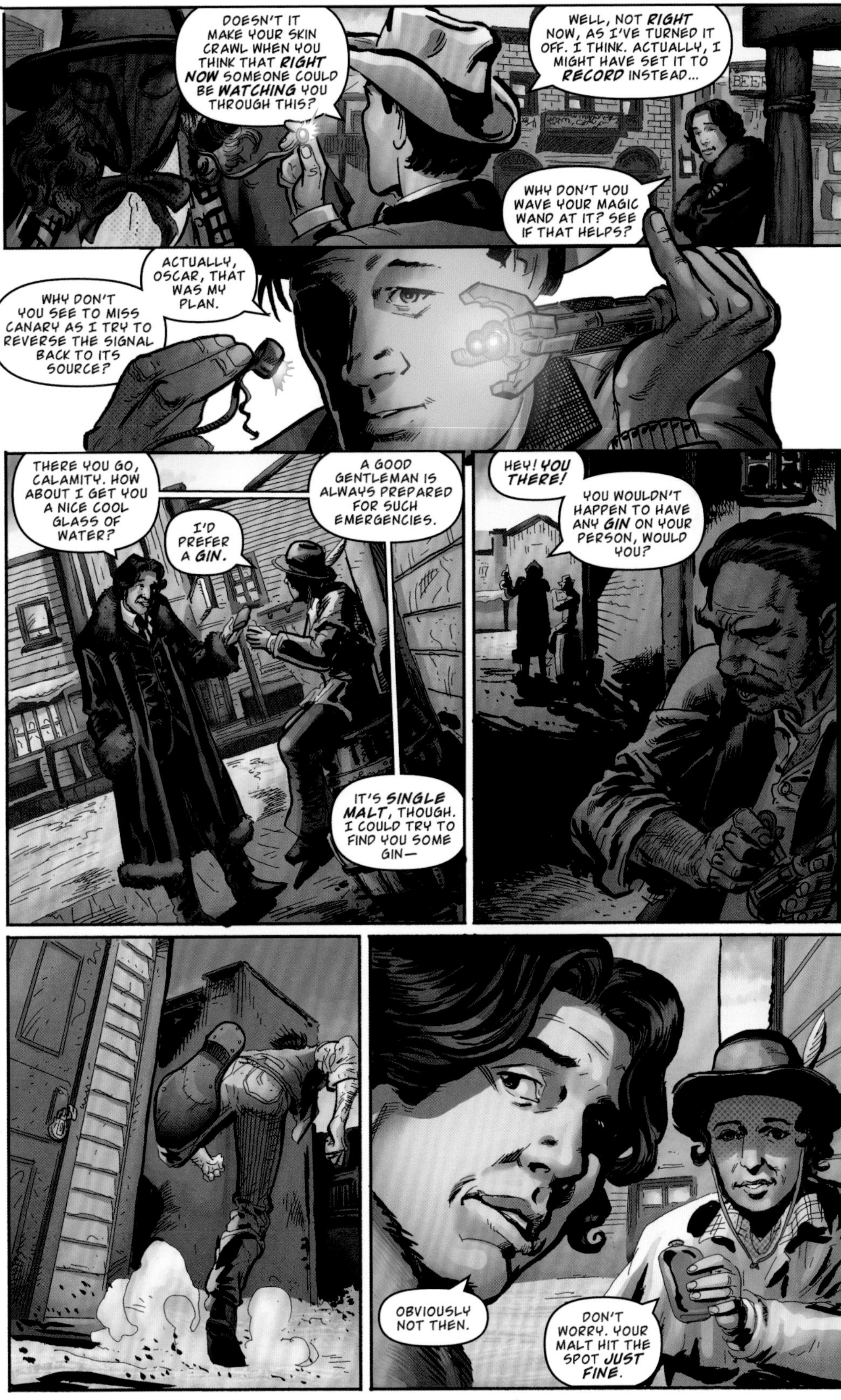
DOESN'T IT MAKE YOUR SKIN CRAWL WHEN YOU THINK THAT **RIGHT NOW** SOMEONE COULD BE **WATCHING** YOU THROUGH THIS?
WELL, NOT **RIGHT** NOW, AS I'VE TURNED IT OFF. I THINK. ACTUALLY, I MIGHT HAVE SET IT TO **RECORD** INSTEAD...
BEER
WHY DON'T YOU WAVE YOUR MAGIC WAND AT IT? SEE IF THAT HELPS?
ACTUALLY, OSCAR, THAT WAS MY PLAN.
WHY DON'T YOU SEE TO MISS CANARY AS I TRY TO REVERSE THE SIGNAL BACK TO ITS SOURCE?
THERE YOU GO, CALAMITY. HOW ABOUT I GET YOU A NICE COOL GLASS OF WATER?
I'D PREFER A **GIN**.
A GOOD GENTLEMAN IS ALWAYS PREPARED FOR SUCH EMERGENCIES.
IT'S **SINGLE MALT**, THOUGH. I COULD TRY TO FIND YOU SOME GIN—
HEY! **YOU THERE!**
YOU WOULDN'T HAPPEN TO HAVE ANY **GIN** ON YOUR PERSON, WOULD YOU?
OBVIOUSLY NOT THEN.
DON'T WORRY. YOUR MALT HIT THE SPOT **JUST FINE**.

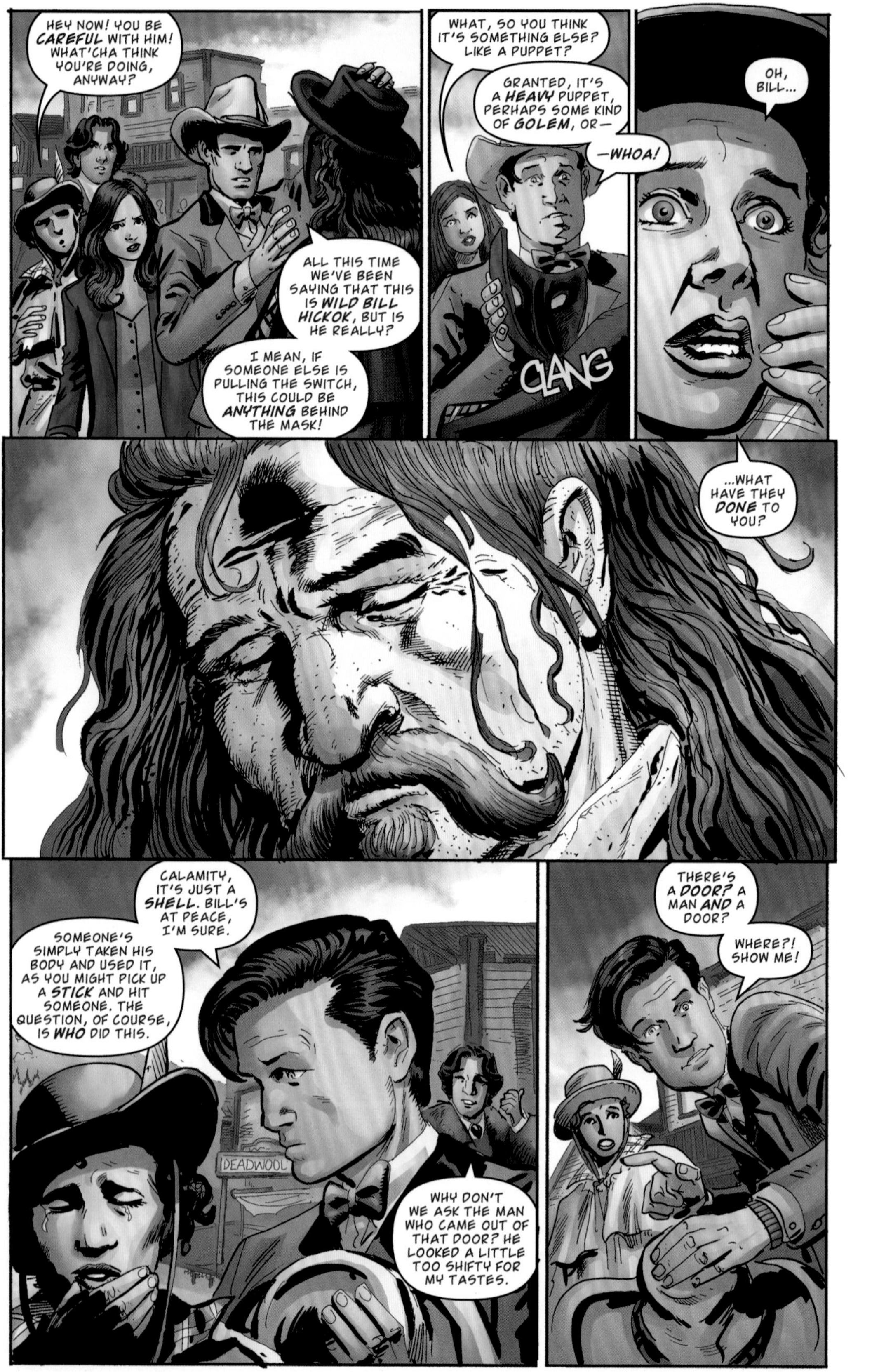
HEY NOW! YOU BE CAREFUL WITH HIM! WHAT'CHA THINK YOU'RE DOING, ANYWAY?
ALL THIS TIME WE'VE BEEN SAYING THAT THIS IS WILD BILL HICKOK, BUT IS HE REALLY?
I MEAN, IF SOMEONE ELSE IS PULLING THE SWITCH, THIS COULD BE ANYTHING BEHIND THE MASK!
WHAT, SO YOU THINK IT'S SOMETHING ELSE? LIKE A PUPPET?
GRANTED, IT'S A HEAVY PUPPET, PERHAPS SOME KIND OF GOLEM, OR—
—WHOA!
CLANG
OH, BILL...
...WHAT HAVE THEY DONE TO YOU?
CALAMITY, IT'S JUST A SHELL. BILL'S AT PEACE, I'M SURE.
SOMEONE'S SIMPLY TAKEN HIS BODY AND USED IT, AS YOU MIGHT PICK UP A STICK AND HIT SOMEONE. THE QUESTION, OF COURSE, IS WHO DID THIS.
DEADWOOD
WHY DON'T WE ASK THE MAN WHO CAME OUT OF THAT DOOR? HE LOOKED A LITTLE TOO SHIFTY FOR MY TASTES.
THERE'S A DOOR? A MAN AND A DOOR?
WHERE?! SHOW ME!

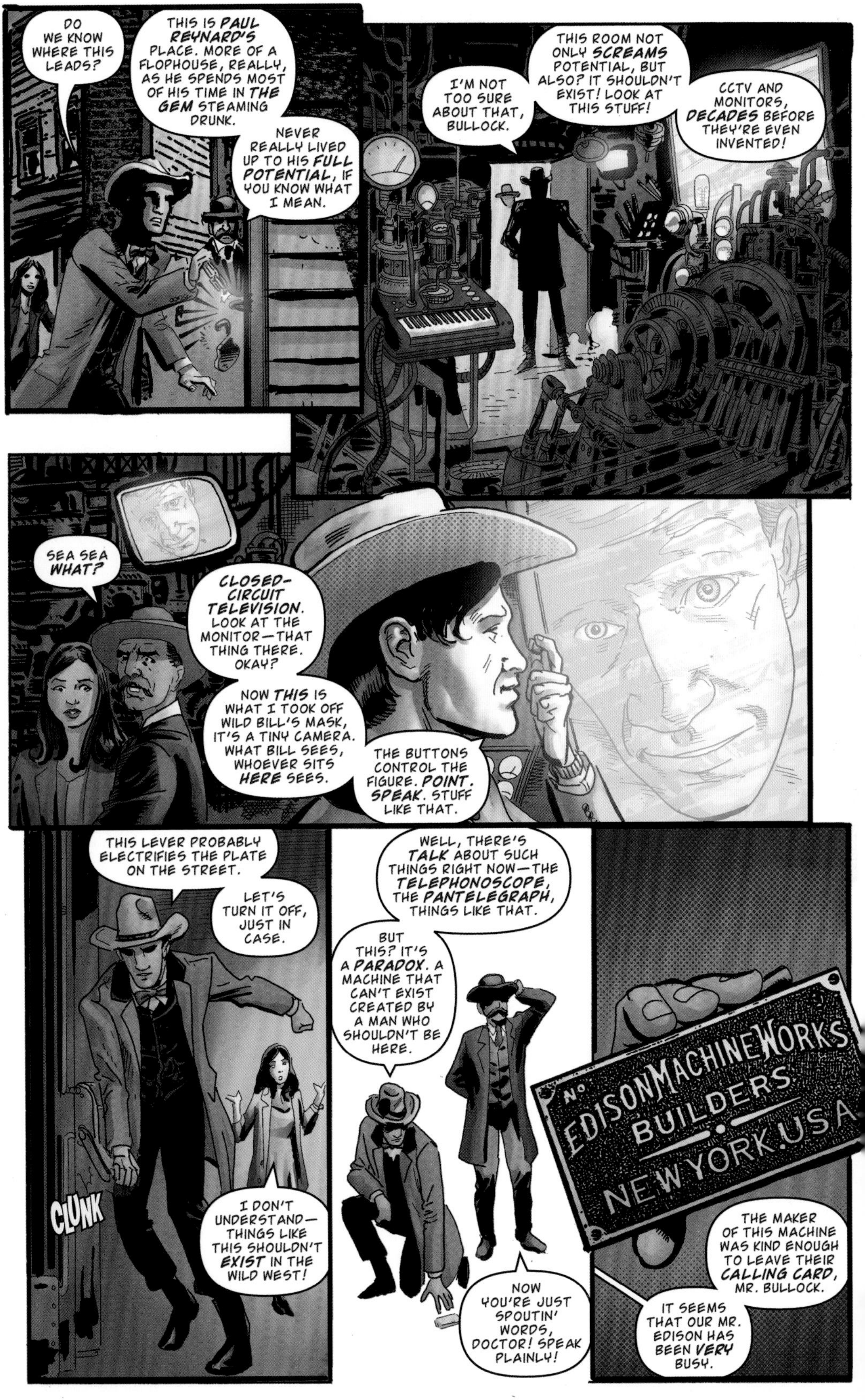
DO WE KNOW WHERE THIS LEADS?
THIS IS PAUL REYNARD'S PLACE. MORE OF A FLOPHOUSE, REALLY, AS HE SPENDS MOST OF HIS TIME IN THE GEM STEAMING DRUNK.
NEVER REALLY LIVED UP TO HIS FULL POTENTIAL, IF YOU KNOW WHAT I MEAN.
I'M NOT TOO SURE ABOUT THAT, BULLOCK.
THIS ROOM NOT ONLY SCREAMS POTENTIAL, BUT ALSO? IT SHOULDN'T EXIST! LOOK AT THIS STUFF!
CCTV AND MONITORS, DECADES BEFORE THEY'RE EVEN INVENTED!
SEA SEA WHAT?
CLOSED-CIRCUIT TELEVISION. LOOK AT THE MONITOR—THAT THING THERE. OKAY?
NOW THIS IS WHAT I TOOK OFF WILD BILL'S MASK, IT'S A TINY CAMERA. WHAT BILL SEES, WHOEVER SITS HERE SEES.
THE BUTTONS CONTROL THE FIGURE. POINT. SPEAK. STUFF LIKE THAT.
THIS LEVER PROBABLY ELECTRIFIES THE PLATE ON THE STREET.
LET'S TURN IT OFF, JUST IN CASE.
CLUNK
I DON'T UNDERSTAND—THINGS LIKE THIS SHOULDN'T EXIST IN THE WILD WEST!
WELL, THERE'S TALK ABOUT SUCH THINGS RIGHT NOW—THE TELEPHONOSCOPE, THE PANTELEGRAPH, THINGS LIKE THAT.
BUT THIS? IT'S A PARADOX. A MACHINE THAT CAN'T EXIST CREATED BY A MAN WHO SHOULDN'T BE HERE.
NOW YOU'RE JUST SPOUTIN' WORDS, DOCTOR! SPEAK PLAINLY!
No EDISON MACHINE WORKS BUILDERS NEW YORK. U.S.A
THE MAKER OF THIS MACHINE WAS KIND ENOUGH TO LEAVE THEIR CALLING CARD, MR. BULLOCK.
IT SEEMS THAT OUR MR. EDISON HAS BEEN VERY BUSY.

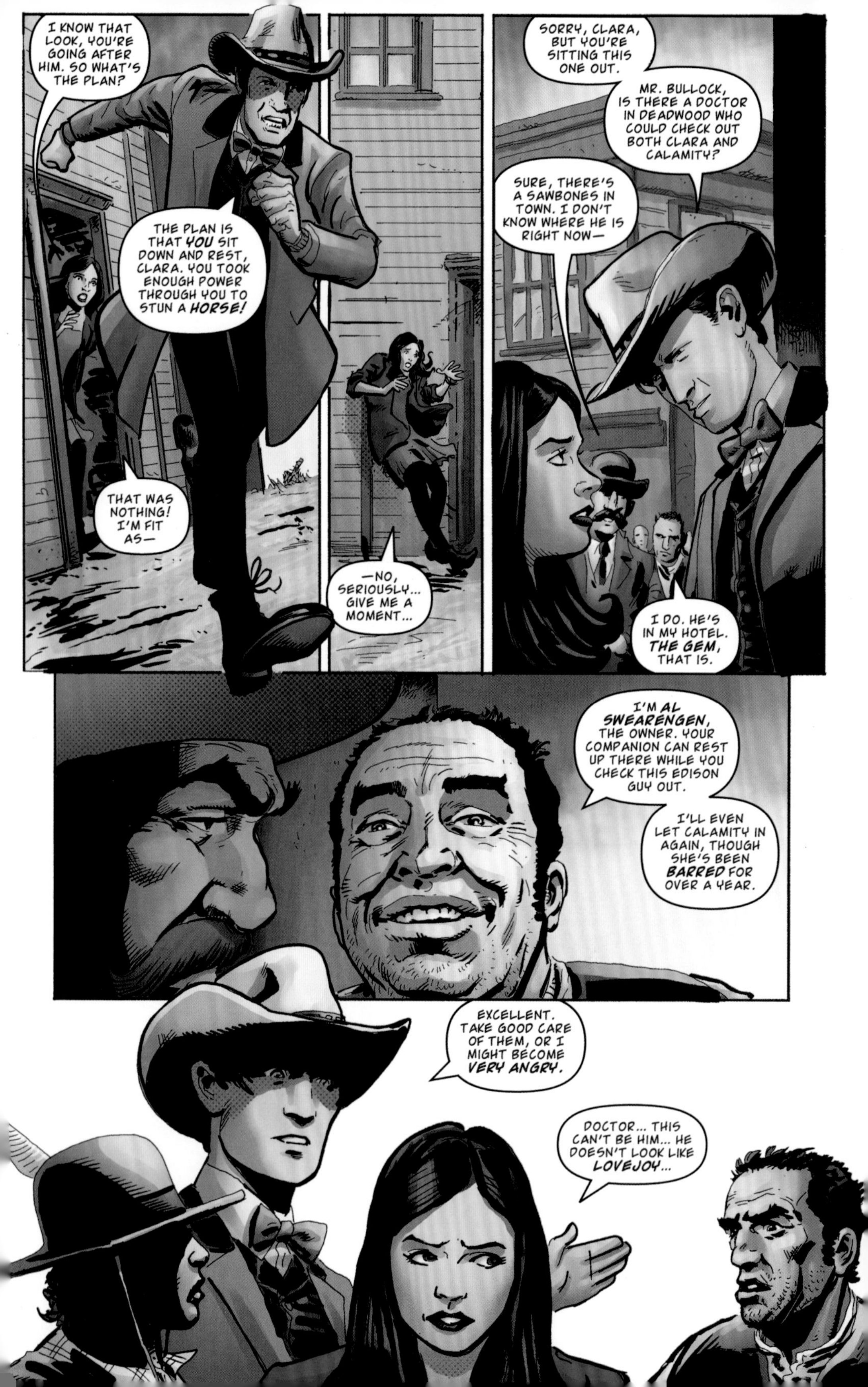
I KNOW THAT LOOK, YOU'RE GOING AFTER HIM. SO WHAT'S THE PLAN?
THE PLAN IS THAT *YOU* SIT DOWN AND REST, CLARA. YOU TOOK ENOUGH POWER THROUGH YOU TO STUN A *HORSE!*
THAT WAS NOTHING! I'M FIT AS—
—NO, SERIOUSLY... GIVE ME A MOMENT...
SORRY, CLARA, BUT YOU'RE SITTING THIS ONE OUT.
MR. BULLOCK, IS THERE A DOCTOR IN DEADWOOD WHO COULD CHECK OUT BOTH CLARA AND CALAMITY?
SURE, THERE'S A SAWBONES IN TOWN. I DON'T KNOW WHERE HE IS RIGHT NOW—
I DO. HE'S IN MY HOTEL. *THE GEM,* THAT IS.
I'M *AL SWEARENGEN,* THE OWNER. YOUR COMPANION CAN REST UP THERE WHILE YOU CHECK THIS EDISON GUY OUT.
I'LL EVEN LET CALAMITY IN AGAIN, THOUGH SHE'S BEEN *BARRED* FOR OVER A YEAR.
EXCELLENT. TAKE GOOD CARE OF THEM, OR I MIGHT BECOME *VERY ANGRY.*
DOCTOR... THIS CAN'T BE HIM... HE DOESN'T LOOK LIKE *LOVEJOY*...

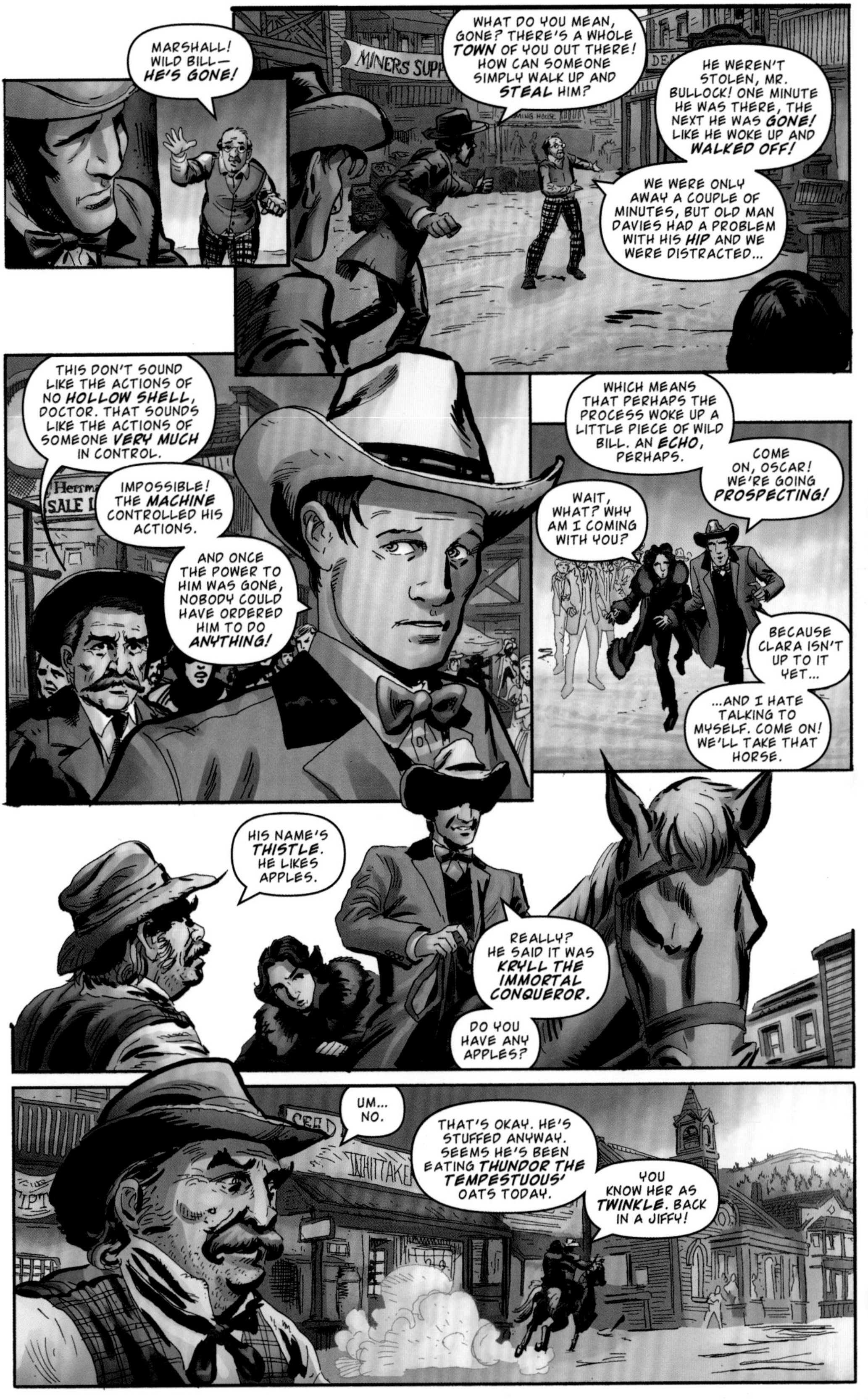
MARSHALL! WILD BILL— HE'S GONE!
WHAT DO YOU MEAN, GONE? THERE'S A WHOLE TOWN OF YOU OUT THERE! HOW CAN SOMEONE SIMPLY WALK UP AND STEAL HIM?
HE WEREN'T STOLEN, MR. BULLOCK! ONE MINUTE HE WAS THERE, THE NEXT HE WAS GONE! LIKE HE WOKE UP AND WALKED OFF!
WE WERE ONLY AWAY A COUPLE OF MINUTES, BUT OLD MAN DAVIES HAD A PROBLEM WITH HIS HIP AND WE WERE DISTRACTED...
MINERS SUPP
THIS DON'T SOUND LIKE THE ACTIONS OF NO HOLLOW SHELL, DOCTOR. THAT SOUNDS LIKE THE ACTIONS OF SOMEONE VERY MUCH IN CONTROL.
IMPOSSIBLE! THE MACHINE CONTROLLED HIS ACTIONS.
AND ONCE THE POWER TO HIM WAS GONE, NOBODY COULD HAVE ORDERED HIM TO DO ANYTHING!
WHICH MEANS THAT PERHAPS THE PROCESS WOKE UP A LITTLE PIECE OF WILD BILL. AN ECHO, PERHAPS.
COME ON, OSCAR! WE'RE GOING PROSPECTING!
WAIT, WHAT? WHY AM I COMING WITH YOU?
BECAUSE CLARA ISN'T UP TO IT YET...
...AND I HATE TALKING TO MYSELF. COME ON! WE'LL TAKE THAT HORSE.
HIS NAME'S THISTLE. HE LIKES APPLES.
REALLY? HE SAID IT WAS KRYLL THE IMMORTAL CONQUEROR.
DO YOU HAVE ANY APPLES?
UM... NO.
THAT'S OKAY. HE'S STUFFED ANYWAY. SEEMS HE'S BEEN EATING THUNDOR THE TEMPESTUOUS' OATS TODAY.
YOU KNOW HER AS TWINKLE. BACK IN A JIFFY!

I STILL DON'T SEE WHY I HAD TO COME ON THIS INSANE JOURNEY. I HAVE AN EVENT IN *SAN FRANCISCO* THAT I SHOULD BE PREPARING FOR.

COME ON, OSCAR, YOU HAVE TO 'PREPARE' FOR A TALK ON INTERIOR DESIGN? *REALLY?*

YOU'VE BEEN OVER HERE FOR THREE MONTHS NOW—WHAT ARE YOU *RUNNING AWAY* FROM?

A *WOMAN.*

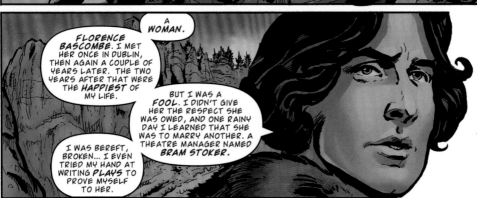

FLORENCE BASCOMBE. I MET HER ONCE IN DUBLIN, THEN AGAIN A COUPLE OF YEARS LATER. THE TWO YEARS AFTER THAT WERE THE *HAPPIEST* OF MY LIFE.

BUT I WAS A *FOOL.* I DIDN'T GIVE HER THE RESPECT SHE WAS OWED, AND ONE RAINY DAY I LEARNED THAT SHE WAS TO MARRY ANOTHER. A THEATRE MANAGER NAMED *BRAM STOKER.*

I WAS BEREFT, BROKEN... I EVEN TRIED MY HAND AT WRITING *PLAYS* TO PROVE MYSELF TO HER.

MY FAITH IN *MYSELF,* IN *GOD,* AND IN *PEOPLE* WAS PUT TO THE TEST OVER THE NEXT FEW YEARS—AND *ALL* FAILED.

I WAS *PAID* TO COME TO AMERICA, DOCTOR. A TOUR RELATED TO A MUSICAL THAT *MOCKS* ME. I HAVE BECOME THE VERY JOKE THAT IT *SAYS* I AM.

SO WHY NOT LOSE MYSELF IN AMERICA? WHY NOT RUN AWAY?

OSCAR, BELIEVE ME WHEN I SAY THAT YOU HAVE SO MUCH TO OFFER THE WORLD. YOUR BOOKS AND PLAYS WILL BE SPOKEN OF A *HUNDRED YEARS* AFTER YOU DIE.

TO WRITE SUCH THINGS I MUST BE INSPIRED, FILLED WITH WONDER. AND *NOTHING* DOES THAT TO ME ANYMORE.

REALLY? *NOTHING?*

NOTHING COMES TO MIND AT ALL?

I... OH, MY.

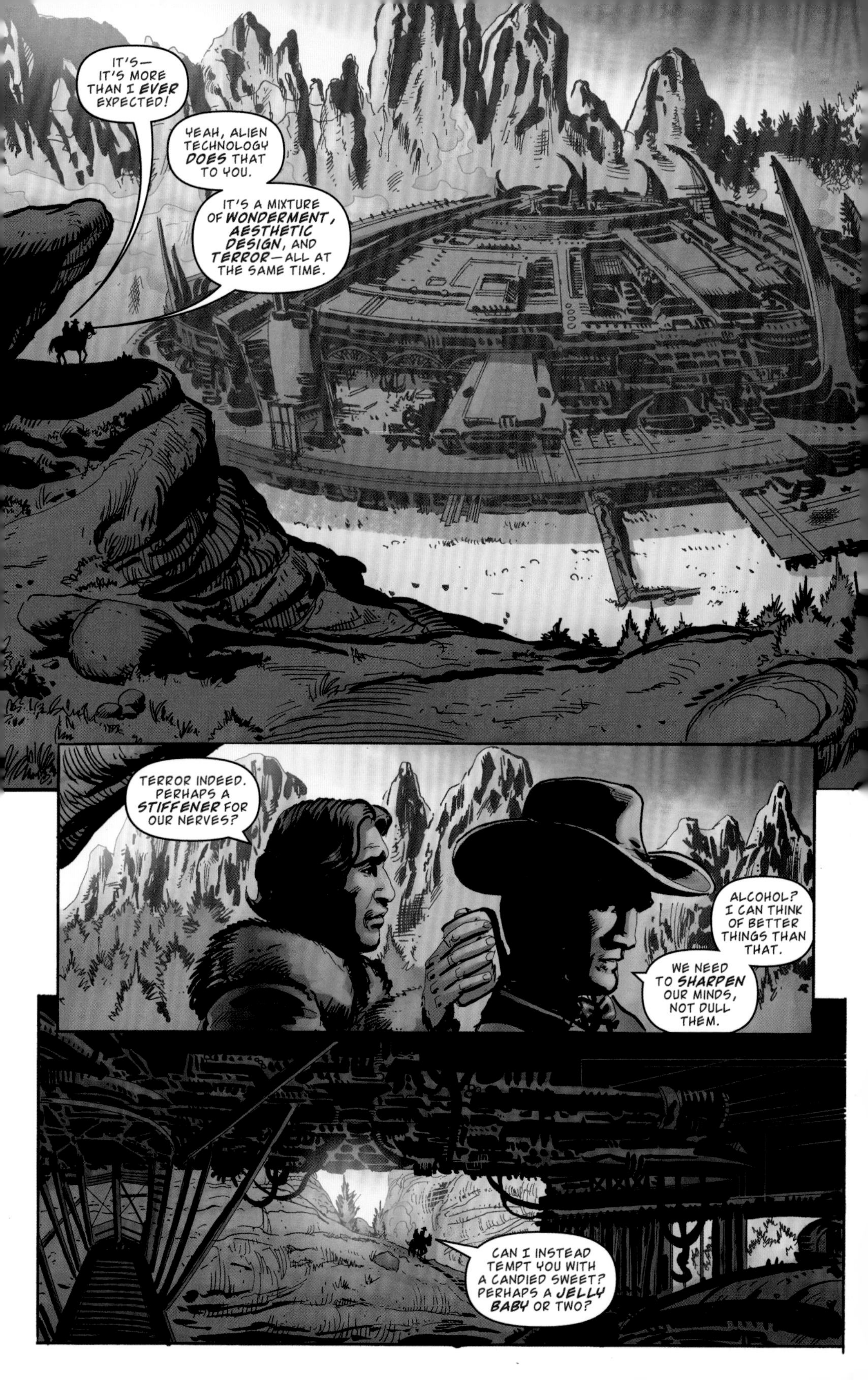
IT'S— IT'S MORE THAN I EVER EXPECTED!
YEAH, ALIEN TECHNOLOGY DOES THAT TO YOU.
IT'S A MIXTURE OF WONDERMENT, AESTHETIC DESIGN, AND TERROR—ALL AT THE SAME TIME.
TERROR INDEED. PERHAPS A STIFFENER FOR OUR NERVES?
ALCOHOL? I CAN THINK OF BETTER THINGS THAN THAT.
WE NEED TO SHARPEN OUR MINDS, NOT DULL THEM.
CAN I INSTEAD TEMPT YOU WITH A CANDIED SWEET? PERHAPS A JELLY BABY OR TWO?

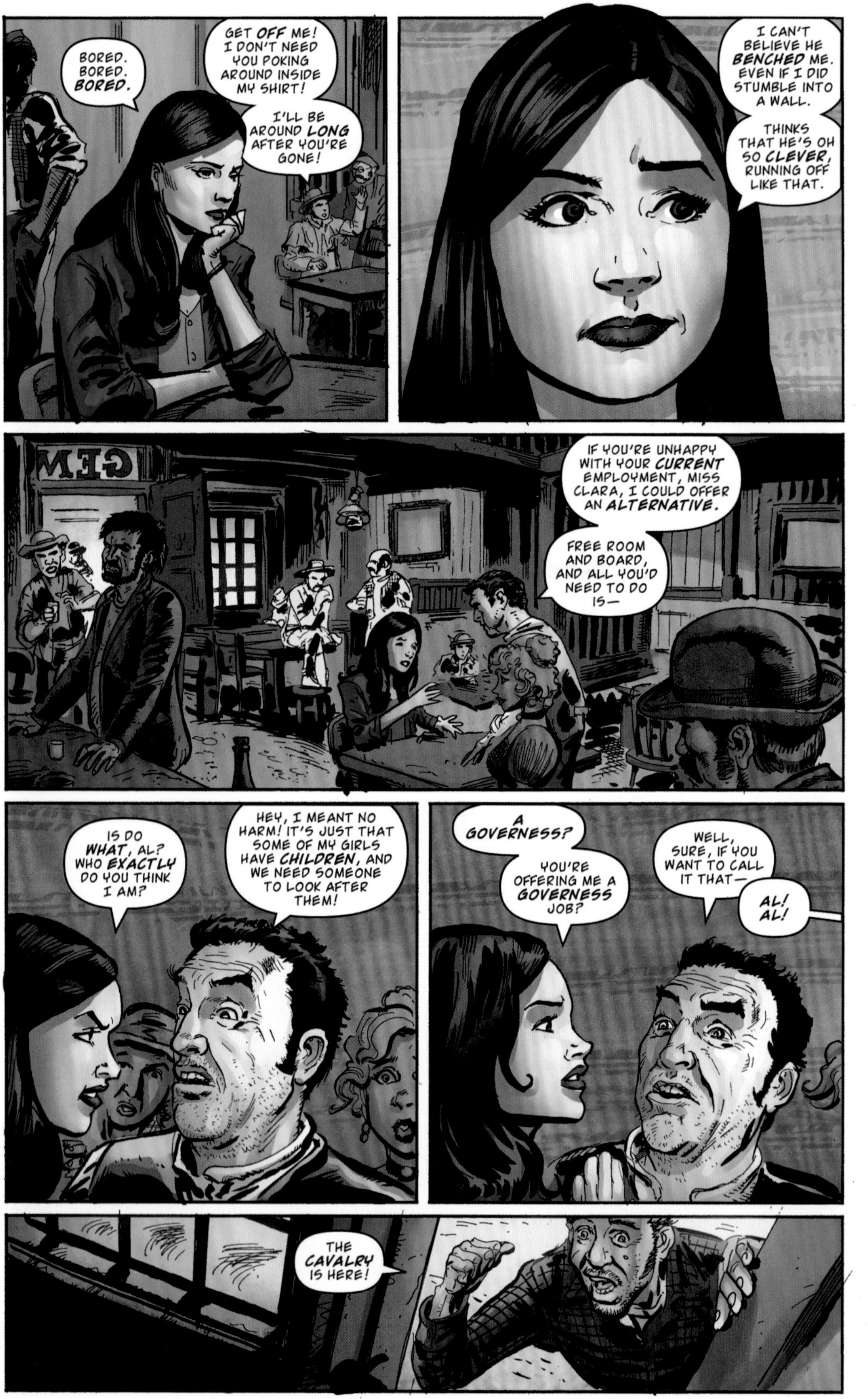
BORED. BORED. BORED.
GET OFF ME! I DON'T NEED YOU POKING AROUND INSIDE MY SHIRT!
I'LL BE AROUND LONG AFTER YOU'RE GONE!
I CAN'T BELIEVE HE BENCHED ME. EVEN IF I DID STUMBLE INTO A WALL.
THINKS THAT HE'S OH SO CLEVER, RUNNING OFF LIKE THAT.
GEM
IF YOU'RE UNHAPPY WITH YOUR CURRENT EMPLOYMENT, MISS CLARA, I COULD OFFER AN ALTERNATIVE.
FREE ROOM AND BOARD, AND ALL YOU'D NEED TO DO IS—
IS DO WHAT, AL? WHO EXACTLY DO YOU THINK I AM?
HEY, I MEANT NO HARM! IT'S JUST THAT SOME OF MY GIRLS HAVE CHILDREN, AND WE NEED SOMEONE TO LOOK AFTER THEM!
A GOVERNESS?
YOU'RE OFFERING ME A GOVERNESS JOB?
WELL, SURE, IF YOU WANT TO CALL IT THAT—
AL! AL!
THE CAVALRY IS HERE!

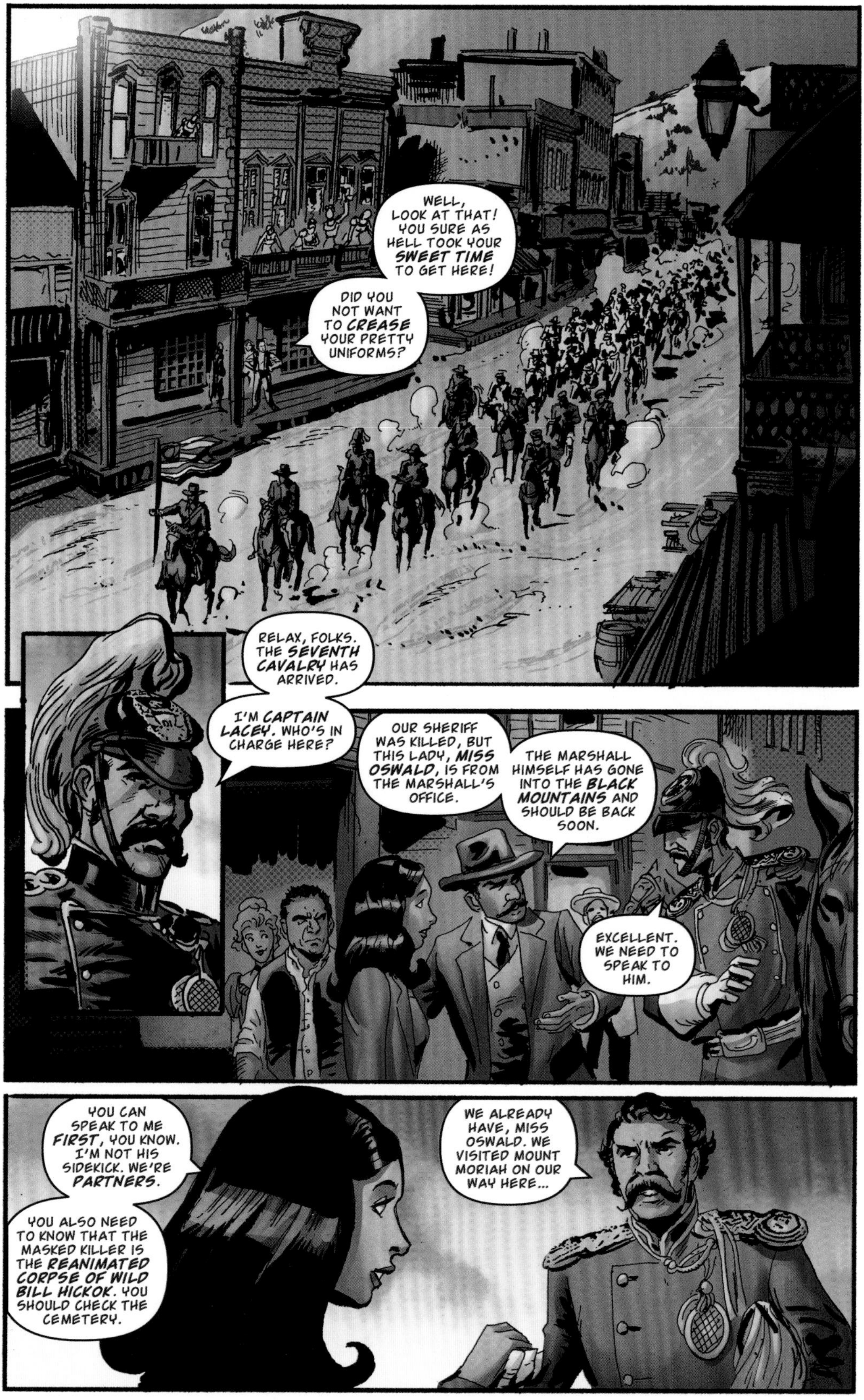
WELL, LOOK AT THAT! YOU SURE AS HELL TOOK YOUR SWEET TIME TO GET HERE!
DID YOU NOT WANT TO CREASE YOUR PRETTY UNIFORMS?
RELAX, FOLKS. THE SEVENTH CAVALRY HAS ARRIVED.
I'M CAPTAIN LACEY. WHO'S IN CHARGE HERE?
OUR SHERIFF WAS KILLED, BUT THIS LADY, MISS OSWALD, IS FROM THE MARSHALL'S OFFICE.
THE MARSHALL HIMSELF HAS GONE INTO THE BLACK MOUNTAINS AND SHOULD BE BACK SOON.
EXCELLENT. WE NEED TO SPEAK TO HIM.
YOU CAN SPEAK TO ME FIRST, YOU KNOW. I'M NOT HIS SIDEKICK. WE'RE PARTNERS.
YOU ALSO NEED TO KNOW THAT THE MASKED KILLER IS THE REANIMATED CORPSE OF WILD BILL HICKOK. YOU SHOULD CHECK THE CEMETERY.
WE ALREADY HAVE, MISS OSWALD. WE VISITED MOUNT MORIAH ON OUR WAY HERE...

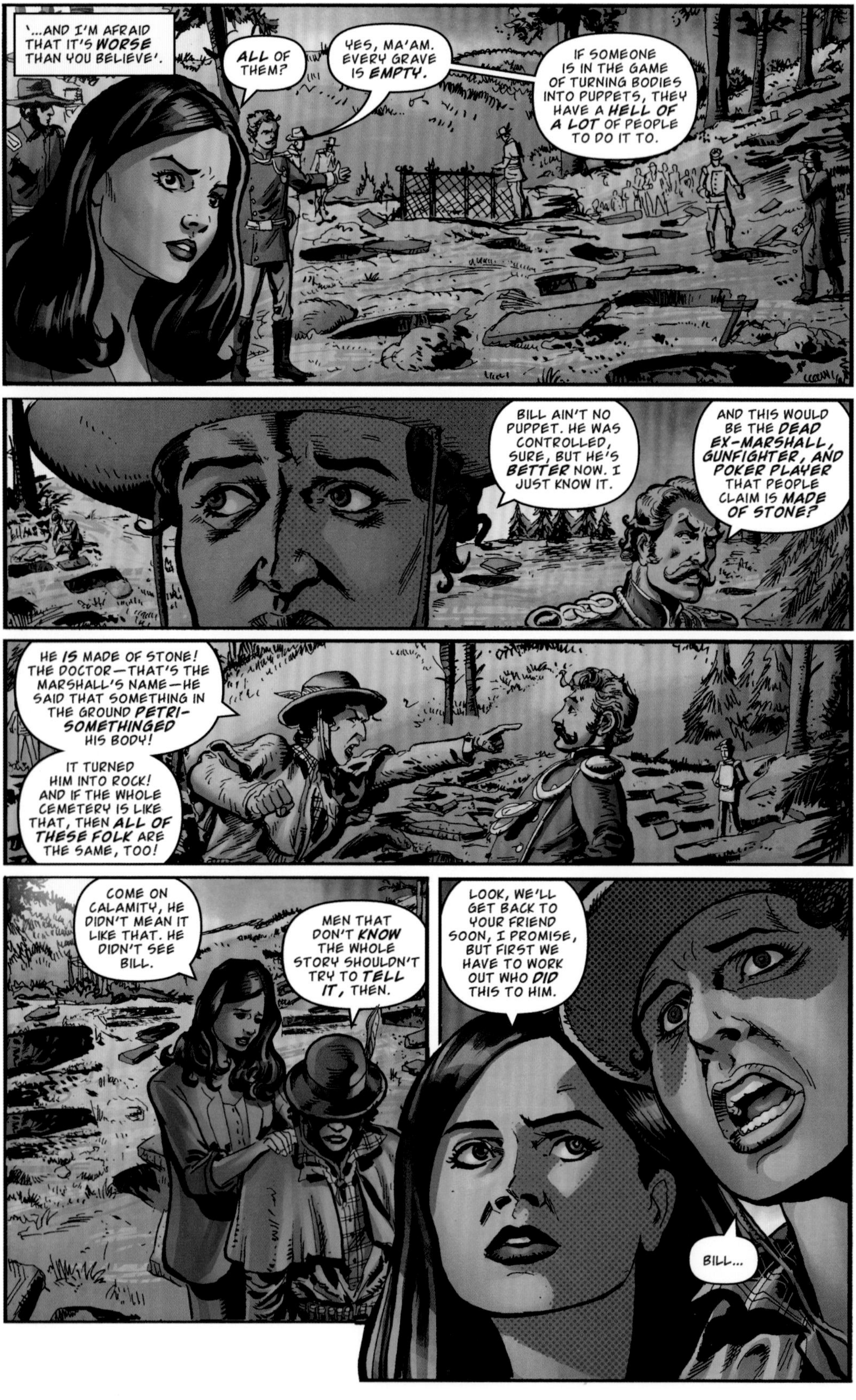
'...AND I'M AFRAID THAT IT'S WORSE THAN YOU BELIEVE'.
ALL OF THEM?
YES, MA'AM. EVERY GRAVE IS EMPTY.
IF SOMEONE IS IN THE GAME OF TURNING BODIES INTO PUPPETS, THEY HAVE A HELL OF A LOT OF PEOPLE TO DO IT TO.
BILL AIN'T NO PUPPET. HE WAS CONTROLLED, SURE, BUT HE'S BETTER NOW. I JUST KNOW IT.
AND THIS WOULD BE THE DEAD EX-MARSHALL, GUNFIGHTER, AND POKER PLAYER THAT PEOPLE CLAIM IS MADE OF STONE?
HE IS MADE OF STONE! THE DOCTOR—THAT'S THE MARSHALL'S NAME—HE SAID THAT SOMETHING IN THE GROUND PETRI-SOMETHINGED HIS BODY!
IT TURNED HIM INTO ROCK! AND IF THE WHOLE CEMETERY IS LIKE THAT, THEN ALL OF THESE FOLK ARE THE SAME, TOO!
COME ON CALAMITY, HE DIDN'T MEAN IT LIKE THAT. HE DIDN'T SEE BILL.
MEN THAT DON'T KNOW THE WHOLE STORY SHOULDN'T TRY TO TELL IT, THEN.
LOOK, WE'LL GET BACK TO YOUR FRIEND SOON, I PROMISE, BUT FIRST WE HAVE TO WORK OUT WHO DID THIS TO HIM.
BILL...

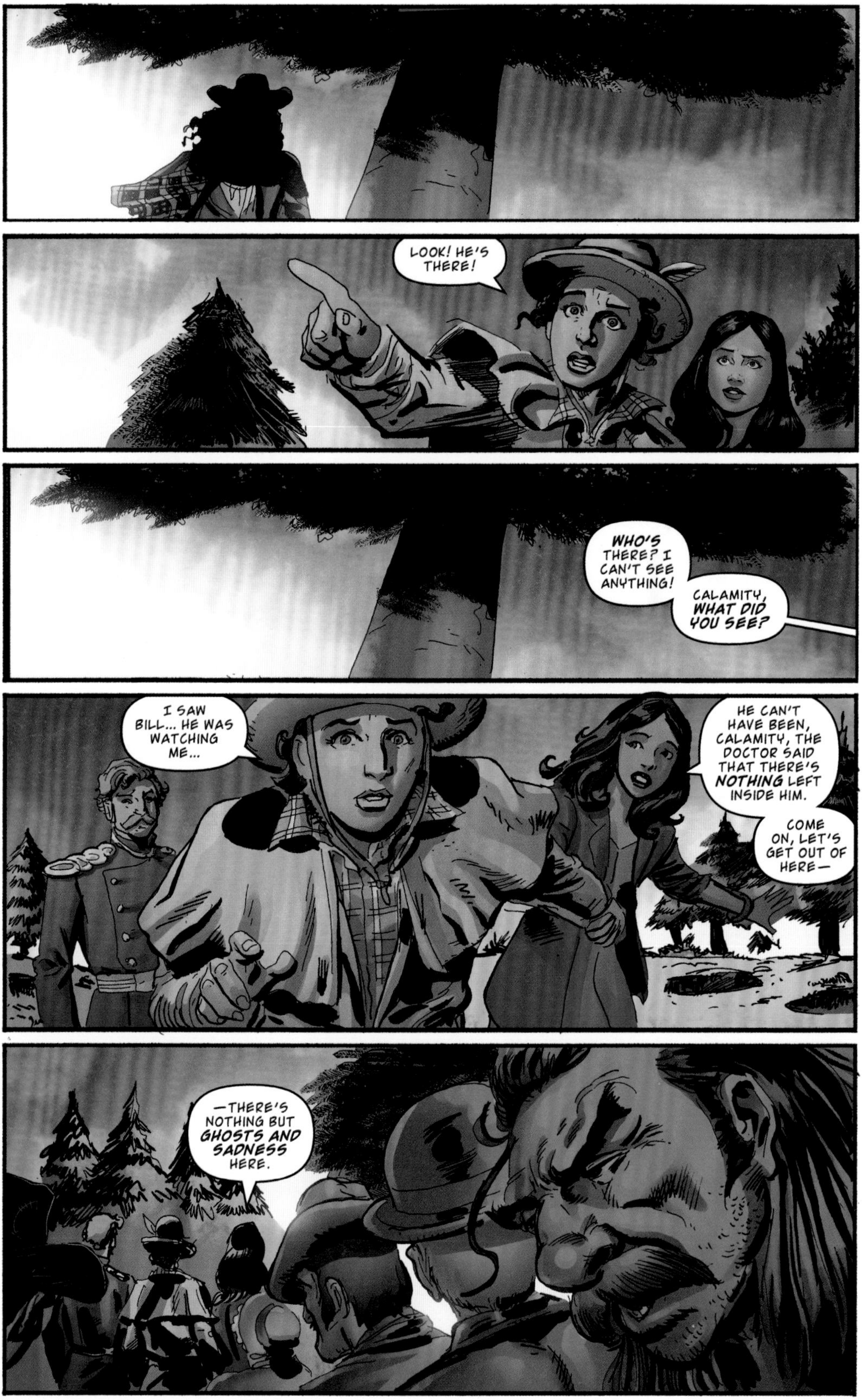
LOOK! HE'S THERE!
WHO'S THERE? I CAN'T SEE ANYTHING!
CALAMITY, WHAT DID YOU SEE?
I SAW BILL... HE WAS WATCHING ME...
HE CAN'T HAVE BEEN, CALAMITY, THE DOCTOR SAID THAT THERE'S NOTHING LEFT INSIDE HIM.
COME ON, LET'S GET OUT OF HERE—
—THERE'S NOTHING BUT GHOSTS AND SADNESS HERE.

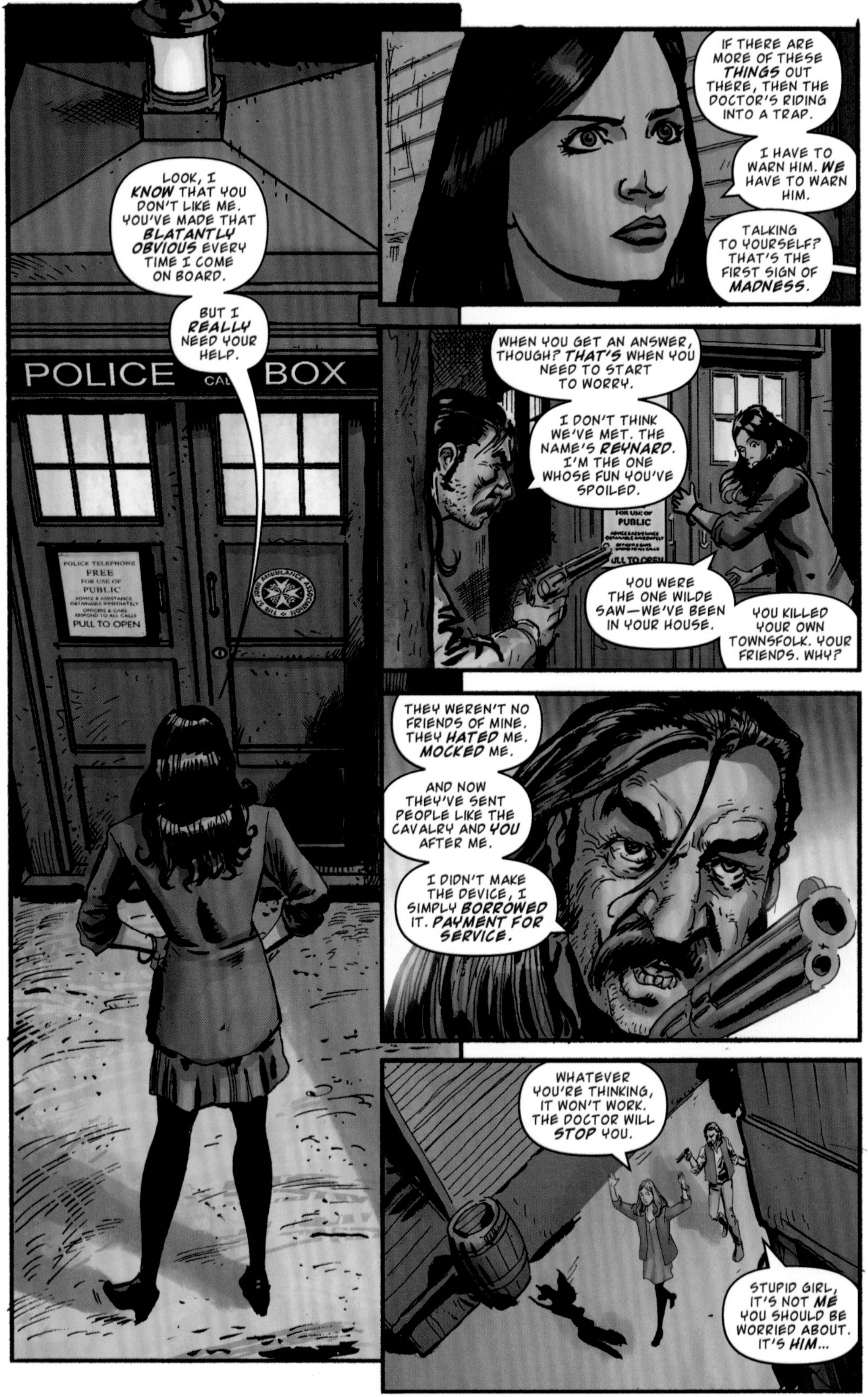
LOOK, I KNOW THAT YOU DON'T LIKE ME. YOU'VE MADE THAT BLATANTLY OBVIOUS EVERY TIME I COME ON BOARD.
BUT I REALLY NEED YOUR HELP.
POLICE CALL BOX
POLICE TELEPHONE FREE FOR USE OF PUBLIC ADVICE & ASSISTANCE OBTAINABLE IMMEDIATELY OFFICERS & CARS RESPOND TO ALL CALLS PULL TO OPEN
IF THERE ARE MORE OF THESE THINGS OUT THERE, THEN THE DOCTOR'S RIDING INTO A TRAP.
I HAVE TO WARN HIM. WE HAVE TO WARN HIM.
TALKING TO YOURSELF? THAT'S THE FIRST SIGN OF MADNESS.
WHEN YOU GET AN ANSWER, THOUGH? THAT'S WHEN YOU NEED TO START TO WORRY.
I DON'T THINK WE'VE MET. THE NAME'S REYNARD. I'M THE ONE WHOSE FUN YOU'VE SPOILED.
YOU WERE THE ONE WILDE SAW—WE'VE BEEN IN YOUR HOUSE.
YOU KILLED YOUR OWN TOWNSFOLK. YOUR FRIENDS. WHY?
THEY WEREN'T NO FRIENDS OF MINE. THEY HATED ME. MOCKED ME.
AND NOW THEY'VE SENT PEOPLE LIKE THE CAVALRY AND YOU AFTER ME.
I DIDN'T MAKE THE DEVICE, I SIMPLY BORROWED IT. PAYMENT FOR SERVICE.
WHATEVER YOU'RE THINKING, IT WON'T WORK. THE DOCTOR WILL STOP YOU.
STUPID GIRL, IT'S NOT ME YOU SHOULD BE WORRIED ABOUT. IT'S HIM...

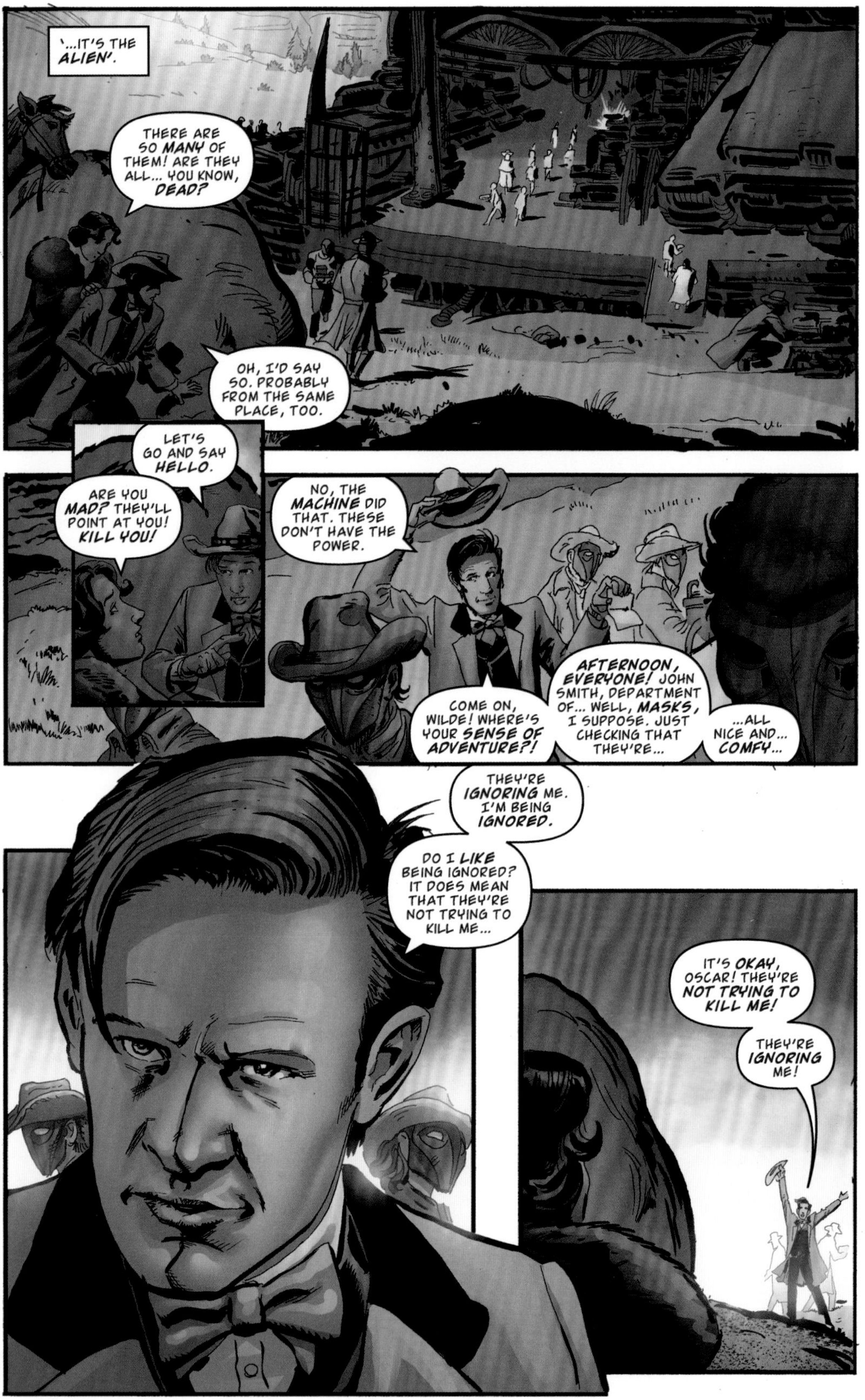
'...IT'S THE ALIEN'.
THERE ARE SO MANY OF THEM! ARE THEY ALL... YOU KNOW, DEAD?
OH, I'D SAY SO. PROBABLY FROM THE SAME PLACE, TOO.
LET'S GO AND SAY HELLO.
ARE YOU MAD? THEY'LL POINT AT YOU! KILL YOU!
NO, THE MACHINE DID THAT. THESE DON'T HAVE THE POWER.
COME ON, WILDE! WHERE'S YOUR SENSE OF ADVENTURE?!
AFTERNOON, EVERYONE! JOHN SMITH, DEPARTMENT OF... WELL, MASKS, I SUPPOSE. JUST CHECKING THAT THEY'RE...
...ALL NICE AND... COMFY...
THEY'RE IGNORING ME. I'M BEING IGNORED.
DO I LIKE BEING IGNORED? IT DOES MEAN THAT THEY'RE NOT TRYING TO KILL ME...
IT'S OKAY, OSCAR! THEY'RE NOT TRYING TO KILL ME!
THEY'RE IGNORING ME!

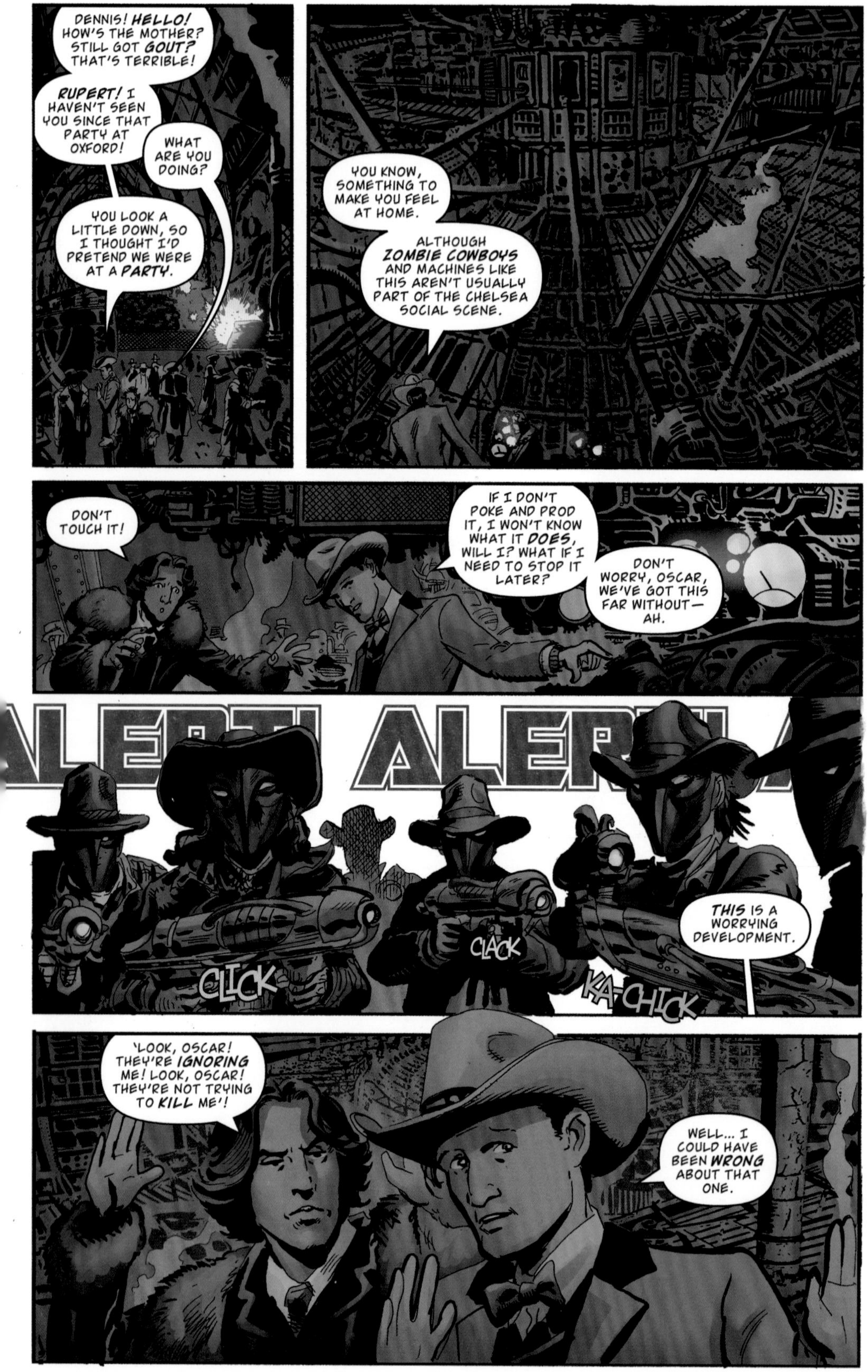
DENNIS! HELLO! HOW'S THE MOTHER? STILL GOT GOUT? THAT'S TERRIBLE!
RUPERT! I HAVEN'T SEEN YOU SINCE THAT PARTY AT OXFORD!
WHAT ARE YOU DOING?
YOU LOOK A LITTLE DOWN, SO I THOUGHT I'D PRETEND WE WERE AT A PARTY.
YOU KNOW, SOMETHING TO MAKE YOU FEEL AT HOME.
ALTHOUGH ZOMBIE COWBOYS AND MACHINES LIKE THIS AREN'T USUALLY PART OF THE CHELSEA SOCIAL SCENE.
DON'T TOUCH IT!
IF I DON'T POKE AND PROD IT, I WON'T KNOW WHAT IT DOES, WILL I? WHAT IF I NEED TO STOP IT LATER?
DON'T WORRY, OSCAR, WE'VE GOT THIS FAR WITHOUT— AH.
ALERT! ALERT!
CLICK
CLACK
KA-CHICK
THIS IS A WORRYING DEVELOPMENT.
'LOOK, OSCAR! THEY'RE IGNORING ME! LOOK, OSCAR! THEY'RE NOT TRYING TO KILL ME'!
WELL... I COULD HAVE BEEN WRONG ABOUT THAT ONE.

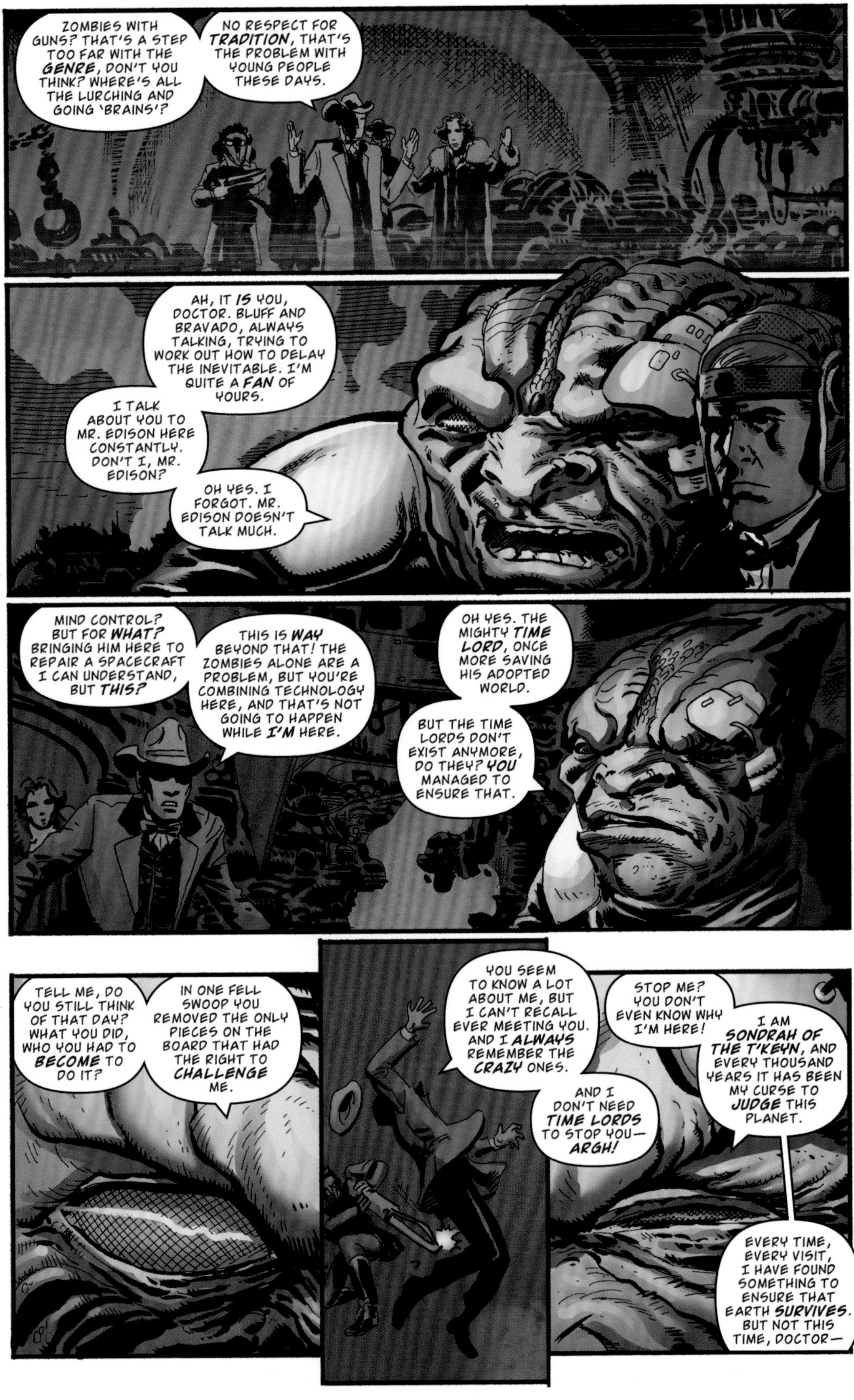
ZOMBIES WITH GUNS? THAT'S A STEP TOO FAR WITH THE GENRE, DON'T YOU THINK? WHERE'S ALL THE LURCHING AND GOING 'BRAINS'?
NO RESPECT FOR TRADITION, THAT'S THE PROBLEM WITH YOUNG PEOPLE THESE DAYS.
AH, IT IS YOU, DOCTOR. BLUFF AND BRAVADO, ALWAYS TALKING, TRYING TO WORK OUT HOW TO DELAY THE INEVITABLE. I'M QUITE A FAN OF YOURS.
I TALK ABOUT YOU TO MR. EDISON HERE CONSTANTLY. DON'T I, MR. EDISON?
OH YES. I FORGOT. MR. EDISON DOESN'T TALK MUCH.
MIND CONTROL? BUT FOR WHAT? BRINGING HIM HERE TO REPAIR A SPACECRAFT I CAN UNDERSTAND, BUT THIS?
THIS IS WAY BEYOND THAT! THE ZOMBIES ALONE ARE A PROBLEM, BUT YOU'RE COMBINING TECHNOLOGY HERE, AND THAT'S NOT GOING TO HAPPEN WHILE I'M HERE.
OH YES. THE MIGHTY TIME LORD, ONCE MORE SAVING HIS ADOPTED WORLD.
BUT THE TIME LORDS DON'T EXIST ANYMORE, DO THEY? YOU MANAGED TO ENSURE THAT.
TELL ME, DO YOU STILL THINK OF THAT DAY? WHAT YOU DID, WHO YOU HAD TO BECOME TO DO IT?
IN ONE FELL SWOOP YOU REMOVED THE ONLY PIECES ON THE BOARD THAT HAD THE RIGHT TO CHALLENGE ME.
YOU SEEM TO KNOW A LOT ABOUT ME, BUT I CAN'T RECALL EVER MEETING YOU. AND I ALWAYS REMEMBER THE CRAZY ONES.
AND I DON'T NEED TIME LORDS TO STOP YOU— ARGH!
STOP ME? YOU DON'T EVEN KNOW WHY I'M HERE!
I AM SONDRAH OF THE T'KEYN, AND EVERY THOUSAND YEARS IT HAS BEEN MY CURSE TO JUDGE THIS PLANET.
EVERY TIME, EVERY VISIT, I HAVE FOUND SOMETHING TO ENSURE THAT EARTH SURVIVES. BUT NOT THIS TIME, DOCTOR—

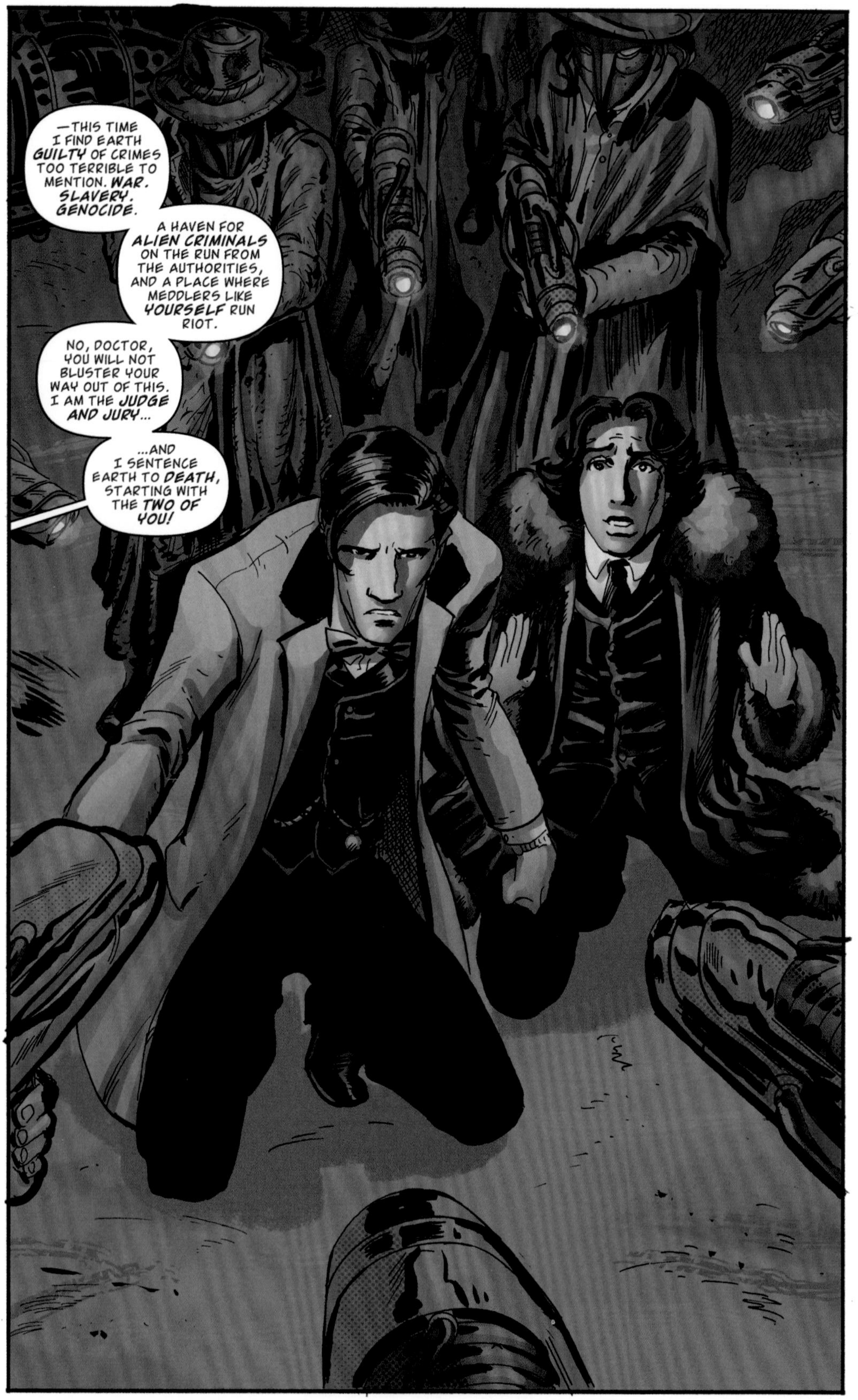
—THIS TIME I FIND EARTH GUILTY OF CRIMES TOO TERRIBLE TO MENTION. WAR. SLAVERY. GENOCIDE.
A HAVEN FOR ALIEN CRIMINALS ON THE RUN FROM THE AUTHORITIES, AND A PLACE WHERE MEDDLERS LIKE YOURSELF RUN RIOT.
NO, DOCTOR, YOU WILL NOT BLUSTER YOUR WAY OUT OF THIS. I AM THE JUDGE AND JURY...
...AND I SENTENCE EARTH TO DEATH, STARTING WITH THE TWO OF YOU!

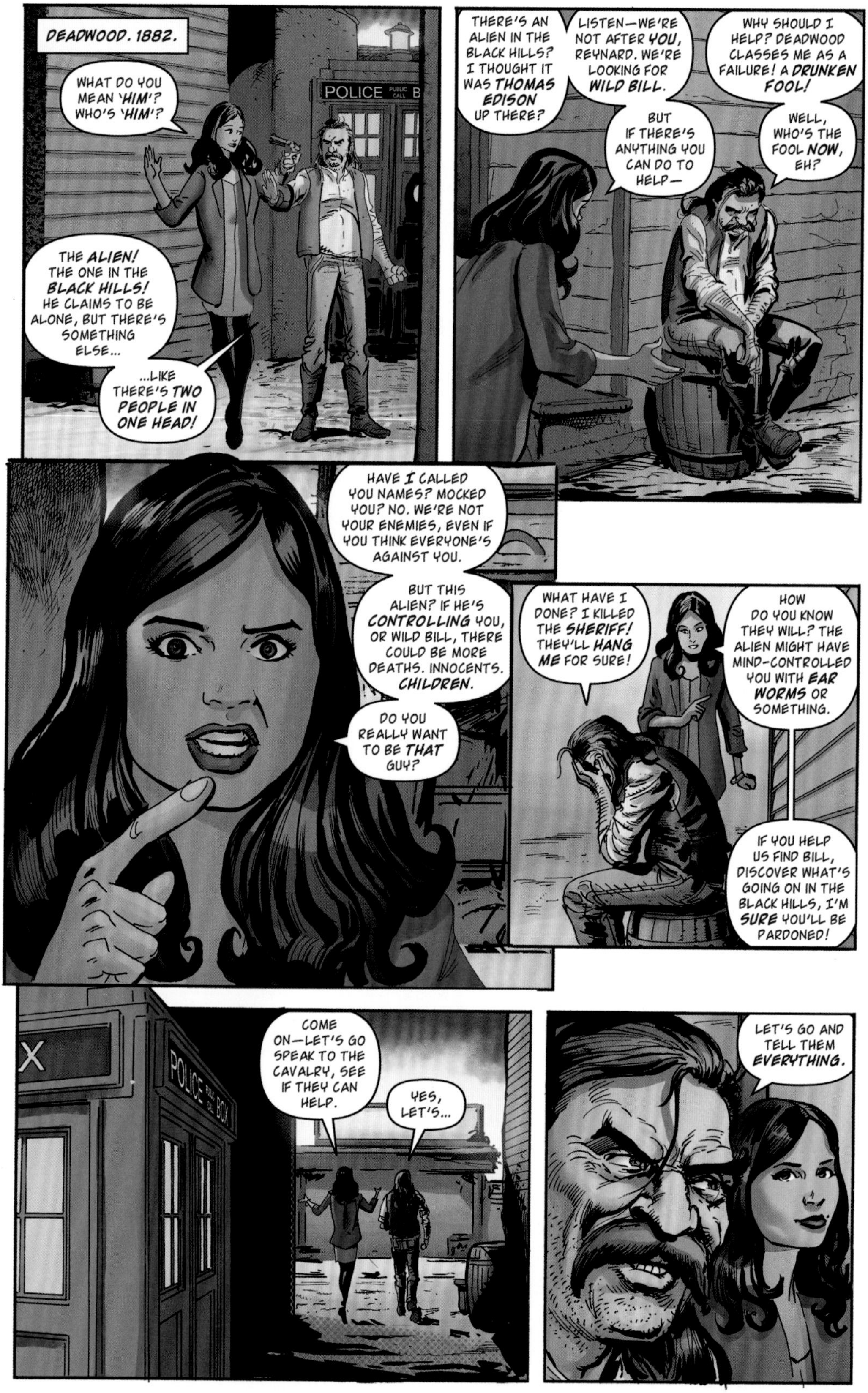
DEADWOOD. 1882.
WHAT DO YOU MEAN 'HIM'? WHO'S 'HIM'?
THE ALIEN! THE ONE IN THE BLACK HILLS! HE CLAIMS TO BE ALONE, BUT THERE'S SOMETHING ELSE...
...LIKE THERE'S TWO PEOPLE IN ONE HEAD!
THERE'S AN ALIEN IN THE BLACK HILLS? I THOUGHT IT WAS THOMAS EDISON UP THERE?
LISTEN—WE'RE NOT AFTER YOU, REYNARD. WE'RE LOOKING FOR WILD BILL.
BUT IF THERE'S ANYTHING YOU CAN DO TO HELP—
WHY SHOULD I HELP? DEADWOOD CLASSES ME AS A FAILURE! A DRUNKEN FOOL!
WELL, WHO'S THE FOOL NOW, EH?
HAVE I CALLED YOU NAMES? MOCKED YOU? NO. WE'RE NOT YOUR ENEMIES, EVEN IF YOU THINK EVERYONE'S AGAINST YOU.
BUT THIS ALIEN? IF HE'S CONTROLLING YOU, OR WILD BILL, THERE COULD BE MORE DEATHS. INNOCENTS. CHILDREN.
DO YOU REALLY WANT TO BE THAT GUY?
WHAT HAVE I DONE? I KILLED THE SHERIFF! THEY'LL HANG ME FOR SURE!
HOW DO YOU KNOW THEY WILL? THE ALIEN MIGHT HAVE MIND-CONTROLLED YOU WITH EAR WORMS OR SOMETHING.
IF YOU HELP US FIND BILL, DISCOVER WHAT'S GOING ON IN THE BLACK HILLS, I'M SURE YOU'LL BE PARDONED!
COME ON—LET'S GO SPEAK TO THE CAVALRY, SEE IF THEY CAN HELP.
YES, LET'S...
LET'S GO AND TELL THEM EVERYTHING.

THE BLACK HILLS.

FOR **CENTURIES** I HAVE WAITED FOR YOU TO MEDDLE IN ONE OF MY **AUDITS**, DOCTOR!

AND NOW, BEFORE I PASS SENTENCE ON THE EARTH, I GET TO **EXECUTE YOU!**

SONDRAH! **WAIT!** YOU SAID YOU'RE OF THE **T'KEYN**, RIGHT?

THEN BY THE **T'KEYN BYLAWS OF THE SHADOW PROCLAMATION'S CONVENTION 15**, I GET TO DEFEND MYSELF IN THE **T'KEYN NEXUS!**

YOU'RE NOT A CONDEMNED RACE! YOU'RE JUST A **TIME LORD!**

AH, BUT AS YOU SAID, I'M THE **LAST** OF THE TIME LORDS. WHICH MEANS THAT IF YOU KILL ME, YOU **END MY RACE.**

WHICH MEANS THAT I GET MY RIGHT TO REPLY, OR THE SHADOW PROCLAMATION WILL **REVOKE** YOUR RIGHT TO AUDIT.

AND BY REVOKE, I MEAN **TERMINATE WITH FORCE.**

THE T'KEYN AND THE TIME LORDS **IGNORED** EACH OTHER PRETTY MUCH, BUT HE KNOWS FAR TOO MUCH ABOUT ME, AND SOMETHING ABOUT HIM IS **FAMILIAR.**

OSCAR, WHILE I'M IN THE NEXUS, I HAVE A SMALL FAVOUR TO ASK OF YOU. AND IT MIGHT JUST SAVE US ALL.

WELL, A **COUPLE** OF SMALL FAVOURS, ACTUALLY.

PERHAPS **BIG** ONES.

HERE, TAKE IT. LET US END THIS. THE T'KEYN NEXUS IS—

—IS A VIRTUAL REALITY LIKE THE **TIME LORD MATRIX**, SONDRAH. I KNOW. I'M NOT AN AMATEUR TO THIS.

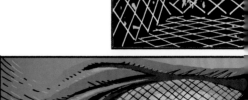

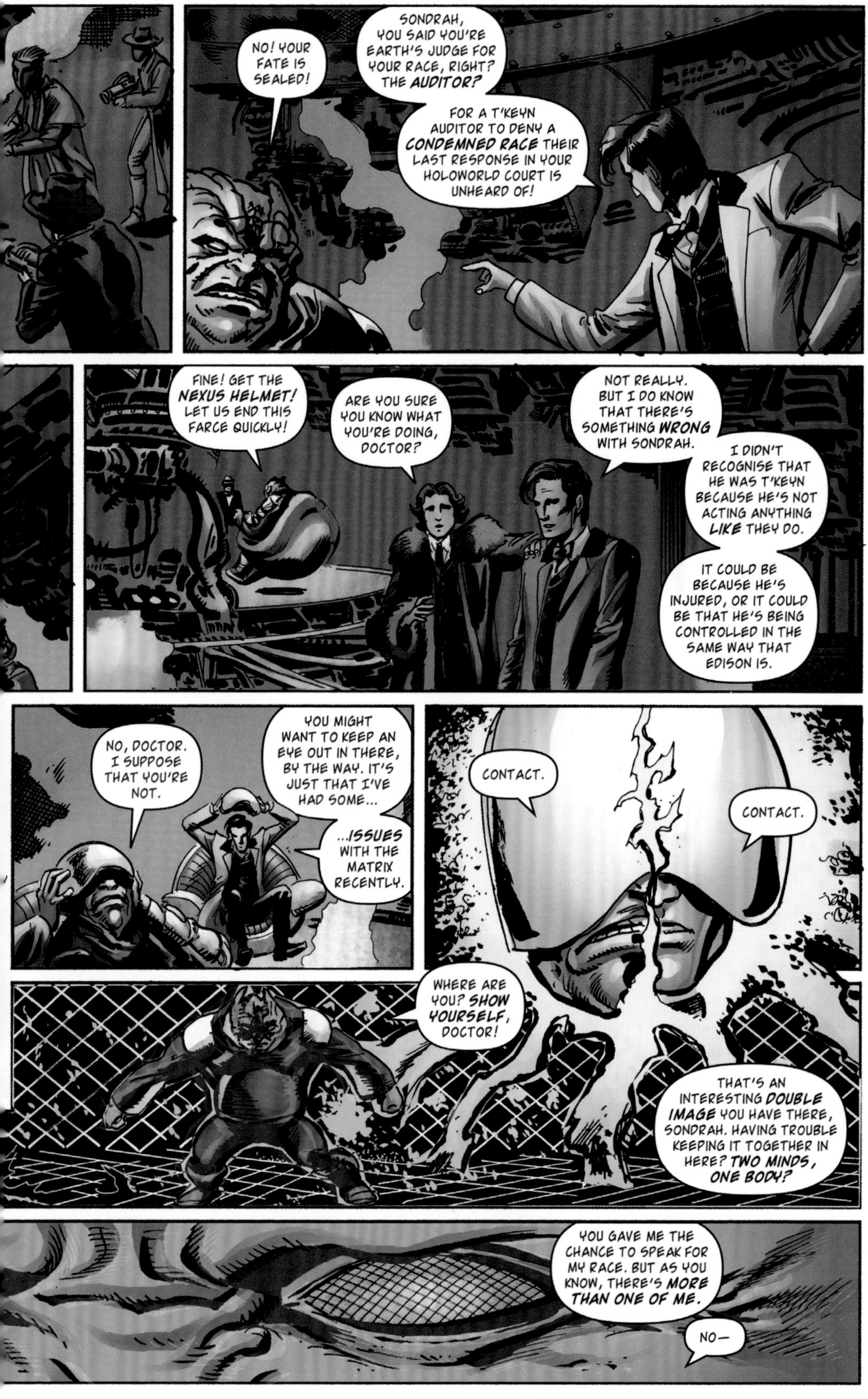

NO! YOUR FATE IS SEALED!
SONDRAH, YOU SAID YOU'RE EARTH'S JUDGE FOR YOUR RACE, RIGHT? THE AUDITOR?
FOR A T'KEYN AUDITOR TO DENY A CONDEMNED RACE THEIR LAST RESPONSE IN YOUR HOLOWORLD COURT IS UNHEARD OF!
FINE! GET THE NEXUS HELMET! LET US END THIS FARCE QUICKLY!
ARE YOU SURE YOU KNOW WHAT YOU'RE DOING, DOCTOR?
NOT REALLY. BUT I DO KNOW THAT THERE'S SOMETHING WRONG WITH SONDRAH.
I DIDN'T RECOGNISE THAT HE WAS T'KEYN BECAUSE HE'S NOT ACTING ANYTHING LIKE THEY DO.
IT COULD BE BECAUSE HE'S INJURED, OR IT COULD BE THAT HE'S BEING CONTROLLED IN THE SAME WAY THAT EDISON IS.
NO, DOCTOR. I SUPPOSE THAT YOU'RE NOT.
YOU MIGHT WANT TO KEEP AN EYE OUT IN THERE, BY THE WAY. IT'S JUST THAT I'VE HAD SOME...
...ISSUES WITH THE MATRIX RECENTLY.
CONTACT.
CONTACT.
WHERE ARE YOU? SHOW YOURSELF, DOCTOR!
THAT'S AN INTERESTING DOUBLE IMAGE YOU HAVE THERE, SONDRAH. HAVING TROUBLE KEEPING IT TOGETHER IN HERE? TWO MINDS, ONE BODY?
YOU GAVE ME THE CHANCE TO SPEAK FOR MY RACE. BUT AS YOU KNOW, THERE'S MORE THAN ONE OF ME.
NO—

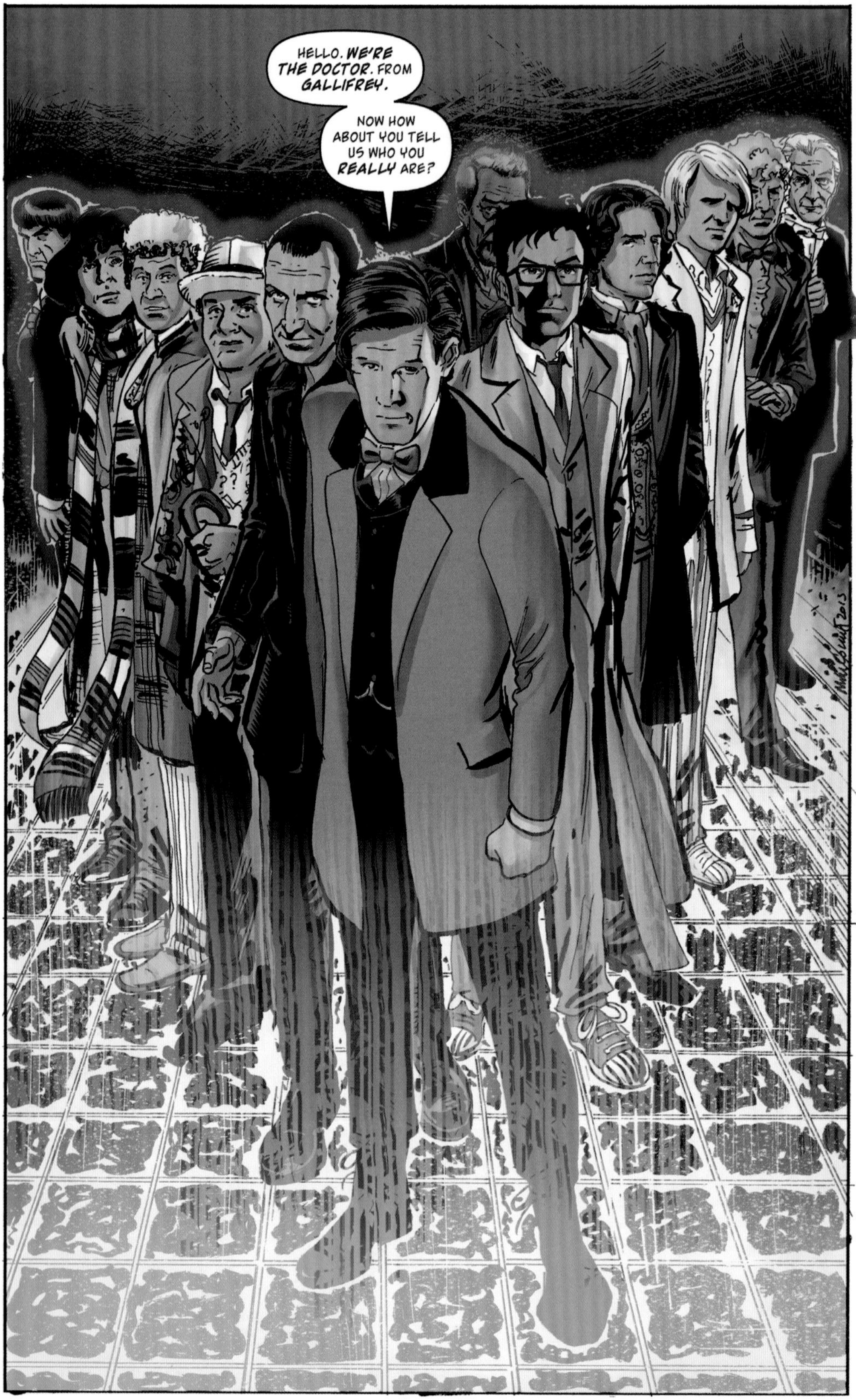
HELLO. WE'RE THE DOCTOR. FROM GALLIFREY.
NOW HOW ABOUT YOU TELL US WHO YOU REALLY ARE?

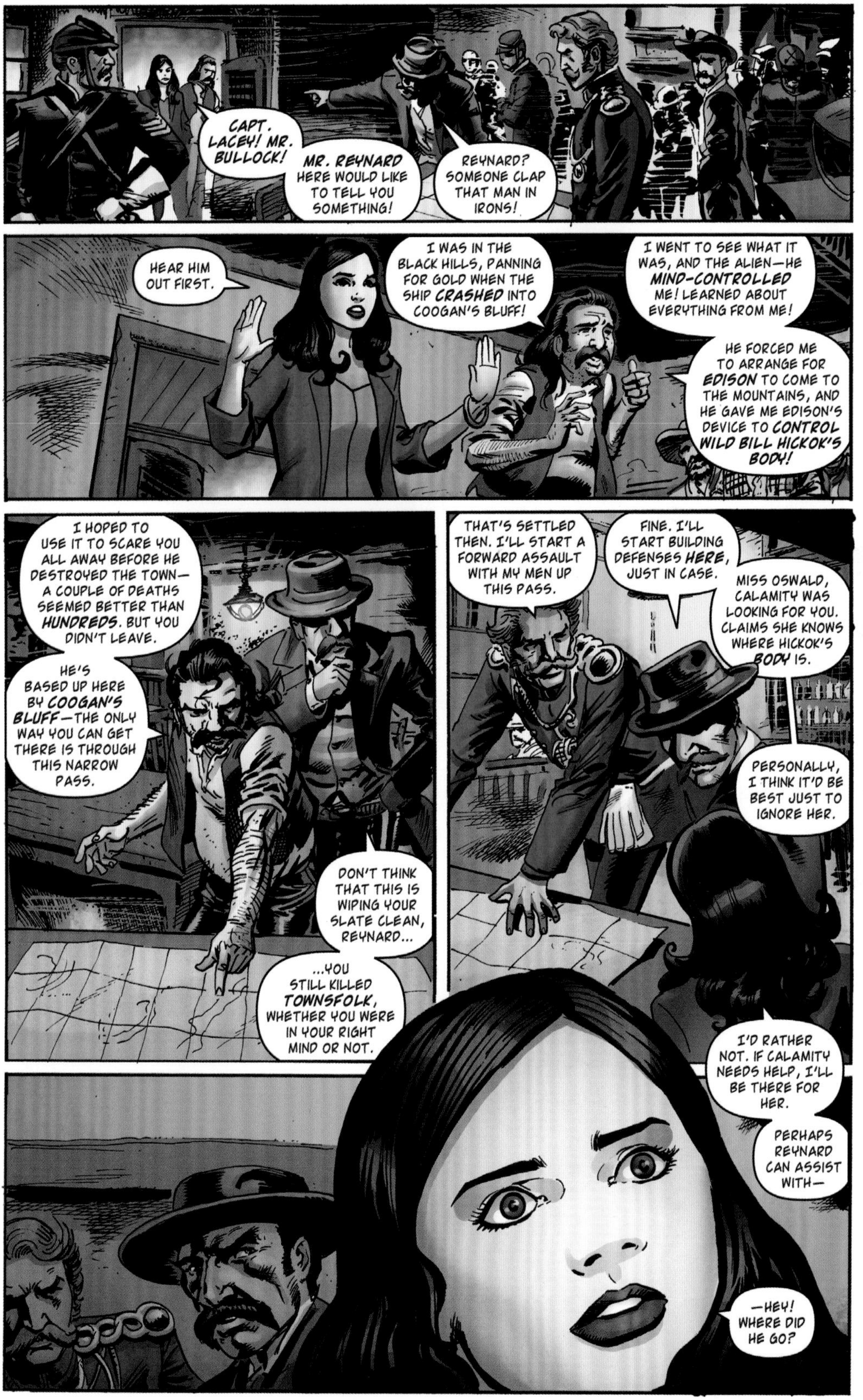
CAPT. LACEY! MR. BULLOCK!
MR. REYNARD HERE WOULD LIKE TO TELL YOU SOMETHING!
REYNARD? SOMEONE CLAP THAT MAN IN IRONS!
HEAR HIM OUT FIRST.
I WAS IN THE BLACK HILLS, PANNING FOR GOLD WHEN THE SHIP CRASHED INTO COOGAN'S BLUFF!
I WENT TO SEE WHAT IT WAS, AND THE ALIEN—HE MIND-CONTROLLED ME! LEARNED ABOUT EVERYTHING FROM ME!
HE FORCED ME TO ARRANGE FOR EDISON TO COME TO THE MOUNTAINS, AND HE GAVE ME EDISON'S DEVICE TO CONTROL WILD BILL HICKOK'S BODY!
I HOPED TO USE IT TO SCARE YOU ALL AWAY BEFORE HE DESTROYED THE TOWN—A COUPLE OF DEATHS SEEMED BETTER THAN HUNDREDS. BUT YOU DIDN'T LEAVE.
HE'S BASED UP HERE BY COOGAN'S BLUFF—THE ONLY WAY YOU CAN GET THERE IS THROUGH THIS NARROW PASS.
DON'T THINK THAT THIS IS WIPING YOUR SLATE CLEAN, REYNARD...
...YOU STILL KILLED TOWNSFOLK, WHETHER YOU WERE IN YOUR RIGHT MIND OR NOT.
THAT'S SETTLED THEN. I'LL START A FORWARD ASSAULT WITH MY MEN UP THIS PASS.
FINE. I'LL START BUILDING DEFENSES HERE, JUST IN CASE.
MISS OSWALD, CALAMITY WAS LOOKING FOR YOU. CLAIMS SHE KNOWS WHERE HICKOK'S BODY IS.
PERSONALLY, I THINK IT'D BE BEST JUST TO IGNORE HER.
I'D RATHER NOT. IF CALAMITY NEEDS HELP, I'LL BE THERE FOR HER.
PERHAPS REYNARD CAN ASSIST WITH—
—HEY! WHERE DID HE GO?

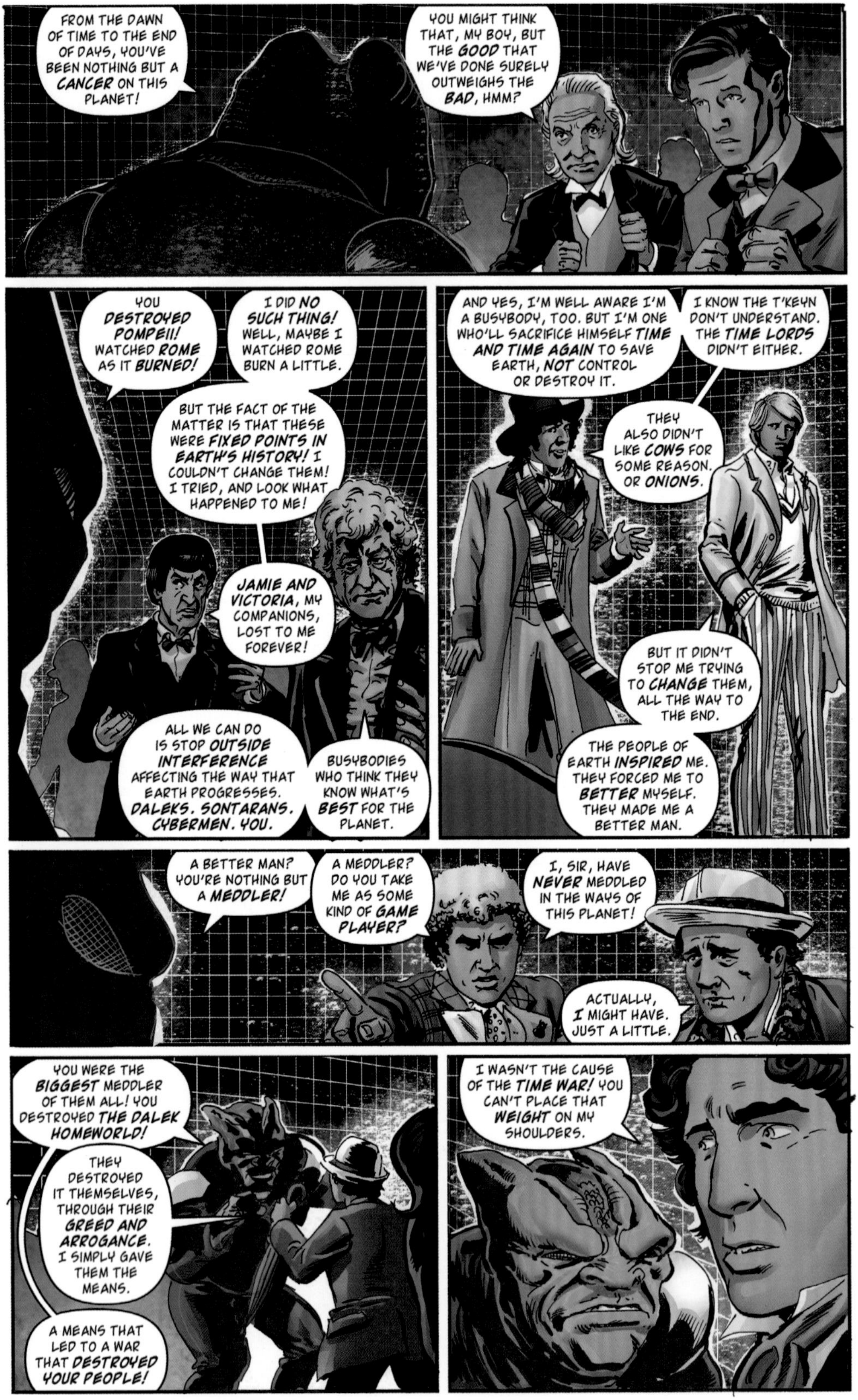
FROM THE DAWN OF TIME TO THE END OF DAYS, YOU'VE BEEN NOTHING BUT A CANCER ON THIS PLANET!
YOU MIGHT THINK THAT, MY BOY, BUT THE GOOD THAT WE'VE DONE SURELY OUTWEIGHS THE BAD, HMM?
YOU DESTROYED POMPEII! WATCHED ROME AS IT BURNED!
I DID NO SUCH THING! WELL, MAYBE I WATCHED ROME BURN A LITTLE.
BUT THE FACT OF THE MATTER IS THAT THESE WERE FIXED POINTS IN EARTH'S HISTORY! I COULDN'T CHANGE THEM! I TRIED, AND LOOK WHAT HAPPENED TO ME!
JAMIE AND VICTORIA, MY COMPANIONS, LOST TO ME FOREVER!
ALL WE CAN DO IS STOP OUTSIDE INTERFERENCE AFFECTING THE WAY THAT EARTH PROGRESSES. DALEKS. SONTARANS. CYBERMEN. YOU.
BUSYBODIES WHO THINK THEY KNOW WHAT'S BEST FOR THE PLANET.
AND YES, I'M WELL AWARE I'M A BUSYBODY, TOO. BUT I'M ONE WHO'LL SACRIFICE HIMSELF TIME AND TIME AGAIN TO SAVE EARTH, NOT CONTROL OR DESTROY IT.
I KNOW THE T'KEYN DON'T UNDERSTAND. THE TIME LORDS DIDN'T EITHER.
THEY ALSO DIDN'T LIKE COWS FOR SOME REASON. OR ONIONS.
BUT IT DIDN'T STOP ME TRYING TO CHANGE THEM, ALL THE WAY TO THE END.
THE PEOPLE OF EARTH INSPIRED ME. THEY FORCED ME TO BETTER MYSELF. THEY MADE ME A BETTER MAN.
A BETTER MAN? YOU'RE NOTHING BUT A MEDDLER!
A MEDDLER? DO YOU TAKE ME AS SOME KIND OF GAME PLAYER?
I, SIR, HAVE NEVER MEDDLED IN THE WAYS OF THIS PLANET!
ACTUALLY, I MIGHT HAVE. JUST A LITTLE.
YOU WERE THE BIGGEST MEDDLER OF THEM ALL! YOU DESTROYED THE DALEK HOMEWORLD!
THEY DESTROYED IT THEMSELVES, THROUGH THEIR GREED AND ARROGANCE. I SIMPLY GAVE THEM THE MEANS.
A MEANS THAT LED TO A WAR THAT DESTROYED YOUR PEOPLE!
I WASN'T THE CAUSE OF THE TIME WAR! YOU CAN'T PLACE THAT WEIGHT ON MY SHOULDERS.

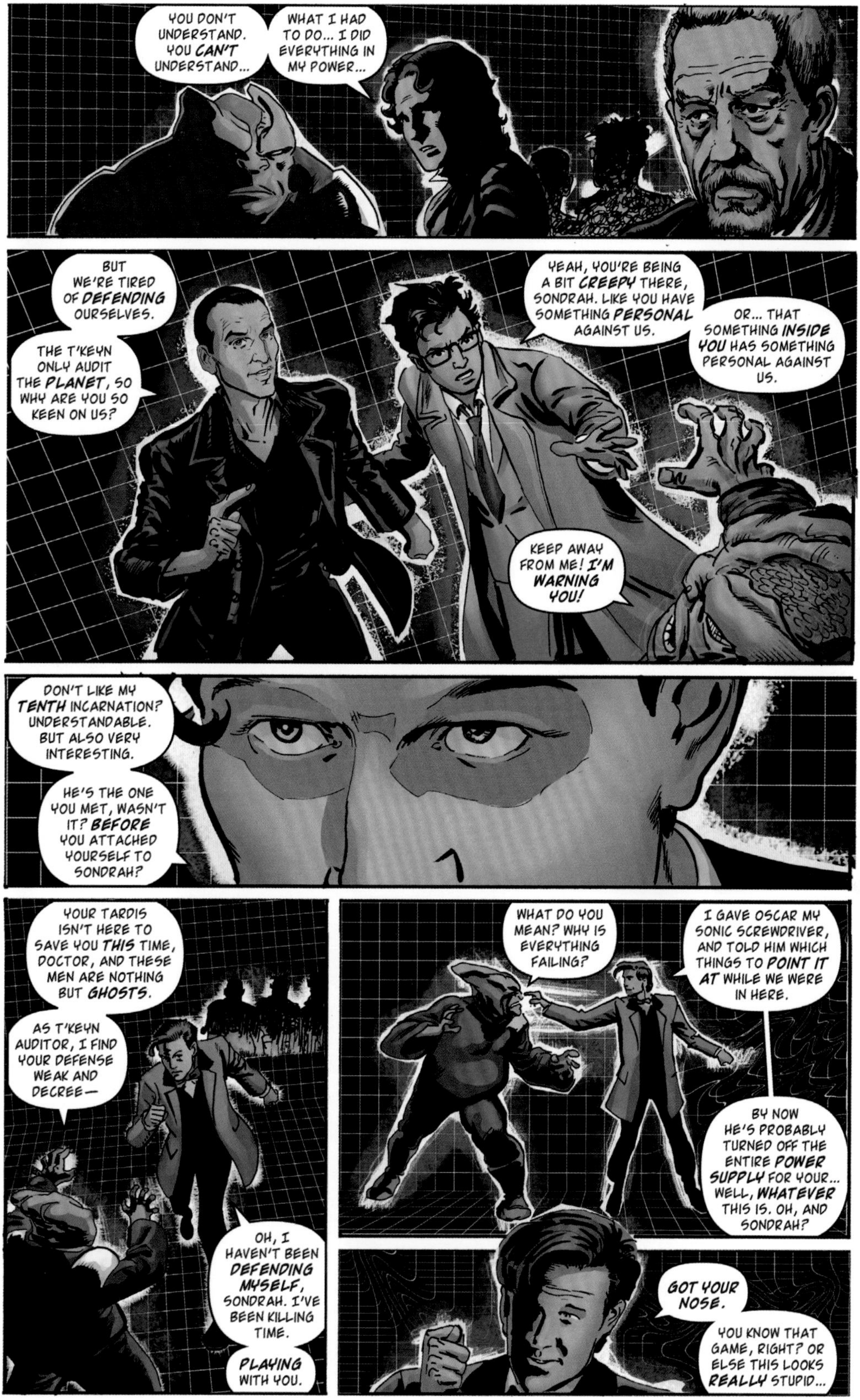
YOU DON'T UNDERSTAND. YOU CAN'T UNDERSTAND...
WHAT I HAD TO DO... I DID EVERYTHING IN MY POWER...
BUT WE'RE TIRED OF DEFENDING OURSELVES.
THE T'KEYN ONLY AUDIT THE PLANET, SO WHY ARE YOU SO KEEN ON US?
YEAH, YOU'RE BEING A BIT CREEPY THERE, SONDRAH. LIKE YOU HAVE SOMETHING PERSONAL AGAINST US.
OR... THAT SOMETHING INSIDE YOU HAS SOMETHING PERSONAL AGAINST US.
KEEP AWAY FROM ME! I'M WARNING YOU!
DON'T LIKE MY TENTH INCARNATION? UNDERSTANDABLE. BUT ALSO VERY INTERESTING.
HE'S THE ONE YOU MET, WASN'T IT? BEFORE YOU ATTACHED YOURSELF TO SONDRAH?
YOUR TARDIS ISN'T HERE TO SAVE YOU THIS TIME, DOCTOR, AND THESE MEN ARE NOTHING BUT GHOSTS.
AS T'KEYN AUDITOR, I FIND YOUR DEFENSE WEAK AND DECREE—
OH, I HAVEN'T BEEN DEFENDING MYSELF, SONDRAH. I'VE BEEN KILLING TIME.
PLAYING WITH YOU.
WHAT DO YOU MEAN? WHY IS EVERYTHING FAILING?
I GAVE OSCAR MY SONIC SCREWDRIVER, AND TOLD HIM WHICH THINGS TO POINT IT AT WHILE WE WERE IN HERE.
BY NOW HE'S PROBABLY TURNED OFF THE ENTIRE POWER SUPPLY FOR YOUR... WELL, WHATEVER THIS IS. OH, AND SONDRAH?
GOT YOUR NOSE.
YOU KNOW THAT GAME, RIGHT? OR ELSE THIS LOOKS REALLY STUPID...

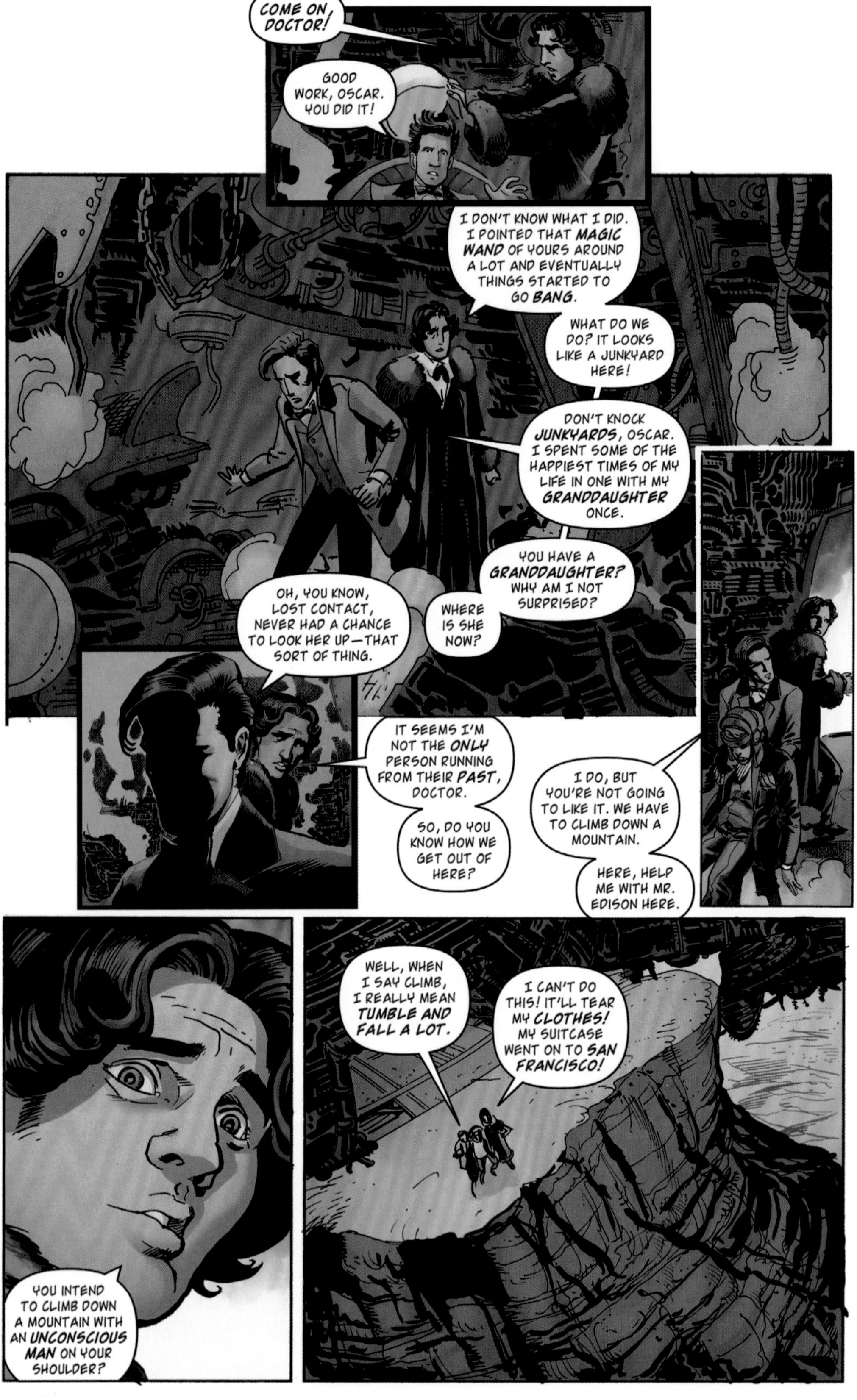
COME ON, DOCTOR!
GOOD WORK, OSCAR. YOU DID IT!
I DON'T KNOW WHAT I DID. I POINTED THAT MAGIC WAND OF YOURS AROUND A LOT AND EVENTUALLY THINGS STARTED TO GO BANG.
WHAT DO WE DO? IT LOOKS LIKE A JUNKYARD HERE!
DON'T KNOCK JUNKYARDS, OSCAR. I SPENT SOME OF THE HAPPIEST TIMES OF MY LIFE IN ONE WITH MY GRANDDAUGHTER ONCE.
YOU HAVE A GRANDDAUGHTER? WHY AM I NOT SURPRISED?
WHERE IS SHE NOW?
OH, YOU KNOW, LOST CONTACT, NEVER HAD A CHANCE TO LOOK HER UP—THAT SORT OF THING.
IT SEEMS I'M NOT THE ONLY PERSON RUNNING FROM THEIR PAST, DOCTOR.
SO, DO YOU KNOW HOW WE GET OUT OF HERE?
I DO, BUT YOU'RE NOT GOING TO LIKE IT. WE HAVE TO CLIMB DOWN A MOUNTAIN.
HERE, HELP ME WITH MR. EDISON HERE.
YOU INTEND TO CLIMB DOWN A MOUNTAIN WITH AN UNCONSCIOUS MAN ON YOUR SHOULDER?
WELL, WHEN I SAY CLIMB, I REALLY MEAN TUMBLE AND FALL A LOT.
I CAN'T DO THIS! IT'LL TEAR MY CLOTHES! MY SUITCASE WENT ON TO SAN FRANCISCO!

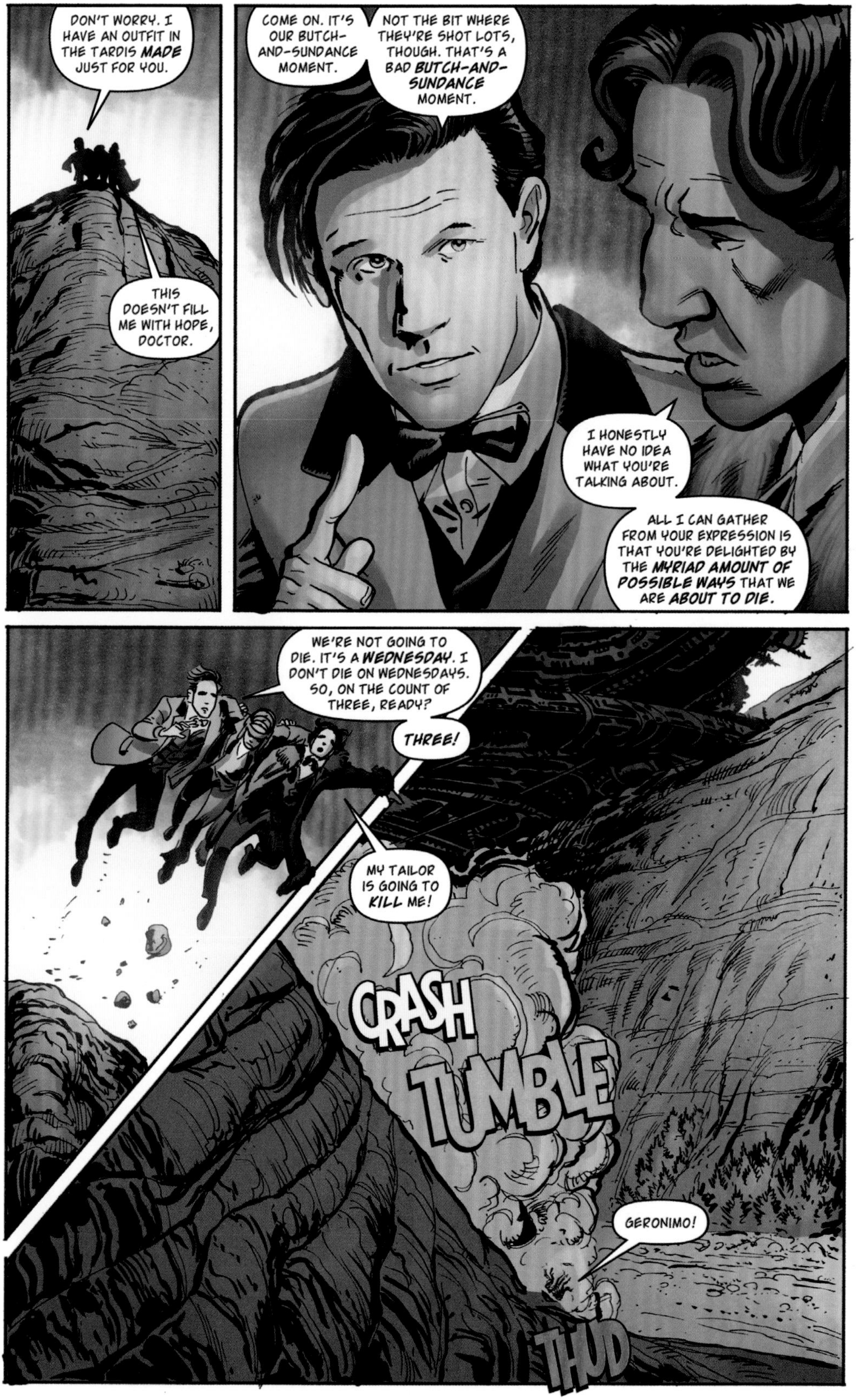
DON'T WORRY. I HAVE AN OUTFIT IN THE TARDIS MADE JUST FOR YOU.
THIS DOESN'T FILL ME WITH HOPE, DOCTOR.
COME ON. IT'S OUR BUTCH-AND-SUNDANCE MOMENT.
NOT THE BIT WHERE THEY'RE SHOT LOTS, THOUGH. THAT'S A BAD BUTCH-AND-SUNDANCE MOMENT.
I HONESTLY HAVE NO IDEA WHAT YOU'RE TALKING ABOUT.
ALL I CAN GATHER FROM YOUR EXPRESSION IS THAT YOU'RE DELIGHTED BY THE MYRIAD AMOUNT OF POSSIBLE WAYS THAT WE ARE ABOUT TO DIE.
WE'RE NOT GOING TO DIE. IT'S A WEDNESDAY. I DON'T DIE ON WEDNESDAYS. SO, ON THE COUNT OF THREE, READY?
THREE!
MY TAILOR IS GOING TO KILL ME!
CRASH
TUMBLE
GERONIMO!
THUD

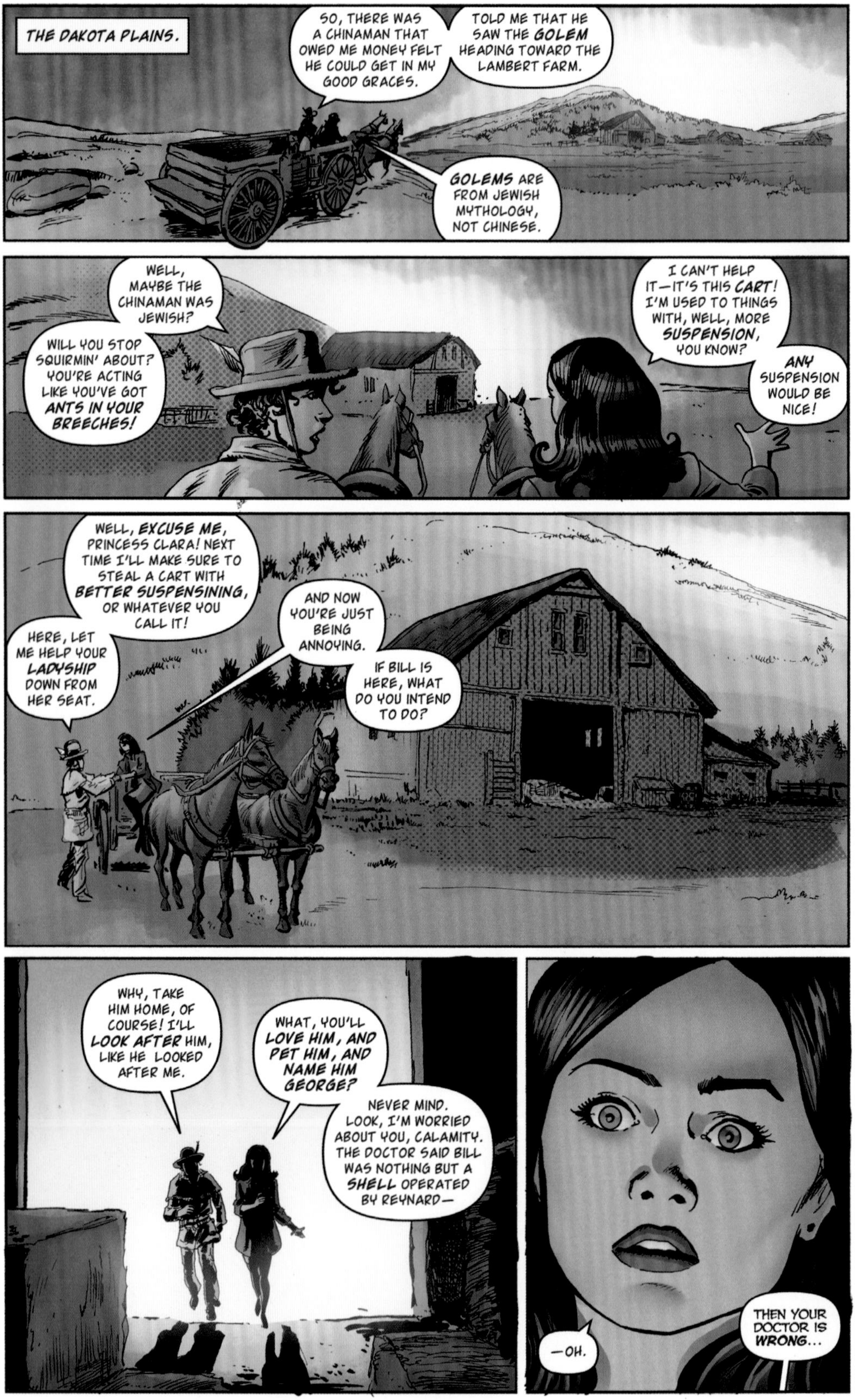
THE DAKOTA PLAINS.
SO, THERE WAS A CHINAMAN THAT OWED ME MONEY FELT HE COULD GET IN MY GOOD GRACES.
TOLD ME THAT HE SAW THE GOLEM HEADING TOWARD THE LAMBERT FARM.
GOLEMS ARE FROM JEWISH MYTHOLOGY, NOT CHINESE.
WELL, MAYBE THE CHINAMAN WAS JEWISH?
WILL YOU STOP SQUIRMIN' ABOUT? YOU'RE ACTING LIKE YOU'VE GOT ANTS IN YOUR BREECHES!
I CAN'T HELP IT—IT'S THIS CART! I'M USED TO THINGS WITH, WELL, MORE SUSPENSION, YOU KNOW?
ANY SUSPENSION WOULD BE NICE!
WELL, EXCUSE ME, PRINCESS CLARA! NEXT TIME I'LL MAKE SURE TO STEAL A CART WITH BETTER SUSPENSINING, OR WHATEVER YOU CALL IT!
HERE, LET ME HELP YOUR LADYSHIP DOWN FROM HER SEAT.
AND NOW YOU'RE JUST BEING ANNOYING.
IF BILL IS HERE, WHAT DO YOU INTEND TO DO?
WHY, TAKE HIM HOME, OF COURSE! I'LL LOOK AFTER HIM, LIKE HE LOOKED AFTER ME.
WHAT, YOU'LL LOVE HIM, AND PET HIM, AND NAME HIM GEORGE?
NEVER MIND. LOOK, I'M WORRIED ABOUT YOU, CALAMITY. THE DOCTOR SAID BILL WAS NOTHING BUT A SHELL OPERATED BY REYNARD—
—OH.
THEN YOUR DOCTOR IS WRONG...

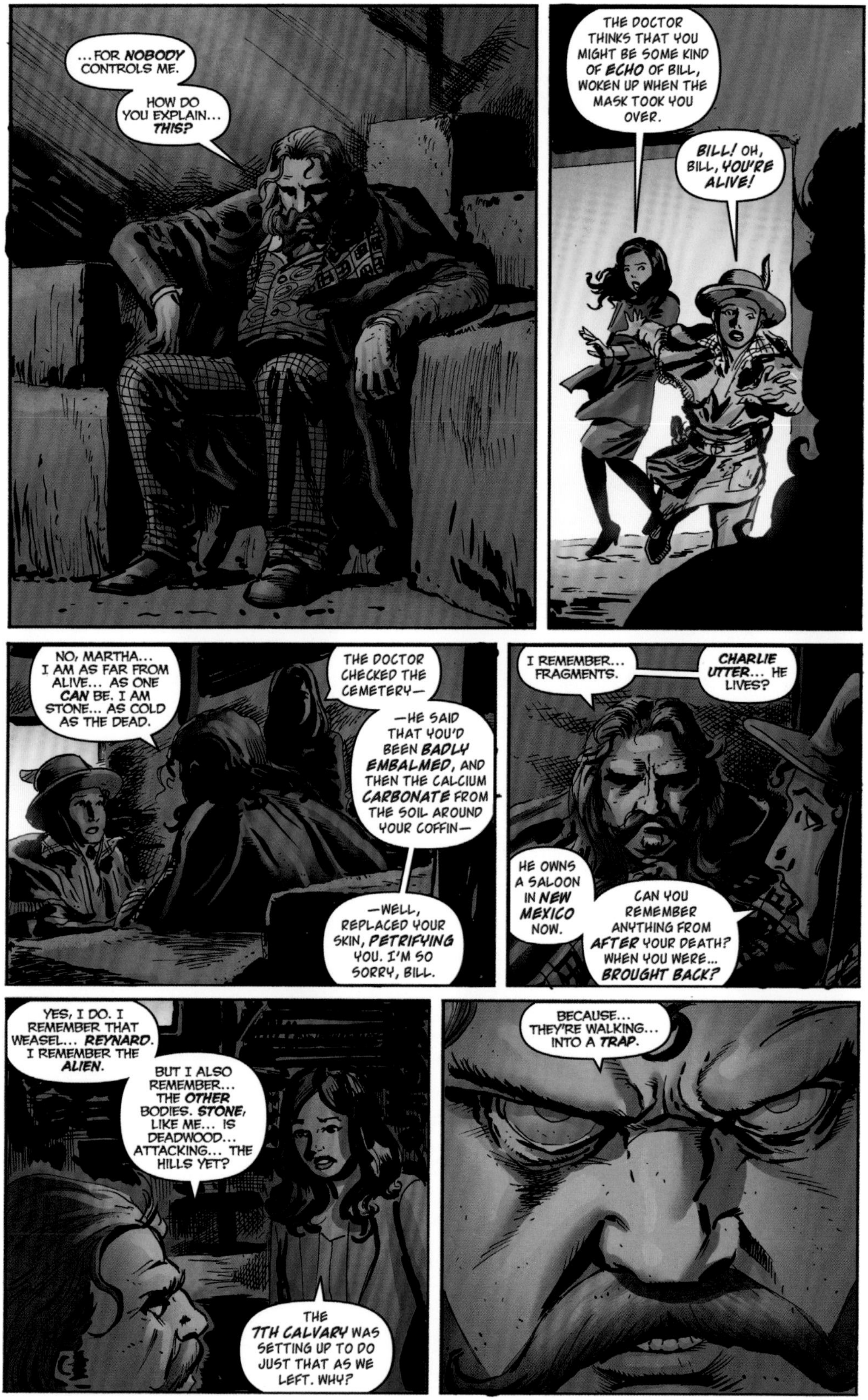
...FOR NOBODY CONTROLS ME.
HOW DO YOU EXPLAIN... THIS?
THE DOCTOR THINKS THAT YOU MIGHT BE SOME KIND OF ECHO OF BILL, WOKEN UP WHEN THE MASK TOOK YOU OVER.
BILL! OH, BILL, YOU'RE ALIVE!
NO, MARTHA... I AM AS FAR FROM ALIVE... AS ONE CAN BE. I AM STONE... AS COLD AS THE DEAD.
THE DOCTOR CHECKED THE CEMETERY—
—HE SAID THAT YOU'D BEEN BADLY EMBALMED, AND THEN THE CALCIUM CARBONATE FROM THE SOIL AROUND YOUR COFFIN—
—WELL, REPLACED YOUR SKIN, PETRIFYING YOU. I'M SO SORRY, BILL.
I REMEMBER... FRAGMENTS.
CHARLIE UTTER... HE LIVES?
HE OWNS A SALOON IN NEW MEXICO NOW.
CAN YOU REMEMBER ANYTHING FROM AFTER YOUR DEATH? WHEN YOU WERE... BROUGHT BACK?
YES, I DO. I REMEMBER THAT WEASEL... REYNARD. I REMEMBER THE ALIEN.
BUT I ALSO REMEMBER... THE OTHER BODIES. STONE, LIKE ME... IS DEADWOOD... ATTACKING... THE HILLS YET?
THE 7TH CALVARY WAS SETTING UP TO DO JUST THAT AS WE LEFT. WHY?
BECAUSE... THEY'RE WALKING... INTO A TRAP.

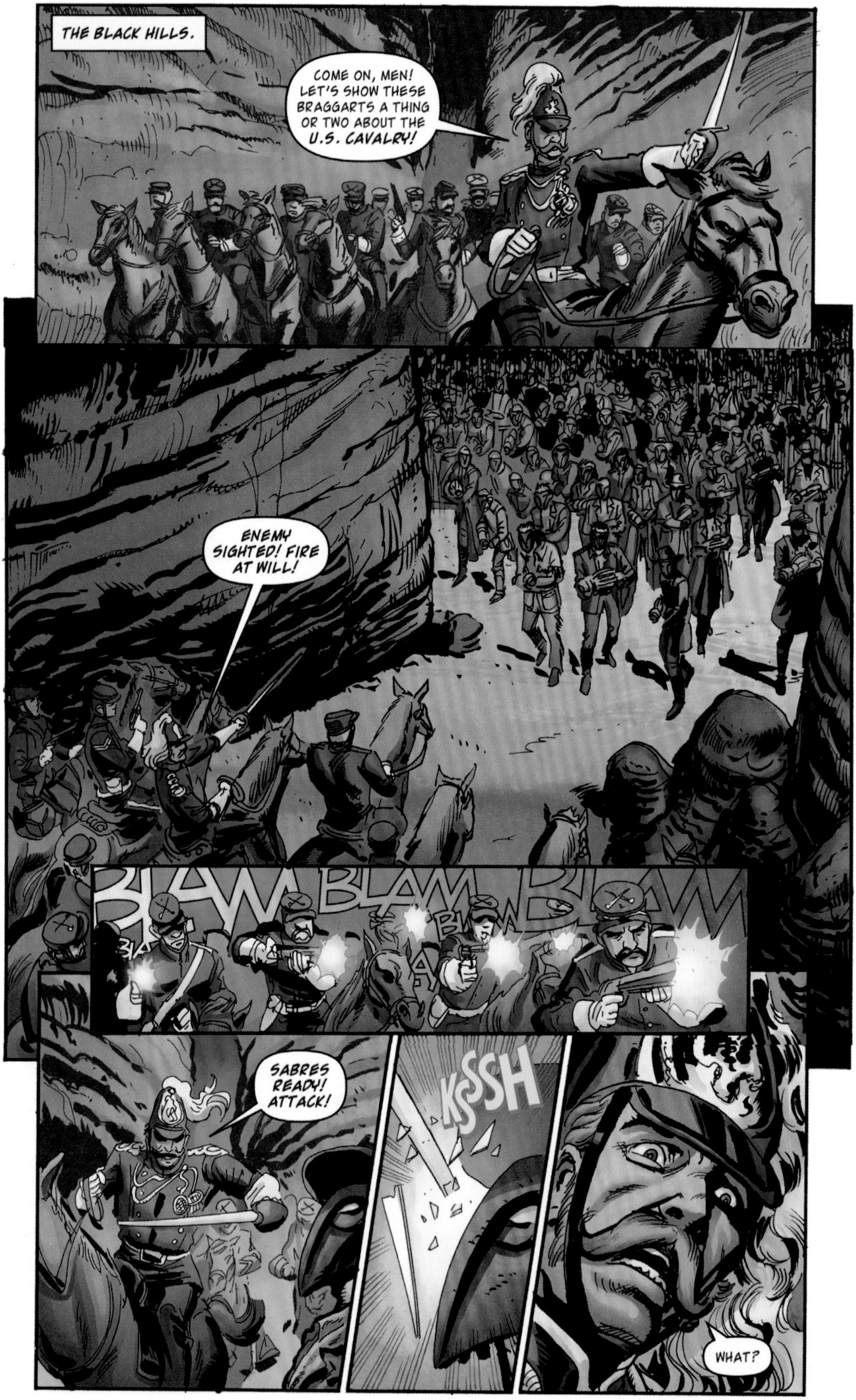
THE BLACK HILLS.
COME ON, MEN! LET'S SHOW THESE BRAGGARTS A THING OR TWO ABOUT THE U.S. CAVALRY!
ENEMY SIGHTED! FIRE AT WILL!
BLAM BLAM BLAM
SABRES READY! ATTACK!
KSSH
WHAT?

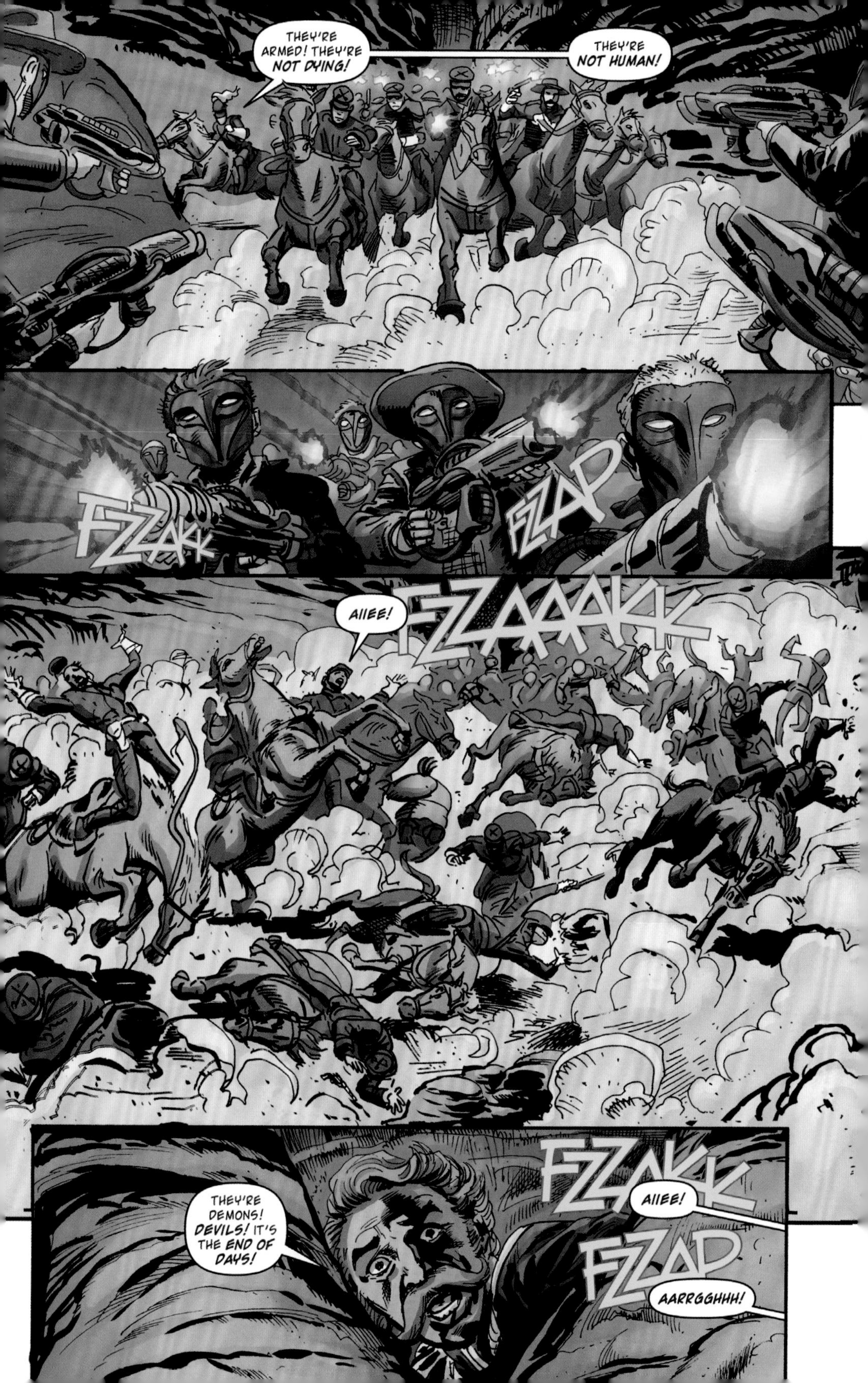
THEY'RE ARMED! THEY'RE NOT DYING!
THEY'RE NOT HUMAN!
FZZAKK
FZZAP
AIIEE!
FZZAAAKK
THEY'RE DEMONS! DEVILS! IT'S THE END OF DAYS!
FZZAKK
AIIEE!
FZZAP
AARRGGHHH!

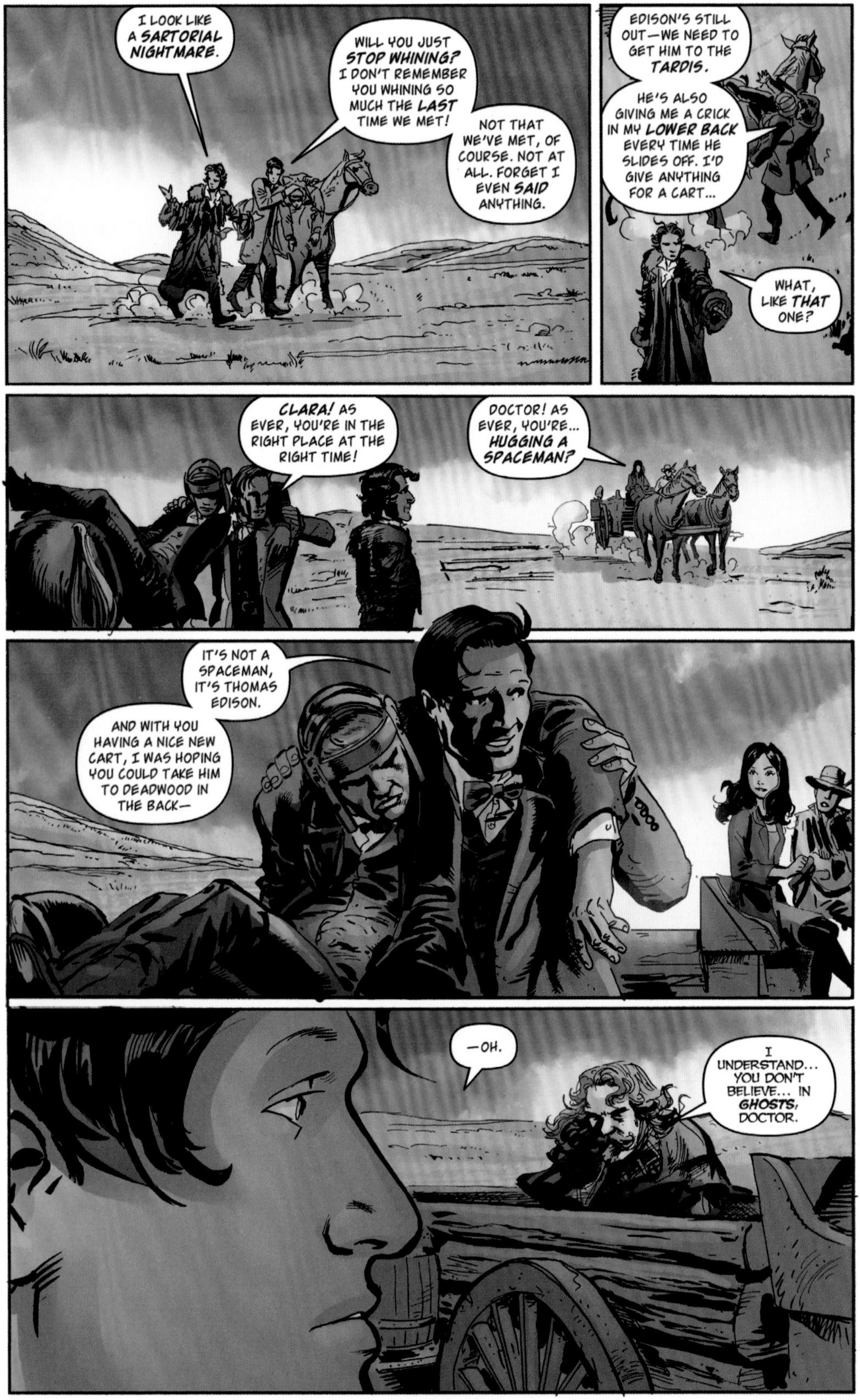
I LOOK LIKE A SARTORIAL NIGHTMARE.
WILL YOU JUST STOP WHINING? I DON'T REMEMBER YOU WHINING SO MUCH THE LAST TIME WE MET!
NOT THAT WE'VE MET, OF COURSE. NOT AT ALL. FORGET I EVEN SAID ANYTHING.
EDISON'S STILL OUT—WE NEED TO GET HIM TO THE TARDIS.
HE'S ALSO GIVING ME A CRICK IN MY LOWER BACK EVERY TIME HE SLIDES OFF. I'D GIVE ANYTHING FOR A CART...
WHAT, LIKE THAT ONE?
CLARA! AS EVER, YOU'RE IN THE RIGHT PLACE AT THE RIGHT TIME!
DOCTOR! AS EVER, YOU'RE... HUGGING A SPACEMAN?
IT'S NOT A SPACEMAN, IT'S THOMAS EDISON.
AND WITH YOU HAVING A NICE NEW CART, I WAS HOPING YOU COULD TAKE HIM TO DEADWOOD IN THE BACK—
—OH.
I UNDERSTAND... YOU DON'T BELIEVE... IN GHOSTS, DOCTOR.

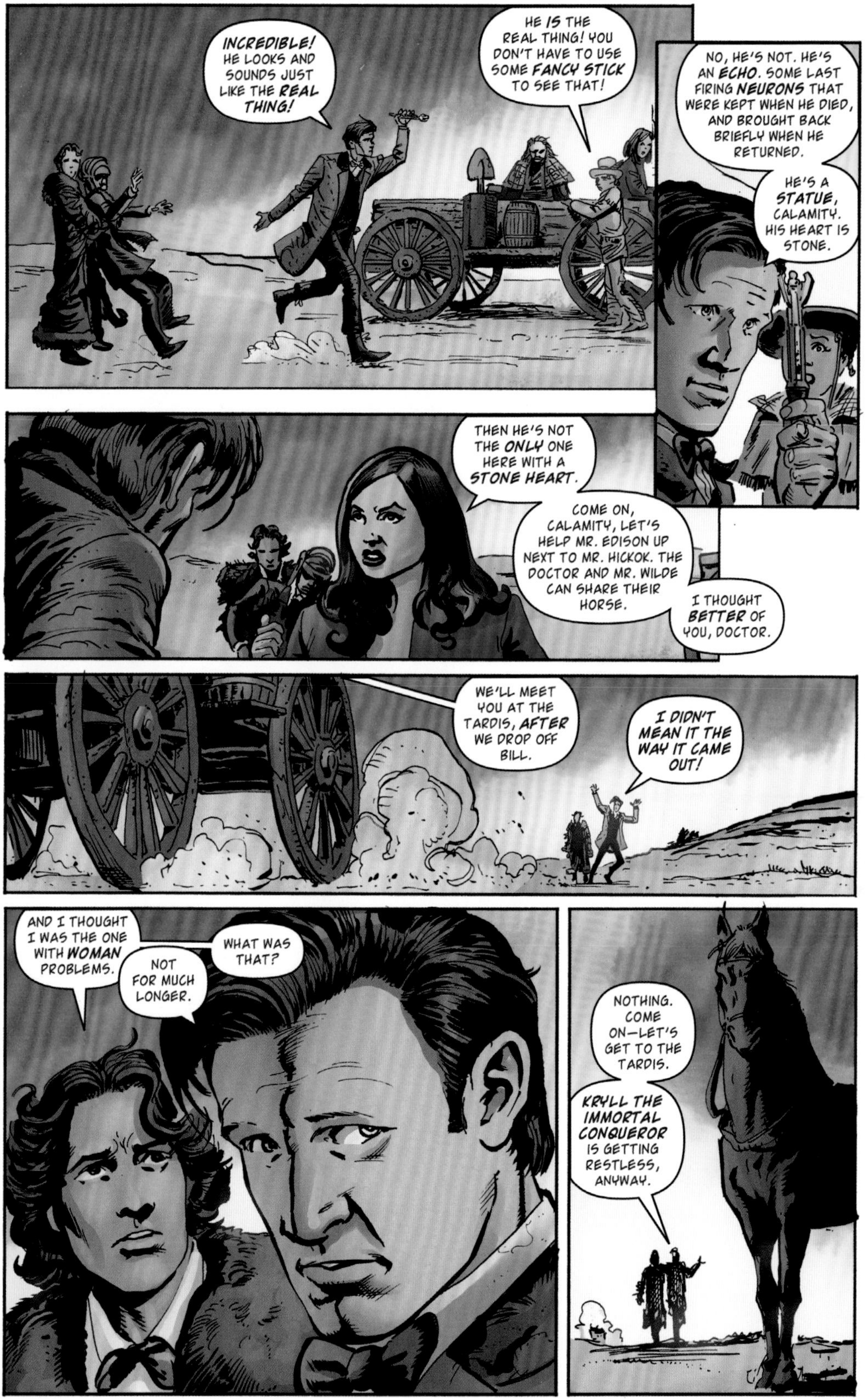
INCREDIBLE! HE LOOKS AND SOUNDS JUST LIKE THE REAL THING!
HE IS THE REAL THING! YOU DON'T HAVE TO USE SOME FANCY STICK TO SEE THAT!
NO, HE'S NOT. HE'S AN ECHO. SOME LAST FIRING NEURONS THAT WERE KEPT WHEN HE DIED, AND BROUGHT BACK BRIEFLY WHEN HE RETURNED.
HE'S A STATUE, CALAMITY. HIS HEART IS STONE.
THEN HE'S NOT THE ONLY ONE HERE WITH A STONE HEART.
COME ON, CALAMITY, LET'S HELP MR. EDISON UP NEXT TO MR. HICKOK. THE DOCTOR AND MR. WILDE CAN SHARE THEIR HORSE.
I THOUGHT BETTER OF YOU, DOCTOR.
WE'LL MEET YOU AT THE TARDIS, AFTER WE DROP OFF BILL.
I DIDN'T MEAN IT THE WAY IT CAME OUT!
AND I THOUGHT I WAS THE ONE WITH WOMAN PROBLEMS.
NOT FOR MUCH LONGER.
WHAT WAS THAT?
NOTHING. COME ON—LET'S GET TO THE TARDIS.
KRYLL THE IMMORTAL CONQUEROR IS GETTING RESTLESS, ANYWAY.

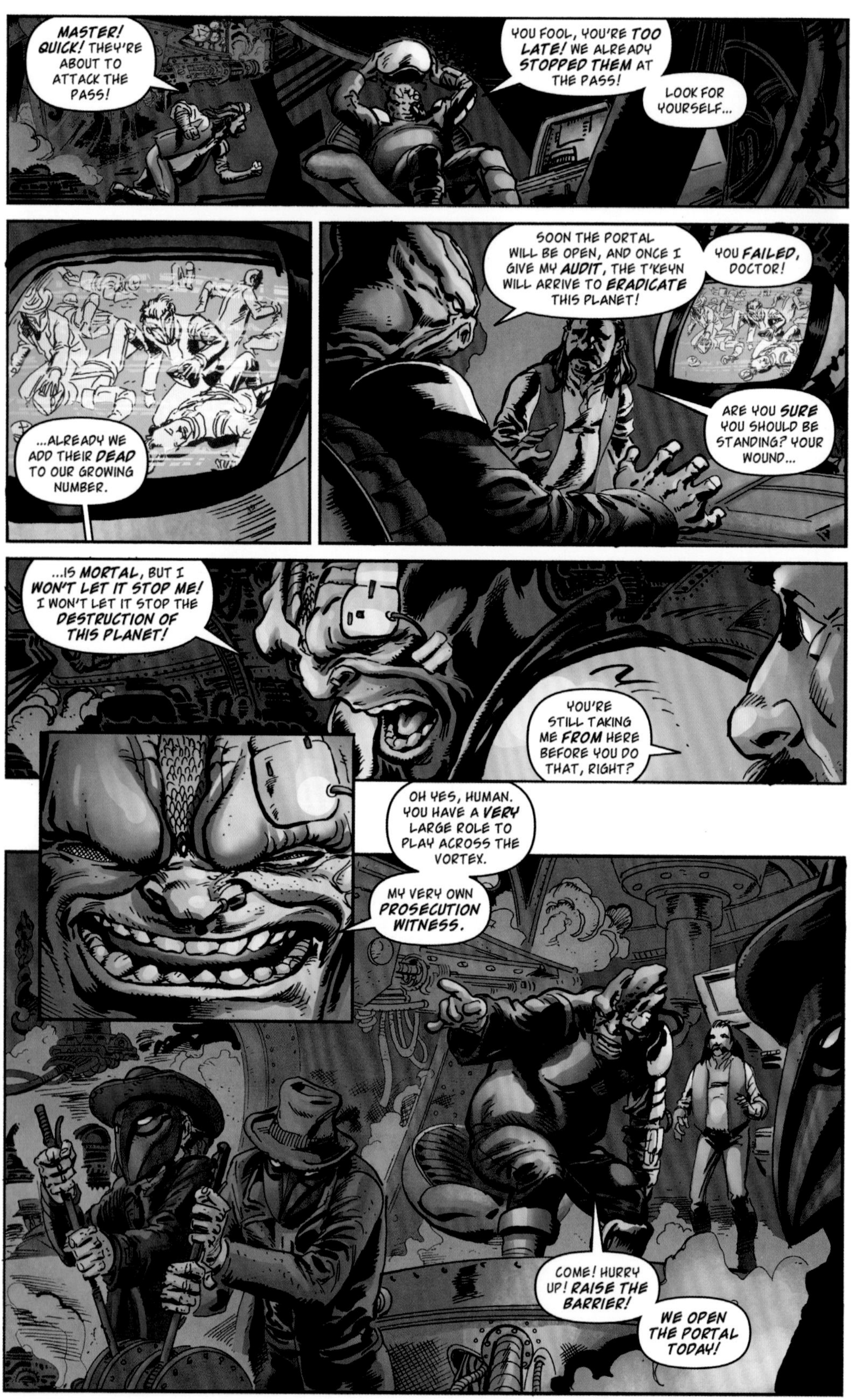
MASTER! QUICK! THEY'RE ABOUT TO ATTACK THE PASS!
YOU FOOL, YOU'RE TOO LATE! WE ALREADY STOPPED THEM AT THE PASS!
LOOK FOR YOURSELF...
...ALREADY WE ADD THEIR DEAD TO OUR GROWING NUMBER.
SOON THE PORTAL WILL BE OPEN, AND ONCE I GIVE MY AUDIT, THE T'KEYN WILL ARRIVE TO ERADICATE THIS PLANET!
YOU FAILED, DOCTOR!
ARE YOU SURE YOU SHOULD BE STANDING? YOUR WOUND...
...IS MORTAL, BUT I WON'T LET IT STOP ME! I WON'T LET IT STOP THE DESTRUCTION OF THIS PLANET!
YOU'RE STILL TAKING ME FROM HERE BEFORE YOU DO THAT, RIGHT?
OH YES, HUMAN. YOU HAVE A VERY LARGE ROLE TO PLAY ACROSS THE VORTEX.
MY VERY OWN PROSECUTION WITNESS.
COME! HURRY UP! RAISE THE BARRIER!
WE OPEN THE PORTAL TODAY!

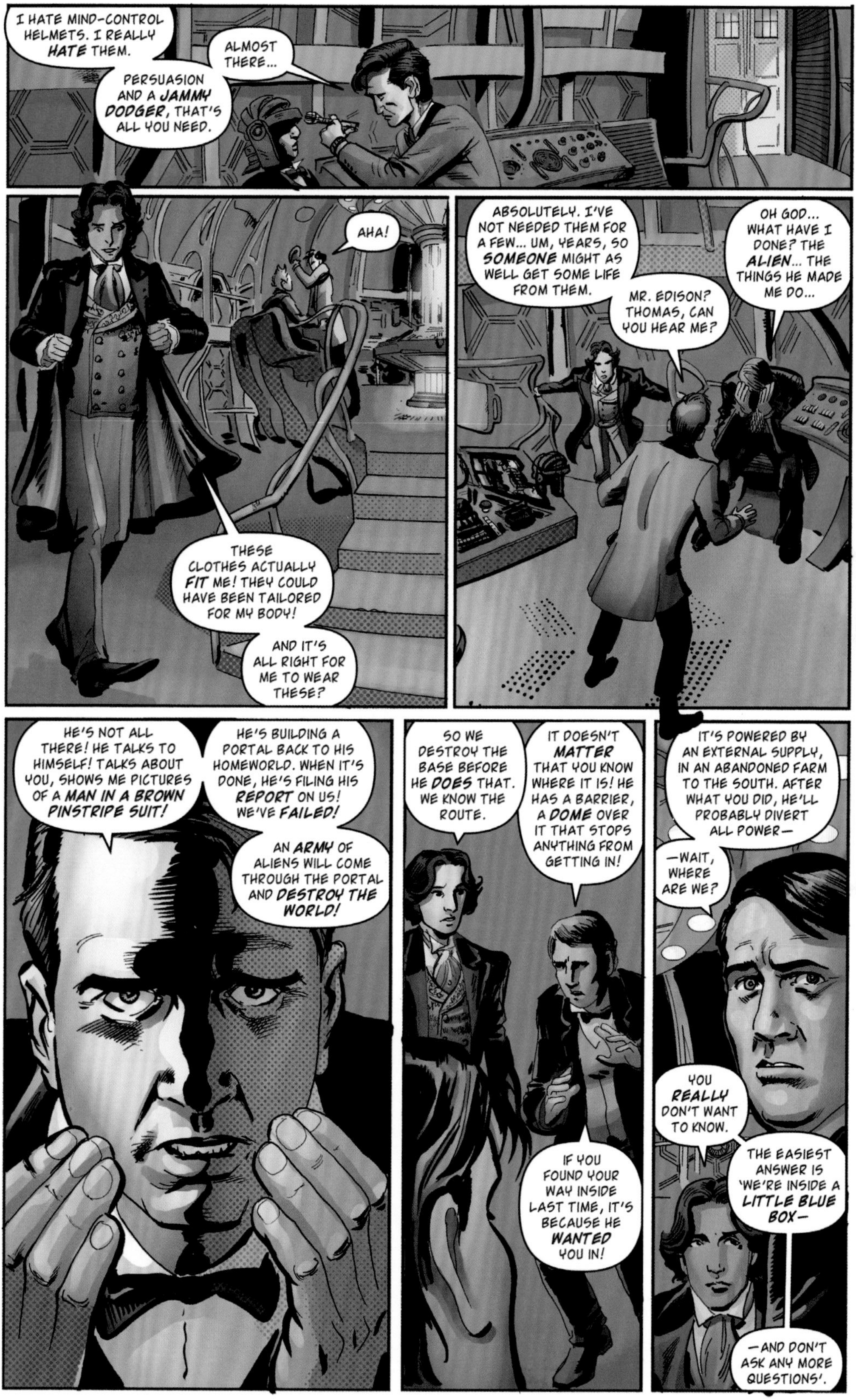
I HATE MIND-CONTROL HELMETS. I REALLY HATE THEM.
PERSUASION AND A JAMMY DODGER, THAT'S ALL YOU NEED.
ALMOST THERE...
AHA!
THESE CLOTHES ACTUALLY FIT ME! THEY COULD HAVE BEEN TAILORED FOR MY BODY!
AND IT'S ALL RIGHT FOR ME TO WEAR THESE?
ABSOLUTELY. I'VE NOT NEEDED THEM FOR A FEW... UM, YEARS, SO SOMEONE MIGHT AS WELL GET SOME LIFE FROM THEM.
MR. EDISON? THOMAS, CAN YOU HEAR ME?
OH GOD... WHAT HAVE I DONE? THE ALIEN... THE THINGS HE MADE ME DO...
HE'S NOT ALL THERE! HE TALKS TO HIMSELF! TALKS ABOUT YOU, SHOWS ME PICTURES OF A MAN IN A BROWN PINSTRIPE SUIT!
HE'S BUILDING A PORTAL BACK TO HIS HOMEWORLD. WHEN IT'S DONE, HE'S FILING HIS REPORT ON US! WE'VE FAILED!
AN ARMY OF ALIENS WILL COME THROUGH THE PORTAL AND DESTROY THE WORLD!
SO WE DESTROY THE BASE BEFORE HE DOES THAT. WE KNOW THE ROUTE.
IT DOESN'T MATTER THAT YOU KNOW WHERE IT IS! HE HAS A BARRIER, A DOME OVER IT THAT STOPS ANYTHING FROM GETTING IN!
IF YOU FOUND YOUR WAY INSIDE LAST TIME, IT'S BECAUSE HE WANTED YOU IN!
IT'S POWERED BY AN EXTERNAL SUPPLY, IN AN ABANDONED FARM TO THE SOUTH. AFTER WHAT YOU DID, HE'LL PROBABLY DIVERT ALL POWER—
—WAIT, WHERE ARE WE?
YOU REALLY DON'T WANT TO KNOW.
THE EASIEST ANSWER IS 'WE'RE INSIDE A LITTLE BLUE BOX—
—AND DON'T ASK ANY MORE QUESTIONS'.

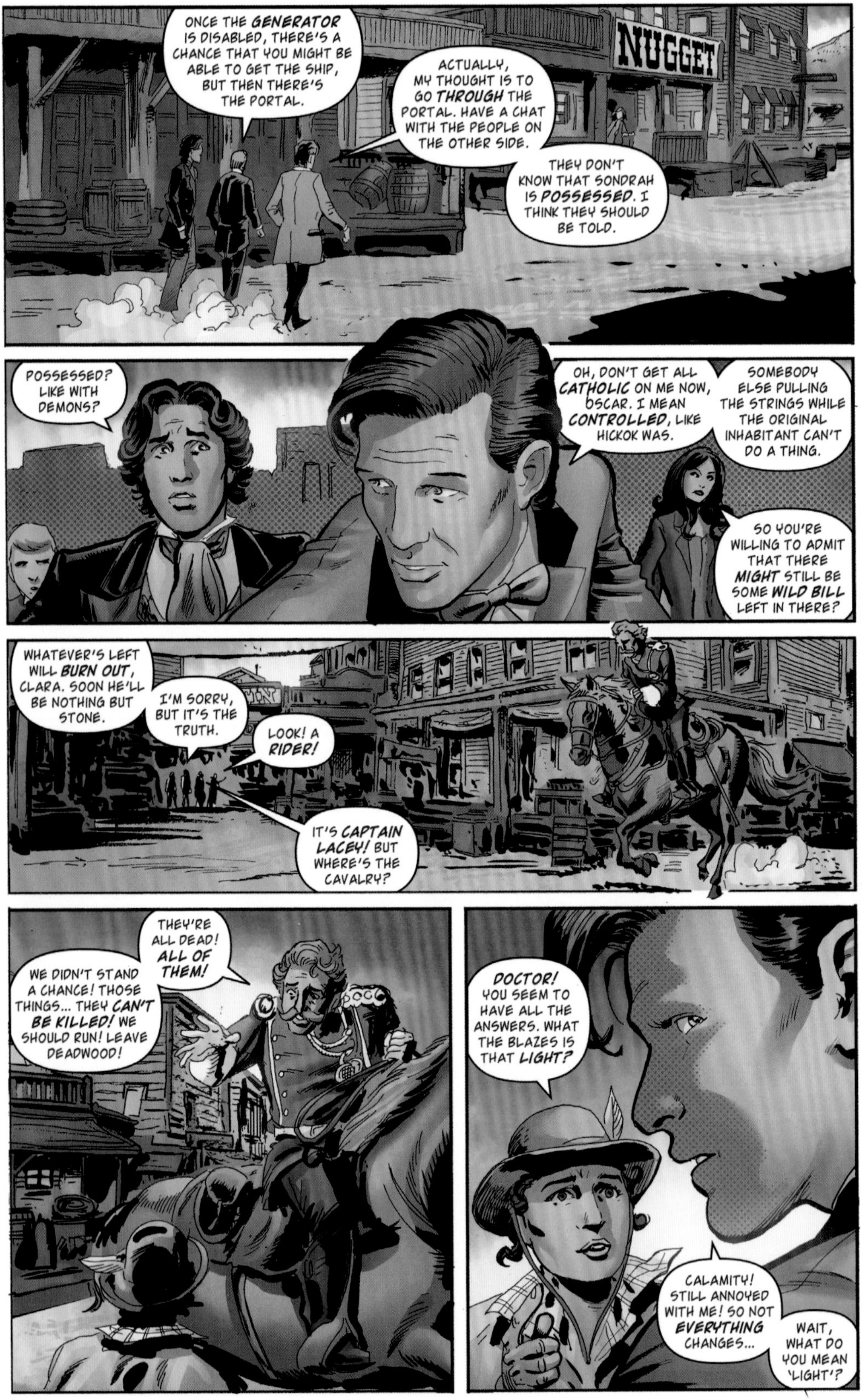
ONCE THE GENERATOR IS DISABLED, THERE'S A CHANCE THAT YOU MIGHT BE ABLE TO GET THE SHIP, BUT THEN THERE'S THE PORTAL.
ACTUALLY, MY THOUGHT IS TO GO THROUGH THE PORTAL. HAVE A CHAT WITH THE PEOPLE ON THE OTHER SIDE.
THEY DON'T KNOW THAT SONDRAH IS POSSESSED. I THINK THEY SHOULD BE TOLD.
NUGGET
POSSESSED? LIKE WITH DEMONS?
OH, DON'T GET ALL CATHOLIC ON ME NOW, OSCAR. I MEAN CONTROLLED, LIKE HICKOK WAS.
SOMEBODY ELSE PULLING THE STRINGS WHILE THE ORIGINAL INHABITANT CAN'T DO A THING.
SO YOU'RE WILLING TO ADMIT THAT THERE MIGHT STILL BE SOME WILD BILL LEFT IN THERE?
WHATEVER'S LEFT WILL BURN OUT, CLARA. SOON HE'LL BE NOTHING BUT STONE.
I'M SORRY, BUT IT'S THE TRUTH.
LOOK! A RIDER!
IT'S CAPTAIN LACEY! BUT WHERE'S THE CAVALRY?
THEY'RE ALL DEAD! ALL OF THEM!
WE DIDN'T STAND A CHANCE! THOSE THINGS... THEY CAN'T BE KILLED! WE SHOULD RUN! LEAVE DEADWOOD!
DOCTOR! YOU SEEM TO HAVE ALL THE ANSWERS. WHAT THE BLAZES IS THAT LIGHT?
CALAMITY! STILL ANNOYED WITH ME! SO NOT EVERYTHING CHANGES...
WAIT, WHAT DO YOU MEAN 'LIGHT'?

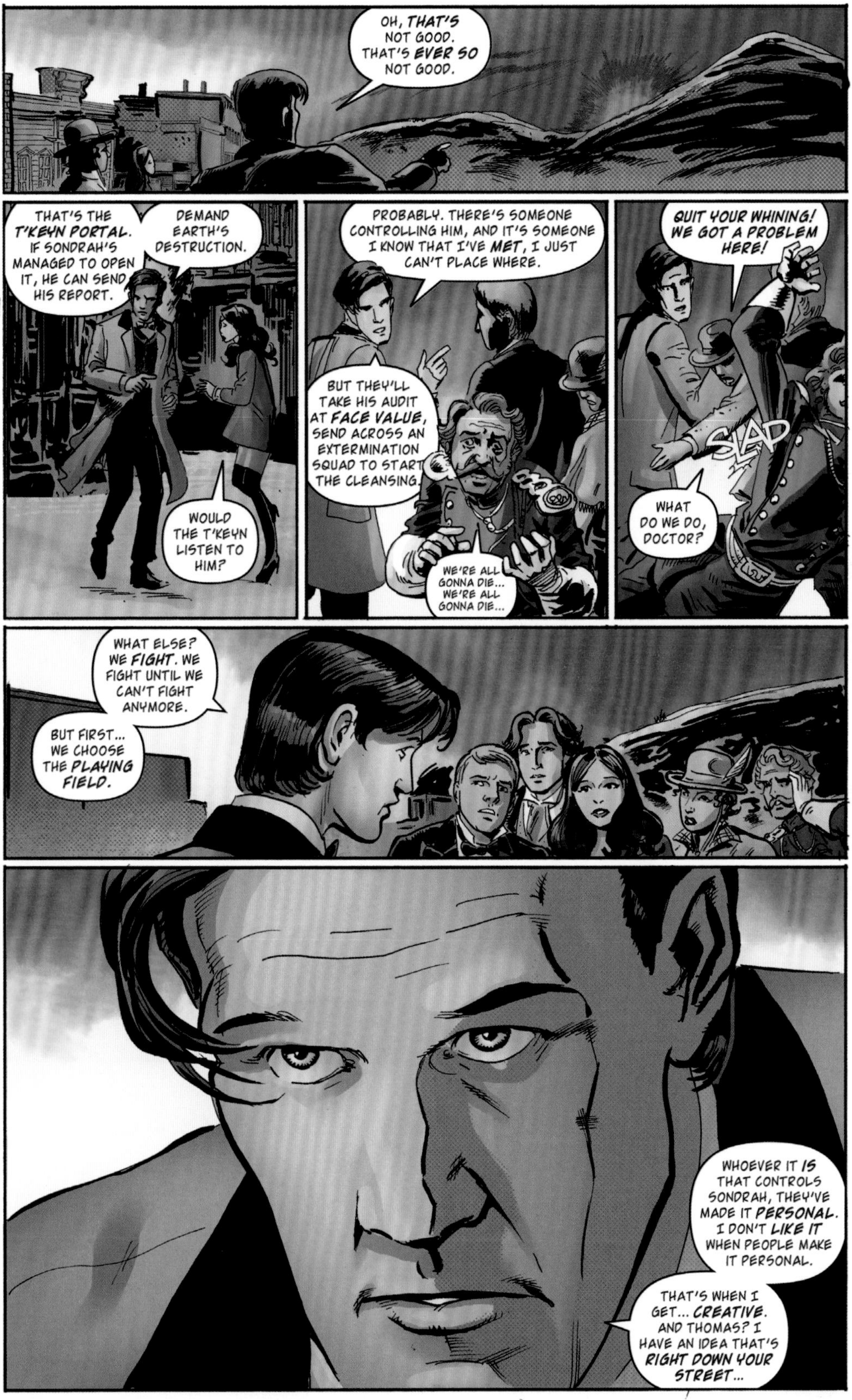

OH, THAT'S NOT GOOD. THAT'S EVER SO NOT GOOD.
THAT'S THE T'KEYN PORTAL. IF SONDRAH'S MANAGED TO OPEN IT, HE CAN SEND HIS REPORT.
DEMAND EARTH'S DESTRUCTION.
WOULD THE T'KEYN LISTEN TO HIM?
PROBABLY. THERE'S SOMEONE CONTROLLING HIM, AND IT'S SOMEONE I KNOW THAT I'VE MET, I JUST CAN'T PLACE WHERE.
BUT THEY'LL TAKE HIS AUDIT AT FACE VALUE, SEND ACROSS AN EXTERMINATION SQUAD TO START THE CLEANSING.
WE'RE ALL GONNA DIE... WE'RE ALL GONNA DIE...
QUIT YOUR WHINING! WE GOT A PROBLEM HERE!
SLAP
WHAT DO WE DO, DOCTOR?
WHAT ELSE? WE FIGHT. WE FIGHT UNTIL WE CAN'T FIGHT ANYMORE.
BUT FIRST... WE CHOOSE THE PLAYING FIELD.
WHOEVER IT IS THAT CONTROLS SONDRAH, THEY'VE MADE IT PERSONAL. I DON'T LIKE IT WHEN PEOPLE MAKE IT PERSONAL.
THAT'S WHEN I GET... CREATIVE. AND THOMAS? I HAVE AN IDEA THAT'S RIGHT DOWN YOUR STREET...

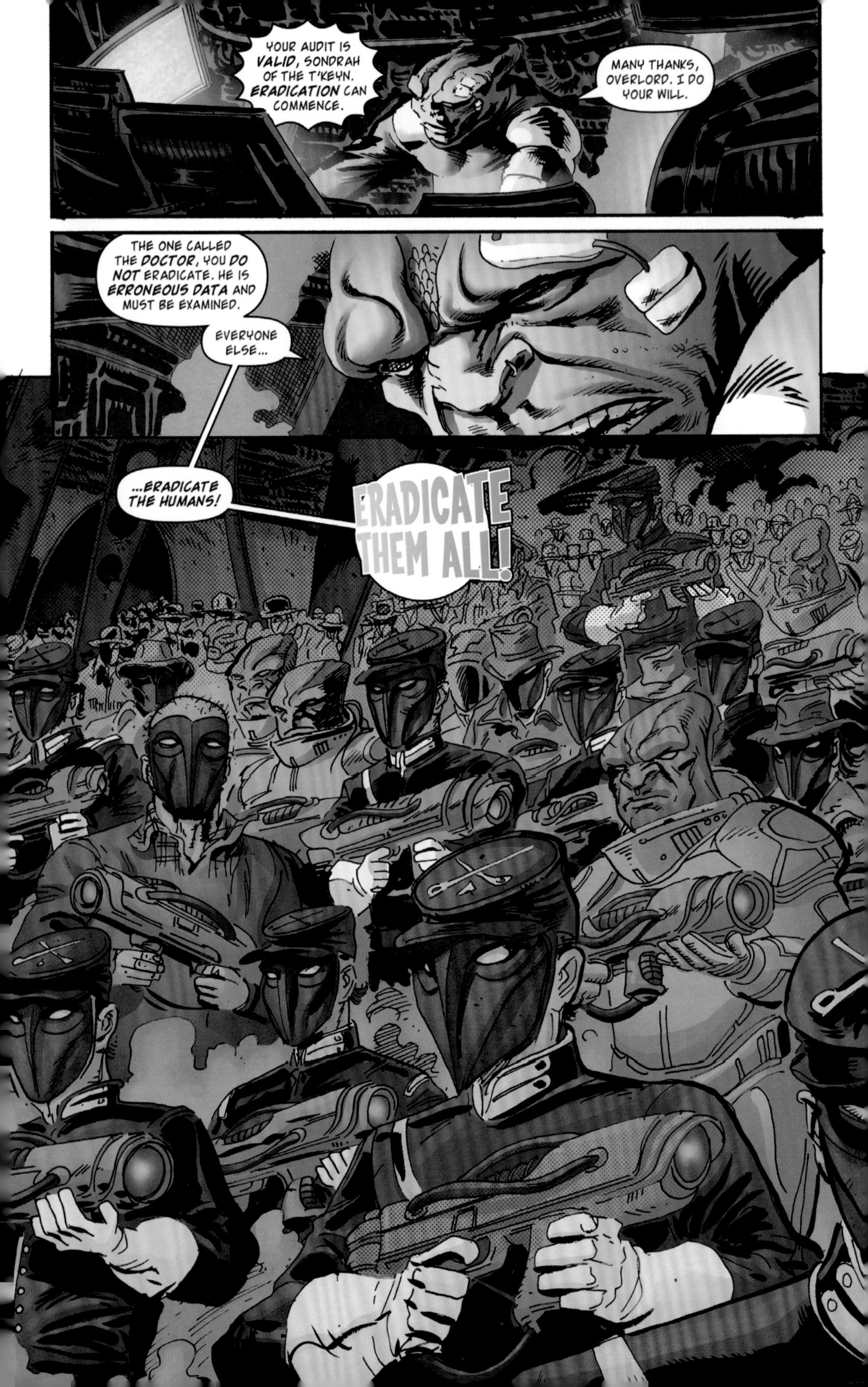
YOUR AUDIT IS VALID, SONDRAH OF THE T'KEYN. ERADICATION CAN COMMENCE.
MANY THANKS, OVERLORD. I DO YOUR WILL.
THE ONE CALLED THE DOCTOR, YOU DO NOT ERADICATE. HE IS ERRONEOUS DATA AND MUST BE EXAMINED.
EVERYONE ELSE...
...ERADICATE THE HUMANS!
ERADICATE THEM ALL!

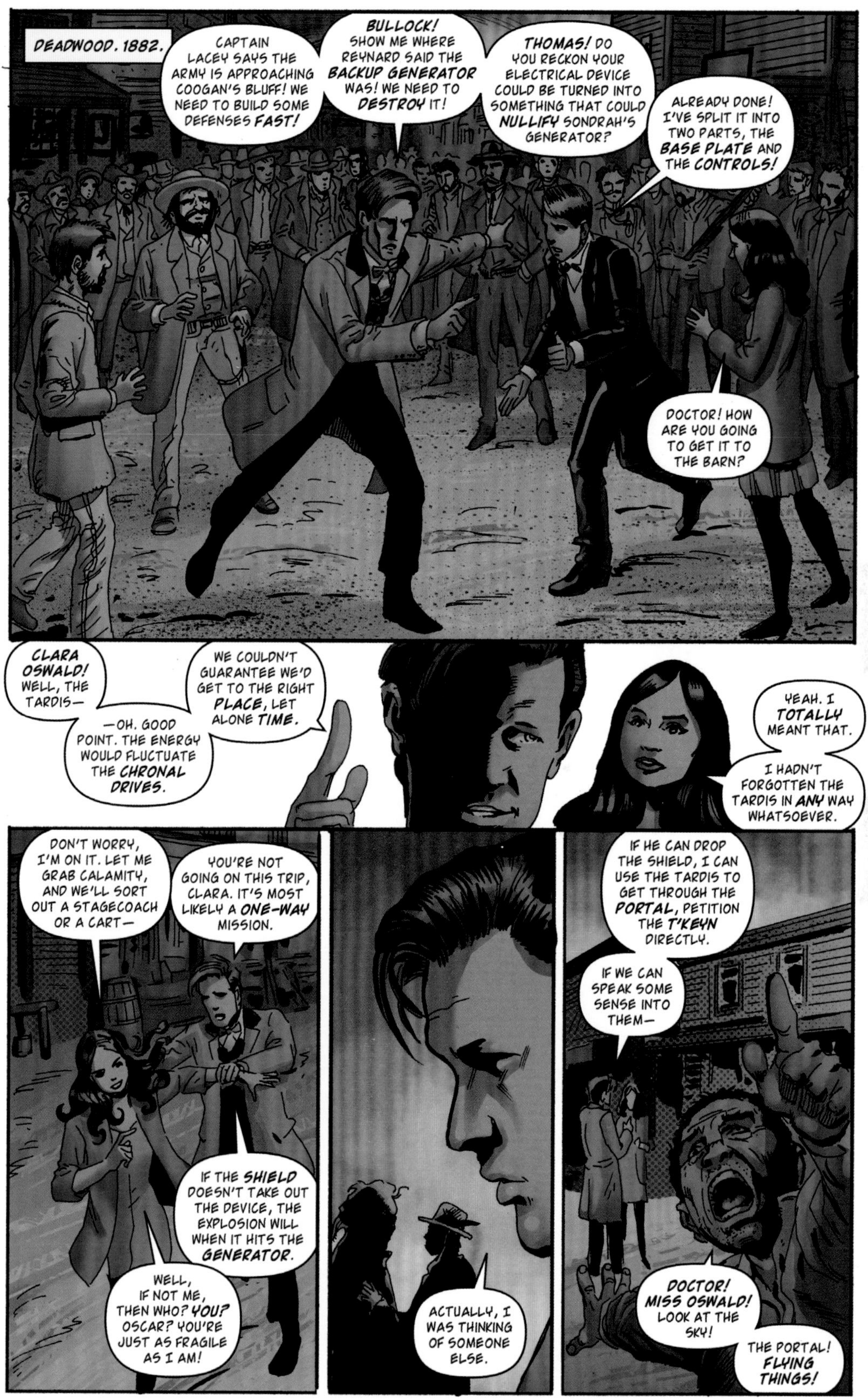

DEADWOOD. 1882.
CAPTAIN LACEY SAYS THE ARMY IS APPROACHING COOGAN'S BLUFF! WE NEED TO BUILD SOME DEFENSES FAST!
BULLOCK! SHOW ME WHERE REYNARD SAID THE BACKUP GENERATOR WAS! WE NEED TO DESTROY IT!
THOMAS! DO YOU RECKON YOUR ELECTRICAL DEVICE COULD BE TURNED INTO SOMETHING THAT COULD NULLIFY SONDRAH'S GENERATOR?
ALREADY DONE! I'VE SPLIT IT INTO TWO PARTS, THE BASE PLATE AND THE CONTROLS!
DOCTOR! HOW ARE YOU GOING TO GET IT TO THE BARN?
CLARA OSWALD! WELL, THE TARDIS—
—OH. GOOD POINT. THE ENERGY WOULD FLUCTUATE THE CHRONAL DRIVES.
WE COULDN'T GUARANTEE WE'D GET TO THE RIGHT PLACE, LET ALONE TIME.
YEAH. I TOTALLY MEANT THAT.
I HADN'T FORGOTTEN THE TARDIS IN ANY WAY WHATSOEVER.
DON'T WORRY, I'M ON IT. LET ME GRAB CALAMITY, AND WE'LL SORT OUT A STAGECOACH OR A CART—
YOU'RE NOT GOING ON THIS TRIP, CLARA. IT'S MOST LIKELY A ONE-WAY MISSION.
IF THE SHIELD DOESN'T TAKE OUT THE DEVICE, THE EXPLOSION WILL WHEN IT HITS THE GENERATOR.
WELL, IF NOT ME, THEN WHO? YOU? OSCAR? YOU'RE JUST AS FRAGILE AS I AM!
ACTUALLY, I WAS THINKING OF SOMEONE ELSE.
IF HE CAN DROP THE SHIELD, I CAN USE THE TARDIS TO GET THROUGH THE PORTAL, PETITION THE T'KEYN DIRECTLY.
IF WE CAN SPEAK SOME SENSE INTO THEM—
DOCTOR! MISS OSWALD! LOOK AT THE SKY!
THE PORTAL! FLYING THINGS!

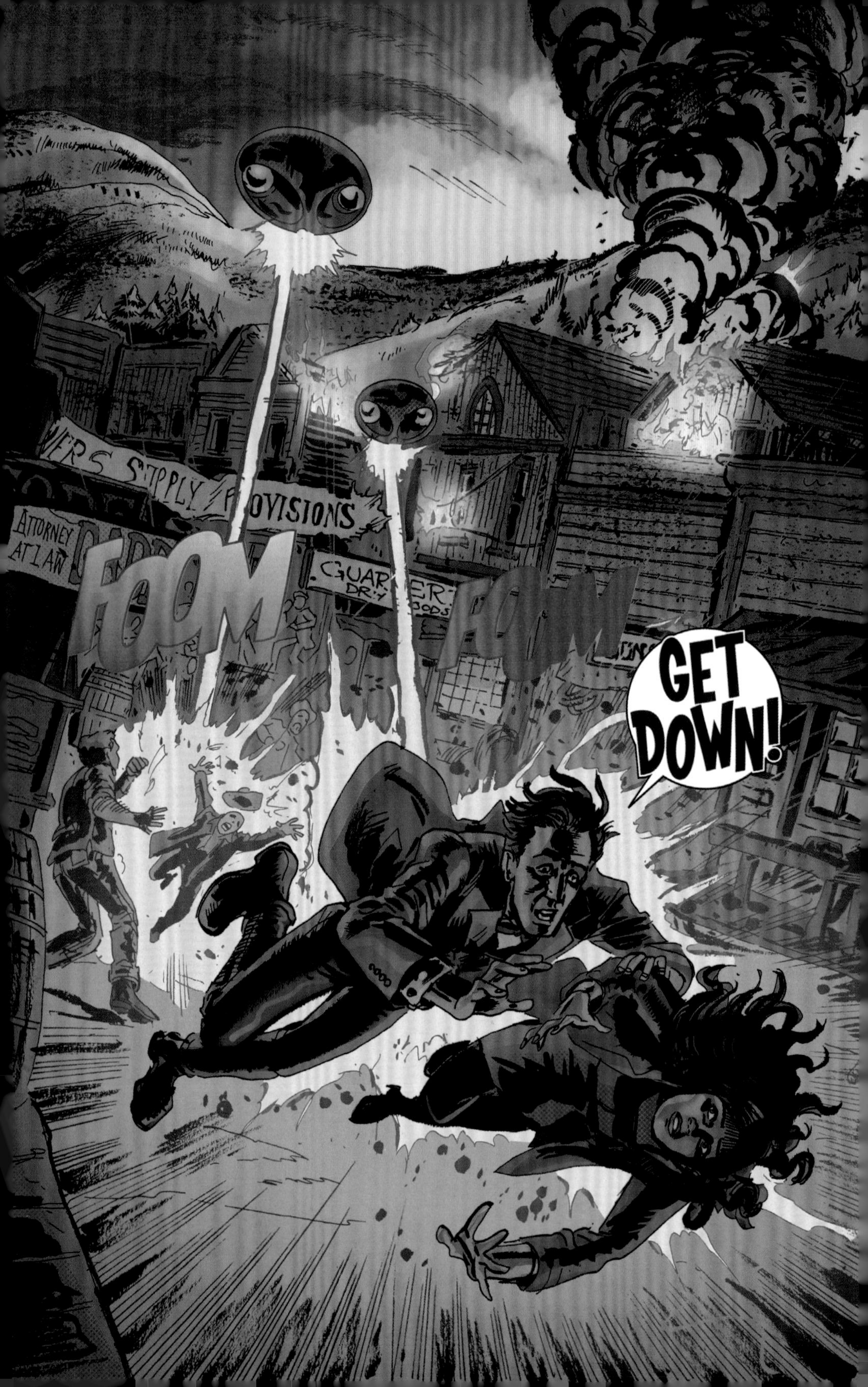
ATTORNEY AT LAW
FOOM
FOOM
GET DOWN!

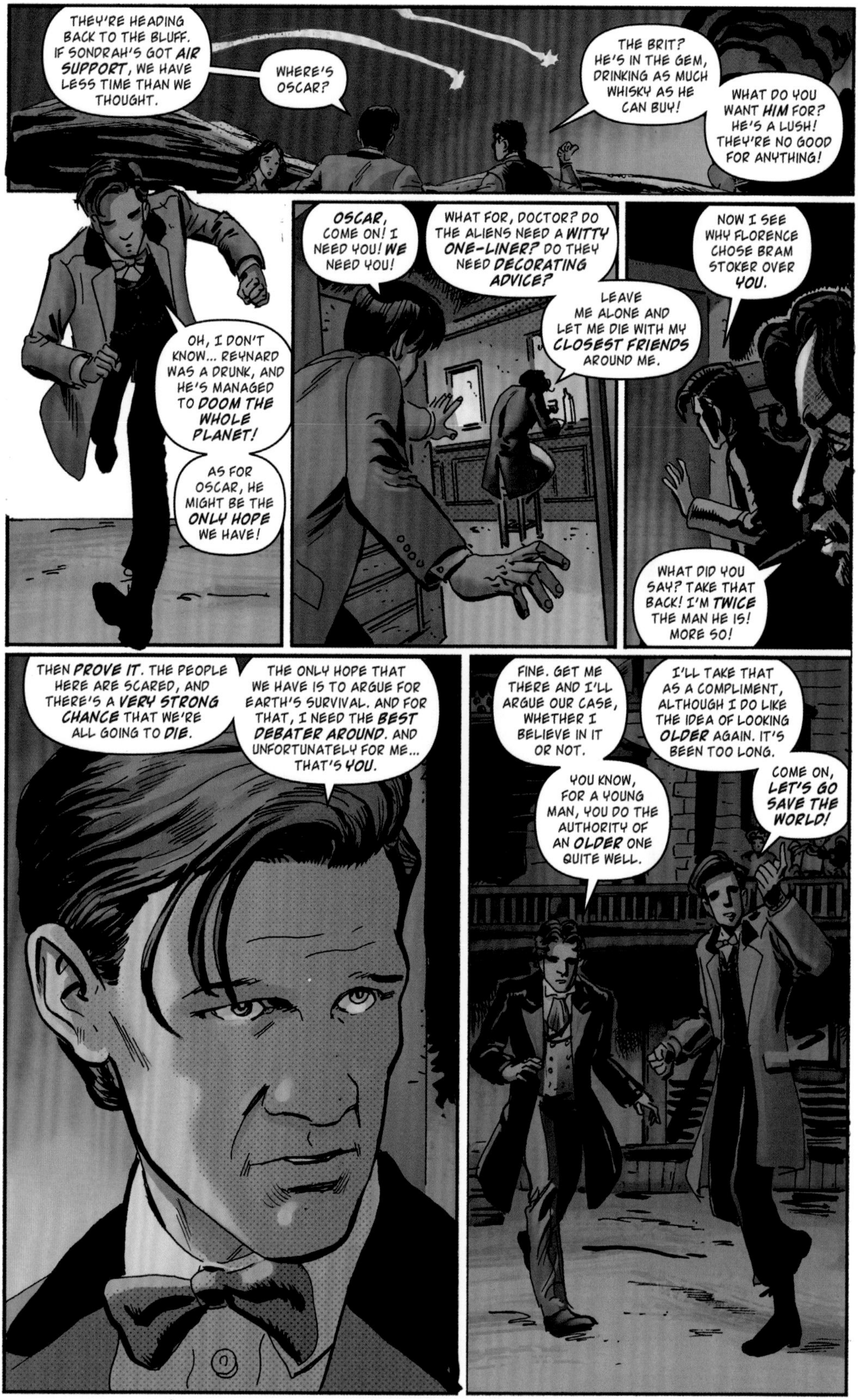
THEY'RE HEADING BACK TO THE BLUFF. IF SONDRAH'S GOT AIR SUPPORT, WE HAVE LESS TIME THAN WE THOUGHT.
WHERE'S OSCAR?
THE BRIT? HE'S IN THE GEM, DRINKING AS MUCH WHISKY AS HE CAN BUY!
WHAT DO YOU WANT HIM FOR? HE'S A LUSH! THEY'RE NO GOOD FOR ANYTHING!
OH, I DON'T KNOW... REYNARD WAS A DRUNK, AND HE'S MANAGED TO DOOM THE WHOLE PLANET!
AS FOR OSCAR, HE MIGHT BE THE ONLY HOPE WE HAVE!
OSCAR, COME ON! I NEED YOU! WE NEED YOU!
WHAT FOR, DOCTOR? DO THE ALIENS NEED A WITTY ONE-LINER? DO THEY NEED DECORATING ADVICE?
LEAVE ME ALONE AND LET ME DIE WITH MY CLOSEST FRIENDS AROUND ME.
NOW I SEE WHY FLORENCE CHOSE BRAM STOKER OVER YOU.
WHAT DID YOU SAY? TAKE THAT BACK! I'M TWICE THE MAN HE IS! MORE SO!
THEN PROVE IT. THE PEOPLE HERE ARE SCARED, AND THERE'S A VERY STRONG CHANCE THAT WE'RE ALL GOING TO DIE.
THE ONLY HOPE THAT WE HAVE IS TO ARGUE FOR EARTH'S SURVIVAL. AND FOR THAT, I NEED THE BEST DEBATER AROUND. AND UNFORTUNATELY FOR ME... THAT'S YOU.
FINE. GET ME THERE AND I'LL ARGUE OUR CASE, WHETHER I BELIEVE IN IT OR NOT.
YOU KNOW, FOR A YOUNG MAN, YOU DO THE AUTHORITY OF AN OLDER ONE QUITE WELL.
I'LL TAKE THAT AS A COMPLIMENT, ALTHOUGH I DO LIKE THE IDEA OF LOOKING OLDER AGAIN. IT'S BEEN TOO LONG.
COME ON, LET'S GO SAVE THE WORLD!

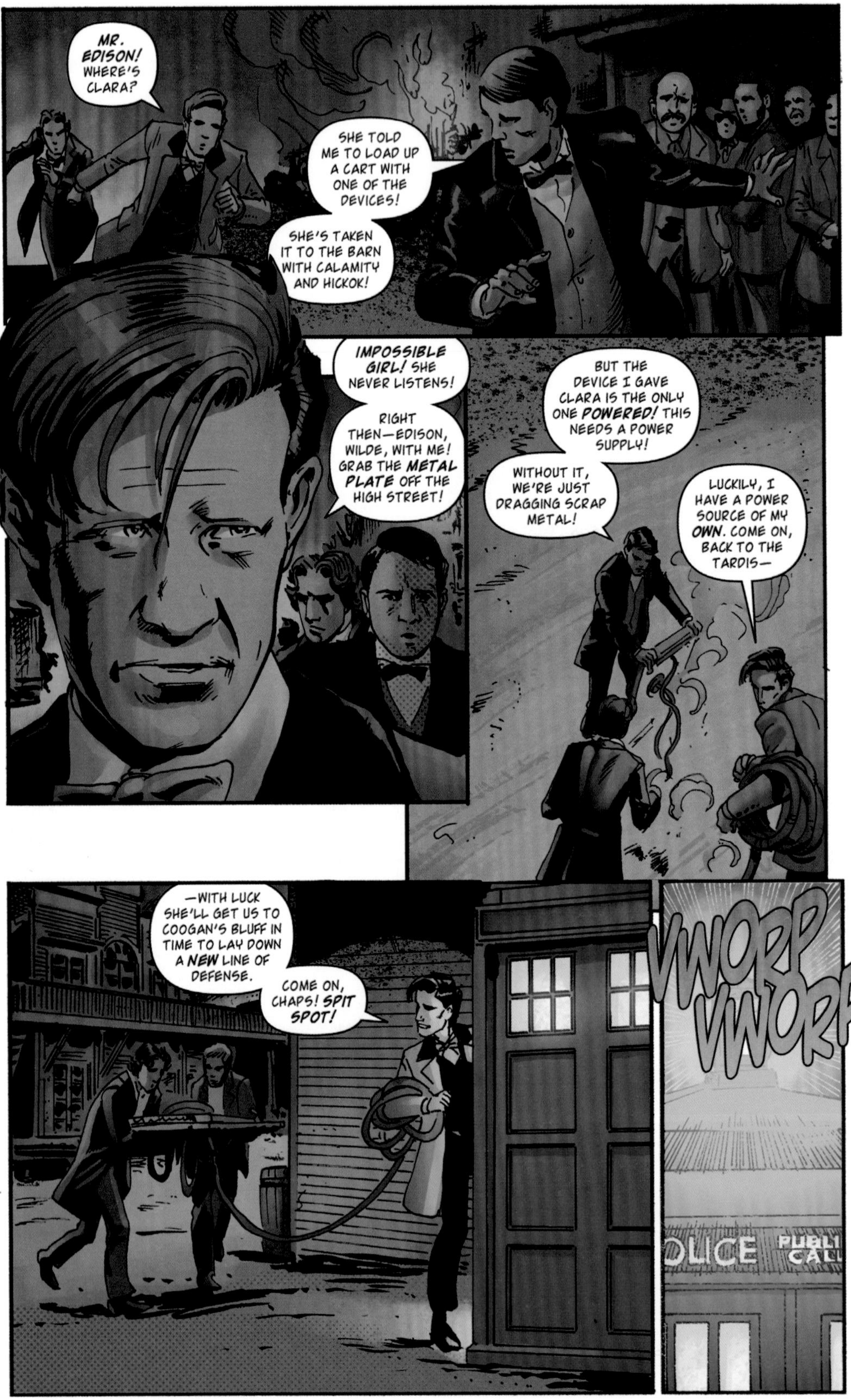

MR. EDISON! WHERE'S CLARA?
SHE TOLD ME TO LOAD UP A CART WITH ONE OF THE DEVICES!
SHE'S TAKEN IT TO THE BARN WITH CALAMITY AND HICKOK!
IMPOSSIBLE GIRL! SHE NEVER LISTENS!
RIGHT THEN—EDISON, WILDE, WITH ME! GRAB THE METAL PLATE OFF THE HIGH STREET!
BUT THE DEVICE I GAVE CLARA IS THE ONLY ONE POWERED! THIS NEEDS A POWER SUPPLY!
WITHOUT IT, WE'RE JUST DRAGGING SCRAP METAL!
LUCKILY, I HAVE A POWER SOURCE OF MY OWN. COME ON, BACK TO THE TARDIS—
—WITH LUCK SHE'LL GET US TO COOGAN'S BLUFF IN TIME TO LAY DOWN A NEW LINE OF DEFENSE.
COME ON, CHAPS! SPIT SPOT!
VWORP VWORP

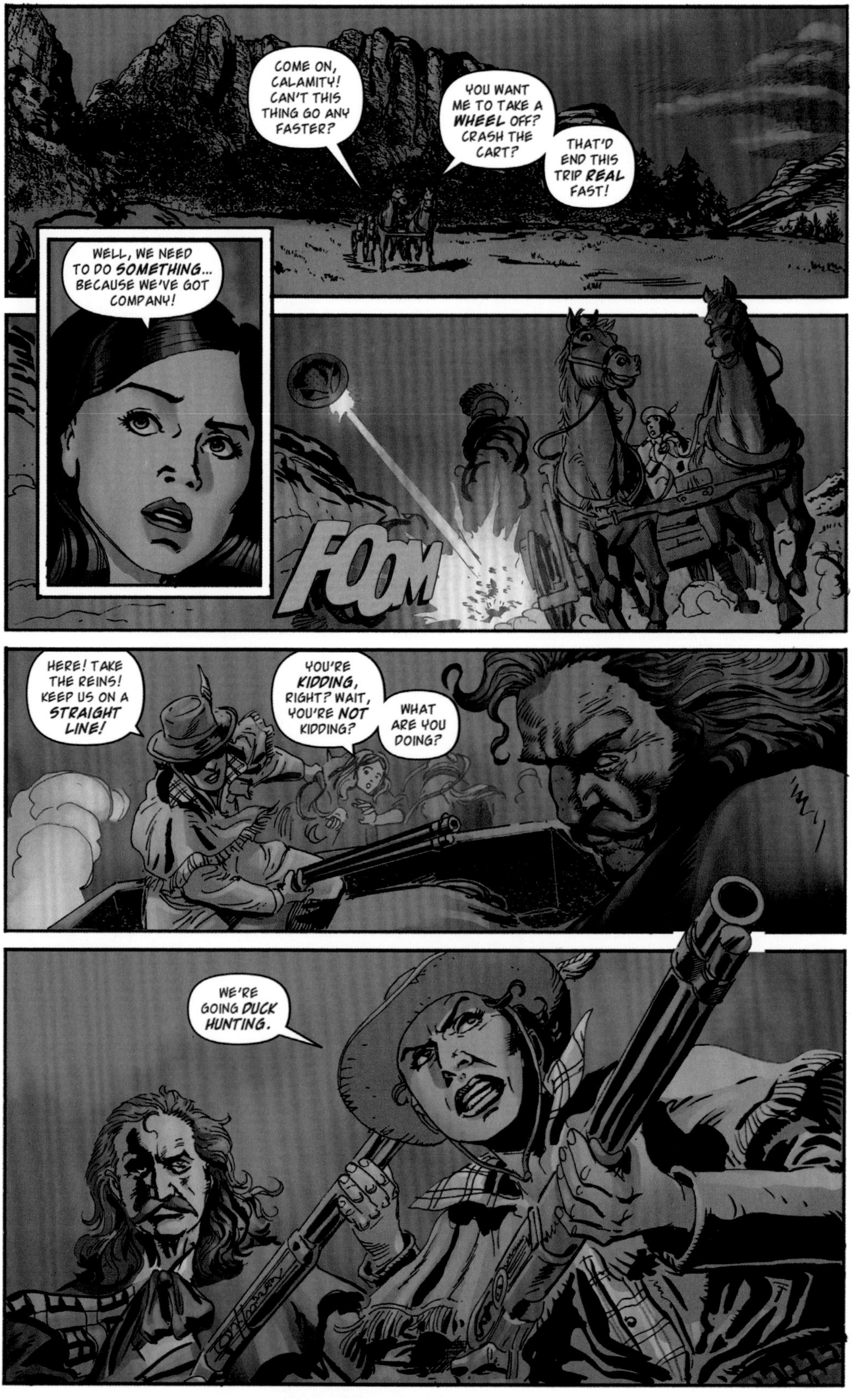
COME ON, CALAMITY! CAN'T THIS THING GO ANY FASTER?
YOU WANT ME TO TAKE A **WHEEL** OFF? CRASH THE CART?
THAT'D END THIS TRIP **REAL** FAST!
WELL, WE NEED TO DO **SOMETHING**... BECAUSE WE'VE GOT COMPANY!
FOOM
HERE! TAKE THE REINS! KEEP US ON A **STRAIGHT LINE!**
YOU'RE **KIDDING**, RIGHT? WAIT, YOU'RE **NOT** KIDDING?
WHAT ARE YOU DOING?
WE'RE GOING **DUCK HUNTING.**

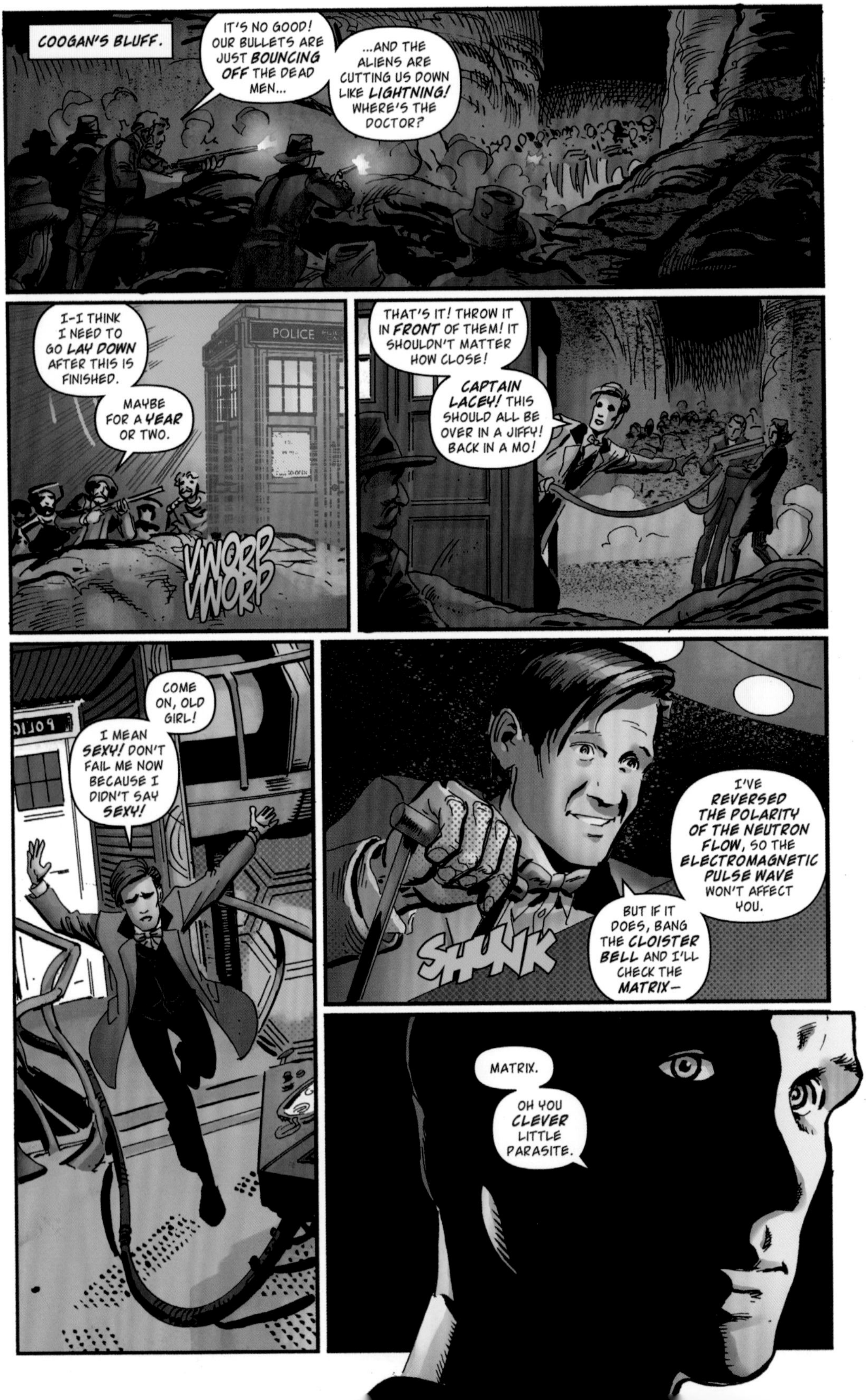

COOGAN'S BLUFF.
IT'S NO GOOD! OUR BULLETS ARE JUST BOUNCING OFF THE DEAD MEN...
...AND THE ALIENS ARE CUTTING US DOWN LIKE LIGHTNING! WHERE'S THE DOCTOR?
I-I THINK I NEED TO GO LAY DOWN AFTER THIS IS FINISHED.
MAYBE FOR A YEAR OR TWO.
POLICE
VWORP VWORP
THAT'S IT! THROW IT IN FRONT OF THEM! IT SHOULDN'T MATTER HOW CLOSE!
CAPTAIN LACEY! THIS SHOULD ALL BE OVER IN A JIFFY! BACK IN A MO!
COME ON, OLD GIRL!
I MEAN SEXY! DON'T FAIL ME NOW BECAUSE I DIDN'T SAY SEXY!
I'VE REVERSED THE POLARITY OF THE NEUTRON FLOW, SO THE ELECTROMAGNETIC PULSE WAVE WON'T AFFECT YOU.
BUT IF IT DOES, BANG THE CLOISTER BELL AND I'LL CHECK THE MATRIX—
SHUNK
MATRIX.
OH YOU CLEVER LITTLE PARASITE.

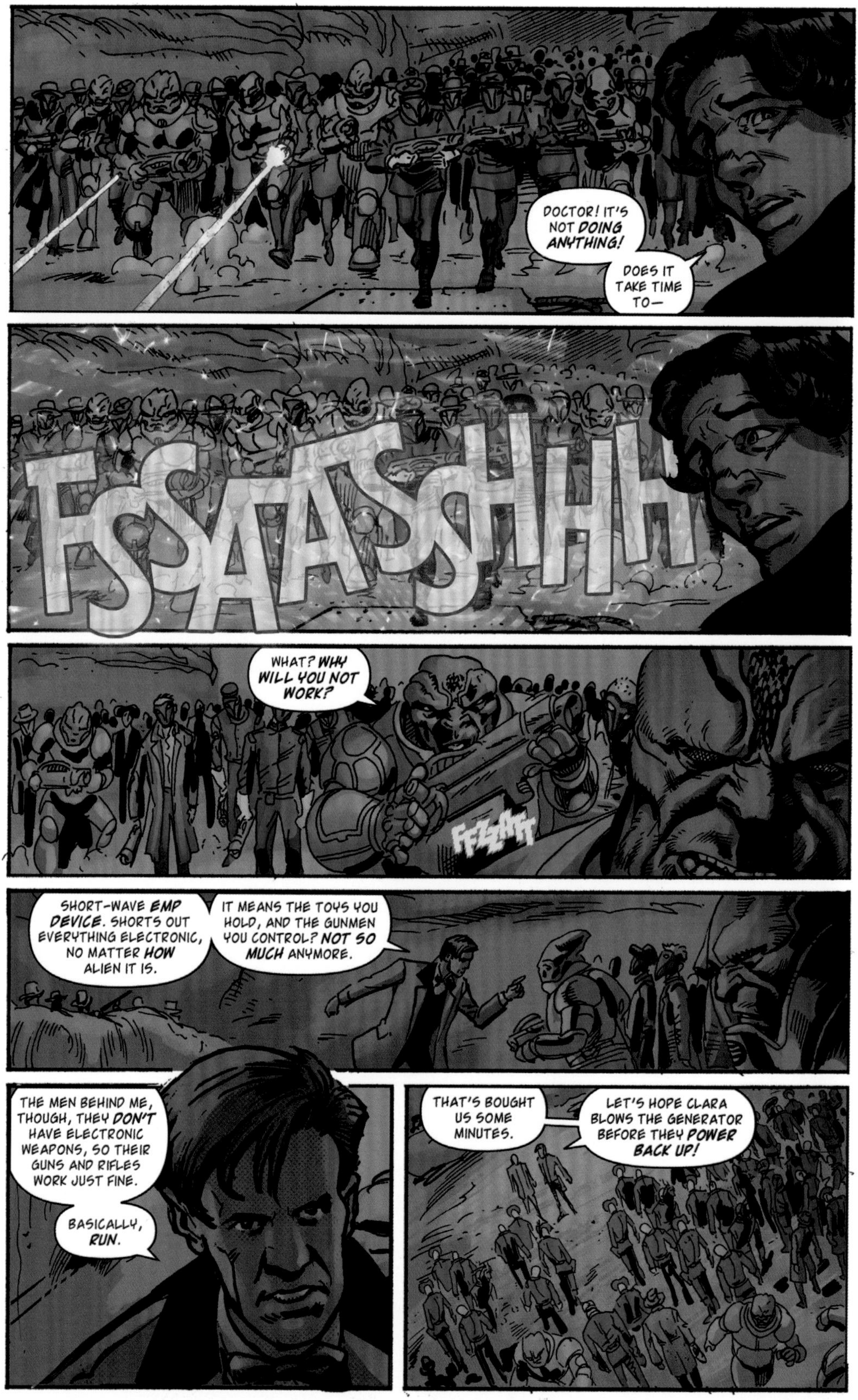
DOCTOR! IT'S NOT DOING ANYTHING!
DOES IT TAKE TIME TO—
FSSASHHH
WHAT? WHY WILL YOU NOT WORK?
FFZZAPT
SHORT-WAVE EMP DEVICE. SHORTS OUT EVERYTHING ELECTRONIC, NO MATTER HOW ALIEN IT IS.
IT MEANS THE TOYS YOU HOLD, AND THE GUNMEN YOU CONTROL? NOT SO MUCH ANYMORE.
THE MEN BEHIND ME, THOUGH, THEY DON'T HAVE ELECTRONIC WEAPONS, SO THEIR GUNS AND RIFLES WORK JUST FINE.
BASICALLY, RUN.
THAT'S BOUGHT US SOME MINUTES.
LET'S HOPE CLARA BLOWS THE GENERATOR BEFORE THEY POWER BACK UP!

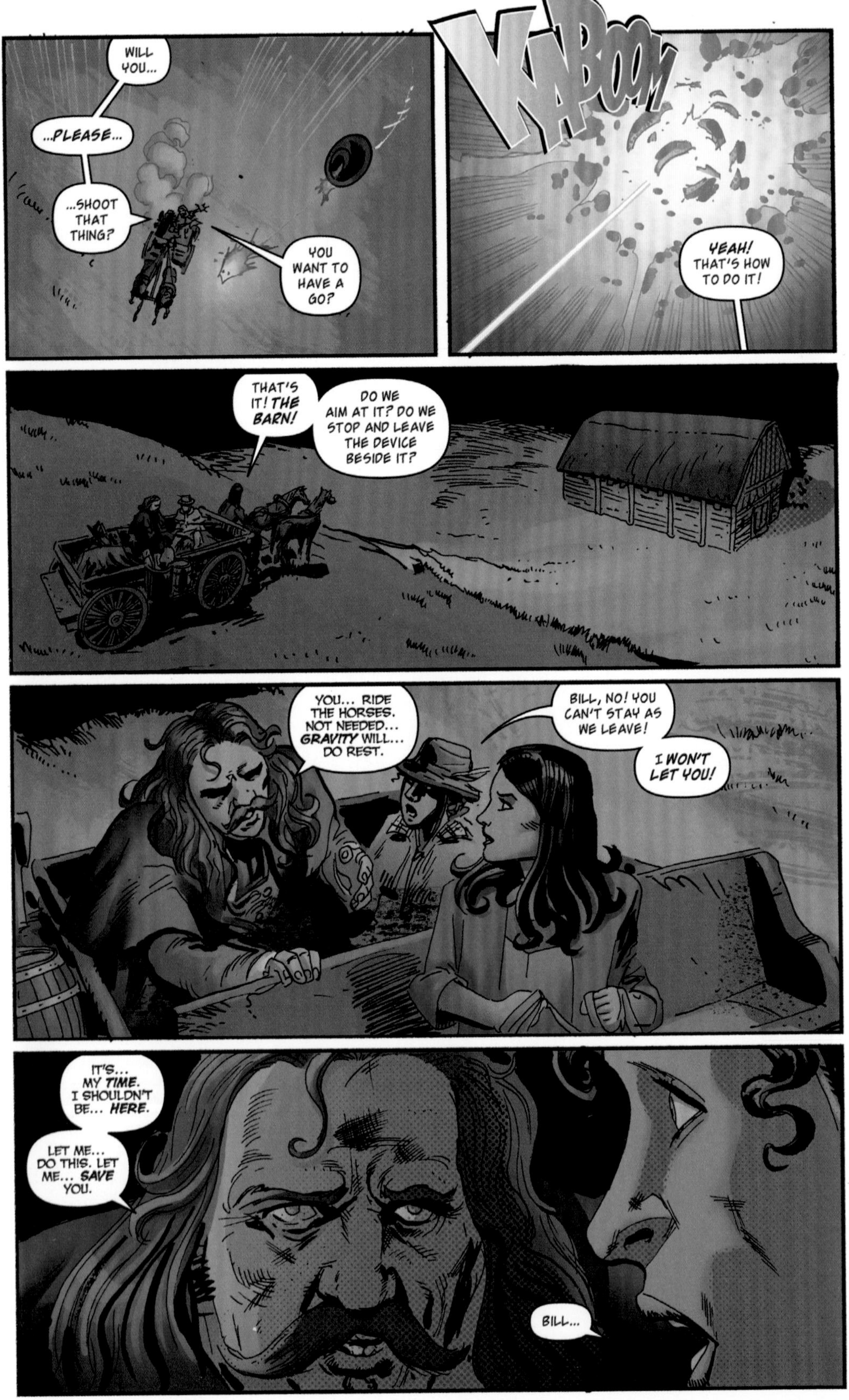
WILL YOU...
...PLEASE...
...SHOOT THAT THING?
YOU WANT TO HAVE A GO?
KABOOM
YEAH! THAT'S HOW TO DO IT!
THAT'S IT! THE BARN!
DO WE AIM AT IT? DO WE STOP AND LEAVE THE DEVICE BESIDE IT?
YOU... RIDE THE HORSES. NOT NEEDED... GRAVITY WILL... DO REST.
BILL, NO! YOU CAN'T STAY AS WE LEAVE!
I WON'T LET YOU!
IT'S... MY TIME. I SHOULDN'T BE... HERE.
LET ME... DO THIS. LET ME... SAVE YOU.
BILL...

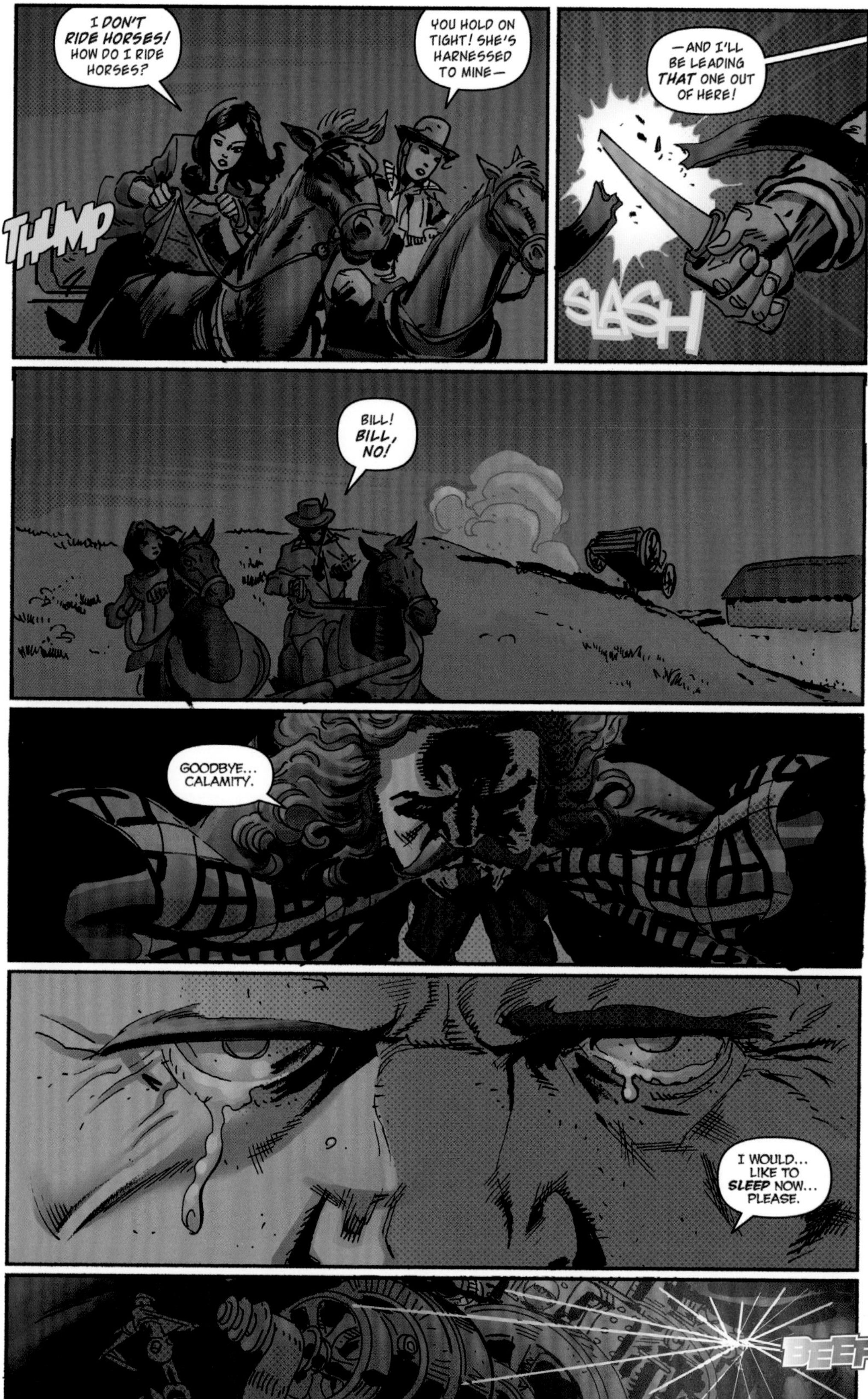
I DON'T RIDE HORSES! HOW DO I RIDE HORSES?
YOU HOLD ON TIGHT! SHE'S HARNESSED TO MINE—
THUMP
—AND I'LL BE LEADING THAT ONE OUT OF HERE!
SLASH
BILL! BILL, NO!
GOODBYE... CALAMITY.
I WOULD... LIKE TO SLEEP NOW... PLEASE.
BEEP

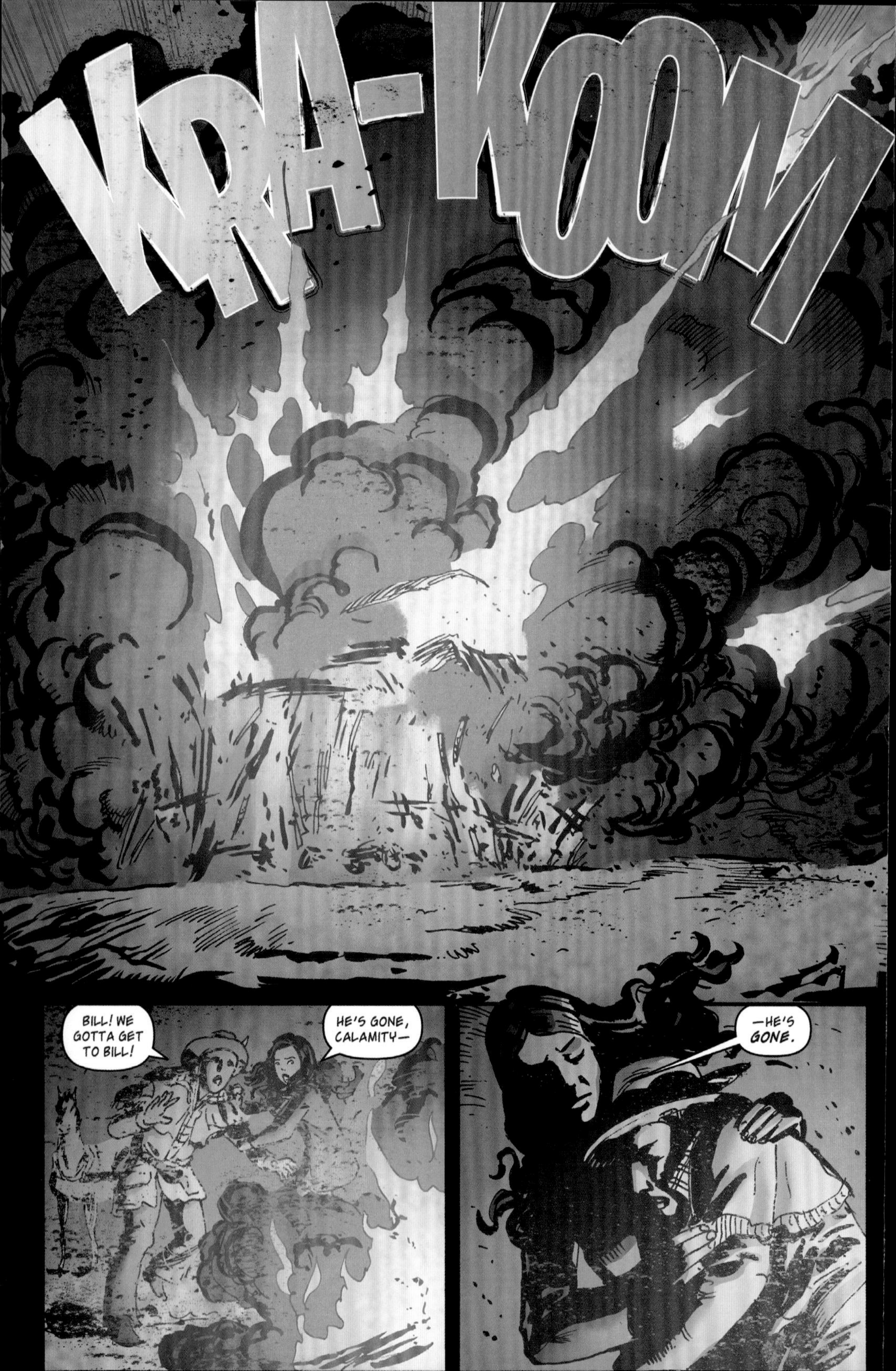
KRA-KOOM
BILL! WE GOTTA GET TO BILL!
HE'S GONE, CALAMITY—
—HE'S GONE.

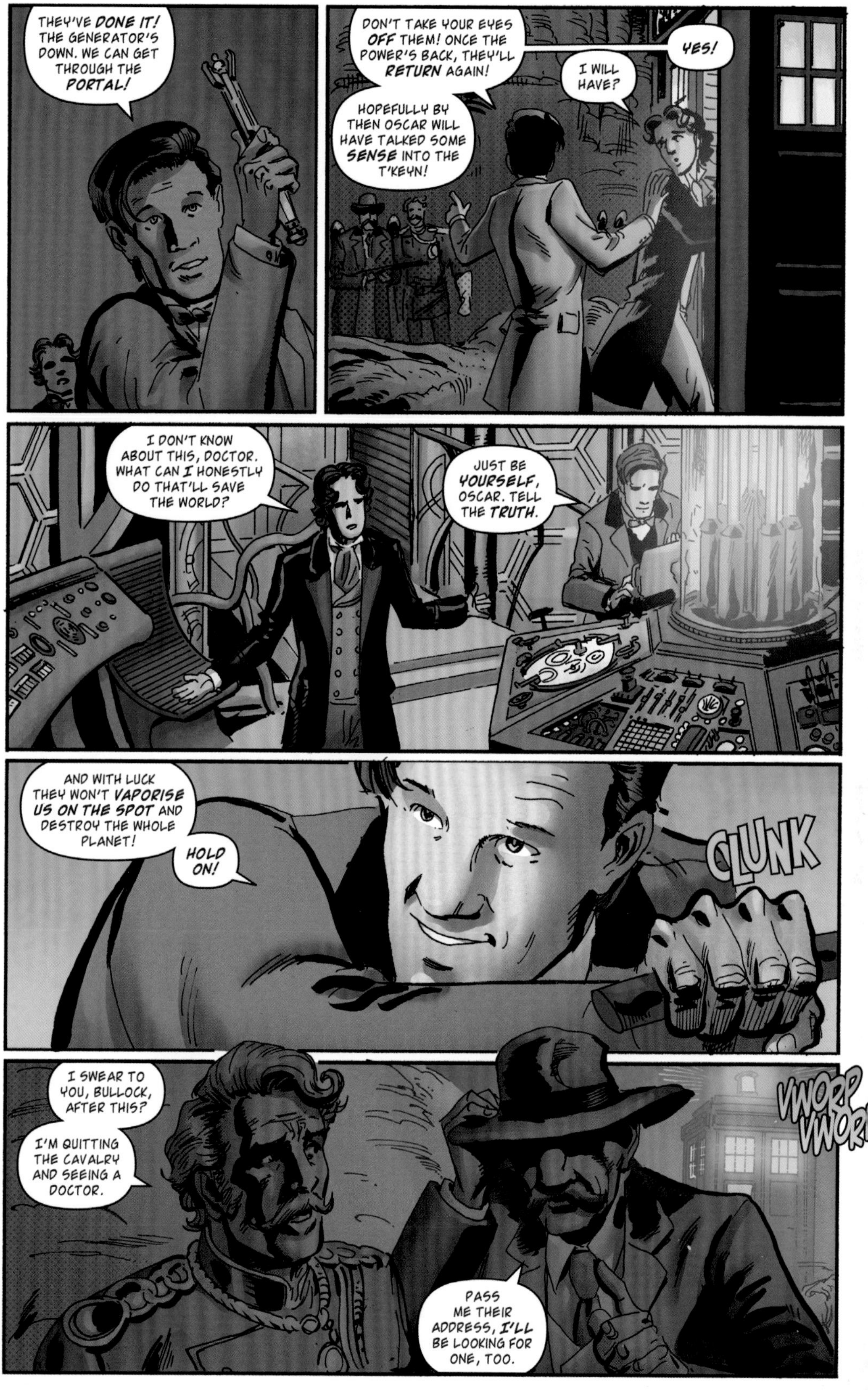
THEY'VE DONE IT! THE GENERATOR'S DOWN. WE CAN GET THROUGH THE PORTAL!
DON'T TAKE YOUR EYES OFF THEM! ONCE THE POWER'S BACK, THEY'LL RETURN AGAIN!
YES!
HOPEFULLY BY THEN OSCAR WILL HAVE TALKED SOME SENSE INTO THE T'KEYN!
I WILL HAVE?
I DON'T KNOW ABOUT THIS, DOCTOR. WHAT CAN I HONESTLY DO THAT'LL SAVE THE WORLD?
JUST BE YOURSELF, OSCAR. TELL THE TRUTH.
AND WITH LUCK THEY WON'T VAPORISE US ON THE SPOT AND DESTROY THE WHOLE PLANET!
HOLD ON!
CLUNK
I SWEAR TO YOU, BULLOCK, AFTER THIS?
I'M QUITTING THE CAVALRY AND SEEING A DOCTOR.
PASS ME THEIR ADDRESS, I'LL BE LOOKING FOR ONE, TOO.

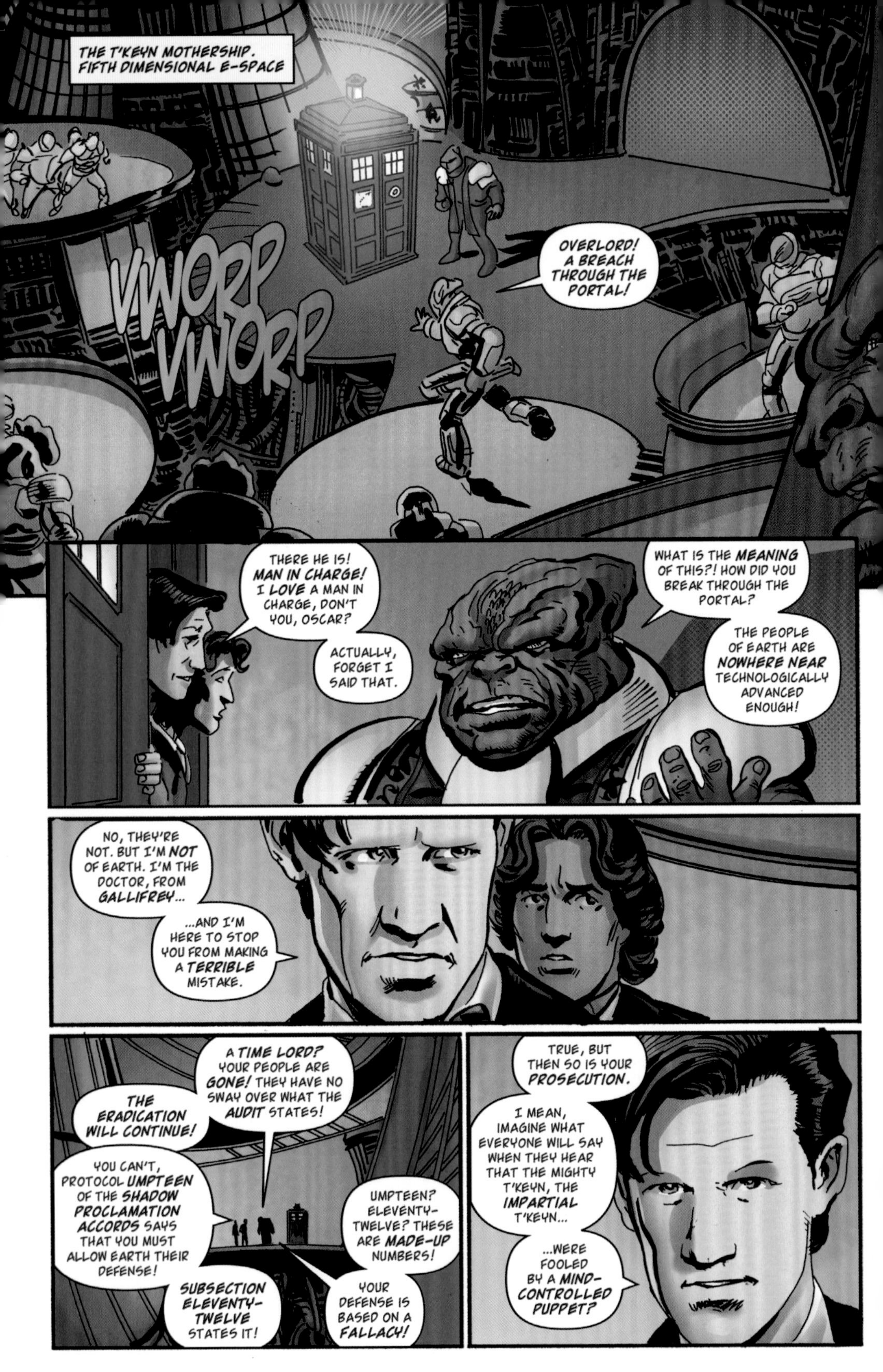
THE T'KEYN MOTHERSHIP. FIFTH DIMENSIONAL E-SPACE
VWORP VWORP
OVERLORD! A BREACH THROUGH THE PORTAL!
THERE HE IS! MAN IN CHARGE! I LOVE A MAN IN CHARGE, DON'T YOU, OSCAR?
ACTUALLY, FORGET I SAID THAT.
WHAT IS THE MEANING OF THIS?! HOW DID YOU BREAK THROUGH THE PORTAL?
THE PEOPLE OF EARTH ARE NOWHERE NEAR TECHNOLOGICALLY ADVANCED ENOUGH!
NO, THEY'RE NOT. BUT I'M NOT OF EARTH. I'M THE DOCTOR, FROM GALLIFREY...
...AND I'M HERE TO STOP YOU FROM MAKING A TERRIBLE MISTAKE.
A TIME LORD? YOUR PEOPLE ARE GONE! THEY HAVE NO SWAY OVER WHAT THE AUDIT STATES!
THE ERADICATION WILL CONTINUE!
YOU CAN'T, PROTOCOL UMPTEEN OF THE SHADOW PROCLAMATION ACCORDS SAYS THAT YOU MUST ALLOW EARTH THEIR DEFENSE!
SUBSECTION ELEVENTY-TWELVE STATES IT!
UMPTEEN? ELEVENTY-TWELVE? THESE ARE MADE-UP NUMBERS!
YOUR DEFENSE IS BASED ON A FALLACY!
TRUE, BUT THEN SO IS YOUR PROSECUTION.
I MEAN, IMAGINE WHAT EVERYONE WILL SAY WHEN THEY HEAR THAT THE MIGHTY T'KEYN, THE IMPARTIAL T'KEYN...
...WERE FOOLED BY A MIND-CONTROLLED PUPPET?

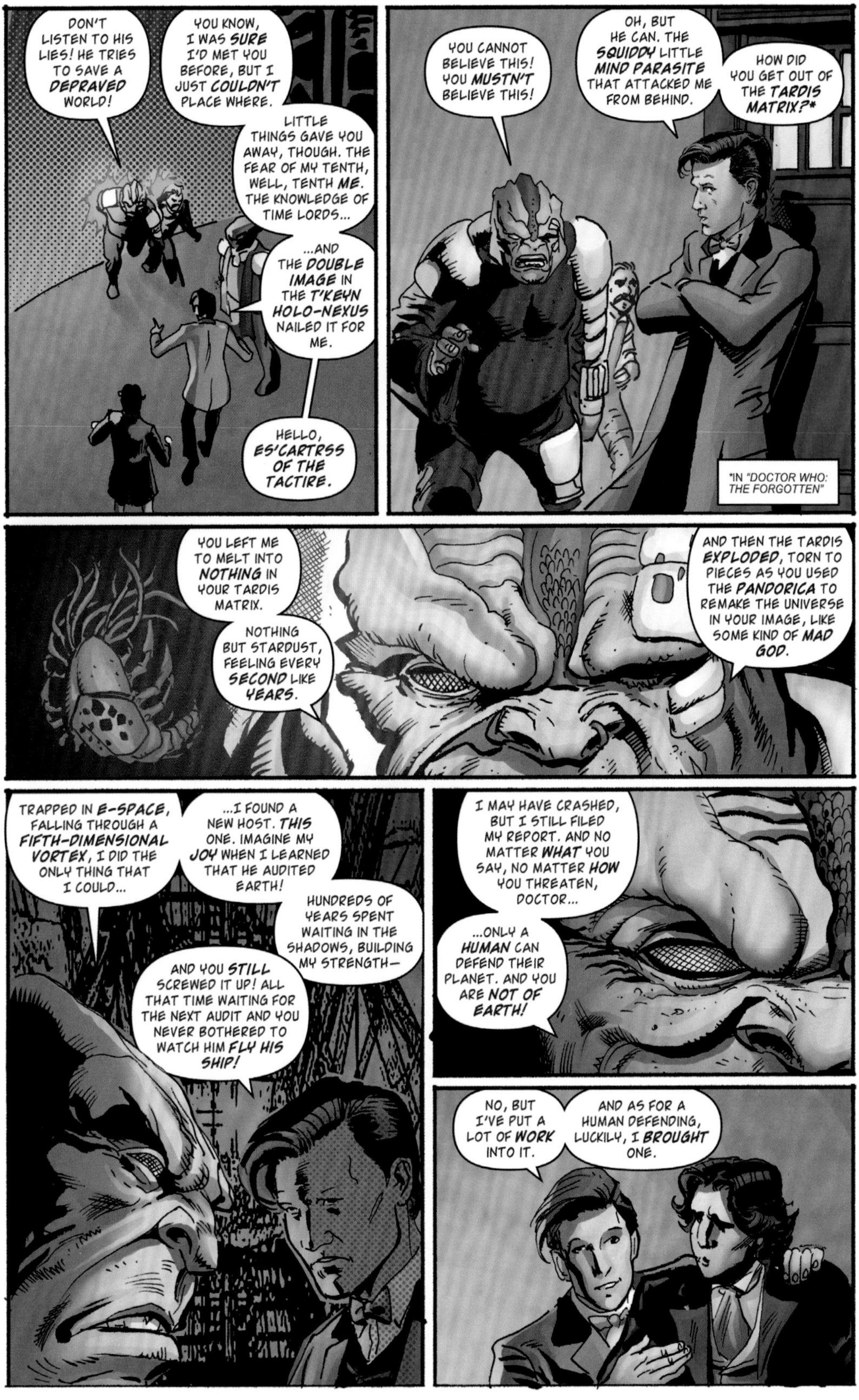
DON'T LISTEN TO HIS LIES! HE TRIES TO SAVE A DEPRAVED WORLD!
YOU KNOW, I WAS SURE I'D MET YOU BEFORE, BUT I JUST COULDN'T PLACE WHERE.
LITTLE THINGS GAVE YOU AWAY, THOUGH. THE FEAR OF MY TENTH, WELL, TENTH ME. THE KNOWLEDGE OF TIME LORDS...
...AND THE DOUBLE IMAGE IN THE T'KEYN HOLO-NEXUS NAILED IT FOR ME.
HELLO, ES'CARTRSS OF THE TACTIRE.
YOU CANNOT BELIEVE THIS! YOU MUSTN'T BELIEVE THIS!
OH, BUT HE CAN. THE SQUIDDY LITTLE MIND PARASITE THAT ATTACKED ME FROM BEHIND.
HOW DID YOU GET OUT OF THE TARDIS MATRIX?*
*IN "DOCTOR WHO: THE FORGOTTEN"
YOU LEFT ME TO MELT INTO NOTHING IN YOUR TARDIS MATRIX.
NOTHING BUT STARDUST, FEELING EVERY SECOND LIKE YEARS.
AND THEN THE TARDIS EXPLODED, TORN TO PIECES AS YOU USED THE PANDORICA TO REMAKE THE UNIVERSE IN YOUR IMAGE, LIKE SOME KIND OF MAD GOD.
TRAPPED IN E-SPACE, FALLING THROUGH A FIFTH-DIMENSIONAL VORTEX, I DID THE ONLY THING THAT I COULD...
...I FOUND A NEW HOST. THIS ONE. IMAGINE MY JOY WHEN I LEARNED THAT HE AUDITED EARTH!
HUNDREDS OF YEARS SPENT WAITING IN THE SHADOWS, BUILDING MY STRENGTH—
AND YOU STILL SCREWED IT UP! ALL THAT TIME WAITING FOR THE NEXT AUDIT AND YOU NEVER BOTHERED TO WATCH HIM FLY HIS SHIP!
I MAY HAVE CRASHED, BUT I STILL FILED MY REPORT. AND NO MATTER WHAT YOU SAY, NO MATTER HOW YOU THREATEN, DOCTOR...
...ONLY A HUMAN CAN DEFEND THEIR PLANET. AND YOU ARE NOT OF EARTH!
NO, BUT I'VE PUT A LOT OF WORK INTO IT.
AND AS FOR A HUMAN DEFENDING, LUCKILY, I BROUGHT ONE.

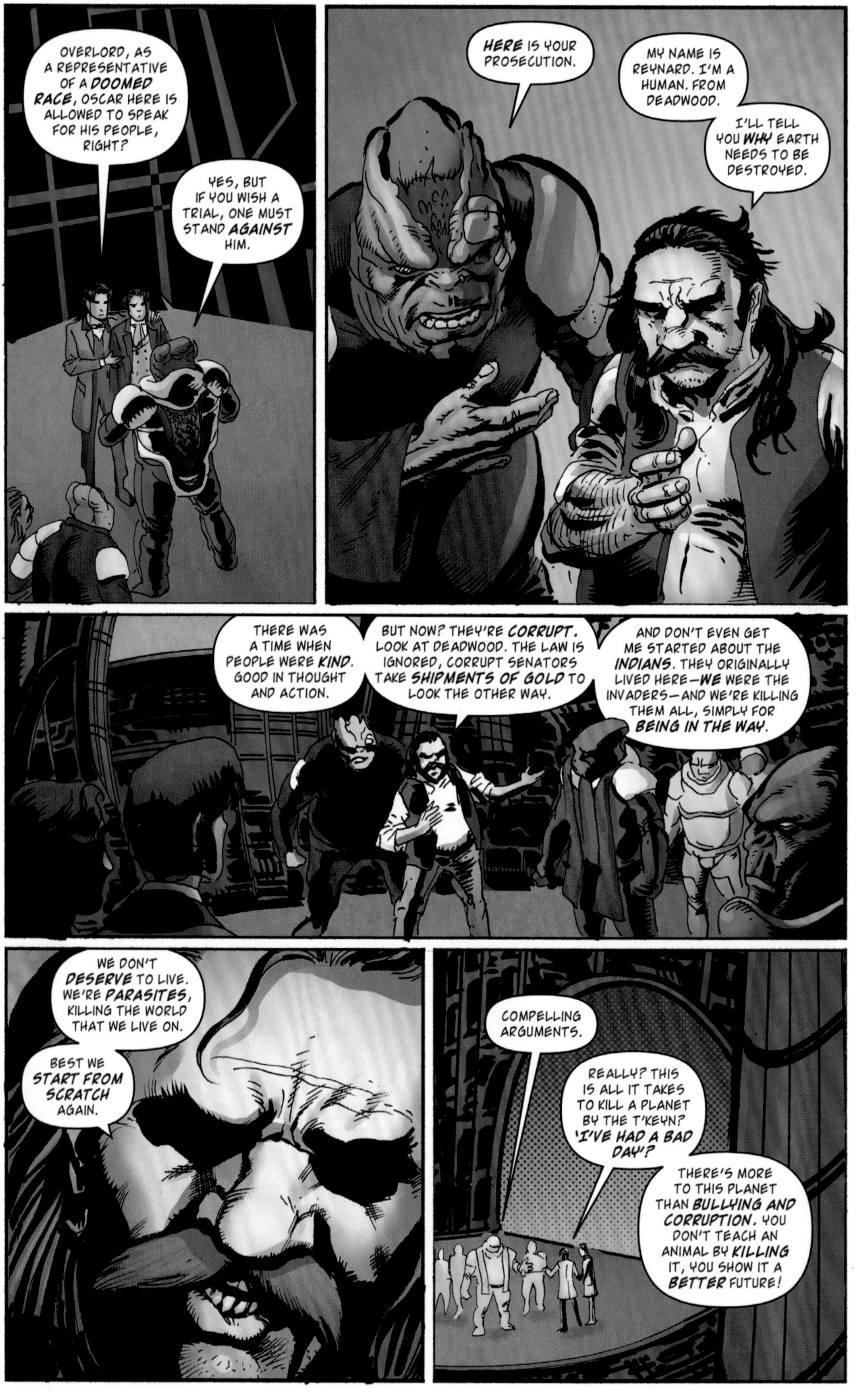
OVERLORD, AS A REPRESENTATIVE OF A DOOMED RACE, OSCAR HERE IS ALLOWED TO SPEAK FOR HIS PEOPLE, RIGHT?
YES, BUT IF YOU WISH A TRIAL, ONE MUST STAND AGAINST HIM.
HERE IS YOUR PROSECUTION.
MY NAME IS REYNARD. I'M A HUMAN. FROM DEADWOOD.
I'LL TELL YOU WHY EARTH NEEDS TO BE DESTROYED.
THERE WAS A TIME WHEN PEOPLE WERE KIND. GOOD IN THOUGHT AND ACTION.
BUT NOW? THEY'RE CORRUPT. LOOK AT DEADWOOD. THE LAW IS IGNORED, CORRUPT SENATORS TAKE SHIPMENTS OF GOLD TO LOOK THE OTHER WAY.
AND DON'T EVEN GET ME STARTED ABOUT THE INDIANS. THEY ORIGINALLY LIVED HERE—WE WERE THE INVADERS—AND WE'RE KILLING THEM ALL, SIMPLY FOR BEING IN THE WAY.
WE DON'T DESERVE TO LIVE. WE'RE PARASITES, KILLING THE WORLD THAT WE LIVE ON.
BEST WE START FROM SCRATCH AGAIN.
COMPELLING ARGUMENTS.
REALLY? THIS IS ALL IT TAKES TO KILL A PLANET BY THE T'KEYN? 'I'VE HAD A BAD DAY'?
THERE'S MORE TO THIS PLANET THAN BULLYING AND CORRUPTION. YOU DON'T TEACH AN ANIMAL BY KILLING IT, YOU SHOW IT A BETTER FUTURE!

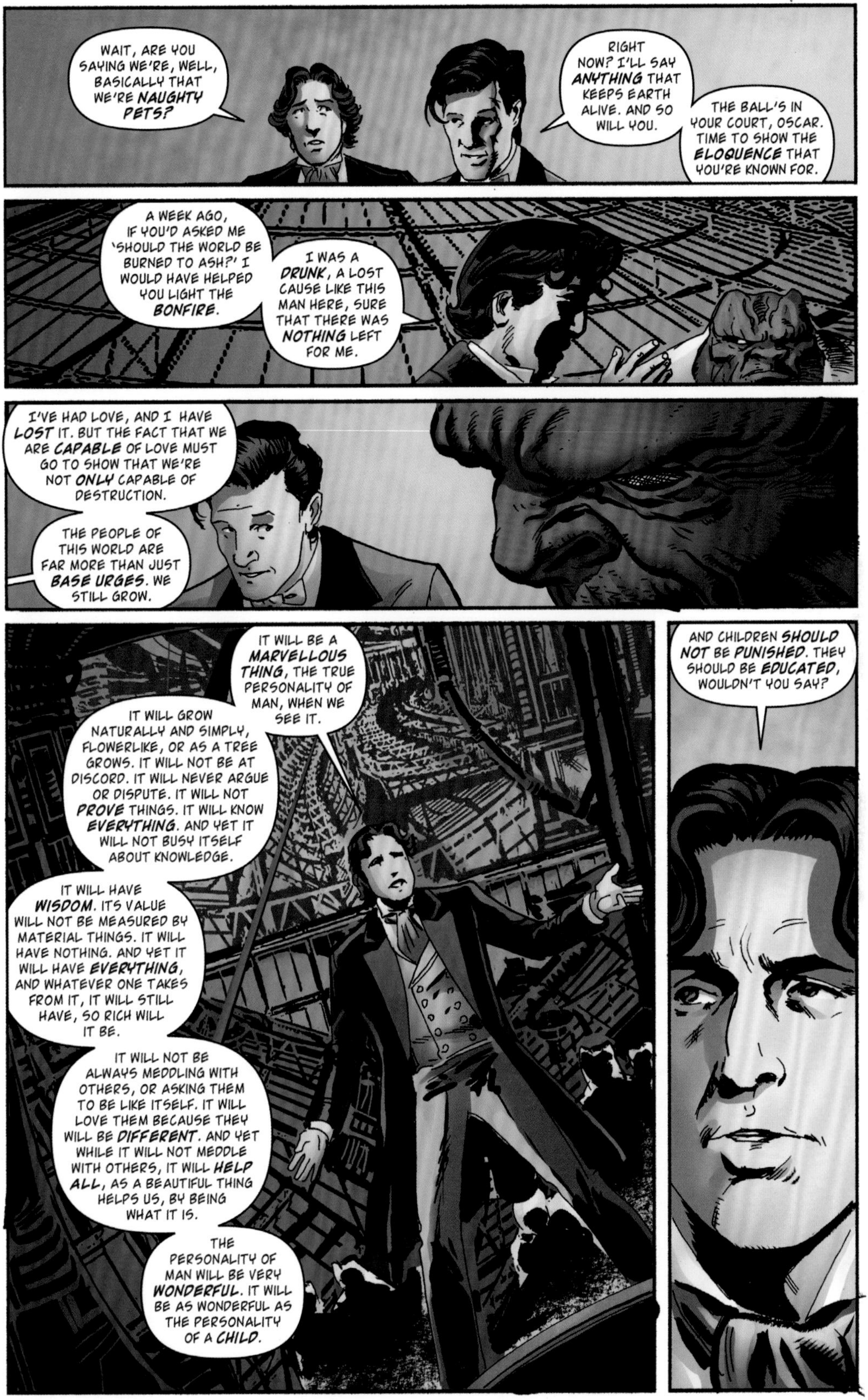
WAIT, ARE YOU SAYING WE'RE, WELL, BASICALLY THAT WE'RE NAUGHTY PETS?
RIGHT NOW? I'LL SAY ANYTHING THAT KEEPS EARTH ALIVE. AND SO WILL YOU.
THE BALL'S IN YOUR COURT, OSCAR. TIME TO SHOW THE ELOQUENCE THAT YOU'RE KNOWN FOR.
A WEEK AGO, IF YOU'D ASKED ME 'SHOULD THE WORLD BE BURNED TO ASH?' I WOULD HAVE HELPED YOU LIGHT THE BONFIRE.
I WAS A DRUNK, A LOST CAUSE LIKE THIS MAN HERE, SURE THAT THERE WAS NOTHING LEFT FOR ME.
I'VE HAD LOVE, AND I HAVE LOST IT. BUT THE FACT THAT WE ARE CAPABLE OF LOVE MUST GO TO SHOW THAT WE'RE NOT ONLY CAPABLE OF DESTRUCTION.
THE PEOPLE OF THIS WORLD ARE FAR MORE THAN JUST BASE URGES. WE STILL GROW.
IT WILL BE A MARVELLOUS THING, THE TRUE PERSONALITY OF MAN, WHEN WE SEE IT.
IT WILL GROW NATURALLY AND SIMPLY, FLOWERLIKE, OR AS A TREE GROWS. IT WILL NOT BE AT DISCORD. IT WILL NEVER ARGUE OR DISPUTE. IT WILL NOT PROVE THINGS. IT WILL KNOW EVERYTHING. AND YET IT WILL NOT BUSY ITSELF ABOUT KNOWLEDGE.
IT WILL HAVE WISDOM. ITS VALUE WILL NOT BE MEASURED BY MATERIAL THINGS. IT WILL HAVE NOTHING. AND YET IT WILL HAVE EVERYTHING, AND WHATEVER ONE TAKES FROM IT, IT WILL STILL HAVE, SO RICH WILL IT BE.
IT WILL NOT BE ALWAYS MEDDLING WITH OTHERS, OR ASKING THEM TO BE LIKE ITSELF. IT WILL LOVE THEM BECAUSE THEY WILL BE DIFFERENT. AND YET WHILE IT WILL NOT MEDDLE WITH OTHERS, IT WILL HELP ALL, AS A BEAUTIFUL THING HELPS US, BY BEING WHAT IT IS.
THE PERSONALITY OF MAN WILL BE VERY WONDERFUL. IT WILL BE AS WONDERFUL AS THE PERSONALITY OF A CHILD.
AND CHILDREN SHOULD NOT BE PUNISHED. THEY SHOULD BE EDUCATED, WOULDN'T YOU SAY?

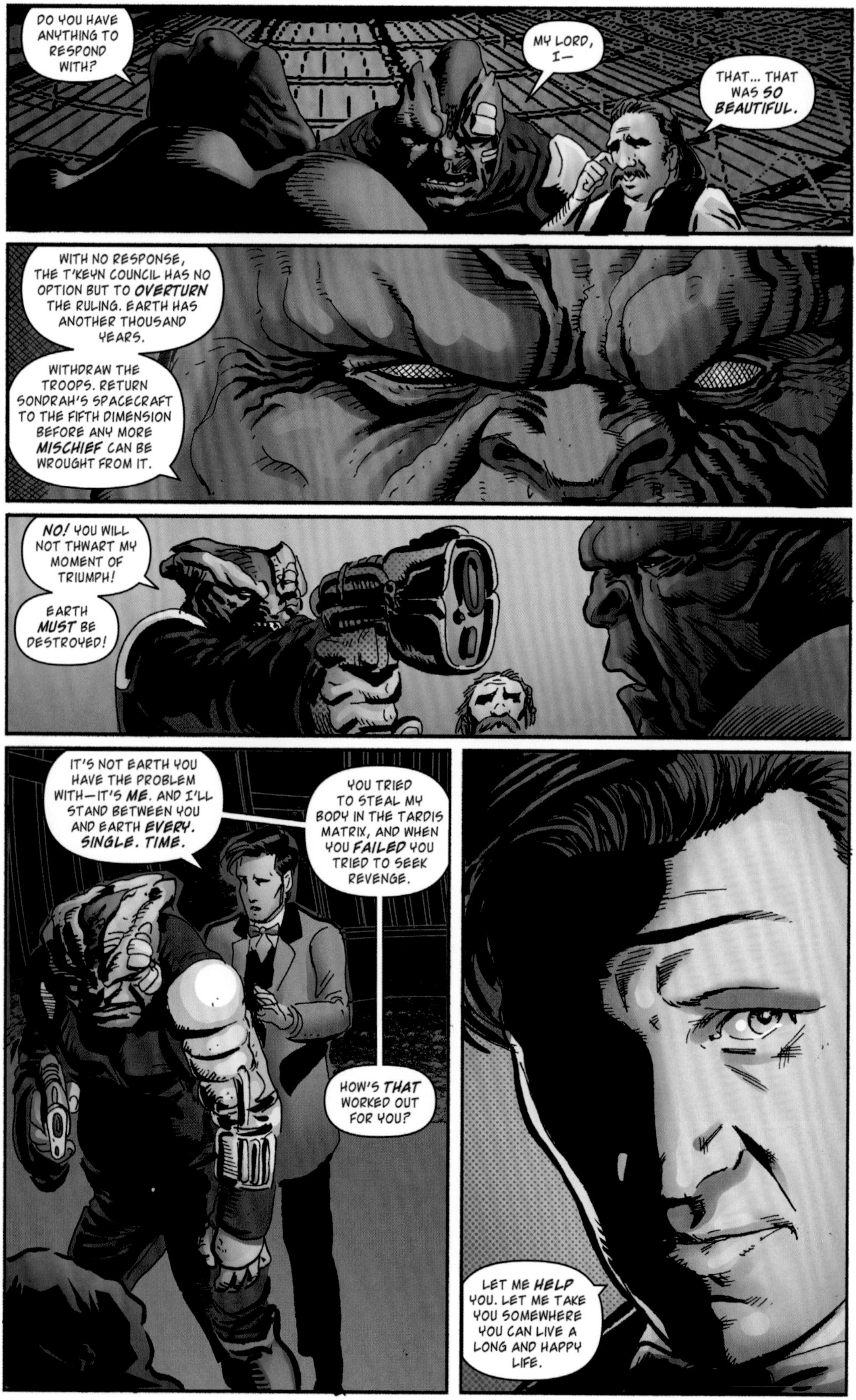
DO YOU HAVE ANYTHING TO RESPOND WITH?
MY LORD, I—
THAT... THAT WAS SO BEAUTIFUL.
WITH NO RESPONSE, THE T'KEYN COUNCIL HAS NO OPTION BUT TO OVERTURN THE RULING. EARTH HAS ANOTHER THOUSAND YEARS.
WITHDRAW THE TROOPS. RETURN SONDRAH'S SPACECRAFT TO THE FIFTH DIMENSION BEFORE ANY MORE MISCHIEF CAN BE WROUGHT FROM IT.
NO! YOU WILL NOT THWART MY MOMENT OF TRIUMPH!
EARTH MUST BE DESTROYED!
IT'S NOT EARTH YOU HAVE THE PROBLEM WITH—IT'S ME. AND I'LL STAND BETWEEN YOU AND EARTH EVERY. SINGLE. TIME.
YOU TRIED TO STEAL MY BODY IN THE TARDIS MATRIX, AND WHEN YOU FAILED YOU TRIED TO SEEK REVENGE.
HOW'S THAT WORKED OUT FOR YOU?
LET ME HELP YOU. LET ME TAKE YOU SOMEWHERE YOU CAN LIVE A LONG AND HAPPY LIFE.

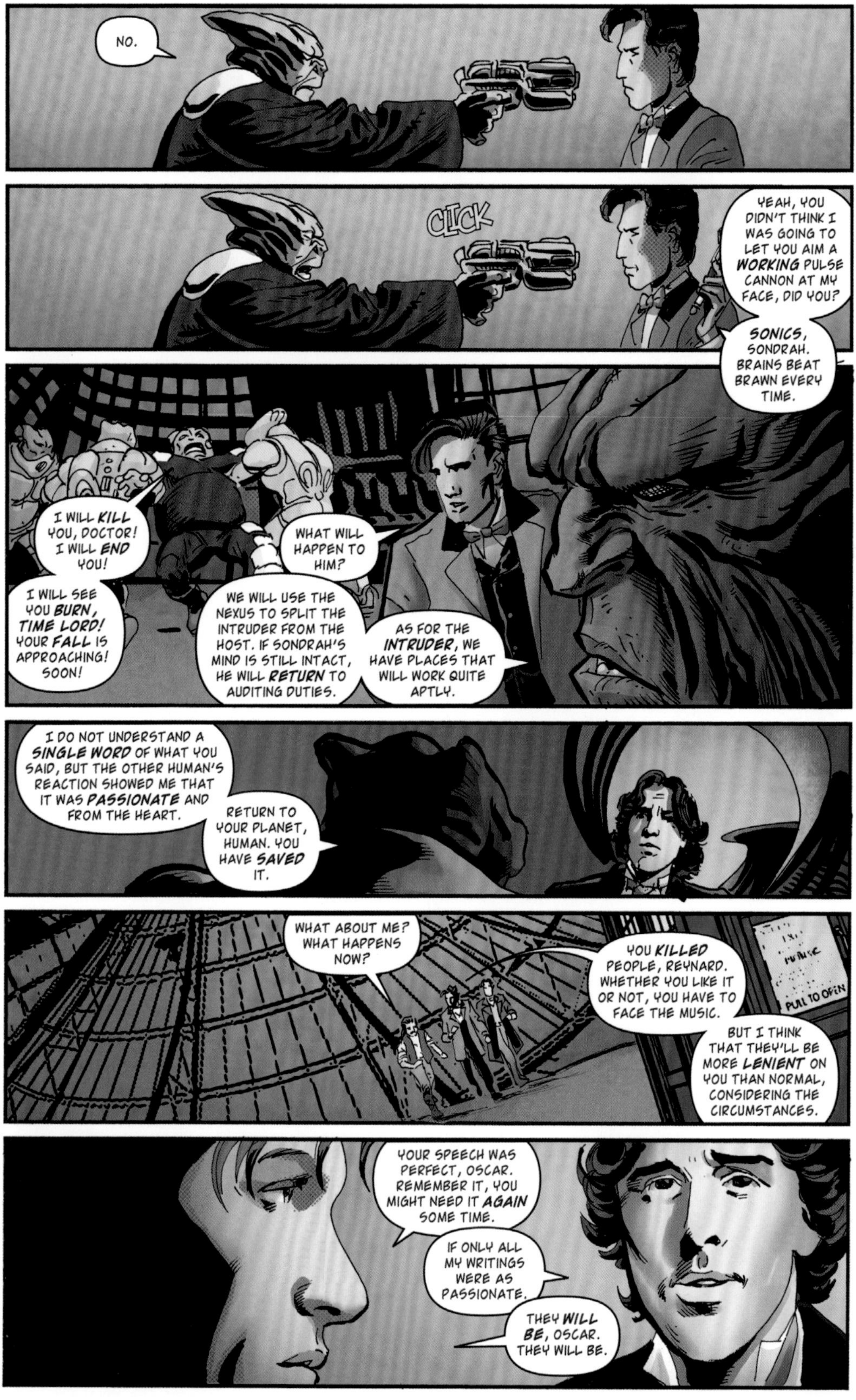
NO.
CLICK
YEAH, YOU DIDN'T THINK I WAS GOING TO LET YOU AIM A WORKING PULSE CANNON AT MY FACE, DID YOU?
SONICS, SONDRAH. BRAINS BEAT BRAWN EVERY TIME.
I WILL KILL YOU, DOCTOR! I WILL END YOU!
I WILL SEE YOU BURN, TIME LORD! YOUR FALL IS APPROACHING! SOON!
WHAT WILL HAPPEN TO HIM?
WE WILL USE THE NEXUS TO SPLIT THE INTRUDER FROM THE HOST. IF SONDRAH'S MIND IS STILL INTACT, HE WILL RETURN TO AUDITING DUTIES.
AS FOR THE INTRUDER, WE HAVE PLACES THAT WILL WORK QUITE APTLY.
I DO NOT UNDERSTAND A SINGLE WORD OF WHAT YOU SAID, BUT THE OTHER HUMAN'S REACTION SHOWED ME THAT IT WAS PASSIONATE AND FROM THE HEART.
RETURN TO YOUR PLANET, HUMAN. YOU HAVE SAVED IT.
WHAT ABOUT ME? WHAT HAPPENS NOW?
YOU KILLED PEOPLE, REYNARD. WHETHER YOU LIKE IT OR NOT, YOU HAVE TO FACE THE MUSIC.
BUT I THINK THAT THEY'LL BE MORE LENIENT ON YOU THAN NORMAL, CONSIDERING THE CIRCUMSTANCES.
PULL TO OPEN
YOUR SPEECH WAS PERFECT, OSCAR. REMEMBER IT, YOU MIGHT NEED IT AGAIN SOME TIME.
IF ONLY ALL MY WRITINGS WERE AS PASSIONATE.
THEY WILL BE, OSCAR. THEY WILL BE.

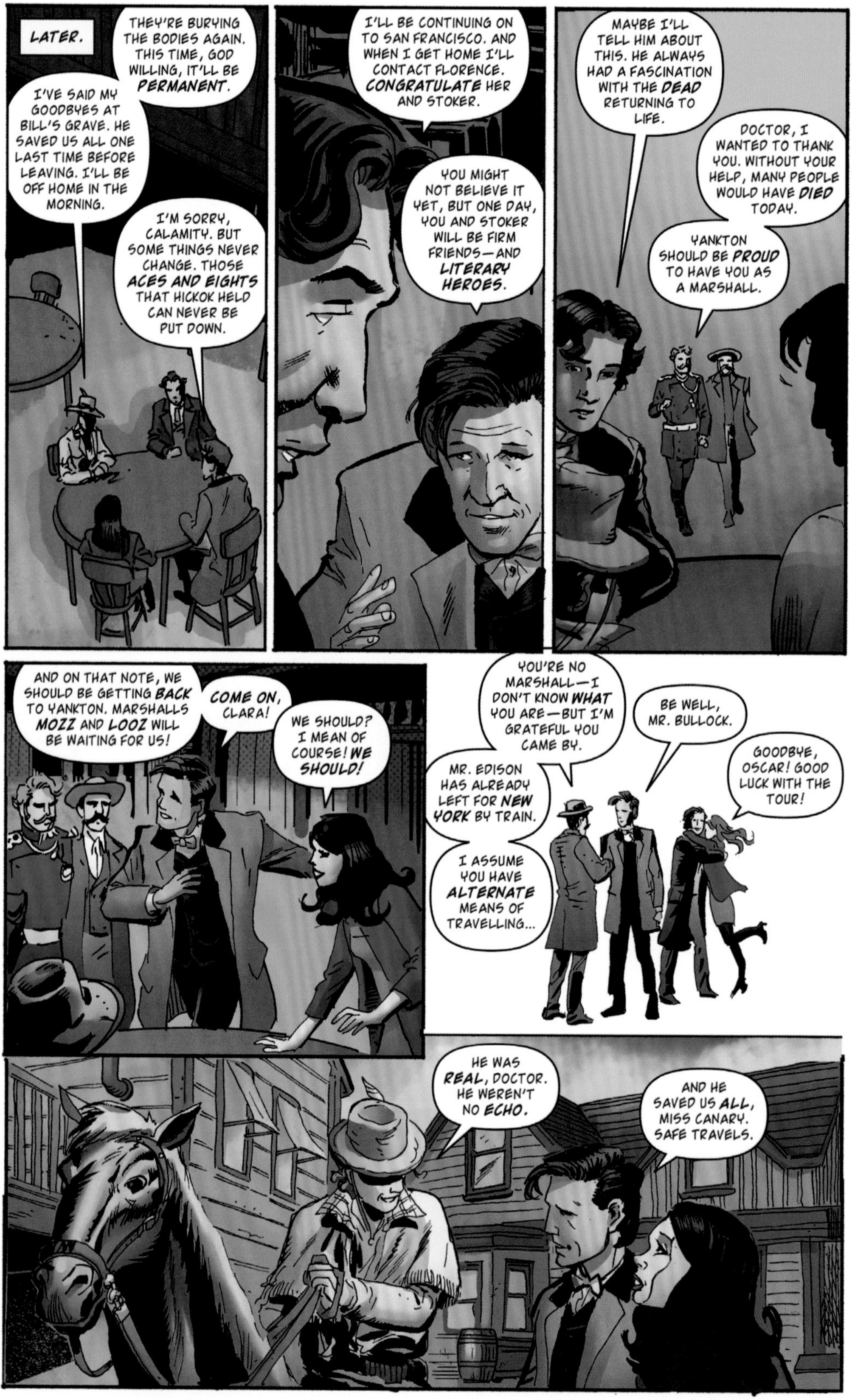
LATER.
THEY'RE BURYING THE BODIES AGAIN. THIS TIME, GOD WILLING, IT'LL BE PERMANENT.
I'VE SAID MY GOODBYES AT BILL'S GRAVE. HE SAVED US ALL ONE LAST TIME BEFORE LEAVING. I'LL BE OFF HOME IN THE MORNING.
I'M SORRY, CALAMITY. BUT SOME THINGS NEVER CHANGE. THOSE ACES AND EIGHTS THAT HICKOK HELD CAN NEVER BE PUT DOWN.
I'LL BE CONTINUING ON TO SAN FRANCISCO. AND WHEN I GET HOME I'LL CONTACT FLORENCE. CONGRATULATE HER AND STOKER.
YOU MIGHT NOT BELIEVE IT YET, BUT ONE DAY, YOU AND STOKER WILL BE FIRM FRIENDS—AND LITERARY HEROES.
MAYBE I'LL TELL HIM ABOUT THIS. HE ALWAYS HAD A FASCINATION WITH THE DEAD RETURNING TO LIFE.
DOCTOR, I WANTED TO THANK YOU. WITHOUT YOUR HELP, MANY PEOPLE WOULD HAVE DIED TODAY.
YANKTON SHOULD BE PROUD TO HAVE YOU AS A MARSHALL.
AND ON THAT NOTE, WE SHOULD BE GETTING BACK TO YANKTON. MARSHALLS MOZZ AND LOOZ WILL BE WAITING FOR US!
COME ON, CLARA!
WE SHOULD? I MEAN OF COURSE! WE SHOULD!
YOU'RE NO MARSHALL—I DON'T KNOW WHAT YOU ARE—BUT I'M GRATEFUL YOU CAME BY.
BE WELL, MR. BULLOCK.
GOODBYE, OSCAR! GOOD LUCK WITH THE TOUR!
MR. EDISON HAS ALREADY LEFT FOR NEW YORK BY TRAIN.
I ASSUME YOU HAVE ALTERNATE MEANS OF TRAVELLING...
HE WAS REAL, DOCTOR. HE WEREN'T NO ECHO.
AND HE SAVED US ALL, MISS CANARY. SAFE TRAVELS.

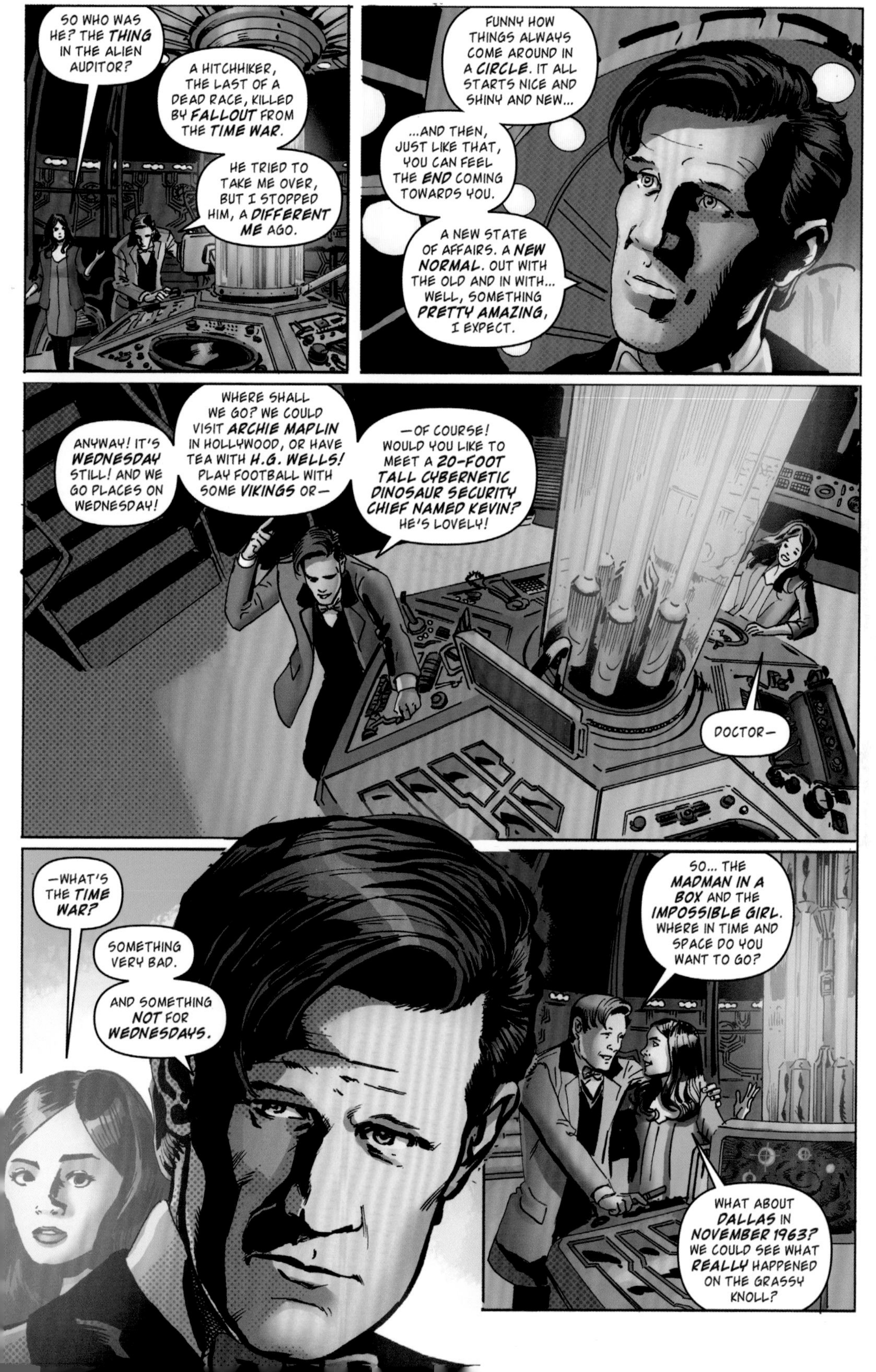
SO WHO WAS HE? THE THING IN THE ALIEN AUDITOR?
A HITCHHIKER, THE LAST OF A DEAD RACE, KILLED BY FALLOUT FROM THE TIME WAR.
HE TRIED TO TAKE ME OVER, BUT I STOPPED HIM, A DIFFERENT ME AGO.
FUNNY HOW THINGS ALWAYS COME AROUND IN A CIRCLE. IT ALL STARTS NICE AND SHINY AND NEW...
...AND THEN, JUST LIKE THAT, YOU CAN FEEL THE END COMING TOWARDS YOU.
A NEW STATE OF AFFAIRS. A NEW NORMAL. OUT WITH THE OLD AND IN WITH... WELL, SOMETHING PRETTY AMAZING, I EXPECT.
ANYWAY! IT'S WEDNESDAY STILL! AND WE GO PLACES ON WEDNESDAY!
WHERE SHALL WE GO? WE COULD VISIT ARCHIE MAPLIN IN HOLLYWOOD, OR HAVE TEA WITH H.G. WELLS! PLAY FOOTBALL WITH SOME VIKINGS OR—
—OF COURSE! WOULD YOU LIKE TO MEET A 20-FOOT TALL CYBERNETIC DINOSAUR SECURITY CHIEF NAMED KEVIN? HE'S LOVELY!
DOCTOR—
—WHAT'S THE TIME WAR?
SOMETHING VERY BAD.
AND SOMETHING NOT FOR WEDNESDAYS.
SO... THE MADMAN IN A BOX AND THE IMPOSSIBLE GIRL. WHERE IN TIME AND SPACE DO YOU WANT TO GO?
WHAT ABOUT DALLAS IN NOVEMBER 1963? WE COULD SEE WHAT REALLY HAPPENED ON THE GRASSY KNOLL?

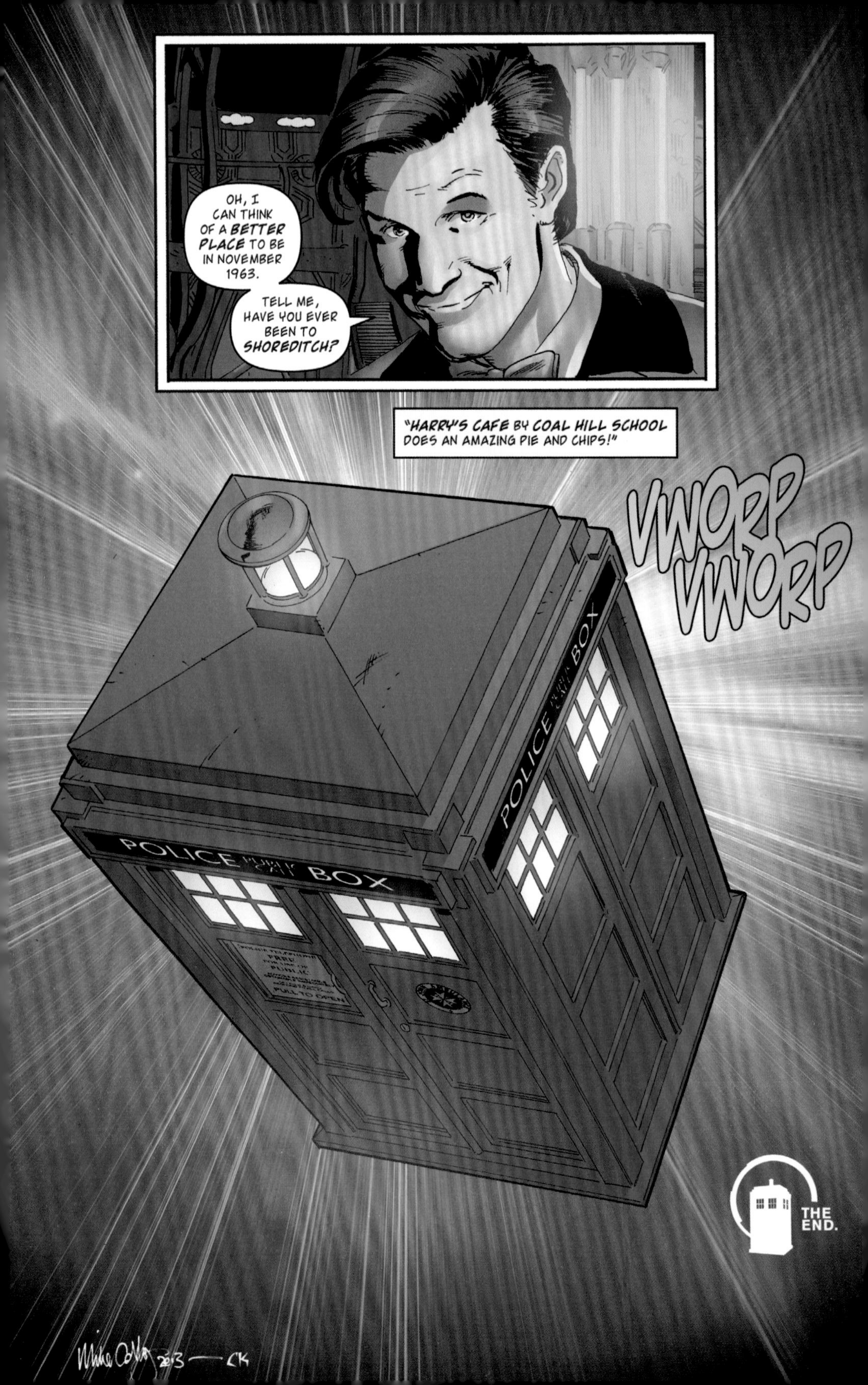

OH, I CAN THINK OF A BETTER PLACE TO BE IN NOVEMBER 1963.
TELL ME, HAVE YOU EVER BEEN TO SHOREDITCH?
"HARRY'S CAFE BY COAL HILL SCHOOL DOES AN AMAZING PIE AND CHIPS!"
VWORP VWORP
POLICE PUBLIC CALL BOX
PULL TO OPEN
THE END.

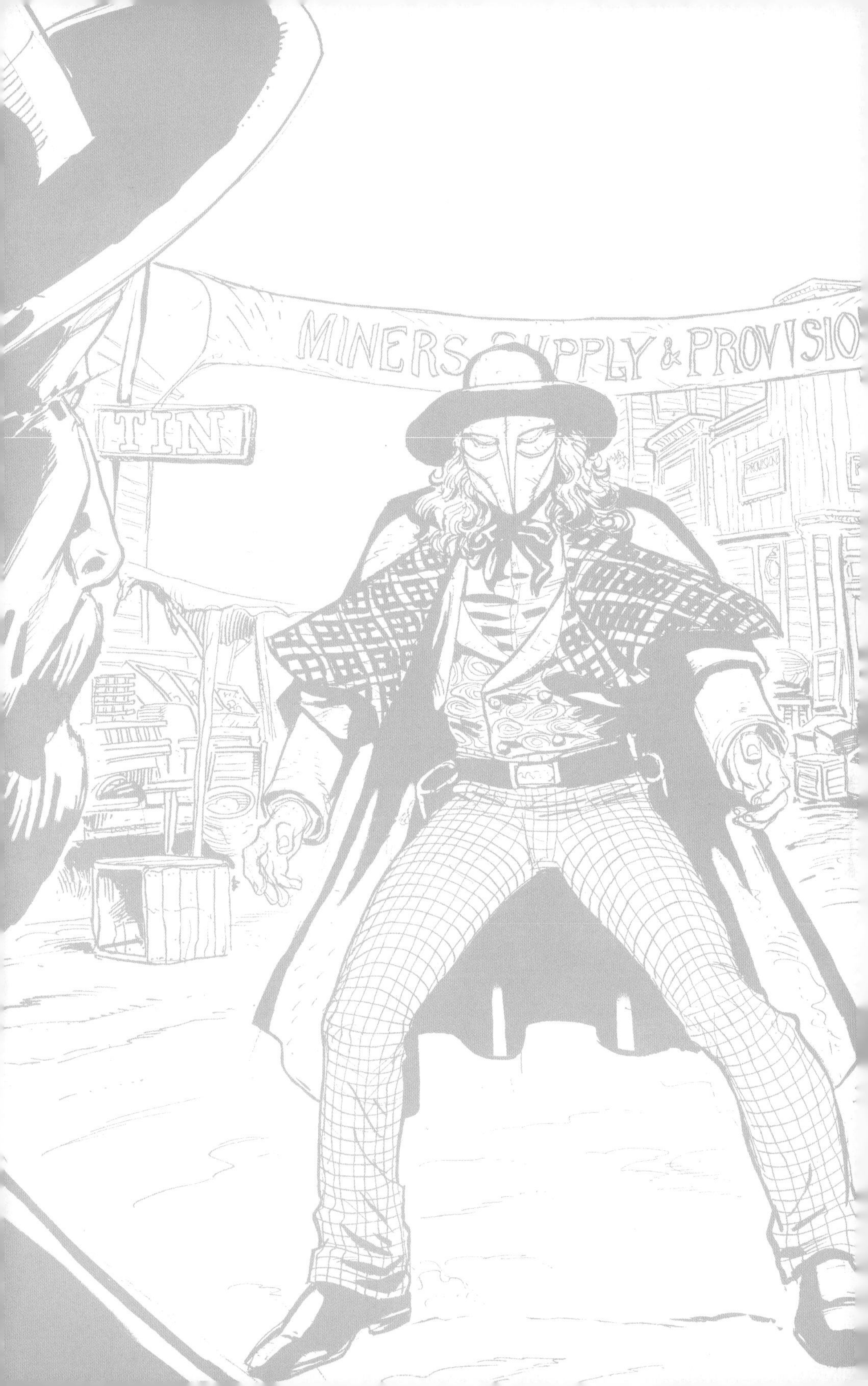
MINERS
TIN
PROVISIONS

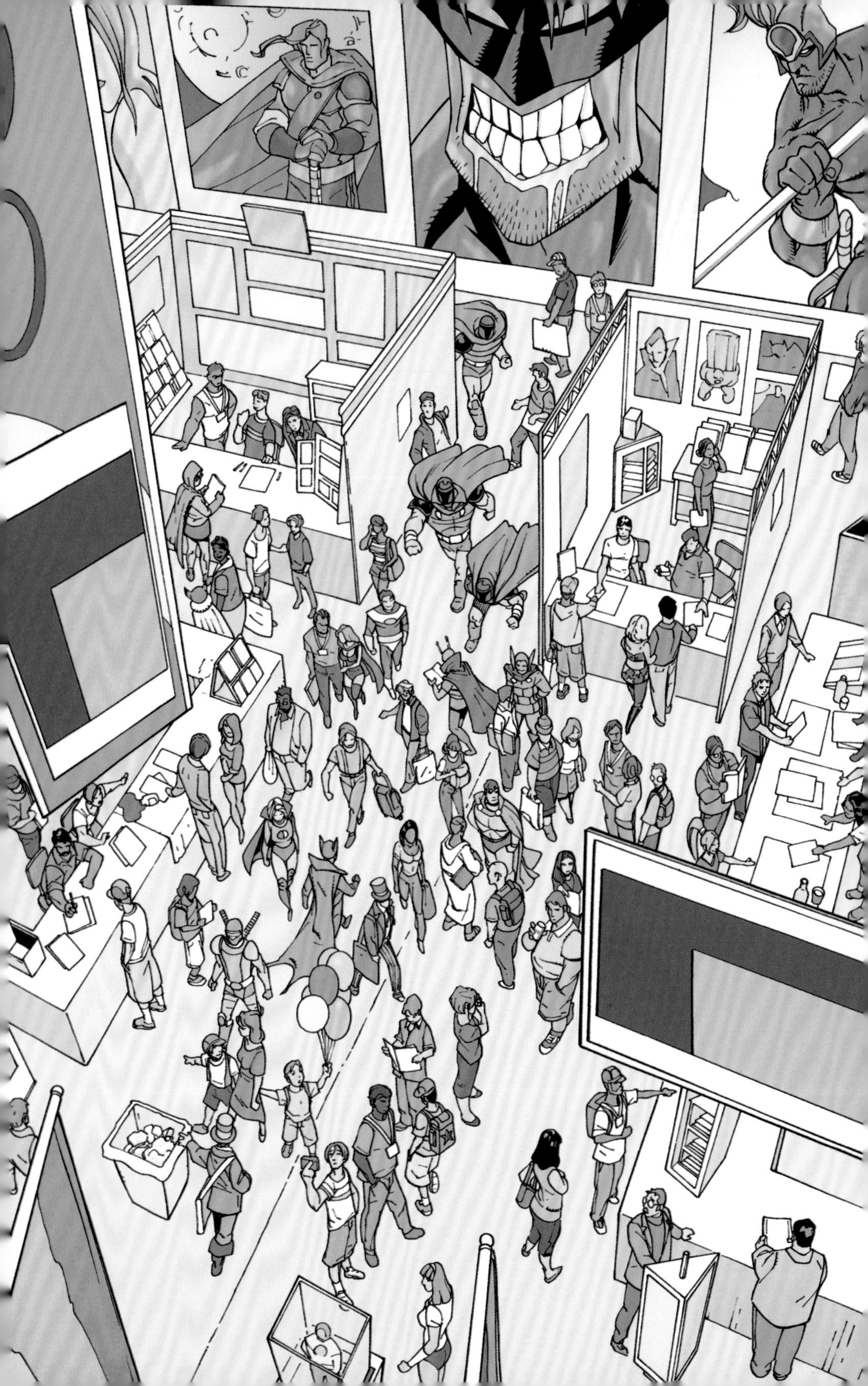

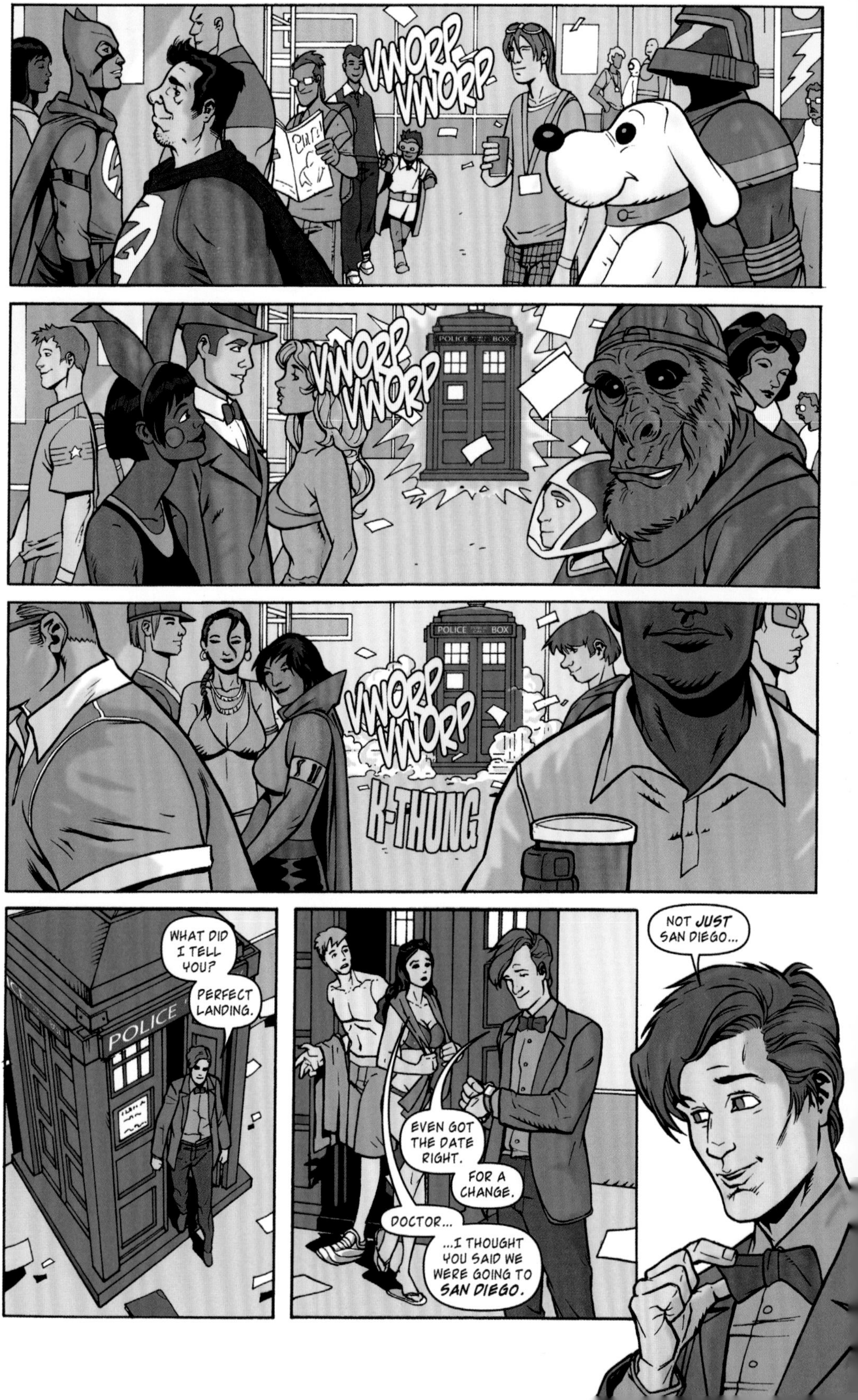
VWORP VWORP
VWORP VWORP
POLICE BOX
POLICE BOX
VWORP VWORP
K-THUNG
WHAT DID I TELL YOU?
PERFECT LANDING.
POLICE
EVEN GOT THE DATE RIGHT.
FOR A CHANGE.
DOCTOR...
...I THOUGHT YOU SAID WE WERE GOING TO SAN DIEGO.
NOT JUST SAN DIEGO...

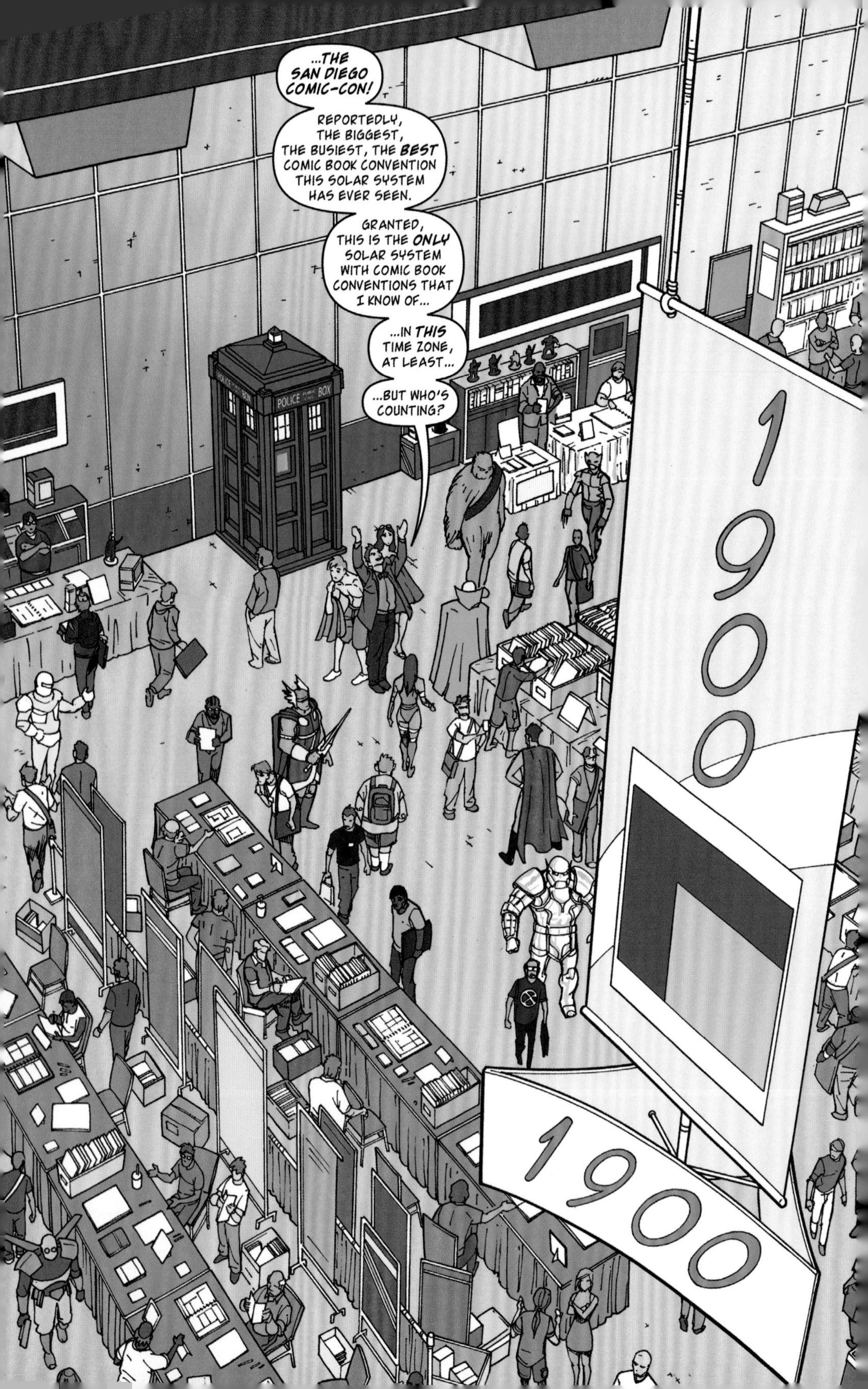

...THE SAN DIEGO COMIC-CON!
REPORTEDLY, THE BIGGEST, THE BUSIEST, THE BEST COMIC BOOK CONVENTION THIS SOLAR SYSTEM HAS EVER SEEN.
GRANTED, THIS IS THE ONLY SOLAR SYSTEM WITH COMIC BOOK CONVENTIONS THAT I KNOW OF...
...IN THIS TIME ZONE, AT LEAST...
...BUT WHO'S COUNTING?
POLICE BOX
1900
1900

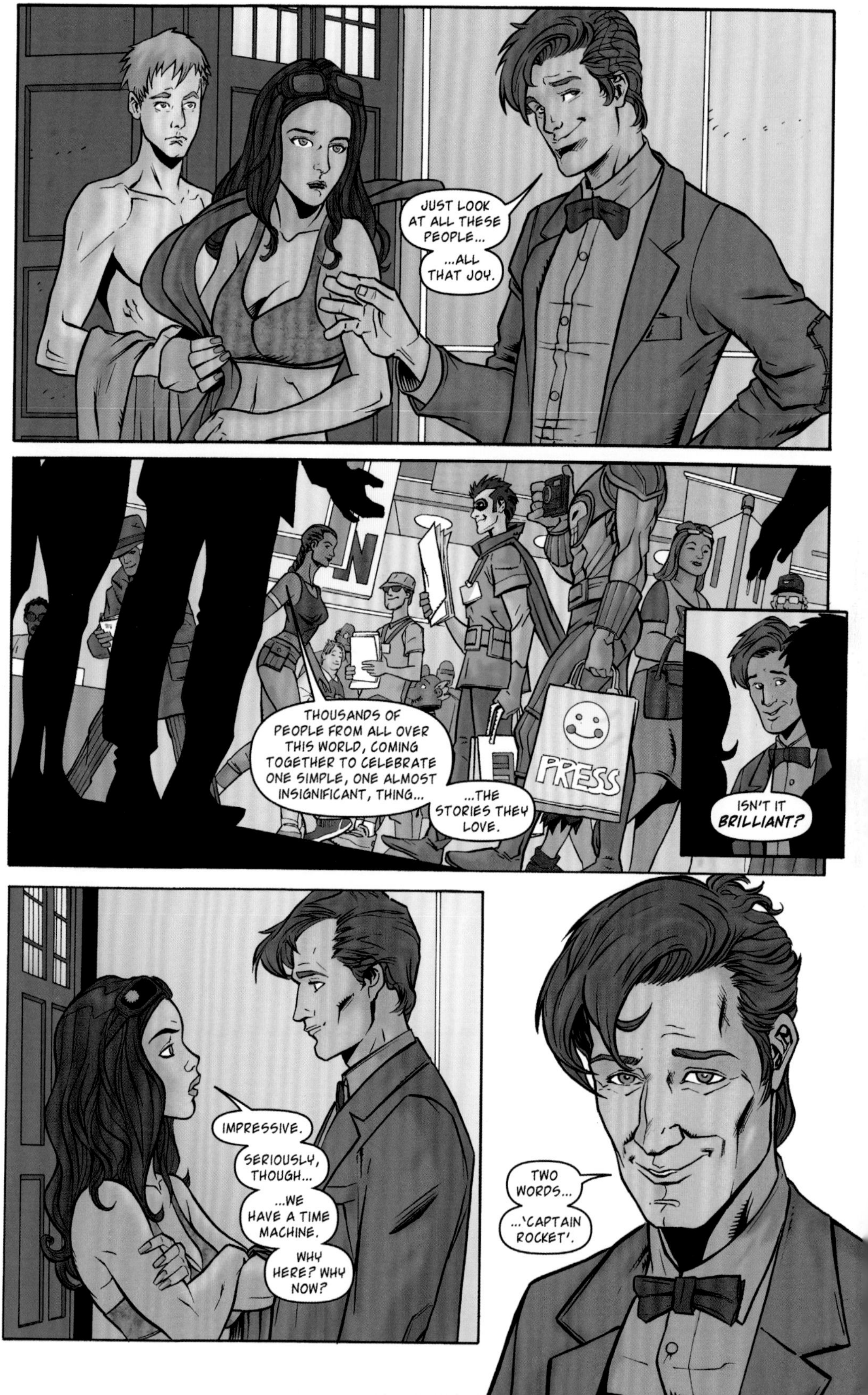
JUST LOOK AT ALL THESE PEOPLE...
...ALL THAT JOY.
THOUSANDS OF PEOPLE FROM ALL OVER THIS WORLD, COMING TOGETHER TO CELEBRATE ONE SIMPLE, ONE ALMOST INSIGNIFICANT, THING...
...THE STORIES THEY LOVE.
PRESS
ISN'T IT BRILLIANT?
IMPRESSIVE.
SERIOUSLY, THOUGH...
...WE HAVE A TIME MACHINE.
WHY HERE? WHY NOW?
TWO WORDS...
...'CAPTAIN ROCKET'.

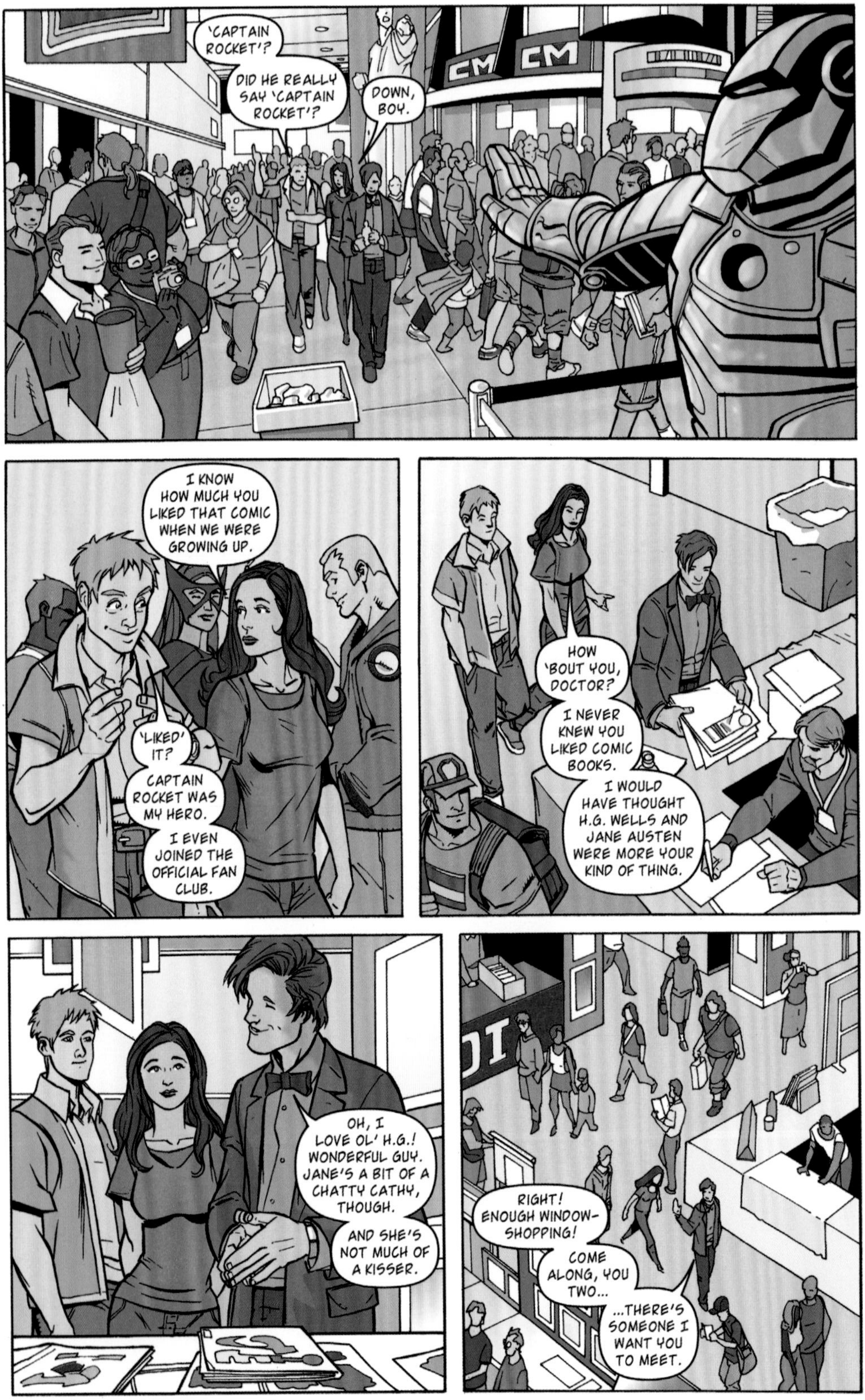
'CAPTAIN ROCKET'?
DID HE REALLY SAY 'CAPTAIN ROCKET'?
DOWN, BOY.
I KNOW HOW MUCH YOU LIKED THAT COMIC WHEN WE WERE GROWING UP.
'LIKED' IT?
CAPTAIN ROCKET WAS MY HERO.
I EVEN JOINED THE OFFICIAL FAN CLUB.
HOW 'BOUT YOU, DOCTOR?
I NEVER KNEW YOU LIKED COMIC BOOKS.
I WOULD HAVE THOUGHT H.G. WELLS AND JANE AUSTEN WERE MORE YOUR KIND OF THING.
OH, I LOVE OL' H.G.! WONDERFUL GUY. JANE'S A BIT OF A CHATTY CATHY, THOUGH.
AND SHE'S NOT MUCH OF A KISSER.
RIGHT! ENOUGH WINDOW-SHOPPING!
COME ALONG, YOU TWO...
...THERE'S SOMEONE I WANT YOU TO MEET.

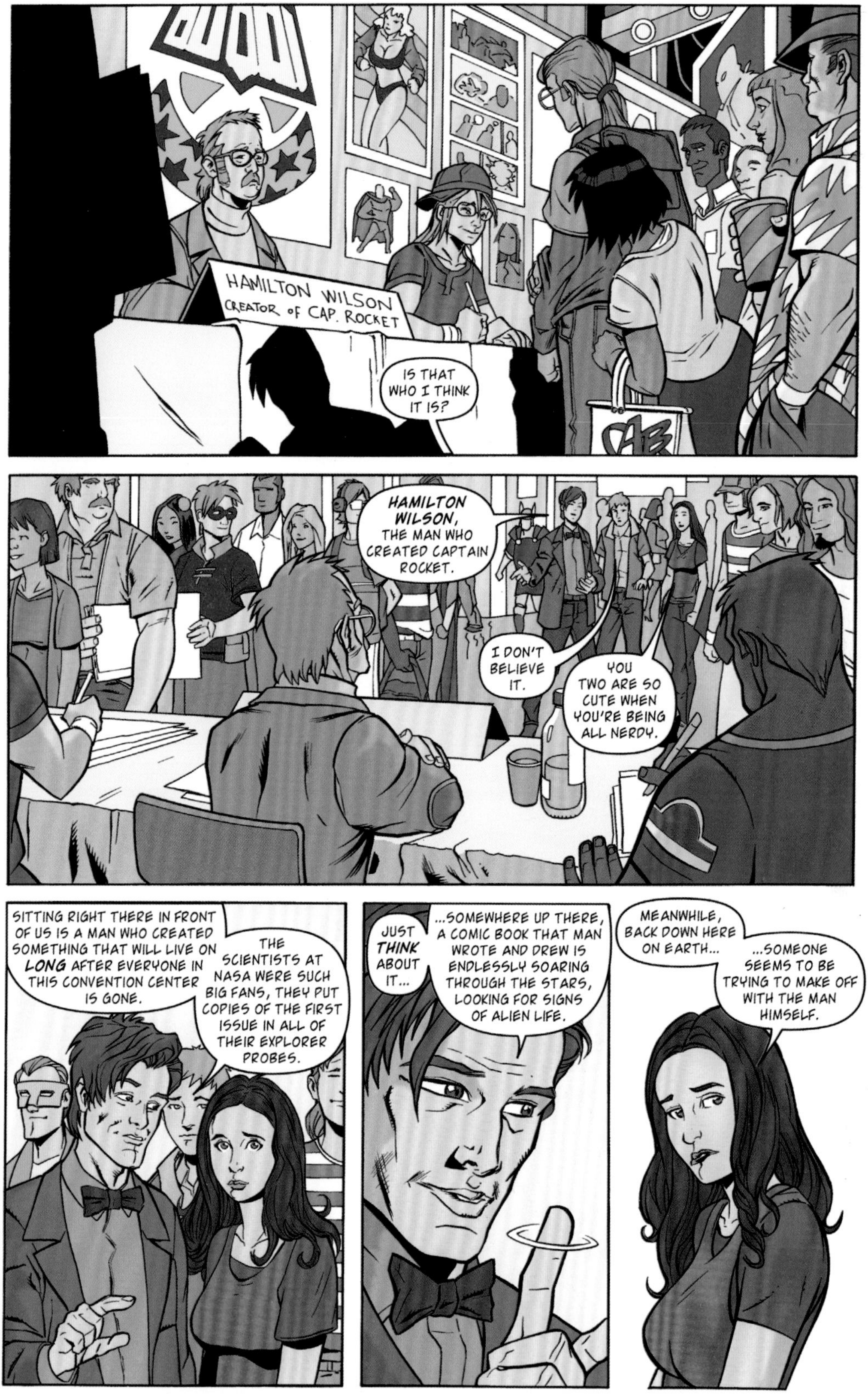
HAMILTON WILSON
CREATOR of CAP. ROCKET
IS THAT WHO I THINK IT IS?
HAMILTON WILSON, THE MAN WHO CREATED CAPTAIN ROCKET.
I DON'T BELIEVE IT.
YOU TWO ARE SO CUTE WHEN YOU'RE BEING ALL NERDY.
SITTING RIGHT THERE IN FRONT OF US IS A MAN WHO CREATED SOMETHING THAT WILL LIVE ON LONG AFTER EVERYONE IN THIS CONVENTION CENTER IS GONE.
THE SCIENTISTS AT NASA WERE SUCH BIG FANS, THEY PUT COPIES OF THE FIRST ISSUE IN ALL OF THEIR EXPLORER PROBES.
JUST THINK ABOUT IT...
...SOMEWHERE UP THERE, A COMIC BOOK THAT MAN WROTE AND DREW IS ENDLESSLY SOARING THROUGH THE STARS, LOOKING FOR SIGNS OF ALIEN LIFE.
MEANWHILE, BACK DOWN HERE ON EARTH...
...SOMEONE SEEMS TO BE TRYING TO MAKE OFF WITH THE MAN HIMSELF.

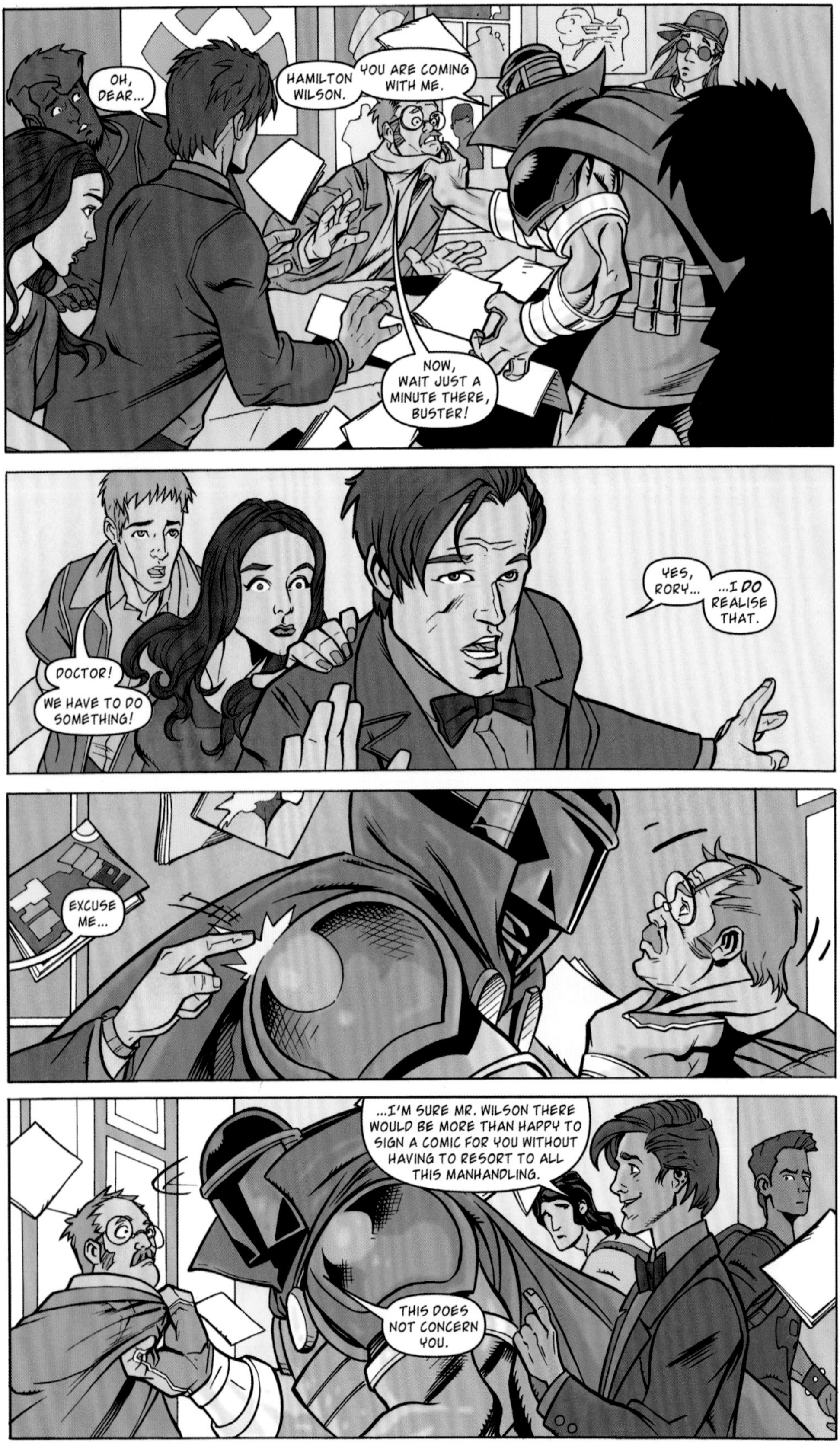
OH, DEAR...
HAMILTON WILSON.
YOU ARE COMING WITH ME.
NOW, WAIT JUST A MINUTE THERE, BUSTER!
DOCTOR!
WE HAVE TO DO SOMETHING!
YES, RORY...
...I DO REALISE THAT.
EXCUSE ME...
...I'M SURE MR. WILSON THERE WOULD BE MORE THAN HAPPY TO SIGN A COMIC FOR YOU WITHOUT HAVING TO RESORT TO ALL THIS MANHANDLING.
THIS DOES NOT CONCERN YOU.

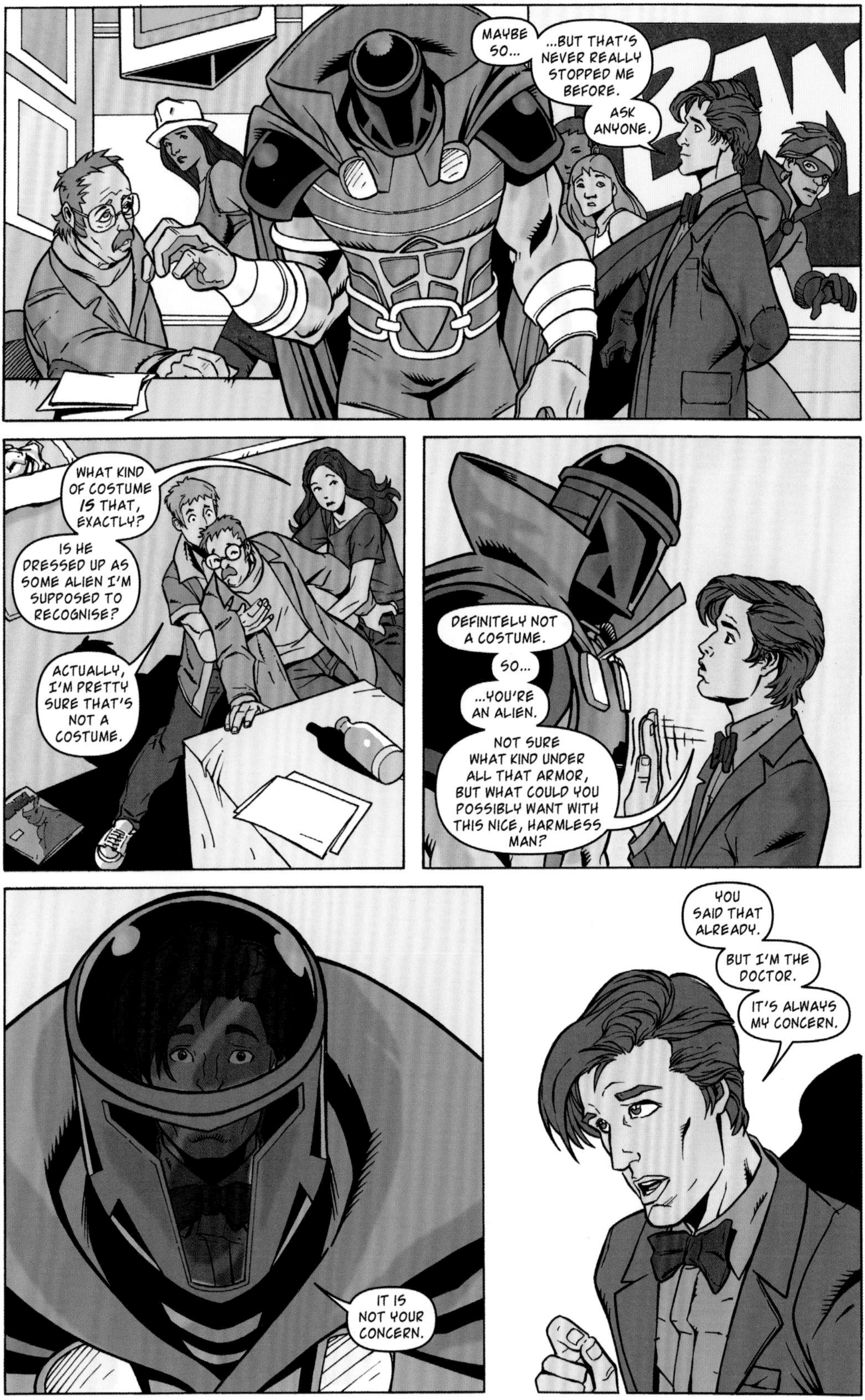
MAYBE SO...
...BUT THAT'S NEVER REALLY STOPPED ME BEFORE.
ASK ANYONE.
WHAT KIND OF COSTUME *IS* THAT, EXACTLY?
IS HE DRESSED UP AS SOME ALIEN I'M SUPPOSED TO RECOGNISE?
ACTUALLY, I'M PRETTY SURE THAT'S NOT A COSTUME.
DEFINITELY NOT A COSTUME.
SO...
...YOU'RE AN ALIEN.
NOT SURE WHAT KIND UNDER ALL THAT ARMOR, BUT WHAT COULD YOU POSSIBLY WANT WITH THIS NICE, HARMLESS MAN?
IT IS NOT YOUR CONCERN.
YOU SAID THAT ALREADY.
BUT I'M THE DOCTOR.
IT'S ALWAYS MY CONCERN.

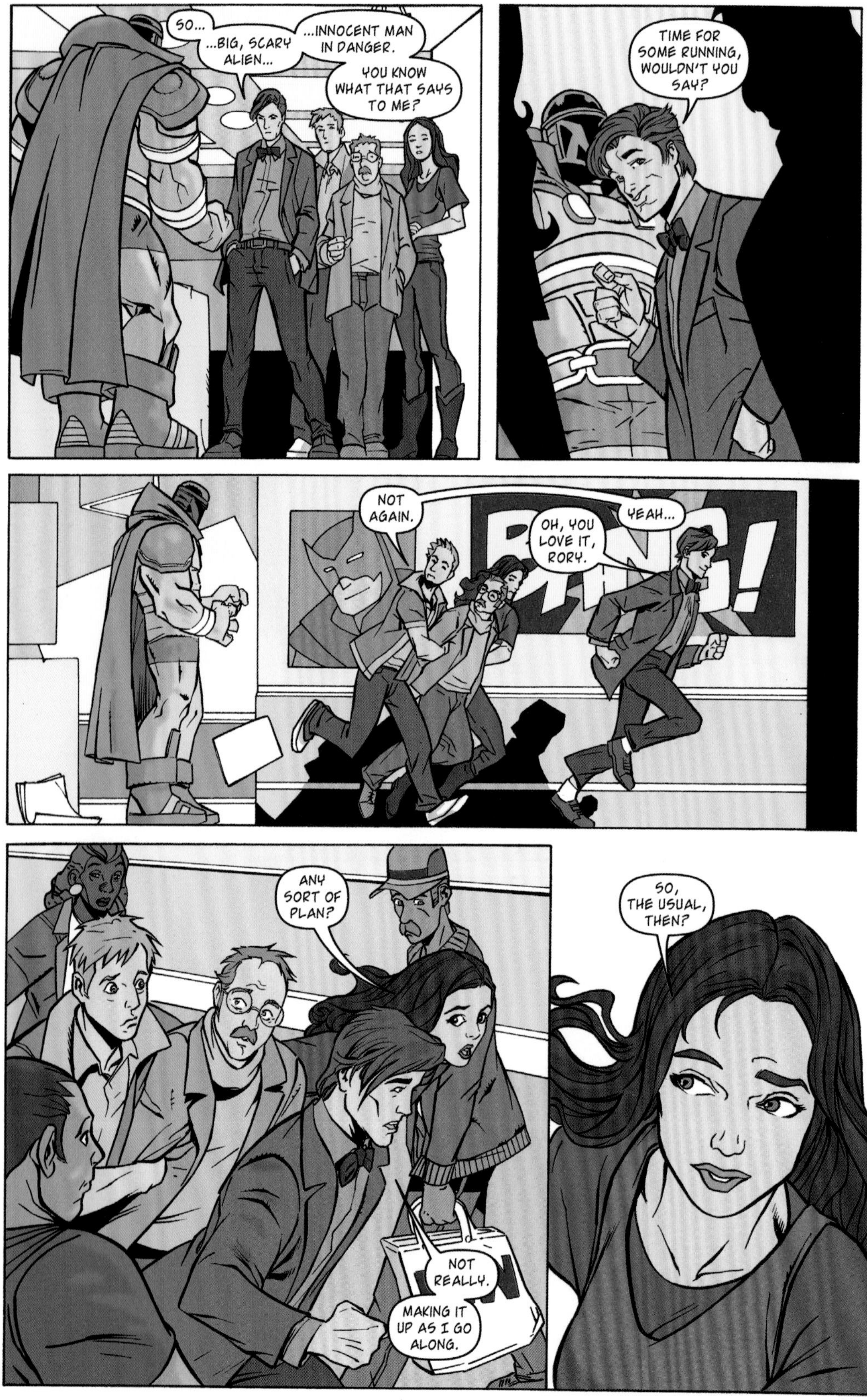
SO...
...BIG, SCARY ALIEN...
...INNOCENT MAN IN DANGER.
YOU KNOW WHAT THAT SAYS TO ME?
TIME FOR SOME RUNNING, WOULDN'T YOU SAY?
NOT AGAIN.
OH, YOU LOVE IT, RORY.
YEAH...
ANY SORT OF PLAN?
NOT REALLY.
MAKING IT UP AS I GO ALONG.
SO, THE USUAL, THEN?

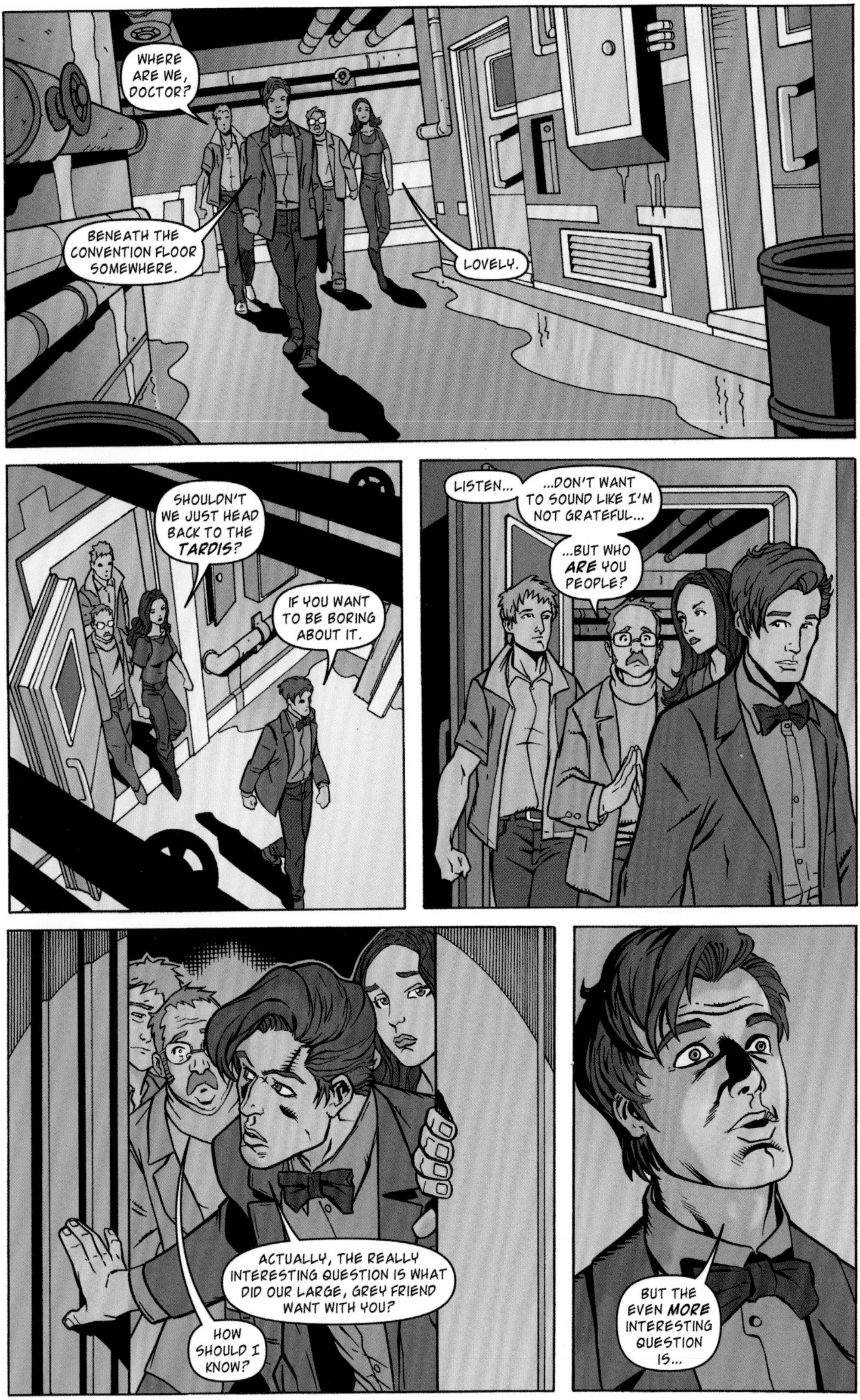
WHERE ARE WE, DOCTOR?
BENEATH THE CONVENTION FLOOR SOMEWHERE.
LOVELY.
SHOULDN'T WE JUST HEAD BACK TO THE *TARDIS*?
IF YOU WANT TO BE BORING ABOUT IT.
LISTEN...
...DON'T WANT TO SOUND LIKE I'M NOT GRATEFUL...
...BUT WHO **ARE** YOU PEOPLE?
ACTUALLY, THE REALLY INTERESTING QUESTION IS WHAT DID OUR LARGE, GREY FRIEND WANT WITH YOU?
HOW SHOULD I KNOW?
BUT THE EVEN **MORE** INTERESTING QUESTION IS...

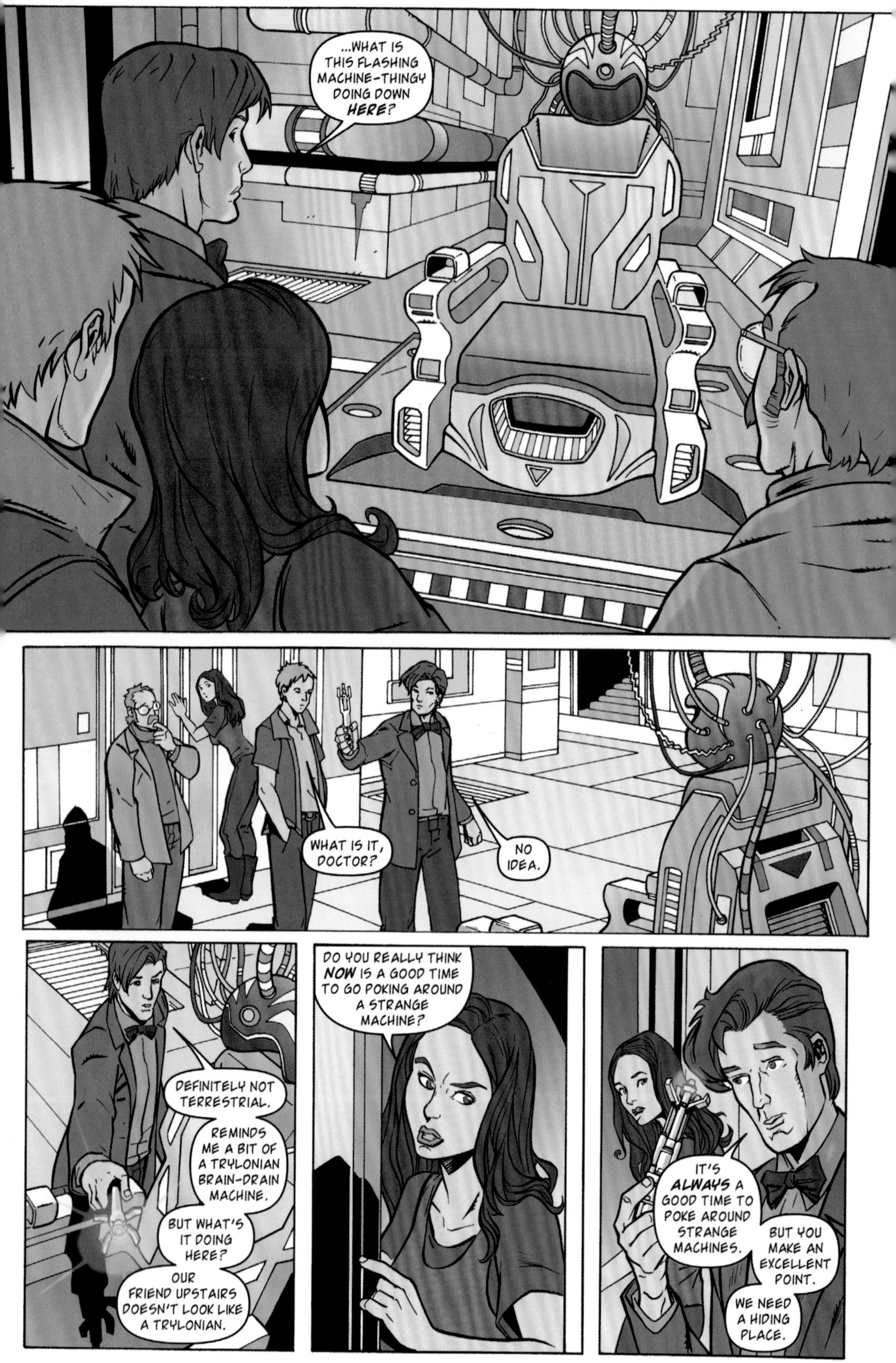
...WHAT IS THIS FLASHING MACHINE-THINGY DOING DOWN HERE?
WHAT IS IT, DOCTOR?
NO IDEA.
DEFINITELY NOT TERRESTRIAL.
REMINDS ME A BIT OF A TRYLONIAN BRAIN-DRAIN MACHINE.
BUT WHAT'S IT DOING HERE?
OUR FRIEND UPSTAIRS DOESN'T LOOK LIKE A TRYLONIAN.
DO YOU REALLY THINK NOW IS A GOOD TIME TO GO POKING AROUND A STRANGE MACHINE?
IT'S ALWAYS A GOOD TIME TO POKE AROUND STRANGE MACHINES.
BUT YOU MAKE AN EXCELLENT POINT.
WE NEED A HIDING PLACE.

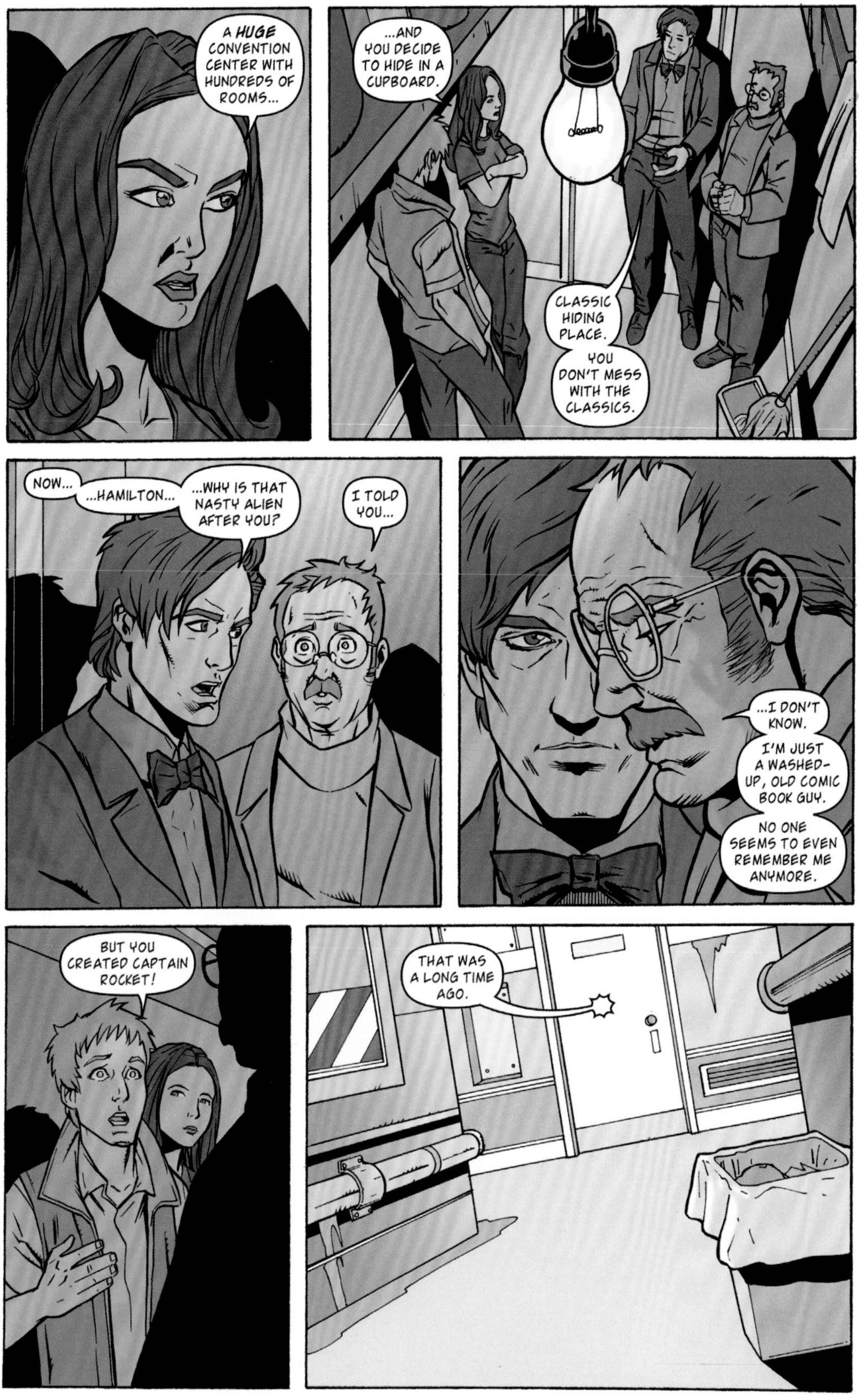
A HUGE CONVENTION CENTER WITH HUNDREDS OF ROOMS...
...AND YOU DECIDE TO HIDE IN A CUPBOARD.
CLASSIC HIDING PLACE.
YOU DON'T MESS WITH THE CLASSICS.
NOW...
...HAMILTON...
...WHY IS THAT NASTY ALIEN AFTER YOU?
I TOLD YOU...
...I DON'T KNOW.
I'M JUST A WASHED-UP, OLD COMIC BOOK GUY.
NO ONE SEEMS TO EVEN REMEMBER ME ANYMORE.
BUT YOU CREATED CAPTAIN ROCKET!
THAT WAS A LONG TIME AGO.

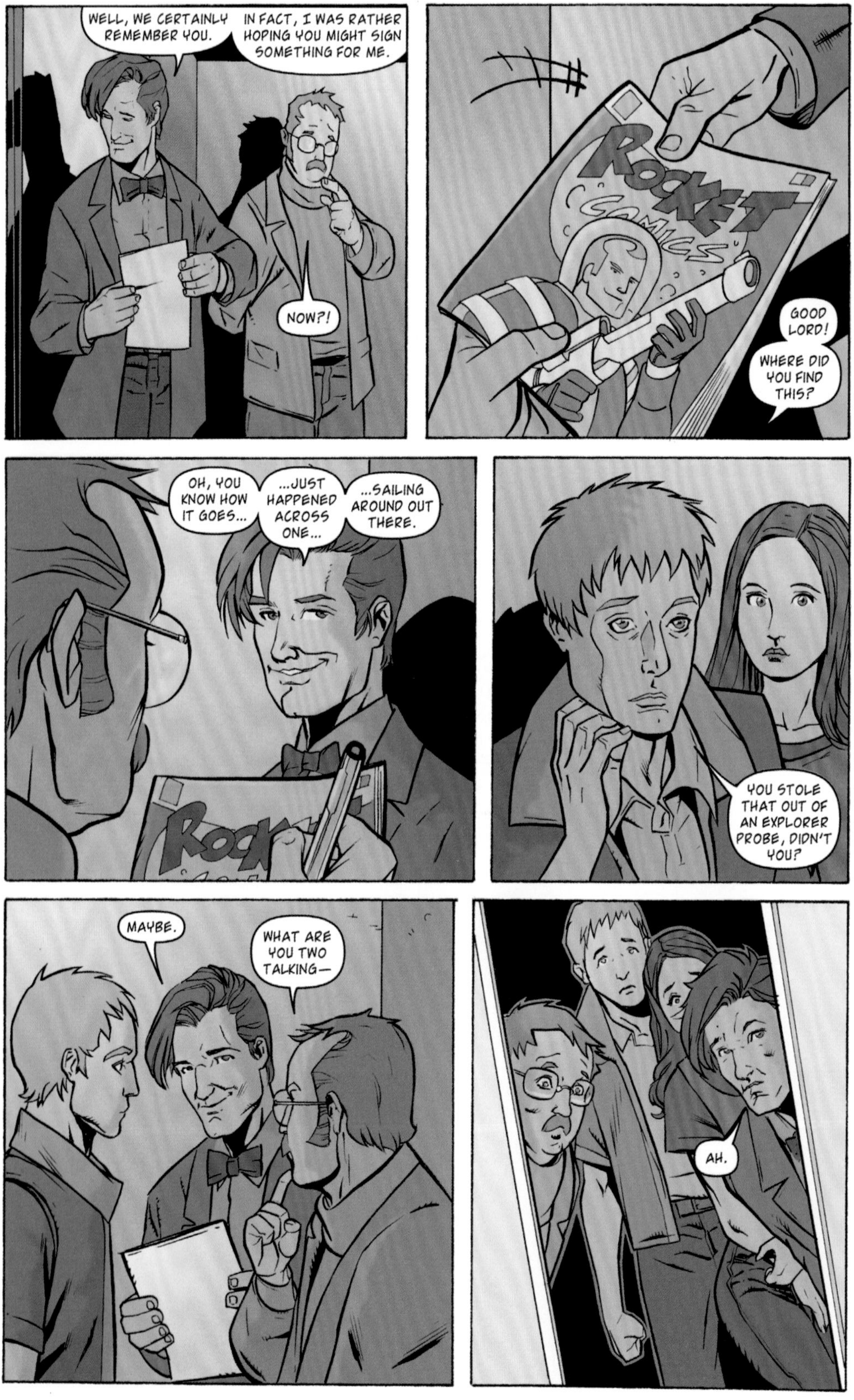
WELL, WE CERTAINLY REMEMBER YOU.
IN FACT, I WAS RATHER HOPING YOU MIGHT SIGN SOMETHING FOR ME.
NOW?!
ROCKET COMICS
GOOD LORD!
WHERE DID YOU FIND THIS?
OH, YOU KNOW HOW IT GOES...
...JUST HAPPENED ACROSS ONE...
...SAILING AROUND OUT THERE.
YOU STOLE THAT OUT OF AN EXPLORER PROBE, DIDN'T YOU?
MAYBE.
WHAT ARE YOU TWO TALKING—
AH.

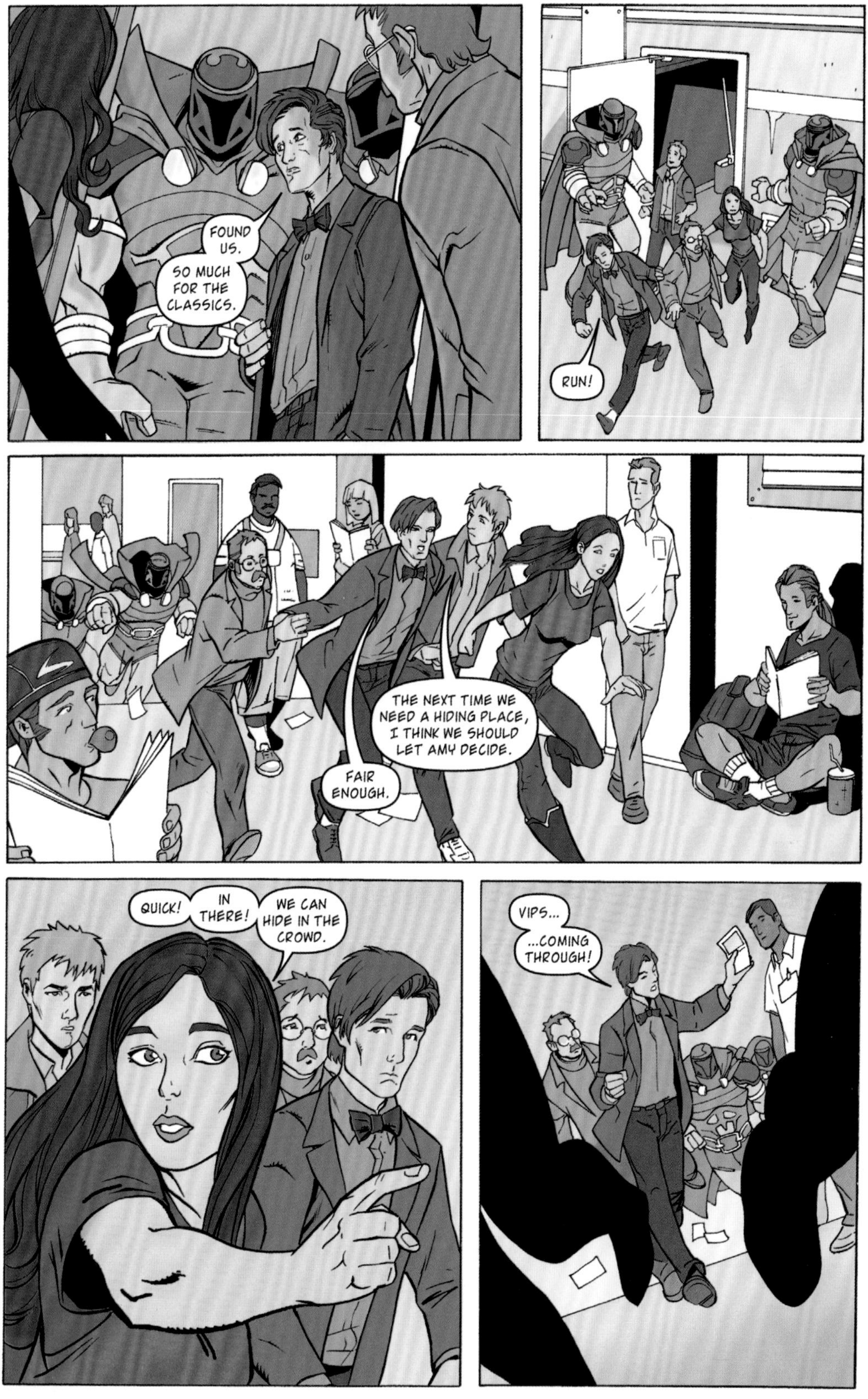
FOUND US.
SO MUCH FOR THE CLASSICS.
RUN!
THE NEXT TIME WE NEED A HIDING PLACE, I THINK WE SHOULD LET AMY DECIDE.
FAIR ENOUGH.
QUICK!
IN THERE!
WE CAN HIDE IN THE CROWD.
VIPS...
...COMING THROUGH!

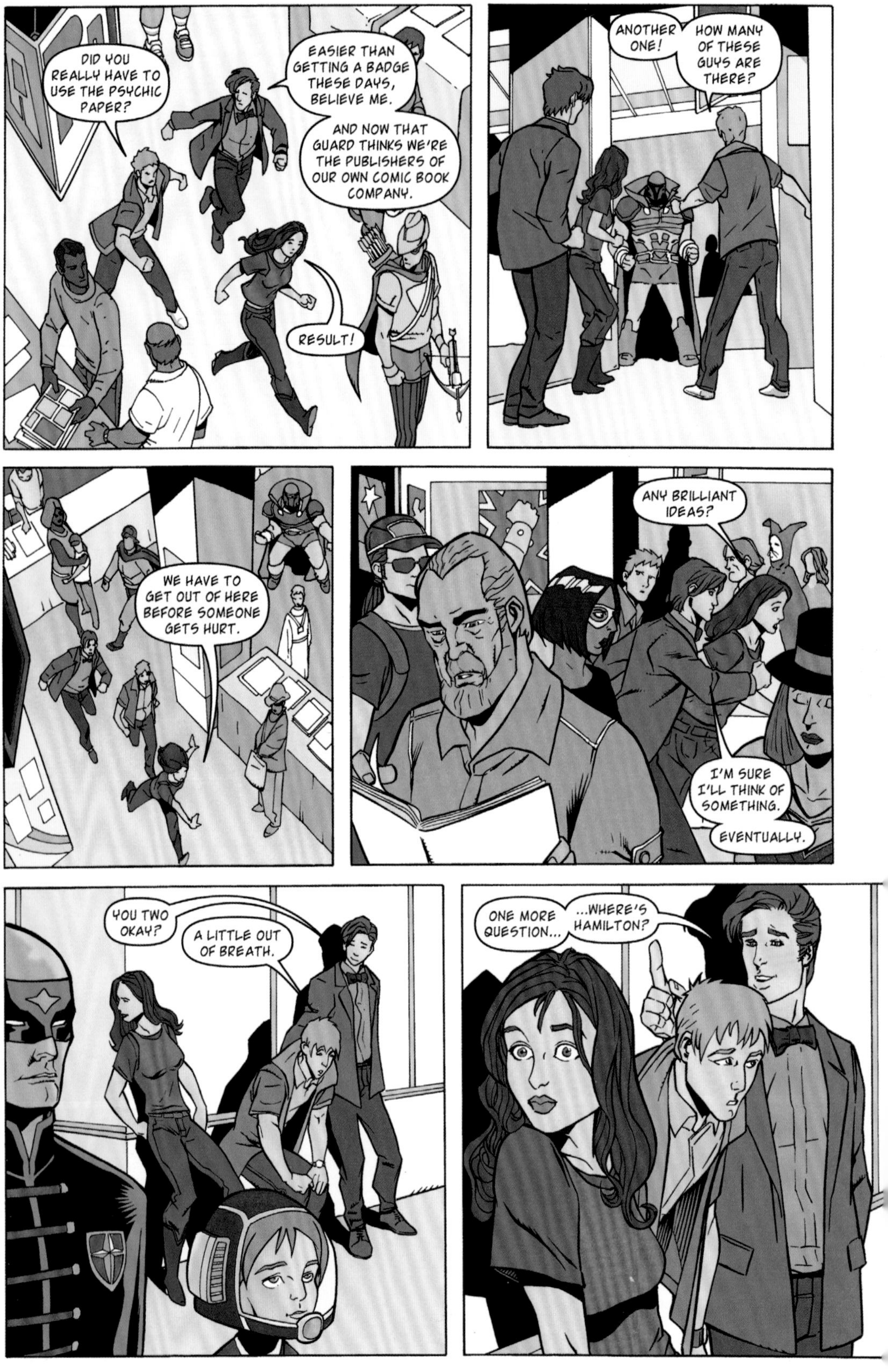
DID YOU REALLY HAVE TO USE THE PSYCHIC PAPER?
EASIER THAN GETTING A BADGE THESE DAYS, BELIEVE ME.
AND NOW THAT GUARD THINKS WE'RE THE PUBLISHERS OF OUR OWN COMIC BOOK COMPANY.
RESULT!
ANOTHER ONE!
HOW MANY OF THESE GUYS ARE THERE?
WE HAVE TO GET OUT OF HERE BEFORE SOMEONE GETS HURT.
ANY BRILLIANT IDEAS?
I'M SURE I'LL THINK OF SOMETHING.
EVENTUALLY.
YOU TWO OKAY?
A LITTLE OUT OF BREATH.
ONE MORE QUESTION...
...WHERE'S HAMILTON?

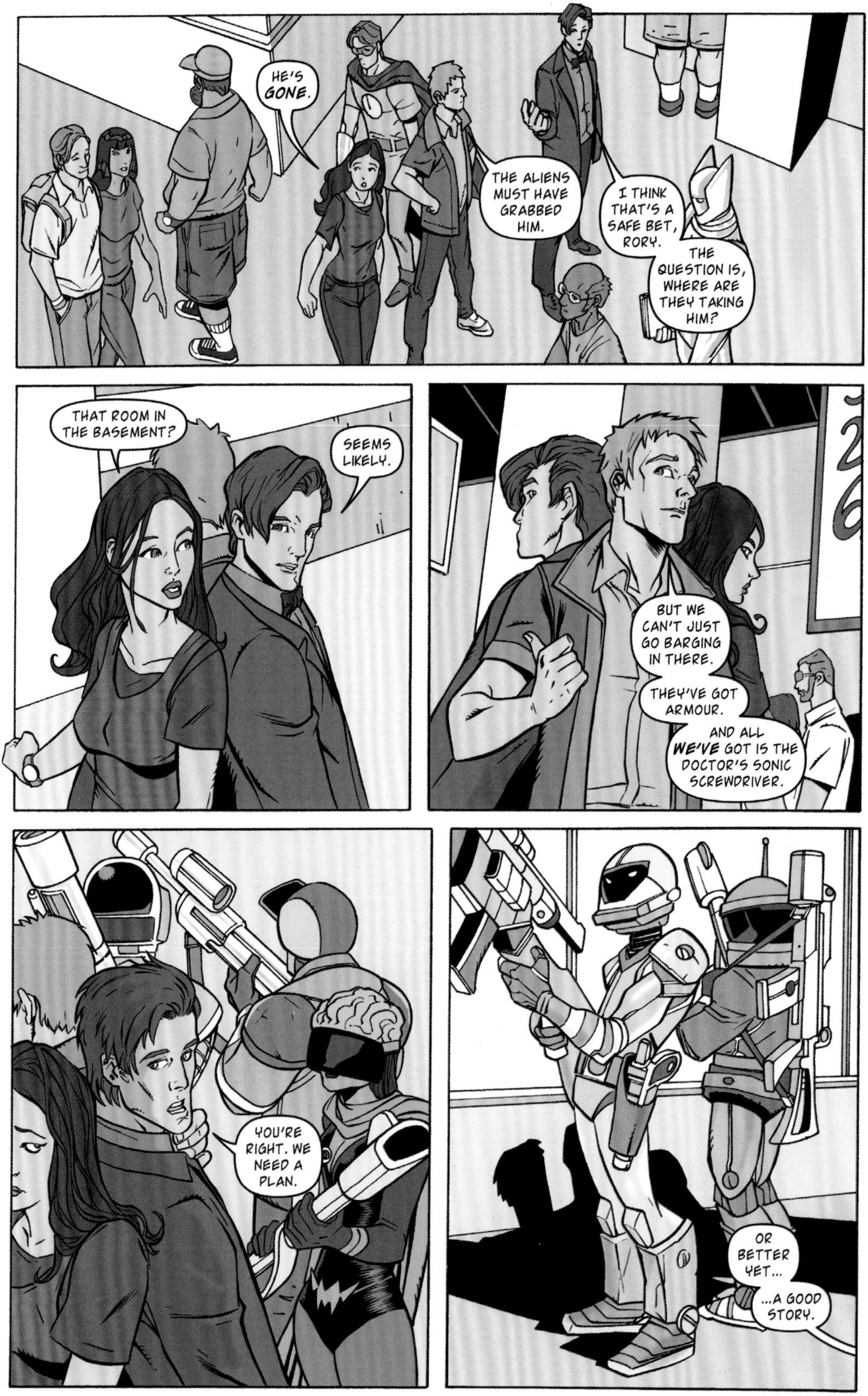
HE'S GONE.
THE ALIENS MUST HAVE GRABBED HIM.
I THINK THAT'S A SAFE BET, RORY.
THE QUESTION IS, WHERE ARE THEY TAKING HIM?
THAT ROOM IN THE BASEMENT?
SEEMS LIKELY.
BUT WE CAN'T JUST GO BARGING IN THERE.
THEY'VE GOT ARMOUR.
AND ALL WE'VE GOT IS THE DOCTOR'S SONIC SCREWDRIVER.
YOU'RE RIGHT. WE NEED A PLAN.
OR BETTER YET...
...A GOOD STORY.

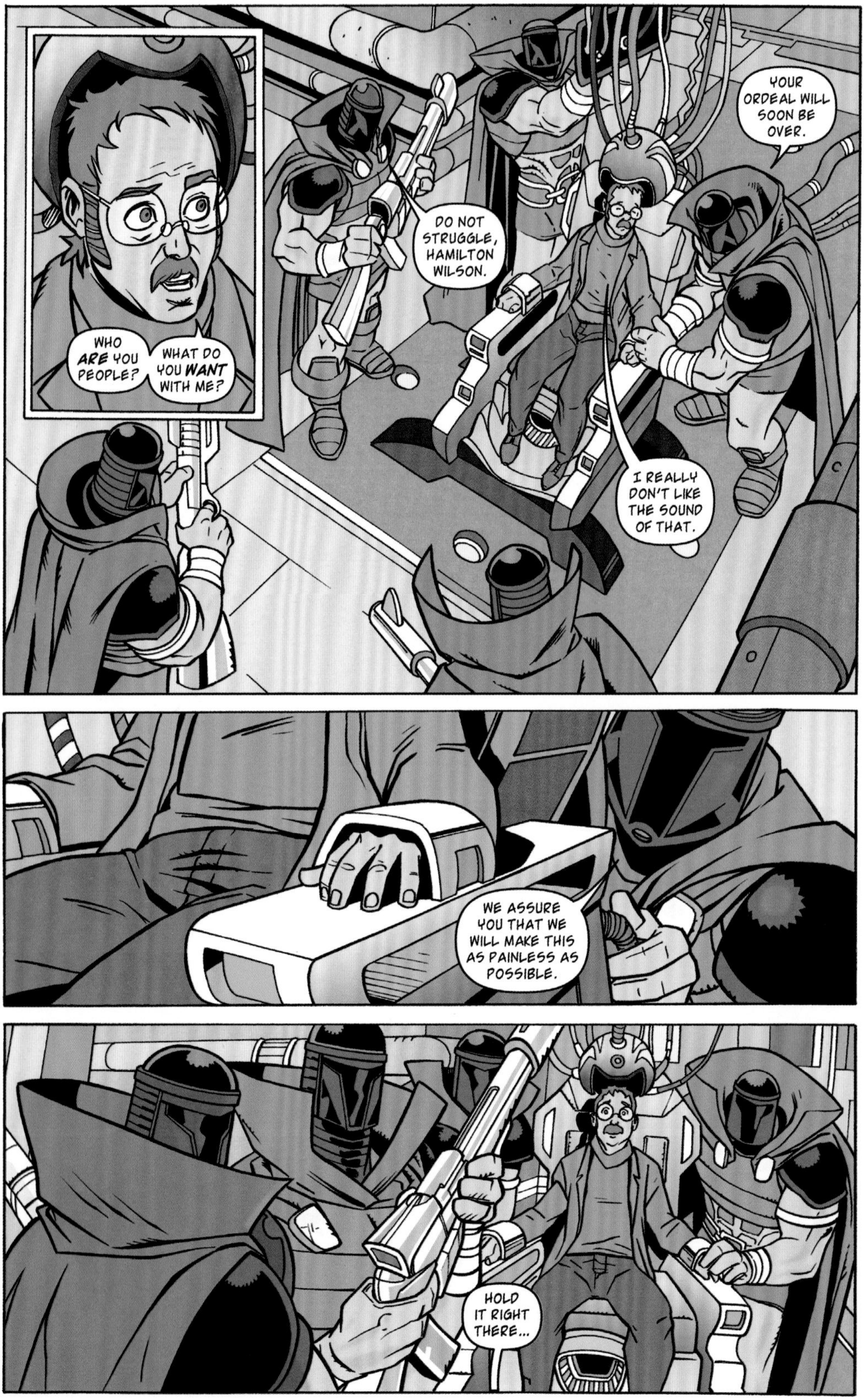

WHO ARE YOU PEOPLE?
WHAT DO YOU WANT WITH ME?
DO NOT STRUGGLE, HAMILTON WILSON.
YOUR ORDEAL WILL SOON BE OVER.
I REALLY DON'T LIKE THE SOUND OF THAT.
WE ASSURE YOU THAT WE WILL MAKE THIS AS PAINLESS AS POSSIBLE.
HOLD IT RIGHT THERE...

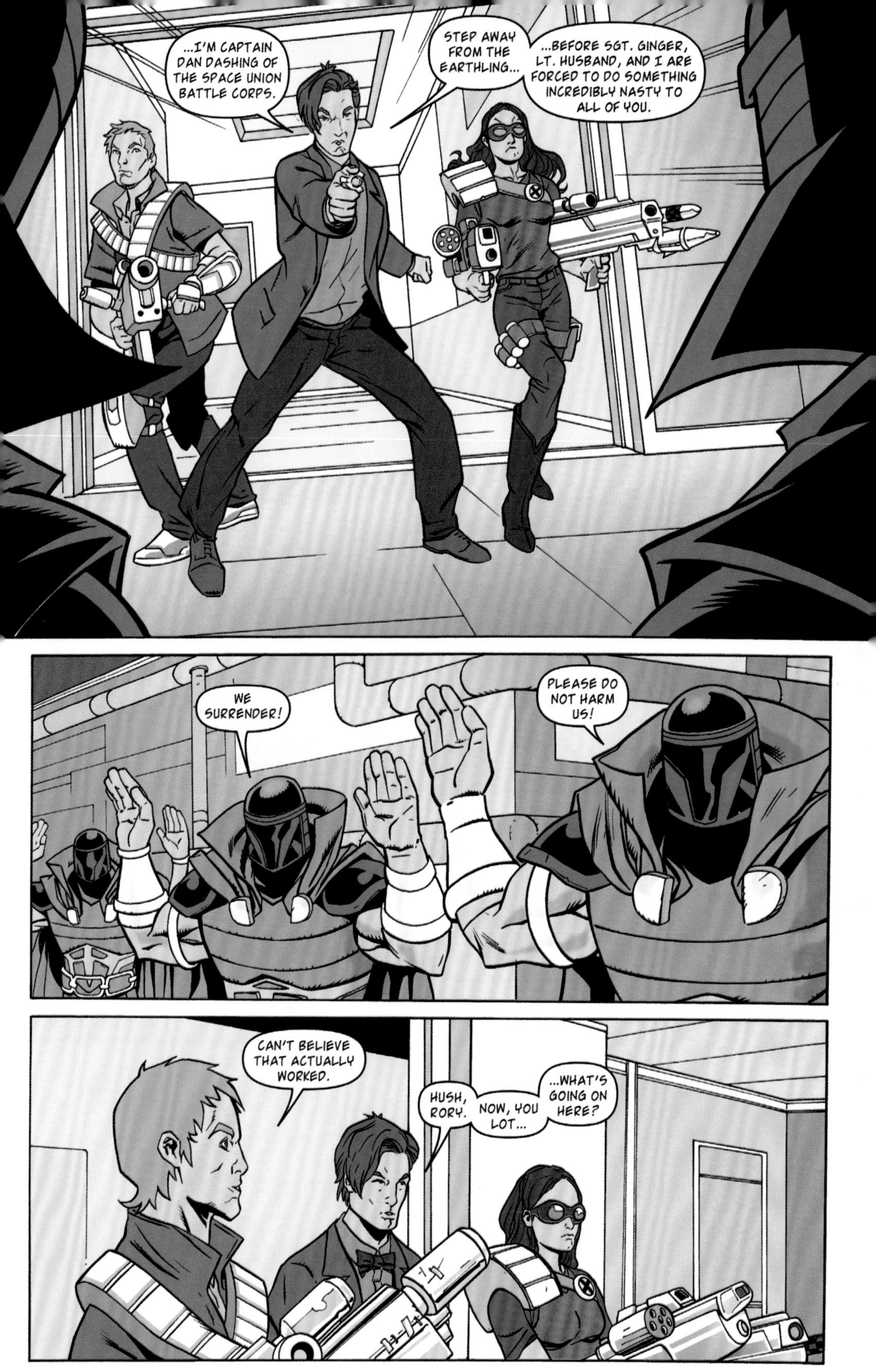
...I'M CAPTAIN DAN DASHING OF THE SPACE UNION BATTLE CORPS.
STEP AWAY FROM THE EARTHLING...
...BEFORE SGT. GINGER, LT. HUSBAND, AND I ARE FORCED TO DO SOMETHING INCREDIBLY NASTY TO ALL OF YOU.
WE SURRENDER!
PLEASE DO NOT HARM US!
CAN'T BELIEVE THAT ACTUALLY WORKED.
HUSH, RORY.
NOW, YOU LOT...
...WHAT'S GOING ON HERE?

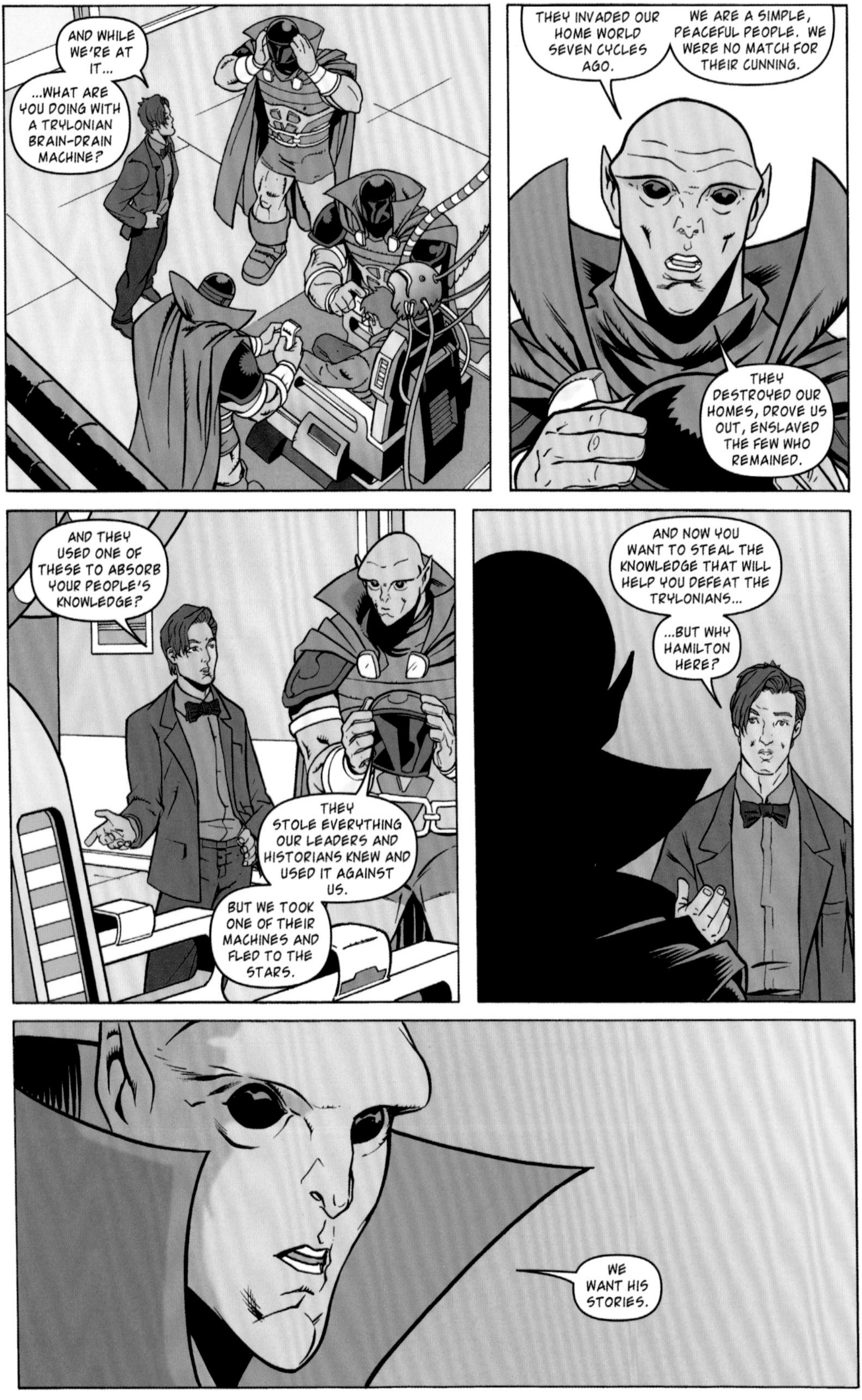
AND WHILE WE'RE AT IT...
...WHAT ARE YOU DOING WITH A TRYLONIAN BRAIN-DRAIN MACHINE?
THEY INVADED OUR HOME WORLD SEVEN CYCLES AGO.
WE ARE A SIMPLE, PEACEFUL PEOPLE. WE WERE NO MATCH FOR THEIR CUNNING.
THEY DESTROYED OUR HOMES, DROVE US OUT, ENSLAVED THE FEW WHO REMAINED.
AND THEY USED ONE OF THESE TO ABSORB YOUR PEOPLE'S KNOWLEDGE?
THEY STOLE EVERYTHING OUR LEADERS AND HISTORIANS KNEW AND USED IT AGAINST US.
BUT WE TOOK ONE OF THEIR MACHINES AND FLED TO THE STARS.
AND NOW YOU WANT TO STEAL THE KNOWLEDGE THAT WILL HELP YOU DEFEAT THE TRYLONIANS...
...BUT WHY HAMILTON HERE?
WE WANT HIS STORIES.

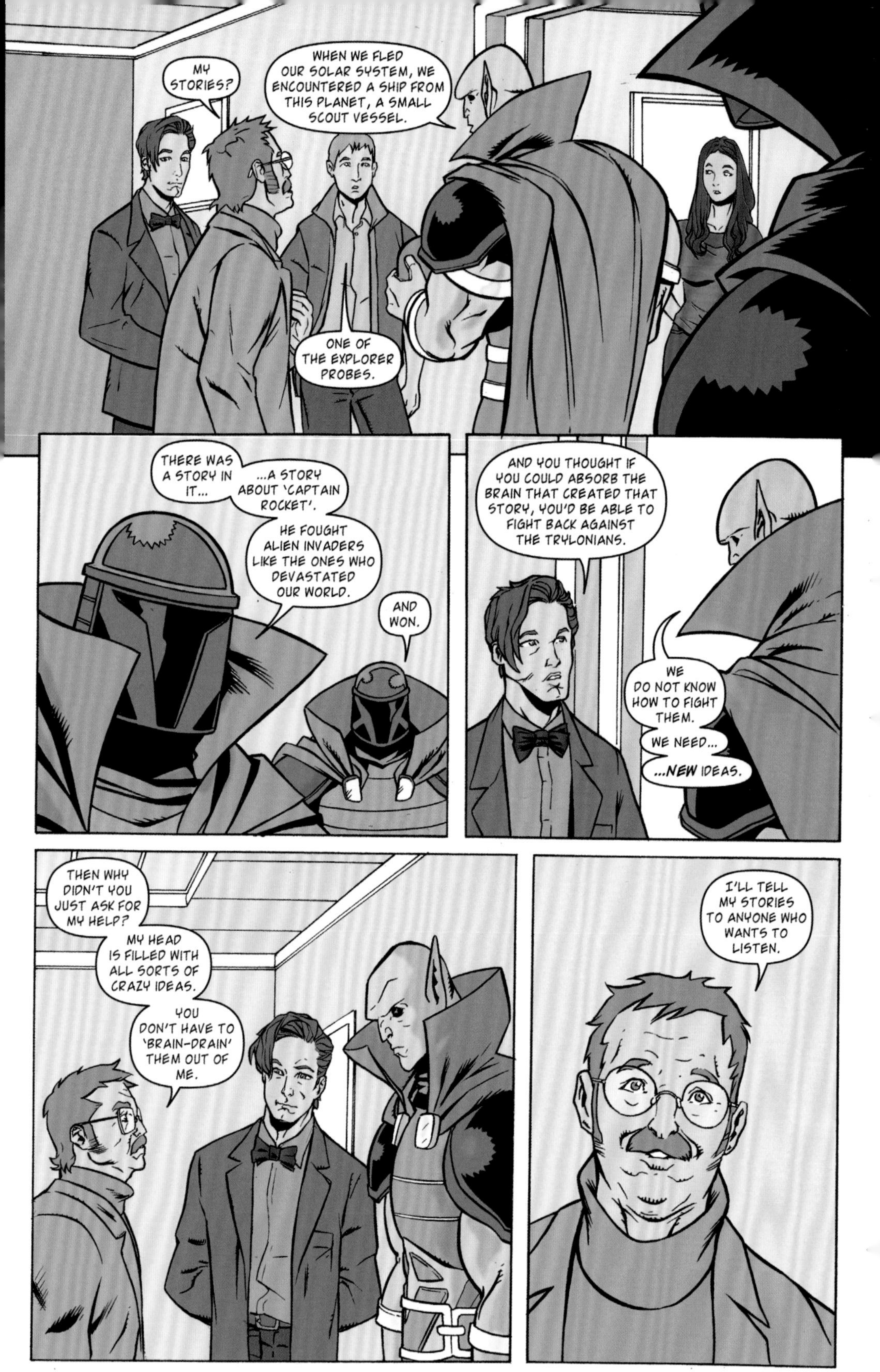
MY STORIES?
WHEN WE FLED OUR SOLAR SYSTEM, WE ENCOUNTERED A SHIP FROM THIS PLANET, A SMALL SCOUT VESSEL.
ONE OF THE EXPLORER PROBES.
THERE WAS A STORY IN IT...
...A STORY ABOUT 'CAPTAIN ROCKET'.
HE FOUGHT ALIEN INVADERS LIKE THE ONES WHO DEVASTATED OUR WORLD.
AND WON.
AND YOU THOUGHT IF YOU COULD ABSORB THE BRAIN THAT CREATED THAT STORY, YOU'D BE ABLE TO FIGHT BACK AGAINST THE TRYLONIANS.
WE DO NOT KNOW HOW TO FIGHT THEM.
WE NEED...
...**NEW** IDEAS.
THEN WHY DIDN'T YOU JUST ASK FOR MY HELP?
MY HEAD IS FILLED WITH ALL SORTS OF CRAZY IDEAS.
YOU DON'T HAVE TO 'BRAIN-DRAIN' THEM OUT OF ME.
I'LL TELL MY STORIES TO ANYONE WHO WANTS TO LISTEN.

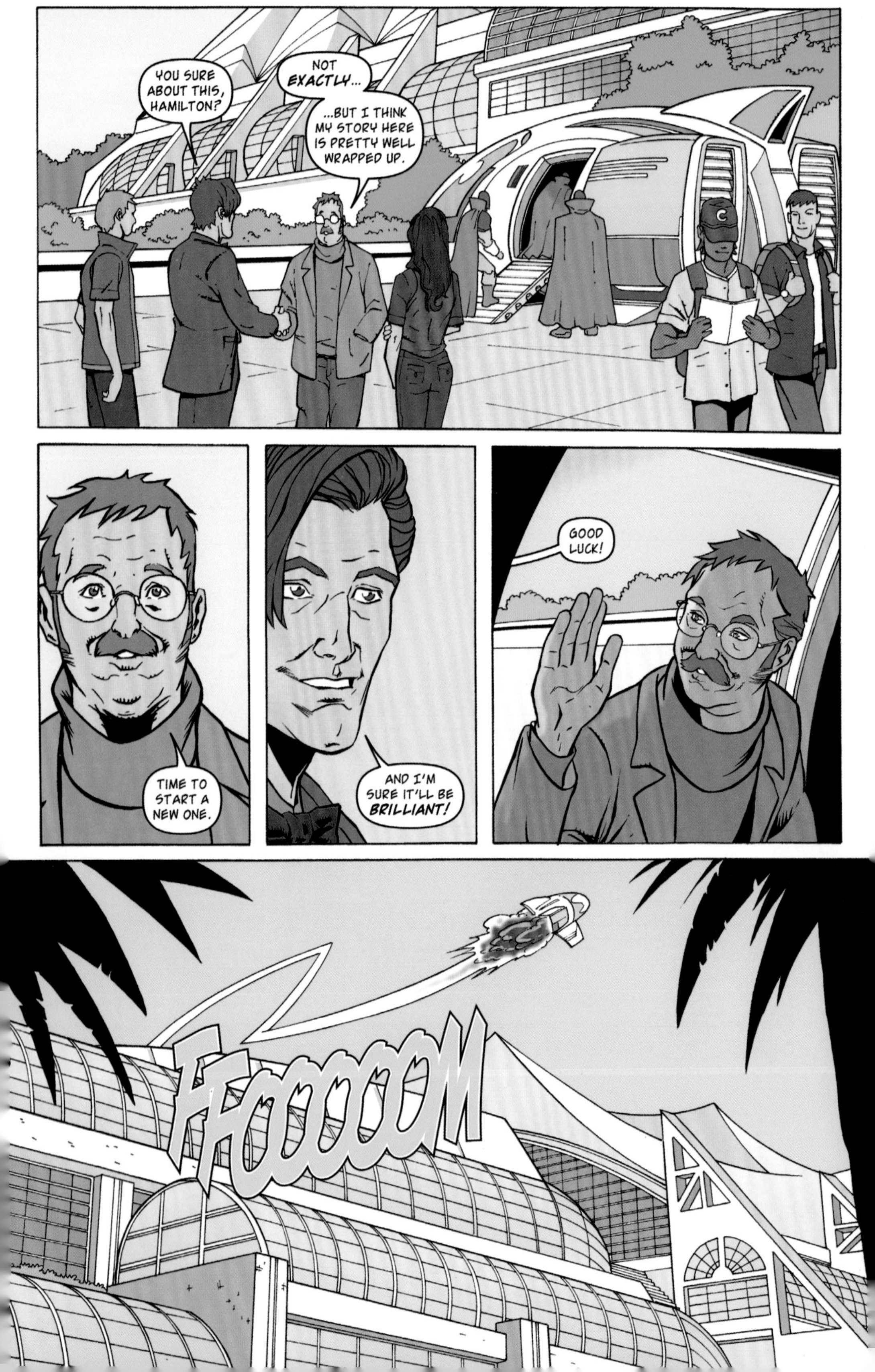
YOU SURE ABOUT THIS, HAMILTON?
NOT EXACTLY...
...BUT I THINK MY STORY HERE IS PRETTY WELL WRAPPED UP.
TIME TO START A NEW ONE.
AND I'M SURE IT'LL BE BRILLIANT!
GOOD LUCK!
FFOOOOOM

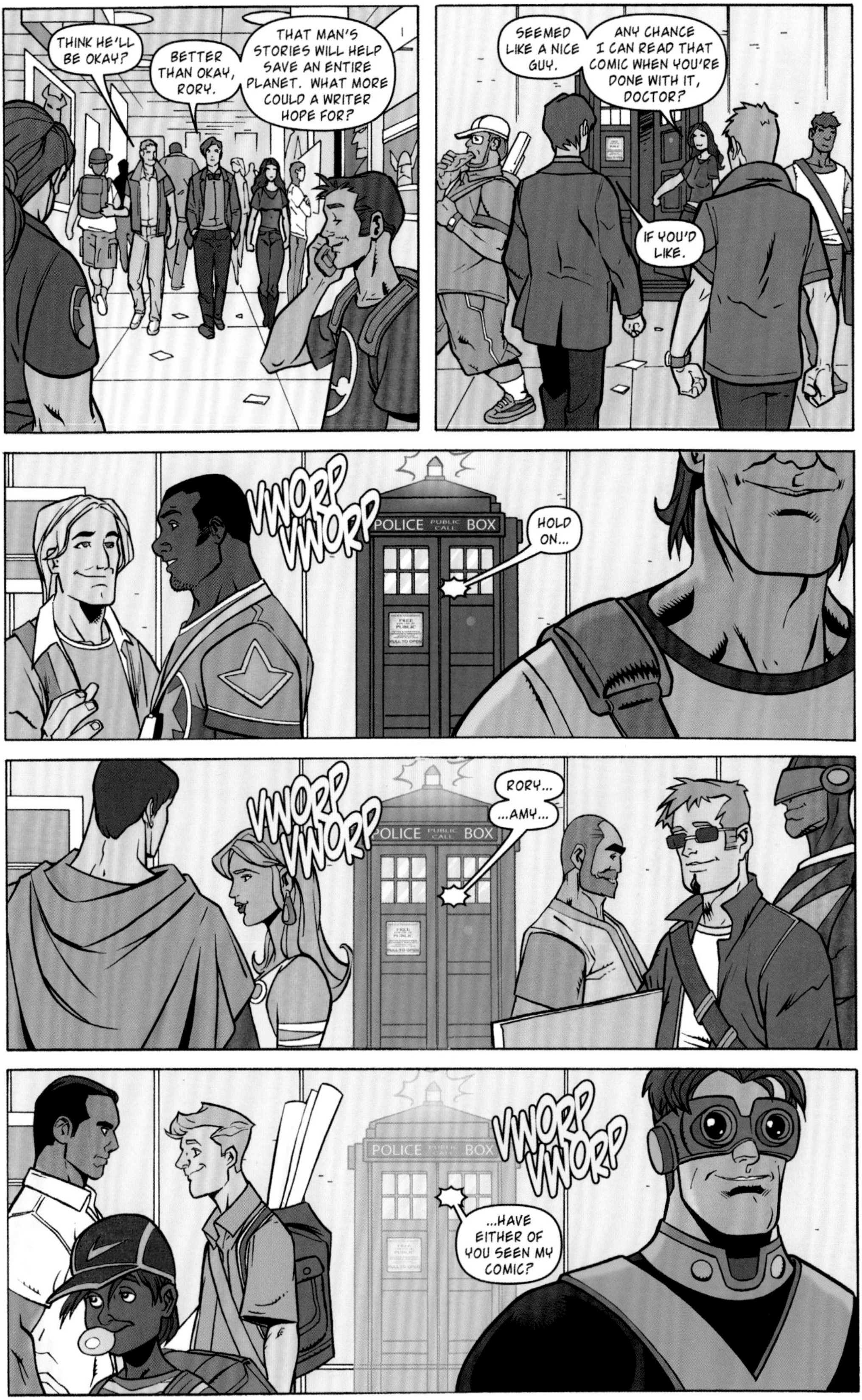
THINK HE'LL BE OKAY?
BETTER THAN OKAY, RORY.
THAT MAN'S STORIES WILL HELP SAVE AN ENTIRE PLANET. WHAT MORE COULD A WRITER HOPE FOR?
SEEMED LIKE A NICE GUY.
ANY CHANCE I CAN READ THAT COMIC WHEN YOU'RE DONE WITH IT, DOCTOR?
IF YOU'D LIKE.
VWORP VWORP
POLICE PUBLIC CALL BOX
HOLD ON...
VWORP VWORP
POLICE PUBLIC CALL BOX
RORY...
...AMY...
POLICE PUBLIC CALL BOX
VWORP VWORP
...HAVE EITHER OF YOU SEEN MY COMIC?

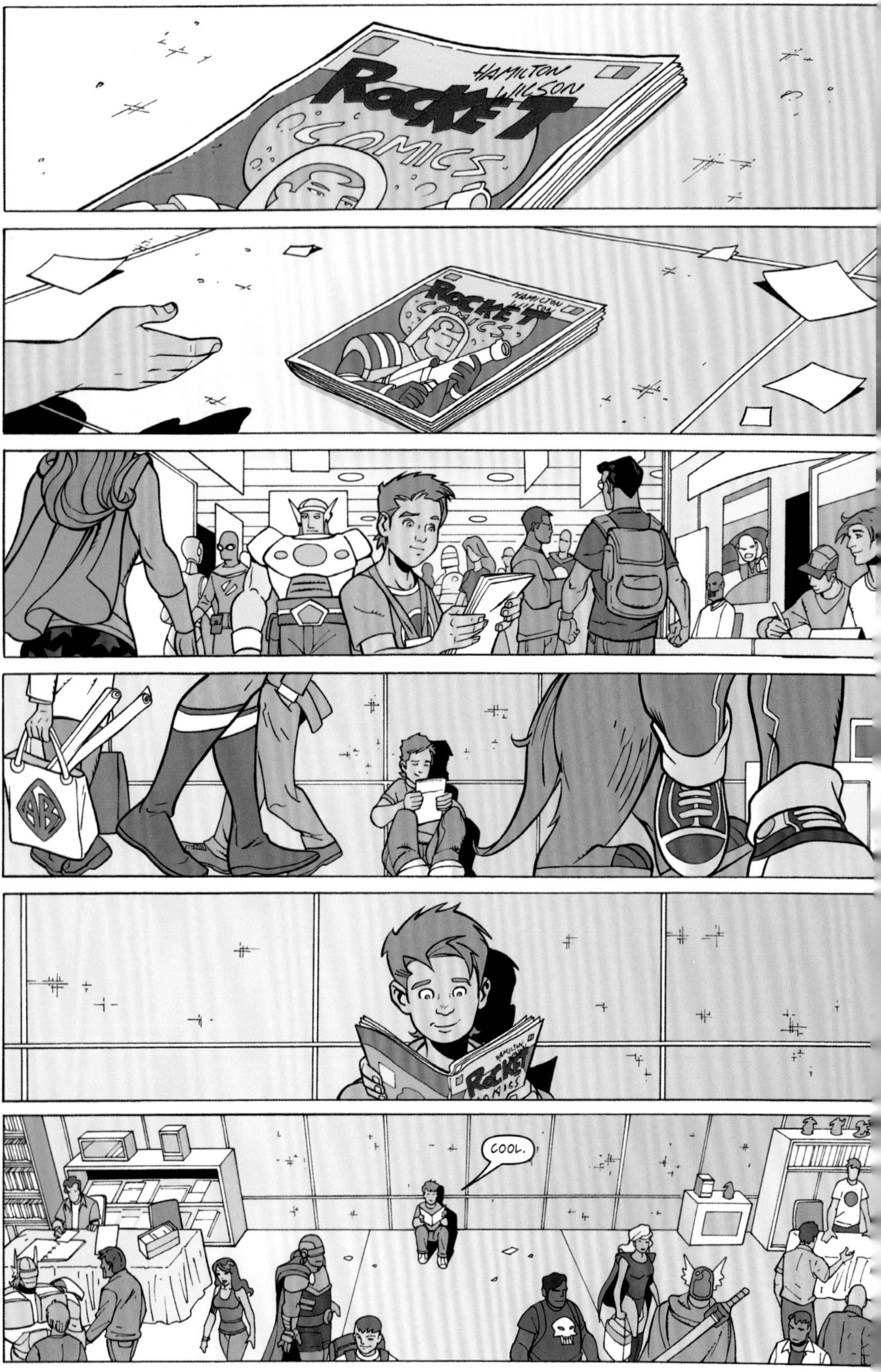
HAMILTON WILSON
ROCKET COMICS
COOL.

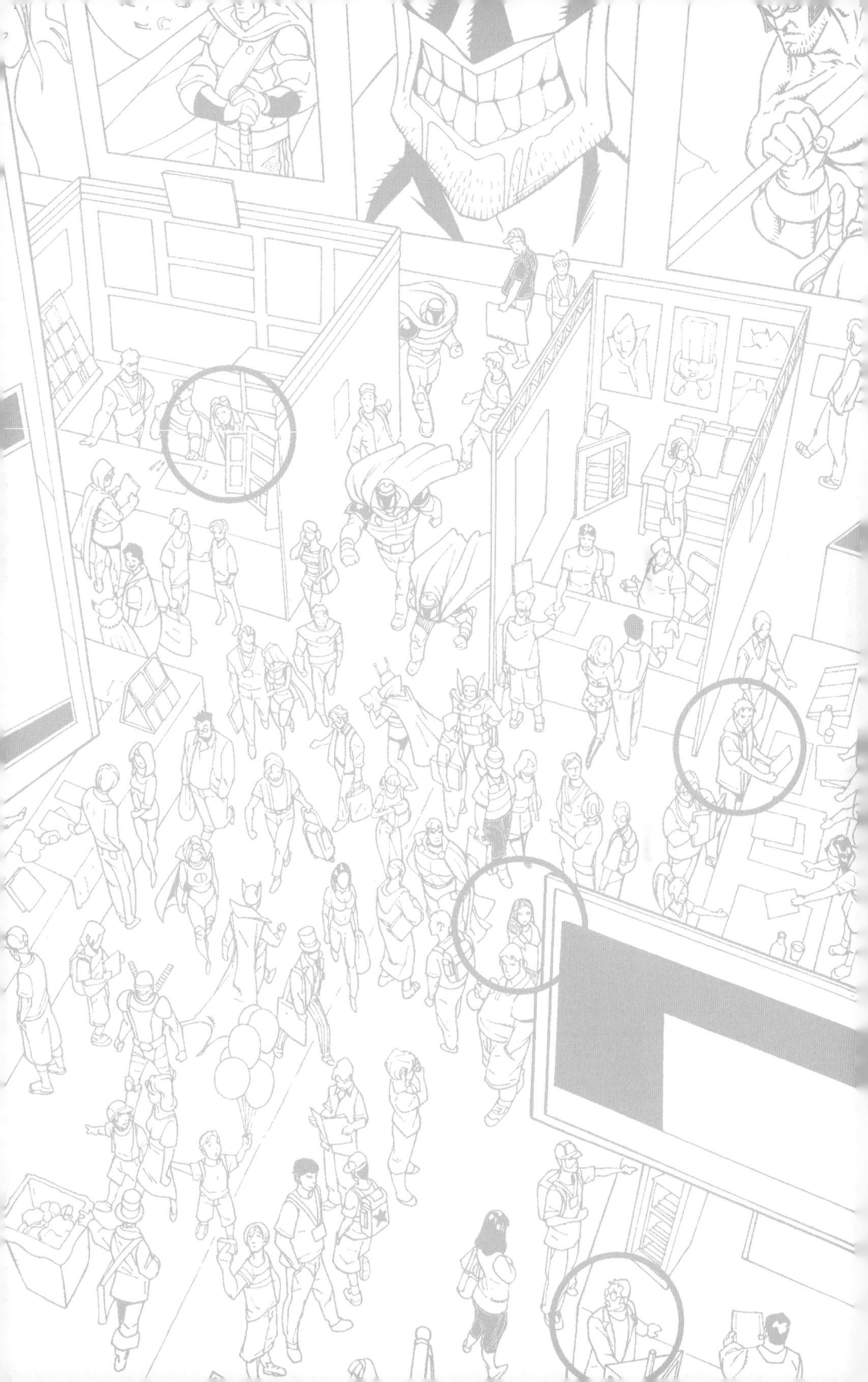

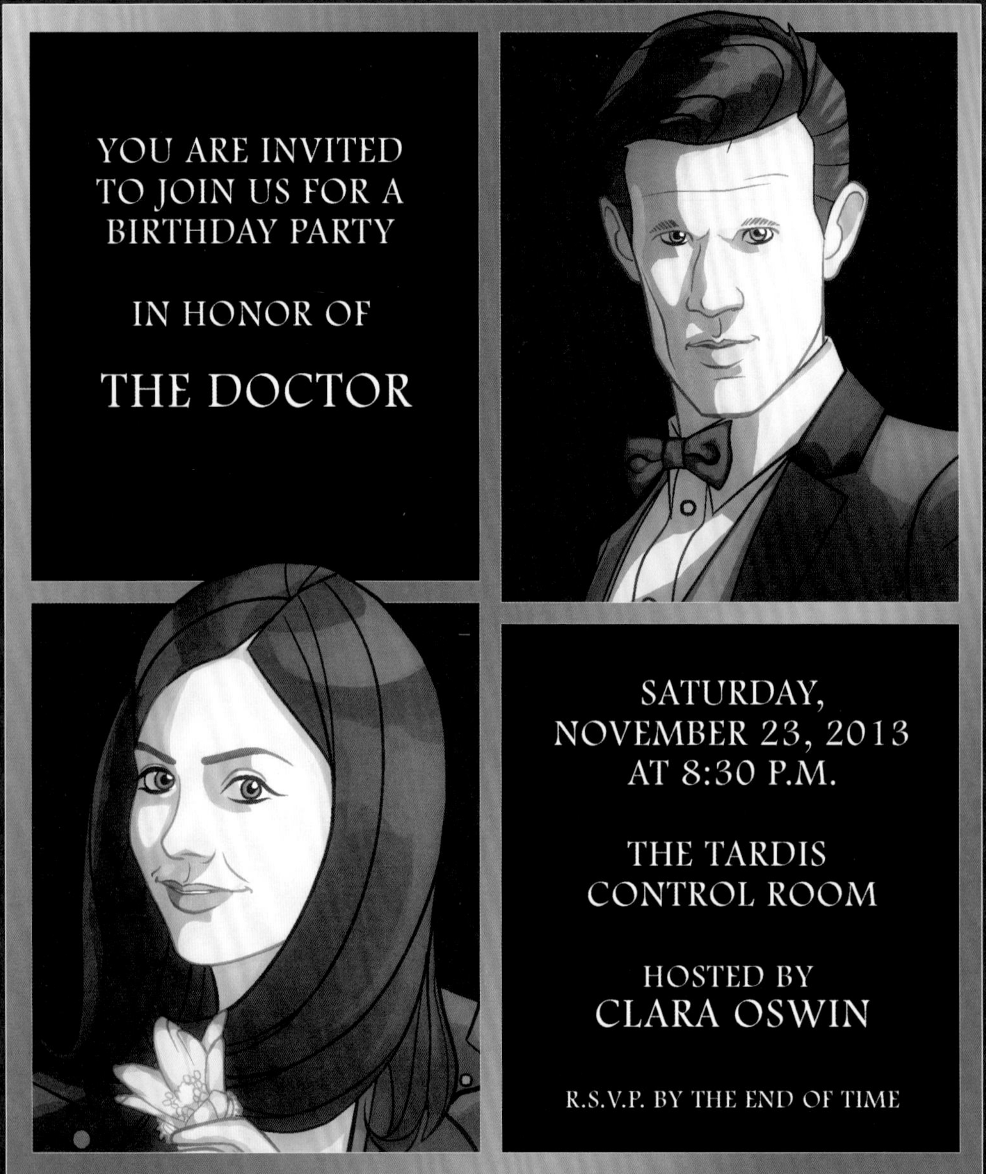
YOU ARE INVITED TO JOIN US FOR A BIRTHDAY PARTY
IN HONOR OF
THE DOCTOR
SATURDAY, NOVEMBER 23, 2013 AT 8:30 P.M.
THE TARDIS CONTROL ROOM
HOSTED BY CLARA OSWIN
R.S.V.P. BY THE END OF TIME

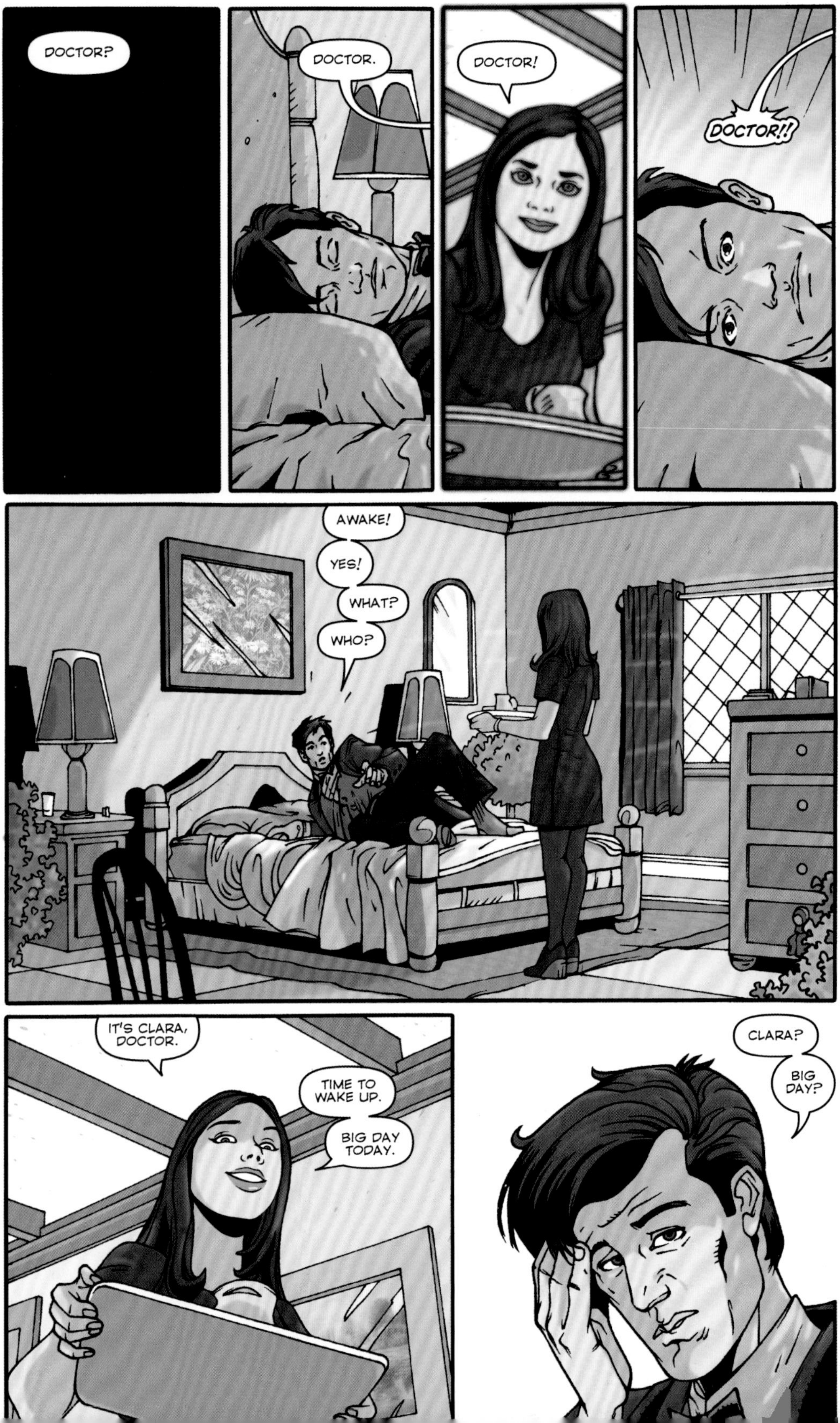
DOCTOR?
DOCTOR.
DOCTOR!
DOCTOR!!
AWAKE!
YES!
WHAT?
WHO?
IT'S CLARA, DOCTOR.
TIME TO WAKE UP.
BIG DAY TODAY.
CLARA?
BIG DAY?

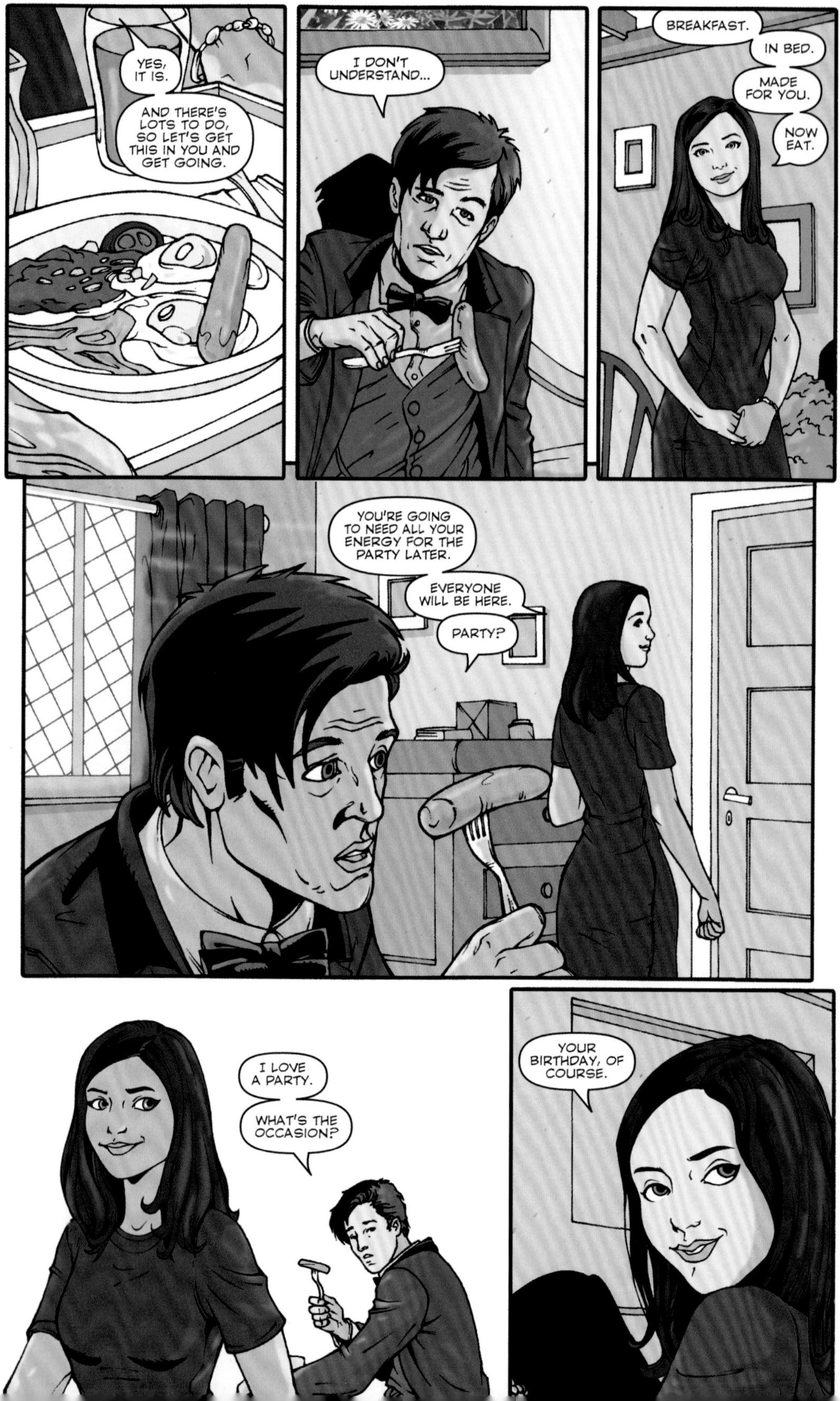
YES, IT IS.
AND THERE'S LOTS TO DO, SO LET'S GET THIS IN YOU AND GET GOING.
I DON'T UNDERSTAND...
BREAKFAST.
IN BED.
MADE FOR YOU.
NOW EAT.
YOU'RE GOING TO NEED ALL YOUR ENERGY FOR THE PARTY LATER.
EVERYONE WILL BE HERE.
PARTY?
I LOVE A PARTY.
WHAT'S THE OCCASION?
YOUR BIRTHDAY, OF COURSE.

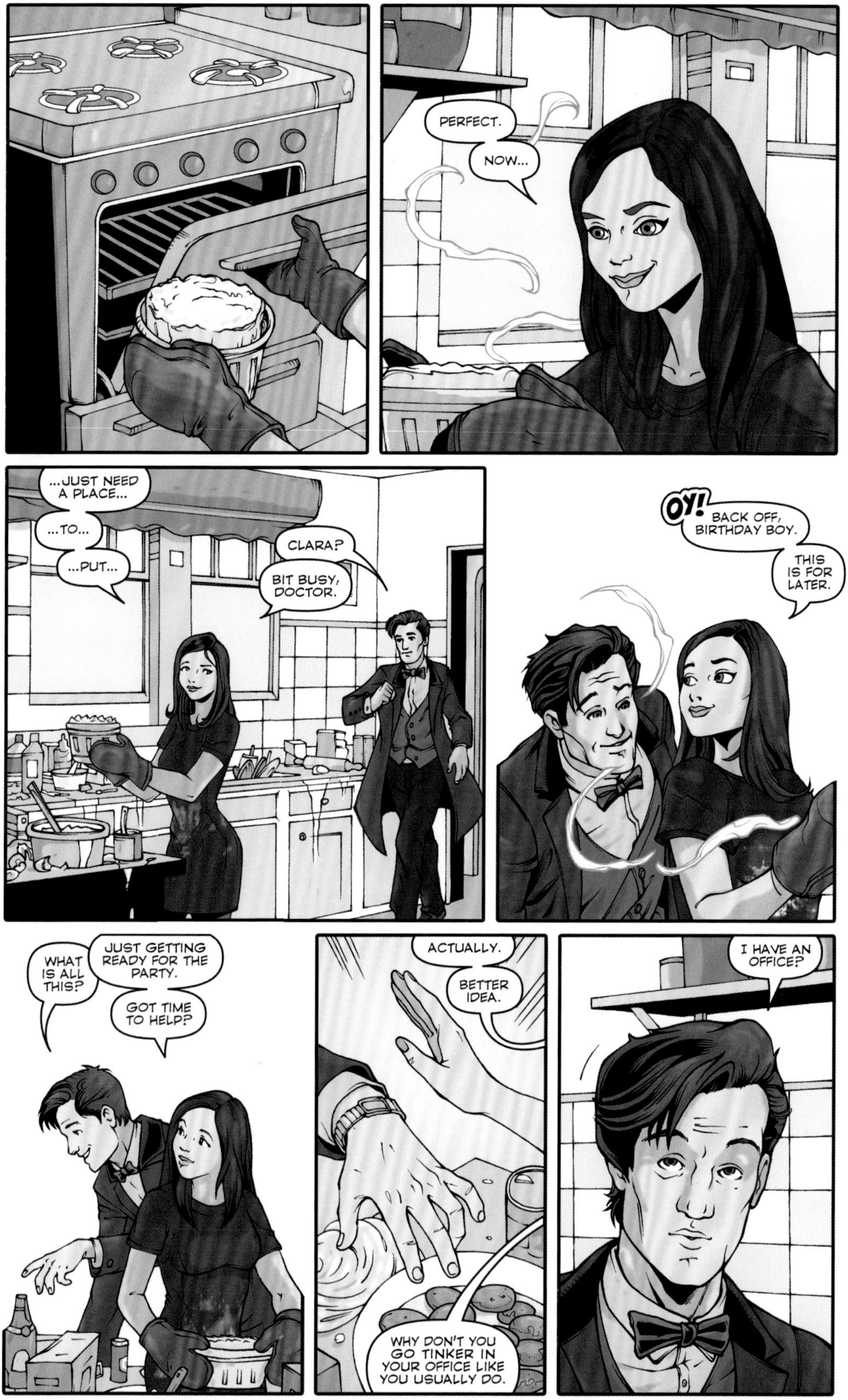
PERFECT.
NOW...
...JUST NEED A PLACE...
...TO...
...PUT...
CLARA?
BIT BUSY, DOCTOR.
OY! BACK OFF, BIRTHDAY BOY.
THIS IS FOR LATER.
WHAT IS ALL THIS?
JUST GETTING READY FOR THE PARTY.
GOT TIME TO HELP?
ACTUALLY.
BETTER IDEA.
WHY DON'T YOU GO TINKER IN YOUR OFFICE LIKE YOU USUALLY DO.
I HAVE AN OFFICE?

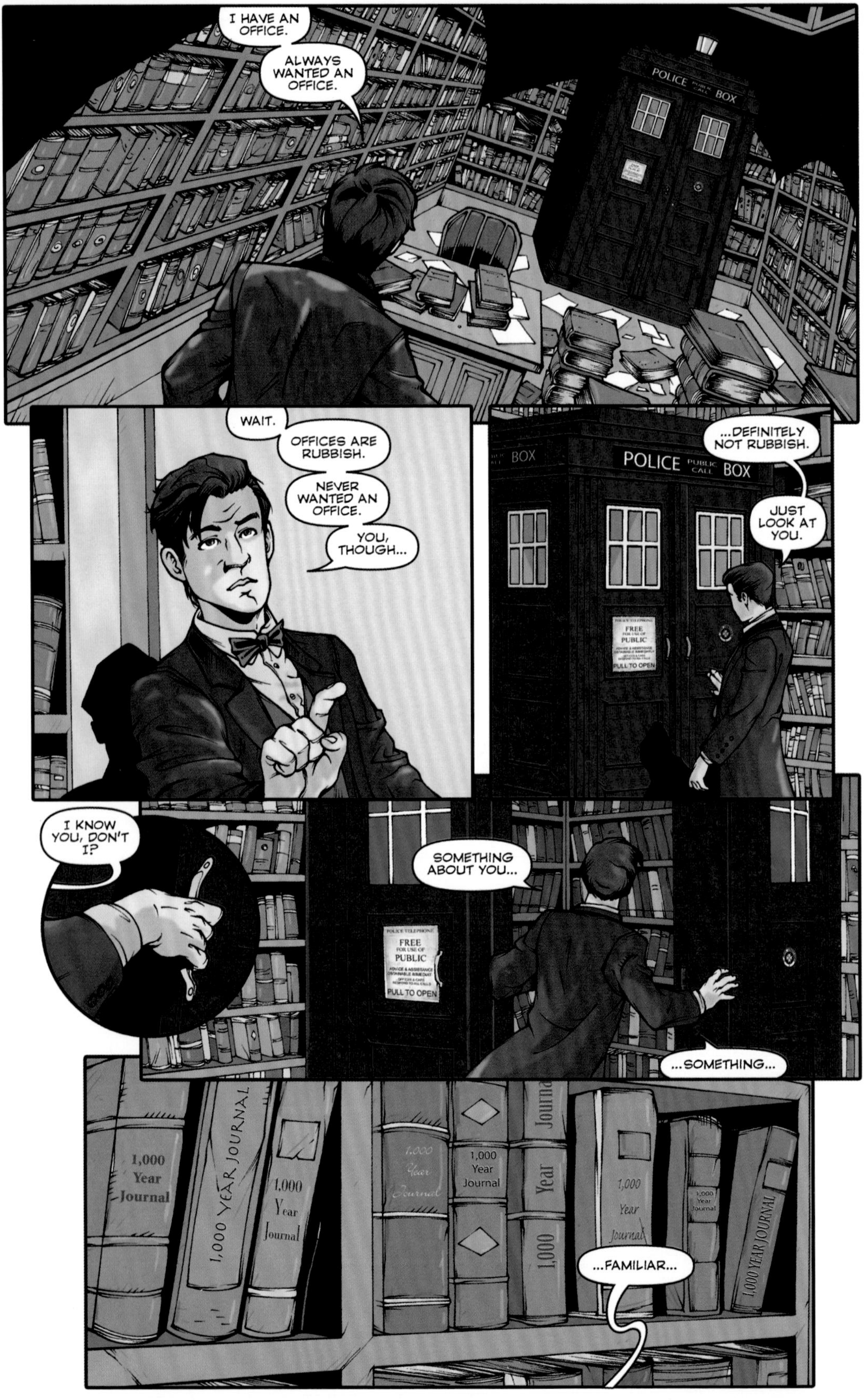
I HAVE AN OFFICE.
ALWAYS WANTED AN OFFICE.
POLICE PUBLIC CALL BOX
WAIT.
OFFICES ARE RUBBISH.
NEVER WANTED AN OFFICE.
YOU, THOUGH...
POLICE PUBLIC CALL BOX
...DEFINITELY NOT RUBBISH.
JUST LOOK AT YOU.
I KNOW YOU, DON'T I?
SOMETHING ABOUT YOU...
FREE FOR USE OF PUBLIC
PULL TO OPEN
...SOMETHING...
1,000 Year Journal
1,000 YEAR JOURNAL
...FAMILIAR...

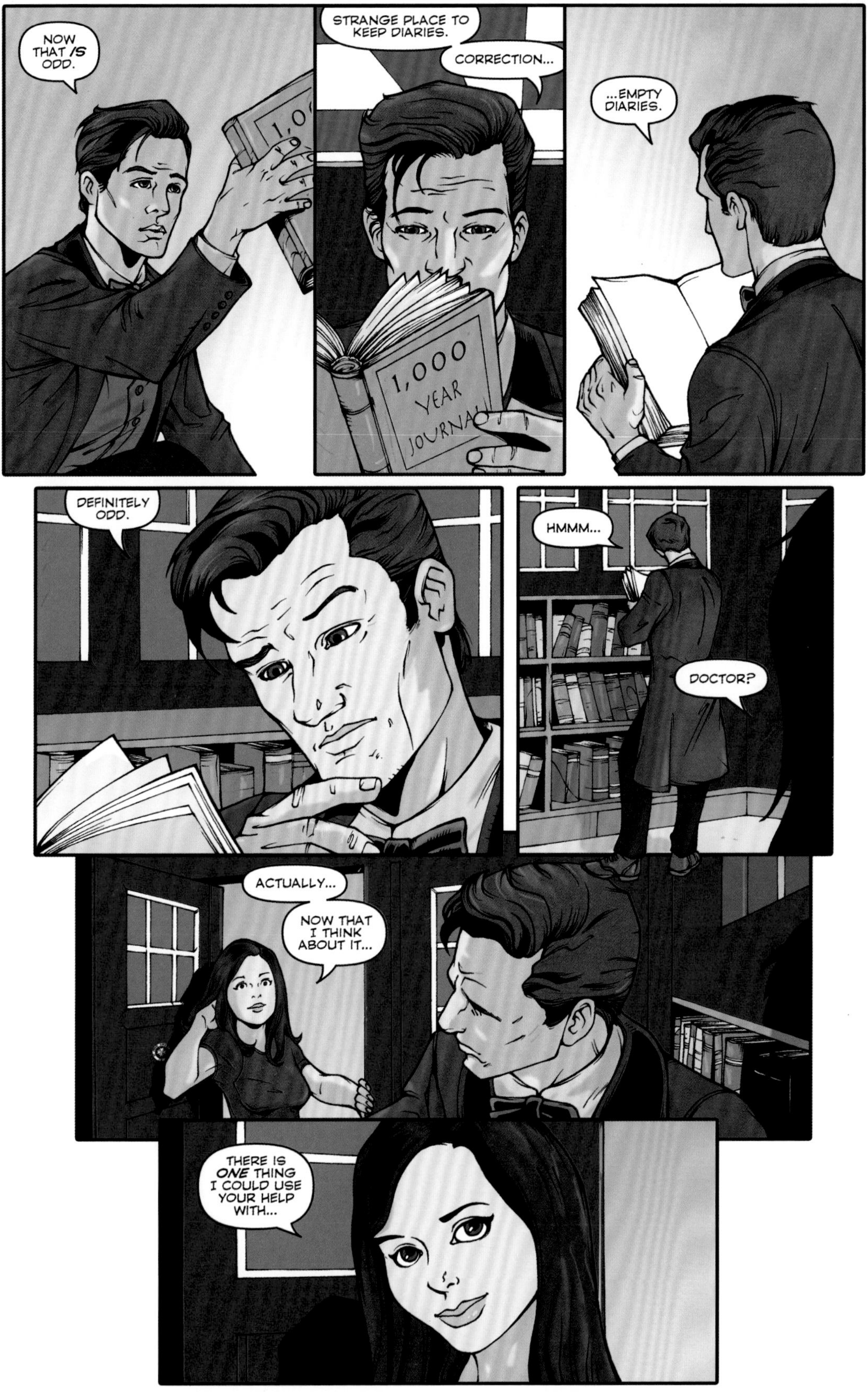
NOW THAT *IS* ODD.
STRANGE PLACE TO KEEP DIARIES.
CORRECTION...
1,000 YEAR JOURNAL
...EMPTY DIARIES.
DEFINITELY ODD.
HMMM...
DOCTOR?
ACTUALLY...
NOW THAT I THINK ABOUT IT...
THERE IS *ONE* THING I COULD USE YOUR HELP WITH...

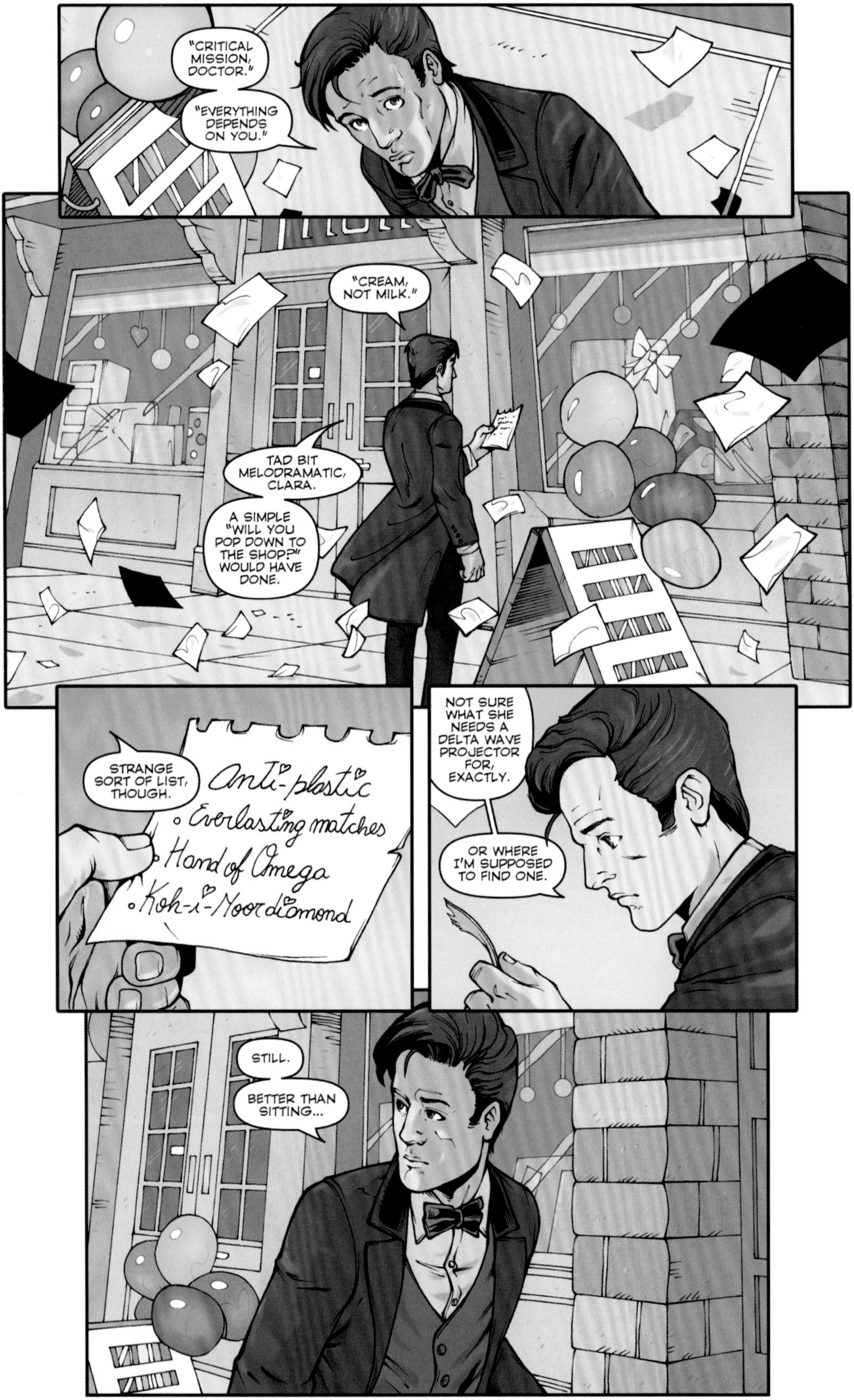
"CRITICAL MISSION, DOCTOR."
"EVERYTHING DEPENDS ON YOU."
"CREAM, NOT MILK."
TAD BIT MELODRAMATIC, CLARA.
A SIMPLE "WILL YOU POP DOWN TO THE SHOP?" WOULD HAVE DONE.
STRANGE SORT OF LIST, THOUGH.
Anti-plastic
Everlasting matches
Hand of Omega
Koh-i-Noor diamond
NOT SURE WHAT SHE NEEDS A DELTA WAVE PROJECTOR FOR, EXACTLY.
OR WHERE I'M SUPPOSED TO FIND ONE.
STILL.
BETTER THAN SITTING...

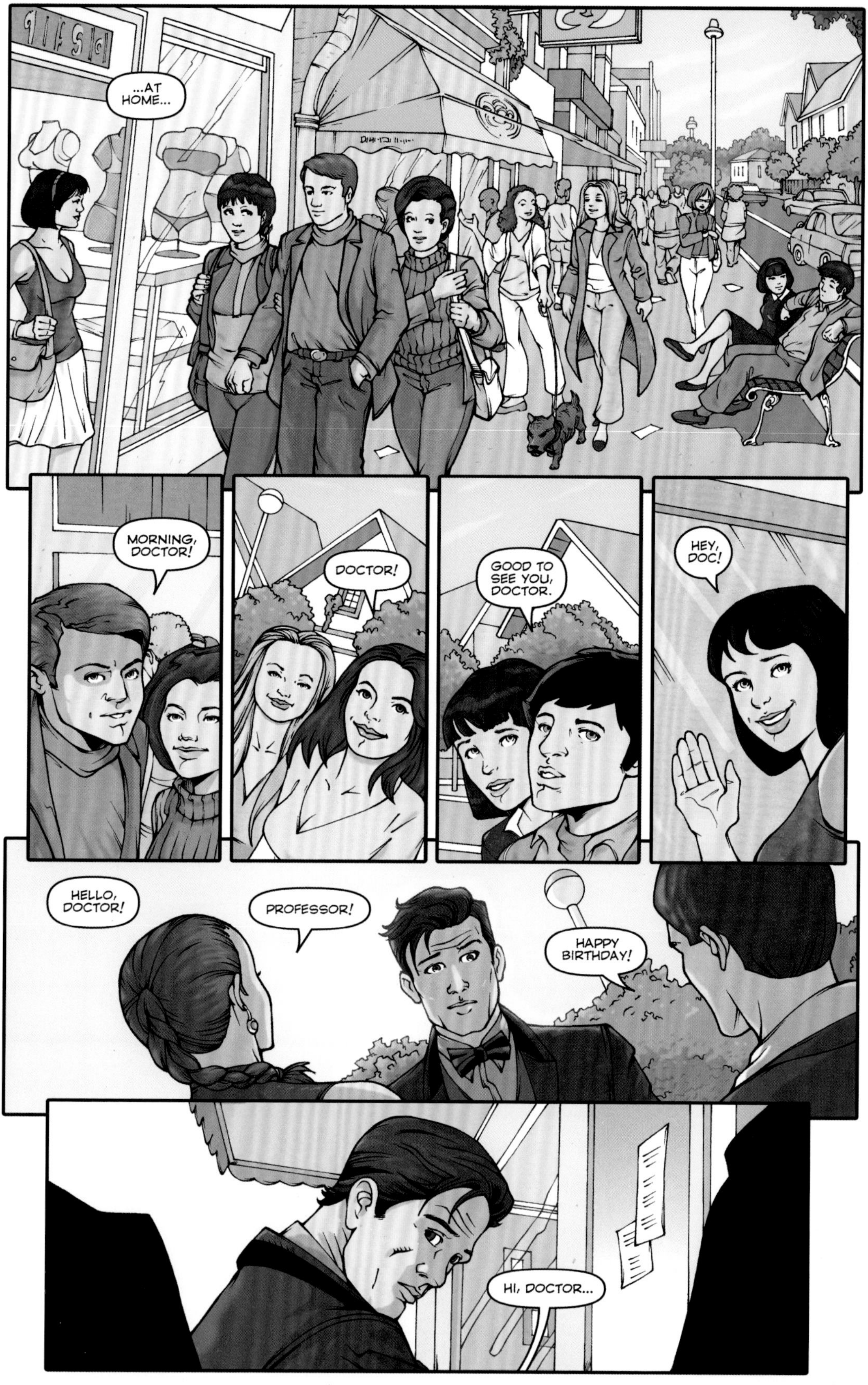
...AT HOME...
MORNING, DOCTOR!
DOCTOR!
GOOD TO SEE YOU, DOCTOR.
HEY, DOC!
HELLO, DOCTOR!
PROFESSOR!
HAPPY BIRTHDAY!
HI, DOCTOR...

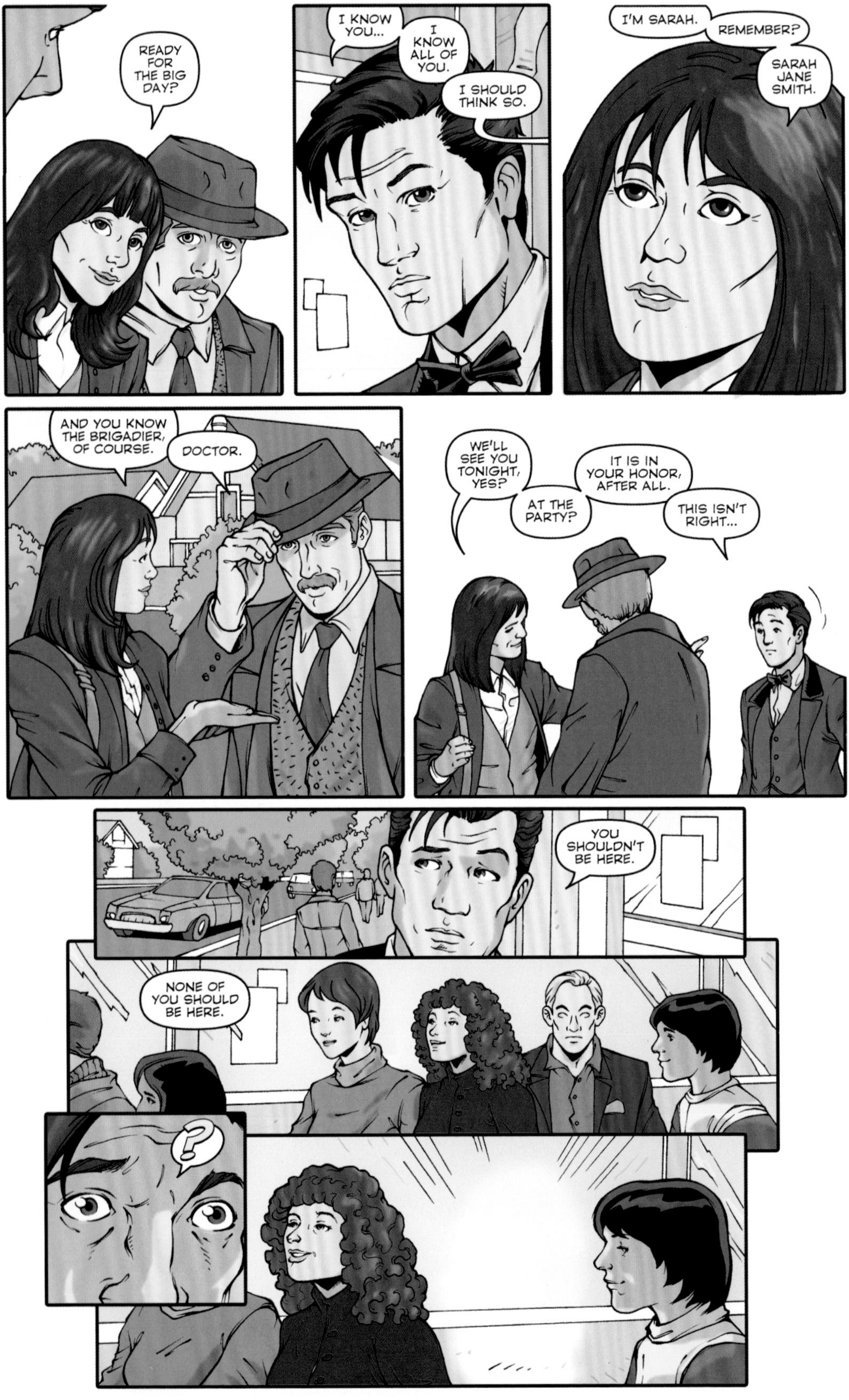
READY FOR THE BIG DAY?
I KNOW YOU...
I KNOW ALL OF YOU.
I SHOULD THINK SO.
I'M SARAH.
REMEMBER?
SARAH JANE SMITH.
AND YOU KNOW THE BRIGADIER, OF COURSE.
DOCTOR.
WE'LL SEE YOU TONIGHT, YES?
AT THE PARTY?
IT IS IN YOUR HONOR, AFTER ALL.
THIS ISN'T RIGHT...
YOU SHOULDN'T BE HERE.
NONE OF YOU SHOULD BE HERE.
?

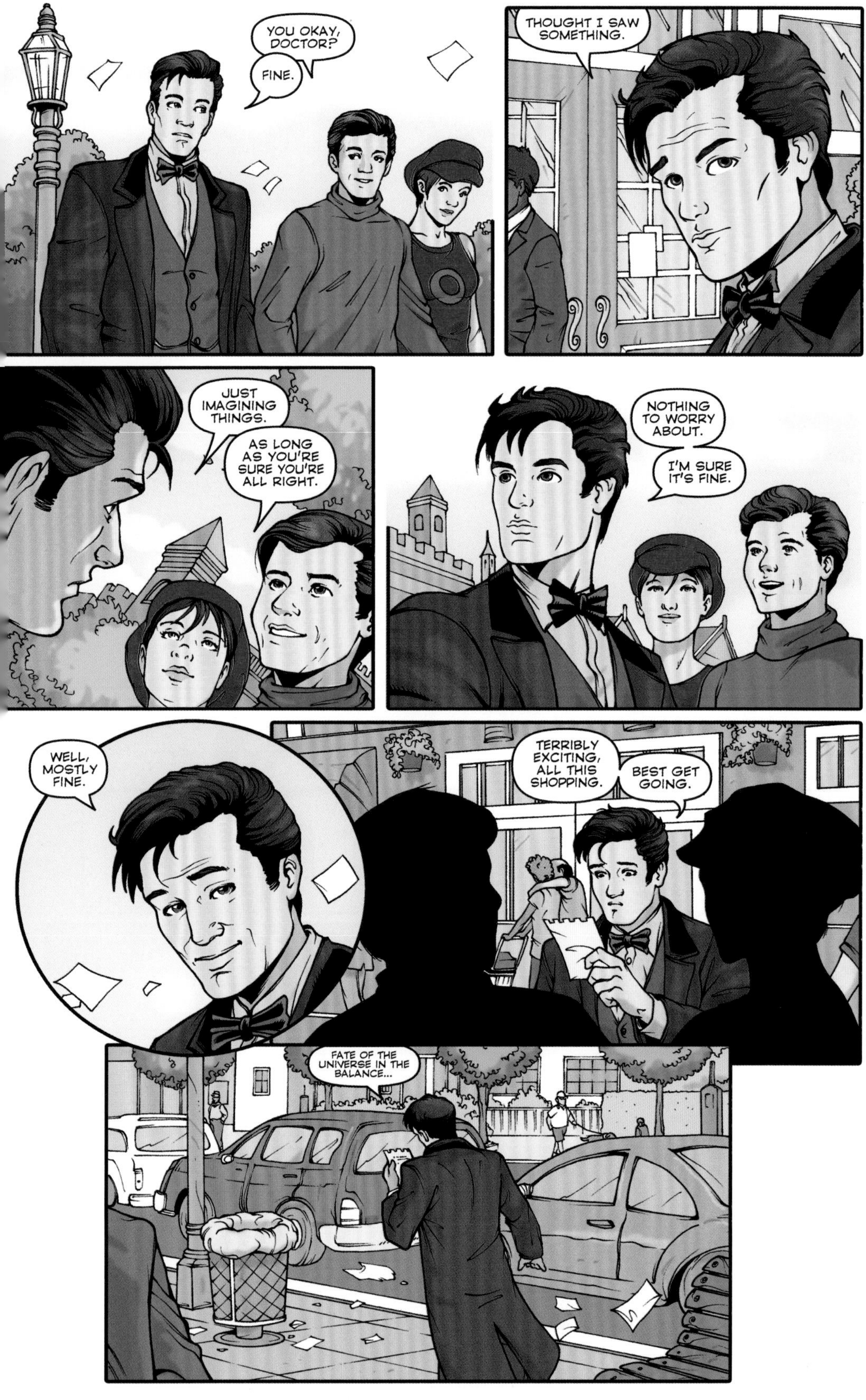
YOU OKAY, DOCTOR?
FINE.
THOUGHT I SAW SOMETHING.
JUST IMAGINING THINGS.
AS LONG AS YOU'RE SURE YOU'RE ALL RIGHT.
NOTHING TO WORRY ABOUT.
I'M SURE IT'S FINE.
WELL, MOSTLY FINE.
TERRIBLY EXCITING, ALL THIS SHOPPING.
BEST GET GOING.
FATE OF THE UNIVERSE IN THE BALANCE...

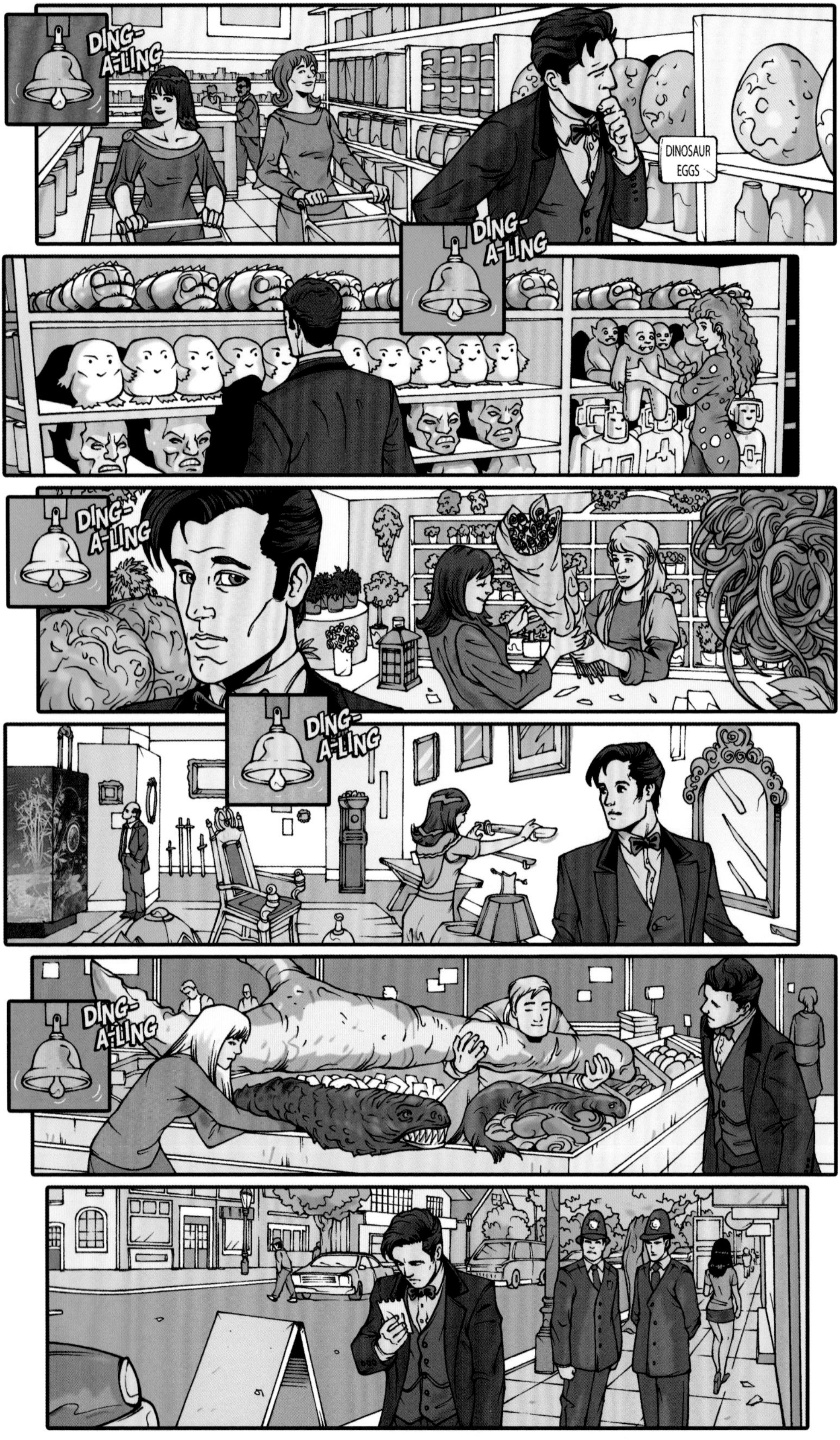
DING-A-LING
DINOSAUR EGGS
DING-A-LING
DING-A-LING
DING-A-LING
DING-A-LING

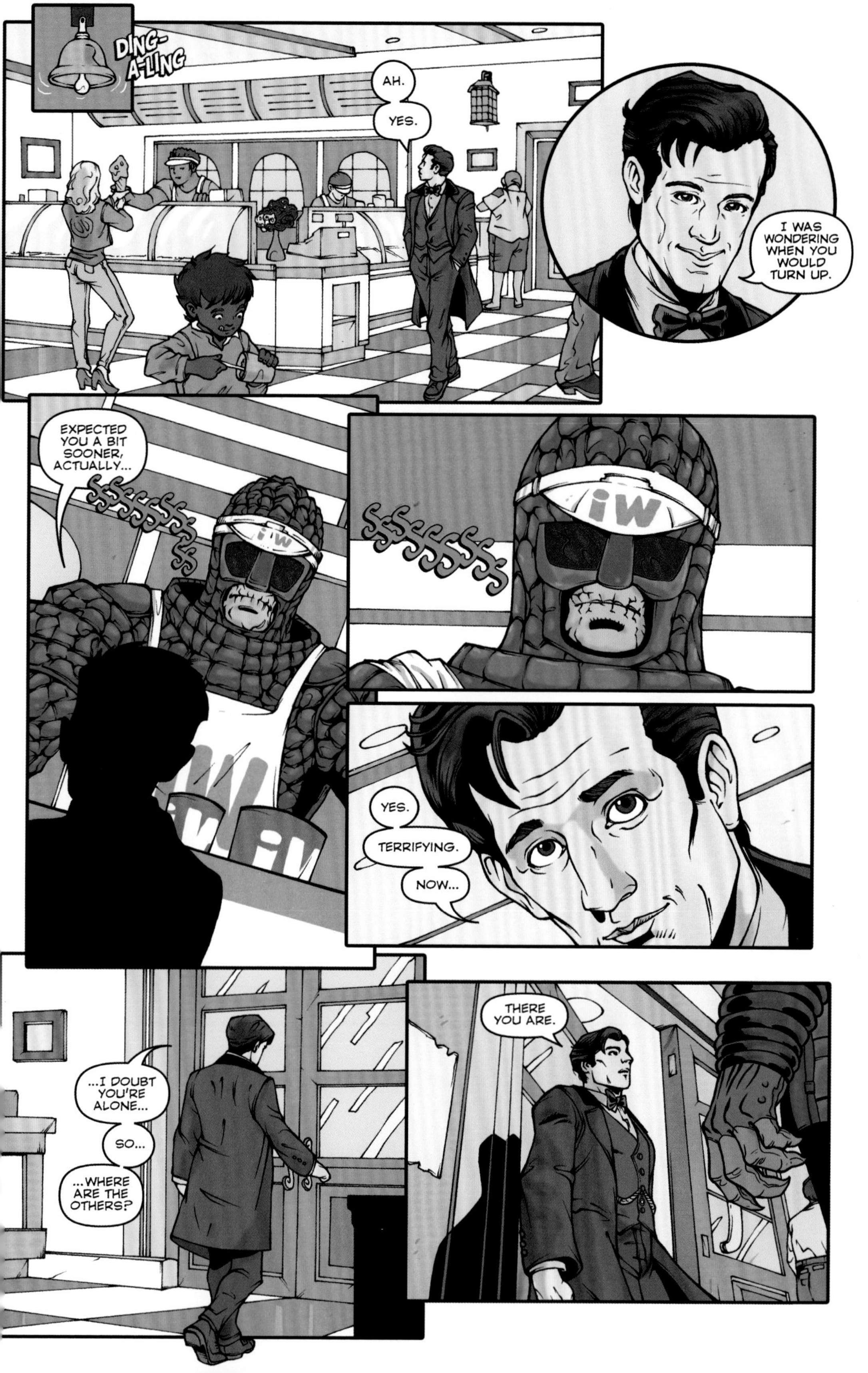
DING-A-LING
AH.
YES.
I WAS WONDERING WHEN YOU WOULD TURN UP.
EXPECTED YOU A BIT SOONER, ACTUALLY...
SSSSSSS
SSSSSSS
YES.
TERRIFYING.
NOW...
...I DOUBT YOU'RE ALONE...
SO...
...WHERE ARE THE OTHERS?
THERE YOU ARE.

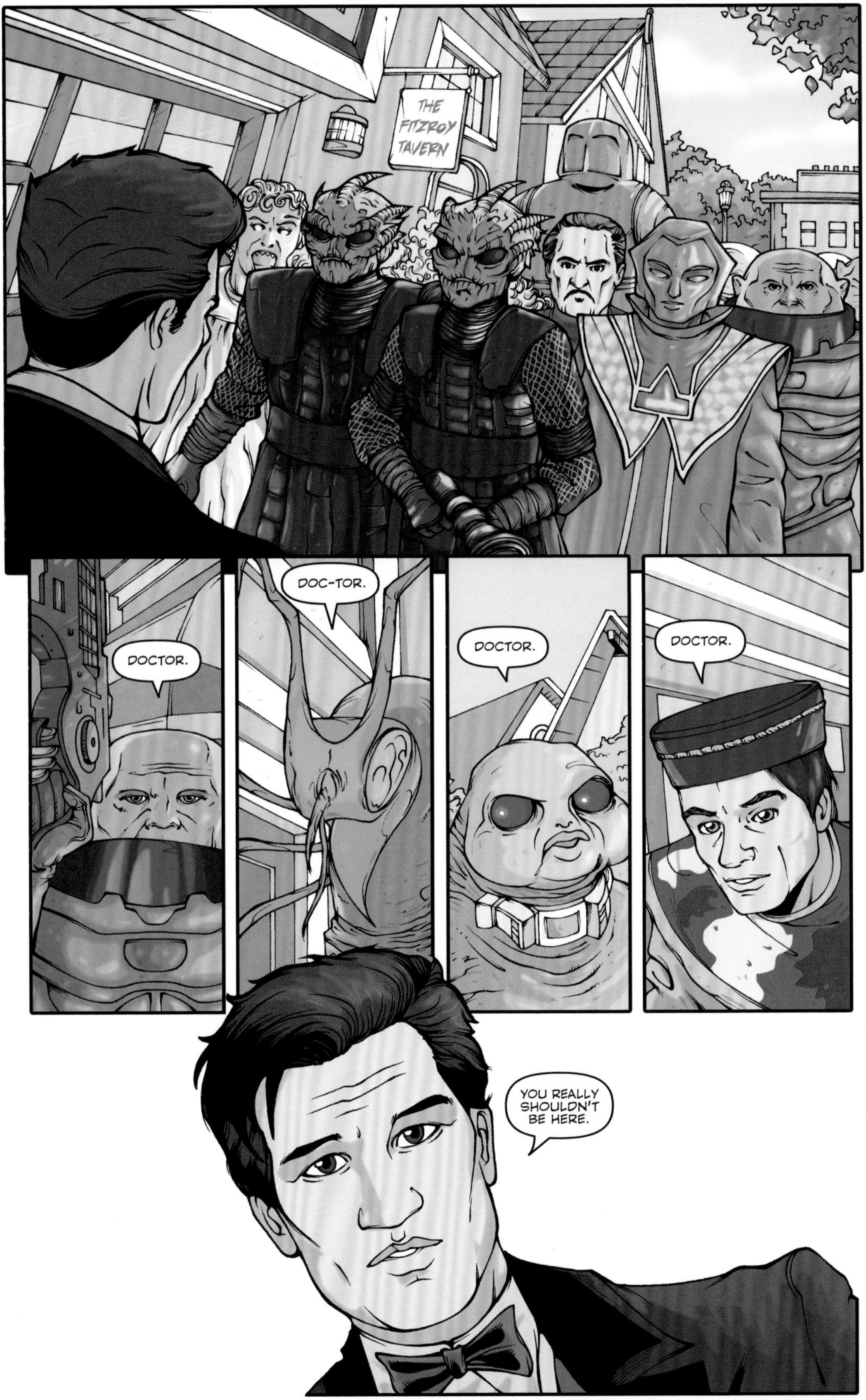
THE FITZROY TAVERN
DOCTOR.
DOC-TOR.
DOCTOR.
DOCTOR.
YOU REALLY SHOULDN'T BE HERE.

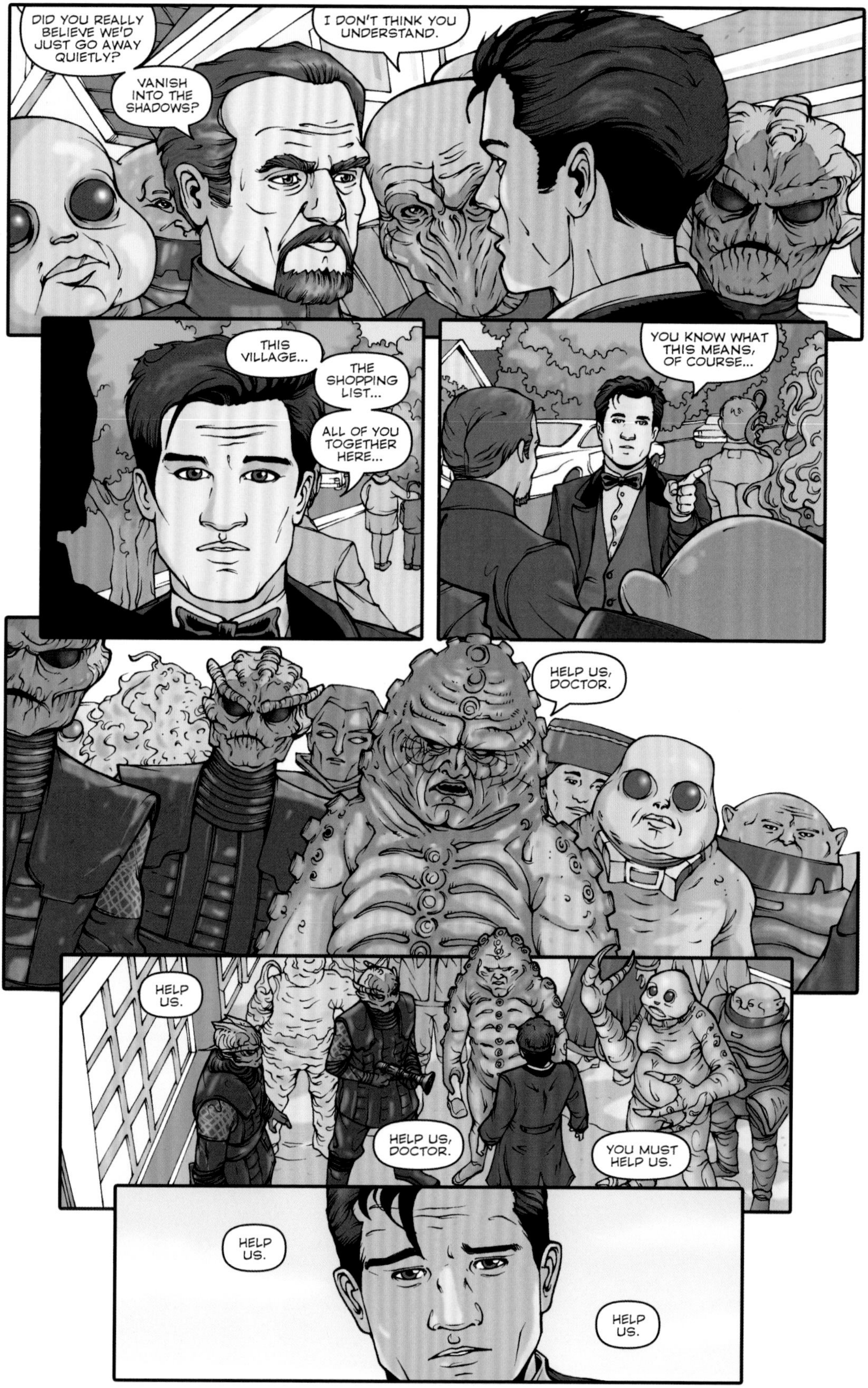
DID YOU REALLY BELIEVE WE'D JUST GO AWAY QUIETLY?
VANISH INTO THE SHADOWS?
I DON'T THINK YOU UNDERSTAND.
THIS VILLAGE...
THE SHOPPING LIST...
ALL OF YOU TOGETHER HERE...
YOU KNOW WHAT THIS MEANS, OF COURSE...
HELP US, DOCTOR.
HELP US.
HELP US, DOCTOR.
YOU MUST HELP US.
HELP US.
HELP US.

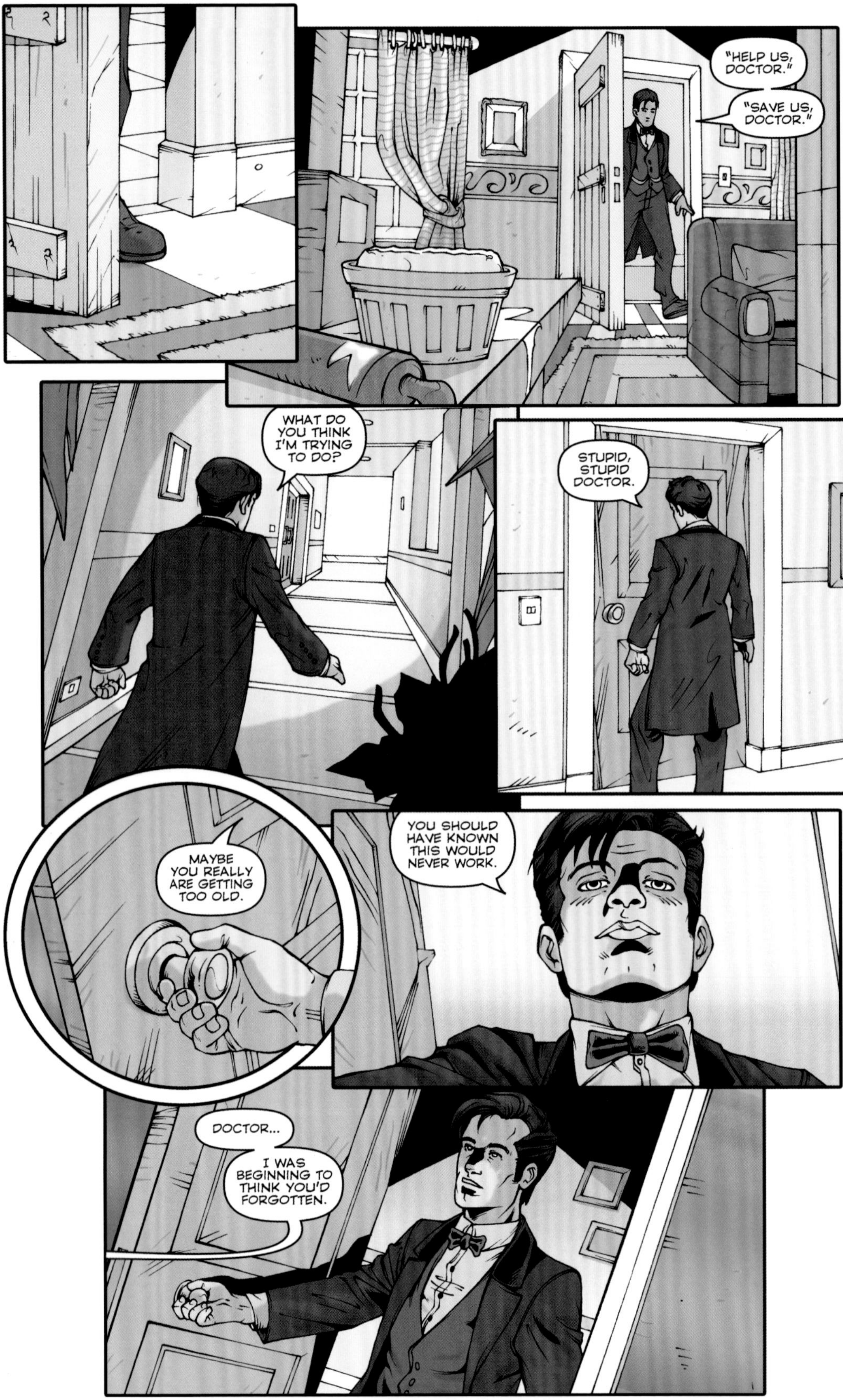
"HELP US, DOCTOR."
"SAVE US, DOCTOR."
WHAT DO YOU THINK I'M TRYING TO DO?
STUPID, STUPID DOCTOR.
MAYBE YOU REALLY ARE GETTING TOO OLD.
YOU SHOULD HAVE KNOWN THIS WOULD NEVER WORK.
DOCTOR...
I WAS BEGINNING TO THINK YOU'D FORGOTTEN.

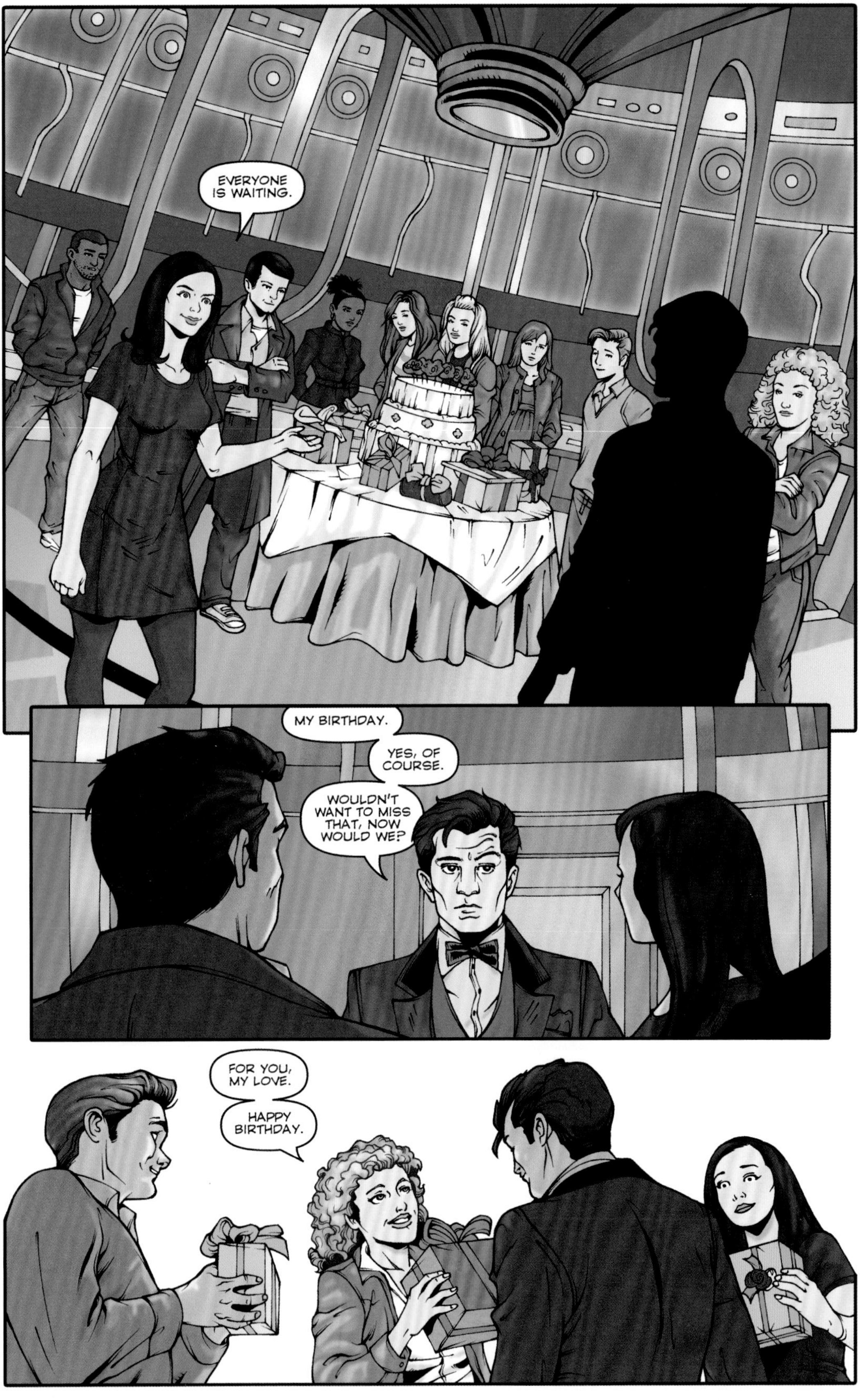
EVERYONE IS WAITING.
MY BIRTHDAY.
YES, OF COURSE.
WOULDN'T WANT TO MISS THAT, NOW WOULD WE?
FOR YOU, MY LOVE.
HAPPY BIRTHDAY.

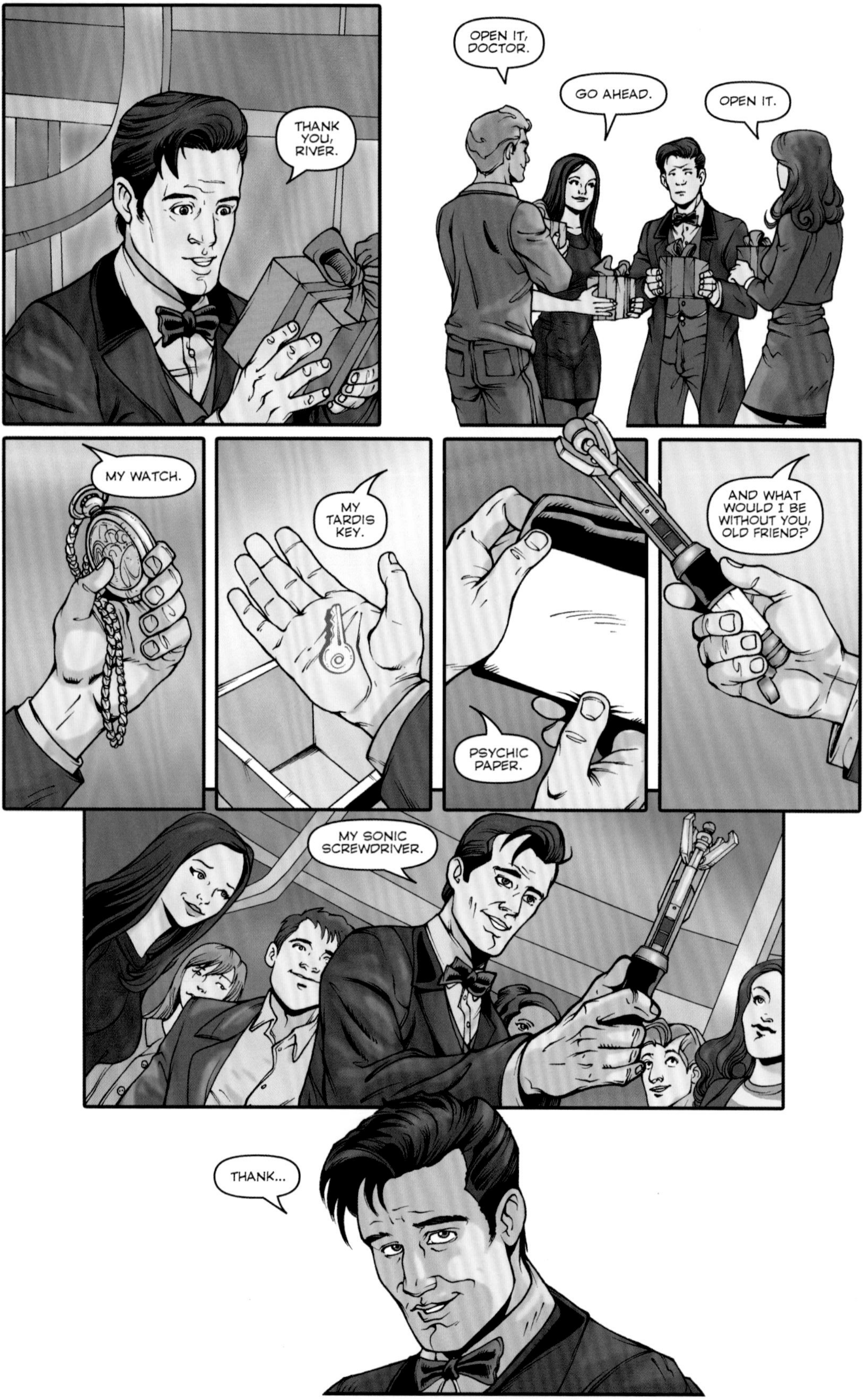
THANK YOU, RIVER.
OPEN IT, DOCTOR.
GO AHEAD.
OPEN IT.
MY WATCH.
MY TARDIS KEY.
PSYCHIC PAPER.
AND WHAT WOULD I BE WITHOUT YOU, OLD FRIEND?
MY SONIC SCREWDRIVER.
THANK...

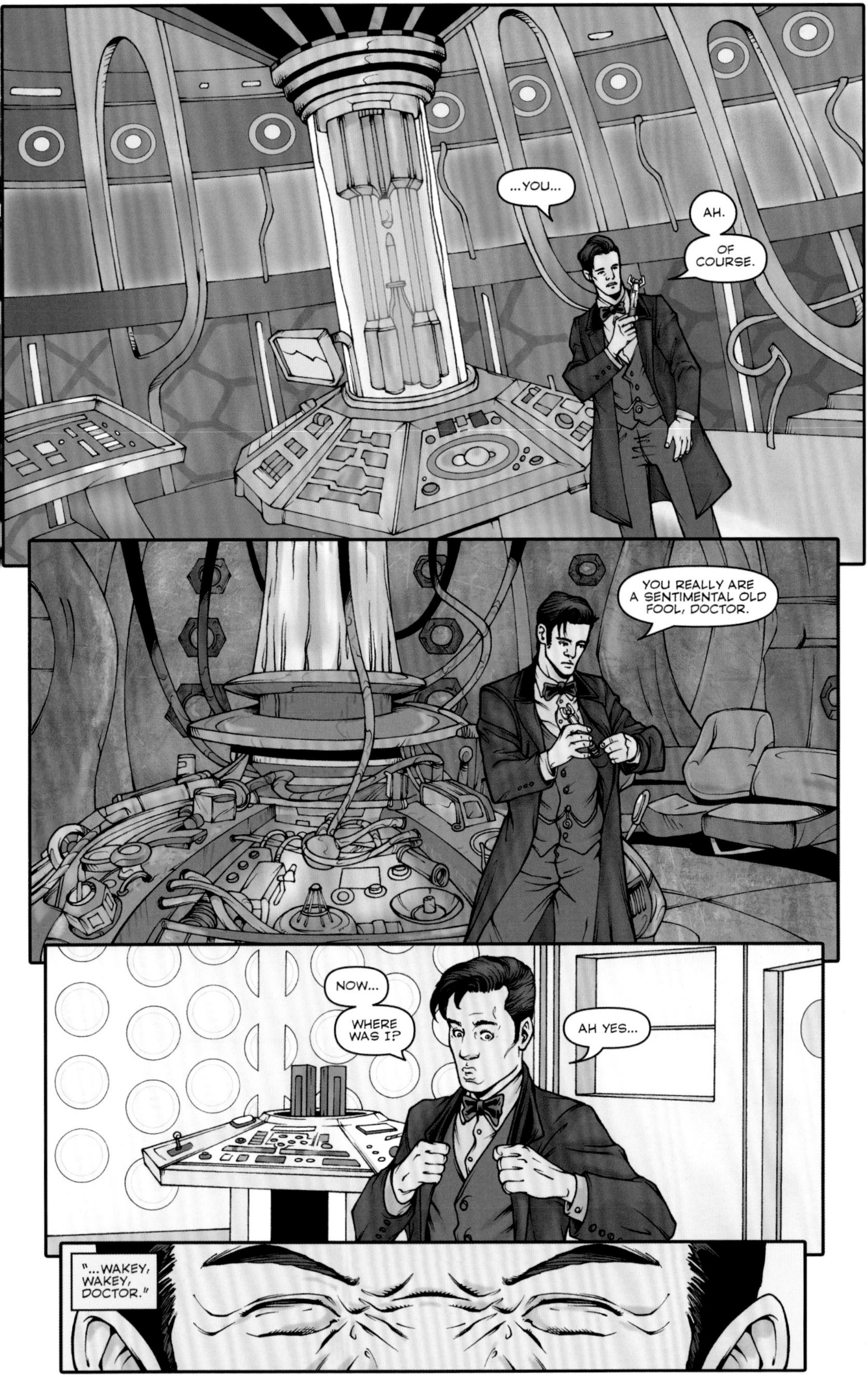
...YOU...
AH.
OF COURSE.
YOU REALLY ARE A SENTIMENTAL OLD FOOL, DOCTOR.
NOW...
WHERE WAS I?
AH YES...
"...WAKEY, WAKEY, DOCTOR."

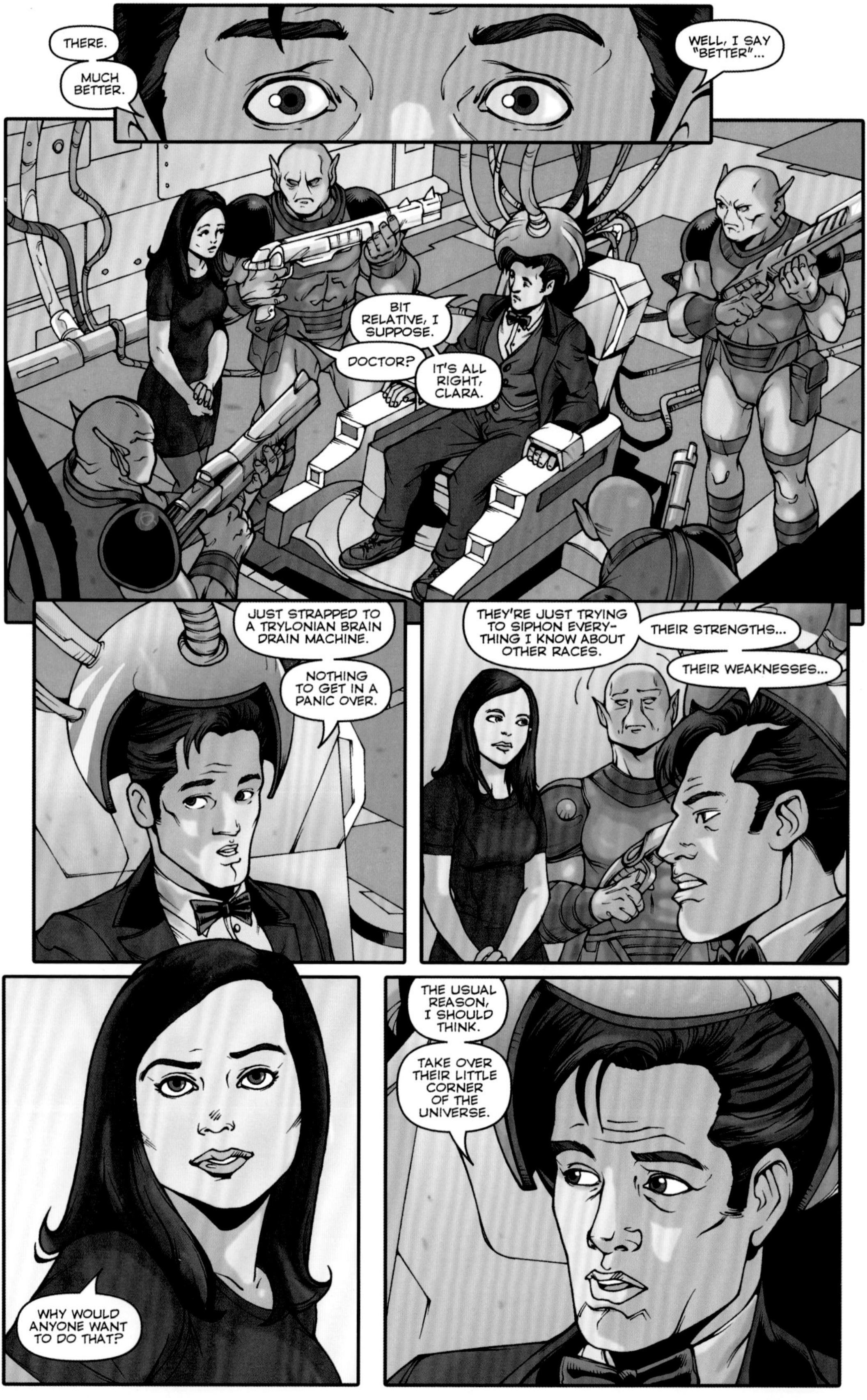
THERE.
MUCH BETTER.
WELL, I SAY "BETTER"...
BIT RELATIVE, I SUPPOSE.
DOCTOR?
IT'S ALL RIGHT, CLARA.
JUST STRAPPED TO A TRYLONIAN BRAIN DRAIN MACHINE.
NOTHING TO GET IN A PANIC OVER.
THEY'RE JUST TRYING TO SIPHON EVERY-THING I KNOW ABOUT OTHER RACES.
THEIR STRENGTHS...
THEIR WEAKNESSES...
WHY WOULD ANYONE WANT TO DO THAT?
THE USUAL REASON, I SHOULD THINK.
TAKE OVER THEIR LITTLE CORNER OF THE UNIVERSE.

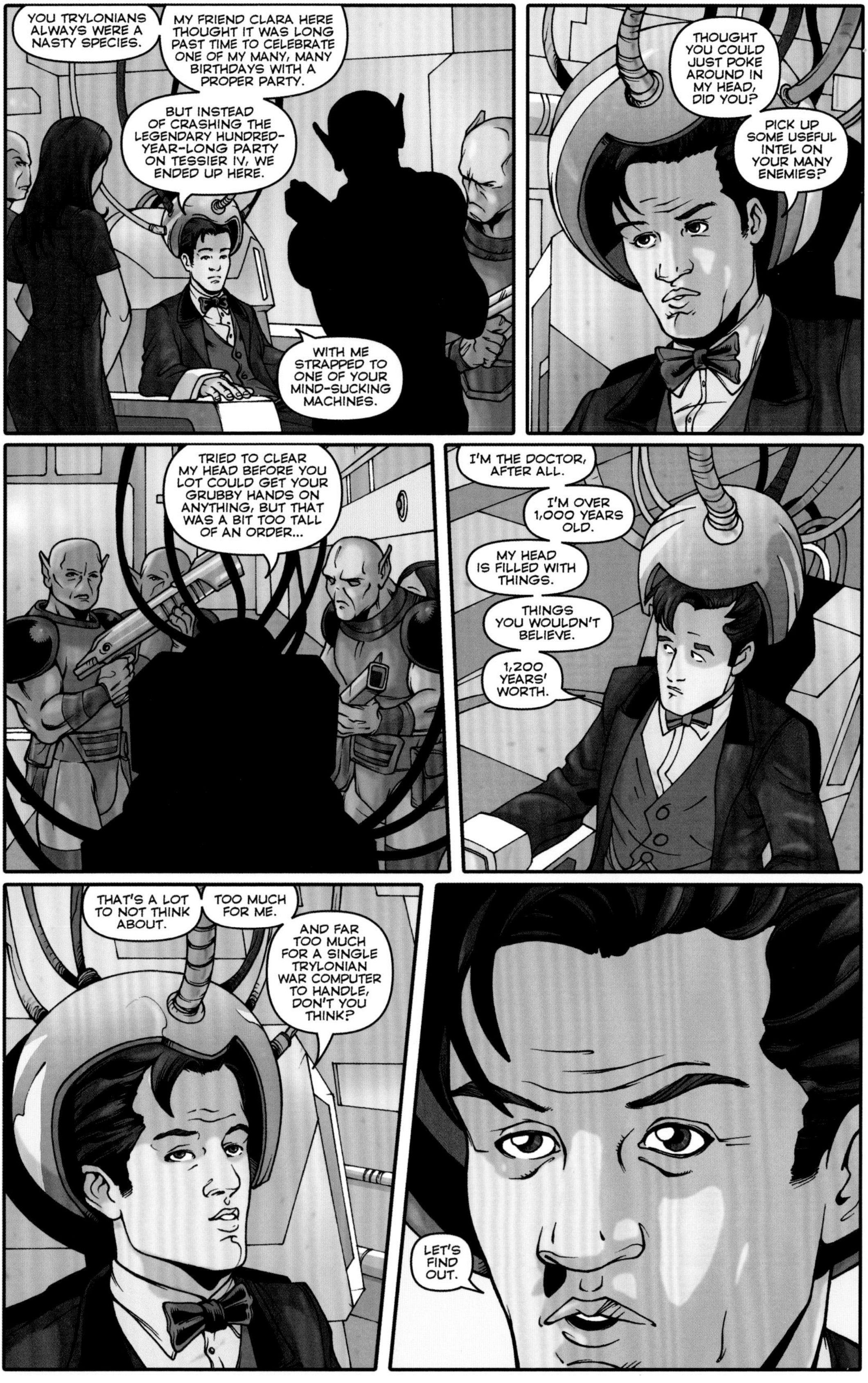

YOU TRYLONIANS ALWAYS WERE A NASTY SPECIES.
MY FRIEND CLARA HERE THOUGHT IT WAS LONG PAST TIME TO CELEBRATE ONE OF MY MANY, MANY BIRTHDAYS WITH A PROPER PARTY.
BUT INSTEAD OF CRASHING THE LEGENDARY HUNDRED-YEAR-LONG PARTY ON TESSIER IV, WE ENDED UP HERE.
WITH ME STRAPPED TO ONE OF YOUR MIND-SUCKING MACHINES.
THOUGHT YOU COULD JUST POKE AROUND IN MY HEAD, DID YOU?
PICK UP SOME USEFUL INTEL ON YOUR MANY ENEMIES?
TRIED TO CLEAR MY HEAD BEFORE YOU LOT COULD GET YOUR GRUBBY HANDS ON ANYTHING, BUT THAT WAS A BIT TOO TALL OF AN ORDER...
I'M THE DOCTOR, AFTER ALL.
I'M OVER 1,000 YEARS OLD.
MY HEAD IS FILLED WITH THINGS.
THINGS YOU WOULDN'T BELIEVE.
1,200 YEARS' WORTH.
THAT'S A LOT TO NOT THINK ABOUT.
TOO MUCH FOR ME.
AND FAR TOO MUCH FOR A SINGLE TRYLONIAN WAR COMPUTER TO HANDLE, DON'T YOU THINK?
LET'S FIND OUT.

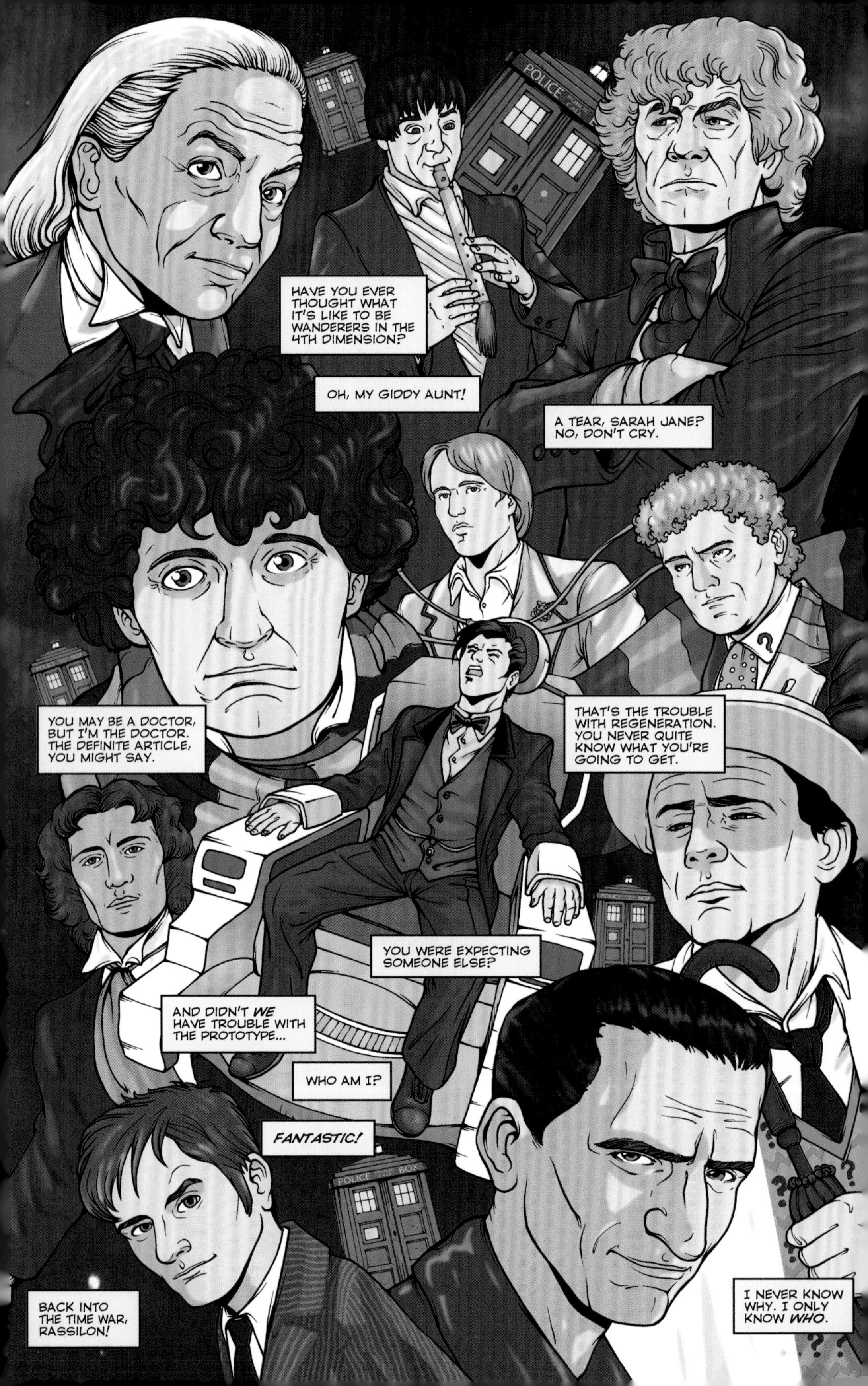
HAVE YOU EVER THOUGHT WHAT IT'S LIKE TO BE WANDERERS IN THE 4TH DIMENSION?
OH, MY GIDDY AUNT!
A TEAR, SARAH JANE? NO, DON'T CRY.
YOU MAY BE A DOCTOR, BUT I'M THE DOCTOR. THE DEFINITE ARTICLE, YOU MIGHT SAY.
THAT'S THE TROUBLE WITH REGENERATION. YOU NEVER QUITE KNOW WHAT YOU'RE GOING TO GET.
YOU WERE EXPECTING SOMEONE ELSE?
AND DIDN'T *WE* HAVE TROUBLE WITH THE PROTOTYPE...
WHO AM I?
FANTASTIC!
BACK INTO THE TIME WAR, RASSILON!
I NEVER KNOW WHY. I ONLY KNOW *WHO*.

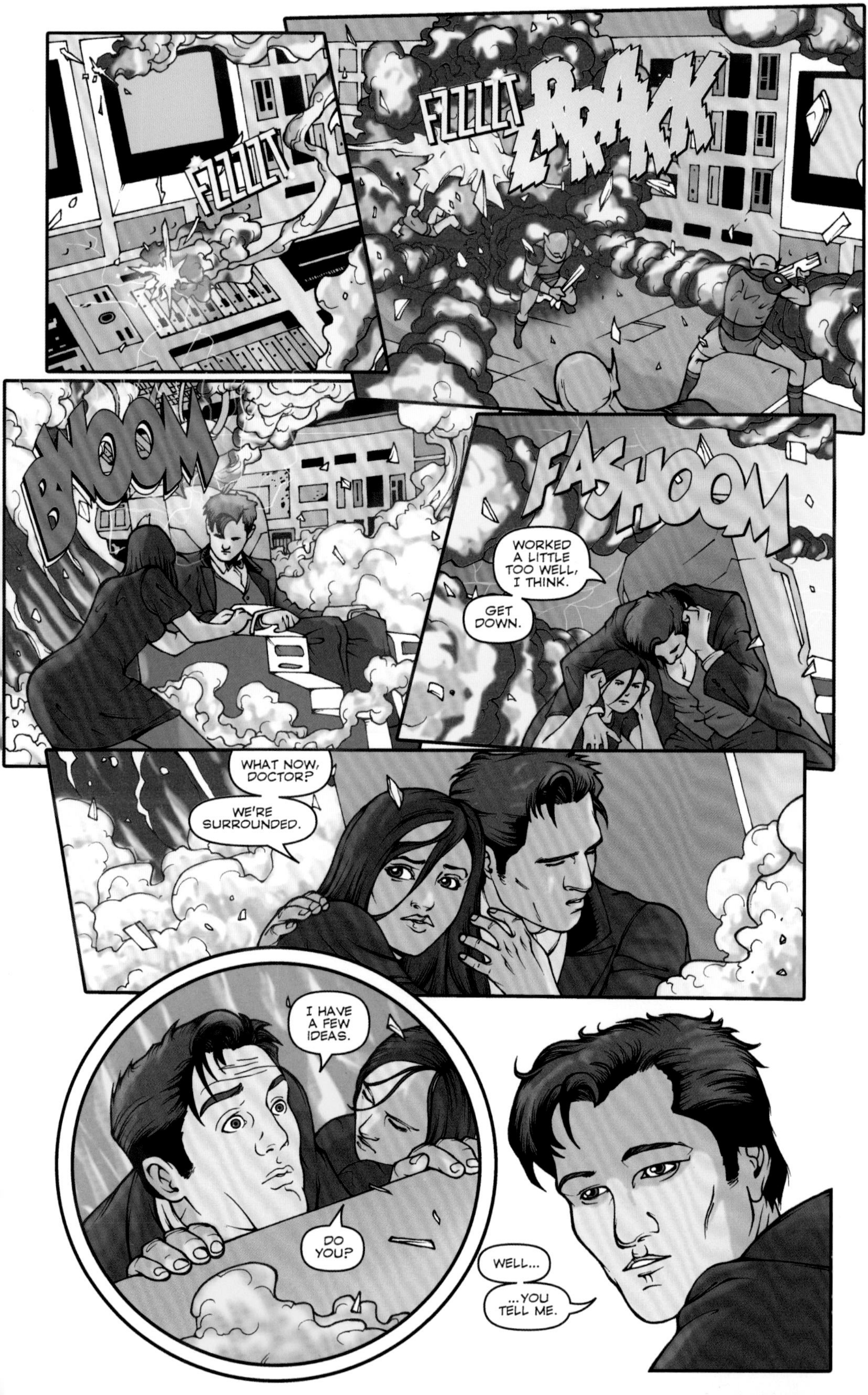
FZZZZT
FZZZZT
ZRAKK
BWOOM
FASHOOM
WORKED A LITTLE TOO WELL, I THINK.
GET DOWN.
WHAT NOW, DOCTOR?
WE'RE SURROUNDED.
I HAVE A FEW IDEAS.
DO YOU?
WELL...
...YOU TELL ME.

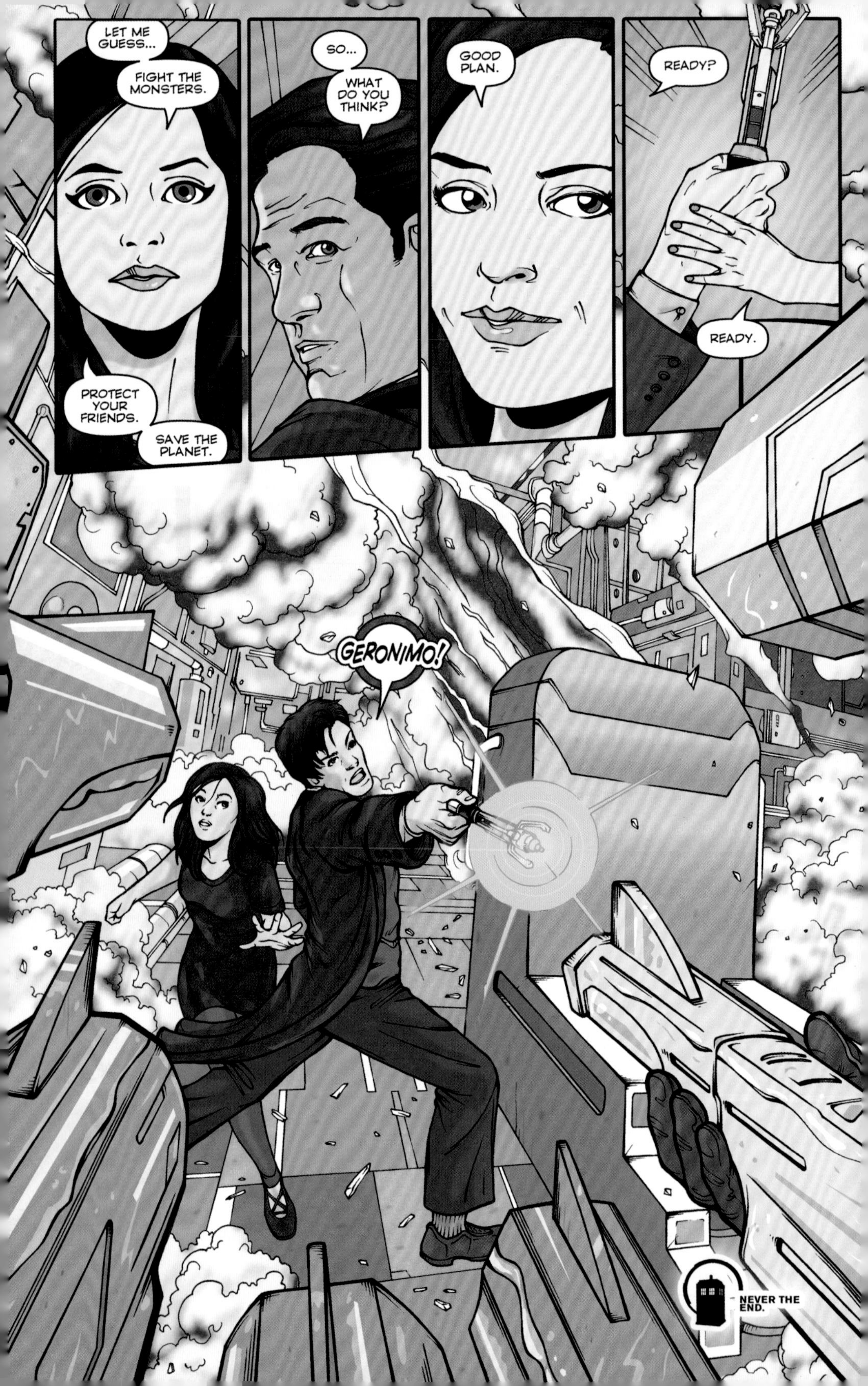
LET ME GUESS...
FIGHT THE MONSTERS.
PROTECT YOUR FRIENDS.
SAVE THE PLANET.
SO...
WHAT DO YOU THINK?
GOOD PLAN.
READY?
READY.
GERONIMO!
NEVER THE END.

ANNOTATIONS

Many companions, friends, and artifacts from the Doctor's past and present appear in the pages of this comic book. Did you spot them all?

PAGE SEVEN

A collection of companions from the Doctor's past. In panel one, from left-to-right: **Peri Brown**, botanist and companion of the Fifth and Sixth Doctors; **Susan Foreman**, the Doctor's granddaughter and traveling companion of the First Doctor; **Ian Chesterton**, Susan's schoolteacher and companion of the First Doctor; **Barbara Wright**, Ian's fellow schoolteacher and another companion of the First Doctor; **Romana I**, Time Lady companion of the Fourth Doctor; **Romana II**, Romana's second regeneration and companion of the Fourth Doctor; **Zoe Herriot**, brilliant astrophysicist and companion of the Second Doctor; **Jamie McCrimmon**, young Scottish piper and companion of the Second Doctor.

In panel six, from left-to-right: **Ace**, a teenager from Earth and traveling companion of the Seventh Doctor; **Turlough**, and exile from the planet Trion who travels with the Fifth Doctor.

PAGE EIGHT

More companions from the Doctor's earlier adventures. In panel one, from left-to-right: **Sarah Jane Smith**, journalist and assistant to the Third and Fourth Doctors; **Brigadier Alistair Gordon Lethbridge-Stewart**, better known simply as 'The Brigadier', head of UNIT and trusted ally of the Doctor (Second Doctor through Fifth Doctor, Seventh Doctor).

In panel seven, from left-to-right: **Tegan Jovanka**, flight attendant and reluctant companion of the Fourth and Fifth Doctors; **Nyssa**, a native of Traken who travels with the Fourth and Fifth Doctors; **Adric**, a young math genius who stows away aboard the TARDIS and travels with the Fourth and Fifth Doctors.

Two more companions. In panel one (left-to-right): **Steven Taylor,** marooned astronaut who ends up traveling with the First Doctor; **Dodo Chaplet,** a teenager from 1960s Earth who travels with the First Doctor.

More companions from the Classic Series. In panel one, from left-to-right: **Katarina,** a young woman from the ancient city of Troy and companion of the First Doctor; **Vicki,** a survivor of a shipwreck on the planet Dido who travels with the First Doctor.

In panel two: **Melanie Bush,** health and fitness enthusiast who travels with the Sixth and Seventh Doctors. On the shelves are **Cybermats** (who first appeared in "Tomb of the Cybermen"), **Adipose** (from "Partners in Crime"), and a **troll doll** (from "Terror of the Autons").

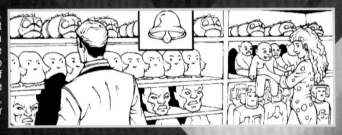

In panel three, from left-to-right: **Sara Kingdom,** a Space Security Agent who helped the First Doctor; **Liz Shaw,** scientist and assistant to the Third Doctor. In the background we see **Wolf Weeds** from "The Creature from the Pit", **Vervoids** from "Terror of the Vervoids", and a **Krynoid** from "The Seeds of Doom".

In panel four: **Victoria Waterfield,** companion of the Second Doctor. She is examining the **scabbard of Excalibur,** from the episode "Battlefield". Also in the background are the **Time Cabinet** from "The Talons of Weng-Chiang", the throne from "Vampires of Venice", and **the Master's TARDIS** from "The Deadly Assassin".

In panel five, from left-to-right: **Polly,** a secretary from the 1960s and traveling companion of the First and Second Doctors; **Ben Jackson,** Royal Navy seaman and companion of the First and Second Doctors. Polly is holding **Prisoner Zero** (from "The Eleventh Hour", and Ben is holding a **Macra claw** (from "The Macra Terror").

In panel six, from left-to-right: **Sergeant Benton,** a UNIT soldier who frequently aided the Doctor (Second through Fourth Doctor): **Captain Mike Yates,** Benton's superior in UNIT and another friend of the Doctor (Third Doctor).

PAGE ELEVEN

Behind the counter is an **Ice Warrior**, a race of Martians who first appeared in "The Ice Warriors".

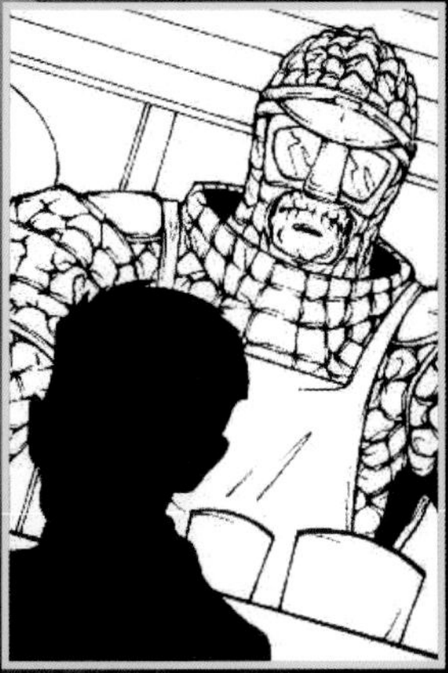

PAGE TWELVE

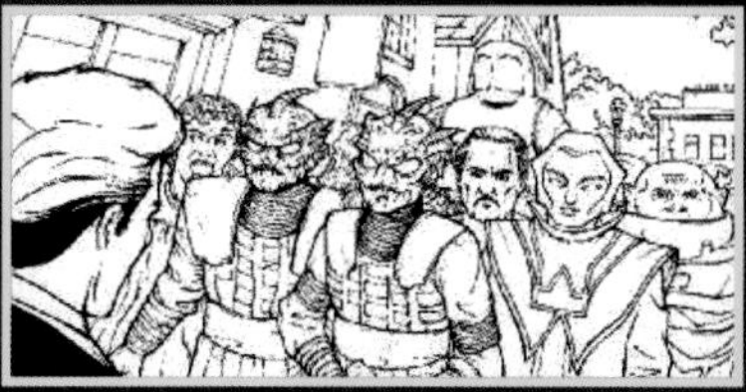

Aliens and monsters from the Doctor's past and present. In the foreground of panel one, from left-to-right: **A Weeping Angel** (first appearance: "Blink"); **Silurians** (first appearance: "Doctor Who and the Silurians"); **The Master** (first appearance: "Terror of the Autons"); **Robot** (from "Robots of Death"); Sontaran (first appearance: "The Time Warrior").

Lurking in the background are an **Axon** (from "The Claws of Axos"), and a **"Mummy" Service Robot** (frovm "The Pyramids of Mars").

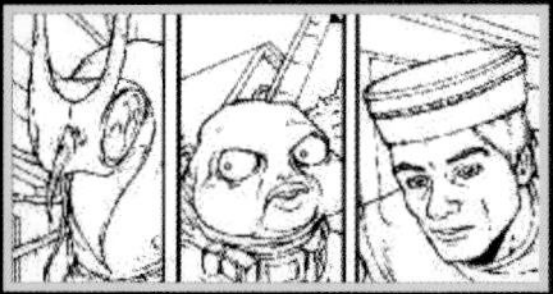

In panel three, we see a **Wirrn** (from "The Ark in Space"); in panel four, a Slitheen (first appearance: "Aliens of London"); in panel five, the **Celestial Toymaker** (from The Celestial Toymaker).

PAGE THIRTEEN

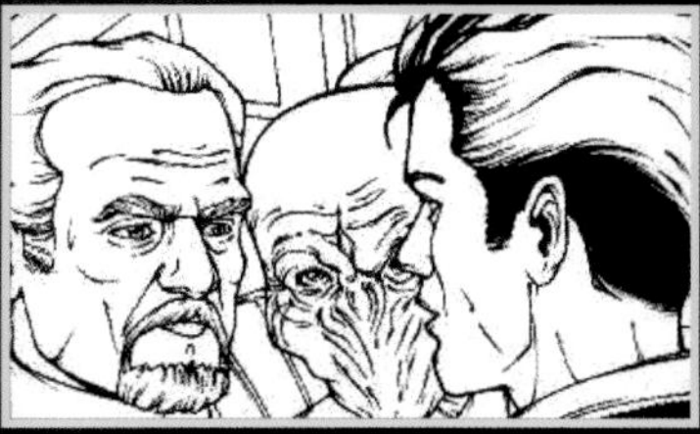

More aliens and monsters from the Doctor's past. In panel one, we see a **Silent** (first appearance: "The Impossible Astronaut"); in panel four, a **Zygon** (first appearance: "Terror of the Zygons").

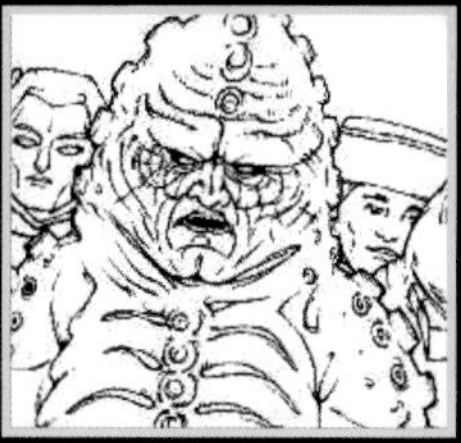

PAGE FIFTEEN

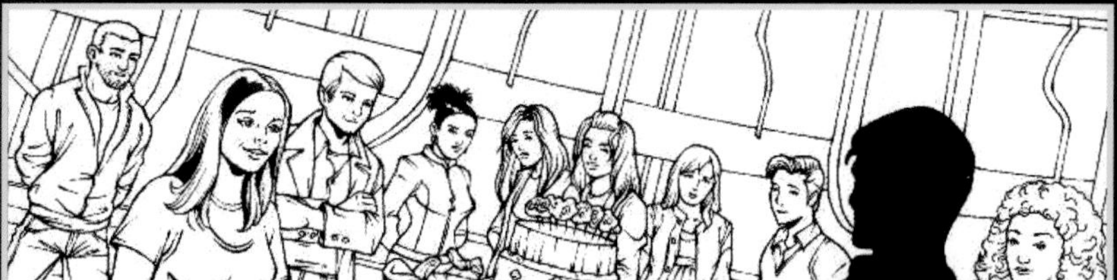

Traveling companions from the Doctor's recent history. In panel one, from left-to-right: **Mickey Smith** (Ninth and Tenth Doctor); **Clara Oswald** (Eleventh Doctor); **Captain Jack Harkness** (Ninth and Tenth Doctor); **Martha Jones** (Tenth Doctor); **Amy Pond** (Eleventh Doctor); **Rose Tyler** (Ninth and Tenth Doctor); **Donna Noble** (Tenth Doctor); **Rory Williams** (Eleventh Doctor); **River Song** (Tenth and Eleventh Doctor).

PAGE SEVENTEEN

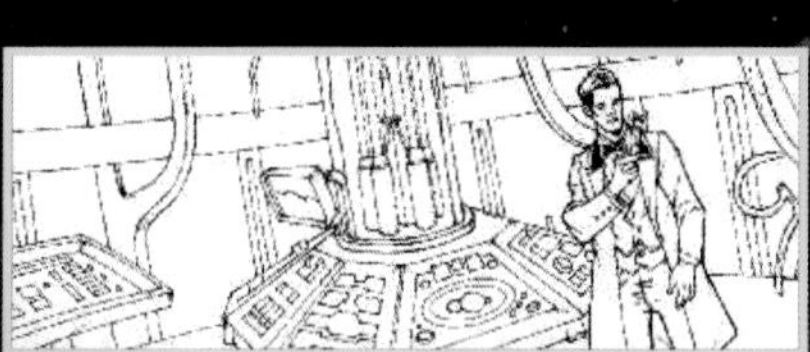

And finally, some of the TARDIS interiors from the past and present: in panel one, we see current TARDIS console room; in panel two, the Ninth and Tenth Doctors' control room; and in panel three, the Fourth Doctor's TARDIS console room.

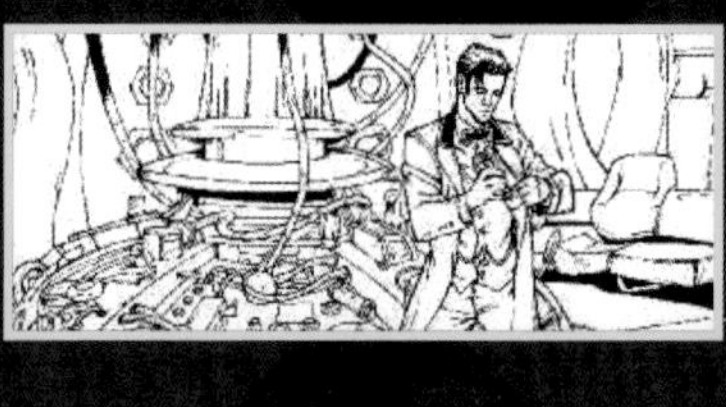

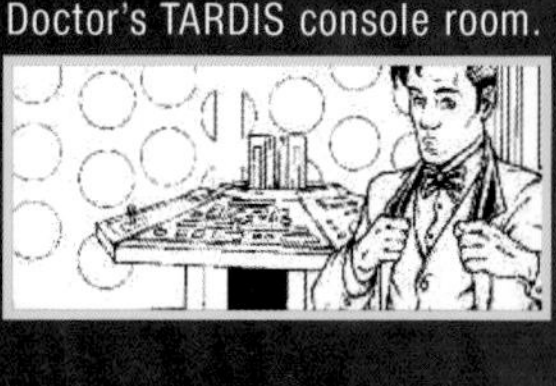

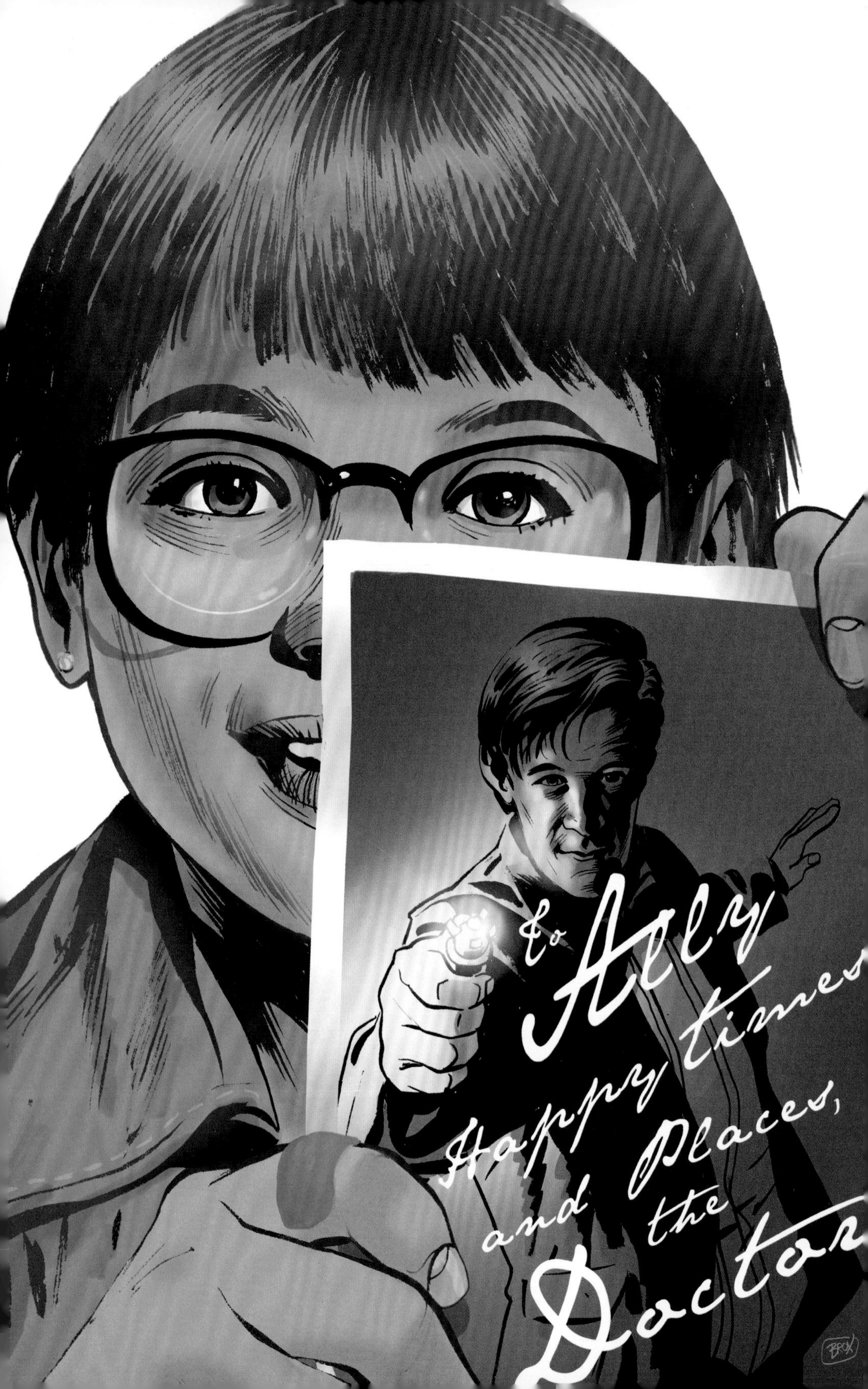
to Ally
Happy times
and Places,
the
Doctor
BROX

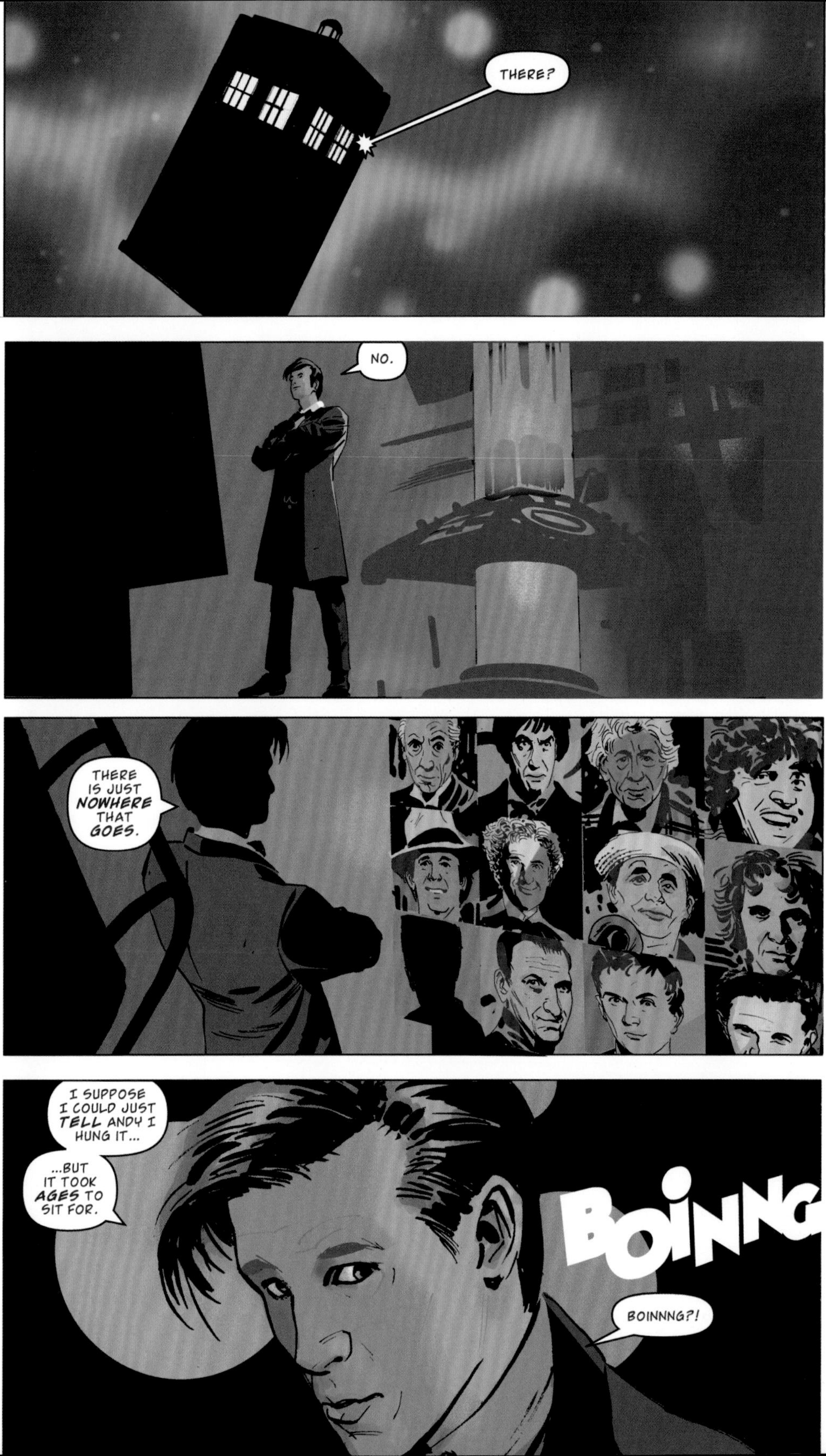
THERE?
NO.
THERE IS JUST NOWHERE THAT GOES.
I SUPPOSE I COULD JUST TELL ANDY I HUNG IT...
...BUT IT TOOK AGES TO SIT FOR.
BOINNG
BOINNNG?!

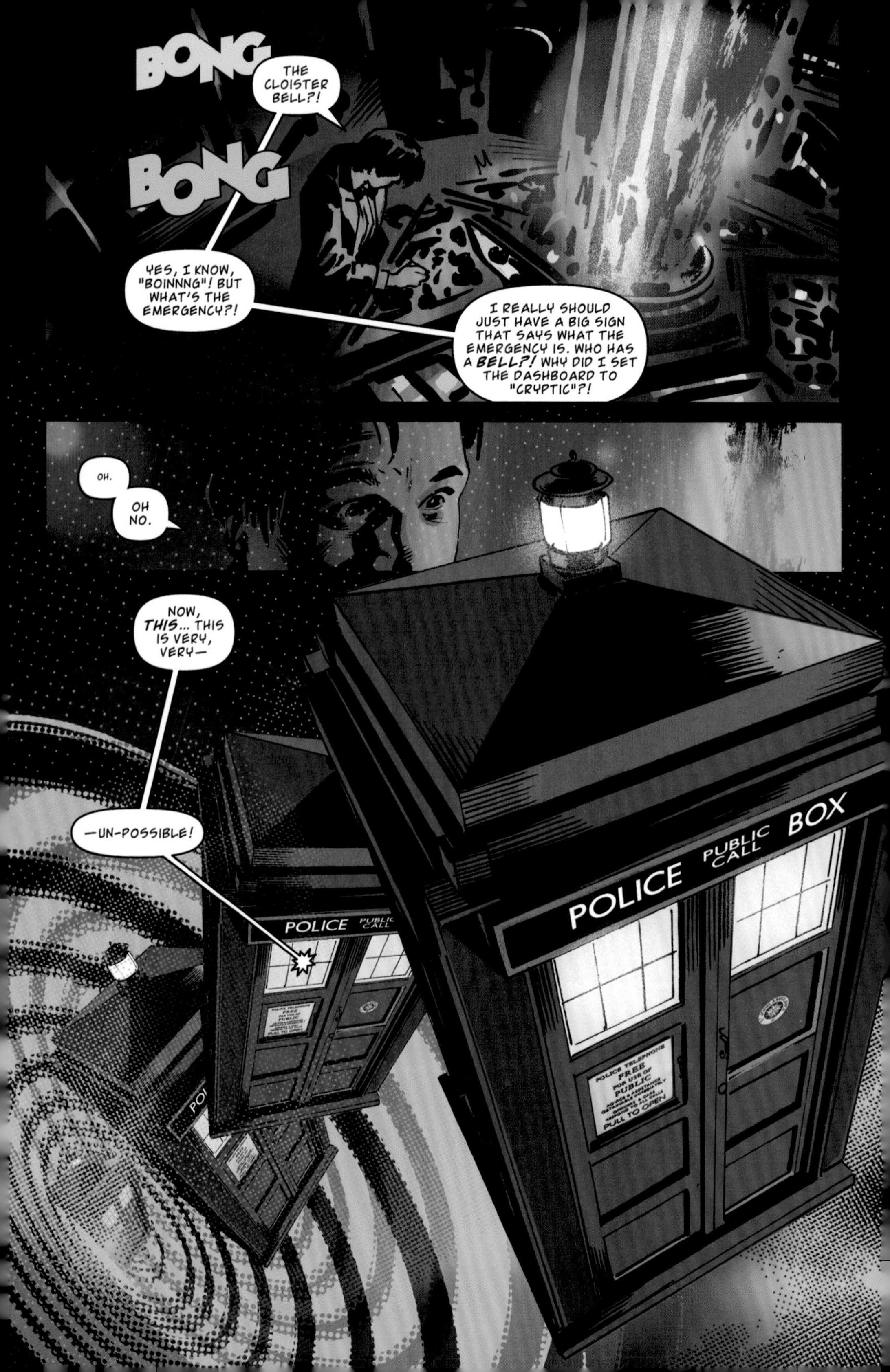
BONG
THE CLOISTER BELL?!
BONG
YES, I KNOW, "BOINNNG"! BUT WHAT'S THE EMERGENCY?!
I REALLY SHOULD JUST HAVE A BIG SIGN THAT SAYS WHAT THE EMERGENCY IS. WHO HAS A *BELL?!* WHY DID I SET THE DASHBOARD TO "CRYPTIC"?!
OH.
OH NO.
NOW, *THIS*... THIS IS VERY, VERY—
—UN-POSSIBLE!
POLICE PUBLIC CALL
POLICE PUBLIC CALL BOX
POLICE TELEPHONE FREE FOR USE OF PUBLIC
PULL TO OPEN

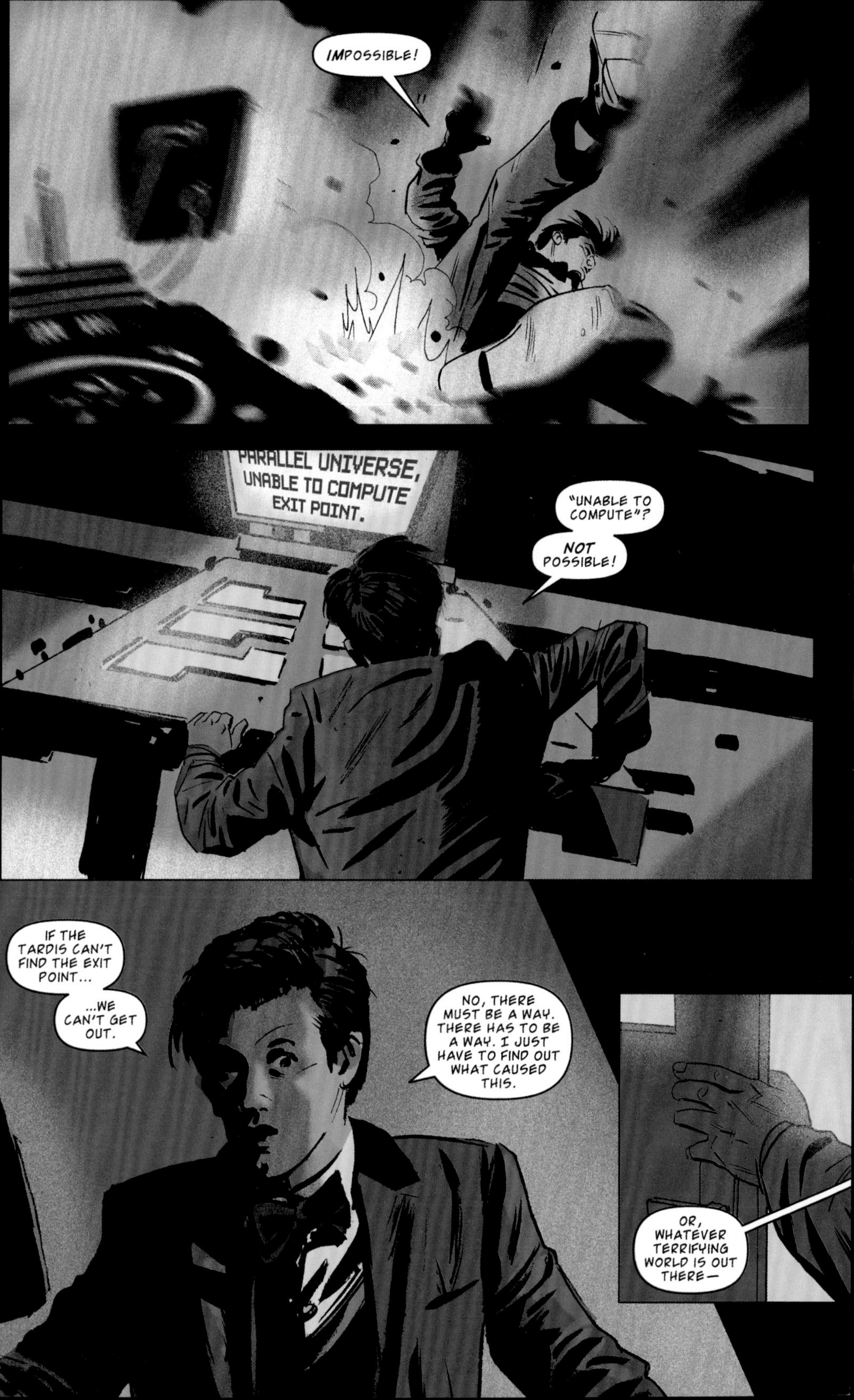
IMPOSSIBLE!
PARALLEL UNIVERSE, UNABLE TO COMPUTE EXIT POINT.
"UNABLE TO COMPUTE"?
NOT POSSIBLE!
IF THE TARDIS CAN'T FIND THE EXIT POINT...
...WE CAN'T GET OUT.
NO, THERE MUST BE A WAY. THERE HAS TO BE A WAY. I JUST HAVE TO FIND OUT WHAT CAUSED THIS.
OR, WHATEVER TERRIFYING WORLD IS OUT THERE—

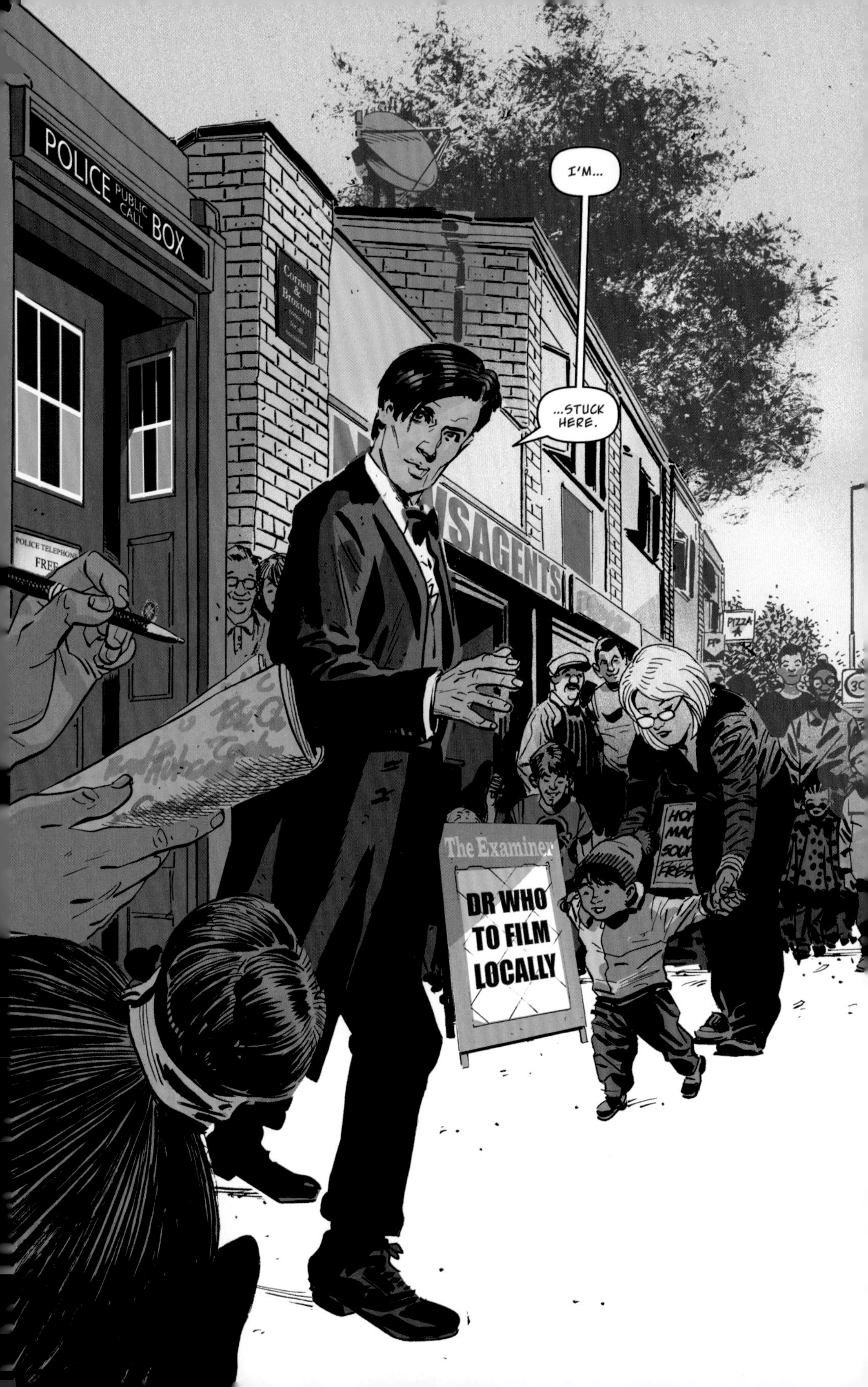
I'M...
...STUCK HERE.
POLICE PUBLIC CALL BOX
Cornell & Broxton
The Examiner
DR WHO TO FILM LOCALLY
PIZZA

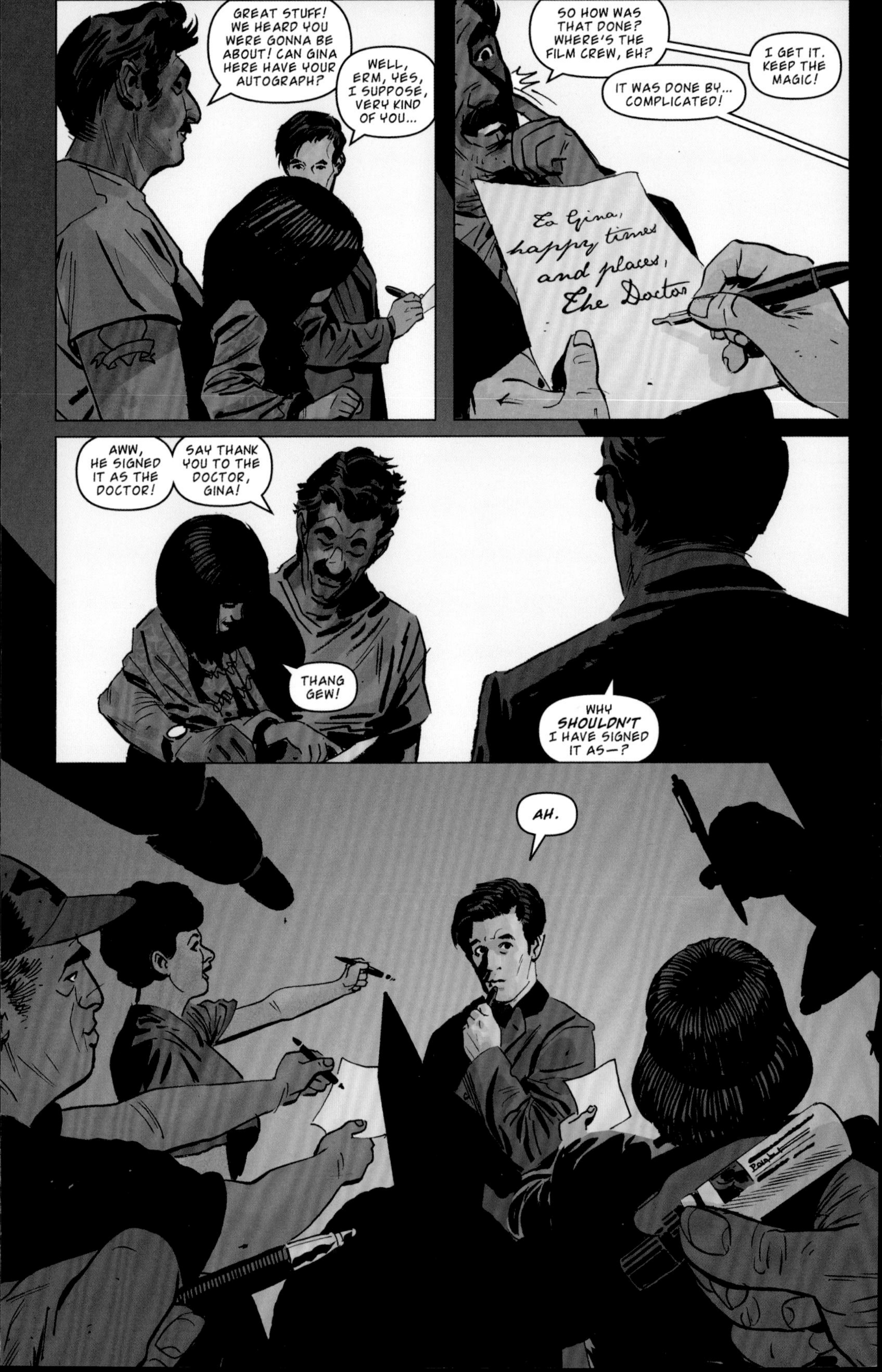
GREAT STUFF! WE HEARD YOU WERE GONNA BE ABOUT! CAN GINA HERE HAVE YOUR AUTOGRAPH?
WELL, ERM, YES, I SUPPOSE, VERY KIND OF YOU...
SO HOW WAS THAT DONE? WHERE'S THE FILM CREW, EH?
I GET IT. KEEP THE MAGIC!
IT WAS DONE BY... COMPLICATED!
To Gina, happy times and places, The Doctor
AWW, HE SIGNED IT AS THE DOCTOR!
SAY THANK YOU TO THE DOCTOR, GINA!
THANG GEW!
WHY SHOULDN'T I HAVE SIGNED IT AS—?
AH.

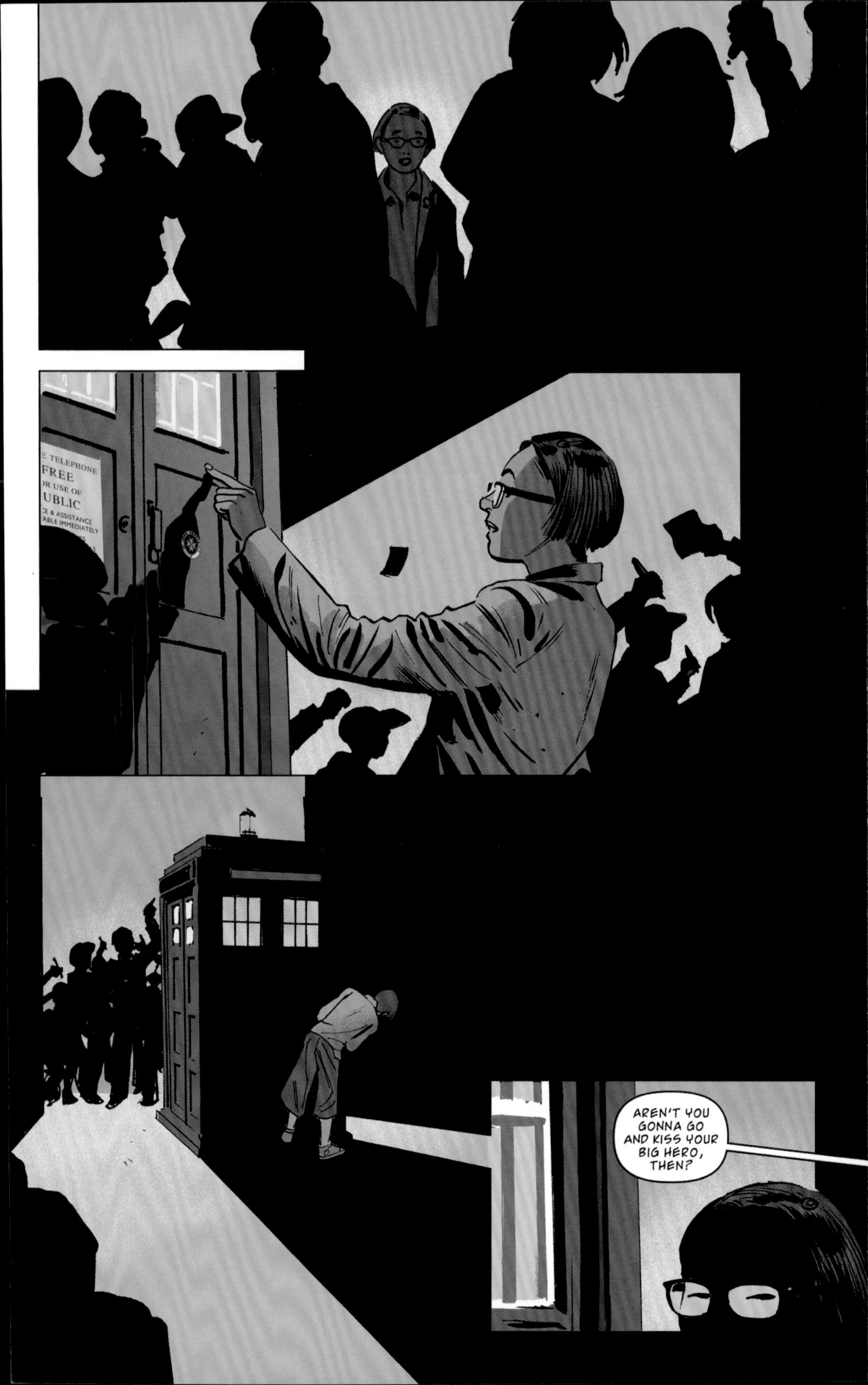
AREN'T YOU GONNA GO AND KISS YOUR BIG HERO, THEN?

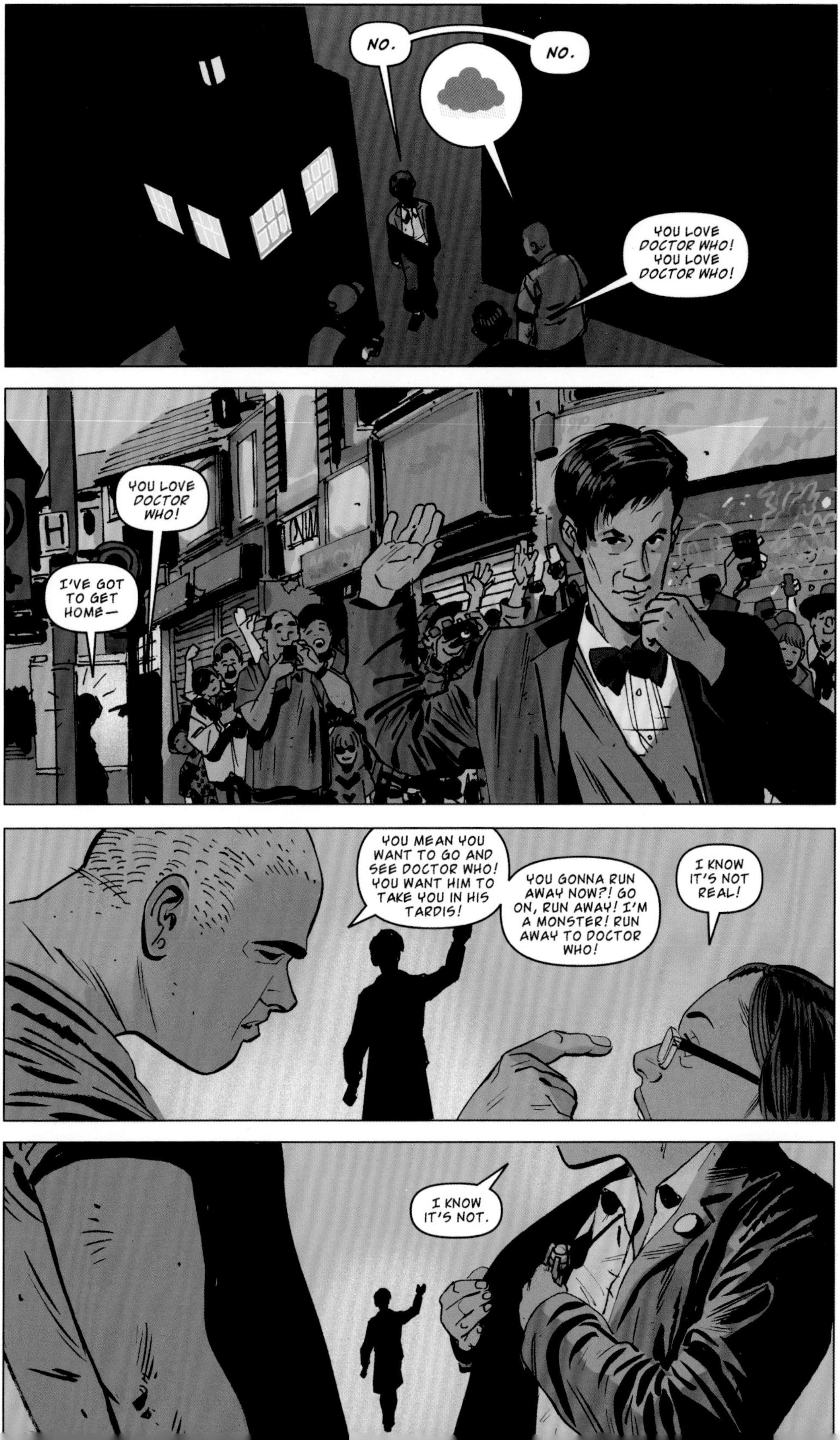
NO.
NO.
YOU LOVE DOCTOR WHO! YOU LOVE DOCTOR WHO!
YOU LOVE DOCTOR WHO!
I'VE GOT TO GET HOME—
YOU MEAN YOU WANT TO GO AND SEE DOCTOR WHO! YOU WANT HIM TO TAKE YOU IN HIS TARDIS!
YOU GONNA RUN AWAY NOW?! GO ON, RUN AWAY! I'M A MONSTER! RUN AWAY TO DOCTOR WHO!
I KNOW IT'S NOT REAL!
I KNOW IT'S NOT.

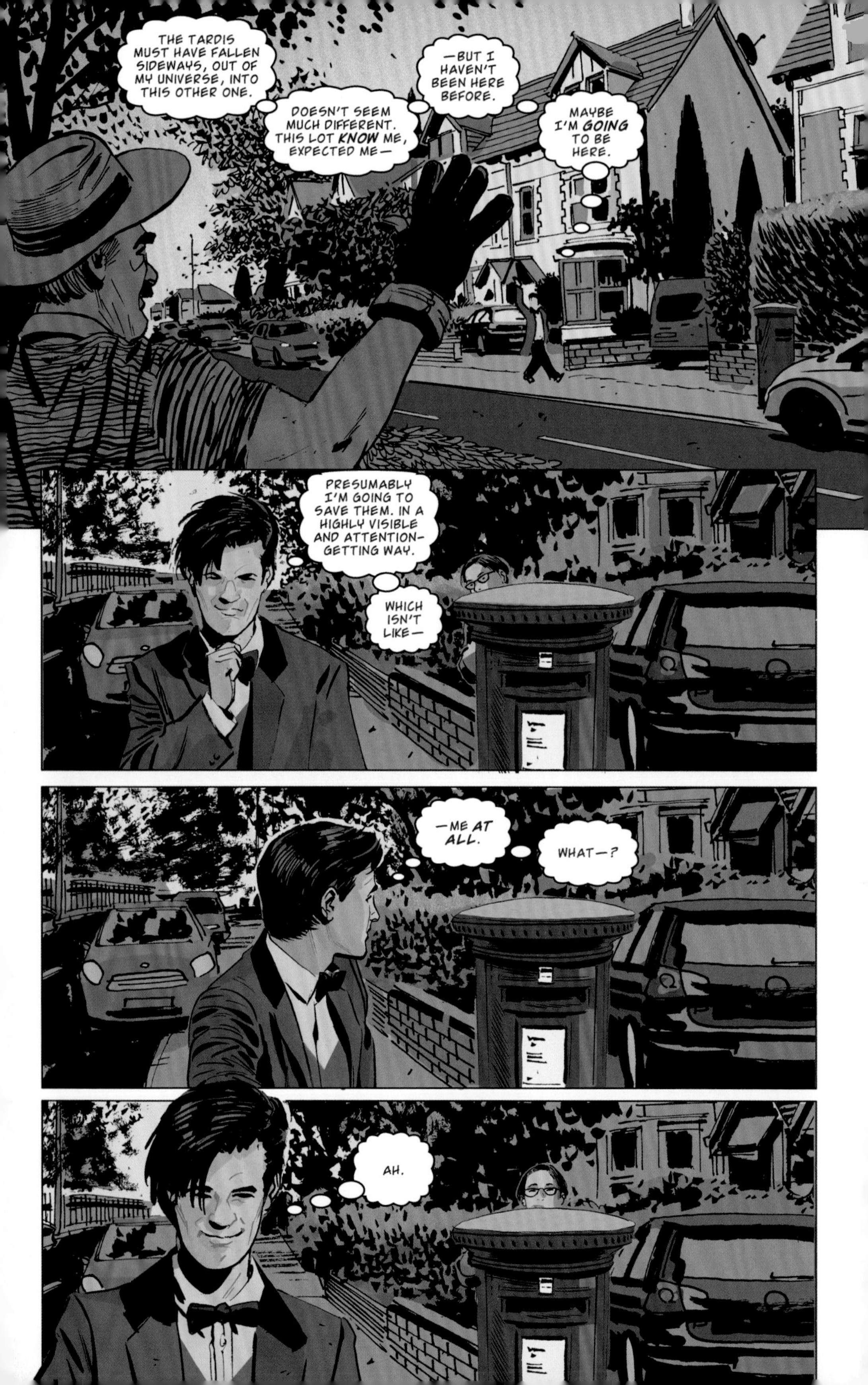
THE TARDIS MUST HAVE FALLEN SIDEWAYS, OUT OF MY UNIVERSE, INTO THIS OTHER ONE.
DOESN'T SEEM MUCH DIFFERENT. THIS LOT KNOW ME, EXPECTED ME—
—BUT I HAVEN'T BEEN HERE BEFORE.
MAYBE I'M GOING TO BE HERE.
PRESUMABLY I'M GOING TO SAVE THEM. IN A HIGHLY VISIBLE AND ATTENTION-GETTING WAY.
WHICH ISN'T LIKE—
—ME AT ALL.
WHAT—?
AH.

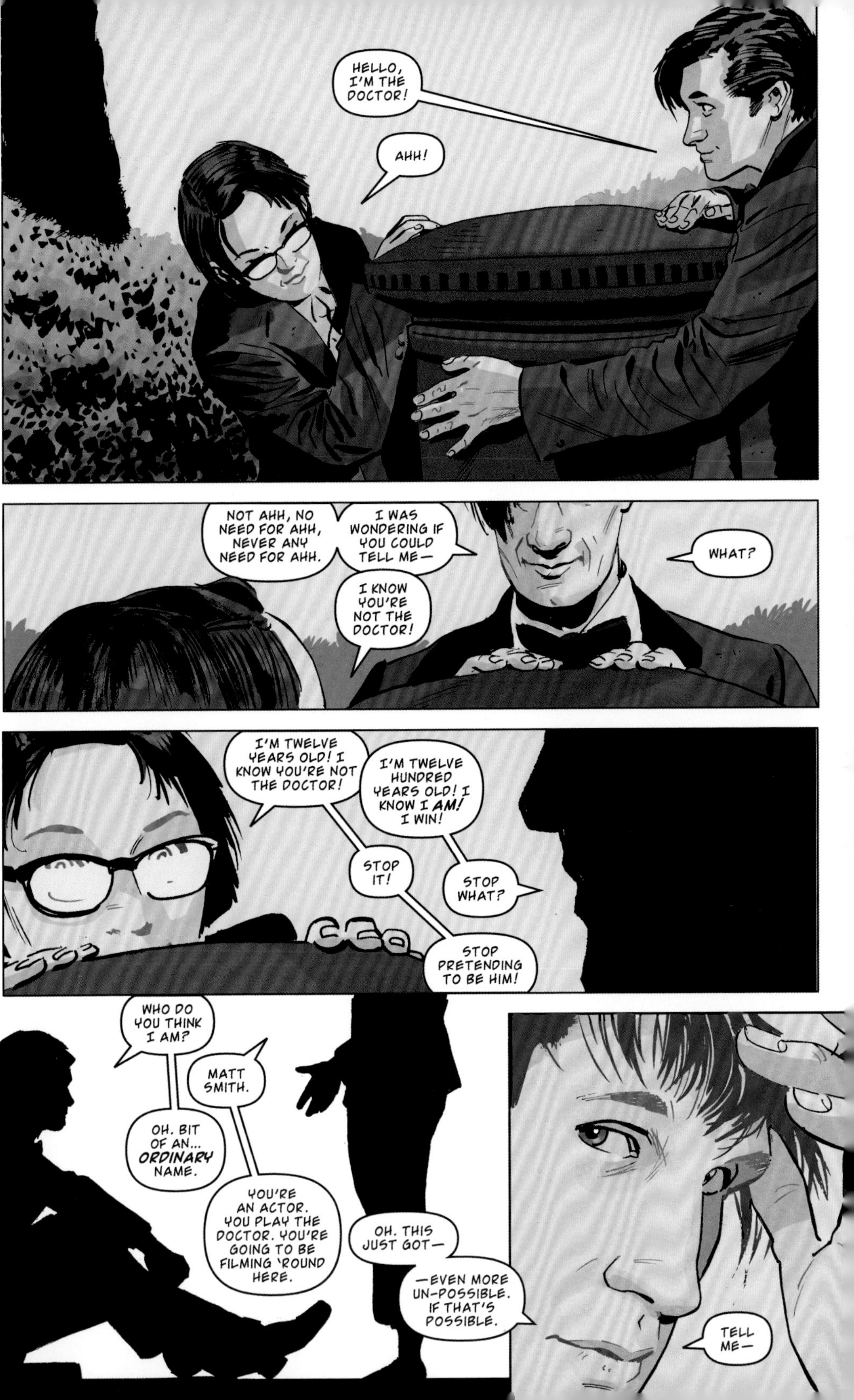
HELLO, I'M THE DOCTOR!
AHH!
NOT AHH, NO NEED FOR AHH, NEVER ANY NEED FOR AHH.
I WAS WONDERING IF YOU COULD TELL ME—
I KNOW YOU'RE NOT THE DOCTOR!
WHAT?
I'M TWELVE YEARS OLD! I KNOW YOU'RE NOT THE DOCTOR!
I'M TWELVE HUNDRED YEARS OLD! I KNOW I AM! I WIN!
STOP IT!
STOP WHAT?
STOP PRETENDING TO BE HIM!
WHO DO YOU THINK I AM?
MATT SMITH.
OH. BIT OF AN... ORDINARY NAME.
YOU'RE AN ACTOR. YOU PLAY THE DOCTOR. YOU'RE GOING TO BE FILMING 'ROUND HERE.
OH. THIS JUST GOT—
—EVEN MORE UN-POSSIBLE. IF THAT'S POSSIBLE.
TELL ME—

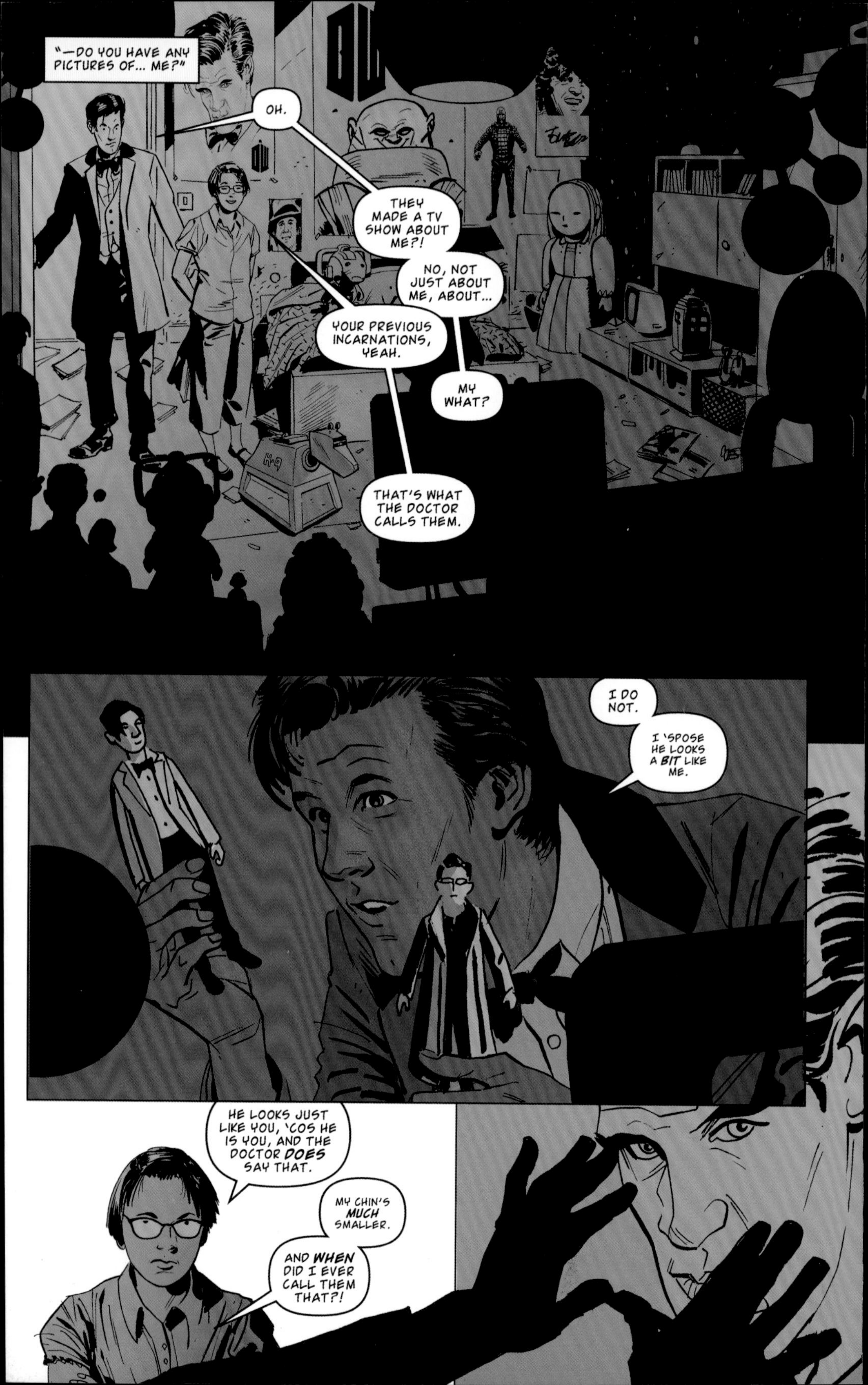
"—DO YOU HAVE ANY PICTURES OF... ME?"
OH.
THEY MADE A TV SHOW ABOUT ME?!
NO, NOT JUST ABOUT ME, ABOUT...
YOUR PREVIOUS INCARNATIONS, YEAH.
MY WHAT?
THAT'S WHAT THE DOCTOR CALLS THEM.
I DO NOT.
I 'SPOSE HE LOOKS A *BIT* LIKE ME.
HE LOOKS JUST LIKE YOU, 'COS HE IS YOU, AND THE DOCTOR *DOES* SAY THAT.
MY CHIN'S *MUCH* SMALLER.
AND *WHEN* DID I EVER CALL THEM THAT?!

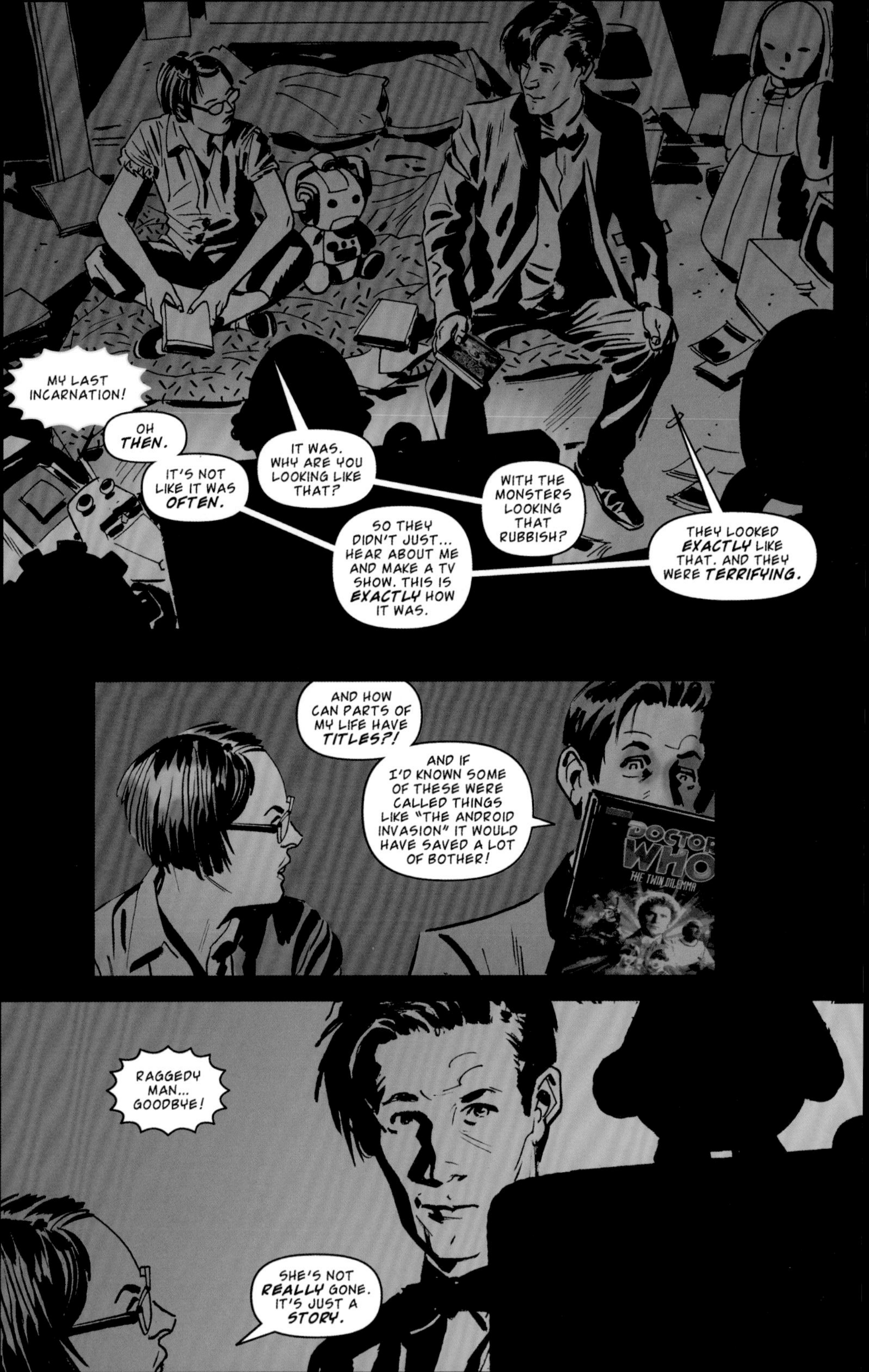
MY LAST INCARNATION!
OH THEN.
IT'S NOT LIKE IT WAS OFTEN.
IT WAS. WHY ARE YOU LOOKING LIKE THAT?
SO THEY DIDN'T JUST... HEAR ABOUT ME AND MAKE A TV SHOW. THIS IS EXACTLY HOW IT WAS.
WITH THE MONSTERS LOOKING THAT RUBBISH?
THEY LOOKED EXACTLY LIKE THAT. AND THEY WERE TERRIFYING.
AND HOW CAN PARTS OF MY LIFE HAVE TITLES?!
AND IF I'D KNOWN SOME OF THESE WERE CALLED THINGS LIKE "THE ANDROID INVASION" IT WOULD HAVE SAVED A LOT OF BOTHER!
DOCTOR WHO
THE TWIN DILEMMA
RAGGEDY MAN... GOODBYE!
SHE'S NOT REALLY GONE. IT'S JUST A STORY.

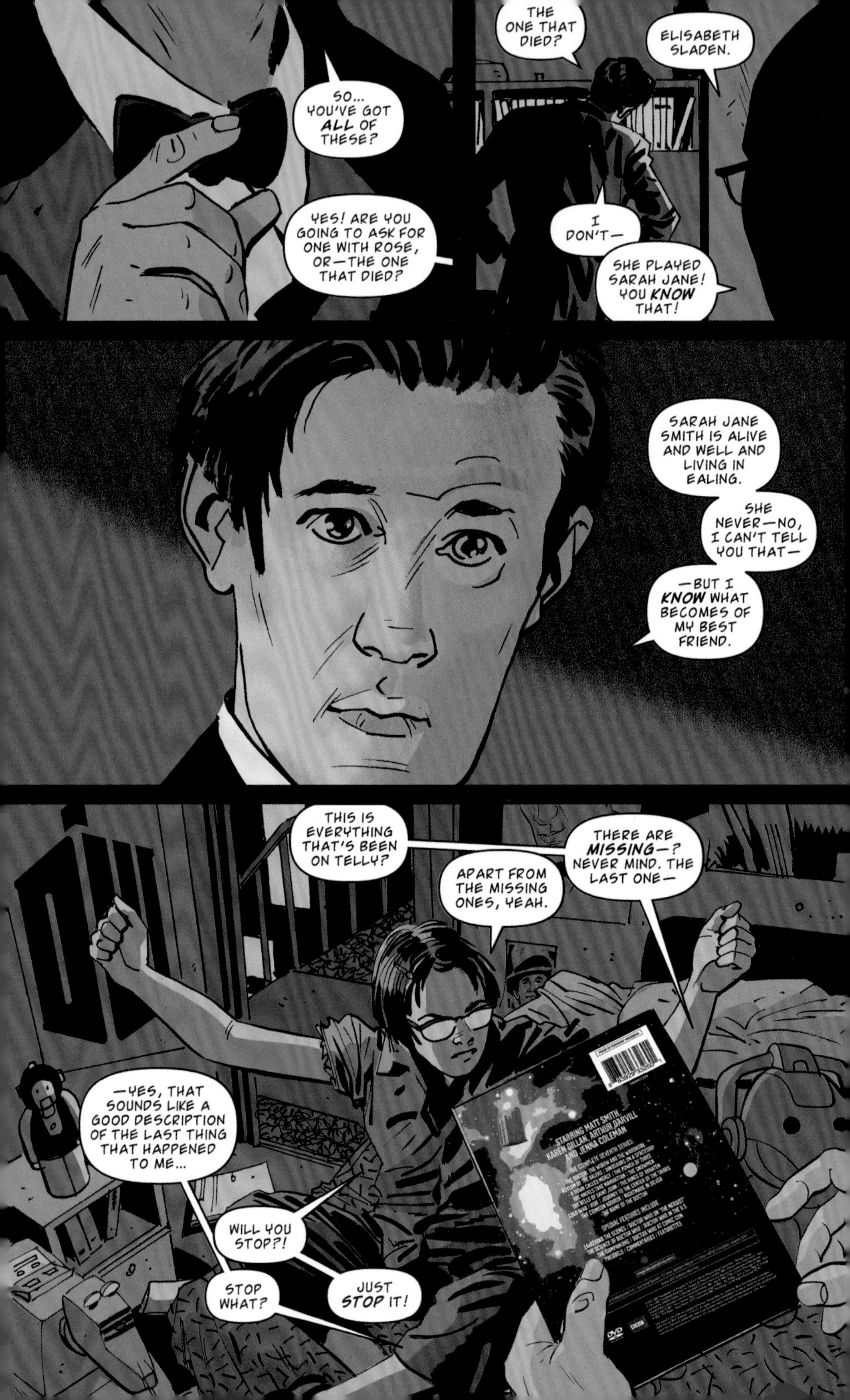
SO... YOU'VE GOT ALL OF THESE?
YES! ARE YOU GOING TO ASK FOR ONE WITH ROSE, OR—THE ONE THAT DIED?
THE ONE THAT DIED?
ELISABETH SLADEN.
I DON'T—
SHE PLAYED SARAH JANE! YOU KNOW THAT!
SARAH JANE SMITH IS ALIVE AND WELL AND LIVING IN EALING.
SHE NEVER—NO, I CAN'T TELL YOU THAT—
—BUT I KNOW WHAT BECOMES OF MY BEST FRIEND.
THIS IS EVERYTHING THAT'S BEEN ON TELLY?
APART FROM THE MISSING ONES, YEAH.
THERE ARE MISSING—? NEVER MIND. THE LAST ONE—
STARRING MATT SMITH, KAREN GILLAN, ARTHUR DARVILL AND JENNA COLEMAN
—YES, THAT SOUNDS LIKE A GOOD DESCRIPTION OF THE LAST THING THAT HAPPENED TO ME...
WILL YOU STOP?!
STOP WHAT?
JUST STOP IT!

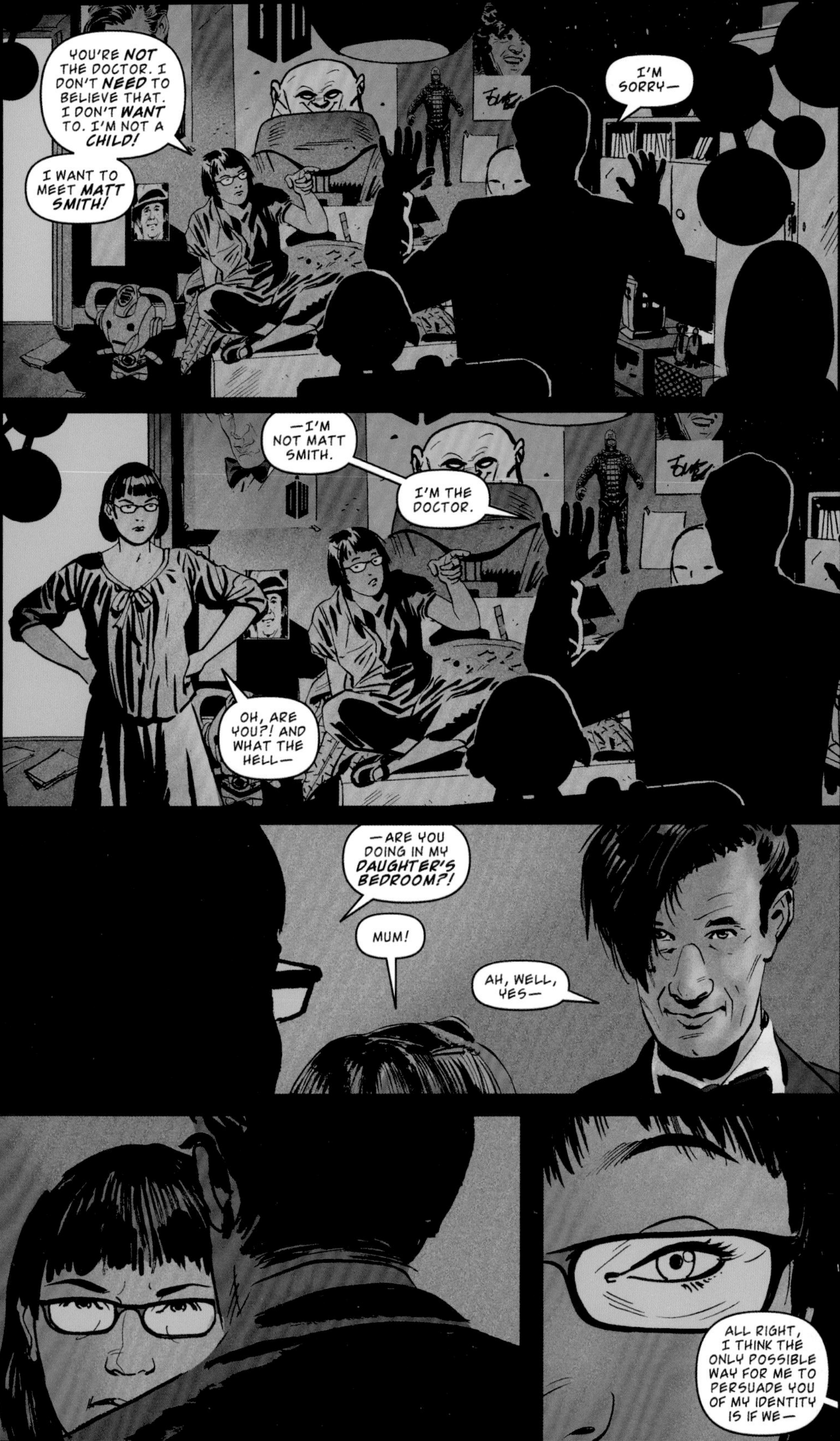
YOU'RE NOT THE DOCTOR. I DON'T NEED TO BELIEVE THAT. I DON'T WANT TO. I'M NOT A CHILD!
I WANT TO MEET MATT SMITH!
I'M SORRY—
—I'M NOT MATT SMITH.
I'M THE DOCTOR.
OH, ARE YOU?! AND WHAT THE HELL—
—ARE YOU DOING IN MY DAUGHTER'S BEDROOM?!
MUM!
AH, WELL, YES—
ALL RIGHT, I THINK THE ONLY POSSIBLE WAY FOR ME TO PERSUADE YOU OF MY IDENTITY IS IF WE—

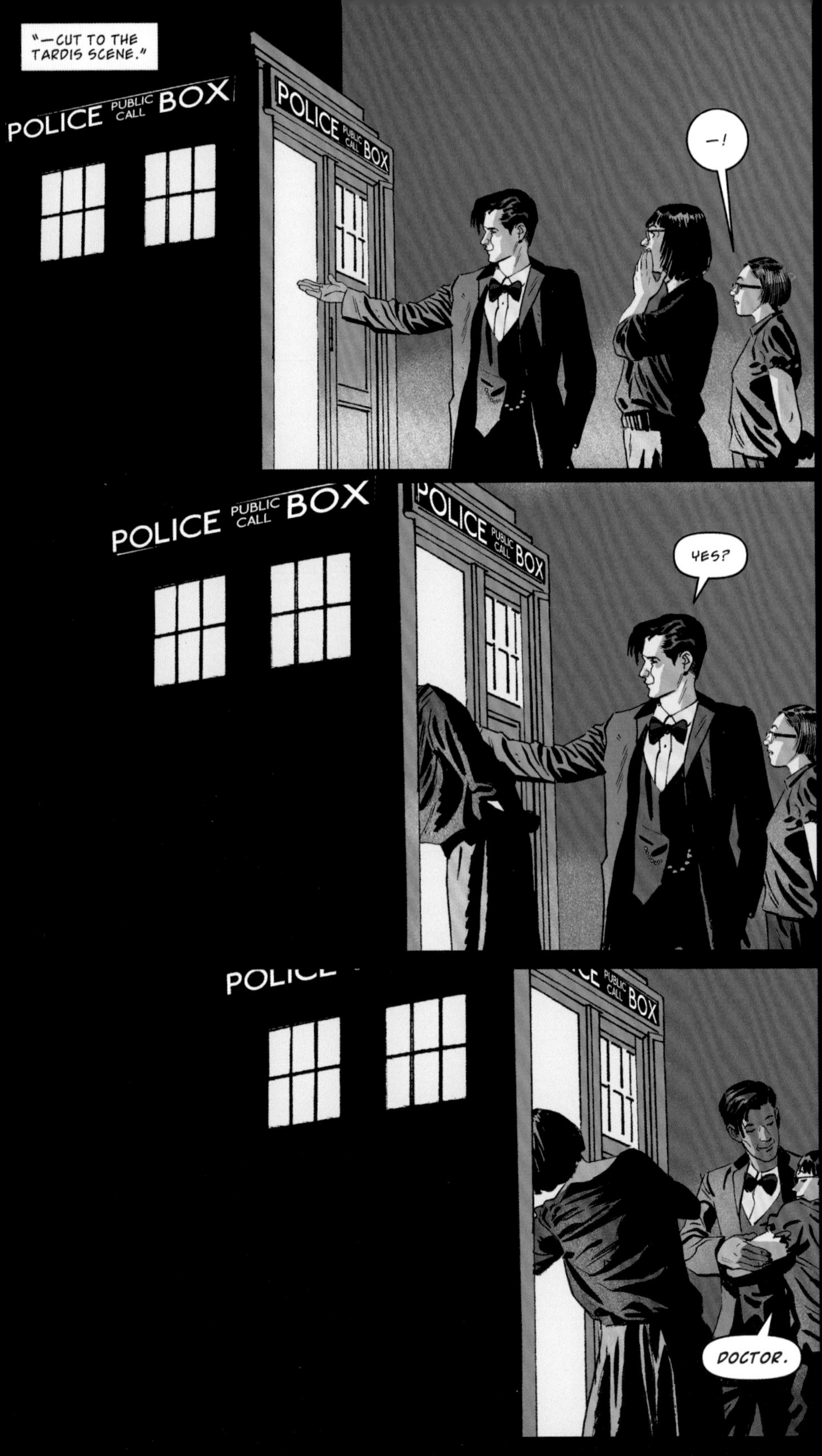
"—CUT TO THE TARDIS SCENE."
POLICE PUBLIC CALL BOX
—!
YES?
DOCTOR.

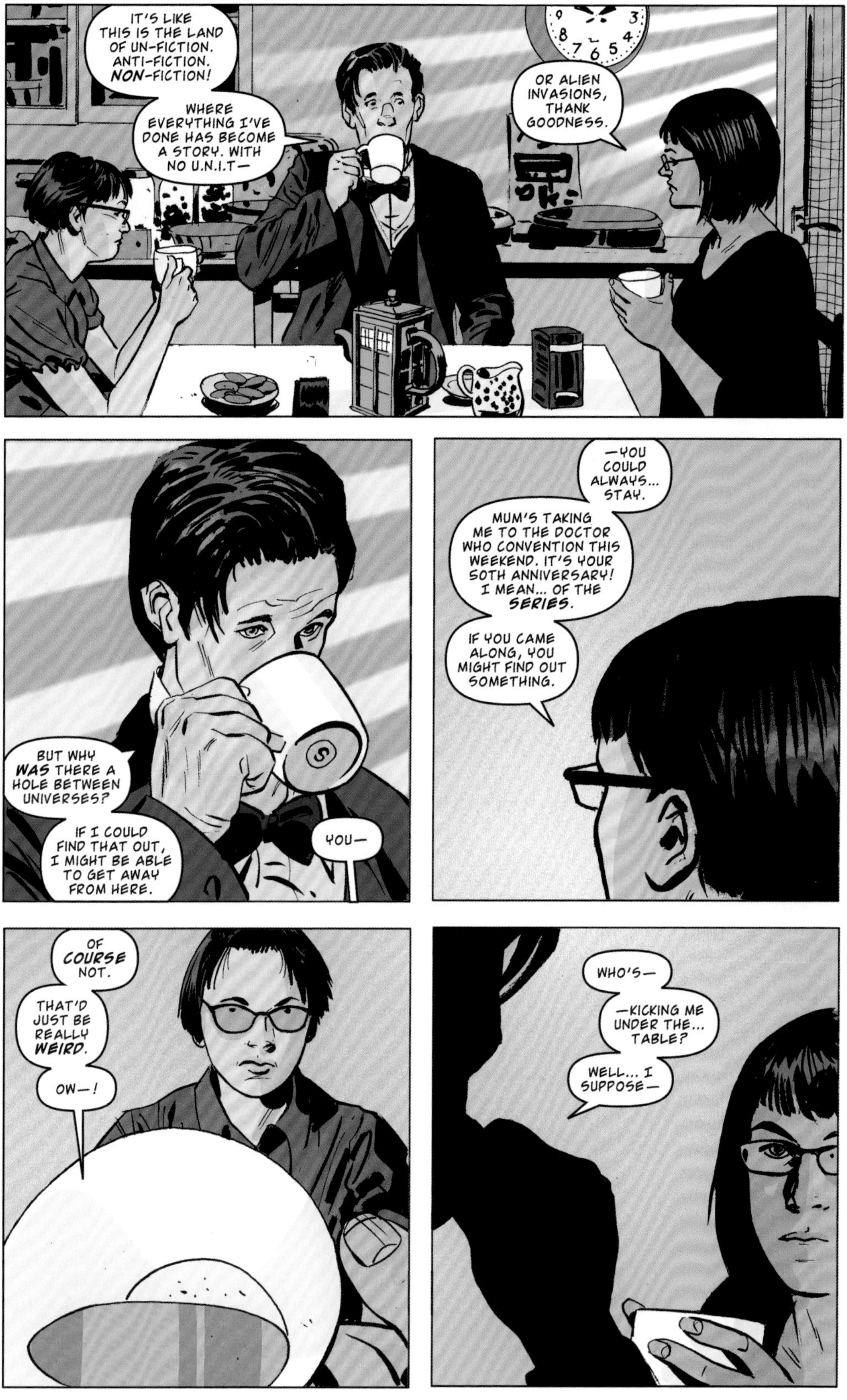

IT'S LIKE THIS IS THE LAND OF UN-FICTION. ANTI-FICTION. NON-FICTION!
WHERE EVERYTHING I'VE DONE HAS BECOME A STORY. WITH NO U.N.I.T—
OR ALIEN INVASIONS, THANK GOODNESS.
BUT WHY WAS THERE A HOLE BETWEEN UNIVERSES?
IF I COULD FIND THAT OUT, I MIGHT BE ABLE TO GET AWAY FROM HERE.
YOU—
—YOU COULD ALWAYS... STAY.
MUM'S TAKING ME TO THE DOCTOR WHO CONVENTION THIS WEEKEND. IT'S YOUR 50TH ANNIVERSARY! I MEAN... OF THE SERIES.
IF YOU CAME ALONG, YOU MIGHT FIND OUT SOMETHING.
OF COURSE NOT.
THAT'D JUST BE REALLY WEIRD.
OW—!
WHO'S—
—KICKING ME UNDER THE... TABLE?
WELL... I SUPPOSE—

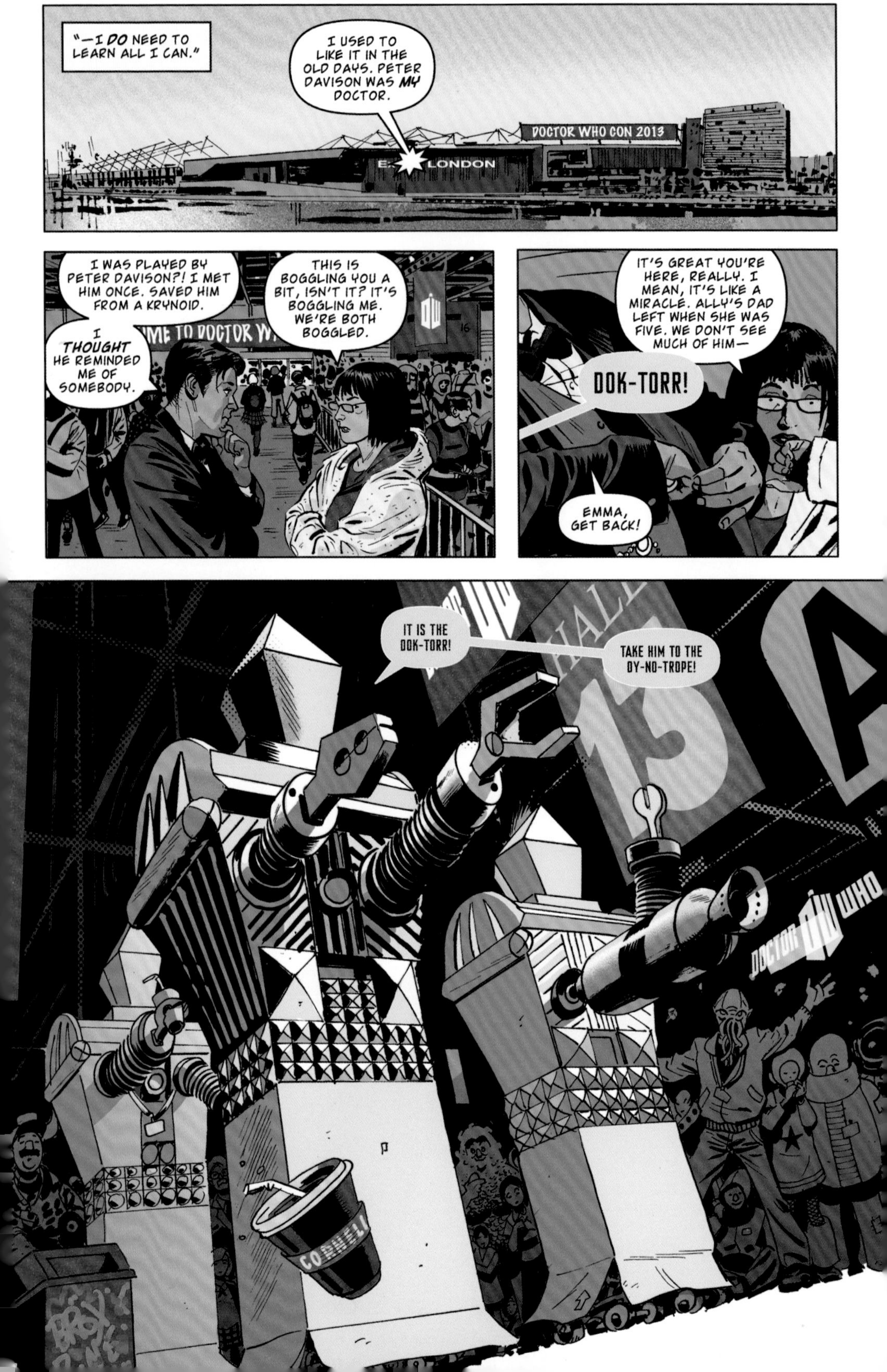
"—I DO NEED TO LEARN ALL I CAN."
I USED TO LIKE IT IN THE OLD DAYS. PETER DAVISON WAS MY DOCTOR.
DOCTOR WHO CON 2013
LONDON
I WAS PLAYED BY PETER DAVISON?! I MET HIM ONCE. SAVED HIM FROM A KRYNOID.
I THOUGHT HE REMINDED ME OF SOMEBODY.
THIS IS BOGGLING YOU A BIT, ISN'T IT? IT'S BOGGLING ME. WE'RE BOTH BOGGLED.
IT'S GREAT YOU'RE HERE, REALLY. I MEAN, IT'S LIKE A MIRACLE. ALLY'S DAD LEFT WHEN SHE WAS FIVE. WE DON'T SEE MUCH OF HIM—
DOK-TORR!
EMMA, GET BACK!
IT IS THE DOK-TORR!
TAKE HIM TO THE OY-NO-TROPE!
DOCTOR WHO

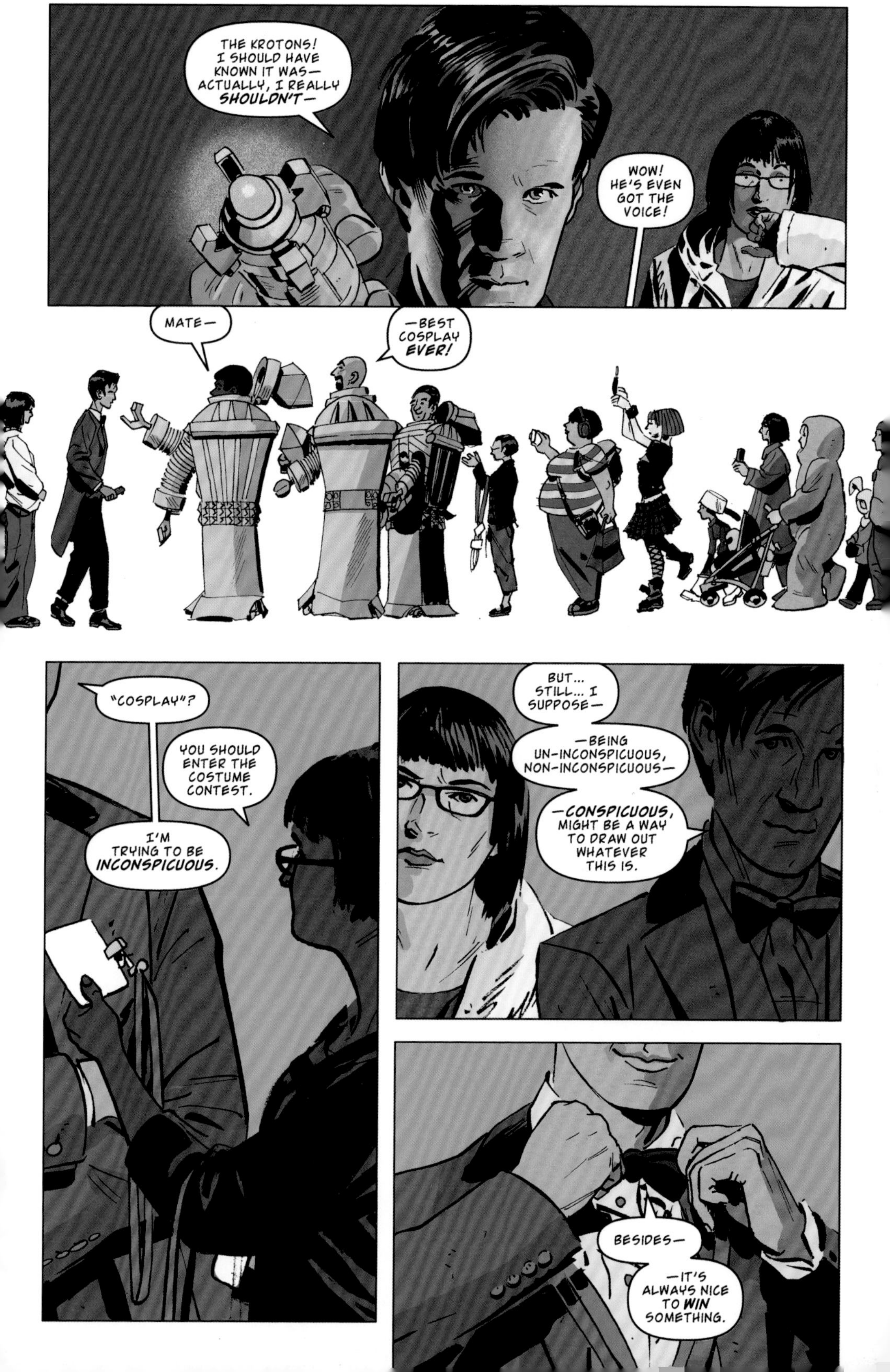
THE KROTONS! I SHOULD HAVE KNOWN IT WAS— ACTUALLY, I REALLY SHOULDN'T—
WOW! HE'S EVEN GOT THE VOICE!
MATE—
—BEST COSPLAY EVER!
"COSPLAY"?
YOU SHOULD ENTER THE COSTUME CONTEST.
I'M TRYING TO BE INCONSPICUOUS.
BUT... STILL... I SUPPOSE—
—BEING UN-INCONSPICUOUS, NON-INCONSPICUOUS—
—CONSPICUOUS, MIGHT BE A WAY TO DRAW OUT WHATEVER THIS IS.
BESIDES—
—IT'S ALWAYS NICE TO WIN SOMETHING.

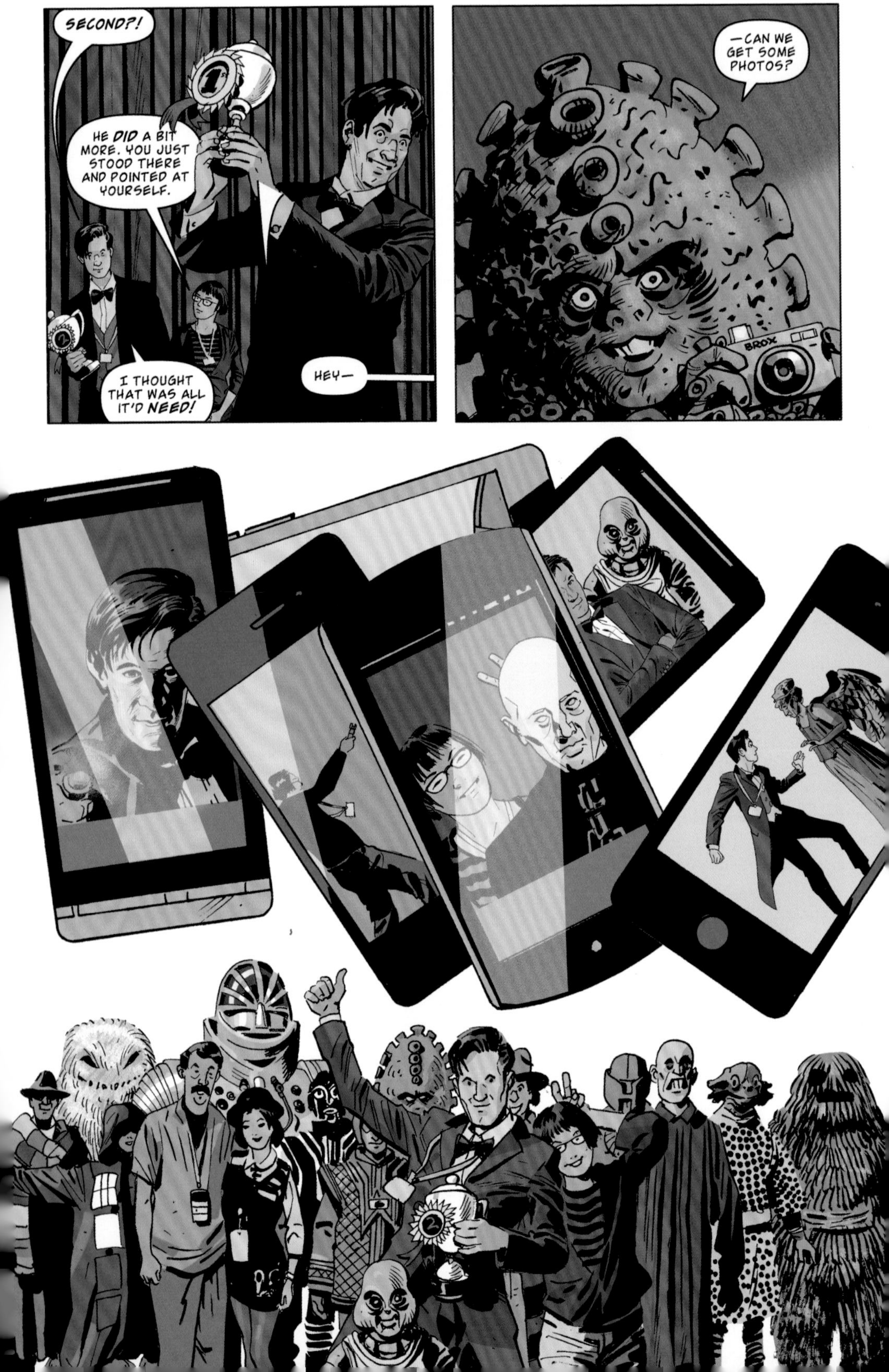
SECOND?!
HE DID A BIT MORE. YOU JUST STOOD THERE AND POINTED AT YOURSELF.
I THOUGHT THAT WAS ALL IT'D NEED!
HEY—
—CAN WE GET SOME PHOTOS?
BROX

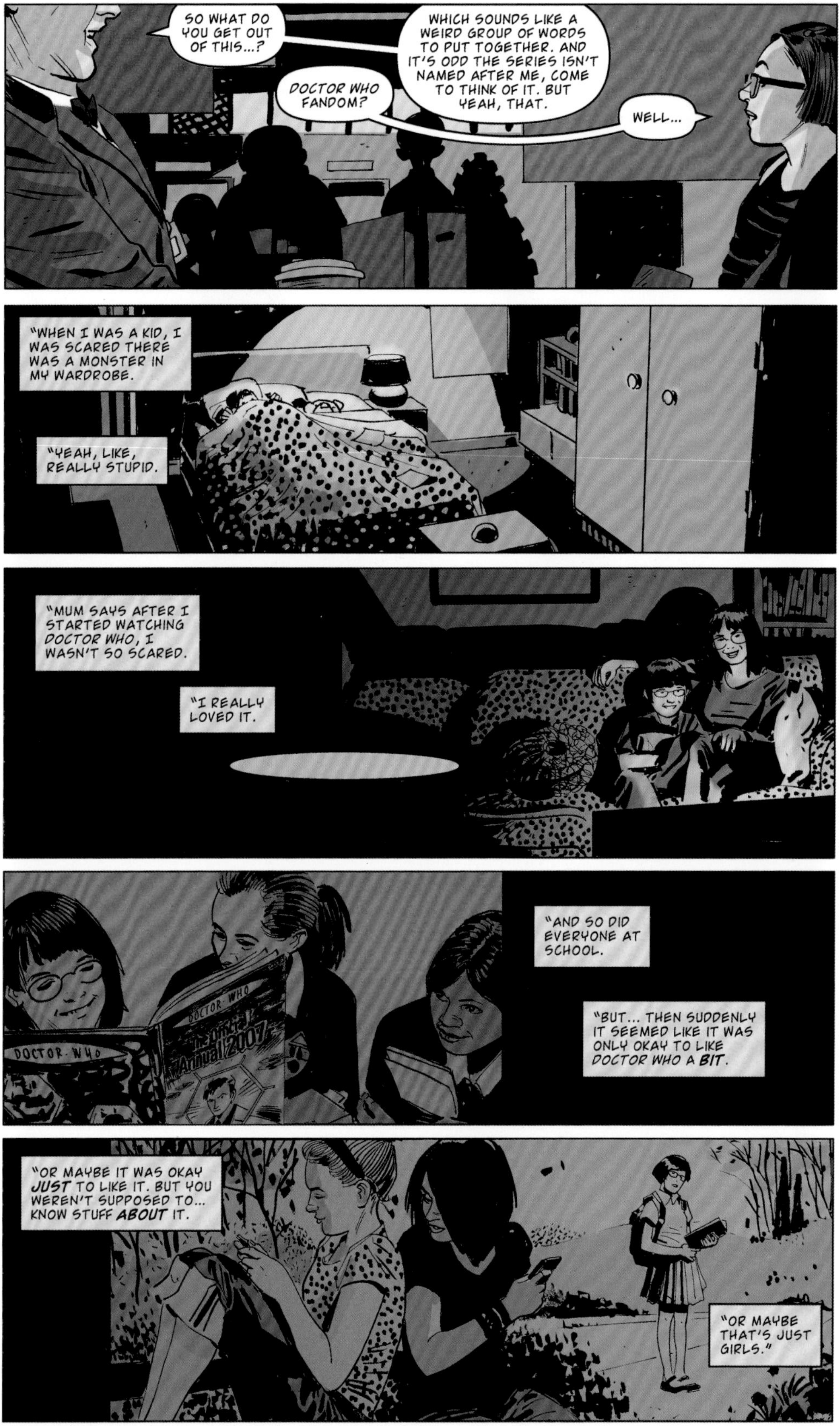
SO WHAT DO YOU GET OUT OF THIS...?
DOCTOR WHO FANDOM?
WHICH SOUNDS LIKE A WEIRD GROUP OF WORDS TO PUT TOGETHER. AND IT'S ODD THE SERIES ISN'T NAMED AFTER ME, COME TO THINK OF IT. BUT YEAH, THAT.
WELL...
"WHEN I WAS A KID, I WAS SCARED THERE WAS A MONSTER IN MY WARDROBE.
"YEAH, LIKE, REALLY STUPID.
"MUM SAYS AFTER I STARTED WATCHING DOCTOR WHO, I WASN'T SO SCARED.
"I REALLY LOVED IT.
DOCTOR WHO
The Official Annual 2007
DOCTOR WHO
"AND SO DID EVERYONE AT SCHOOL.
"BUT... THEN SUDDENLY IT SEEMED LIKE IT WAS ONLY OKAY TO LIKE DOCTOR WHO A BIT.
"OR MAYBE IT WAS OKAY JUST TO LIKE IT. BUT YOU WEREN'T SUPPOSED TO... KNOW STUFF ABOUT IT.
"OR MAYBE THAT'S JUST GIRLS."

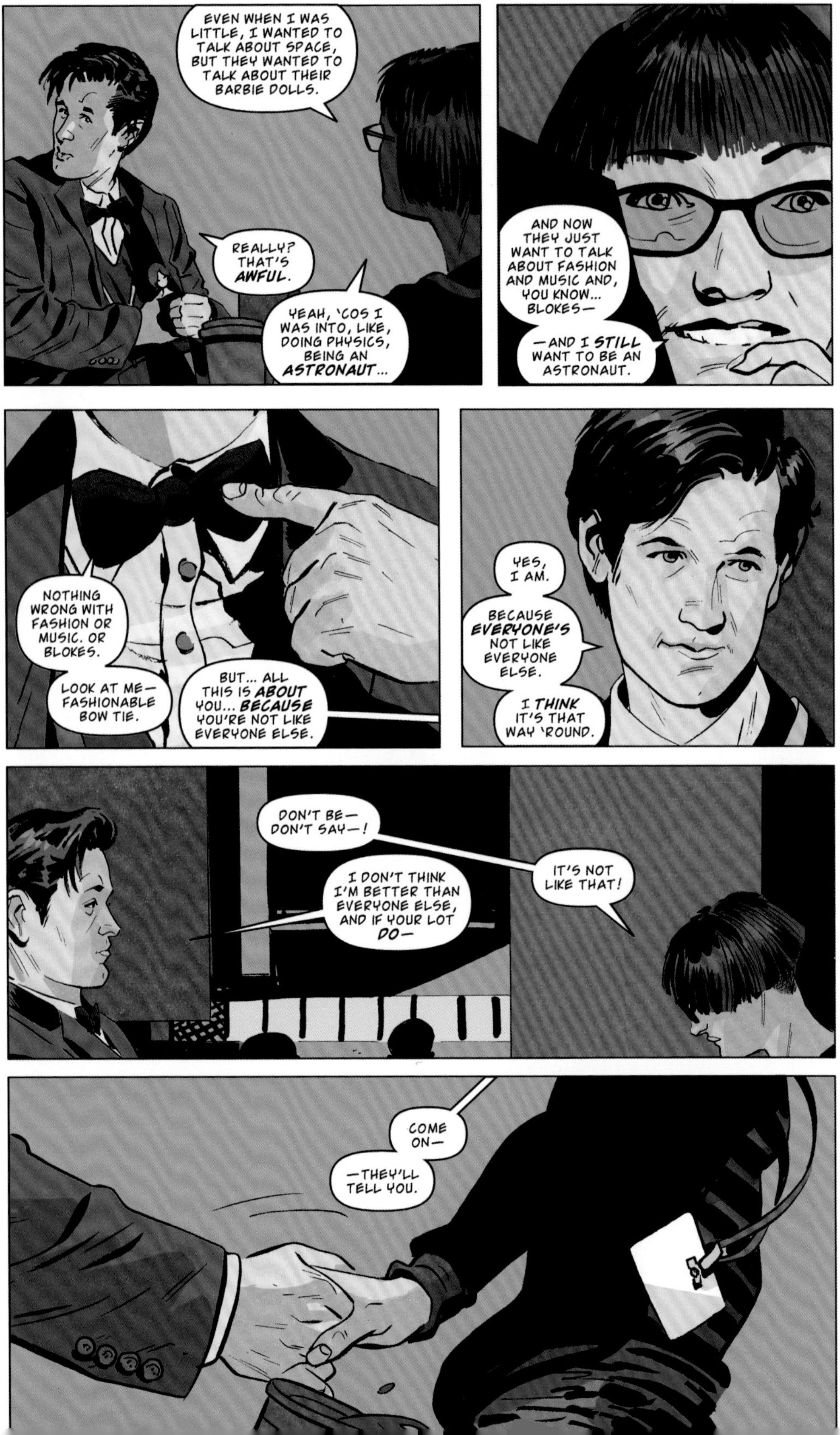
EVEN WHEN I WAS LITTLE, I WANTED TO TALK ABOUT SPACE, BUT THEY WANTED TO TALK ABOUT THEIR BARBIE DOLLS.
REALLY? THAT'S AWFUL.
YEAH, 'COS I WAS INTO, LIKE, DOING PHYSICS, BEING AN ASTRONAUT...
AND NOW THEY JUST WANT TO TALK ABOUT FASHION AND MUSIC AND, YOU KNOW... BLOKES—
—AND I STILL WANT TO BE AN ASTRONAUT.
NOTHING WRONG WITH FASHION OR MUSIC. OR BLOKES.
LOOK AT ME—FASHIONABLE BOW TIE.
BUT... ALL THIS IS ABOUT YOU... BECAUSE YOU'RE NOT LIKE EVERYONE ELSE.
YES, I AM.
BECAUSE EVERYONE'S NOT LIKE EVERYONE ELSE.
I THINK IT'S THAT WAY 'ROUND.
DON'T BE—DON'T SAY—!
I DON'T THINK I'M BETTER THAN EVERYONE ELSE, AND IF YOUR LOT DO—
IT'S NOT LIKE THAT!
COME ON—
—THEY'LL TELL YOU.

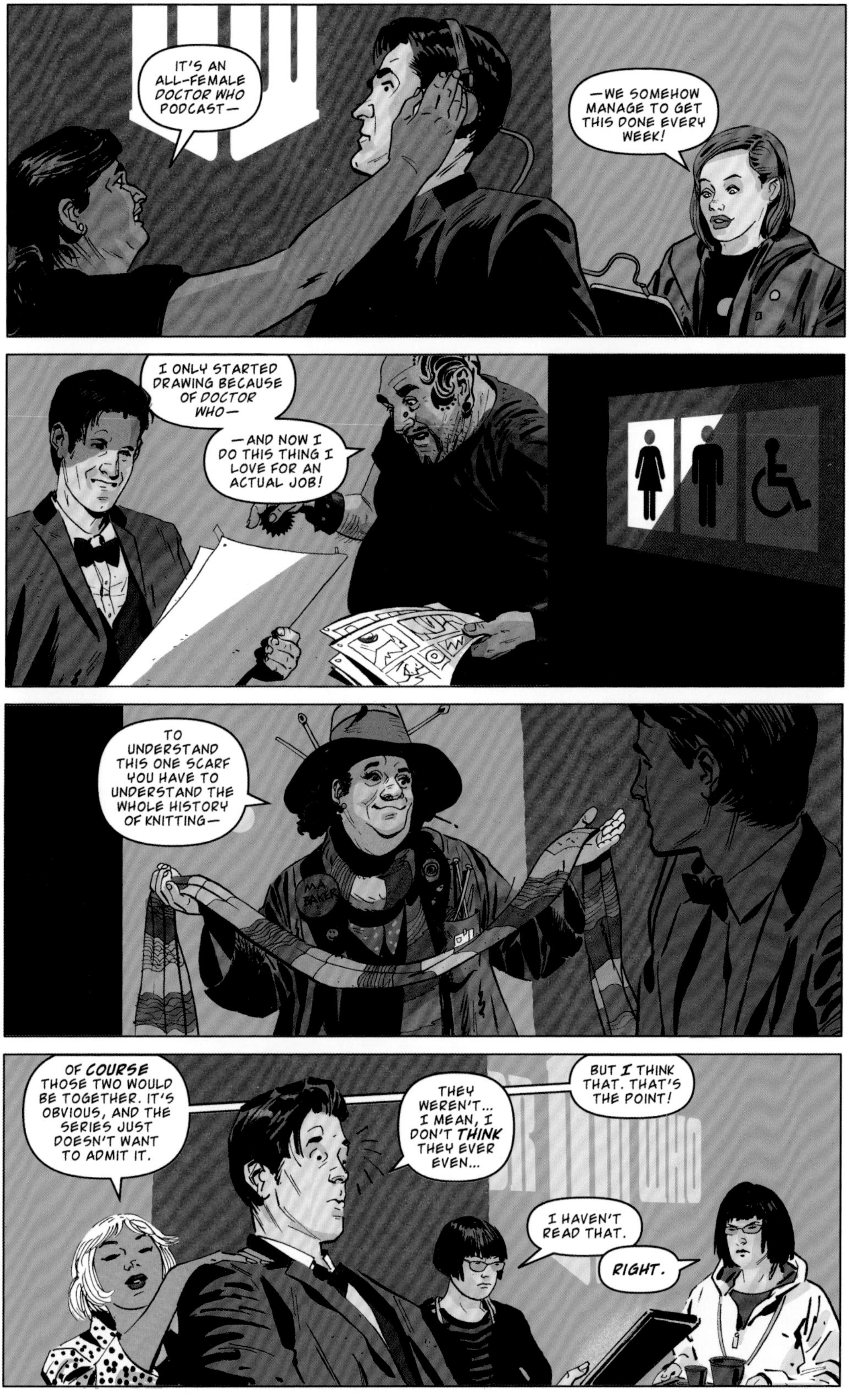
IT'S AN ALL-FEMALE DOCTOR WHO PODCAST—
—WE SOMEHOW MANAGE TO GET THIS DONE EVERY WEEK!
I ONLY STARTED DRAWING BECAUSE OF DOCTOR WHO—
—AND NOW I DO THIS THING I LOVE FOR AN ACTUAL JOB!
TO UNDERSTAND THIS ONE SCARF YOU HAVE TO UNDERSTAND THE WHOLE HISTORY OF KNITTING—
MA BAKER
OF COURSE THOSE TWO WOULD BE TOGETHER. IT'S OBVIOUS, AND THE SERIES JUST DOESN'T WANT TO ADMIT IT.
THEY WEREN'T... I MEAN, I DON'T THINK THEY EVER EVEN...
BUT I THINK THAT. THAT'S THE POINT!
I HAVEN'T READ THAT.
RIGHT.

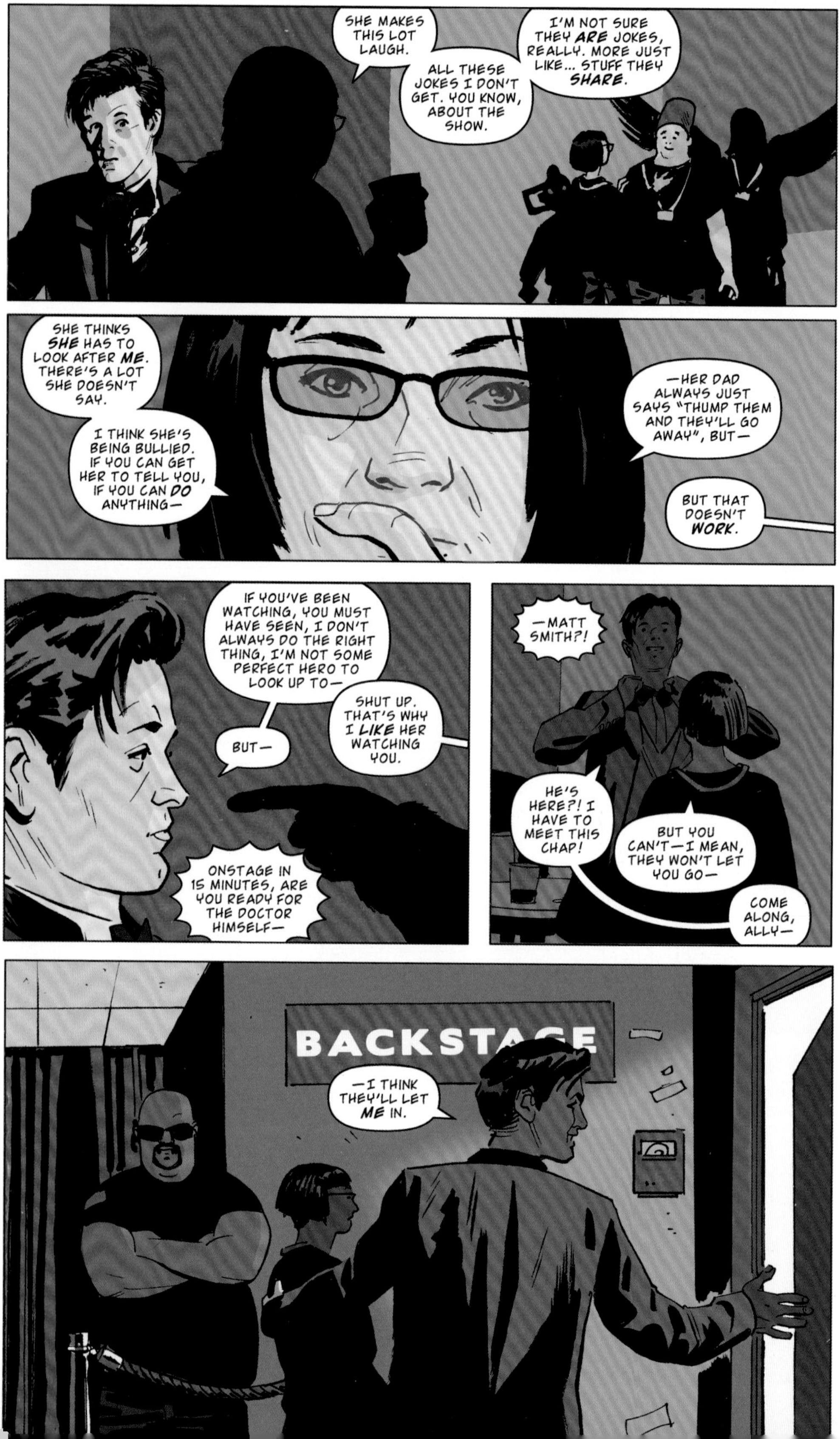
SHE MAKES THIS LOT LAUGH.
ALL THESE JOKES I DON'T GET. YOU KNOW, ABOUT THE SHOW.
I'M NOT SURE THEY ARE JOKES, REALLY. MORE JUST LIKE... STUFF THEY SHARE.
SHE THINKS SHE HAS TO LOOK AFTER ME. THERE'S A LOT SHE DOESN'T SAY.
I THINK SHE'S BEING BULLIED. IF YOU CAN GET HER TO TELL YOU, IF YOU CAN DO ANYTHING—
—HER DAD ALWAYS JUST SAYS "THUMP THEM AND THEY'LL GO AWAY", BUT—
BUT THAT DOESN'T WORK.
IF YOU'VE BEEN WATCHING, YOU MUST HAVE SEEN, I DON'T ALWAYS DO THE RIGHT THING, I'M NOT SOME PERFECT HERO TO LOOK UP TO—
BUT—
SHUT UP. THAT'S WHY I LIKE HER WATCHING YOU.
ONSTAGE IN 15 MINUTES, ARE YOU READY FOR THE DOCTOR HIMSELF—
—MATT SMITH?!
HE'S HERE?! I HAVE TO MEET THIS CHAP!
BUT YOU CAN'T—I MEAN, THEY WON'T LET YOU GO—
COME ALONG, ALLY—
BACKSTAGE
—I THINK THEY'LL LET ME IN.

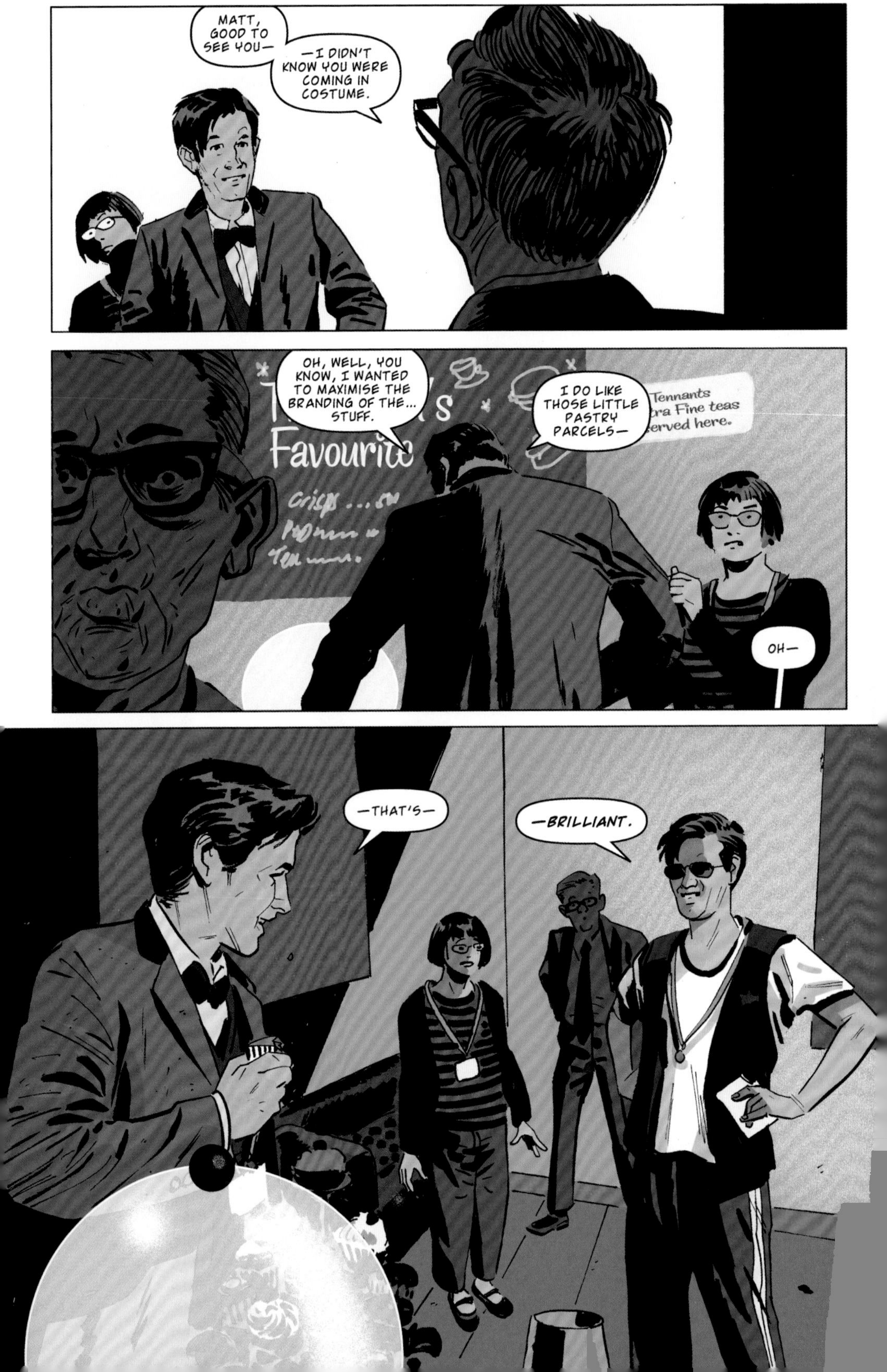
MATT, GOOD TO SEE YOU—
—I DIDN'T KNOW YOU WERE COMING IN COSTUME.
OH, WELL, YOU KNOW, I WANTED TO MAXIMISE THE BRANDING OF THE... STUFF.
Favourite
I DO LIKE THOSE LITTLE PASTRY PARCELS—
Tennants
OH—
—THAT'S—
—BRILLIANT.

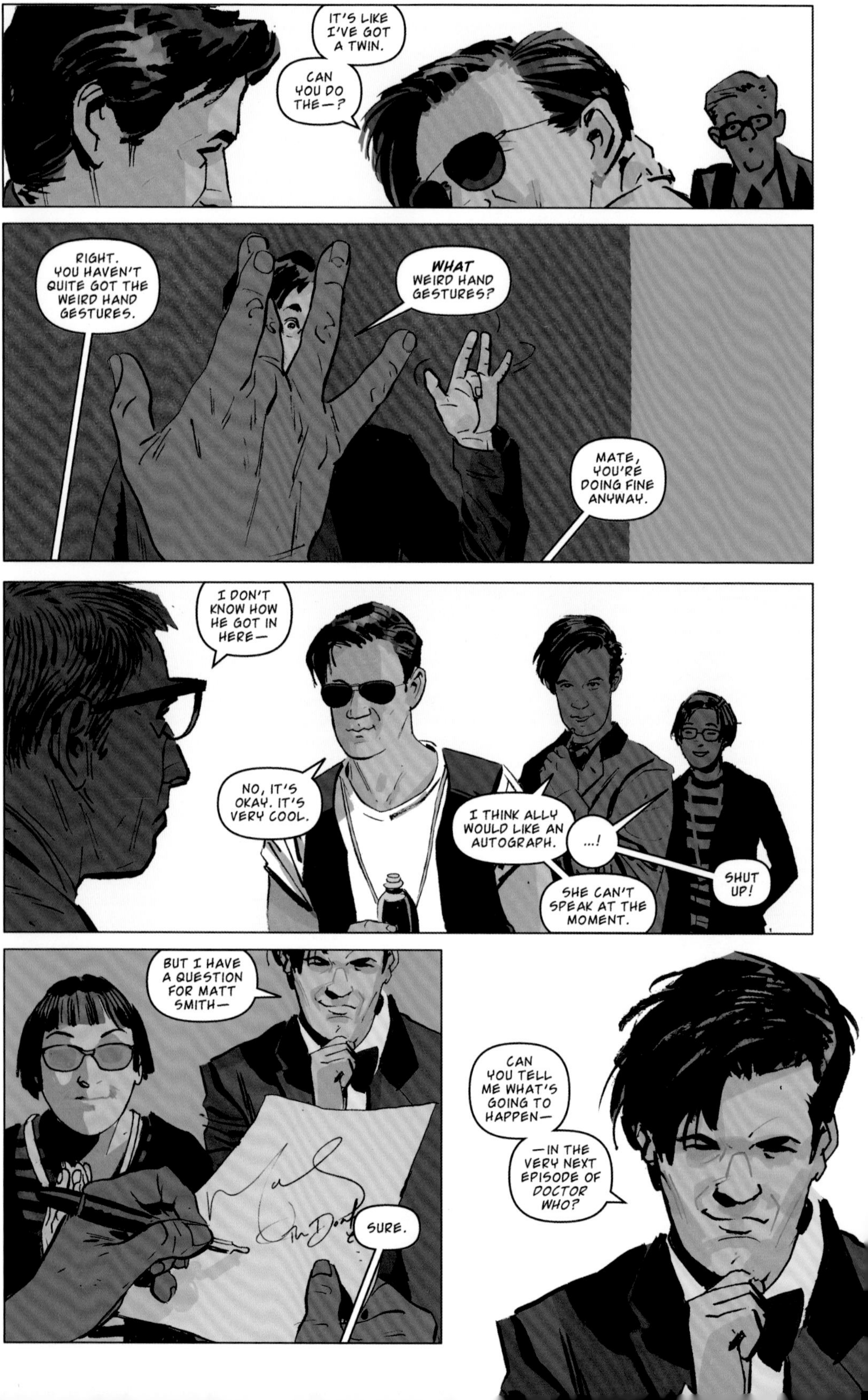
IT'S LIKE I'VE GOT A TWIN.
CAN YOU DO THE—?
RIGHT. YOU HAVEN'T QUITE GOT THE WEIRD HAND GESTURES.
WHAT WEIRD HAND GESTURES?
MATE, YOU'RE DOING FINE ANYWAY.
I DON'T KNOW HOW HE GOT IN HERE—
NO, IT'S OKAY. IT'S VERY COOL.
I THINK ALLY WOULD LIKE AN AUTOGRAPH.
...!
SHE CAN'T SPEAK AT THE MOMENT.
SHUT UP!
BUT I HAVE A QUESTION FOR MATT SMITH—
SURE.
CAN YOU TELL ME WHAT'S GOING TO HAPPEN—
—IN THE VERY NEXT EPISODE OF DOCTOR WHO?

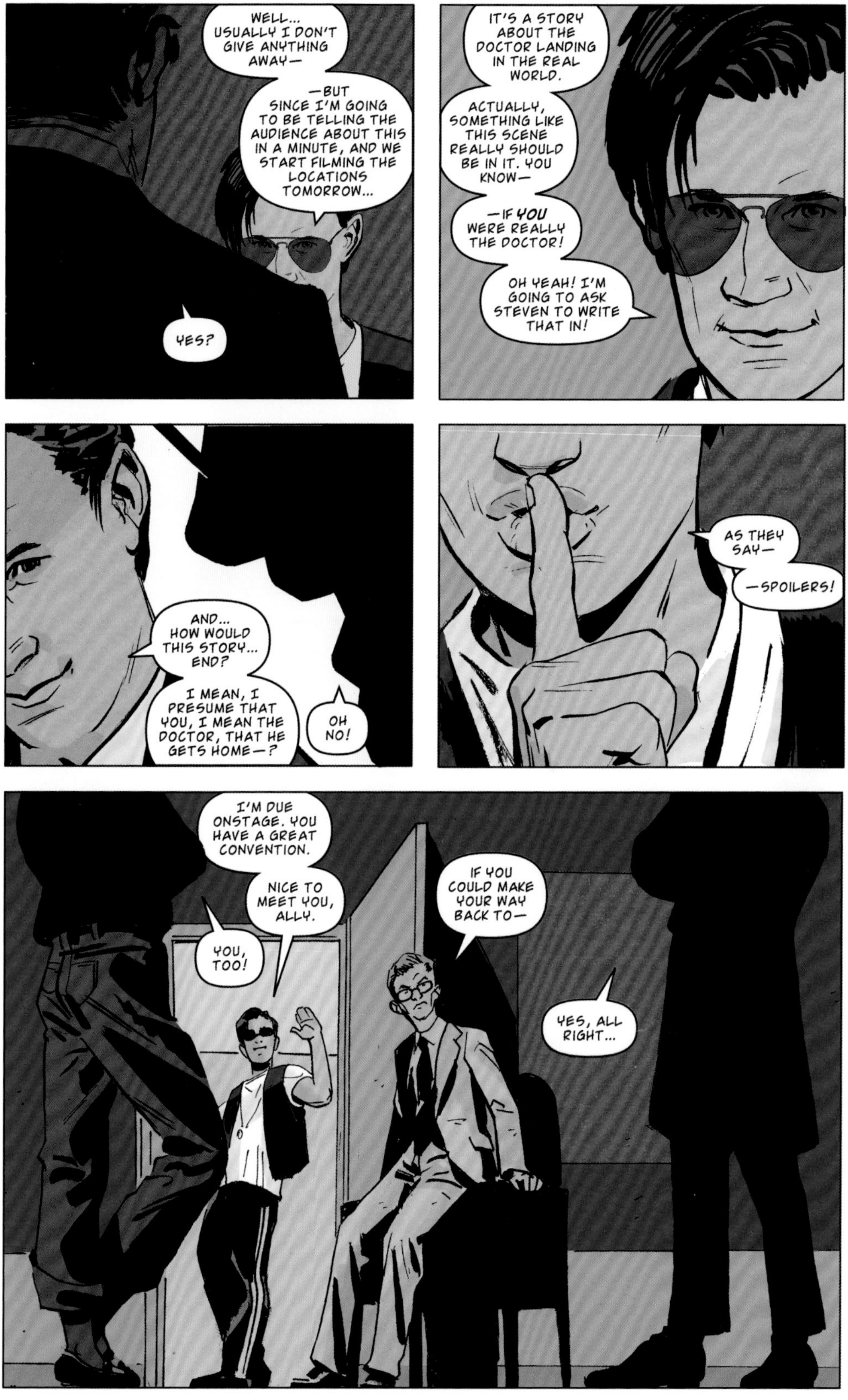
WELL... USUALLY I DON'T GIVE ANYTHING AWAY—
—BUT SINCE I'M GOING TO BE TELLING THE AUDIENCE ABOUT THIS IN A MINUTE, AND WE START FILMING THE LOCATIONS TOMORROW...
YES?
IT'S A STORY ABOUT THE DOCTOR LANDING IN THE REAL WORLD.
ACTUALLY, SOMETHING LIKE THIS SCENE REALLY SHOULD BE IN IT. YOU KNOW—
—IF YOU WERE REALLY THE DOCTOR!
OH YEAH! I'M GOING TO ASK STEVEN TO WRITE THAT IN!
AND... HOW WOULD THIS STORY... END?
I MEAN, I PRESUME THAT YOU, I MEAN THE DOCTOR, THAT HE GETS HOME—?
OH NO!
AS THEY SAY—
—SPOILERS!
I'M DUE ONSTAGE. YOU HAVE A GREAT CONVENTION.
NICE TO MEET YOU, ALLY.
YOU, TOO!
IF YOU COULD MAKE YOUR WAY BACK TO—
YES, ALL RIGHT...

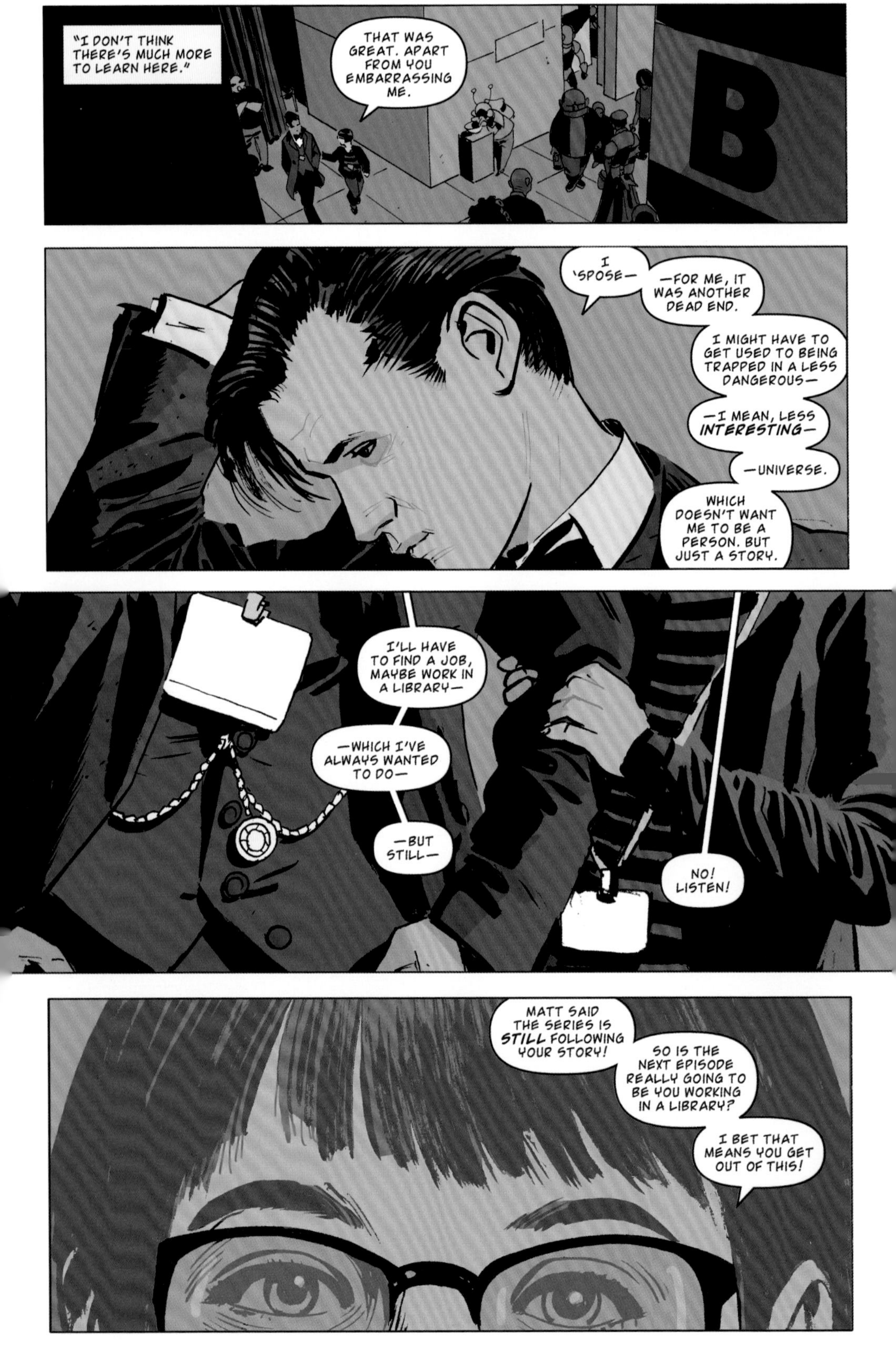
"I DON'T THINK THERE'S MUCH MORE TO LEARN HERE."
THAT WAS GREAT. APART FROM YOU EMBARRASSING ME.
I 'SPOSE—
—FOR ME, IT WAS ANOTHER DEAD END.
I MIGHT HAVE TO GET USED TO BEING TRAPPED IN A LESS DANGEROUS—
—I MEAN, LESS *INTERESTING*—
—UNIVERSE.
WHICH DOESN'T WANT ME TO BE A PERSON. BUT JUST A STORY.
I'LL HAVE TO FIND A JOB, MAYBE WORK IN A LIBRARY—
—WHICH I'VE ALWAYS WANTED TO DO—
—BUT STILL—
NO! LISTEN!
MATT SAID THE SERIES IS *STILL* FOLLOWING YOUR STORY!
SO IS THE NEXT EPISODE REALLY GOING TO BE YOU WORKING IN A LIBRARY?
I BET THAT MEANS YOU GET OUT OF THIS!

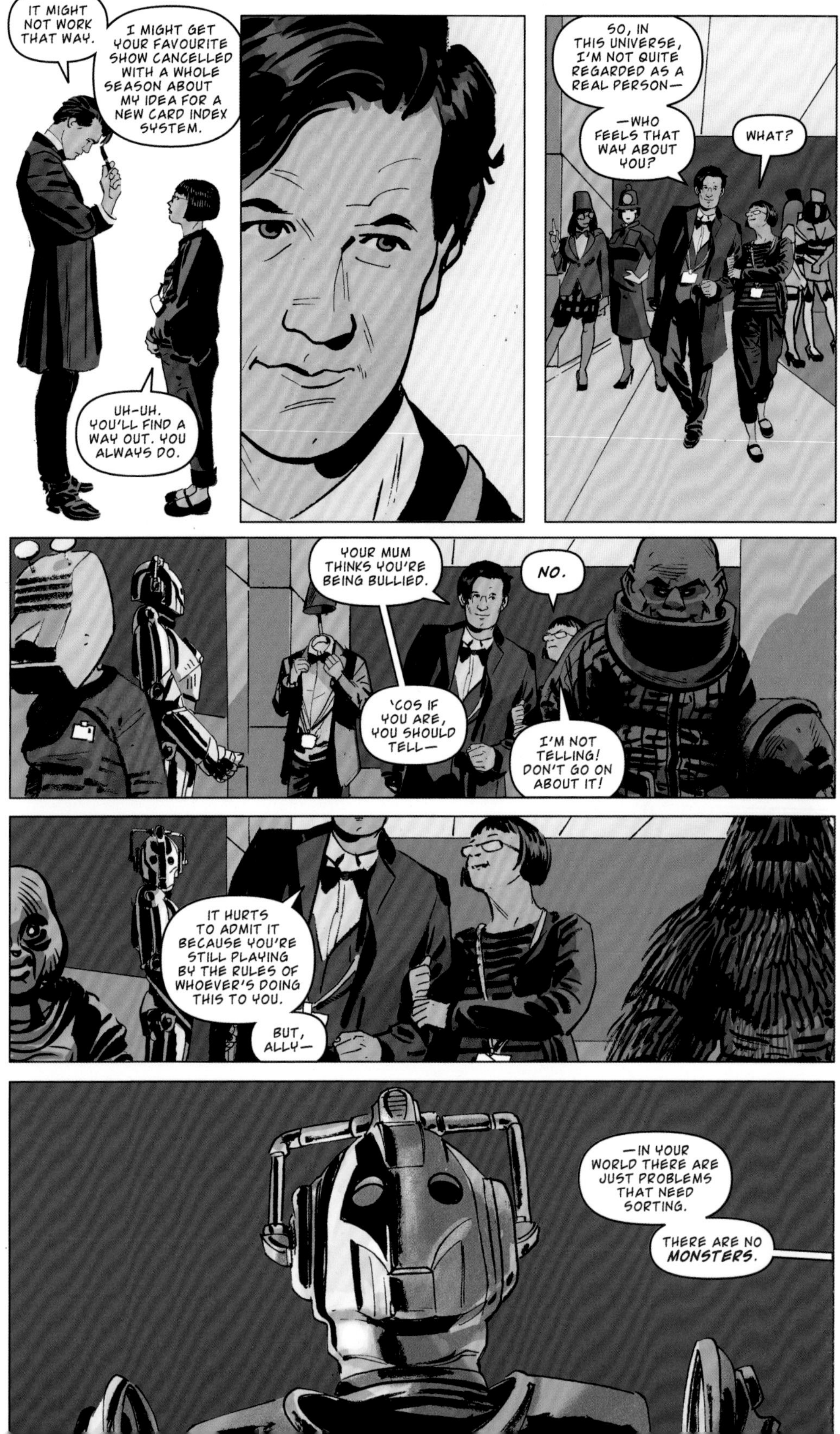
IT MIGHT NOT WORK THAT WAY.
I MIGHT GET YOUR FAVOURITE SHOW CANCELLED WITH A WHOLE SEASON ABOUT MY IDEA FOR A NEW CARD INDEX SYSTEM.
UH-UH. YOU'LL FIND A WAY OUT. YOU ALWAYS DO.
SO, IN THIS UNIVERSE, I'M NOT QUITE REGARDED AS A REAL PERSON—
—WHO FEELS THAT WAY ABOUT YOU?
WHAT?
YOUR MUM THINKS YOU'RE BEING BULLIED.
NO.
'COS IF YOU ARE, YOU SHOULD TELL—
I'M NOT TELLING! DON'T GO ON ABOUT IT!
IT HURTS TO ADMIT IT BECAUSE YOU'RE STILL PLAYING BY THE RULES OF WHOEVER'S DOING THIS TO YOU.
BUT, ALLY—
—IN YOUR WORLD THERE ARE JUST PROBLEMS THAT NEED SORTING.
THERE ARE NO MONSTERS.

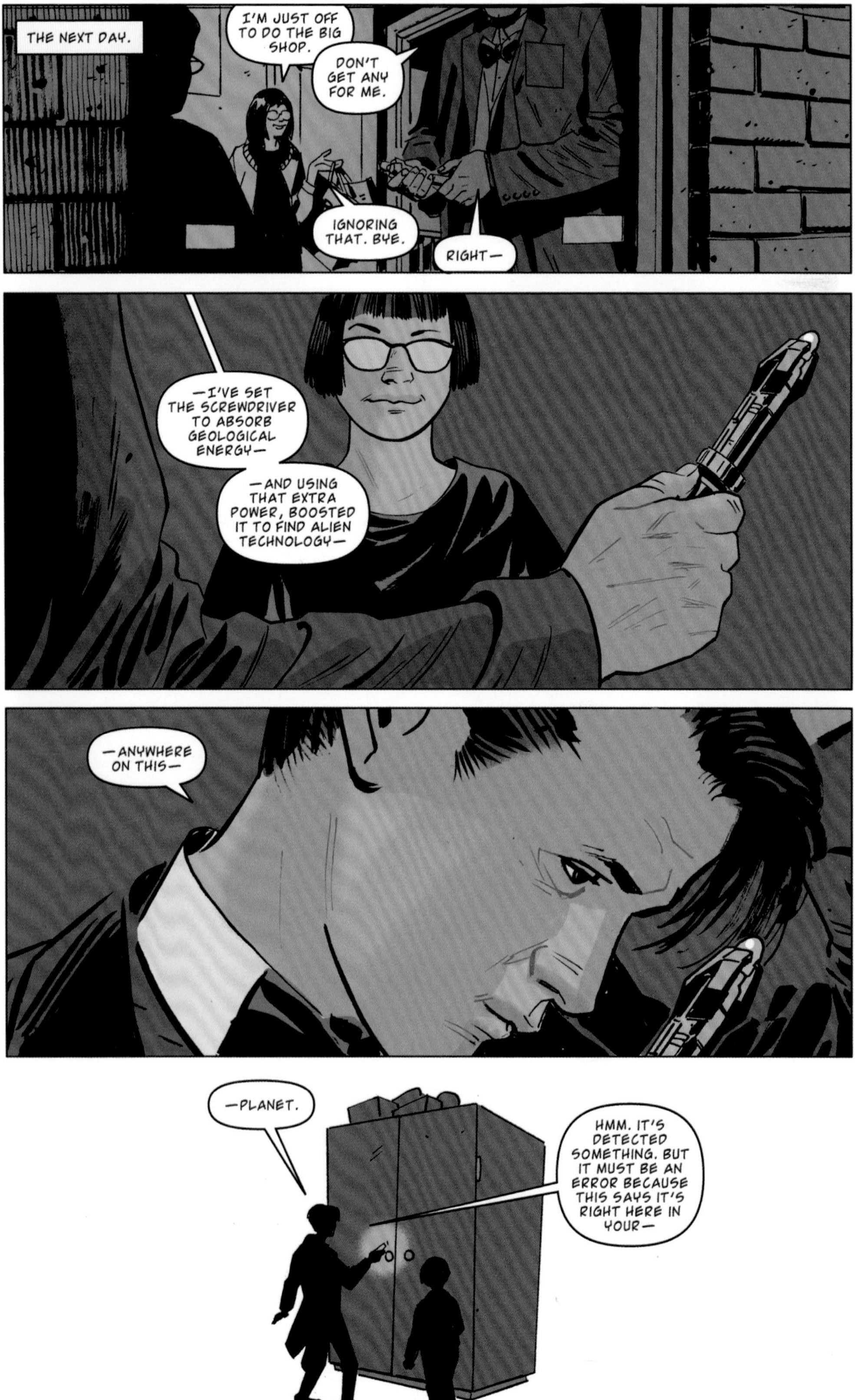
THE NEXT DAY.
I'M JUST OFF TO DO THE BIG SHOP.
DON'T GET ANY FOR ME.
IGNORING THAT. BYE.
RIGHT—
—I'VE SET THE SCREWDRIVER TO ABSORB GEOLOGICAL ENERGY—
—AND USING THAT EXTRA POWER, BOOSTED IT TO FIND ALIEN TECHNOLOGY—
—ANYWHERE ON THIS—
—PLANET.
HMM. IT'S DETECTED SOMETHING. BUT IT MUST BE AN ERROR BECAUSE THIS SAYS IT'S RIGHT HERE IN YOUR—

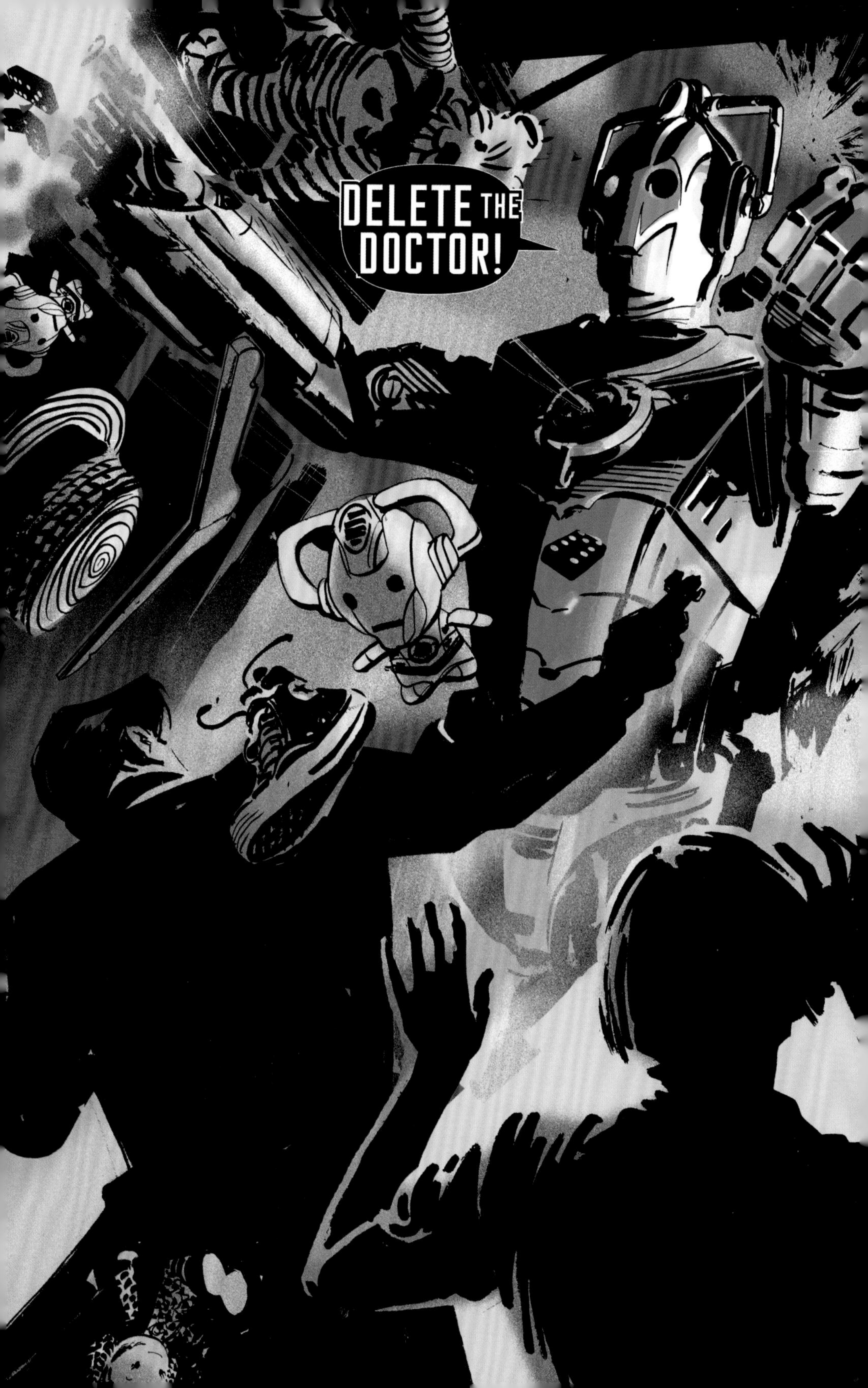
DELETE THE DOCTOR!

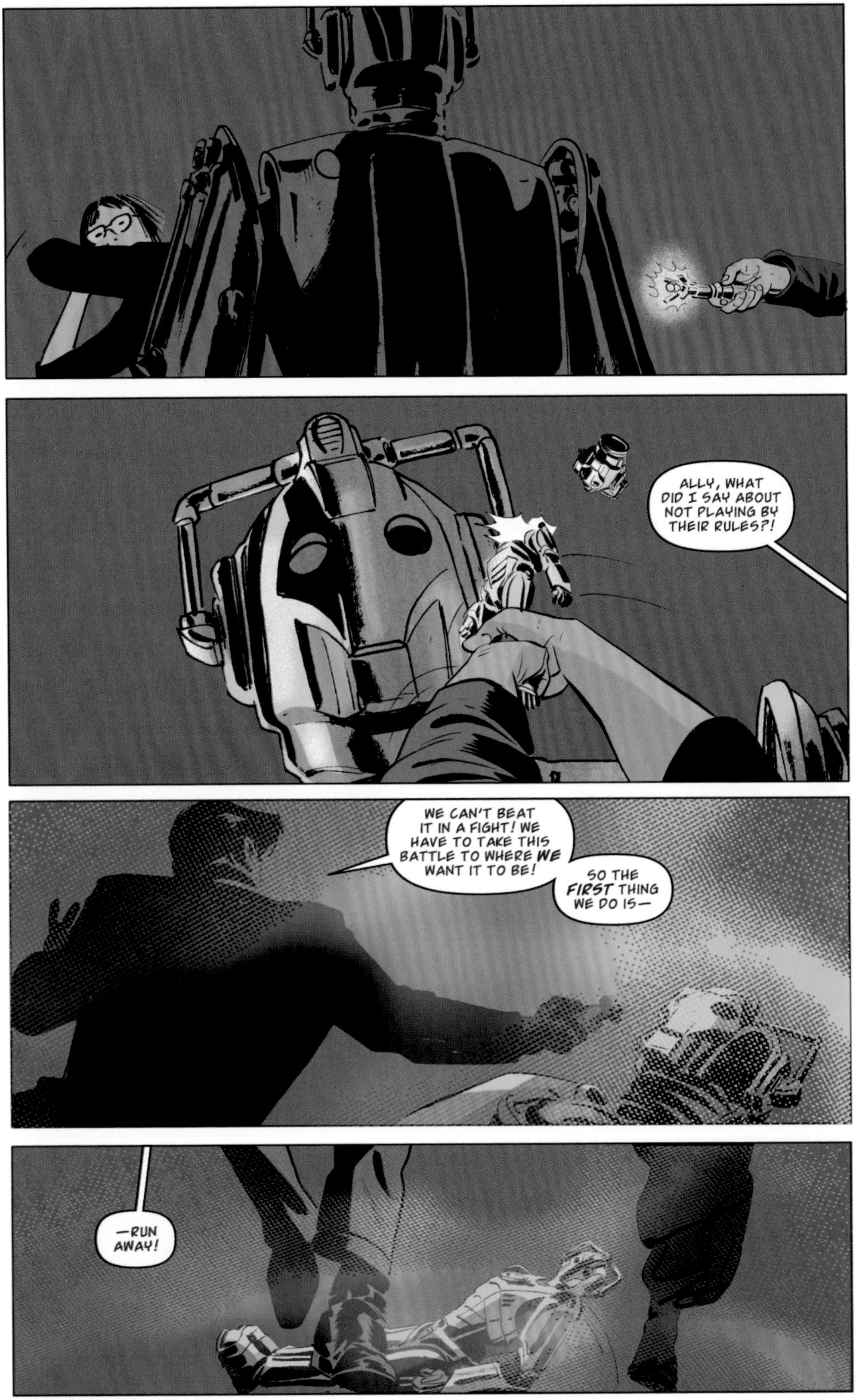
ALLY, WHAT DID I SAY ABOUT NOT PLAYING BY THEIR RULES?!
WE CAN'T BEAT IT IN A FIGHT! WE HAVE TO TAKE THIS BATTLE TO WHERE WE WANT IT TO BE!
SO THE FIRST THING WE DO IS—
—RUN AWAY!

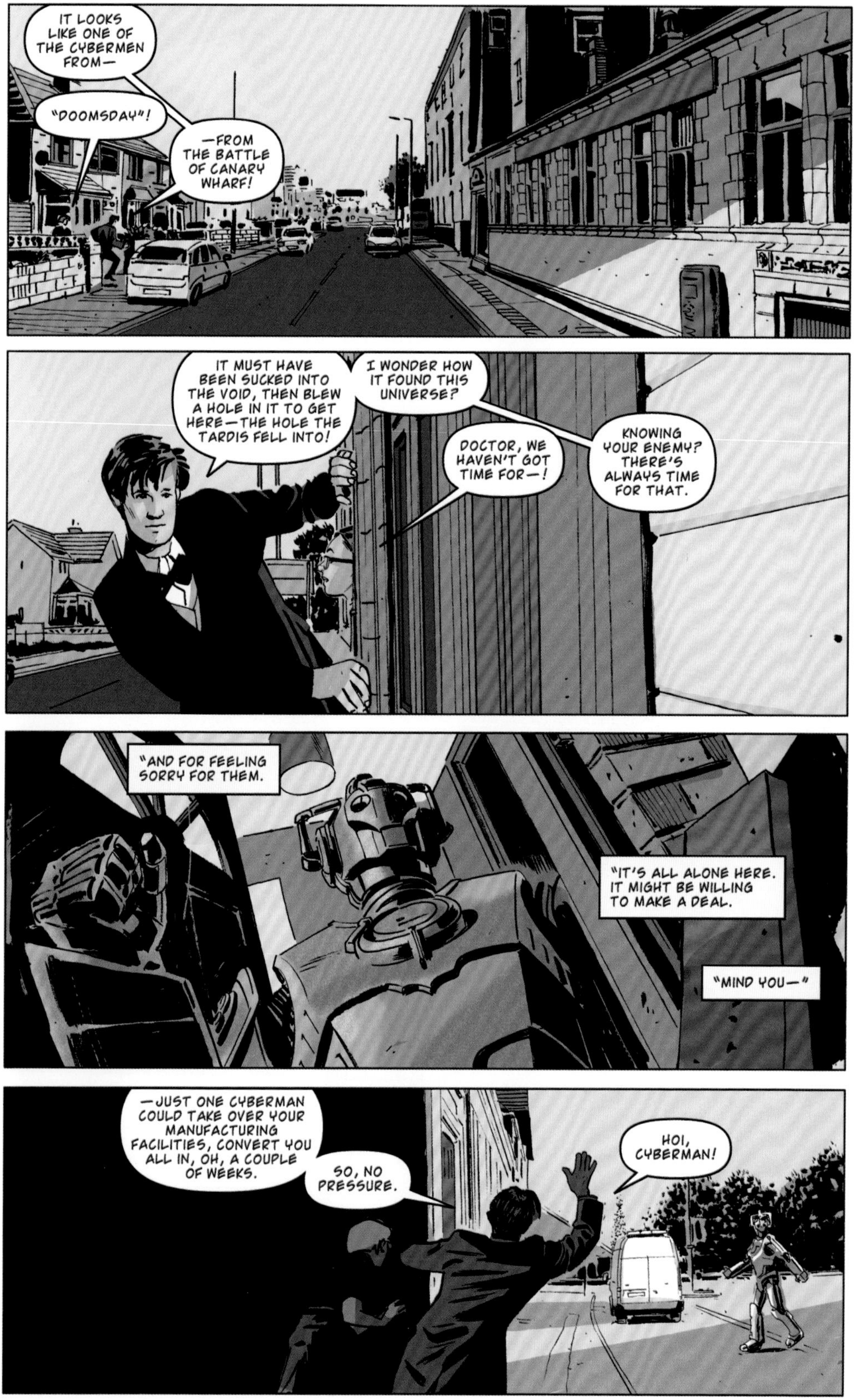
IT LOOKS LIKE ONE OF THE CYBERMEN FROM—
"DOOMSDAY"!
—FROM THE BATTLE OF CANARY WHARF!
IT MUST HAVE BEEN SUCKED INTO THE VOID, THEN BLEW A HOLE IN IT TO GET HERE—THE HOLE THE TARDIS FELL INTO!
I WONDER HOW IT FOUND THIS UNIVERSE?
DOCTOR, WE HAVEN'T GOT TIME FOR—!
KNOWING YOUR ENEMY? THERE'S ALWAYS TIME FOR THAT.
"AND FOR FEELING SORRY FOR THEM.
"IT'S ALL ALONE HERE. IT MIGHT BE WILLING TO MAKE A DEAL.
"MIND YOU—"
—JUST ONE CYBERMAN COULD TAKE OVER YOUR MANUFACTURING FACILITIES, CONVERT YOU ALL IN, OH, A COUPLE OF WEEKS.
SO, NO PRESSURE.
HOI, CYBERMAN!

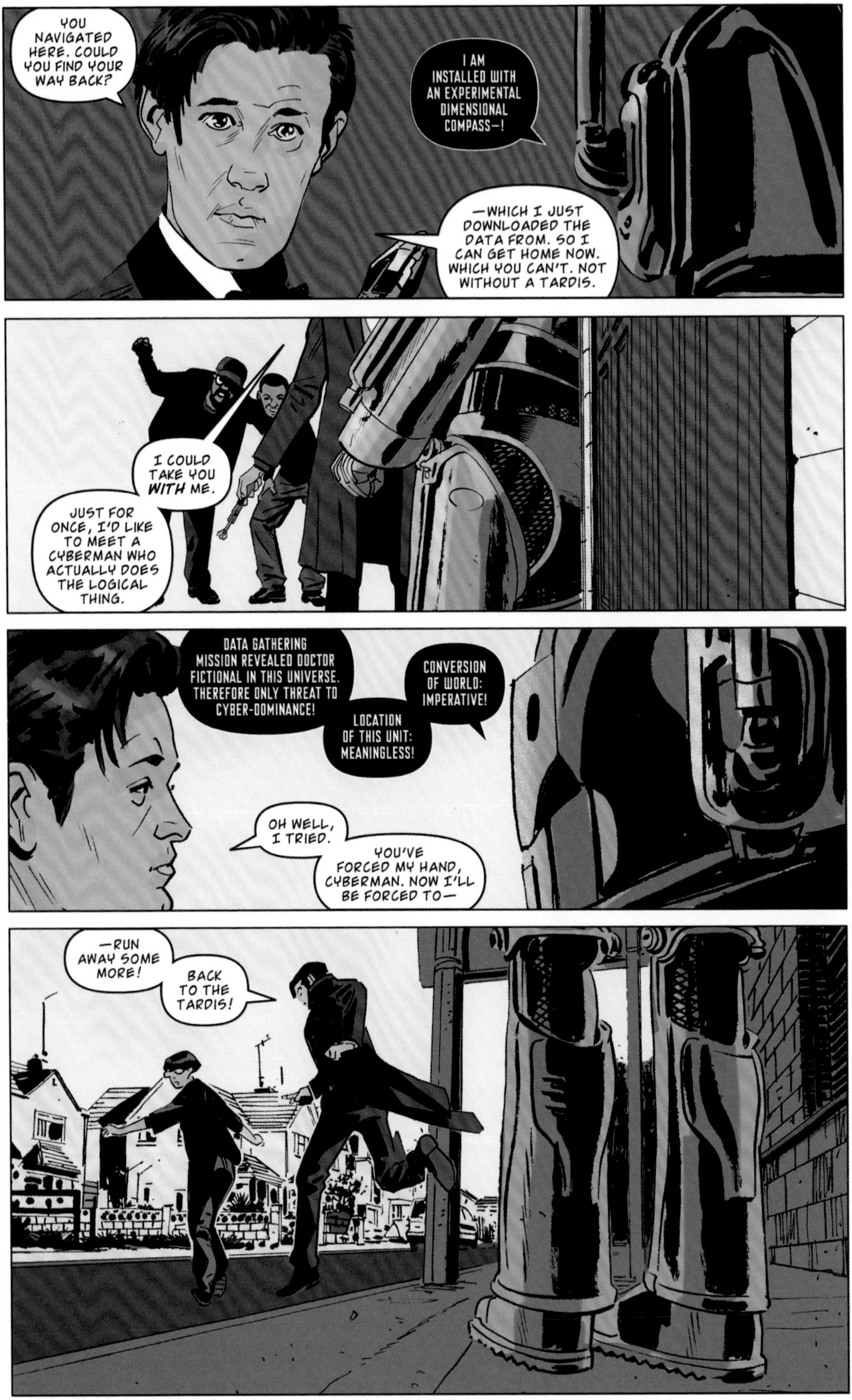
YOU NAVIGATED HERE. COULD YOU FIND YOUR WAY BACK?
I AM INSTALLED WITH AN EXPERIMENTAL DIMENSIONAL COMPASS—!
—WHICH I JUST DOWNLOADED THE DATA FROM. SO I CAN GET HOME NOW. WHICH YOU CAN'T. NOT WITHOUT A TARDIS.
I COULD TAKE YOU WITH ME.
JUST FOR ONCE, I'D LIKE TO MEET A CYBERMAN WHO ACTUALLY DOES THE LOGICAL THING.
DATA GATHERING MISSION REVEALED DOCTOR FICTIONAL IN THIS UNIVERSE. THEREFORE ONLY THREAT TO CYBER-DOMINANCE!
CONVERSION OF WORLD: IMPERATIVE!
LOCATION OF THIS UNIT: MEANINGLESS!
OH WELL, I TRIED.
YOU'VE FORCED MY HAND, CYBERMAN. NOW I'LL BE FORCED TO—
—RUN AWAY SOME MORE!
BACK TO THE TARDIS!

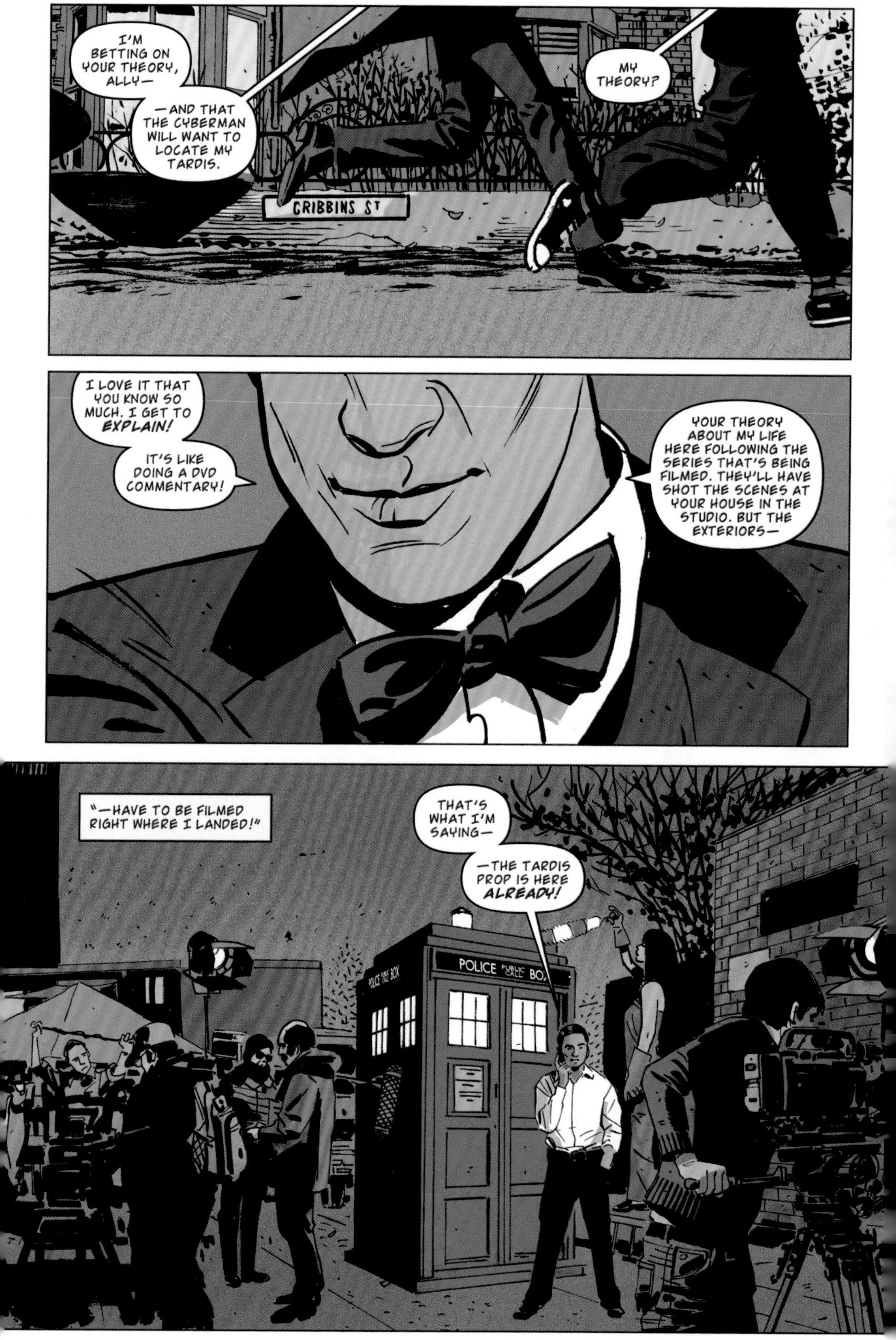
I'M BETTING ON YOUR THEORY, ALLY—
—AND THAT THE CYBERMAN WILL WANT TO LOCATE MY TARDIS.
MY THEORY?
CRIBBINS ST
I LOVE IT THAT YOU KNOW SO MUCH. I GET TO EXPLAIN!
IT'S LIKE DOING A DVD COMMENTARY!
YOUR THEORY ABOUT MY LIFE HERE FOLLOWING THE SERIES THAT'S BEING FILMED. THEY'LL HAVE SHOT THE SCENES AT YOUR HOUSE IN THE STUDIO. BUT THE EXTERIORS—
"—HAVE TO BE FILMED RIGHT WHERE I LANDED!"
THAT'S WHAT I'M SAYING—
—THE TARDIS PROP IS HERE ALREADY!
POLICE PUBLIC CALL BOX

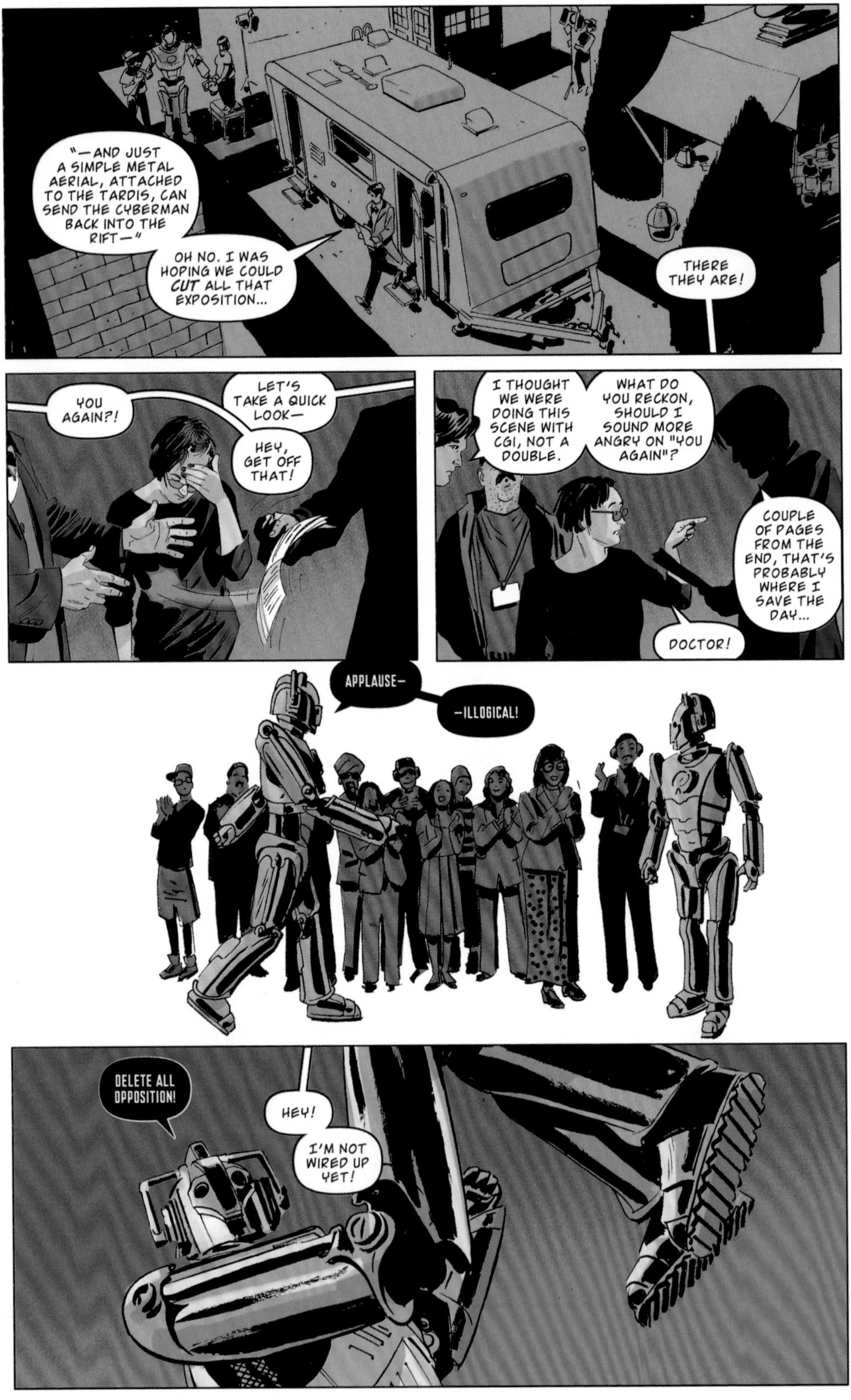
"—AND JUST A SIMPLE METAL AERIAL, ATTACHED TO THE TARDIS, CAN SEND THE CYBERMAN BACK INTO THE RIFT—"
OH NO. I WAS HOPING WE COULD CUT ALL THAT EXPOSITION...
THERE THEY ARE!
YOU AGAIN?!
LET'S TAKE A QUICK LOOK—
HEY, GET OFF THAT!
I THOUGHT WE WERE DOING THIS SCENE WITH CGI, NOT A DOUBLE.
WHAT DO YOU RECKON, SHOULD I SOUND MORE ANGRY ON "YOU AGAIN"?
COUPLE OF PAGES FROM THE END, THAT'S PROBABLY WHERE I SAVE THE DAY...
DOCTOR!
APPLAUSE—
—ILLOGICAL!
DELETE ALL OPPOSITION!
HEY!
I'M NOT WIRED UP YET!

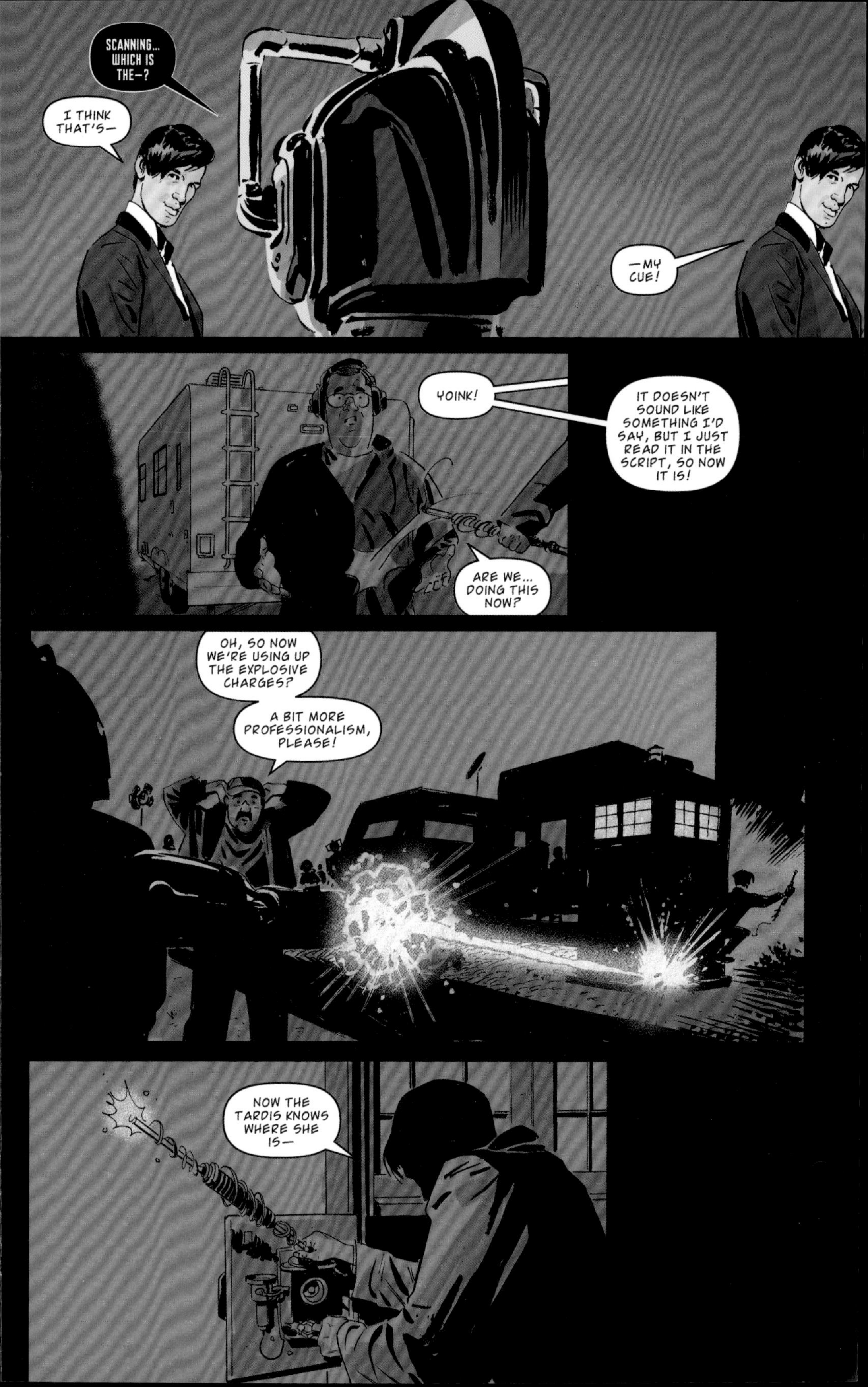
SCANNING... WHICH IS THE—?
I THINK THAT'S—
—MY CUE!
YOINK!
IT DOESN'T SOUND LIKE SOMETHING I'D SAY, BUT I JUST READ IT IN THE SCRIPT, SO NOW IT IS!
ARE WE... DOING THIS NOW?
OH, SO NOW WE'RE USING UP THE EXPLOSIVE CHARGES?
A BIT MORE PROFESSIONALISM, PLEASE!
NOW THE TARDIS KNOWS WHERE SHE IS—

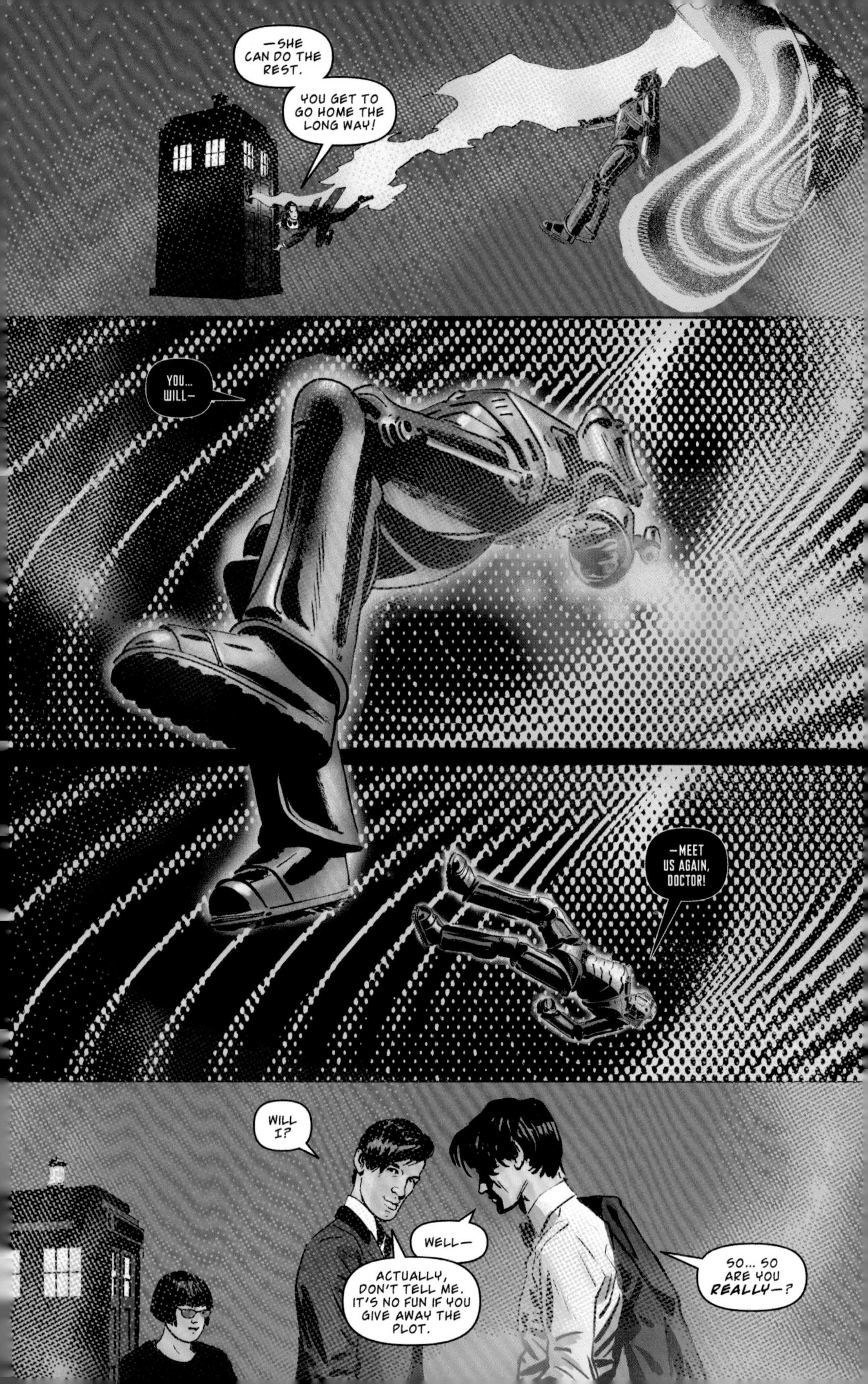
—SHE CAN DO THE REST.
YOU GET TO GO HOME THE LONG WAY!
YOU... WILL—
—MEET US AGAIN, DOCTOR!
WILL I?
WELL—
ACTUALLY, DON'T TELL ME. IT'S NO FUN IF YOU GIVE AWAY THE PLOT.
SO... SO ARE YOU *REALLY*—?

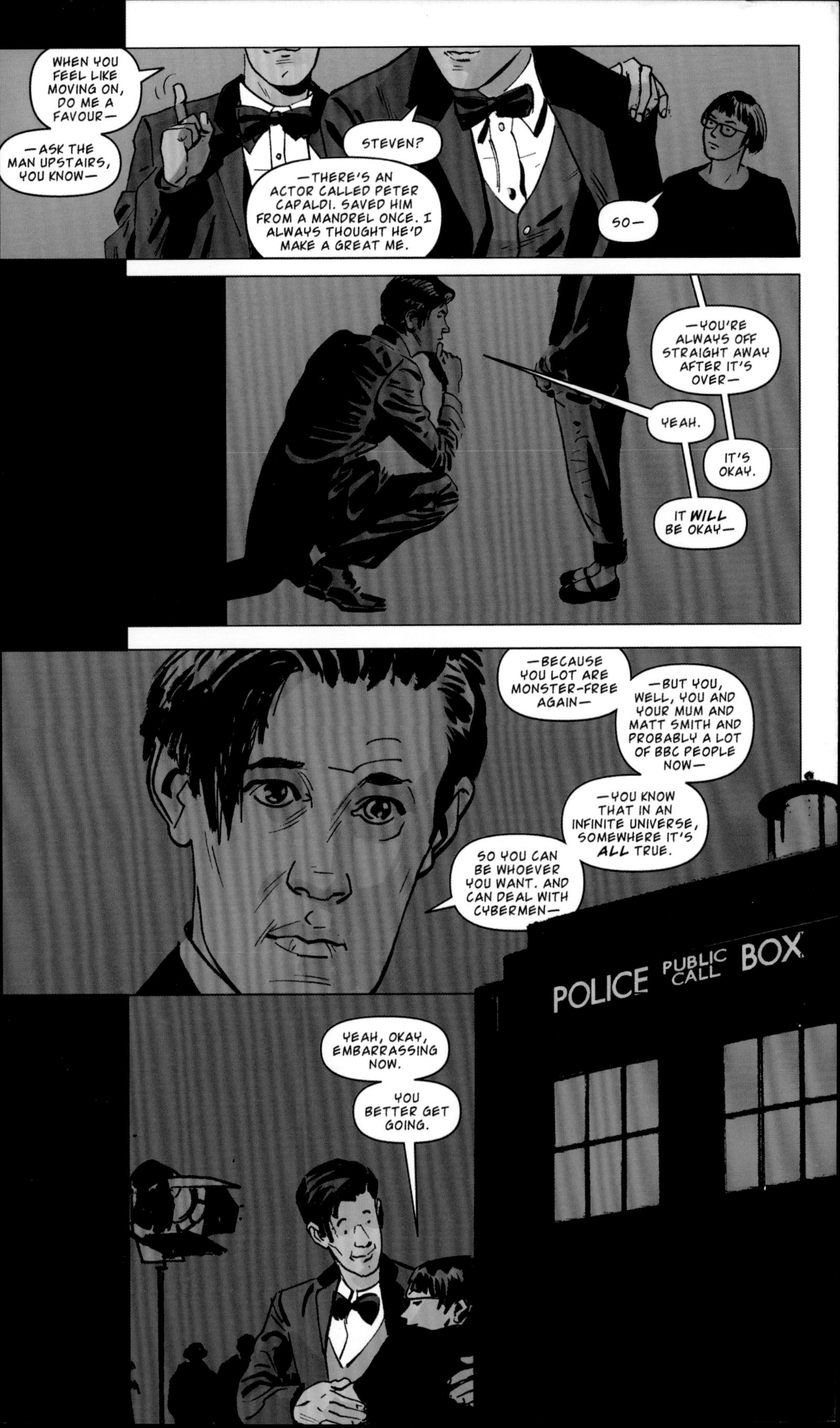
WHEN YOU FEEL LIKE MOVING ON, DO ME A FAVOUR—
—ASK THE MAN UPSTAIRS, YOU KNOW—
STEVEN?
—THERE'S AN ACTOR CALLED PETER CAPALDI. SAVED HIM FROM A MANDREL ONCE. I ALWAYS THOUGHT HE'D MAKE A GREAT ME.
SO—
—YOU'RE ALWAYS OFF STRAIGHT AWAY AFTER IT'S OVER—
YEAH.
IT'S OKAY.
IT WILL BE OKAY—
—BECAUSE YOU LOT ARE MONSTER-FREE AGAIN—
—BUT YOU, WELL, YOU AND YOUR MUM AND MATT SMITH AND PROBABLY A LOT OF BBC PEOPLE NOW—
—YOU KNOW THAT IN AN INFINITE UNIVERSE, SOMEWHERE IT'S ALL TRUE.
SO YOU CAN BE WHOEVER YOU WANT. AND CAN DEAL WITH CYBERMEN—
POLICE PUBLIC CALL BOX
YEAH, OKAY, EMBARRASSING NOW.
YOU BETTER GET GOING.

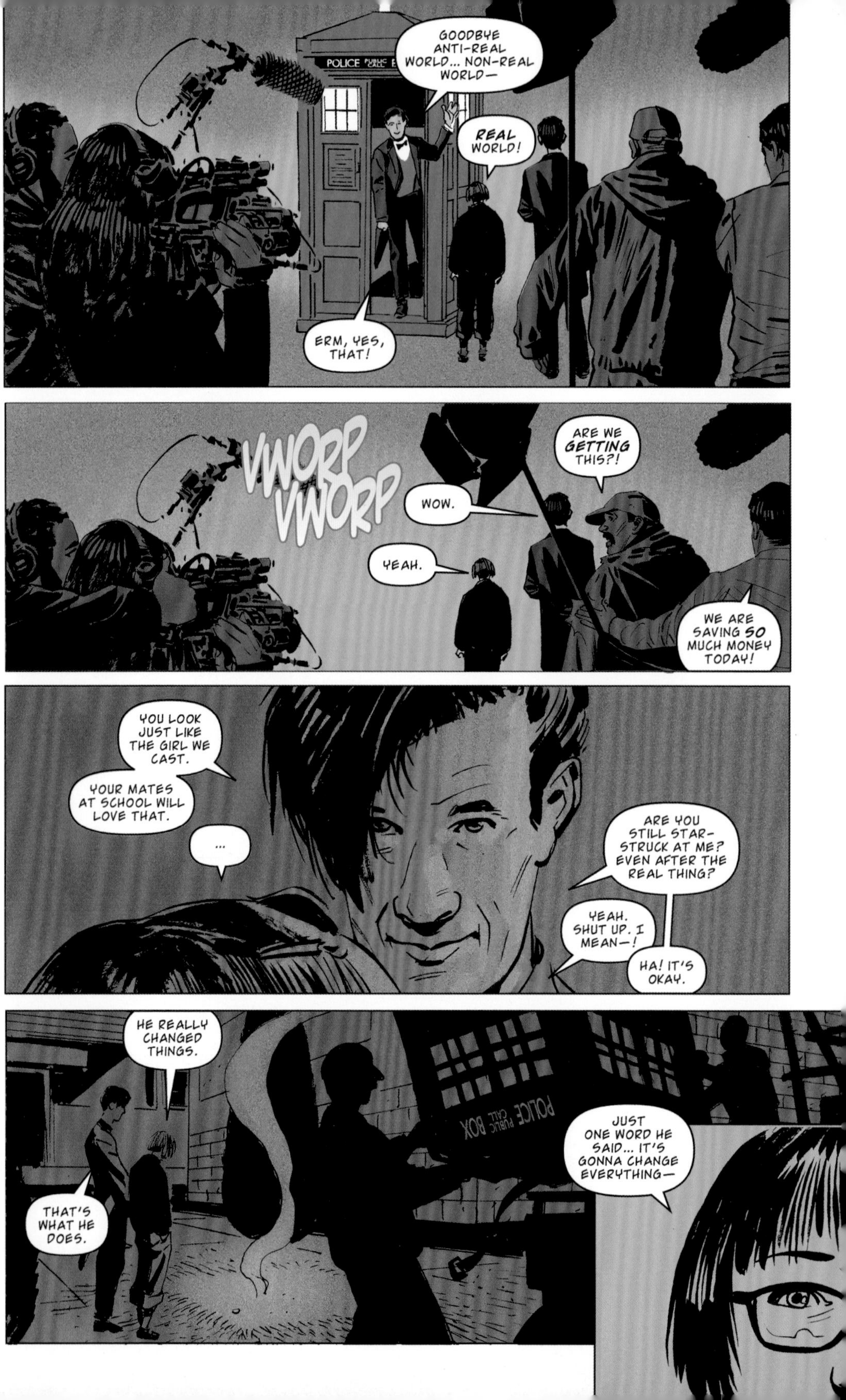
GOODBYE ANTI-REAL WORLD... NON-REAL WORLD—
REAL WORLD!
ERM, YES, THAT!
POLICE PUBLIC CALL BOX
VWORP VWORP
ARE WE GETTING THIS?!
WOW.
YEAH.
WE ARE SAVING SO MUCH MONEY TODAY!
YOU LOOK JUST LIKE THE GIRL WE CAST.
YOUR MATES AT SCHOOL WILL LOVE THAT.
...
ARE YOU STILL STAR-STRUCK AT ME? EVEN AFTER THE REAL THING?
YEAH. SHUT UP. I MEAN—!
HA! IT'S OKAY.
HE REALLY CHANGED THINGS.
THAT'S WHAT HE DOES.
POLICE PUBLIC CALL BOX
JUST ONE WORD HE SAID... IT'S GONNA CHANGE EVERYTHING—

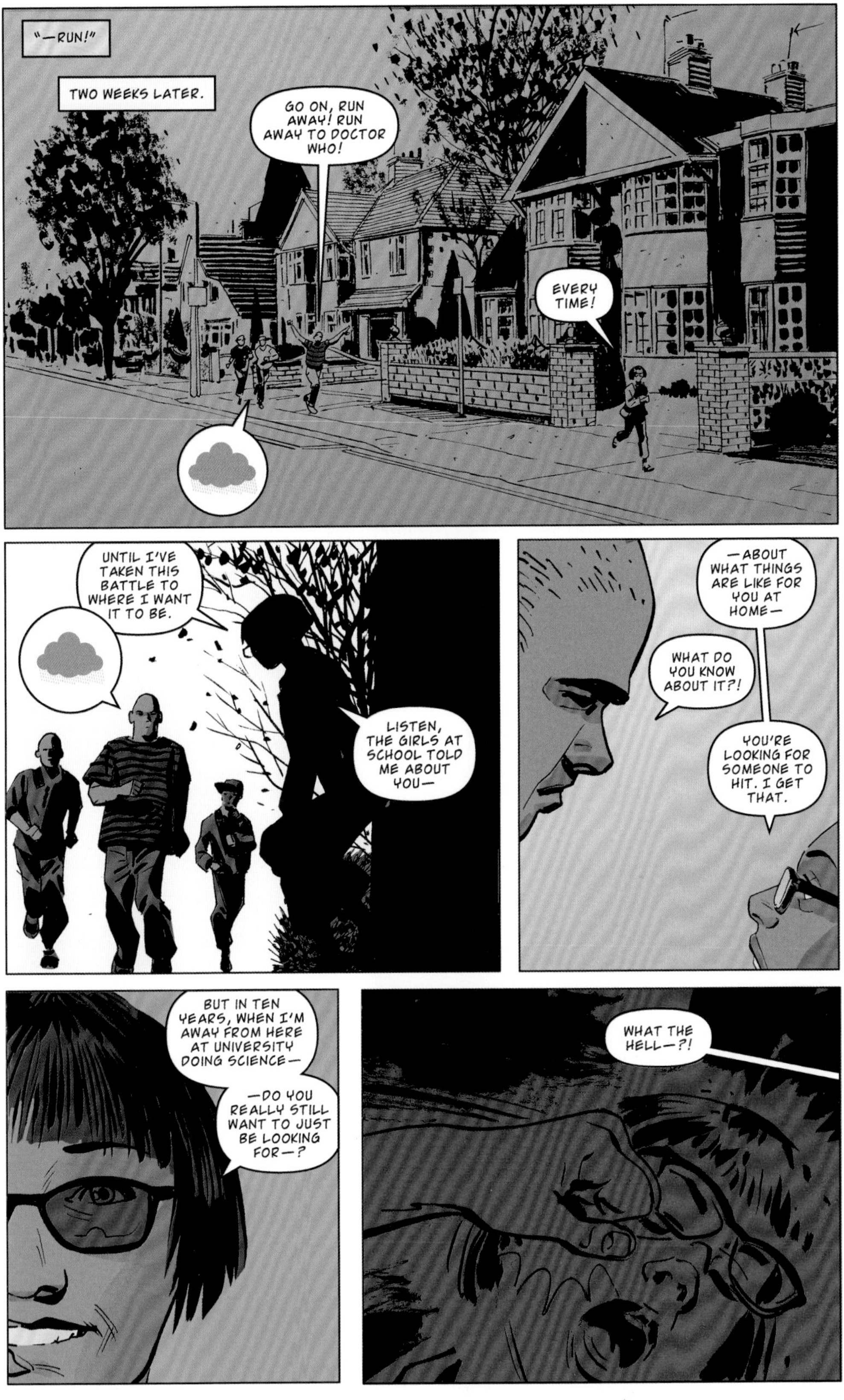
"—RUN!"
TWO WEEKS LATER.
GO ON, RUN AWAY! RUN AWAY TO DOCTOR WHO!
EVERY TIME!
UNTIL I'VE TAKEN THIS BATTLE TO WHERE I WANT IT TO BE.
LISTEN, THE GIRLS AT SCHOOL TOLD ME ABOUT YOU—
—ABOUT WHAT THINGS ARE LIKE FOR YOU AT HOME—
WHAT DO YOU KNOW ABOUT IT?!
YOU'RE LOOKING FOR SOMEONE TO HIT. I GET THAT.
BUT IN TEN YEARS, WHEN I'M AWAY FROM HERE AT UNIVERSITY DOING SCIENCE—
—DO YOU REALLY STILL WANT TO JUST BE LOOKING FOR—?
WHAT THE HELL—?!

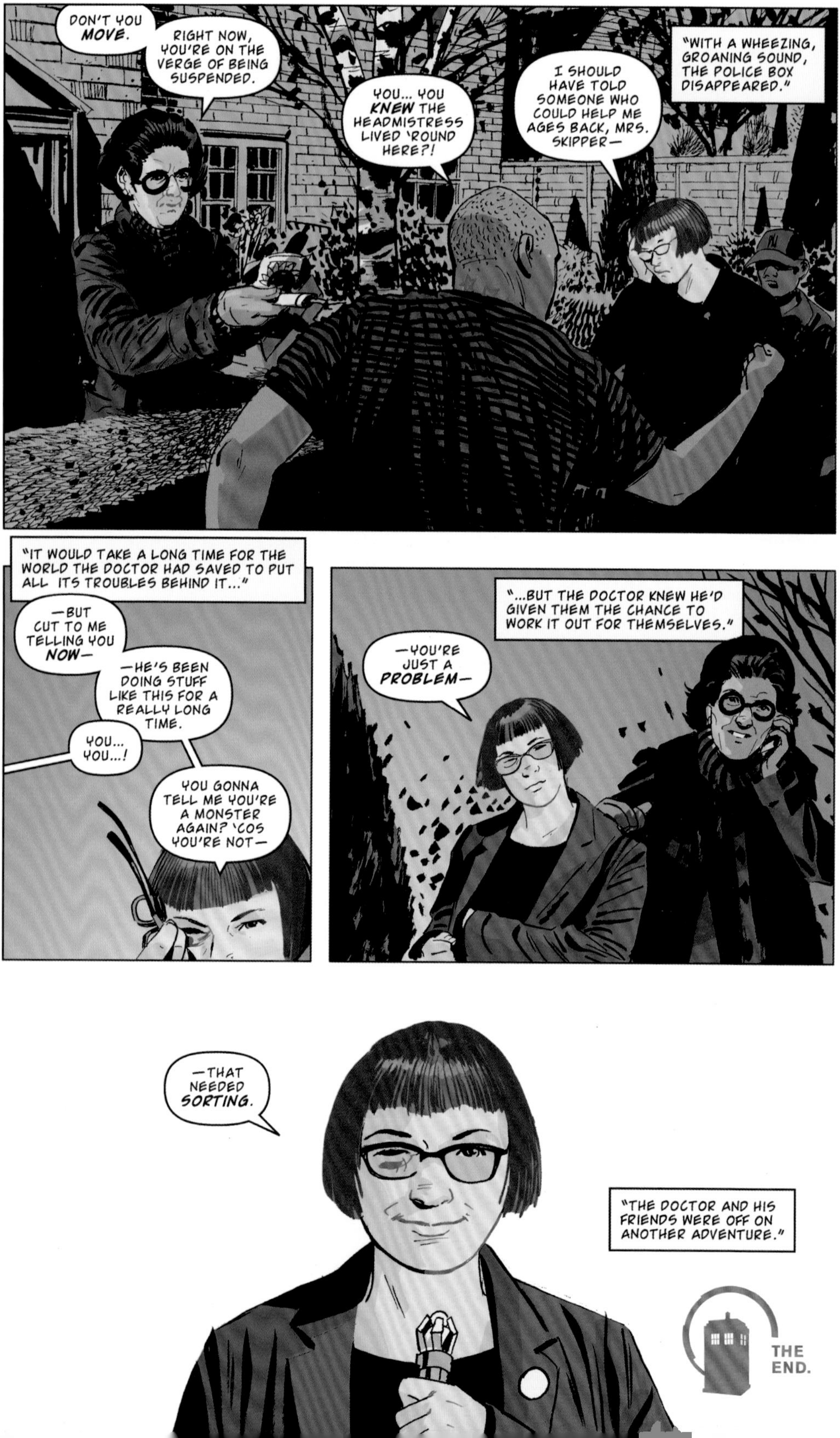
DON'T YOU MOVE.
RIGHT NOW, YOU'RE ON THE VERGE OF BEING SUSPENDED.
YOU... YOU KNEW THE HEADMISTRESS LIVED 'ROUND HERE?!
I SHOULD HAVE TOLD SOMEONE WHO COULD HELP ME AGES BACK, MRS. SKIPPER—
"WITH A WHEEZING, GROANING SOUND, THE POLICE BOX DISAPPEARED."
"IT WOULD TAKE A LONG TIME FOR THE WORLD THE DOCTOR HAD SAVED TO PUT ALL ITS TROUBLES BEHIND IT..."
—BUT CUT TO ME TELLING YOU NOW—
—HE'S BEEN DOING STUFF LIKE THIS FOR A REALLY LONG TIME.
YOU... YOU...!
YOU GONNA TELL ME YOU'RE A MONSTER AGAIN? 'COS YOU'RE NOT—
"...BUT THE DOCTOR KNEW HE'D GIVEN THEM THE CHANCE TO WORK IT OUT FOR THEMSELVES."
—YOU'RE JUST A PROBLEM—
—THAT NEEDED SORTING.
"THE DOCTOR AND HIS FRIENDS WERE OFF ON ANOTHER ADVENTURE."
THE END.

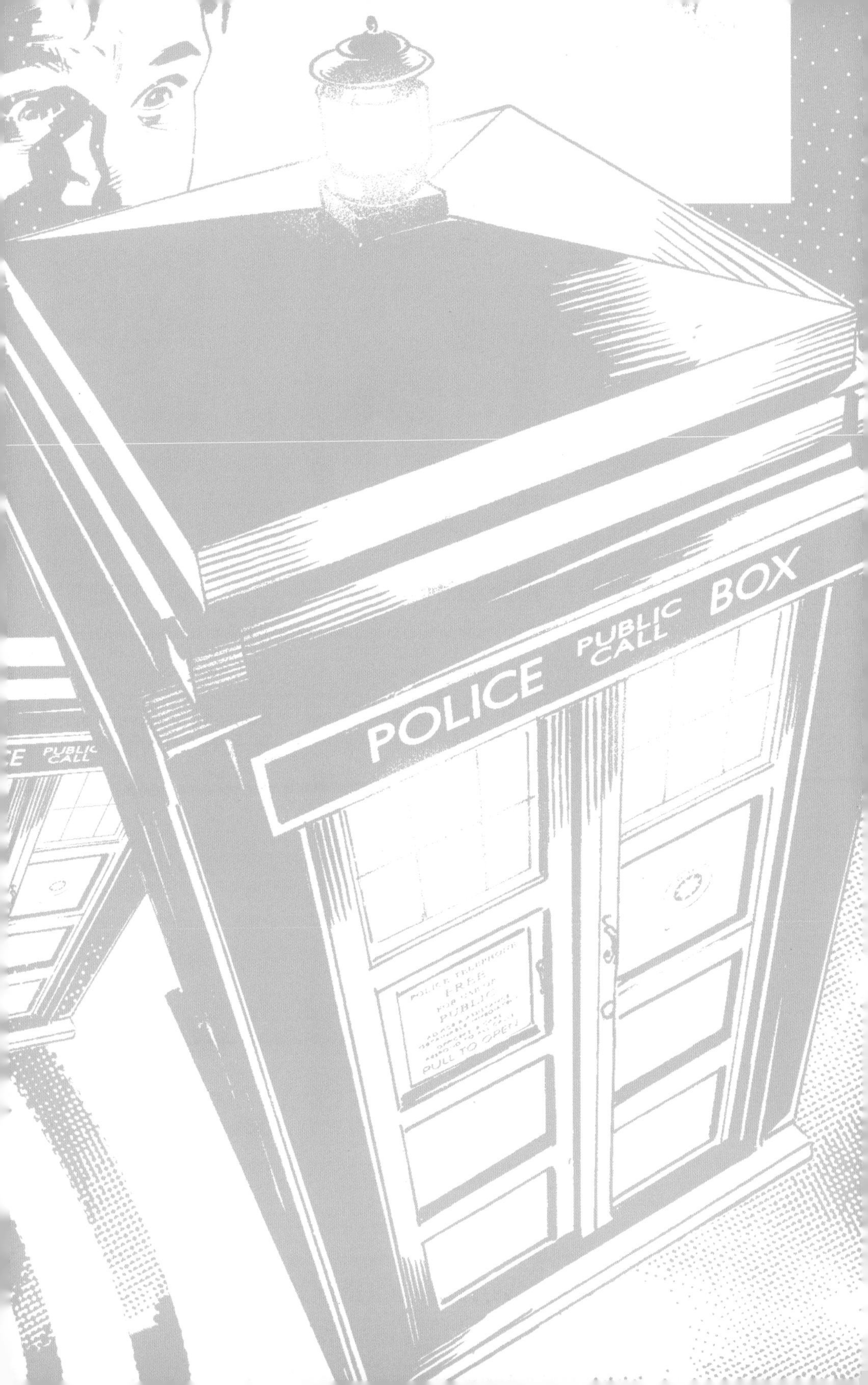
POLICE PUBLIC CALL BOX
FREE
PUBLIC
PULL TO OPEN
PUBLIC CALL

FOLLOW YOUR FAVORITE INCARNATIONS ACROSS THESE FANTASTIC COLLECTIONS!

DOCTOR WHO: THE TWELFTH DOCTOR VOL. 1: TERRORFORMER

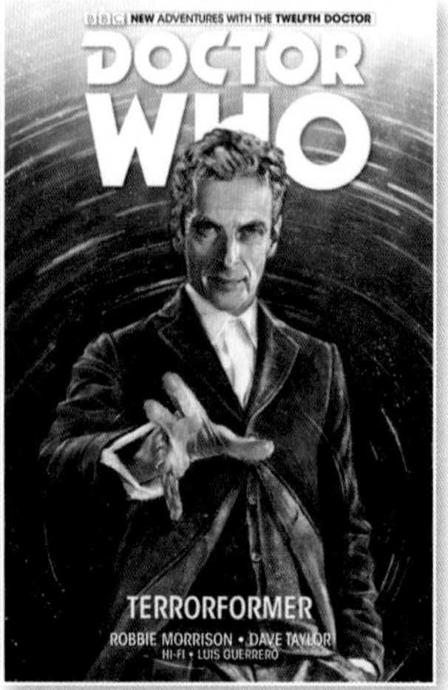
BBC NEW ADVENTURES WITH THE TWELFTH DOCTOR
DOCTOR WHO
TERRORFORMER
ROBBIE MORRISON • DAVE TAYLOR
HI-FI • LUIS GUERRERO

ON SALE NOW ISBN: 9781782761778
$19.99 / $22.95 CAN / £10.99
(UK EDITION ISBN: 9781782763864)

DOCTOR WHO: THE TWELFTH DOCTOR VOL. 2: FRACTURES

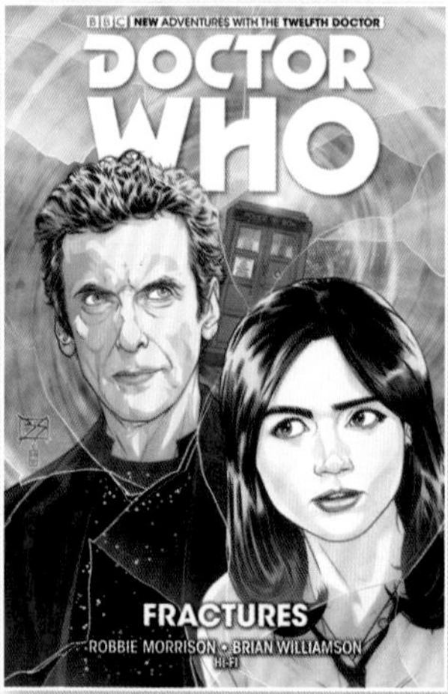
BBC NEW ADVENTURES WITH THE TWELFTH DOCTOR
DOCTOR WHO
FRACTURES
ROBBIE MORRISON • BRIAN WILLIAMSON
HI-FI

ON SALE NOW ISBN: 9781782763017
$19.99 / $25.99 CAN / £10.99
(UK EDITION ISBN: 9781782766599)

DOCTOR WHO: THE TWELFTH DOCTOR VOL. 3: HYPERION

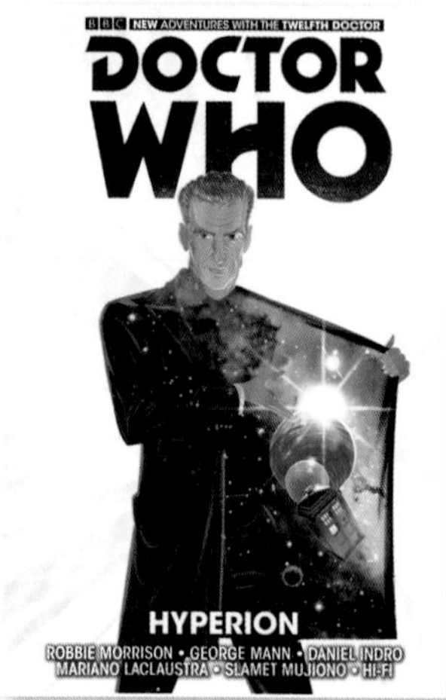
BBC NEW ADVENTURES WITH THE TWELFTH DOCTOR
DOCTOR WHO
HYPERION
ROBBIE MORRISON • GEORGE MANN • DANIEL INDRO
MARIANO LACLAUSTRA • SLAMET MUJIONO • HI-FI

COMING SOON ISBN: 9781782767473
$19.99 / $25.99 CAN / £10.99
(UK EDITION ISBN: 97817827674442)

DOCTOR WHO: THE TENTH DOCTOR VOL. 1: REVOLUTIONS OF TERROR

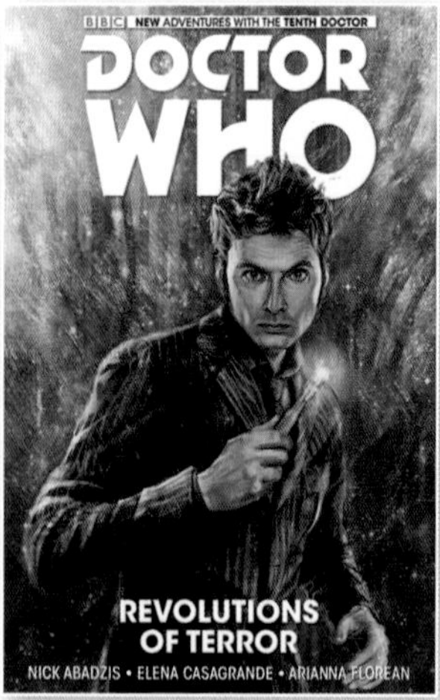
BBC NEW ADVENTURES WITH THE TENTH DOCTOR
DOCTOR WHO
REVOLUTIONS OF TERROR
NICK ABADZIS • ELENA CASAGRANDE • ARIANNA FLOREAN

ON SALE NOW ISBN: 9781782761730
$19.99 / $22.95 CAN / £10.99
(UK EDITION ISBN: 9781782763840)

DOCTOR WHO: THE TENTH DOCTOR VOL. 2: THE WEEPING ANGELS OF MONS

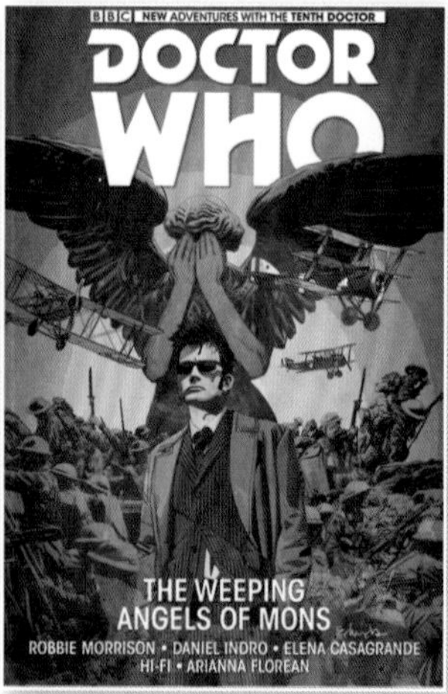
BBC NEW ADVENTURES WITH THE TENTH DOCTOR
DOCTOR WHO
THE WEEPING ANGELS OF MONS
ROBBIE MORRISON • DANIEL INDRO • ELENA CASAGRANDE
HI-FI • ARIANNA FLOREAN

ON SALE NOW ISBN: 9781782761754
$19.99 / $25.99 CAN / £10.99
(UK EDITION ISBN: 9781782766575)

DOCTOR WHO: THE TENTH DOCTOR VOL. 3: THE FOUNTAINS OF FOREVER

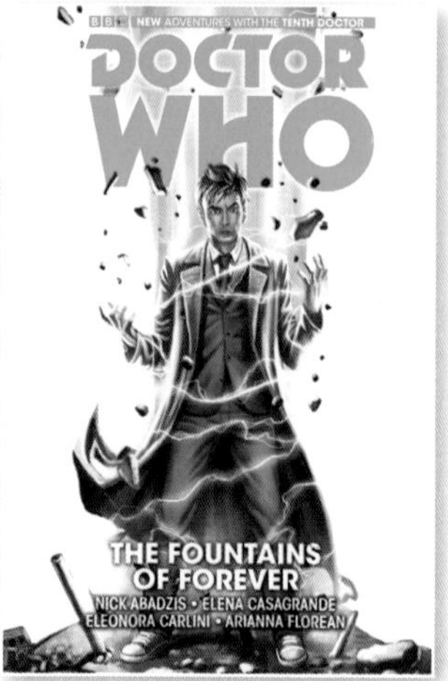
BBC NEW ADVENTURES WITH THE TENTH DOCTOR
DOCTOR WHO
THE FOUNTAINS OF FOREVER
NICK ABADZIS • ELENA CASAGRANDE
ELEONORA CARLINI • ARIANNA FLOREAN

ON SALE NOW ISBN: 9781782763024
$19.99 / $25.99 CAN/ £10.99
(UK EDITION ISBN: 9781782767404)

TITAN COMICS

For information on how to subscribe to our great Doctor Who titles, or to purchase them digitally for your favorite device, visit:

WWW.TITAN-COMICS.COM

JOIN THE ELEVENTH DOCTOR FOR ALL-NEW ADVENTURES – AND COMPLETE YOUR ARCHIVES!

DOCTOR WHO: THE ELEVENTH DOCTOR VOL. 1: AFTER LIFE

ON SALE NOW ISBN: 9781782761747
$19.99 / $22.95 CAN / £10.99
(UK EDITION ISBN: 9781782763857)

DOCTOR WHO: THE ELEVENTH DOCTOR VOL. 2: SERVE YOU

ON SALE NOW ISBN: 9781782761754
$19.99 / $25.99 CAN / £10.99
(UK EDITION ISBN: 9781782766582)

DOCTOR WHO: THE ELEVENTH DOCTOR VOL. 3: CONVERSION

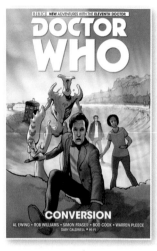

ON SALE NOW ISBN: 9781782763024
$19.99 / $25.99 CAN / £10.99
(UK EDITION ISBN: 9781782767435)

DOCTOR WHO: THE ELEVENTH DOCTOR ARCHIVES VOL. 1

ON SALE NOW ISBN: 9781782767688
$24.99 / $32.99 CAN / £18.99

DOCTOR WHO: THE ELEVENTH DOCTOR ARCHIVES VOL. 2

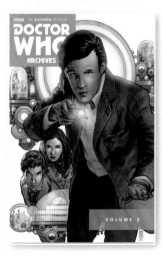

ON SALE NOW ISBN: 9781782767695
$24.99 / $32.99 CAN / £18.99

DOCTOR WHO: PRISONERS OF TIME ARCHIVES

COMING SOON ISBN: 9781782767749
$24.99 / $32.99 CAN / £18.99

AVAILABLE IN ALL GOOD COMIC STORES, BOOK STORES, AND DIGITAL PROVIDERS!

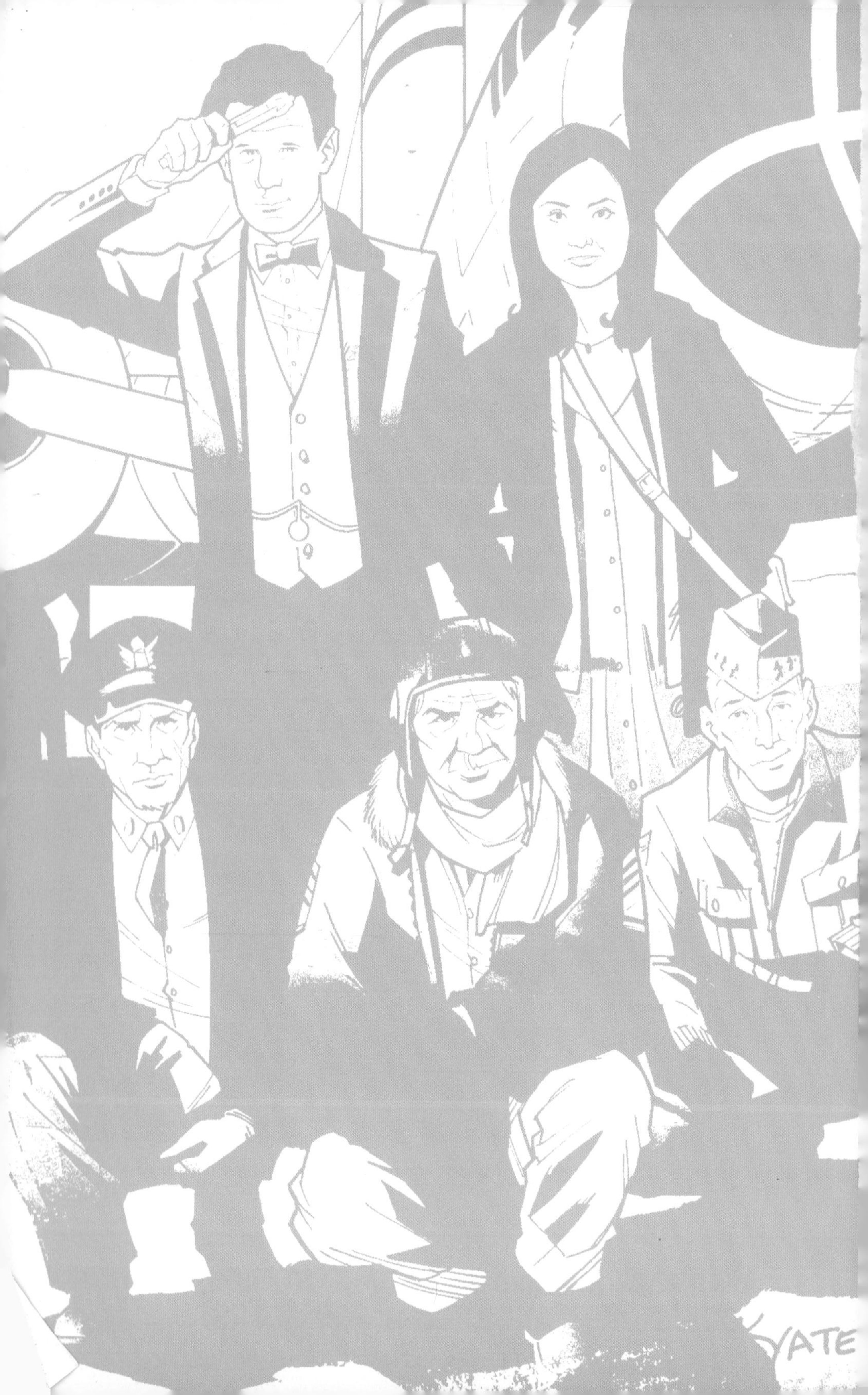